EVOLUTION OF A FEDERALIST

WILLIAM LOUGHTON SMITH
by *Gilbert Stuart*

"He is truly an excellent member—a ready, clear speaker, of a sound analytic head, and the justest views. I know no man whose loss from the House would be more severely felt by the good cause."

Alexander Hamilton

Evolution of a

FEDERALIST

WILLIAM LOUGHTON SMITH

OF CHARLESTON (1758-1812)

George C. Rogers, junior

UNIVERSITY OF SOUTH CAROLINA PRESS
Columbia

iv

To
Helen Bean Rogers
and
George Calvin Rogers

PREFACE

DURING a visit to the Rosenbach Foundation in Philadelphia in 1955 the librarian, William H. McCarthy, junior, showed me the William Loughton Smith Papers that the Foundation had recently acquired. Among the papers were Smith's journals of his travels in 1790, 1791, and 1793, which Mr. McCarthy suggested I might like to edit. Although a South Carolinian and a student of American history, I knew very little about William Loughton Smith. After some research into Smith's life, I came upon two curious facts that seemed to warrant explanation, and in attempting to explain these two facts I abandoned the job of editing, at least temporarily, and devoted myself to a full-scale study of the man and his times. Smith was sent abroad at the age of eleven in 1770 and returned in December 1783, having spent the intervening years studying in England and Switzerland. In spite of this long absence, which encompassed the years of the Revolution, Smith was elected in November 1788 to be the first congressman from Charleston District to the national House of Representatives. The second fact of unusual interest was that Smith was re-elected in 1794, despite his being openly opposed by the Rutledges and the Pinckneys, who have been considered the principal leaders of the Federalist party in South Carolina. These two facts, his election in 1788 and his re-election in 1794, suggested that Smith drew his strength from old tories and British merchants. My purpose, therefore, has been to analyze Smith's political support, and my study has revealed a group of arch-Federalists to the right of the Rutledges and the Pinckneys, who were moderate Federalists.

Recalling that, with the one exception of the letters of Henry Laurens, the private papers of South Carolina's eighteenth-century leaders have been dispersed (fire, climate, and war have played havoc with such collections), I decided to make a thorough search of northern libraries and historical societies, hoping that I could assemble a body of documents that would help me tell the story in detail. Since southerners wrote their northern friends and northern collections of this period have been more generally kept intact, the search promised to be a fruitful one. The bibliography of primary sources indicates the extent of my search, which was most successful—a significant body of new material has been unearthed from which to write the history of South Carolina. These private documents have been supplemented by abundant public documents in

vii

the South Carolina Archives Department. Eighteenth-century spelling is notoriously variable; names used in the text are spelled as they are in the source cited.

I have endeavored to write this story with no personal bias injected, but perhaps my readers should know that I was born in Charleston, attended public school there, and was graduated from the College of Charleston. My first interest in South Carolina history was stimulated by my school teachers, particularly Miss Lucia Hutchinson (now Mrs. Henry O. Withington), who through the use of historical novels made the past a vibrant reality. The teacher to whom I owe the greatest debt of gratitude is the late J. Harold Easterby, who taught me at the College of Charleston and who later read and discussed this manuscript with me. It was also he who suggested that I continue my historical training at the University of Chicago. I wrote my master's thesis and my doctoral dissertation under the direction of Avery Craven, William T. Hutchinson, and Alan Simpson, who helped me widen my historical horizon—to understand the South, the nation, and the Anglo-American world. To study with them and their colleagues was an enriching experience. A year at the University of Edinburgh, where I had the good fortune to be able to study with the late Richard Pares, further sharpened my historical perspectives.

Many persons assisted me in the writing of this book. Mr. McCarthy of the Rosenbach Foundation suggested the subject. The librarians and staff of the following institutions opened their collections to me: American Antiquarian Society, Boston Public Library, John Carter Brown Library, Connecticut Historical Society, Colonial Williamsburg, Duke University Library, Essex Institute, the Federal Records Center in East Point, Georgia, Henry E. Huntington Library, Library of Congress, Library Company of Philadelphia, Long Island Historical Society, Massachusetts Historical Society, National Archives, North Carolina Department of Archives and History, New-York Historical Society, New York Public Library, Historical Society of Pennsylvania, Pierpont Morgan Library, Southern Historical Collection in Chapel Hill, North Carolina, University of Virginia Library, William L. Clements Library, and Yale University Library. Miss Geraldine Beard of the New-York Historical Society was particularly helpful in answering questions about New York leaders with South Carolina connections.

In Charleston it was my pleasure to work at the South Carolina Historical Society, the Charleston Library Society, and the College of Charleston Library. Mrs. Granville T. Prior, executive secretary of the South Carolina Historical Society, patiently answered many questions and devoted much time to ferreting out obscure documents. Miss Virginia Rugheimer, of the Charleston Library Society, and her staff, particularly Mrs. Minnie Pringle Haigh, were equally cooperative. Since I was an undergraduate, Miss Mary V. Powers, librarian at the College of Charleston, has been helping me locate just the right volume.

I found in Columbia at the South Carolina Archives Department much unworked material. Dr. Easterby first introduced me to these public documents, and Charles Lee, the present director, has continued Dr. Easterby's tradition of making important suggestions and pausing in the midst of his own work for lengthy discussions. I am most grateful for the time that Miss Mary Crawford, Francis M. Hutson, Mrs. Florence M. Law, William McDowell, and Miss Wylma Wates of the Archives staff have given me. Miss Ruth Green was especially helpful—teaching me a great deal about eighteenth-century South Carolinians and also instructing me in the intricacies of index-making.

The South Caroliniana Library is a repository of private records pertaining to South Carolina history comparable to the Archives in the richness of its untapped resources. E. L. Inabinett, the director, who is himself the authority on Ralph Izard, took an especial interest in this work, pointing out from time to time still other unexplored materials. Mrs. Clara Mae Jacobs in the manuscript room and James F. Ellsworth in the reading room were always ready to fulfill my frantic requests for papers and books. I would also like to commend Alfred Rawlinson and his staff of the libraries of the University of South Carolina, who though overworked, always render expert service.

My colleagues in the department of history at the University of South Carolina have endured much talk about the South Carolina Federalists, and I appreciate their tolerance of my enthusiasm. Robert D. Ochs read a portion of the manuscript and made helpful suggestions. Bradley D. Bargar took time from his work on Lord Dartmouth to consider my inquiries. Daniel W. Hollis, who has shared an office with me, put up with a great deal of extraneous chatter and let me test some of my insights against his own knowledge of South Carolina history. And William A. Foran has always been ready to challenge my theories about Carolina history.

George S. McCowen, of Wofford College, read the manuscript and helped me understand the eighteenth century.

The greatest pleasure that comes from being a Charlestonian is that one has life-long friends. I must acknowledge the patience of Joan, Henrietta, Desmond, Priestley, George, and Harriet, for they have listened to my hopes over the years and have encouraged me in the dark moments. And thanks are due Porter, above all, who took the time to read the manuscript at one point in the many stages of rewriting and give incisive criticism.

No manuscript should see the light of publication day without the amputations and emendations of able editors. Mrs. Louise Jones DuBose and Miss Frances Porcher have done their best to make this a good book. Where it falls short, I must assume the responsibility.

The Research Committee of the University of South Carolina made funds available for typing the manuscript and for subsidizing part of the original printing costs. For these grants I am most grateful. Without the expert typing of Mrs. Roberta Hamm and Mrs. Dorothy Knight the delay in publication would have been even greater than it has been.

Miss Helen McCormack, director of the Gibbes Art Gallery, helped me locate and select the portraits used as illustrations. Mrs. Mary L. Wilson and Mrs. Kate L. Farnsworth of Ladson Farm, Horseshoe, North Carolina, kindly gave me permission to use the portrait of Benjamin Smith by John Wollaston.

This book is dedicated to my Mother and Father, who have been the most patient of all.

G. C. R., JUNIOR

August 1962

CONTENTS

ILLUSTRATIONS

ABBREVIATIONS

abbrev.	title
AAS	American Antiquarian Society, Worcester, Mass.
AHR	*American Historical Review*
BPL	Boston Public Library, Boston, Mass.
CHS	The Connecticut Historical Society, Hartford, Conn.
CJ	Manuscript Journals of the Council of South Carolina, South Carolina Archives Department, Columbia, S. C.
CLS	Charleston Library Society, Charleston, S. C.
CW	Colonial Williamsburg, Williamsburg, Va.
DAB	*Dictionary of American Biography*, eds. Allen Johnson and Dumas Malone, New York, 1928-1936
DNB	*Dictionary of National Biography*, eds. Leslie Stephens and Sidney Lee, London, 1885-1900
DUL	Duke University Library, Durham, N. C.
EI	Essex Institute, Salem, Mass.
FO	Copies of the Manuscript Records of the Foreign Office in the British Public Record Office, which are in the Library of Congress, Washington, D. C.
FRC Georgia	Federal Records Center, East Point, Ga.
HEHL	Henry E. Huntington Library, San Marino, Calif.
JCBL	The John Carter Brown Library, Brown University, Providence, R. I.
JCHA	Manuscript Journals of the Commons House of Assembly, South Carolina Archives Department, Columbia, S. C.
JHR	Manuscript Journals of the House of Representatives of South Carolina, South Carolina Archives Department, Columbia, S. C.
LC	Library of Congress, Washington, D. C.
LCP	The Library Company of Philadelphia, Philadelphia, Pa.
LIHS	Long Island Historical Society, Brooklyn, N. Y.
MHS	Massachusetts Historical Society, Boston, Mass.
National Archives	National Archives, Washington, D. C.
NC Archives	Department of Archives and History, State of North Carolina, Raleigh, N. C.
NYHS	The New-York Historical Society, New York, N. Y.
NYPL	The New York Public Library, New York, N. Y.
PHS	The Historical Society of Pennsylvania, Philadelphia, Pa.
PML	The Pierpont Morgan Library, New York, N. Y.
PRO	Copies of the Manuscript Records in the British Public Record Office Relating to South Carolina, which are in the South Carolina Archives Department, Columbia, S. C.
RC	Collections of the Philip H. & A. S. W. Rosenbach Foundation, Philadelphia, Pa.
SC Archives	South Carolina Archives Department, Columbia, S. C.
SCHGM	*South Carolina Historical and Genealogical Magazine*
SCHS	South Carolina Historical Society, Charleston, S. C.
SCL	South Caroliniana Library, The University of South Carolina, Columbia, S. C.
SC Statutes	*Statutes at Large of South Carolina*, eds. Thomas Cooper and David J. McCord, Columbia, S. C., 1837-1841
SHC	Southern Historical Collection, The University of North Carolina Library, Chapel Hill, N. C.
UVL	University of Virginia Library, Charlottesville, Va.
WLCL	William L. Clements Library, The University of Michigan, Ann Arbor, Mich.
YL	Yale University Library, New Haven, Conn.

I

THE SCHENCKINGH-SMITHS

ANNE ASHBY MANIGAULT, wife of the great merchant-banker, Gabriel Manigault, who was reputed to be the wealthiest man in colonial Carolina, kept a journal in which she recorded the activities of her family and friends: births and deaths, sailings and landings, plantation visits, social calls. For almost thirty years she noted entrances and exits from the Carolina stage. Among the entries, which were always brief, was the following for the year 1758: "Oct. 2. Mrs. Ben: Smith l[ay in] a son."[1] William Smith, the son of Benjamin and Anne Loughton Smith, was born.

Birthdates are difficult to document for the eighteenth century, and without the jottings of a Mrs. Manigault many of the vital statistics of South Carolina's early leaders would have been lost. Benjamin Smith, the father, however, did verify the fact of his son's birth in the postscript to a letter written in May 1766 to his Boston cousin, the Reverend William Smith: "Your namesake my son William is a very fine boy takes his learning very well and will be eight years old next October."[2] Additional proof of the birthdate came in an unusual fashion. After the birth of William's second son on October 2, 1808, another Mrs. Manigault, Margaret, the wife of Gabriel Manigault, II, wrote her mother Mrs. Ralph Izard that the boy had been born fifty years to the day after his father's birth.[3]

William Smith was a very commonplace name with which to live. Its owner, however, bore it honorably and long as a sufficient designation of his individuality until a politician of the same name—but opposite political persuasion—appeared in the backcountry.[4]

It was on his return to Carolina after an absence of six years in Europe that William Smith decided to add as a middle name his

[1] "Extracts from the Journal of Mrs. Ann Manigault, 1754-1781," ed. Mabel L. Webber, *SCHGM*, XX (1919), 131. Mrs. Manigault's name is spelled "Anne" in letters to her from her grandson Gabriel. *See* letters for 1775 and 1776 in *Manigault Papers*, SCL.
[2] Benjamin Smith to Reverend William Smith, May 16, 1766, *Smith-Carter Papers*, MHS.
[3] Margaret Manigault to Alice Izard, November 29, 1808, *Izard Papers*, LC.
[4] The subject of this biography has often been confused with William Smith, a representative from Pinckney and Washington District in Congress, 1797-1799, and a senator from South Carolina, 1816-1823, 1826-1831. J. G. deR. Hamilton, "William Smith, 1762-1840," *DAB. Also see* John Belton O'Neall, *Biographical Sketches of the Bench and Bar of South Carolina*, Charleston, 1859, I, 106-120.

[1]

mother's maiden name, Loughton. On February 1, 1804, in the columns of the *Courier*, a newspaper just commenced to revive the drooping spirits of the Federalist party, he announced that henceforth he would be known as William Loughton Smith.[5] The name was undoubtedly in honor of his mother, yet it must have also reflected devotion to the memory of his beloved elder brother, Thomas Loughton, who died in 1773 at the age of thirty-three. Perhaps, too, in 1804 plain William Smith was simply too plain. For a Federalist in the days of Jefferson, "William Loughton Smith" had an aristocratic ring, suggesting something of defiance of the new order.

THROUGH HIS FATHER, William Smith was descended from the Schenckingh-Smiths, a family which represented in Carolina the crossing of two lines of colonial migration. The Schenckinghs were planters who had come from Barbados; the Smiths were merchants and ship captains from New England.

Carolina was an off-shoot of British West Indian colonization. Although the English had not made their first settlement in the West Indies until 1624, some of their islands, particularly Barbados, felt the pressure of population upon land by the middle of the 1640's. Migration from Barbados was first to the neighboring islands of Antigua, Montserrat, and Tobago and, after 1655, to Jamaica. The plight of the planters grew worse after the Restoration. By the Navigation Act of 1660 sugar was placed on the enumerated list, which meant that it, from then on, had to be shipped directly to England. The home market was to be reserved for the English colonies, but this advantage for Barbados was diminished by the mounting competition from Jamaica. Labor costs were rising, as the African Company had been given a monopoly of the slave trade in 1660, and the second Anglo-Dutch War (1664-1667) cut off their supplies and thereby increased costs. The planters, faced with these conditions, could profit only if they merged their holdings into larger units. A writer in 1667 explained that at least 12,000 former landholders and tradesmen had gone off, "wormed out of theire small settlements by theire more suttle and greedy neighbours."[6]

John Colleton and John Yeamans were two of these planters

[5] *Charleston Courier*, February 1, 1804. In keeping with this, the author refers to him as William Smith until 1804, and William Loughton Smith from then on.

[6] Vincent T. Harlow, *A History of Barbados, 1625-1685*, Oxford, 1926, p. 340. Richard Pares, *Merchants and Planters*, Cambridge, 1960, pp. 4, 16-17. The legislature of Barbados tried to halt this process by an act against depopu-

looking for fresh lands. They had fought for the King in the 1640's and had fled to Barbados in the 1650's. They therefore became in the early 1660's claimants at court.[7] As petitioners of the Crown, the Barbadians came in touch quite naturally with noble patrons such as George Monck, Duke of Albemarle, and Edward Hyde, Earl of Clarendon, as well as the rising statesman, Sir Anthony Ashley Cooper. The result of this combination of forces was the granting of the Carolina Charters of 1663 and 1665. The real fruit, however, was the founding of Charles Town in 1670.

The expedition to settle Charles Town sailed from England in the late summer of 1669, stopped at Barbados to pick up Sir John Yeamans and others, and arrived at the mouth of the Ashley River in the spring of 1670.[8] This route, which swung down through the region of the northeast trades to touch the West Indian Islands before catching the Gulf Stream, was the customary one for vessels sailing to America. In 1679 and 1680 another group of Barbadian planters came to Carolina; many of them settled on Goose Creek, the first important settlement outside of Charles Town. Among these planters was Bernard Schenckingh. His growing family and the distressing condition of the island's economy must have forced him to undertake a move to fresher lands. His plans were deliberate (a contemporary described him as "sharpsighted and a wise fox"), and good land along Goose Creek was obtained prior to his departure.[9] According to the records of St. Michael's Parish, Barbados, his daughter Elizabeth, who was to be the maternal ancestor of the Smiths of Carolina, was eight years old at the time of her baptism in January 1679. In the spring of 1751, when Elizabeth Schenckingh Smith died, the *South-Carolina Gazette* noted that she was in her eighty-first year, having lived upwards of seventy years in the province "with an unblemished Reputation."[10] It is from

---

lation in 1671, *ibid.*, p. 19. For the effect of the navigation act of 1660, *see ibid.*, p. 26.

[7] For the tendency of the leaders to migrate, *see ibid.*, p. 17. John Colleton was created a baronet after the Restoration. "The Colleton Family in South Carolina," *SCHGM*, I (1900), 327. John Yeamans was created a baronet on January 12, 1665. John Andrew Doyle, "Sir John Yeamans," *DNB.*

[8] Sir John Yeamans actually left the expedition in Bermuda. Edward McCrady, *The History of South Carolina under the Proprietary Government, 1670-1719*, New York, 1897, pp. 123-124.

[9] McCrady, *op. cit.*, pp. 182, 327-329. *Warrants for Lands in South Carolina, 1672-1679*, ed. A. S. Salley, Jr., Columbia, 1910, p. 202. John Stewart to William Dunlop, June 23, 1690, *SCHGM*, XXXII (1931), 97.

[10] *The Original Lists of Persons of Quality*, ed. John Camden Hotten, New York, 1931, p. 490. *South-Carolina Gazette*, April 8, 1751.

such fragments that the story of the Schenckinghs must be pieced together.

The Schenckinghs quickly assumed a place of importance among the Carolina planters. Bernard Schenckingh's lands, which extended along the north side of Goose Creek, amounted to several thousand acres. When the colony was divided in 1682 into the three counties of Craven, Berkeley, and Colleton, Schenckingh was appointed sheriff of Berkeley, the county in which his lands lay.[11] His son Benjamin, when the Anglican Church was established in 1706, gave a hundred acres as a glebe for the parish of St. James Goose Creek, and in 1712 he presented the communion plate.[12] The Schenckinghs were Anglican planters whose position was high enough to command a seat at the council board, Benjamin being appointed to this honor before the end of the proprietary period.[13]

As SOON AS the planters produced enough to export, the merchants appeared—some from the islands, some from England, and some from the northern colonies. New England, after the breaking of the home market in 1640 at the end of the Great Migration, had found the West Indies the answer to her trade problems; it was there that New Englanders obtained coin and commodities to exchange for English goods. They peddled the products of the New England farm, forest, and sea in the islands, stopping also to trade in the southern continental colonies. Thomas Smith, merchant and victualer of Charles Town, Massachusetts, was one of those who sent his sons to weave a web of commerce across the southern seas. Thomas Smith, who had married Sarah Boylston in 1662, had three sons who grew to manhood. William for many years ran a business house in Nevis, although he ultimately returned to Boston, where his granddaughter Abigail was to meet and marry John Adams. John was a mariner who died in Jamaica. Thomas, the eldest, was a captain, who in plying his West Indian routes must have touched oc-

[11] Bernard Schenckingh in 1679 took out warrants for 1,950 acres and for "one towne lott in the Oyster pointe." *Warrants for Lands in South Carolina, 1672-1679*, ed. A. S. Salley, Jr., Columbia, 1910, pp. 202, 206, 211. In the 1680's he took out warrants for 1,466 acres and seven town lots. *Warrants for Lands in South Carolina, 1680-1692*, ed. A. S. Salley, Jr., Columbia, 1911, pp. 16, 24, 44, 59-60, 72-73, 146, 159, 202. According to the "Abstracts of Land Grants" these grants were laid out along the north side of Goose Creek. *Record Book*, SC Archives, XXXVIII, 64, 222. McCrady, *op. cit.*, p. 237.

[12] Joseph Ioor Waring, *St. James Church, Goose Creek, S. C.*, Charleston, [1909], pp. 7, 26. Benjamin Schenckingh received a grant of 1,040 acres in Berkeley County along the north side of Goose Creek in 1702. *Record Book*, SC Archives, XXXVIII, 412.

[13] *CJ*, I, 130.

casionally at Charles Town.[14] There on June 23, 1690, he married Elizabeth, the daughter of Bernard Schenckingh.[15] The marriage was of but short duration, for Thomas died at sea on September 8, 1690, leaving his young wife with child. This child, a boy born on April 22, 1691,[16] and named Thomas after his father, was heir to Barbadian planters and New England ship captains, a fitting lineage for a native-born Carolinian.

Elizabeth Schenckingh Smith married again, and to the despair of historians and genealogists, her second husband was also named Smith.[17] William Smith was a factor, or commission merchant, probably a recent arrival from Barbados or Jamaica, islands with which he had close connections during his Charles Town career.[18] While Elizabeth Schenckingh's first husband was a ship captain who bought and sold for himself in each port that he visited, her second husband carried on all of his business in Charles Town. The role of the resident factor was more specialized and remunerative than that of the ship captain. The factor could give a ship a quicker turn-round by preparing her cargoes beforehand and staying to collect the outstanding debts after she had been dispatched. He could therefore charge a higher commission for his services.[19] William Smith assembled cargoes of skins and furs for England and provisions for the West Indies and sold the goods brought by the

[14] "Letters from the Schenckingh Smiths of South Carolina to the Boylston Smiths of Massachusetts," ed. A. S. Salley, Jr., SCHGM, XXXV (1934), 2, 12.
[15] John Stewart to William Dunlop, June 23, 1690, SCHGM, XXXII (1931), 97.
[16] "Letters from the Schenckingh Smiths of South Carolina to the Boylston Smiths of Massachusetts," ed. A. S. Salley, Jr., SCHGM, XXXV (1934), 12.
[17] For evidence that Elizabeth Schenckingh married twice, see n. 30 by Mabel L. Webber, SCHGM, XXXII (1931), 97. For a more complete discussion, see "Letters from the Schenckingh Smiths of South Carolina to the Boylston Smiths of Massachusetts," ed. A. S. Salley, Jr., SCHGM, XXXV (1934), 1-12.
[18] On March 4, 1693, Richard Walter, of Barbados, appointed his "Loveing friend William Smith Marcht:" his true and lawful attorney for purpose of collecting debts. "Abstracts from the Records of the Court of Ordinary of the Province of South Carolina," ed. A. S. Salley, Jr., SCHGM, VIII (1907), 202. On January 13, 1694, "William Smith, of Charles Town, merchant," executed a bond for Capt. George Duncan of Barbados, ibid., IX (1908), 75. On August 26, 1701, Smith filed a bill of complaint in the court of chancery for Jacob Mears, a Jamaica merchant. Records of the Court of Chancery of South Carolina, 1671-1779, ed. Anne King Gregorie, Washington, 1950, p. 75. Smith may have been one of the West Indian factors squeezed out by the changing economic situation in those islands. Both K. G. Davies and Richard Pares agree that the factors and merchants were disappearing, but give different explanations. K. G. Davies, "The Origin of the Commission System in the West India Trade," Transactions of the Royal Historical Society, fifth series, II (1952), 89-107. Pares, op. cit., pp. 33-37.
[19] Ibid., p. 30.

ships that carried them. The commissions that he earned permitted him to trade on his own and become a merchant in his own right, for he was usually referred to in the records as "William Smith, merchant."[20]

William Smith played an active part in the Assembly after it was set up as a separate house of the legislature in 1692. He was primarily concerned with matters of trade and navigation, assisting in the setting of the weight and value of foreign coins, the fixing of the pilots' charges, the protection of the wharves, and the making of Sullivan's Island "more remarkable to marriners."[21] The merchants in the Assembly eventually used their power to wrest control of the Indian trade from the proprietors. An act of 1707 setting up an Indian board to regulate trade named William Smith first secretary to the board.[22] Smith died in 1710, however, before the board began to function, so his name appears only three times in the official records of the commissioners.[23]

HISTORIANS AND GENEALOGISTS have debated whether Thomas Smith (1691-1724) was the son of Elizabeth Schenckingh's first or second husband. The facts clearly indicate that he was the son of the first, Thomas Smith the New England ship captain: he did not receive any property from his step-father;[24] nor indeed did he receive any property from the New England Smiths, but in 1714 he signed a release to any claim he might have had on his grandmother's estate in Boston.[25] His worldly possessions came from his grandfather Schenckingh, for Thomas Smith resided on a Goose Creek plantation the lands of which had originally been granted to Bernard Schenckingh. In 1718 he wrote to his uncle William Smith in Boston that he was then living in sight of his uncle Benjamin Schenckingh,

---

[20] *See* n. 18 above.

[21] *JCHA, January 30, 1696-March 17, 1696*, ed. A. S. Salley, Jr., Columbia, 1908, pp. 20-29. *JCHA, October 30, 1700-November 16, 1700*, ed. A. S. Salley, Jr., Columbia, 1924, p. 25. *JCHA, February 4, 1701-March 1, 1701*, ed. A. S. Salley, Jr., Columbia, 1925, p. 8.

[22] By section xxx of the act, Smith was to receive 20 shillings for each trader who secured a license and instructions and 10 shillings per day for each day he attended the commissioners. *SC Statutes*, II, 316. *Also see* Verner W. Crane, *The Southern Frontier, 1670-1732*, Ann Arbor, 1956, pp. 120-121.

[23] *Journals of the Commissioners of the Indian Trade, 1710-1718*, ed. W. L. McDowell, Columbia, 1955, pp. 3, 5, 19.

[24] William and Elizabeth Smith had six children. A. S. Salley, Jr., "William Smith and Some of His Descendants," *SCHGM*, IV (1903), 240. Thomas Smith (1691-1724) apparently possessed only Schenckingh lands. "Letters from the Schenckingh Smiths of South Carolina to the Boylston Smiths of Massachusetts," ed. A. S. Salley, Jr., *SCHGM*, XXXV (1934), 12.

[25] Thomas Smith to William Smith, March 5, 1714, *ibid.*, pp. 1-2.

whose home was the prosperous center of a community of ninety souls.[26] This uncle must have been more of a father to him than his step-father, for Thomas named his first-born Benjamin.

Thomas Smith confused the Smith family genealogical ties further by marrying Sabina Smith, a daughter of the second Landgrave Thomas Smith. His wife brought him lands in the parish of St. James Goose Creek, but Thomas was still a small planter approaching only remotely the status of his father-in-law who already had obvious claims to be a Carolina aristocrat.[27]

Thomas and Sabina Smith had three children: Benjamin, born in 1717; Thomas, born in 1720; and Anne, the middle child, whose year of birth is unknown and who died at an early age.[28] Little is known of the family life of Thomas Smith except what can be gleaned from a few letters written to his New England cousins. In 1718 he wrote of his quiet life in the country, interrupted occasionally by alarms of pirates on the coast and of Indians on the frontier.[29] In 1724 he wrote a letter of introduction for young Josiah Smith, Sabina's first cousin, who was then entering Harvard.[30] The picture is that of a planter living in comparative quiet with his small family amid an extending cousinry.

When Thomas Smith died in 1724, he left a modest estate of 4,000 acres and six slaves. Benjamin received the home plantation of 2,000 acres and two slaves. Thomas also got 2,000 acres and two slaves, while Anne was to have £700 sterling out of income from the estate, "if possible," and two slaves.[31] Benjamin and Thomas Smith, as heirs to land originally granted to their great-grandfathers Bernard Schenckingh and the first Landgrave Thomas Smith, were in the planting tradition, but they forsook the land for commerce as the best means of augmenting their small fortunes.

[26] Thomas Smith to William Smith, July 1, 1718, *ibid.*, p. 5.
[27] A. S. Salley, Jr., "William Smith and Some of His Descendants," *SCHGM,* IV (1903), 243.
[28] *Ibid.*, p. 244.
[29] Thomas Smith to William Smith, July 1, 1718, "Letters from the Schenckingh Smiths of South Carolina to the Boylston Smiths of Massachusetts," ed. A. S. Salley, Jr., *SCHGM,* XXXV (1934), 4-5.
[30] Thomas Smith to William Smith, junior, February 3, 1724, *ibid.*, pp. 9-10.
[31] *Will Book, 1722-1724, Charleston County, S. C.,* SC Archives, p. 307.

II

BENJAMIN SMITH, MERCHANT

THE SYSTEM OF COLONIAL TRADE in its purest and simplest form, especially in the staple-producing colonies, was controlled by three figures: the British merchant, the colonial factor (or commission merchant), and the planter. The British merchant who possessed capital would purchase manufactured goods at home and send them to the colony, preferably in his own ship. In the colonial port the factor received these goods and disposed of them to planters on a commission basis. The planter would pay for these goods with the produce of his soil—sugar in the West Indies, tobacco in Virginia, and rice or indigo in Carolina. The factor took these crops and freighted the returning vessel with them, for which he charged the merchant a commission somewhat less than for the disposal of his goods. The merchant in Britain ultimately sold the crops and replenished his capital. If the planter produced more than he bought, he might have large sums at his command in Britain. If, on the other hand, he bought more than he sold, he would be in debt to the merchant. These debts would be collected for the merchant by his agent, the factor.

The history of the factor is different in each of the three staple-producing areas. In the West Indies he largely disappeared. Planters who had survived into the eighteenth century were big enough to become absentee landlords, to live in England, and to deal directly with merchants. The disappearance of the factor and the absenteeism of the planter help to explain the loyalty of the West Indies during the Revolution. Sugar nabobs bought seats in Parliament and were in this way represented directly, not virtually, as some Englishmen believed the continental colonies to be.

In Virginia, tobacco planters never became absentee landlords, although some were big enough to assume the functions of the factor and to save the commissions for themselves. Factors were therefore present until the eve of the Revolution, always pressing the planters for the payment of debts.

In South Carolina, factors in many instances soon ceased to be factors for others and became merchants in their own right. There was a general tendency in the colonies for this to happen, but the likelihood was greater in the important colonial ports where many small rivulets merged into the principal streams of commerce. "Handling large sums of other people's money; knowing and seizing the opportunities for a good bargain; forced, very often, to take cargoes to himself and pay for them on the spot because it was so immensely difficult to get the planters to pay cash down, the factor—the agent of the merchant in Europe—was necessarily tempted to set up for himself as an entrepreneur."[1] Benjamin Smith was an excellent example of a factor who became a merchant.

BENJAMIN SMITH was quite fortunate when he entered the house of James Crokatt in Charles Town to learn the rudiments of trade, for he thereby attached himself to a rising figure in Anglo-American commerce. Crokatt was a principal merchant in the Carolina Indian trade,[2] he had West Indian connections,[3] and he was well-known in London. By 1738 he had accumulated a fortune, which permitted him to withdraw from the colony and set himself up as a London merchant. A number of Charles Town boys served apprenticeships with him in London, among them Henry Laurens, who even hoped to be taken in as a partner but was not—for reasons still unknown.[4] In 1748 Crokatt was instrumental in securing passage of the parliamentary act placing a bounty on the production of indigo; in recognition of this signal service to the colony he was appointed agent, a position he held from 1749 to 1756.[5] By 1750 Crokatt was rich enough to purchase a fine seat, Luxborough, in Essex, for £19,500 sterling and to spend £10,000 more on repairs and furnishings. Peter Manigault, who was studying at the Inns of Court, spent a week end at the new estate and after dining with twenty-five at his table thought Crokatt had "Grandour enough for his Money."[6] For over fifty years James Crokatt and after him his son-in-law

---

[1] Richard Pares, *Merchants and Planters*, Cambridge, 1960, p. 31.

[2] "Memorial of the merchants engaged in the Indian trade," July 4, 1735, *PRO*, XVII, 412-421. *Also see* Verner W. Crane, *The Southern Frontier, 1670-1732*, Ann Arbor, 1956, p. 121.

[3] Crokatt in 1737 shipped 80 tons of logwood from the Bay of Honduras to Europe. *Journal of the Commons House of Assembly, 1736-1739*, ed. J. H. Easterby, Columbia, 1951, p. 426.

[4] David Duncan Wallace, *The Life of Henry Laurens*, New York, 1915, pp. 15-19.

[5] Crokatt was paid £215/9/2 sterling for expenses in securing the passage of the act. *Journal of the Commons House of Assembly, 1749-1750*, eds. J. H. Easterby and Ruth S. Green, Columbia, 1961, pp. 52-53. Crokatt was appointed agent by an ordinance of the Assembly, June 1, 1749, *ibid.*, p. 276. Ella Lonn, *The Colonial Agents of the Southern Colonies*, Chapel Hill, 1945, p. 395.

[6] "Peter Manigault's Letters," ed. Mabel L. Webber, *SCHGM*, XXXI (1930), 272-273.

John Nutt were to look after the English interests, both business and personal, of Benjamin Smith and his family.

Benjamin Smith was "at Mr. Crokatt's" as early as June 1735.[7] His opportunity came in 1738 when Crokatt retired to London. Smith and Ebenezer Simmons, who had also been in the house of Crokatt, signed on February 3, 1738, articles of partnership with Crokatt, in which the three agreed to be equally concerned "in the trade and business of Merchandizing," the agreement to be effective for seven years beginning September 1, 1738.[8] Simmons, Smith and Company announced on October 19, 1738, the arrival of a very large assortment of European and East Indian goods just imported from London—blankets, linseys, scotch plaid, nails, hoes, spades, pickles, raisins, currants, shoes, gloves, and wigs. These were offered on the same terms that Crokatt had given. Produce would be taken in payment, but credit would also be given—though for a limited time since they were "unable to be longer out of their Money than 2 years."[9] A shipment arrived from London in April 1744 consisting of mahogany desks, tables, chairs, couches, and chests of drawers to be sold for good rice, at the market price, until the first of May next.[10] In 1743 they acquired a wharf with warehouse for the storage of rice received in payment while it awaited transshipment to England.[11]

In 1738, Simmons, Smith and Company had been made responsible for collecting the debts due Crokatt and for shipping the funds in specie to London. They retained James Wright as attorney to prosecute delinquents,[12] and another life-long association of great importance in the career of Benjamin Smith was thereby established. Wright was appointed attorney general of the province by

[7] *South-Carolina Gazette*, June 28, 1735. The earliest Benjamin Smith letter that has come to light is dated February 5, 1736. He was writing to his Boston great-uncle William Smith, hoping to establish commercial ties as well as to re-establish family ties. Benjamin Smith to William Smith, February 5, 1736, *Smith-Carter Papers*, MHS.

[8] James Crokatt's power of attorney was drawn in London, January 3, 1749, to George Austin, Henry Lawrence [Laurens], merchants, and Robert Raper, gentleman, to settle with Ebenezer Simmons and Benjamin Smith all affairs relating to the partnership of Simmons, Smith and Company. *Miscellaneous Records, 1749-1751*, SC Archives, pp. 92-94. Indenture of three parts made August 29, 1749, between James Crokatt by his attorneys, George Austin and Robert Raper, and Ebenezer Simmons and Benjamin Smith, *ibid.*, pp. 293-301.

[9] *South-Carolina Gazette*, October 19, 1738. *Also see ibid.*, June 9, 1739, March 12, 1741, and May 2, 1743.

[10] *Ibid.*, April 9, 1744.

[11] *Ibid.*, September 5, 1743.

[12] *Ibid.*, October 19, 1738, January 25, 1739, January 12, 1740, January 25, 1746.

Governor James Glen in 1744, a position he held until the Assembly selected him to replace Crokatt as provincial agent in London in 1757.[13] When Wright was leaving the province in 1757 he turned over his affairs in Carolina to his "esteemed friend," Benjamin Smith.[14] In 1760 the King appointed him royal governor of Georgia.[15] In 1767, when Wright needed nine slaves, Smith bought them from Joshua Lockwood and shipped them to Savannah.[16]

The partnership of Simmons, Smith and Company was dissolved on September 1, 1745, according to notice in writing reciprocally circulated among the partners.[17] The business connections of the three men were not, however, completely severed. They had already taken shares in one vessel and were to take shares in another after this date, taking advantage of opportunities provided by King George's War to buy vessels condemned in the local vice-admiralty court. On January 14, 1745, Benjamin Smith registered the two-hundred-ton *Flamborough Prize* which had been taken by HMS *Flamborough* from the French. The owners were Ebenezer Simmons, Benjamin Smith, William Hopton, Thomas Smith of Charles Town, and James Crokatt of London. Then on March 11, 1746, Benjamin Smith swore before Governor Glen and Collector of the Customs Hector Berenger de Beaufain that the brigantine *Charming Nancy* of Charles Town, "a square stern'd vessel of 100 tons," had been built in Rhode Island, captured by the Spaniards, retaken by HMS *Tartar*, and condemned in the court of vice-admiralty on June 6, 1745. Smith had bought the brigantine in partnership with Ebenezer Simmons, Thomas Smith, Edmund Cossens of Charles Town, and James Crokatt of London. The *Charming Nancy* was thereby registered according to the navigation acts, being American-built and owned by Anglo-American merchants.[18]

Benjamin Smith and John Palmer entered into a five-year partnership and announced in March 1747 that the new house of Smith and Palmer would be located on Broad Street. Smith and Palmer

[13] For appointment as attorney general on July 6, 1744, *see Miscellaneous Records, 1743-1746*, SC Archives, pp. 90-91. For appointment as agent *see JCHA*, XXXI, part 2, 18. *Also see* Lonn, *op. cit.*, p. 395.

[14] James Wright's power of attorney, July 15, 1757, *Miscellaneous Records, 1758-1763*, SC Archives, pp. 18-19.

[15] W. W. Abbot, *The Royal Governors of Georgia, 1754-1775*, Chapel Hill, 1959, p. 84.

[16] *Miscellaneous Records, 1763-1767*, SC Archives, pp. 729-730.

[17] *See* n. 8 above.

[18] *Ship Register, 1734-1765*, SC Archives, pp. 17, 319-320.

sold European and East Indian goods, including many fine "Brocades, Sattins and other Silks."[19]

By the end of King George's War (the cessation of hostilities was proclaimed in Charles Town in August 1748),[20] Smith had amassed a fortune which was probably in excess of £10,000 sterling. When the assets of Simmons, Smith and Company were divided as of August 1, 1749, each partner received £33,361/6/7 current money of South Carolina. The bonds still held by the company were divided into categories designated "good," "dubious," and "bad," and each category was then divided into three piles for which the men drew lots. In addition, Benjamin Smith held bonds whose face value was £42,866/12/3 on which there was no probability of payment, but, in case of any returns, the proceeds were to be divided equally among the three partners.[21] As the ratio of South Carolina current money to sterling was seven:one, Benjamin Smith received in 1749 well over £5,000 sterling as his share of the old partnership. Counting the capital he had invested in Smith and Palmer, in several vessels, and personal property, a conservative estimate of his fortune would be £10,000 sterling in 1749. Benjamin Smith was certainly by this time a principal merchant of Charles Town.

THE RICHEST of the Carolina merchants were often importers of slaves, and the most successful of the early slave merchants were the brothers Samuel and Joseph Wragg. With the great expansion of rice culture in the 1730's the demand for slaves had risen rapidly.[22] Out of sixty-seven cargoes of slaves advertised in the *South-Carolina Gazette* from 1733 to 1740 the company of Joseph Wragg handled twenty-two, far more than any other house. Joseph Wragg's obituary in the *Gazette* June 1751 described him as "an eminent Merchant of this Town, who formerly dealt pretty largely in the Slave Trade. . . ."[23]

[19] *South-Carolina Gazette*, March 30, 1747, April 7, 1749, November 19, 1750.

[20] *Ibid.*, August 15, 1748.

[21] *See* n. 8 above. It took time to settle these accounts. In November 1746, Simmons, Smith and Company had warned their debtors to settle by January 1, 1747, or be sued. *South-Carolina Gazette*, November 17, 1746.

[22] *Documents Illustrative of the History of the Slave Trade to America*, ed. Elizabeth Donnan (cited hereafter as *Documents*, ed. Donnan), Washington, 1935, IV, 255. Elizabeth Donnan, "The Slave Trade into South Carolina Before the Revolution," *AHR*, XXXIII (1927-1928), 807.

[23] *Documents*, ed. Donnan, IV, 278-280, 296. *South-Carolina Gazette*, June 24, 1751.

At first slaves had been exchanged for rice, but by the end of the 1730's a system of credit had grown up. The factor gave the planter eighteen months' credit and promised to remit to England two-thirds of the value of slaves sold in twelve months' time and the other third within two years after the date of sale. The factor took upon himself the responsibility of making good all debts; this meant he had to give security (to have capital) in England in order to trade. Since his business depended on such security, it was imperative that he not impair his financial standing. Factors insisted upon prompt payment by planters.

By 1738 importations were running at the rate of 2,600 to 2,800 a year. The temptation of eighteen months' credit had been too much for the planters: "Negroes may be said to be the Bait proper for catching a Carolina Planter, as certain as Beef to catch a Shark."[24] Natural disasters caused the failure of two crops and put the planters in debt to the value of three crops. The solution was to levy a prohibitive tax on slaves, effective from July 1741. This was planned to halt the flow of specie from the colony and make it easier for planters to get out of debt. Another reason for this 1740 act was the Stono uprising of September 1739 which had enhanced the fears of a servile insurrection. The tax was to be in effect for three years. Four shiploads were imported during the latter half of 1744; then the prohibition was re-established in April 1745 for five years. The trade, however, was actually reopened in 1749 to remain open until January 1, 1766. The number of slaves brought in mounted year after year until in 1765, 7,184 were imported.[25]

In 1749 Charles Town was on the threshold of her golden age. Eliza Lucas Pinckney had so successfully experimented with indigo that Governor Glen was prompted to inform the Assembly in January 1748 that "our success in indigo seems to be certain."[26] Prosperity was assured by the granting of a bounty on indigo by the British Parliament in 1748. Indigo was an excellent complement to rice, for it was grown on high, dry ground, while rice took up the swamp and marsh lands. South Carolina thus had two great staples.

---

[24] A letter to Mr. Timothy, March 9, 1738, quoted in *Documents,* ed. Donnan, IV, 291-294.

[25] *Ibid.,* pp. 296-301. Elizabeth Donnan, "The Slave Trade into South Carolina Before the Revolution," *AHR,* XXXIII (1927-1928), 807.

[26] Harriott Horry Ravenel, *Eliza Pinckney,* New York, 1928, pp. 102-106. The governor's speech was printed in *South-Carolina Gazette,* January 25, 1748. Indigo was a difficult crop to prepare for the market, demanding great skill on the part of the planter. *See* Pares, *op. cit.,* p. 22.

With the end of King George's War in 1748 and the opening of the slave trade in 1749 the colony entered a new era.

Benjamin Smith wanted to take advantage of the new prospects and in Henry Laurens he had a good example to follow. Laurens, after arranging for security in the amount of £10,000 sterling in England, returned to Charles Town in 1749 and formed a partnership with George Austin. Austin and Laurens were ready to do business when the slave trade was reopened.[27] The early fifties were so prosperous that their business was almost on a cash basis. At least the Laurens firm regularly cleared its books by the first of each year (March 25 until the calendar change of 1752).[28]

Benjamin Smith made a trip to England in 1752 to make arrangements for extending his commercial operations. The affairs of Smith and Palmer were wound up during the winter of 1751-1752, which permitted Smith to sail with his family early in March 1752 on the ship *Edinburgh,* Captain Russell, for London.[29] Two of their fellow passengers were Joseph Pickering of the house of Inglis, Pickering, and Waxall, and James Lennox of the house of Lennox and Deas.[30] In the company of such merchants and with James Crokatt, his old employer and former partner, the Carolina agent in London, Smith's introduction to English commercial life was assured. Although it is impossible to discover what Benjamin Smith did in England, one may assume that he selected a new supply of goods, arranged for security, and perhaps, as an indulgence to his family, frequented some fashionable watering spot. He returned to Carolina in the fall—escaping the great hurricane of that year—to launch his new business. On December 11, 1752, in a three-column spread in the largest type—the boldest advertisement that had yet appeared in the *Gazette*—he announced the formation of BENJAMIN SMITH & COMPANY. A large assortment of European and East Indian goods,

[27] Henry Laurens to Foster Cunliffe, January 20, 1749, *Documents,* ed. Donnan, IV, 303-304. *Also see* Laurens to Wells, Wharton, and Doran, May 27, 1755, *ibid.,* p. 320.

[28] Henry Laurens to Smith and Clifton, May 26, 1755, *ibid.,* p. 318.

[29] While abroad Smith intended to put his house servants to work: "Mr. Smith has a good washer-woman, a seamstress, & 2 house wenches to hire, by the month or year." *South-Carolina Gazette,* December 20, 1751, March 2, 9, 1752. *Also see* Charles Pinckney to Peter Manigault, March 5, 1752, *Manigault Papers,* SCL.

[30] Joseph Pickering and George Inglis were closely associated with Smith in trade, especially in the purchase of prizes in 1757 and 1758. *Ship Register, 1734-1765,* SC Archives, pp. 150-152, 154, 163. James Lennox, William Lennox, David Deas, and John Deas were important Scottish merchants in Charles Town and close friends of Benjamin Smith. *See* will of George Seaman, "South Carolina Gleanings in England," *SCHGM,* VIII (1907), 211-216.

including silks and head-lace, was to be found at the store on Broad Street lately possessed by Smith and Palmer.[31] The new firm did not import slaves until 1754. Perhaps it took that long for the arrangements of 1752 to bear fruit.

In May 1754, Benjamin Smith and Company in conjunction with Benjamin Stead advertised two hundred Coast-of-Guinea Negroes for sale. In July, Benjamin Smith and Company advertised thirty "choice, healthy, grown slaves" from Gambia that had come via Jamaica.[32] The profits on these sales were high. Governor Glen wrote the Board of Trade on August 24, 1754, that the prices were £250, £260, and £270 currency for men, which was a great advance over the £170 and £180 of "some years agoe." And the more recent shipments had been sold "for ready money!" The governor continued: "As Negroes are sold at higher prices here than in any part of the King's Dominions we have them sent from Barbados, the Leeward Islands, Jamaica, Virginia, and New York. This I think is a plain proof that this Province is in a flourishing condition."[33] Under boom conditions all efforts were being devoted to the staples, indigo and rice. Corn and peas were no longer produced for sale in the West Indies or for consumption at home. In order to feed their slaves, planters were beginning to draw for provisions on the backcountry, which in the 1750's was being filled by a flood of settlers from the North. This crop specialization created a huge demand for slaves.[34]

The Atlantic community was never long at peace during the eighteenth century. Trade was highly speculative, and clever merchants learned to ride the waves of world affairs with infinite skill. During 1755 the war that had begun in the Ohio Valley between England and France was on the verge of breaking out in Europe, and the price of slaves skyrocketed. In a letter to a Liverpool company of September 26, 1755, Laurens noted that the four best men in a recent cargo went for £330 currency: "The nearer we seem to a warr the more mad some of our people seem to be after slaves."[35] Prices fell sharply in the fall, declining in one month from £330 to £275. This drop was due to the low price of rice, which was in turn due to a rise in the cost of insurance on rice being shipped to

[31] *South-Carolina Gazette,* December 11, 1752.
[32] *Documents,* ed. Donnan, IV, 310.
[33] Governor James Glen to Lords of Trade, August 26, 1754, *ibid.,* p. 313.
[34] Henry Laurens to Smith and Clifton, May 26, 1755, *ibid.,* p. 318.
[35] Henry Laurens to Thomas Mears and Company, September 26, 1755, *ibid.,* p. 334.

Britain. It was thought that a war with France or Spain would affect adversely the rice trade, for the market south of Cape Finisterre was an important one. During the winter of 1755-1756 Laurens for the first time found that he was unable to complete his remittances by January.[36] In March 1756 he was even forced to draw upon his security in Bristol to make remittances.[37] None of the 1,305 slaves imported in 1755 were brought in by Benjamin Smith and Company.

The spring of 1756 was a slack time. The war in Europe that was declared on May 18 in London was announced in Charles Town on July 3.[38] This news caused a temporary stop to trade. To make matters worse, a drought "almost totally demolished" the indigo crop and Negro provisions.[39] During this war, however, unlike the preceding one, trade continued to flourish; it even expanded after the seizure of French and Spanish colonies. Benjamin Smith and Benjamin Stead were lucky enough to hit the first upturn of activity. The cargo of the *Sylvia* from Africa was sold on October 7 and "went off something brisker than those that preceded."[40] News of the loss of Fort St. Philip in Minorca and Fort Oswego on Lake Ontario not only dampened the spirits of the adventurers, but caused prices to go down.[41] But these were temporary fluctuations. The ultimate prosperity of the province depended on the demand for rice and indigo, and as the war continued, that held up far better than expected. In fact, the demand increased, beginning in 1759 with the British capture of Guadeloupe; Martinique and Havana were taken in 1762, and these islands, too, became markets for South Carolina rice. The stimulus this gave to rice cultivation was reflected in the slave imports for 1760, when 3,740 slaves were sold, the largest number up to that time.[42]

In 1757 only four cargoes were advertised, and in two of these Benjamin Smith had an interest. On March 8, two hundred Negroes from Barbados were sold by Benjamin Smith and Company. The

[36] Henry Laurens to Law, Satterthwaite, and Jones, December 14, 1755, *ibid.*, pp. 335-336.
[37] Henry Laurens to Devonshire, Reeve, and Lloyd, March 3, 1756, *ibid.*, p. 345.
[38] Henry Laurens to Richard Oswald, July 10, 1756, *ibid.*, p. 357.
[39] Laurens and Austin to Robert and John Thompson and Company, July 24, 1756, *ibid.*, p. 358.
[40] Henry Laurens to Richard Oswald and Company, November 22, 1756, *ibid.*, pp. 363-364.
[41] *Ibid.*
[42] Elizabeth Donnan, "The Slave Trade into South Carolina Before the Revolution," *AHR*, XXXIII (1927-1928), 807.

prices were so good that Laurens referred to the sale as a definite indication of the rising spirits of the planters. Most of the Negroes were Calabars—a most unpopular type—and yet they sold for £280 current money, and most of them had been sold "for very short pay."[43]

In the summer of 1757 Smith formed a new partnership with Miles Brewton, his wife's half-brother;[44] the speculative nature of wartime trade demanded that the risks be more extensively shared. Smith and Brewton sold a cargo of Gambia slaves late in the summer of 1757, but not another until October 15, 1760, when they disposed of a cargo of three hundred fifty slaves from Angola at Ashley Ferry.[45] Thomas Loughton Smith, Benjamin's eldest son, joined the firm in 1761, and the new firm of Smith, Brewton, and Smith brought in two cargoes in 1761 and one in 1762.[46] At the end of 1762 Benjamin Smith retired from active participation in the firm, which then continued as Brewton and Smith.[47]

Although Benjamin Smith had withdrawn from active trade, he continued to lend his prestige to the firm of Brewton and Smith. During 1764 and 1765 Brewton and Smith was exceedingly busy. In 1764 the company handled three of the sixteen slave cargoes and in 1765 seven of the fifty.[48] Laurens, who had also retired, assisted Brewton and Smith by turning over the consignments he continued to receive from his English connections: Henry Bright of Bristol, John Knight of Liverpool, and Richard Oswald of London.[49] When Captain McKie brought in the *Jenny* with two hundred ninety-two slaves from Whydah consigned by John Knight to Laurens, with the understanding that they should be signed over to Shirley and

[43] *South-Carolina Gazette*, February 24, 1757. Henry Laurens to Capt. Thomas Hinde, March 21, 1757, *Documents*, ed. Donnan, IV, 369.

[44] *South-Carolina Gazette*, August 25, 1757. A. S. Salley, Jr., "Col. Miles Brewton and Some of His Descendants," *SCHGM*, II (1901), 131, 142-143.

[45] *South-Carolina Gazette*, October 11, 1760.

[46] *Ibid.*, August 1, September 5, 1761, August 21, 1762.

[47] According to the newspaper advertisements, Benjamin Smith retired in October 1762. The last advertisement of Smith, Brewton, and Smith appeared in August; the first of Brewton and Smith in October. The local practice was to put the senior partner's name first. Brewton and Smith had for sale in October Madeira wines and Negro cloth and in November "2 neat London-made riding chairs." *South-Carolina Gazette*, August 14-November 27, 1762.

[48] In 1765, Brewton and Smith were the third most active house, just behind Brailsford and Chapman with 10 cargoes and Middleton, Liston, and Hope with nine. *Documents*, ed. Donnan, IV, 386, 411-413.

[49] Laurens wrote Oswald on February 15, 1763, that his partners had gone and that he was curtailing his business activities. *Ibid.*, p. 382. Laurens had purchased Mepkin plantation, a retreat on the Cooper River, from John Colleton, on June 4, 1762. Wallace, *op. cit.*, p. 125.

Martin if Laurens did not know of a better firm, Laurens bypassed the firm of Shirley and Martin for that of Brewton and Smith. Laurens favored Brewton and Smith because "of the Elder Mr. Smith . . . whose extensive acquaintance and ability in dispatch of business as well as influence with the Planters are at least equal to those of any other Man in the Province." Martin was a new man and then alone: "consequently not so capable of going through business of this importance."[50]

Martin might have done better if there had been no slave ships in port, but Laurens wrote that "when the *Jenny* arrived there was also in port the *Sally* of Bristol with _____ slaves on board for Brewton and Smith, a small cargo of 90 to Middleton, Liston, and Hope, the sales of both to come on within these eight days, besides several little scattered parcels from West Indies and more daily expected, as well as a cargo of 500 from Angola which B and S have late advice of and hourly expect its arrival." The implication was that Brewton and Smith and Middleton, Liston, and Hope were "too powerful opponents for [any] new house." There was something of a trend towards a monopoly. Laurens thought that "if all [slave sales] were confined to one house then that house could maintain prices much better and I am morally sure it will have that effect in the present case."[51]

By 1763 Benjamin Smith and Henry Laurens were among South Carolina's greatest merchants, both rich enough to retire from trade. Although the two had never been partners in the same house, they had always worked closely together. In 1757 and 1758 the members of the firms of Smith and Brewton; Austin, Laurens, and Appleby; and Inglis and Pickering had taken shares in five prizes purchased after condemnation in the vice-admiralty court.[52] By

---

[50] Henry Laurens to John Knight, June 12, 1764, *ibid.*, pp. 391-394.
[51] *Ibid.*
[52] Benjamin Smith took an oath on February 12, 1757, that the snow *Friendship*, 100 tons, was taken March 1756 from the French and ordered sold by the vice-admiralty court. The owners were Benjamin Smith, George Austin, Henry Laurens, William Bampfield, Miles Brewton, George Inglis, Joseph Pickering, Thomas Smith, junior, and Joseph Nutt. Henry Laurens took an oath on February 15, 1757, that the brigantine *Spy*, 40 tons, was built at Diton in Massachusetts in 1756. The owners were George Austin, George Inglis, Joseph Pickering, Benjamin Smith, Thomas Smith, junior, and Henry Laurens. Benjamin Smith took an oath on February 21, 1757, that the snow *Planter*, 100 tons, was taken March 1756 from the French and ordered sold by the vice-admiralty court. The owners were Benjamin Smith, George Austin, Henry Laurens, George Inglis, Joseph Pickering, Thomas Smith, junior, William Bampfield, Joseph Nutt, and Miles Brewton. Henry Laurens took an oath on March 30, 1757, that the ship *Cooper River*, 200 tons, was taken March 1756 from the French and ordered sold by the vice-admiralty court. The owners

1764 Austin and Appleby had retired to England[53] and Pickering had died;[54] Brewton and Smith was apparently falling heir to the interests of these other firms. Thomas Loughton Smith, Benjamin's son who ran the firm with Miles Brewton, married the daughter of George Inglis, thus cementing still further economic interests by marriage.[55] It was not that a monopoly in any strict sense existed, but business did tend to gravitate more and more to a favored few. There was a gap, gradually widening, between the great merchants and those of a lesser rank.

THIS TENDENCY towards control of the important branches of trade by a few can be seen in those areas where public business blended with private business. Benjamin Smith had taken a seat in the Commons House of Assembly in 1747 and had been elected speaker in 1755, a position which he still held in 1763.[56] He was therefore able to use political influence.

The story of the control of Indian presents is an interesting one. The Cherokees, entrenched in the "over hills" of the Alleghanies, and the Creeks, located in the region south and west of the mountains, were the chief danger to the colony and were being stirred up by the French on the Ohio and the Spanish in Florida. Peace with the Indians was essential, and it was bought by presents, paid for by Crown and colony. Each annual appropriation of the Assembly had its section of sums allotted for Indian presents. During the years 1756, 1757, 1758, and 1759 the biggest supplier of presents was John McQueen and Co. Second in the list, although for more modest sums, was Smith and Brewton. Other firms—McCartan and Campbell, Alexander Petrie, Laurens and Motte, Austin and

---

were Henry Laurens, George Austin, George Inglis, Benjamin Smith, Miles Brewton, Thomas Smith, William Bampfield, George Appleby, and Joseph Pickering. Henry Laurens took an oath on January 4, 1758, that the ship *Nelly*, 180 tons, had been condemned as a prize at New Providence. The owners were Henry Laurens, George Austin, Benjamin Smith, Miles Brewton, George Inglis, Thomas Smith, junior, George Appleby, William Bampfield, and the executors of Joseph Pickering. *Ship Register, 1734-1765*, SC Archives, pp. 150-152, 154, 163.

[53] Governor Thomas Boone wrote the Lords of Trade on September 14, 1762, that Austin wanted to resign his Council seat. *PRO*, XXIX, 241. George Appleby sailed from Charles Town in May 1764. *South-Carolina Gazette*, October 8, 1764.

[54] Pickering died in 1757. *Ship Register, 1734-1765*, SC Archives, pp. 150-152, 154, 163.

[55] The wedding was May 29, 1763. A. S. Salley, Jr., "William Smith and Some of His Descendants," *SCHGM*, IV (1903), 251.

[56] *Journal of the Commons House of Assembly, 1746-1747*, eds. J. H. Easterby and Ruth S. Green, Columbia, 1958, pp. 238-239, 402. *South-Carolina Gazette*, April 17, 1755.

Laurens—shared to a lesser extent.[57] In February 1759, a committee in charge of receiving accounts challenged the items supplied by John McQueen and Co. and Smith and Brewton.

> Your committee are not able to judge of many of the charges in all these accounts for Indian Affairs, unless they could see the articles to judge of their quality; and are farther of opinion that if the commissary was directed, whenever any Indian presents are wanted, to stick up a List (as near as he can judge) of the Articles, under the Watch House and Vendue House, supposing such list could not remain there above one hour before the things were to be collected and dispatched. The Public would reap a very considerable advantage by such a Method, and its Favours more equally distributed among the Inhabitants.

This demand was accepted by the Assembly and so ordered on March 15.[58] A tendency towards the control of this trade by a few firms was therefore thwarted.

The above-mentioned firms were also the principal suppliers for the troops. Lieutenant Colonel Henry Bouquet arrived in Charles Town in June 1757 with five companies of royal Americans and two companies of provincial troops raised in Virginia. These troops remained in South Carolina until February 1758. Although the pay and armament were furnished by Great Britain, the barracks and incidentals were to be paid for by the provincial legislature. Benjamin Stead supplied rum, duffels, and brown rolls and charged £6,643/5/9 current money of South Carolina. Smith and Brewton supplied blankets, rolls, and pepper for £2,350/10/4. James Laurens charged £1,772/5/10 for blankets and other articles; Inglis and Pickering £341/17/6 for rum, glass, and nails. At the same time John McQueen was charging £4,319/0/6 and Smith and Brewton £1,271/8/6 for supplies for the troops in the frontier garrisons of Fort George and Fort Loudoun.[59]

In order to pay his soldiers and to purchase food for them Bouquet had told his superiors to ship him specie, but he had been sent bills of exchange on London instead that had to be negotiated locally. Smith offered his services for a two per cent commission. Even at that figure, Bouquet wrote Colonel Hunter, Smith was "the only Man of Credit I could find that would do it." Bouquet, after waiting four months—from June to October—hoping for better

---

[57] JCHA, XXXI, part 2, 121-122. JCHA, XXXII, part 1, 214. JCHA, XXXII, part 2, 210-211.

[58] JCHA, XXXII, part 2, 115, 121, 160.

[59] Lt. Col. Henry Bouquet to the Earl of Loudoun, June 23, 1757, Papers of Lt. Col. Henry Bouquet, LC. JCHA, XXXII, part 1, 207, 211.

terms, felt that he had to accept, for the local merchants had "agreed together not to take these bills under 2 per cent." When the crops of indigo and rice came to market in November and December there would be available many bills on London making it even more difficult to negotiate his own.[60] Bouquet must have accepted Smith's offer for in December he was doing other business with Smith, securing funds to send to Governor James Wright for the troops stationed in Georgia.[61]

The evidence begins to mount up and reveals Benjamin Smith standing at the very center of Charles Town's economic life, more than a great merchant—a merchant-banker. The modern banker evolved out of the great merchant, but the merchant-bankers were rare in the colonies. Only one man apparently surpassed Smith's position—Gabriel Manigault. Henry Laurens wrote Samuel and William Vernon of Rhode Island on June 12, 1756, that "Mr. Manigault is a Gentleman [who] can at all times advance Sums of Money without any inconvenience to himself."[62] Gabriel Manigault had been public treasurer from 1735 to 1743, when he had been succeeded by Jacob Motte.[63] It was perfectly legal for the public treasurer to use the public funds for his private profit; this was in lieu of salary.[64] Manigault had first been banker for the province in a public way; he was in the 1750's its banker in a private way. Smith, Manigault, and Motte each had more funds readily available than any other merchant in the colony.[65]

In 1760 Benjamin Smith lent his name to the government. Parliament had appropriated in July 1760, £50,000 sterling to reimburse the colonies for expenditures made in supplying the troops. South Carolina's share was £9,624/10/10 sterling. James Wright, Carolina's agent, received it and deposited it with John Beswick and John Nutt of London who then permitted Benjamin Smith, Henry Laurens, and John McQueen to draw upon them for that amount.

[60] Lt. Col. Henry Bouquet to Col. John Hunter, October 16, 1757, *Papers of Lt. Col. Henry Bouquet*, LC.

[61] Lt. Col. Henry Bouquet to Governor Henry Ellis, December 10, 1757, *Papers of Lt. Col. Henry Bouquet*, LC.

[62] Henry Laurens to Samuel and William Vernon, June 12, 1756, quoted in Elizabeth Donnan, "The Slave Trade into South Carolina Before the Revolution," *AHR*, XXXIII (1927-1928), 815.

[63] *Journal of the Commons House of Assembly, 1742-1744*, ed. J. H. Easterby, Columbia, 1954, p. 312.

[64] See "value of the office of public treasurer in 1776," *SCHGM*, XIII (1912), 229-230.

[65] Manigault and Smith had been part owners of the ship *St. Phillip*, and Smith and Motte had been part owners of the ship *Charles Town*. *Ship Register, 1734-1765*, SC Archives, pp. 34, 38-39.

These gentlemen sold bills of exchange on London and turned over on May 21, 1761, £67,371/15/10 currency to the colonial treasurer, Jacob Motte.[66] Wright was Crokatt's old attorney and John Nutt was Crokatt's son-in-law—the connections that had been established in the 1730's still stood![67]

BENJAMIN SMITH was the greatest of the native-born Charles Town merchants. By the end of the Great War for the Empire, to use a more recent designation for the French and Indian War, Smith had accumulated a vast fortune.[68] As shopkeeper, Indian trader, slave trader, shareholder in several vessels, and banker, Smith's interests extended in various directions. Was he speaker of the Commons House of Assembly because he was rich, or was he rich because he was speaker? Neither question is fair. The two roles in a colony like South Carolina neatly blended together. He was one of a group, many of whom could retire at the end of the war. Benjamin Stead, who had married the daughter of Governor Robert Johnson, sold slaves with Benjamin Smith, and acted as colonial agent in Carolina for the English contractors supplying the army, was able to return to London in 1759 and establish himself there as a principal merchant. Some of his profit had been invested in rice plantations; the rest was put back into trade. His London home became a center for Carolinians traveling abroad.[69] George Austin and George Appleby, partners of Henry Laurens, returned to England after the war and set themselves up as country squires.[70] While there were those who went back to England, others like Benjamin Smith and

[66] JCHA, XXXIV, 73-74, 85.

[67] Joseph Hunter, "Familiae Minorum Gentium," Harleian Society Publications, XXXVII-XL, 745 (pagination continuous for the four volumes). Joseph Nutt, John Nutt's brother, was appointed by Governor Lyttelton commissary for all the forces to be employed against the Cherokees in the fall of 1759. Miscellaneous Records, 1758-1763, SC Archives, p. 226. Joseph Nutt was also a shareholder in two vessels with Benjamin Smith. Ship Register, 1734-1765, SC Archives, pp. 150-152.

[68] It would be impossible to give an estimate of Benjamin Smith's fortune, but it was vast enough to establish his family as one of the first families of South Carolina.

[69] Benjamin Stead, "an eminent merchant of this town," married Mary Johnson, daughter of the late Governor Johnson, "an agreeable young lady, with a sufficient fortune and other accomplishments to render the nuptial state perfectly happy." South-Carolina Gazette, November 21, 1748. For Benjamin Stead as contractor, see petition of Lt. Col. Henry Bouquet to the Assembly, January 19, 1758, Papers of Lt. Col. Henry Bouquet, LC. Stead and his family went in the fleet in May 1759. South-Carolina Gazette, May 21, 1759.

[70] Laurens visited his old partners in 1772, both of whom were living in Shropshire. Henry Laurens to James Laurens, May 13, 1772; Henry Laurens to Thomas Smith, September 24, 1772, Laurens Letter-Book, 1771-1772, SCHS.

Henry Laurens remained in South Carolina. Yet all the merchants looked for a step up the social ladder; their ideal was the titled landed gentleman.

WAS THERE NO STIGMA attached to those who had made their fortune in the slave trade? None. Pelatiah Webster, a Connecticut Yankee, Yale graduate, and Philadelphia merchant, was in Charles Town in June 1765 peddling "northward flour" in the southern market, which he finally sold through Thomas Liston of Middleton, Liston, and Hope. In the course of his stay he met most of the slave merchants, and rode, visited, and dined with Benjamin and Thomas Smith, but there is no hint from him of any stigma attached to the slave merchant.[71] Captains of slaving vessels, a rough lot, were welcome at merchants' homes, admittedly for the sake of the valuable commissions they controlled. Yet, if there were any stigma, it was upon the captains, not upon the merchants. One pleasant June afternoon Webster rode seven miles into the country with young Thomas Loughton Smith to visit "the country seat" of his father. In his journal Webster wrote that Colonel Benjamin Smith was "a Gent. of about 50, cheerful, easy & generous [who] has a great fortune & declines business, having turned over his mercantile affairs into the hands of his son Tho."[72]

[71] "Journal of a Voyage to Charlestown in So. Carolina by Pelatiah Webster in 1765," ed. T. P. Harrison, *Publications of the South Carolina Historical Society*, Charleston, 1898, p. 12. The partners of Middleton, Liston, and Hope were Thomas Middleton, Thomas Liston, and William Hope. Henry Laurens to William Reeve, October 2, 1767, "Correspondence of Henry Laurens," ed. Joseph W. Barnwell, *SCHGM*, XXVIII (1927), 212. *Also see* Langdon Cheves, "Middleton of South Carolina," *SCHGM*, I (1900), 260-262.

[72] "Journal of Pelatiah Webster," *op. cit.*, pp. 8-9.

III

BENJAMIN SMITH, SELF-MADE ARISTOCRAT

IN COLONIAL SOCIETY, aristocracy was quite frankly based on wealth, and the quickest way to the top was through commerce. Once at the top, however, the colonial began to think in terms of English society, and his dearest wish was to found a family. Thus marriage was the institution by which social position could be consolidated. Benjamin Smith and Thomas Smith, his brother, each had twelve children, more than half of whom were to marry and establish families of their own. In the expansion of these two family circles one can see the Carolina aristocracy forming and consolidating, a process which was well underway by the 1760's. Indeed, as one moves from the generation of Benjamin Smith to that of his children, one moves from self-made aristocrats to born aristocrats.

IN 1740, BENJAMIN SMITH married Anne Loughton, the daughter and stepdaughter of lesser colonial officials, William Loughton and Robert Brewton.[1] Edward Loughton, her grandfather, the first of that name in Carolina, was in Charles Town by 1684, possibly one of the English Dissenters.[2] He was granted a town lot in 1692.[3] In 1700 he tried to secure a warrant with Richard Tranter to search for and to develop silver mines "beyond the Appalesean Mountains."[4] In this effort he was certainly connected with James Moore, a leading Dissenter and principal Indian trader.[5] In 1706 and 1707 he was elected to the Commons House of Assembly.[6] Edward Loughton's wife, Sarah, died in Barbados in 1700. There is a family tradition that William Loughton, the son of Sarah and Edward

[1] A. S. Salley, Jr., "William Smith and Some of His Descendants," *SCHGM*, IV (1903), 244.

[2] Edward Loughton and his brother-in-law David Maybank were "house carpenters." Edward Randolph to "your lordship," March 22, 1699, *Records in the British Public Record Office Relating to South Carolina, 1698-1700*, ed. A. S. Salley, Columbia, 1946, p. 78.

[3] Henry A. M. Smith, "Charleston—The Original Plan and the Earliest Settlers," *SCHGM*, IX (1908), 25.

[4] "Memorial of Edward Loughton and Richard Tranter," *Records in the British Public Record Office Relating to South Carolina, 1698-1700*, ed. A. S. Salley, Columbia, 1946, pp. 194-196.

[5] Edward McCrady, *The History of South Carolina under the Proprietary Government, 1670-1719*, New York, 1897, pp. 347-348.

[6] A. S. Salley, Jr., "Members of the Commons House of Assembly, 1702-1711," *SCHGM*, XXVII (1926), 171.

Loughton, was born on board ship coming out from England. It may be that he was born on the first leg of a voyage in 1700 and that his mother died subsequently in Barbados.[7] William Loughton served as deputy provost marshal, 1721-1725, and died in 1727.[8] His widow, Mary Griffith Loughton, married on April 17, 1729, Robert Brewton, the son of Michael Brewton, who was colonial powder receiver from 1717 to 1745. Robert Brewton succeeded his father in this position in 1745 and held the office until 1759. Mary and Robert Brewton's son Miles Brewton, the great merchant, was Benjamin Smith's half-brother-in-law.[9]

Thomas Loughton Smith, Benjamin and Anne Loughton Smith's first child, was born in 1741.[10] He became a partner of his father and of Miles Brewton, whom he called uncle, in 1761. Two years later he married Elizabeth Inglis, a daughter of George Inglis, who was for thirty years an eminent Charles Town merchant.[11] George Inglis was closely connected in trade with Robert Pringle in the 1740's and with Joseph Pickering in the 1750's.[12] On at least six occasions he and Benjamin Smith had shares in the same vessels.[13] In the 1760's he set up his nephew Alexander Inglis in Savannah, where Alexander assembled Georgia produce for shipment through Charles Town. In the years before the Revolution Alexander Inglis and Thomas Loughton Smith were closely associated in trade. Alexander Inglis married a daughter of David Deas, who like Robert Pringle was a Scottish merchant long resident in Charles Town.[14]

[7] "South Carolina Gleanings in England," SCHGM, IV (1903), 288. Note on a family tree in the handwriting of William Smith in the William Loughton Smith Papers, RC.

[8] W. Roy Smith, South Carolina as a Royal Province, 1719-1776, New York, 1903, p. 412. The will, proved August 10, 1728, mentions his wife Mary and two daughters, Mary (later Mrs. Mathews) and Anne (later Mrs. Benjamin Smith). Will Book, 1727-1729, Charleston County, S. C., SC Archives, p. 118.

[9] A. S. Salley, Jr., "Col. Miles Brewton and Some of His Descendants," SCHGM, I (1901), 131, 142-143. For Brewtons as powder receivers see W. Roy Smith, op. cit., p. 411.

[10] A. S. Salley, Jr., "William Smith and Some of His Descendants," SCHGM, IV (1903), 249.

[11] Ibid. George Inglis died on September 6, 1775. "Records Kept by Colonel Isaac Hayne," SCHGM, X (1909), 222.

[12] Inglis made a trip to the island of Providence for Robert Pringle in the summer of 1746. "Journal of Robert Pringle, 1746-1747," ed. Mabel L. Webber, SCHGM, XXVI (1925), 24, 29. Joseph Pickering and George Inglis bought the schooner Spy, 46 tons, in 1754. Ship Register, 1734-1765, SC Archives, p. 133.

[13] Ibid., pp. 38-39, 150-154, 163.

[14] South-Carolina Gazette, April 5, May 31, 1773. Alexander Inglis married Mary Deas, April 27, 1773. "Records Kept by Colonel Isaac Hayne," SCHGM, XI (1910), 100. Also see "Petition of Mary Deas Inglis to the Senate," 1783, Confiscated Estates, SC Archives.

Anne, affectionately nicknamed Nancy by her father, was born on April 18, 1745. In 1763 she married Isaac Motte, the son of Jacob Motte, the public treasurer from 1743 to 1770. Jacob Motte was also a partner in the firm of Laurens and Motte, the Laurens being James, the brother of Henry.[15] This marriage established a family tie between Benjamin Smith and Jacob Motte, who were next to Gabriel Manigault the two biggest merchant-bankers of the day.

Susannah, the second daughter, was the first child to marry into a planting family. In 1775 she married Barnard Elliott who had extensive plantations near Beaufort—another center of rich planters.[16] Lord Charles Montagu recommended Elliott in 1769 for the royal Council. He took the oath as councilor on September 26, 1772, and attended the board with some regularity until November 1774.[17]

William, the third son (John, the second son, had died at birth), was born on October 2, 1758.[18] William's mother remains a shadowy figure. She died on February 29, 1760, after an inoculation for small-pox—just sixteen months after his birth. Catherine, her sixth child, was buried two days after her mother, having succumbed to the same disease.[19] The preventive was almost as dangerous as the disease in the eighteenth century. A lesser man than Benjamin Smith might have set his face henceforth against these crude attempts to advance medicine. He did, as he wrote Isaac Smith, ever after shudder at the very mention of inoculation, yet he was "well convinced of the propriety of the act from general experience."[20] This bespoke the sane and sensible temper of the man, one who could rise above personal grief, perceiving the general good. Such was the father of William, the father who was to have just twelve years to mold his son.

More accustomed to the ceaseless ebb and flow of life than present generations, Benjamin put his sorrows behind him and married again in the fall of 1760. It was on William's second birthday, October 2, 1760, that Benjamin and Mary Wragg, the daughter of

[15] A. S. Salley, Jr., "William Smith and Some of His Descendants," SCHGM IV (1903), 249.
[16] Ibid. The first Mrs. Barnard Elliott died in December 1774. South-Carolina Gazette, December 19, 1774. John Laurens to Gabriel Manigault, II, April 5, 1776, Manigault Papers, SCL.
[17] Montagu to Hillsborough, March 1, 1769, PRO, XXXII, 74. For his attendance see the Council records, CJ, passim.
[18] See page O.
[19] Register of St. Philip's Parish, Charles Town, or Charleston, S. C., 1754-1810, eds. D. E. Huger Smith and A. S. Salley, Jr., Charleston, 1927, p. 293.
[20] Benjamin Smith to Isaac Smith, May 24, 1764, Smith-Carter Papers, MHS.

Joseph Wragg, were wed.[21] This marriage joined two of the most important families engaged in the colonial slave trade, for the Smiths were the great traders in the 1760's as the Wraggs had been in the 1730's. In nine years this union of Mary Wragg and Benjamin Smith was blessed with six children. A boy and two girls died in childhood, but Judith and Mary, the oldest girls, and Joseph Allen, the younger boy, grew to maturity.[22]

Benjamin's brother Thomas entered trade in 1742.[23] Except for taking shares in vessels from time to time with Benjamin, Thomas followed an independent career, which by the early 1760's had brought him an equally large fortune. On August 2, 1744, he and Sarah Moore, a great granddaughter of Governor James Moore and a granddaughter of Colonel William Rhett, were married. Sarah Moore Smith bore twelve children of whom seven married and had families.[24]

Thomas Smith has left a pen-portrait of his growing family in a letter of May 17, 1764.[25] Roger Moore, the eldest son, was then at work by his father's side in the family "compting house." Roger had been for several years at the academy of a Dissenter in England but had returned at the end of the war, coming out in the first great fleet which brought so many new English factors to Charles Town.[26] Although Thomas hoped to retire when Roger reached the age of twenty on August 4, 1765, he remained active during the stormy scenes of the winter of 1765-1766, and in the spring of 1766 turned control of the firm over to Roger.[27] Shortly thereafter Roger married Mary Rutledge, the sister of John, Hugh, and Edward Rutledge.[28]

[21] A. S. Salley, Jr., "William Smith and Some of His Descendants," *SCHGM*, IV (1903), 245. The sisters of the second Mrs. Smith married Peter Manigault, John Poaug, William Wragg, and Christopher Gadsden. See Wragg genealogical chart in Henry A. M. Smith, "Wragg of South Carolina," *SCHGM*, XIX (1918), facing 121. Gadsden did not marry Anne Wragg until 1776. Robert L. Meriwether, "Christopher Gadsden," *DAB*.

[22] A. S. Salley, Jr., "William Smith and Some of His Descendants," *SCHGM*, IV (1903), 251.

[23] Thomas Smith to Isaac Smith, January 31, 1763, *Smith-Carter Papers*, MHS.

[24] Barnwell Rhett Heyward, "The Descendants of Col. William Rhett, of South Carolina," *SCHGM*, IV (1903), 38, 41-42.

[25] Thomas Smith to Isaac Smith, May 17, 1764, *Smith-Carter Papers*, MHS. The descriptions of the children that follow are from this letter.

[26] For further information on Roger's schooling see Thomas Smith to Reverend William Smith, February 20, 1766, *ibid*. For Roger's return see *South-Carolina Gazette*, February 5, 1763.

[27] Thomas Smith to Reverend William Smith, February 20, 1766, *Smith-Carter Papers*, MHS.

[28] Barnwell Rhett Heyward, "The Descendants of Col. William Rhett, of South Carolina," *SCHGM*, IV (1903), 41.

Sarah, Thomas and Sarah Moore Smith's eldest daughter, was "a child of a mild good disposition rather too bashful but it is a good fault." This child "with the red hair" married first John Mackenzie, who with Thomas Lynch and Christopher Gadsden was one of the early leaders of the patriot cause. On his death in May 1771 the *Gazette* eulogized Mackenzie as "that jealous, disinterested and unshaken Patriot—that true Friend to *America* and the *English* Constitution."[29] The widowed Sarah married on March 16, 1773, Thomas Bee, a young gentleman, according to her father, "that I think will make her and all of us happy."[30]

Peter, in his tenth year, had "a black complection, made more so by the sun" but was "good natured, lively and indeed very wild" and therefore would "require great attention." Peter was sent to the Reverend Jacob Duché's in Philadelphia for his education, but as he was destined for trade, was soon brought home to the family firm.[31] His wife was Mary Middleton, a daughter of the enormously wealthy Ashley River planter Henry Middleton. Charles Cotesworth Pinckney and Edward Rutledge also married daughters of Henry Middleton, so Peter, like his brother Roger, acquired connections with South Carolina's most famous lawyers and patriot leaders.[32]

Benjamin, with "red hair" and "freckled face," was eight in 1764. He was "a good natured passionate little fellow . . . the last we endeavour to rectifye and hope to accomplish it as he has a good capacity." The training at home and at the Reverend Jacob Duché's could not stamp out the passion, for Benjamin was the family's lone military hero. During the war he was an aide to General Washington and rose to the rank of general. After the war he settled in North Carolina; there he married Sarah Dry, whose father, although originally from Goose Creek, was for many years collector of the port of Brunswick and member of the royal Council of North Carolina. In time Benjamin became a United States senator and governor of North Carolina.[33]

[29] Sarah married John Mackenzie on April 3, 1769. *See ibid.*, p. 41, n. 3. *South-Carolina Gazette*, May 30, 1771.

[30] Thomas Smith to Isaac Smith, senior, March 29, 1773, *Smith-Carter Papers*, MHS.

[31] Peter was brought home in 1772. Thomas Smith to Isaac Smith, senior, April 11, 1772, *ibid.* John Pringle to William Tilghman, July 30, 1774, *Preston Davie Papers*, SHC.

[32] Barnwell Rhett Heyward, "The Descendants of Col. William Rhett, of South Carolina," *SCHGM*, IV (1903), 41.

[33] The inscriptions on the tombstones in the churchyard of old St. Philip's at the site of colonial Brunswick on the Cape Fear River still tell the story of Benjamin Smith and the Drys. Notes taken by the author.

James, though only three, was "a fine boy," and Polly, born only "last February," was "a fine girl." James, after studying at the Inns of Court, married Mariana Gough and became the father of the Smiths who changed their name to Rhett.[34] Polly married the lawyer, later judge, John Faucheraud Grimké and was the mother of Sarah and Angelina Grimké, the noted abolitionists.[35]

The children of Benjamin and Thomas Smith had married members of the most important local merchant, planter, and lawyer families. The Inglises and Mottes were merchants; the Elliotts and Middletons were planters; and the Rutledges, Pinckneys, Bees, and Grimkés were lawyers. In the 1760's the most prominent of the merchants, planters, and lawyers were being knit year by year more closely together by intermarriage. A local aristocracy was being formed, the members of which took pride in their new status. This aristocracy was not primarily a landed aristocracy until after the Revolution. Of Benjamin Smith's children who married after 1776, none married the son or daughter of a merchant. Judith married Captain James Ladson of the First South Carolina Regiment in 1778. Mary married John Gibbes in 1787. William and Joseph Allen both married daughters of Ralph Izard.[36] The Ladson, Gibbes, and Izard families were rooted quite firmly in the Goose Creek land.[37]

BENJAMIN AND THOMAS SMITH must have sold their Goose Creek inheritance to gain funds for a start in commerce, but by the time of their retirement they were once again plantation owners. In 1749 Benjamin bought seventy-one and a half acres on Ashley River seven miles up from Charles Town.[38] In 1765 Thomas Smith inherited Broom Hall plantation (eight hundred forty acres on Goose Creek) nineteen miles from town. Peter Taylor, who left it to him, was by the curious course of eighteenth-century marriages both an uncle

[34] Barnwell Rhett Heyward, "The Descendants of Col. William Rhett, of South Carolina," *SCHGM*, IV (1903), 42, 48-50. Laura A. White, *Robert Barnwell Rhett; Father of Secession*, New York, 1931, p. 4.

[35] The story of Sarah (1792-1873) and Angelina (1805-1879) has been told by Catherine H. Birney, *The Grimké Sisters*, Boston, 1885. Ann, the youngest child of Thomas and Sarah Moore Smith, was born in 1765 after the writing of the above letter. She married in 1783 Hugh Rutledge, brother of John and Edward Rutledge. Barnwell Rhett Heyward, "The Descendants of Col. William Rhett, of South Carolina," *SCHGM*, IV (1903), 42.

[36] A. S. Salley, Jr., "William Smith and Some of His Descendants," *SCHGM*, IV (1903), 251, 253, 256.

[37] McCrady, *op. cit.*, p. 327, n. 2.

[38] Benjamin Smith had bought the southwest corner of Henry Izard's Stock Prior plantation. At Benjamin's death Roger Smith bought it in. Henry A. M. Smith, "Charleston and Charleston Neck," *SCHGM*, XIX (1918), 42.

and a brother-in-law of Thomas Smith.[39] Benjamin and Thomas each had a house on Broad Street, and they divided their time between the town and the country. The annual sojourn on the plantations from April to August was for rest and relaxation; the remainder of the year was spent in town to attend to both private and public business. Thomas explained the extent of his retirement to his New England cousin in a letter of February 1766: "Not that I expect to be free from business, for the necessary care of a large family and raising an income from what Estate I have acquired with some services to the public will engross a good deal of my time while I am in Town which will be two thirds of my time."[40]

The Smith plantations were not worked for profit. Thomas wrote that he kept only thirty slaves, just enough to satisfy the needs of his family![41] The brothers lived off their investments; the largest part of their fortune was out on loan, commanding approximately eight per cent return.[42] They also owned tenements and warehouses which were rented[43] and acted as administrators of the estates of friends. Benjamin Smith confessed that he would have traveled more often except that he was kept at home by having under his care "large concerns as Executor to deceased friends."[44] Thomas

[39] Broom Hall had originally belonged to Benjamin Gibbes, but had passed by his second marriage to Amarinthia Smith, daughter of William and Elizabeth Schenckingh Smith. Amarinthia Smith Gibbes had then married Peter Taylor. After Amarinthia's death Peter Taylor married Ann Moore, the sister of Thomas Smith's wife. Peter Taylor left the plantation for life to Thomas Smith with reversion to his namesake Peter Smith. Thomas turned the plantation over to Peter in 1779. Henry A. M. Smith, "Goose Creek," SCHGM, XXIX (1928), 275-276.

[40] Thomas Smith to Reverend William Smith, February 20, 1766, Smith-Carter Papers, MHS.

[41] Ibid.

[42] For 8% interest see Bull to Hillsborough, November 30, 1770, PRO, XXXII, 402. The law was passed in 1748. SC Statutes, III, 709-712.

[43] Thomas Smith built brick tenements which he began to rent in May 1763. South-Carolina Gazette, April 2, 1763. Benjamin Smith had three brick tenements at the time of his death. Will Book, 1767-1771, Charleston County, S. C., SC Archives, pp. 831-837. Thomas Loughton Smith and Roger Smith owned the Bear Inn on the Broad Road, as the continuation of King Street up the Neck was called. South-Carolina Gazette, June 27, 1771.

[44] Benjamin Smith to Reverend William Smith, May 16, 1766, Smith-Carter Papers, MHS. The newspapers constantly reveal Smith acting as administrator. South-Carolina Gazette, February 27, 1744, February 23, 1747, January 24, February 4, 1761, February 24, 1767, July 11, 1768. When he left the province in 1763 he appointed Thomas Smith of Broad Street, Miles Brewton, and Thomas Loughton Smith as attorneys "who will transact any business for me, or the estates I am concerned for, during my absence." Ibid., July 23, 1763. Also see Records of the Court of Chancery of South Carolina, 1671-1779, ed. Anne King Gregorie, Washington, 1950, pp. 499-501, 505, 524. Benjamin Smith was one of three guardians of Sarah Izard, who was worth £50,000 current money at the time of her marriage to Lord William Campbell. See marriage settlement in Miscellaneous Records, 1763-1767, SC Archives, pp. 24-27.

Bee told Josiah Quincy in 1773 that Benjamin Smith had made "10,000 Sterling and more" in this way.[45]

Both brothers gave a great deal of time to the government of the town. Benjamin served as commissioner of the market, of the streets, and of the work house, and as firemaster.[46] These were civic duties which a man of his position could not shirk.

BENJAMIN SMITH'S POSITION in Carolina society can also be gauged by his prominence in the local Masonic movement. The Charles Town factors and merchants had cooperated in the introduction of Freemasonry into South Carolina. Solomon's Lodge of the Ancient and Honorable Society of Free and Accepted Masons was opened in 1736 and James Wright, James Crokatt, and Benjamin Smith served as masters of Solomon's Lodge in succession.[47] In December 1742 Benjamin Smith was elected provincial grand master, the highest office in the gift of the Masons.[48] For a number of years the Masonic movement languished, but it was revived in the 1750's when Peter Leigh came out with an appointment from England to be provincial grand master. In 1761 when Leigh died, Benjamin Smith was named Leigh's successor by Lord Aberdour, grand master of the English Masons.[49] Smith was installed on St. John the Evangelist's Day in 1761 amid impressive ceremonies. Benjamin Yarnold, the organist at St. Philip's Church, composed for the occasion a Masonic "anthem and an ode for voices and instruments."[50] The celebration of the feast of St. John the Evangelist became an annual affair surrounded by much pageantry. In December 1764 Lord Adam Gordon, Lieutenant Governor William Bull, and many other distinguished gentlemen accompanied Smith and the Masons to St. Philip's where a discourse was delivered by the Reverend Charles Martyn, rector of St. Andrew's, and afterwards the gentlemen dined together.[51]

---

[45] "Journal of Josiah Quincy, Junior, 1773," *Proceedings of the Massachusetts Historical Society*, XLIX (1915-1916), 448-449.

[46] Elections for these positions were held each April. Every April from 1749 to 1770 Benjamin Smith's name appeared in the lists. See *South-Carolina Gazette*.

[47] Albert G. Mackey, *The History of Freemasonry in South Carolina, From its Origin in the Year 1736 to the Present Time*, Columbia, 1861, pp. 10, 12, 16.

[48] *Ibid.*, p. 20.

[49] *Ibid.*, pp. 39-40.

[50] George W. Williams, "Eighteenth-Century Organists of St. Michael's, Charleston," *SCHGM*, LIII (1952), 149.

[51] Mackey, *op. cit.*, pp. 39-40. Smith indicated that he would resign in 1767. Egerton Leigh succeeded him and was installed in 1770. *Ibid.*, pp. 42, 51.

The Masonic movement added color to the life of Benjamin Smith, but it was not a substitute for religion. Benjamin and his brother Thomas were parishioners of St. Philip's Church, and both sat for many years on the vestry. Thomas professed himself "an Established Church Man," yet he sent his son Roger to England to a Dissenting academy. For the average Carolina Anglican in the eighteenth century the differences between Churchmen and Dissenters were blurred and unimportant. Thomas expressed the common attitude in writing to his New England cousin, the Reverend William Smith, a Congregationalist: "for my part I look on the difference [as] of so little consequence that could I not conveniently communicate with the one I should with the other."[52] The proper course, as Governor Glen told the Archbishop of Canterbury in praising Alexander Garden for his thirty-four years of service in the colony, was to steer "between the dangers of deism on one side, and of enthusiasm on the other."[53]

Even though Benjamin and Thomas themselves steered clear of enthusiasm they revered and loved that passionate man, the Reverend Richard Clarke, who was rector of St. Philip's from 1755 to 1759.[54] According to Ramsay, Clarke "was admired as a preacher, both in Charles Town and London. His eloquence captivated persons of taste—his serious preaching and personal piety procured for him the love and esteem of all good men. When he preached, the church was crowded, and the effects of it were visible in the reformed lives of many of his hearers, and the increased number of serious communicants." While in Charles Town, Clarke and Mr. William Hutson, the minister of the Congregational Church, started a religious and literary society of which Benjamin Smith, Henry and James Laurens, Gabriel Manigault, Christopher Gadsden, and other distinguished gentlemen were members. "The Society met once a month in the evening at the houses of the respective members. One of the clergymen opened the meeting with a short prayer, and they then discussed some literary or religious topic which had been previously agreed on, without, however, being so strictly confined to it, but that other matters not inconsistent with the intention of the

    [52] Thomas Smith to Reverend William Smith, February 20, 1766, *Smith-Carter Papers*, MHS. On the academies of Dissenters, *see* J. H. Plumb, *Sir Robert Walpole*, London, 1956, p. 67.
    [53] Governor James Glen to the Archbishop of Canterbury, April 1754, *CJ*, XXIII, 183.
    [54] Frederick Dalcho, *An Historical Account of the Protestant Episcopal Church in South Carolina*, Charleston, 1820, pp. 166-184.

meeting might be introduced."[55] Clarke was an attractive and compelling personality, yet there was a rather curious streak in his nature, a mystical quality, for he was wont to foretell the end of the world. Governor William Henry Lyttelton described the Reverend Clarke's departure in a letter to the Lords of Trade, September 1, 1759: "In the month of February last the Reverend Mr. Clarke, Rector of one of the parishes in this town, a clergyman of much learning but of an overheated imagination, preached some sermons in which he asserted that the world wou'd very soon be at an end, and that in this month of September some great calamity wou'd befall this province. At length this enthusiasm rose to such a height that he let his beard grow and run about the streets crying, Repent, Repent for the Kingdom of Heaven is at hand, but on the 25th of March he resigned his Benefice and embarked for England."[56] In spite of this rather odd exit Benjamin Smith obviously still respected the Reverend Richard Clarke, for in 1770 he sent his son William to live and study in his home near London.[57]

Besides being a longtime parishioner of St. Philip's, Benjamin Smith was one of the principal founders of St. Michael's. In 1751 it had been necessary to divide the expanding town into two parishes. The lower half of the city was carved out of St. Philip's Parish to form the parish of St. Michael, named perhaps after the Barbadian parish from which many Carolinians had originally come. Benjamin Smith was on the board of commissioners to superintend the building of St. Michael's Church on the site of the first St. Philip's, and the subscription lists for pews were kept at his home on Broad Street.[58] In 1759 he was elected to the vestry of the new parish, but declined to serve, having on the same day been elected once again to the vestry of St. Philip's.[59] Smith was as interested in the beauty of the service as he was in the stateliness of the church edifice; in 1752 while abroad he secured the services of Benjamin Yarnold as organist for St. Philip's. Yarnold returned to South Carolina with Smith and remained at St. Philip's until 1764 when he

[55] David Ramsay, *History of South Carolina, From its First Settlement in 1670 to the Year 1808*, Newberry, 1858, II, 251.
[56] Lyttelton to Lords of Trade, September 1, 1759, *PRO*, XXVIII, 213.
[57] *See* Chapter V.
[58] George W. Williams, *St. Michael's, Charleston, 1751-1951*, Columbia, 1951, pp. 13, 129-130.
[59] *Ibid.*, pp. 16-17.

moved to St. Michael's.[60] In his will Smith left £50 sterling as a subscription to buy a new organ for St. Philip's.[61]

HAVING ATTAINED AFFLUENCE by their own efforts, Benjamin and Thomas Smith sought to establish their family's claim to respectability and social prominence. In an attempt to unravel their lineage, they again got in touch with their Boston cousins after a silence of twenty-six years. Thomas wrote Isaac Smith of Boston on April 17, 1762, that he and Benjamin had taken the coat of arms of their mother's father, the second Landgrave Thomas Smith, who, there was "good reason to believe," was "of the same Family as my Father's father,"[62] and in July 1763, as soon as peace was declared after the French and Indian War, Benjamin set sail with his family for New England to meet their cousins and find out more about their family.[63]

In Boston Smith "enjoyed the company of so many relations," and he moved among men of his own rank. Captain John Erving was one of the most eminent merchants and a member of the Council for twenty years. His son, John Erving, junior, who married a daughter of Governor William Shirley, was a mandamus councilor in 1774 and an addresser of Hutchinson in the same year. Both Henry Lloyd and Ralph Inman were addressers of Gage in 1775, and Mr. Hubbard and Mr. Gould were later loyalists. After meeting and mingling with these conservative Boston merchants, Smith returned by way of Philadelphia. He left there on November 11, and after a pretty boisterous ten-day passage ("Mrs. Smith was very sea sick during the whole voyage") arrived in Charles Town.[64]

At the close of 1763 Benjamin Smith had every reason to feel satisfied. He was able to live handsomely on returns from his invested fortune; through his large and growing family he was becoming connected with most of the important Carolina families; and in each sphere of local government he had held the highest offices. He was highly respected in the town, in the parish, and in

[60] George W. Williams, "Early Organists at St. Philip's, Charleston," *SCHGM*, LIV (1953), 87.

[61] *Will Book, 1767-1771, Charleston County, S. C.*, SC Archives, p. 489.

[62] Thomas Smith to Isaac Smith, April 17, 1762, *Smith-Carter Papers*, MHS.

[63] He sailed on the *Britannia*, Captain Saltonstall, for New England. *South-Carolina Gazette*, July 16, 1763.

[64] Benjamin Smith to Isaac Smith, January 21, 1764, *Smith-Carter Papers*, MHS. Benjamin had asked Isaac to thank the above-mentioned gentlemen for their hospitality. For the future careers of these men, *see* Lorenzo Sabine, *The American Loyalists*, Boston, 1847, pp. 274, 331, 371, 381, 426; James H. Stark, *The Loyalists of Massachusetts*, Salem, 1910, p. 298.

the province. Lieutenant Governor Bull had appointed him commissioner for building up the curtain line;[65] the parishioners of St. Philip's had repeatedly elected him to the vestry; for eight years the members of the Assembly had honored him with the speakership; and since 1761 he had been provincial grand master of the Masons.

When Lord Adam Gordon visited Charles Town during the winter of 1763-1764, he gained the distinct impression that the planters and merchants of Carolina were closely tied to the mother country. The most opulent planters really preferred to live in England, and almost all of the men of business had made at least one trip "home." His conviction was that South Carolina was much more firmly attached to England than were those colonies to the northward whose prosperity depended so largely on smuggling molasses and other contraband commodities.[66] If these were the facts of Carolina society and this the impression of Lord Adam Gordon, why then did Benjamin Smith and his family, indeed his whole circle of friends, take the path to revolution?

[65] *Miscellaneous Records, 1758-1763*, SC Archives, p. 332.
[66] "Journal of an Officer's Travels in America and the West Indies, 1764-1765," *Travels in the American Colonies*, ed. Newton D. Mereness, New York, 1916, pp. 397-398. Lord Adam Gordon traveled to the northward with Ralph Izard who certainly at this time preferred to live abroad. *South-Carolina Gazette*, March 9, 1765. When Izard made out a power of attorney to Peter Manigault on June 3, 1763, he listed himself as of the "parish of St. Paul Covent Garden in the county of Middlesex." *Miscellaneous Records, 1758-1763*, SC Archives, pp. 633-635.

IV

BENJAMIN SMITH, MODERATE PATRIOT

THE STRUCTURE OF SOCIETY in South Carolina, although far from being rigidly fixed, was hierarchical. At the top were the governor and other royal officials who found their principal local support among the Carolina members of the royal Council. Next came the merchants, planters, and lawyers, largely native-born, who spoke through the Commons House of Assembly. The voice of the mechanics, just beginning to be audible, came out of the taverns and from under the Liberty Tree. Last, and virtually unheard, were the farmers in the backcountry, Indians on the frontier, and slaves in the fields.

The Revolution in South Carolina is the story of the separation of a Carolina society from a British society. The patriot leaders of the merchant, planter, and lawyer class drove out the royal placemen (most of whom by the eve of the Revolution were British-born) and seized power for themselves. They skillfully managed to pull their society away from England without letting power slip through their hands to mechanics, farmers, Indians, or slaves. No Robespierre, no Toussaint L'Ouverture, no Lenin appeared! Yet the patriot leaders were themselves split into moderate and radical wings. The moderate men, mainly merchants like Benjamin Smith, desired self-rule, not in the interest of all men, but in their own self-interest. If self-rule could have been secured within the empire, they would have had no desire for revolution. The radicals—men like Christopher Gadsden—believed more sincerely in the right of all men to rule themselves. They were therefore willing to reach down and invite the aid of the mechanics: to risk all in revolution. Whether a patriot leader was a moderate or a radical depended upon his personal commitment, his view of human nature. The pessimist, who had little faith in the mass of men, was a moderate. The optimist, who believed that the majority was always right, was a radical.

The royal governors of South Carolina, from James Glen, who arrived in 1743, to Lord William Campbell, who fled Charles Town in September 1775, were placemen sent out from England. Glen, William Henry Lyttelton, Thomas Boone, Lord Charles Montagu, and Lord William Campbell were not an unusually able group nor were they very sympathetic to the aspirations of the self-made Carolina aristocrats.[1] The royal officials during the first half of the eighteenth century had usually been native Carolinians, but by the 1760's men were being sent out from England to fill vacancies.

The careers of Peter Leigh and his son Egerton offer the best examples of the fortunes of placemen. Peter Leigh came out in 1753 with a royal mandamus to be chief justice, replacing thereby Charles Pinckney, the father of Charles Cotesworth and Thomas Pinckney. The Pinckneys never forgave the Leighs. C. C. Pinckney recalled as late as 1819, "The removal of my father . . . carries me near to my first recollections."[2] Egerton Leigh, with the support of his father's influence, made his way quite quickly, becoming in swift succession surveyor-general (1755), justice of the peace (1756), councilor (1759), and judge of the vice-admiralty court (1762).[3] In June 1765 Egerton Leigh not only brought out the news of the Stamp Act but also a royal mandamus to be attorney general, replacing John Rutledge who held a temporary appointment from Lieutenant Governor Bull.[4] Plural office-holding was bad enough, but when it was common knowledge that Egerton Leigh had seduced his own sister-in-law (who happened to be the niece of Henry Laurens), such appointments became odious, and the British authorities could not be forgiven.[5] The Leighs deserve great credit for pushing the Pinckneys, the Rutledges, and the Laurenses along the road toward revolution.

[1] W. Roy Smith, *South Carolina as a Royal Province, 1719-1776*, New York, 1903, pp. 410-411.

[2] Charles Cotesworth Pinckney to _____, September 8, 1819, *Pinckney Papers*, LC. McCrady emphasized this episode. Edward McCrady, *The History of South Carolina under the Proprietary Government, 1670-1719*, New York, 1897, p. 36. Hale Bellot in his sketch of the Leighs tried hard to indicate that the Pinckneys were not disappointed, but he failed to convince the reader even with his own evidence. H. Hale Bellot, "The Leighs of South Carolina," *Transactions of the Royal Historical Society*, fifth series, VI (1956), 171-173.

[3] *Ibid.*, pp. 175-176.

[4] Bull to Lords of Trade, October 8, 1764, *PRO*, XXX, 200. Bull appointed John Rutledge on September 17, 1764, "during pleasure." *Miscellaneous Records, 1763-1767*, SC Archives, pp. 155-156. The King issued letters patent to Leigh on January 31, 1765, in place of David Graeme whose position Rutledge was temporarily holding. These letters patent were passed under the seal of the province of South Carolina by Bull in the Council chamber on June 5, 1765. *Ibid.*, pp. 277-278. Leigh had just arrived in June from England. *South-Carolina Gazette*, June 1, 1765.

[5] Bellot accepts the story of seduction and admits that this cost Leigh the friendship of Laurens. H. Hale Bellot, "The Leighs of South Carolina," *Transactions of the Royal Historical Society*, fifth series, VI (1956), 175-176. Bellot states that after the seduction episode Leigh's law practice slipped into the hands of John Rutledge, who took his place as one of the leading lawyers. Leigh was appointed attorney general after this episode. *Ibid.*

A seat on the royal Council had been looked upon as a step up
for the members of the Assembly, but the expulsion of William
Wragg from the Council by Governor Lyttelton in 1756 brought
about a change in attitude towards the Council. William Wragg
had been appointed to the Council in 1753.[6] Since his father (Samuel Wragg) and his uncle (Joseph Wragg) had been members,
he no doubt thought in terms of an almost hereditary right to sit
in the Council.[7] Governor Lyttelton, however, could not tolerate
Wragg's outspokenness, and he removed him from office without
giving any cause.[8] After Wragg's summary removal none of the
local magnates would readily accept a seat at the Council board.
Lieutenant Governor Bull recommended as councilors in July 1760
Peter Taylor, Benjamin Smith, Gabriel Manigault, Ralph Izard,
Henry Hyrne, and Rawlins Lowndes, "being Gentlemen of loyalty
to His Majesty, Estates in this province, well acquainted with our
Public Affairs, and of undoubted Integrity."[9] When Bull, however,
asked these gentlemen to accept a temporary appointment, all
declined.[10]

This attitude prevailed until the Revolution. Henry Laurens and
David Deas actually refused appointments by the Crown,[11] and
Henry Middleton resigned his seat in September 1770 after serving
for fourteen years.[12] Bull wrote the Earl of Hillsborough in 1770
to explain that it had been very difficult to prevail on gentlemen

[6] William Wragg was recommended by Lords of Trade to the King, December 22, 1752, PRO, XXV, 138. Wragg presented his mandamus to the governor
and took the oaths on July 3, 1753, JC, XXI, part 2, 498.
[7] Samuel Wragg was sworn as member of the proprietary Council in 1717,
CJ, I, 114. Joseph Wragg was a member of the royal Council. Edward
McCrady, The History of South Carolina under the Royal Government, 1719-
1776, New York, 1899, pp. 801-802.
[8] Wragg's views can be understood by reading the following documents:
Lyttelton to Lords of Trade, December 6, 1756, PRO, XXVII, 201-204. Lords
of Trade to Lyttelton, February 10, 1757, ibid., p. 251. Lyttelton to Lords of
Trade, June 11, 1757, ibid., pp. 279-281. The King confirmed the suspension
on December 6, 1757, ibid., pp. 326, 329-330, 338. Lyttelton merely asked
that a minute be placed in the journal that he had suspended Wragg. No reason
is given there. CJ, XXV, 404.
[9] Bull to Lords of Trade, July 2, 1760, PRO, XXVIII, 370-371.
[10] Bull to Lords of Trade, January 28, 1761, PRO, XXIX, 14-15.
[11] Laurens was named as a councilor in the instructions to Montagu, February 19, 1766, PRO, XXX, 309-210. For the fact that Laurens declined, see
Montagu to Hillsborough, March 1, 1769, PRO, XXXII, 74. David Deas was
recommended in Bull to Lords of Trade, May 16, 1764, PRO, XXX, 143-144.
Also in Bull to Lords of Trade, October 16, 1770, PRO, XXXII, 337. The
Lords of Trade recommended Deas to the King, April 26, 1771, PRO, XXXIII,
6. For Deas's reluctance to accept, see Montagu to Hillsborough, September
26, 1771, PRO, XXXIII, 85.
[12] Middleton's resignation letter, dated September 14, 1770, was read before
the Council, September 19, 1770, CJ, XXXV, 156.

of spirit and ability to accept a seat at the Council board ever since William Wragg had been suddenly suspended "without any cause known here deserving of such mark of disgrace." Bull continued: "The Assembly pretend to justify the slight regard shown the Council, by their being a dependent body, removable at pleasure, that they must obsequiously follow the dictates of an imperious governor, or be immediately suspended; where if, say they, the Council were constituted like the House of Lords, Hereditary, or even for life, the Council might more safely be confided in." If the Council were "on a more respectable footing," the merchants and the planters would accept seats.[13] Thus in the 1760's the royal Council consisted for the most part of placemen.

THE PRETENSIONS of the Commons House of Assembly had grown with the increasing wealth of its merchant, planter, and lawyer members. By 1750 the Assembly had won from the royal governors almost complete control over the finances of the colony, the kind of victory that Parliament had won over the Crown in 1688. During the 1750's the Assembly was therefore busy consolidating and institutionalizing its growing power.

Benjamin Smith, as warden of St. Philip's Parish, had managed elections for members of the Assembly in 1742 and 1743, making returns to the Commons House according to the election law of 1721.[14] He first took his seat for St. Philip's on May 15, 1747, winning a by-election to fill the place of Alexander Vanderdussen, who had been appointed a royal councilor.[15] In each succeeding election until the time of the Stamp Act crisis Smith was returned from St. Philip's, although in 1749 he decided to represent St. George Dorchester when he was returned by both parishes.[16] His steady devotion to the work of the Assembly won him the

[13] Bull to Hillsborough, October 20, 1770, *PRO*, XXXII, 343-344.
[14] *Journal of the Commons House of Assembly, 1742-1744*, ed. J. H. Easterby, Columbia, 1954, pp. 7, 32-33, 464.
[15] *Journal of the Commons House of Assembly, 1746-1747*, eds. J. H. Easterby and Ruth S. Green, 1958, pp. 201, 238-239, 402.
[16] Elected January 7 and 8, 1748. *Journal of the Commons House of Assembly, 1748*, eds. J. H. Easterby and Ruth S. Green, Columbia, 1961, p. 9. Elected March 15 and 16, 1749, from St. Philip's and St. George Dorchester, *Journal of the Commons House of Assembly, 1749-1750*, eds. J. H. Easterby and Ruth S. Green, Columbia, 1962, pp. 4, 6, 11, 15. Elected October 22 and 23, 1751. *JCHA*, XXVII, part 1, 8. Elected October 29 and 30, 1754, *JCHA*, XXX, part 1, 1-2. Elected September [?], 1757, *JCHA*, XXXII, 3-4. Elected September 23 and 24, 1760, *JCHA*, XXXIII, part 2, 3. Elected February 9 [?], 1761, *JCHA*, XXXIV, 1-2. Elected December 28 [?], 1761, *JCHA*, XXXV, 1-2. Elected September 14 [?], 1762, *JCHA*, XXXV, 1-2 (second pagination).

temporary speakership in April 1755 after Henry Middleton resigned because of illness.[17] When Middleton was moved up to the Council board in the place of Alexander Vanderdussen, Smith was confirmed in his position as speaker at the next regular election in October 1757. Peter Manigault offered his name: "that as Mr. Smith had acquitted himself in that office to the general sattisfaction of the late Assembly" he took the liberty to move that Mr. Smith take the chair. Benjamin Smith protested "that there were several members in the House who had had longer experience in the Business of the Assembly than he had and therefore desired the Gentlemen would consider of some other person for this important trust." But the House unanimously approved, and Peter Manigault and Rawlins Lowndes, themselves to be speakers in succession to Smith, escorted him to the chair.[18]

Smith had the support and respect of the whole House. On one occasion when he had broken his arm in a fall from a horse and was unable to attend the Assembly in the State House, the members adjourned to the speaker's house to transact public business.[19] Smith was subsequently re-elected speaker four times, holding this position until the fall of 1763.[20]

As speaker, Smith endeavored to uphold the rights and privileges of the members as well as to pay proper respect to the governors. At the beginning of each General Assembly the speaker and the House attended the governor in the Council chamber where the speaker traditionally claimed the ancient rights of the members of the Assembly. Governor Lyttelton in 1757 was pleased to recognize "all their Ancient Rights and Privileges in as ample a manner as any of their Predecessors ever enjoyed them: particularly that they, their servants and estates shou'd be free from arrests and all molestation, that they should have freedom of Speech and have Access to his person on all proper occasions."[21] Smith's respect for governors was exhibited on two important occasions. On April 1, 1757, he broke a tie in the House, committing the House to offer a dinner

[17] *JCHA*, XXX, part 2, 417.
[18] *JCHA*, XXXII, 4-5.
[19] *JCHA*, XXXI, part 2, 126.
[20] Nominated by William Roper and elected, *nemine contradicente*, October 8, 1760, *JCHA*, XXXIII, part 2, 5. Nominated by William Roper and elected, *nemine contradicente*, March 27, 1761, *JCHA*, XXXIV, 3. Nominated by William Roper and elected, *nemine contradicente*, February 11, 1762, *JCHA*, XXXV, 3. Nominated by William Scott and elected, *nemine contradicente*, October 25, 1762, *JCHA*, XXXV, part 2, 3.
[21] *JCHA*, XXXII, 5.

to the new Governor Lyttelton.[22] Again in December 1761 upon
the arrival of Lyttelton's successor, Governor Thomas Boone, there
was a deadlock over whether the Assembly should draw up an
address to congratulate Boone on his safe arrival. Smith broke the
tie in favor of offering the address.[23]

The Assembly's desire to consolidate its power in the 1750's was
symbolized by the physical arrangements which were made to
house the Assembly. Benjamin Smith, who had been appointed in
1752 to the committee to draw the plans for the State House, took
an active part in overseeing the construction of this, by far the largest building that had been erected in the colony. It was ready for
use by the Assembly in March 1756.[24] His firm sold "crimson dam-
ask" for the chairs and "taffaty" for the curtains, and when it was
nearly completed, Benjamin Smith and Company ordered a gown
for the clerk, robes for the speaker, and a mace for the Assembly.[25]
The symbols of power were to be as grand as any possessed by the
English Parliament. The Commons House of Assembly obviously
wanted to keep abreast of all developments in their English model,
for Smith was authorized to purchase the printed journals of the
House of Commons for the State-House library.[26] Later he was
asked to obtain the more recent issues and an index, if one had been
printed.[27]

Smith was undoubtedly satisfied with the *status quo* as long as
he and his friends received the respect which their pretensions demanded. He was not a trouble-maker and therefore must have found
himself in an equivocal position during the controversy over the
election of Christopher Gadsden.[28]

When Governor Thomas Boone arrived in December 1761, he

---

[22] *JCHA*, XXXI, part 2, 88-89.
[23] *JCHA*, XXXIV, 271.
[24] *JCHA*, XXVI, 77; XXXI, part 1, 139, 149; XXXII, part 2, 200.
[25] *JCHA*, XXXII, 216; XXXIII, part 2, 336; XXXI, part 1, 128. The mace
was made in London in 1756, the year the new State House was completed.
It was of solid silver with a gold burnishing which carried the arms of the
House of Hanover and of the province of Carolina and cost 90 guineas sterling.
A. S. Salley, Jr., "The Mace of the House of Representatives of the State of
South Carolina," *Bulletin of the Historical Commission of South Carolina*,
number 3 (1917), p. 3.
[26] Smith delivered to the Assembly in 1756, 20 volumes of the printed *Journals of the House of Commons* and two volumes of Camden's *Britannia* and
charged the colony £49/18/3 sterling. *JCHA*, XXXI, part 1, 107.
[27] *JCHA*, XXXIII, part 2, 12. He was later paid £248/12/6 currency. *JCHA*,
XXXVI, 193.
[28] For an excellent recent article *see* Jack P. Greene, "The Gadsden Election
Controversy and the Revolutionary Movement in South Carolina," *Mississippi
Valley Historical Review*, XLVI (1959), 469-492.

brought news of the royal disallowance of the election law of 1759. As the Assembly then sitting had been elected under that law, Governor Boone dissolved it and called for new elections. When the new Assembly met, Boone was determined to stick to the letter of the old election law of 1721. Under cloak of his right to tender the oath to new members, he undertook to judge the qualifications of the members. The governor and the Assembly came to a deadlock over the election of Christopher Gadsden from St. Paul's Parish. Boone refused to tender the oath to Gadsden on the grounds that the wardens of St. Paul's, who had managed the poll, had not taken the oath required by the old law. The Assembly claimed that a special oath was unnecessary as all wardens upon assuming office swore to uphold the government and that this was sufficient. Moreover it was the undoubted right of the Assembly to be the judge of the qualifications of its own members. As neither side would give way, the governor once again called for elections. Gadsden was again elected, and the Assembly took his cause as its own. It based its right on "the known and ancient Constitution of our Mother Country," which right had been confirmed by the Charter of 1663.[29] When the governor still refused to bend, the Assembly would do no further business with him, and none was done from December 1762 until May 1764 when Boone was finally recalled.

It is impossible to fathom Smith's thoughts at this time. The one fact that looms large, however, upon the political horizon is that Rawlins Lowndes, not Smith, was elected speaker in September 1763. The explanation for the change was that Smith was "off the Province,"[30] but when he returned from New England, there was no attempt to make him speaker. Lowndes on January 4, 1764, went through the motions of returning the thanks of the house to Smith for his "constant attendance" and "faithful discharge" of duties which had been "to the Universal Satisfaction of the House." Smith thanked the Assembly for "the Great Honor" they did him, but this polite exchange was mere form.[31] Smith may have wanted to retire from politics as he had already retired from business, but there is also the possibility, and here it is impossible to be certain, that Smith was removed because of his moderation. It is evident that by the spring of 1764 the members of the Assembly were divided into moderate and radical wings. Benjamin Smith wrote

[29] JCHA, XXXV, part 2, 27, 42.
[30] JCHA, XXXVI, 12 (first pagination).
[31] JCHA, XXXVI, 4 (second pagination).

Isaac Smith on May 24, 1764, that there was a division in the Assembly over the proper attitude to adopt towards the Sugar Act: ". . . whether our Assembly will order the Agent to join the Nor. agents about the Sugar Act I cannot tel for *we are pretty much divided with respect to the effect it has on us.*"[32] Smith was still a member of the Assembly, but a moderate.

THE STAMP ACT CRISIS brought out more clearly the differences in attitude that existed at each level in the local hierarchy. The lieutenant governor and royal officials were determined, to the full extent of their power, to uphold the Stamp Act. Lieutenant Governor William Bull took the oath to carry out the law.[33] George Saxby and Caleb Lloyd, the stamp agents, meant to distribute the stamps.[34] The royal Council, the chief justice, the attorney general, and the clerk of the pleas were determined that all official documents should be stamped.[35] If they were not, the port and the courts would remain closed.

The merchants, planters, and lawyers took the lead in fighting the Stamp Act *with words.* Christopher Gadsden, a merchant, Thomas Lynch, a planter, and John Rutledge, a lawyer, were sent by the Assembly to the Stamp Act Congress in New York.[36] The journal of the Assembly reveals no opposition to the sending of the delegation although this apparently was not a unanimous action. Richard Barry, whose facts in his biography of John Rutledge must be accepted tentatively because of the almost impossible task of checking them, says that there were five dissenting voices.[37] Wallace, who speaks with more authority, documents his statement that Henry Laurens voted against the sending of the delegation.[38] Benjamin Smith's name appears in the record only in connection with harbor improvements; he was on a committee to prevent the harbor from being "choked up" and on another to plan a cut through the lands of William Elliot to improve the navigation of

---

[32] Benjamin Smith to Isaac Smith, May 24, 1764, *Smith-Carter Papers,* MHS.
[33] Bull took the oath before the Council, October 19, 1765, *CJ,* XXXII, 628.
[34] *CJ,* XXXII, 649-650.
[35] *CJ,* XXXII, 709, 727-765.
[36] John Rutledge in November 1764, while attorney general, had drawn up a list of legal documents that might be stamped and had sent the list to Grenville, yet in August 1765 he accepted an appointment to go to the Stamp Act Congress. Being replaced by Leigh as attorney general in June must have been an important factor in his change of mind. The list is enclosed in Bull to Halifax, November 14, 1764, *PRO,* XXX, 208-213.
[37] Richard Barry, *Mr. Rutledge of South Carolina,* New York, 1942, p. 100.
[38] David Duncan Wallace, *The Life of Henry Laurens,* New York, 1915, p. 122.

Wappoo Creek.[39] Despite the fact that all the merchants, planters, and lawyers did not approve of the Stamp Act Congress, their representatives were part of the Congress that drew up and sent to England four documents stating the colonial grievances.

The mechanics, aided by sailors in port, protested *by deeds*. When Peter Timothy printed in his *Gazette* news of the riots in Boston and Newport, the Charles Town mob took heart and in their search for stamps even ransacked the home of Henry Laurens.[40] When the mob did not distinguish between the homes of the stamp distributors and the home of a prominent merchant, the men of property had second thoughts.

The Stamp Act was to go into effect on November 1, 1765. The authorities, however, afraid to use the stamps, closed the port and the courts. It was very difficult for a whole society to sit still for four months waiting for news from England, especially when each incoming vessel brought sailors who were forced into idleness. Lieutenant Governor Bull had to call the masters of the vessels before the Council and urge them to keep their sailors on board.[41] The situation became more dangerous when Bull received news of an intended slave revolt. Since the slave trade had been forbidden after January 1, 1766, the merchants, trying to beat the deadline, had imported 7,184 slaves during 1765; this was three times the annual average. As Christmas—the dangerous season, since slaves were given a measure of freedom for festivities—approached, Bull found it necessary to call on the masters of the vessels again, this time to arrange for the arming of sailors in case of a slave insurrection. The insurrection did not come off, but runaway slaves hiding in the swamps might still have sparked a revolt. To recapture these fugitives, forty-five Catawba Indians were brought down from the frontier; armed with their scalping knives, they struck terror into the hearts of all slaves. The Catawbas tracked down seven slaves, were thanked by the Council, and sent home with presents.[42] It was above this seething society that the Commons House of Assembly dared to challenge the King by adopting the resolutions of the Stamp Act Congress.

On November 26, Gadsden reported to the Assembly the resolu-

[39] *JCHA*, XXXVI, 49, 165.
[40] Bull blamed the riots on the news from the North. Bull to Lords of Trade, November 3, 1765, *PRO*, XXX, 281-289.
[41] This was done on October 24, 1765, *CJ*, XXXII, 638.
[42] Bull to Lords of Trade, December 17, 1765, *PRO*, XXX, 298-301, and December 17, 25, 1765, February 27, 1766, *CJ*, XXXII, 680-682, 727.

tions agreed to in New York. The Assembly adopted a similar set of resolutions with only William Wragg voting against adoption. Some members, however, were absent. Among these were Benjamin Smith, who did not take his seat as a representative of St. James Goose Creek until January 22, 1766.[43]

Pressure was soon brought to bear upon the lieutenant governor and Council to open the port. Gadsden raised the question of whether the lieutenant governor had ever officially received the news of the Stamp Act, the assumption being that if he had not, he might disregard the act.[44] The governor had not been officially notified, but Bull consulted his Council, who by a vote of five to two advised him nevertheless to continue to enforce the act.[45] Merchants thereupon consulted Beaufain, the collector, and Peter Randolph, the surveyor-general of the customs, and discovered that ports to the north were open, clearances being given without stamps but with a "permit" for which the merchant paid what the stamps would have cost. The merchants petitioned that the port of Charles Town be opened on the same basis. The Assembly transmitted this petition to Bull and urged him not to listen to "a few Place Men" who had an interest in their opinions. Bull thereupon yielded and the port was opened.[46]

The next clash between royal placemen and patriot leaders occurred in the spring of 1766 when the merchants petitioned to open the courts without stamps.[47] Chief Justice Charles Shinner, an Irishman who had received his appointment through the influence of Lord Halifax's mistress, refused. The merchants thereupon asked Bull to appoint three new assistant judges. Bull issued commissions to Rawlins Lowndes, a planter, Benjamin Smith, a merchant, and Daniel Doyley, a merchant, who joined Robert

---

[43] *JCHA*, XXXVII, part 1, 15, 29-31. "American Loyalists," *Southern Quarterly Review*, IV (1843), 118. Benjamin Smith, who had long represented St. Philip's Parish, took his seat on January 22, 1766, for the parish of St. James Goose Creek. *JCHA*, XXXVII, part 1, 45.

[44] *JCHA*, XXXVII, part 1, 49.

[45] *JCHA*, XXXVII, part 1, 52-53. On January 27, 1766, the Council voted five to two not to open the port. Othniel Beale, Egerton Leigh, Thomas Skottowe, and John Burn most probably voted against; Henry Middleton for. Beale was a consistent supporter of the government over a long period. Leigh, Skottowe, and Burn were placemen. Middleton eventually resigned from the board because of disagreement over policy. The other two members present on this day were John Drayton and Daniel Blake, both natives of the province. One of them probably voted for opening the port. *CJ*, XXXII, 709.

[46] *JCHA*, XXXVII, part 1, 58-60.

[47] Gadsden presented the petition on March 6. The Assembly voted 19 to 15 not to take up the petition. *JCHA*, XXXVII, part 1, 79-81.

Pringle, a merchant, to make four assistant judges. None was trained in the law, but all were men respected in the colony. When the court convened on March 3, 1766, Thomas Bee, lawyer for the plaintiff, argued that a judgment should be entered in the records in the case of *Jordan* v. *Law,* as the defendant had not pursued his cause. The attorney general for the Crown, Egerton Leigh, argued that the judgment should not be entered, since stamped paper was not available. On the return day, April 1, the assistant judges voted to record the decision; the chief justice opposed. When the clerk of the pleas, Dougal Campbell, refused to record the decision, the assistant judges called upon a bystander to do so. The assistant judges then appealed to the lieutenant governor to suspend Campbell, but Bull after consulting his Council refused. Thereupon the assistant judges fined Campbell £100 currency, which fine the lieutenant governor immediately suspended. It was in the middle of this impasse that the news of the repeal of the Stamp Act arrived, clearing the air.[48] The chief justice was eventually suspended and his removal recommended by the Council, of which he was a member, for incompetence and ignorance of the law.[49]

On May 16, 1766, Benjamin Smith summed up his thoughts on the crisis for the Reverend William Smith:

> With what pleasure and satisfaction must every true lover of his country receive the late most interesting and agreeable intelligence, "The Repeal of the Stamp Act." England as well as the colonys have great reason to rejoice and be thankful that it pleased God to inspire the Parliament with wisdom to see the true interest of both. And may we in America rejoice, and be thankful to that God who ruleth the hearts of all men, and who was pleased to raise us up so many friends to liberty and our happy constitution—how must your Governor and all your high Prerogative Men, look now. Those I mean who were at all events for cramming down the Stamp Act and preached up Non-Resistance and Passive Obedience. Had the colonys submitted, they would soon have been—carried on from one degree of slavery to another—I hope we shall, I mean all the colonys unite in a general address of thanks to our most gracious Sovereign and to both houses of Parliament, and may each individual do all in his power to promote peace and quietness in our respective provinces—for I am afraid some of the lower class who have been made men of consequence in the late comotions, will

[48] February 27 to May 16, 1766, *CJ*, XXXII, 727-765.
[49] The Council on May 11, 1767, unanimously gave as their opinion that the chief justice "was ignorant of the Law and very unfit for filling the important office he was appointed to in this province." They advised suspension until His Majesty's pleasure might be known. *CJ*, XXXIII, 143-144.

not readily endeavour to promote peace as their consequence is now sunk into nothing.[50] This letter is excellent evidence of the three-part struggle within the colonies. At one extreme were "your Governor and all your high Prerogative Men" which in Carolina would have described the royal officials. At the other extreme were "some of the lower class who have been made men of consequence in the late comotions." This was a reference to local politics and was undoubtedly aimed at Gadsden and his mechanic supporters. In the middle were the "friends to liberty and our happy constitution," the group with which Smith identified himself. These three groups, placemen, moderate patriots, and radical patriots, were present in every crisis until the Revolution.

THE PROHIBITION on the importation of slaves was to run for three years. During the interim the Smiths reorganized their commercial interests. The partnership of Miles Brewton and Thomas Loughton Smith was dissolved in the summer of 1766. The stores at Bacon's Bridge at the head of the Ashley River, which had served as a country outlet, were sold, as was the twenty-ton schooner *Jonathan,* which was used to bring in country produce. Miles Brewton intended to make a visit to England and upon his return to set up for himself.[51] Thomas Loughton Smith joined with his cousin Roger to establish a new house behind which their fathers stood with large financial resources and advice.[52] This reorganization was accomplished in sufficient time to take advantage of the reopening of the slave trade on January 1, 1769. Laurens in anticipation of the reopening of the trade favored the new house of Smith

[50] Benjamin Smith to Reverend William Smith, May 16, 1766, *Smith-Carter Papers,* MHS.

[51] A good dwelling-house, front and back stores, convenient out-buildings, with 70 acres were for sale at Bacon's Bridge. *South-Carolina Gazette,* October 27, 1766. The schooner *Jonathan,* of 20 tons, was built in the province in 1746 and was registered on February 8, 1763, under the joint ownership of Miles Brewton and Thomas Loughton Smith. *Ship Register, 1734-1765,* SC Archives, p. 211. Brewton and Smith traded as far north as Portsmouth, New Hampshire. They continued to make use of the services of John Nutt in London. Brewton and Smith to Messrs. Moffatt and Meserves, September 30, 1768, *Miscellaneous Manuscripts,* SCL. Also see *South-Carolina Gazette,* August 18, 1766.

[52] In June 1767, Thomas and Roger Smith advertised a new Italian riding chair and a Windsor chair. *South-Carolina Gazette,* June 29, 1767. When Thomas Loughton Smith was going abroad in 1769, Laurens wrote: "He leaves in his absence two excellent substitutes his own and his partner's father." Henry Laurens to Henry Bright and Company, June 2, 1769, *Documents Illustrative of the History of the Slave Trade to America,* ed. Elizabeth Donnan, Washington, 1935, IV, 432.

over that of Brewton: "The connexions capital and application to business of those younger gentlemen together with the aid of their fathers and other able friends will give them an ascendant over some houses and enable them to do as much for the interest of their constituents in the African branch as any House in the place, both in obtaining good prices and making faithful remittances."[53] These fine prospects were blunted by a new crisis.

On July 2, 1767, Parliament, acting under the direction of Charles Townshend, placed a duty on lead, paint, glass, and tea which was to raise £35- to £40,000 sterling, part of which was to be used to pay the salaries of governors and judges where these officials had been dependent upon colonial assemblies. At the same time the English government overhauled its machinery for collecting colonial duties by establishing a board of commissioners in Boston with authority to supervise all customs officials in North America. In 1768 superior vice-admiralty courts were established in Boston, Philadelphia, and Charles Town—one had existed at Halifax since 1764—with each court having appellate jurisdiction over the local vice-admiralty courts in its district as well as an original jurisdiction.[54] It was this further reorganization of the old colonial system, with its increased burdens of new taxes and new officials, that pinched the colonials. Oliver M. Dickerson has pointed out that these new arrangements permitted the royal officials to engage in what he has convincingly labeled "customs racketeering." Many moderate merchants were thereby driven into the arms of radical leaders: John Hancock into the arms of Samuel Adams; Henry Laurens into the arms of Christopher Gadsden.[55]

The crisis came when Massachusetts sent out its Circular Letter of February 11, 1768, asking the other colonies to join once again in protest. With many merchants now feeling the brunt of the new system one would have expected South Carolina to act with more unity and dispatch. There was, however, much hesitation. Peter Manigault, speaker of the Commons House of Assembly, did not

[53] Henry Laurens to Ross and Mill, September 2, 1768, *Laurens Letter-Book, 1767-1771* SCHS.

[54] Carl Ubbelohde, *The Vice-Admiralty Courts and the American Revolution,* Chapel Hill, 1960, pp. 130-131. Augustus Johnston, the stamp distributor for Rhode Island who had been roughed up by the Newport mob, was appointed judge of the new superior vice-admiralty court in Charles Town. For his arrival in South Carolina, *see* Montagu to Hillsborough, May 25, 1769, PRO, XXXII, 76. Ubbelohde, *op. cit.,* pp. 150-151.

[55] Oliver M. Dickerson, *The Navigation Acts and the American Revolution,* Philadelphia, 1951, pp. 211-212.

reply to Thomas Cushing, speaker of the Massachusetts house, until July 30 and then only to say that he would not be able to present the letter to the Carolina Assembly until after the fall elections.[56] Charles Town mechanics, especially printers, painters, and glaziers, who were particularly affected by the new duties, were more eager to press for immediate cooperation with Massachusetts.[57] They made determined efforts to send men to the Assembly from St. Philip's and St. Michael's parishes who would reflect their point of view.[58]

When the Assembly met on November 17, public opinion in Charles Town was strongly in favor of supporting Massachusetts. The King's instructions to the royal governors to dissolve the assemblies if they discussed the Massachusetts letter, caught members of the Assembly between the threat of the dissolution by the governor and the mechanics' disapproval. The twenty-six members present thought they had a right to discuss the letter, so they did, and the governor consequently dissolved the Assembly. The "unanimous 26" won the plaudits of the multitude.[59]

McCrady notes that since forty-five were elected and only twenty-six attended, some must have stayed away in disapproval of what they knew would happen.[60] Wallace disagrees, pointing out that scant attendance, particularly at the beginning of a session, was not unusual.[61] The strongest point in McCrady's defense is that of the nineteen who did not sit, six actually appeared before the Assembly and refused to qualify: Joseph Allston, Peter Sinklair, William Wragg, John Freer, Rawlins Lowndes, and Daniel Heyward.[62] Wragg pointedly disapproved of the pressure upon the Assembly by the mechanics. Lowndes had been speaker, so his refusal to attend at this moment is odd. On the motives of the others it is impossible to speculate. Another point in McCrady's favor is that when, in 1772, Governor Lord Charles Montagu called the As-

[56] *South-Carolina Gazette*, September 12, 1768. Manigault received the letter from Cushing on July 26. See Peter Manigault to [Thomas Cushing], July 26, 1768, *Manigault Papers*, SCL. Manigault certainly wanted reconciliation. See also Peter Manigault to Peyton Randolph, August 23, 1769, *Manigault Papers*, SCL.
[57] Richard Walsh, *Charleston's Sons of Liberty, A Study of the Artisans, 1763-1789*, Columbia, 1959, p. 44.
[58] *South-Carolina Gazette*, October 3, 10, 1768.
[59] *JCHA*, XXXVII, part 2, 5-6, 9-22.
[60] Edward McCrady, *The History of South Carolina under the Royal Government, 1719-1776*, New York, 1899, p. 609.
[61] Wallace, *op. cit.*, pp. 155-156.
[62] The list of members with reference to whether they qualified or not precedes page one of the journal for this session. *JCHA*, XXXVII, part 2.

sembly to meet in Beaufort, a very difficult place to reach, thirty-seven of the forty-two elected members turned up on the first day.[63] It is apparent that although the Carolinians talked of the "unanimous 26" there was a division among the colonial leaders. It is worth noting that Henry Laurens, Charles Pinckney, John Rutledge, and Peter Manigault were among the "unanimous 26." Basically moderate in their outlook, their part in this episode is apparently one of trying to maintain control of the local situation—to guide and direct, to keep open alternatives, without being adamant and unyielding as a Wragg would have been. They were the politicians.

THE DIVISION between moderates and radicals was evident again in 1769 in South Carolina's attempt to set up non-importation agreements. Some of the merchants had looked forward eagerly to the reopening of the slave trade on January 1, 1769. The profits, however, were not as great as had been expected. Thomas Loughton and Roger Smith imported four hundred slaves direct from Africa, "but there were not," as Laurens wrote, "so many planters appeared as used in former days to appear at such sales nor did they discover that eagerness for buying as might be expected from the abundance of their crops and the high prices obtained for them." Thomas Loughton Smith feared that his sales would not average much above £31 or £32 sterling "and yet both cargoes were very fine and no house in town more capable of selling negroes to advantage."[64] Since preparations had been made and cargoes were expected, slave merchants were reluctant to accept the non-importation agreement of July 1769 which was finally engineered under great pressure from the mechanic class. Concessions, however, were obtained—the slave trade from the West Indies would be stopped only after October 1 and that from Africa only after January 1, 1770. A committee of thirty-nine was appointed to enforce this agreement, the merchants, planters, and mechanics each having thirteen representatives.[65] This committee began to put pressure upon all to sign an association promising not to import.

If some men like Wragg could not stomach an Assembly that

---

[63] Edward McCrady, *The History of South Carolina under the Royal Government, 1719-1776*, New York, 1899, pp. 697-698.

[64] Henry Laurens to Ross and Mill, March 31, 1769, *Laurens Letter-Book, 1767-1771*, SCHS. Roger Smith not only dealt in slaves but also had white indentured servants. *See* his advertisement for "a white indented *Servant Lad,* named Brunswick Cumberland Perry" who has gone "towards the back parts of the province." *South-Carolina Gazette*, September 26, 1768.

[65] Roger Smith was in the list of 13 merchants. *Ibid.*, July 27, 1769.

seemed to reflect the wishes of the mechanics, how could they listen to a committee on which the mechanics had a third of the voices and which was a completely extra-legal body? This committee was an innovation, an ominous development, for it was the first time that the mechanics had been given a formal voice. William Henry Drayton, the son of councilor John Drayton, wrote in the *South-Carolina Gazette* that no man who could "boast of having a liberal education would consult on public affairs with men who never were in any way to study, or to advise upon any points, but rules how to cut up a beast in the market to the best advantage, cobble an old shoe in the neatest manner, or to build a necessary house."[66] Of course, what Wragg and Drayton feared was that in opposing the royal authority, power might slip into the hands of the mechanics.

Christopher Gadsden and Thomas Lynch evidently did not share this fear for they were determined to keep the association alive. Bull described the two radical leaders:

> The first movers in the grand machine are Mr. Thomas Lynch who, tho' a man of sense, is very obstinate in urging to extremity any opinion he has once adopted. Mr. Christopher Gadsden is a very violent enthusiast in the cause, he views every object of British moderation and measures with a suspicious and jaundiced eye, and maintains with great vehemence the most extravagant claims of American exemptions. . . . These are the most determined leaders, and are meer tribunes of the people. At public meetings whether in taverns or under liberty tree, they direct the motions as they previously settle the matter.[67]

"Meer tribunes of the people"—that is what Drayton and Wragg did not want to be.

One of the central issues in the Revolutionary crisis was the question of representation. This question divided Americans from Britons; it also divided moderate Americans from radical Americans. Of the former division the Gadsden election controversy is a good example; of the latter the objections of Drayton and Wragg to the mechanics are good examples. Wragg connected the right to speak forth on public affairs with the right to property: "Had I no other resources than what a plantation afforded, I would endure every thing, rather than have the freedom of my will or understanding limited by the humors or capricious proscription of men not having authority."[68] It was his ownership of a plantation protected by the

---

[66] *Ibid.*
[67] Bull to Hillsborough, December 5, 1770, *PRO*, XXXII, 416.
[68] "American Loyalists," *Southern Quarterly Review*, IV (1843), 119.

natural right to property that afforded Wragg a platform. The King had to respect Wragg's right to speak forth as did the mechanics. This explains both why Wragg got in trouble as a councilor in 1756 and why he opposed the committee of thirty-nine in 1769. Gadsden, of course, could understand Wragg's opposition to royal authority, but he was willing to go further and listen to the voices of all free men. "Numbers" counted as well as plantation-owners. Gadsden was therefore willing to be a "tribune of the people." It was the importance of the question of representation that made John Wilkes a hero in America; it was the many-sidedness of that question that made it possible for both a Wragg and a Gadsden to see something of their own position in Wilkes's stand.

JOHN WILKES had had to flee England after the publication of the famous issue of the *North Briton,* number 45, in 1763. He dared to return to England in the spring of 1768, even though he had been declared an outlaw, and successfully stood for Parliament from the County of Middlesex. Afterwards Wilkes surrendered himself to the authorities and was lodged in King's Bench prison. A mob assembled outside on May 10, 1768, and when the troops tried to disburse the crowd, they were forced to fire, killing six. More notoriously, the troops who were chasing a ringleader, swooped into a house and cut down an innocent man in cold blood. English public opinion was horrified and rebounded to Wilkes's support. From America came a flood of letters and gifts.[69]

In February 1769, Parliament refused to seat Wilkes. Three times he was re-elected and each time they refused to seat him. After the second refusal the wealthiest supporters of Wilkes formed the Society of the Supporters of the Bill of Rights to aid his cause, mainly by paying his debts. Quite obviously Wilkes was championing the right of the people freely to choose their own representatives. In December 1769 the South Carolina Assembly, out of sympathy for Wilkes's cause, voted to send £1,500 sterling to the society.[70]

This gesture infuriated the King. On April 14, 1770, an instruction was sent to the governor forbidding him under penalty of removal from office to give assent henceforth to any bill appropriating money for other than provincial expenses, except on a special requi-

[69] For Wilkes's story *see* the appropriate chapters in Raymond Postgate, *That Devil Wilkes*, London, 1930.

[70] Edward McCrady, *The History of South Carolina under the Royal Government, 1719-1776,* New York, 1899, pp. 662-663.

sition from the King. This was a direct challenge to the Assembly's control of the purse. This contest between King and colony over the appropriation for the Wilkes Fund was never settled. Even after the repeal of the Townshend duties and the breaking of the non-importation agreement, this question kept the crisis in South Carolina simmering.[71]

DURING THIS SECOND CRISIS involving opposition to the Townshend duties and the controversy over the Wilkes Fund, Benjamin Smith took a back seat. He sat for St. James Goose Creek in the General Assembly of 1765-1768, but he was not re-elected in October 1768.[72] There was a minor revolution in that parish in 1768 when a number of men came down from Saxe Gotha and Beaver Creek to cast votes. Aaron Loocock and Moses Kirkland were elected, and both of these were connected with the backcountry. A question of whether Loocock and Kirkland had been properly elected was raised in the Assembly, but the story can be carried no further.[73] Benjamin Smith was passed over again in the elections of March 1769, but was returned in September 1769 from St. John's Colleton, which had consistently returned William Wragg and definitely had the marks of a conservative constituency.[74] Had Benjamin Smith lost his support in the town and then, after seeking support in St. James Goose Creek, been unseated by an influx of Regulators from the backcountry and, therefore, finally forced to look for support among the conservative planters in the Beaufort neighborhood? This is a speculative question, but the facts clearly indicate that Benjamin Smith was not an ardent leader of the opposition to the Crown. Even his brother, Thomas Smith of Broad Street, who had the respect of the Charles Town mechanics, preferred to represent the more conservative constituency of St. Helena.[75] Benjamin and Thomas Smith were certainly a step behind Henry Laurens, Peter Manigault, and Charles Pinckney in the fight to uphold the rights of Englishmen. Yet Benjamin Smith was still a supporter of that cause as the following letter, written on December 12, 1769, to Isaac Smith, his Boston cousin, indicates:

[71] Bull wrote that the resolutions were broken on December 13, 1770. Bull to Hillsborough, December 13, 1770, *PRO*, XXXII, 434.

[72] *JCHA*, XXXVII, part 1, 45.

[73] See list preceding page one, *JCHA*, XXXVII, part 2. *Also see JCHA*, XXXVII, part 2, 7.

[74] *South-Carolina Gazette*, March 16, 1769. Benjamin Smith received 48 votes, Charles Cotesworth Pinckney 42, and James Brisbane 12 in the poll in St. John's Colleton. The two highest were elected. *Ibid.*, September 21, 1769.

[75] *Ibid.*, March 16, 1769.

The whole continent of America have great reason to speak the praises of your countrymen, tho greatly oppressed they have shewn a manly behaviour consistent with the true sons of Liberty—and by their example the other provinces have at last been led to their true interest. We in this province have entered into the Non importation scheme with great spirit (there being very few who have not subscribed the Resolutions). And if the colonies stick close to this— we shall I make no doubt soon be relieved from all unconstitutional acts of Parliament. . . . Our Assembly has ordered £ 1,500 sterling to be immediately remitted to G. B. in bills of exchange to the Committee for the support of the Bill of Rights, in this I believe we are the first Assembly that have contributed.[76]

After reading this letter it might be better to say that Benjamin Smith's declining political importance was due to his declining health rather than to any excessive moderation in the cause. The true answer probably lies somewhere between. In this same letter he wrote that "in last August and September I was very ill with my old complaint in my bowels" and hinted that the next summer he would give his ailing body a rest in the cooler climate of New England.[77] He, undoubtedly because of his health, failed to take his seat in the Assembly until January 17, 1770.[78] He died the following summer, and Miles Brewton was elected to represent St. John's Colleton.[79]

MANY CAROLINA MERCHANTS and planters were now rich enough to make an annual pilgrimage during the hot summer months to northern resorts, of which Newport, prior to the Revolution, was the most important. The first to seek the cool cliffs of Newport had been the British West Indian planters, but Carolinians soon outnumbered all other summer residents. During the eight years 1767 through 1774, according to one account, there were two hundred sixty-six visitors from Charles Town, ninety-two from Philadelphia, fifty-four from Jamaica, twenty-five from Georgia, with a sprinkling of others from North Carolina and the British West Indies.[80] Benjamin Smith was among the Carolina visitors in 1770. Desiring comfort, Benjamin chartered the brigantine *William and John*, Captain Rog-

[76] Benjamin Smith to Isaac Smith, December 12, 1769, *Smith-Carter Papers,* MHS.

[77] *Ibid.*

[78] *JCHA,* XXXVIII, part 2, 223. Smith had therefore taken no active part in the discussion leading to the contribution to the Wilkes Fund.

[79] *South-Carolina Gazette,* September 20, 1770.

[80] Carl Bridenbaugh, "Colonial Newport as a Summer Resort," *Rhode Island Historical Society Collections,* XXVI (1933), 23. Brewster was wrong in starting his story in 1790. Lawrence Fay Brewster, *Summer Migrations and Resorts of South Carolina Low Country Planters,* Durham, 1947, pp. 1-2.

ers, to take his family and servants, thereby becoming the first summer visitor to sail for Newport in the grand manner—by privately chartered yacht. Benjamin's wealth, however, was no guard against disaster. A violent storm cast him, his wife, four of his children, and four servants—ashore near New London. "Happily," as the Newport *Mercury* quaintly put it, "there was no Person lost except the Mate, who was drowned."[81]

At Newport the Smiths took lodging in the house of Charles Bardin. Benjamin was first placed under the care of Doctor William Hunter but when his strength began to ebb Doctor Thomas Moffat was fetched from New London, and he remained in constant attendance.[82] A premonition of death moved Benjamin to add a final codicil to his will on July 5. He remembered his church, St. Philip's, with a subscription of £50 sterling for a new organ, and to his wife he left his coach and chaise with all harnesses, as well as three horses, Peacock, Possett, and York.[83] When Benjamin Smith died on the 29th, "after a painful illness of five weeks," Isaac Smith, junior, was with the family, having come down from Boston to be of service to his cousins. Benjamin was buried in Trinity Churchyard after a funeral service attended by a great number of the principal inhabitants.[84] In the fall he was reinterred in Charles Town.[85] Thomas Smith expressed the feelings of the family when he wrote that it was "one of the greatest calamities that could befal me in life, the death of my dear, my only, my most affectionate Brother. He had got over all the storms and tempests of this life and I have no doubt is in peace and happiness. The remainder of my journey I must travel without his most agreable company—I am resigned to the divine dispensation, tho' I must feel the wound as long as I live."[86]

[81] Quoted in Carl Bridenbaugh, "Charlestonians at Newport, 1767-1775," *SCHGM*, XLI (1940), 45.

[82] Charles Bardin to Isaac Smith, July 13, 1770, *Smith-Carter Papers*, MHS. Dr. William Hunter, whose fine house faced the harbor, was a member of the Newport Junto along with Howard and Moffat. These three had been roughly handled by the mob at the time of the Stamp Act crisis. David S. Lovejoy, *Rhode Island Politics and the American Revolution, 1760-1776*, Providence, 1958, pp. 49, 107. The letters of Dr. Thomas Moffat on the Newport riots were reprinted in the *South-Carolina Gazette*, August 30, 1773.

[83] *Will Book, 1767-1771, Charleston County, S. C.*, SC Archives, p. 489.

[84] *South-Carolina Gazette*, August 16, 1770.

[85] *South-Carolina Gazette*, October 18, November 1, 1770.

[86] Thomas Smith to Isaac Smith, junior, August 20, 1770, *Smith-Carter Papers*, MHS.

V

THE EDUCATION OF WILLIAM SMITH, 1770-1783

AFTER THE NON-IMPORTATION AGREEMENT was broken in South Carolina in December 1770, trade boomed. By May 1771 the shops of Charles Town were once more stocked with goods.[1] The price of rice doubled between the spring of 1771 and the summer of 1772. With their profits the planters bought vast numbers of slaves, 6,471 being imported between November 1, 1772, and July 26, 1773. The consequent great demand for Negro provisions brought boom times to the backcountry as well.[2] In the lull between the repeal of the Townshend duties and the Boston Tea Party, South Carolina experienced her greatest prosperity. On April 11, 1772, Thomas Smith of Broad Street wrote: "The desires of the planters increase faster than their riches. Coaches, chariots, and English horses pour in fast upon us since the Resolutions were broken through. Houses and lands and everything for luxury sell high."[3]

THE SMITHS, particularly the younger generation, were living amid great luxury. When Josiah Quincy, junior, arrived in Charles Town in February 1773, fortified with letters of introduction from the Boston Smiths to the Charles Town Smiths, he recorded in detail the extent of the new prosperity:

> Dined with Mr. Thomas Smith; several gentlemen and ladies; decent and plenteous table of meats: the upper cloth removed, a compleat table of puddings, pies, tarts, custards, sweetmeats, oranges, macarones, etc., etc.,—profuse. Excellent wines—no politicks.
> Dined with Mr. Roger Smith, son to Mr. Thomas Smith: good deal of company, elegant table, and the best provisions I have seen in this town. One cloth removed, a handsome desert of most kinds of nicknacks. Good wines and much festivity. Two ladies being called on for toasts, the one gave, 'Delicate pleasures to susceptable minds.' The other, 'When passions rise may reason be the guide.'

[1] *South-Carolina Gazette,* May 30, 1771.
[2] *Ibid.,* March 7, 1771, May 25, 1772. Elizabeth Donnan, "The Trade into South Carolina Before the Revolution," *AHR,* XXXIII (1927-1928), 809. George Rogers Taylor, "Wholesale Commodity Prices at Charleston, S. C.," *Journal of Economic and Business History,* IV (1932), 366, 372.
[3] Thomas Smith to Isaac Smith, junior, April 11, 1772, *Smith-Carter Papers,* MHS.

The same indulgence in food and in light, frivolous conversation was found in the home of Thomas Loughton Smith.

> This day was to have been spent with Thomas Loughton Smith Esqr. at his country seat. Bad weather prevents, and I take what is called a family dinner with him. A prodigious fine pudding made of what they call rice flour. Nick-nacks brought on table after removal of meats. Ladies ask the gentlemen to drink a glass of wine with them: Upon a gentleman's asking a lady to do the like, she replies 'G__ bless you, I thought you never would ask. I have been waiting for you this half hour.' First toast, Our Boston friend and your good health. Sir: the unmarried lady (of nineteen) at my right, 'your good health and best affections Sir!' Miss _____ your toast, madam. 'Love and friendship and they who feel them!' Toasts called for from the guests, etc., till coffee, etc. Mr. Smith's house, furniture, pictures, plate etc. very elegant—wines very fine. Mrs. Smith shewed me a most beautiful white satin and very richly embroidered lady's work-bag, designed as a present for a lady in London. Miss Catherine Ingliss, her sister, a still more finely embroidered festoon (as they called it) of flowers. Both their own work; and far surpassing anything of the kind I ever saw.

Several days later Quincy went to Thomas Loughton Smith's country seat.

> At eleven set off *in state* for the Retreat of T. L. Smith Esqr. Dined there and spent remainder of the day. This day spent the most agreeably of any since my arrival in Charlestown. A most delightful place indeed!

The ultimate in extravagant living was to be found at the home of Miles Brewton, the former partner of Benjamin and Thomas Loughton Smith.

> Dined with considerable company at Miles Brewton, Esqr's, a gentleman of very large fortune: a most superb house said to have cost him 8,000 £ sterling. The grandest hall I ever beheld, azure blue satin window curtains, rich blue paper with gilt, mashee borders, most elegant pictures, excessive grand and costly looking glasses etc. . . . A most elegant table, three courses, nick-nacks, jellies, preserves, sweetmeats, etc. After dinner, two sorts of nuts, almonds, raisins, three sorts of olives, apples, oranges, etc. By odds the richest wine I ever tasted: Exceeds Mr. Hancock's, Vassall's, Phillips's and others much in flavour, softness, and strength. . . . At Mr. Brewton's side board was very magnificent plate: a very large exquisitely wrought Goblet, most excellent workmanship and singularly beautiful. A very fine bird kept familiarly playing over the room, under our chairs and the table, picking up the crumbs, etc., and perching on the window, side board and chairs: vastly pretty![4]

[4] "Journal of Josiah Quincy, Junior, 1773," *Proceedings of the Massachusetts Historical Society*, XLIX (1915-1916), 443-450.

THERE WAS A NEW TONE to society which dismayed the older generation. It could be traced in part to the young men of inherited wealth who were attempting to ape the manners, accent, and style of living of the English aristocracy. Thomas Loughton, who had just returned from England, and Roger were far more willing to embrace the new ways than was Thomas Smith of Broad Street. The returning student was, of course, quite often the carrier of this new disease. As Timothy Ford was to say later, the sons came back "much more dissipated than they went."[5] Thomas Heyward, a student at the Middle Temple, wrote his father an eight-page letter in February 1767 devoted almost entirely to recounting the pleasures of London. His excuse for not writing more often was that his time was so divided and used up "between the courts at Westminster Hall, the Parliament, my private tutors, my closet and my friends." But amusements more than public affairs were spread across his letter paper. Grenville, Townshend, and Conway were debating in Parliament but their speeches were not sufficient to brighten the dull London winter. Heyward admitted that he indulged in the play-house because "Cicero and Quintillian both recommend it" and had eagerly tried skating in the park. But it was the return of the *beau monde,* or people of quality, at the end of January from their dissipations at Bath who brightened the London season. Heyward commented: "They spend their time here in as much indolence and luxury as did the Romans at the decline of their empire."[6]

At the time of the non-importation agreement there had been a serious attempt to find an alternative to sending young colonials abroad to school. Several boys were sent in 1769 to the Reverend Jacob Duché's in Philadelphia, but this city was not a completely satisfactory place for the young since it was well-known for its yellow fever epidemics.[7] The real solution was to set up a provincial school system and cap it with a college. Plans were formulated by Bull in 1770 and presented to the Assembly, but the controversy with the Crown prevented any further action. Benjamin Smith left £500 sterling in his will to the new college, and John Mackenzie, Thomas Smith's son-in-law, left £1,000 sterling and eight hundred

[5] "Diary of Timothy Ford, 1785-1786," *SCHGM,* XIII (1912), 192.

[6] Thomas Heyward to [Daniel Heyward], February 11, 1767, *Emmet Collection,* NYPL.

[7] *South-Carolina Gazette,* August 24, 1769. Among those who had gone to Philadelphia were John Pringle, Peter and Ben Smith, Jack Harleston, Tom Mitchell, Archy Gamble, and James Ferguson. John Pringle to William Tilghman, July 30, September 15, 1774, *Preston Davie Papers,* SHC.

books. These initial bequests did eventually help to establish a college but not until after the Revolution.[8] No American college or school could equal those in Europe, so in spite of the interest in keeping the boys at home, many were still shipped off to the mother country. The sons of the Carolina merchants and planters formed the largest group of American students abroad on the eve of the Revolution.[9] An English education fostered a unique Carolina aristocracy.[10]

IT IS IMPOSSIBLE to ascertain the precise date of William Smith's departure for England. He was sent abroad by his father when he "was a little more than 11 years of age" and this was just "a few months" before his father's death.[11] This places the time somewhere in the spring of 1770. Perhaps William's departure was the last matter attended to before Benjamin set sail with the rest of his family for a New England vacation. Young William was undoubtedly met by his older brother Thomas Loughton, who had gone over in June 1769.[12] Although Thomas Loughton was busy with personal and public affairs, he found time to be a charming companion for his younger brother. Henry Laurens, knowing Thomas Loughton quite well, wrote him in August 1769 the following advice: "Don't spend your whole time in pleasures, ease and studying the easiest way for amassing a great estate for your children. Apply a portion of it to the service of your country and do every thing in your power to procure the repeal or amendment of bad laws and the enacting of such as are more salutary in order to secure to them in their own right and as their own property such estates whether

[8] J. H. Easterby, *A History of the College of Charleston*, n.p., 1935, pp. 10-13.

[9] Pares wrote that "the rice planters of Carolina were already, in 1776, rather better able" to send their sons abroad "than the tobacco planters of Virginia." Pares did not distinguish between the sons of Carolina planters and Carolina merchants. *See* Richard Pares, *Merchants and Planters*, Cambridge, 1960, p. 81, n. 1. *Also see* William L. Sachse, *The Colonial American in Britain*, Madison, 1956, pp. 47-69.

[10] These boys may have brought home a new accent, which became the peculiar Charleston speech. They presumably learned elocution from Thomas Sheridan, the father of the playwright. John Rutledge wrote his brother Edward in 1769: "I believe Sheridan is the only lecturer, in England, upon oratory; and, I think, it would be advisable to attend him, and mark well his observations. He reads with propriety, though he is much too stiff, and his voice exceeding bad." John Rutledge to Edward Rutledge, July 30, 1769, John Belton O'Neall, *Biographical Sketches of the Bench and Bar of South Carolina*, Charleston, 1858, II, 122.

[11] William Smith to Gentlemen, November 22, 1788, William Smith folder, *Personal Papers, Miscellaneous*, LC.

[12] *South-Carolina Gazette*, June 22, 1769.

great or small as you may leave them."[13] Thomas Loughton used his influence in favor of the repeal of the Townshend duties, but the evidence that remains indicates that he was busier with more trivial affairs, such as arranging to ship the statue of William Pitt which had been commissioned by the colony to be placed at the intersection of Broad and Meeting streets, as well as obtaining subscriptions from the Crokatt family, John Nutt, Benjamin Stead, and others for the bells for St. Michael's.[14]

With the death of Benjamin Smith, Thomas Loughton was called home to assist in the filing and proving of his father's will. William was placed in the home of the Reverend Richard Clarke, formerly rector of St. Philip's in Charles Town, but then living near Colebrooke's Row in Islington. John Nutt, "a right down London merchant," who, according to Thomas Smith of Broad Street, "had as much religion in him as merchants of London in general have," was to keep in touch with William and supply him with funds.[15]

By the terms of his father's will, William inherited £15,000 currency which was to be placed out at interest within three months, as well as part of a lot in Broad Street with two brick tenements, then rented to Troup and Courtonne. There were also four slaves: Belinda and her son Peter, and Lucy and her son Dick. After his step-mother's death William was to have the family pew at St. Phillip's. This fortune, ample for his education, was to be managed by Thomas Loughton Smith, Thomas Smith of Broad Street, Isaac Motte, and Miles Brewton. They were instructed to carry out Benjamin's last wish that his children "be Religiously brought up, and that they have a Liberal Education."[16]

Thomas Loughton, who had inherited £9,000 sterling, took this opportunity to quit the "Store business." He bought in his father's Broad Street mansion for £3,150 sterling and began to live according to the new fashion, quite ostentatiously.[17] In the summer of

[13] Henry Laurens to Thomas Loughton Smith, August 8, 1769, *Laurens Letter-Book, 1767-1771*, SCHS.

[14] Thomas Loughton Smith wanted to pay the freight of the statue as a compliment to the province. Charles Garth to the Committee of Correspondence, March 10, 1770, "Correspondence of Charles Garth," ed. Joseph W. Barnwell, SCHGM, XXVIII (1927), 89. George W. Williams, *St. Michael's, Charleston, 1751-1951*, Columbia, 1951, p. 247.

[15] Thomas Smith to Reverend William Smith, February 20, 1766; Thomas Smith to Isaac Smith, junior, August 20, 1770, *Smith-Carter Papers*, MHS.

[16] *Will Book, 1767-1771, Charleston County, S.C.*, SC Archives, p. 489.

[17] Thomas Smith to Isaac Smith, junior, April 11, 1772, *Smith-Carter Papers*, MHS.

1772 he made the northern tour.[18] He had taken his seat in the Assembly, representing St. Michael's Parish, on September 18, 1771, and his loyalty to the royal government was such that Lord Charles Montagu recommended him for the Council board on August 2, 1772.[19] Thomas Smith, who lived nearby, watched his nephew's progress with disapproval. Roger had now been left alone in the family business, although Peter would soon join him. Thomas Smith thought the Carolinians were growing rich too fast: "Luxury, vice and immorality are thus introduced."[20]

The social whirl was at its height during race week in February. Expensive horses were being imported; the stakes were high. Quincy saw in 1773 "a prodigious fine collection of excellent, though very high-priced horses," and recorded that £2,000 sterling was "won and lost at the Race."[21] The death of Thomas Loughton Smith in April 1773 may have been symbolic. He fell from his horse on Monday; he died on Friday. He was only thirty-three. The fast pace had overwhelmed him.[22] After the death of this nephew, Thomas Smith of Broad Street took the principal interest in educating his younger brother William.

HENRY LAURENS, after his wife died in May 1770, considered the possibility of sending his three sons, John, Harry, and James, to England to be educated. Laurens consulted Thomas Smith, who recommended that he send them to Clarke. Clarke had written of his financial losses and had asked Smith to secure additional students·for him. When Laurens called to console Thomas upon the death of his brother Benjamin, Thomas gave Henry Laurens one of Clarke's printed advertisements of his plans as schoolmaster.[23] Robert Williams, a Charles Town distiller, who returned in January 1771 from placing his own son at Clarke's, told Laurens that Clarke

[18] Thomas Loughton Smith and his wife sailed for Philadelphia in August and returned by land before Christmas. *South-Carolina Gazette,* August 13, December 24, 1772. They intended to visit Boston, for Thomas Smith wrote a letter of introduction to Isaac Smith, senior, August 4, 1772, *Smith-Carter Papers,* MHS.

[19] *JCHA,* XXXVIII, part 3, 519-520. He had been elected in the place of Benjamin Dart who had been appointed joint-public-treasurer. *South-Carolina Gazette,* April 18, 1771. He was re-elected in December 1772. *Ibid.,* December 17, 1772. Montagu to Hillsborough, August 2, 1772, *PRO,* XXXIII, 171.

[20] Thomas Smith to Isaac Smith, junior, April 11, 1772, *Smith-Carter Papers,* MHS.

[21] "Journal of Josiah Quincy, Junior, 1773," *op. cit.,* p. 451.

[22] *South-Carolina Gazette,* April 19, 1773.

[23] Henry Laurens to Reverend Richard Clarke, August 25, 1770, March 16, April 6, 1771, *Laurens Letter-Book, 1767-1771,* SCHS.

had fixed upon a plan of education that limited his scholars to twelve, a number which Williams thought he would have no trouble in securing. Laurens therefore quickened his preparations.[24] Harry, his second son, was sent off in the spring, but Clarke was instructed that if his quota were filled to see that Harry was properly inoculated and then placed with the Reverend Mr. Hockley, formerly the rector of St. John's Berkeley in Carolina, whom Miles Brewton had recommended. Above all, Laurens warned Clarke to keep Harry "within narrow bounds" because he had been informed "by a Gentleman lately from London that he frequently met Billy Smith and others of your scholars, rambling the streets of the City, in half Holy days as he called them."[25]

There must have been some doubt in Laurens' mind about the Clarke school for he decided to go to London and to see for himself. He set sail in July with John and James and with Jacky Petrie, the ward of his brother James Laurens and the son of Alexander Petrie, late of the firm of Hawkins, Petrie and Company.[26] Laurens and the schoolboys sailed first for Philadelphia, where they added Billy Fisher to their party; he was the son of William Fisher, an important Quaker merchant with whom Laurens had done business for many years.[27] While in Philadelphia Laurens visited the Reverend Jacob Duché's to see how Peter and Benjamin Smith, the sons of Thomas, were getting along. In commenting on Ben's promising start Laurens set forth his views on the education of the sons of merchants:

> If you mean to let him go forward in the study of language and science, in order to qualify him for one of the learned professions— next year will be a very proper time to remove him, from America to Winchester, Westminster, or Eton—(I should not prefer West-minster)—as preparatory to his entry at one of the Universities which I know is very much his desire. If Ben is designed for trade,—you and I if I remember right, are agreed in this point, that the first Rudiments may be gained in as great a degree of certainty and clearness, in Charles Town, as can be acquired in any Counting House in London without making any remarks, on the advantages

[24] Williams opened a distillery in 1754. *South-Carolina Gazette*, November 17, 1754. Williams had taken his son to England in May 1770. *Ibid.*, May 10, 1770, January 31, 1771.

[25] Henry Laurens to Reverend Richard Clarke, March 16, April 6, 1771, *Laurens Letter-Book, 1767-1771*, SCHS.

[26] Alexander Petrie was a brother-in-law of James Laurens. David Duncan Wallace, *The Life of Henry Laurens*, New York, 1915, p. 502. Mr. Hawkins, obviously the London agent of Hawkins, Petrie and Company, took care of the boy's financial arrangements. Henry Laurens to James Laurens, February 17, 1774, *Laurens Letter-Book, 1772-1774*, SCHS.

[27] Wallace, *op. cit.*, pp. 183-184.

resulting from a knowledge of local customs, and an acquaintance with people of the province, or on the difference of expence of money and morals.[28]

The Laurens party sailed from New York in September for Falmouth. By the end of October Laurens was at Chelsea near Clarke's and in November was firmly settled with Robert Deane in Fulyer Street, Westminster. He placed all of his sons with Clarke and then began to inquire of his effectiveness as a schoolmaster. He consulted John Nutt about Billy Smith's progress and was alarmed by Nutt's description of the economy and manners of Clarke's house.[29] When Laurens talked to Thomas Corbet, who had been asked to keep an eye on young Robert Williams, certain of Corbet's questions "roused my attention too." An "honest man at Chelsea merely from kindness and regard" gave Laurens several hints "that it was not a proper place, for Gentlemen's children."[30] In spite of these warnings, Laurens thought he knew the goodness of Clarke's heart and his abilities as a tutor, and he therefore permitted himself more time in which to observe the fruits of Clarke's efforts.

The boys spent their weekends with Laurens, and from what he could remember of Billy Smith, he thought him greatly improved. He was "too much inclined to fat" but, as John Laurens told his father, "greatly improved in English, Latin, and French" and "a smart hand in fencing." Laurens wrote Thomas Smith that since William's brother intended him "to have quite an English education" to prepare him for the bar he thought the sooner he was sent to a public school the better. He suggested moving him the following May (1772) to Winchester or Eton.[31]

Laurens made an effort to entertain the boys. He invited all the boys ("among whom I have desired Billy Smith") to watch the

[28] Henry Laurens to Thomas Smith, December 28, 1771, *Laurens Letter-Book, 1771-1772.* SCHS.

[29] *Ibid.*

[30] Henry Laurens to James Laurens, January 1, 1772, *Laurens Letter-Book, 1771-1772,* SCHS. Thomas Corbet had been an eminent lawyer in Charles Town. He embarked for England in 1750 with Peter Manigault, who lived in his London home for four years while studying law. Peter Manigault to Gabriel Manigault, I, June 23, 1750, "Peter Manigault's Letters," ed. Mabel L. Webber, *SCHGM,* XXXI (1930), 172. Peter Manigault to Gabriel Manigault, I, August 7, 1750, "Six Letters of Peter Manigault," *SCHGM,* XV (1914), 119. Corbet bought, in 1753, the office of high bailiff of Westminster, which he held until his death in 1796. He was accustomed to receive in his house the sons of the leading Carolina merchants and planters while they were at school or at the Inns of Court. H. Hale Bellot, "The Leighs in South Carolina," *Transactions of the Royal Historical Society,* fifth series, VI (1956), 170.

[31] Henry Laurens to James Laurens, December 5, 1771; Henry Laurens to Thomas Smith, December 28, 1771, *Laurens Letter-Book, 1771-1772,* SCHS.

lord mayor's show in November "from Mr. Hawkins's."[32] For Christmas he had Jacky Petrie, Billy Smith, and his three sons along with John Faucheraud Grimké, who was down from Cambridge, for the holidays. Laurens saw to it that they heard a good sermon at the Asylum Chapel as well as serious talk in his rooms. Grimké particularly distinguished himself in the eyes of Laurens. Laurens wrote his father, John Paul Grimké:

> He is truly modest and diffident—but very ready and sensible when he delivers his sentiments upon any occasion—I had an opportunity of knowing so much by an argument held at my rooms between a gentleman of letters and experience and himself and tho' it was chiefly musick in which Mr. Grimké must be allowed to have advantages—yet the other Gentleman, is not behind him in knowledge in that science, but the manner in which your son supported and defended his principles and opinions was very pleasing—and discovered that modesty and good sense which I have declared him to be possessed of.[33]

Matters got worse rather than better at Clarke's. Harry came home with a "horrible burn" on his cheek from a candle "wantonly and maliciously thrust into his face, by a vagabond brother of Mrs. Clarke's who had defrauded and eloped from some tradesmen" and was now entertained by his sister. "If an eye had been struck, it must have perished." Even after this the idler was allowed to remain in the house "in spite of his history and his language." Nor did any word come from Clarke on this occasion. The fathers of the boys had agreed to pay a high rate, £70 sterling a year plus additional expenses for clothing and pocket money, if Clarke would limit his students to twelve so that there could be close supervision of their studies and their morals. Clarke was not living up to his contract. John Laurens, whose word could always be trusted, said that Clarke did not keep "a proper discipline" and that he was not strict enough with the boys. Those who voluntarily did their work would learn, but "those of duller genius" would remain slack or backward. There had been frequent omissions of lessons for a day or two and once for an entire week. Discipline was the crux of the problem.[34] Laurens was torn between his friendship for Clarke, which must have been strong to stand up under these severe failures in performance, and his duty to his own sons. If Laurens

[32] Henry Laurens to James Laurens, November 6, 1771, *Laurens Letter-Book, 1771-1772,* SCHS.

[33] Henry Laurens to John Paul Grimké, December 30, 1771, *Laurens Letter-Book, 1771-1772,* SCHS.

[34] Henry Laurens to James Laurens, January 1, 1772, *Laurens Letter-Book, 1771-1772,* SCHS.

removed the boys, he would undoubtedly deprive Clarke of his school and of his livelihood. He therefore delayed.

There were six Carolina boys at Clarke's in 1772. John Laurens and Alexander McQueen studied together in their chambers; Jacky Petrie, Billy Smith, and Robert Williams were in a class together; Harry Laurens, the youngest, was by himself.[35] The boys were tutored by Clarke and an usher in a classical program which was to prepare them for the professions rather than for commerce. Petrie was considering the ministry and had the choice of going on to Edinburgh or to Geneva, if he desired to follow the religion of his father, or to Winchester and Oxford, if he wanted to be of the Established Church.[36] Smith and Williams were intended for the law.[37] John Laurens preferred any of the professions to trade, for, he confessed to his uncle: "I never loved Merchandise, nor can I now."[38]

The boys all lived together in the Clarke house in Islington. Because it was over-crowded and stuffy, Clarke promised Laurens in the spring of 1772 that he would move to Chinkford in Essex, about eleven miles from London. With this prospect of a change, Laurens relaxed and took his sons off to visit his old partner, George Austin, near Shrewsbury in Shropshire.[39] It was on this tour to the Midlands that James, the youngest Laurens boy, was placed with Mr. Howel, at Winson Green near Birmingham.[40] One can imagine Laurens' chagrin upon his return to find that Clarke had not moved. Even worse Laurens suddenly had to deal with a duel.

A son of Samuel Brailsford, who had retired from the Carolina

[35] John Laurens to James Laurens, April 17, 1772, *Laurens Papers*, LIHS. The fathers of these boys were Henry Laurens, John McQueen, Benjamin Smith, Alexander Petrie, and Robert Williams. The first four were merchants; Williams was a distiller. All had been prominent in the supply of goods for the Indians and the soldiers during the French and Indian War. *JCHA*, XXXII, part 1, 207-214.

[36] Henry Laurens to James Laurens, August 19, 1772, *Laurens Letter-Book, 1771-1772*, SCHS.

[37] Henry Laurens to Thomas Smith, December 28, 1771, *Laurens Letter-Book, 1771-1772*, SCHS.

[38] John Laurens to James Laurens, April 17, 1772, *Laurens Papers*, LIHS. In his will, John McQueen, senior, had made provision for his three sons to be "severally brought up in the study of the law, Physick, or in the business of a Merchant, or some Genteel profession or business." Alexander McQueen became a merchant. Walter Charlton Hartridge, *The Letters of Don Juan McQueen to His Family*, Columbia, 1943, p. xxii.

[39] Henry Laurens to James Laurens, December 5, 1771, *Laurens Letter-Book, 1771-1772*, SCHS. *Also see* John Laurens to James Laurens, April 17, 1772, *Laurens Papers*, LIHS.

[40] Henry Laurens to James Laurens, May 13, 1772, *Laurens Letter-Book, 1771-1772*, SCHS.

trade in 1767 and had since then been living in Bristol, was a former pupil of Clarke's.[41] Young Brailsford was on his way to Amsterdam with his father to begin serving a clerkship in a counting house there. Alexander McQueen had apparently, on seeing his former schoolmate again, revived an old school quarrel and the boys with their seconds had arranged a meeting with swords in Hyde Park. When Laurens heard of the intended affair, he frantically exerted himself to prevent it, walking eight or ten miles and riding twelve in an effort to find the culprits. Fortunately, the seconds had persuaded the contestants to accommodate the matter, and Laurens caught up with them as they were coming off the field of honour. They confirmed what they called the "late act of amnesty" and permitted Laurens "to join their hands" to end the foolish affair which forced Laurens to deliver Brailsford to his father and lecture McQueen sternly.[42]

This was the last straw. Laurens removed John and Harry from Clarke's in June 1772 and took them to Switzerland—Geneva had been highly recommended to him. He could not remove Petrie without James Laurens' consent, nor could he remove Smith without consulting Thomas Smith. Over the other two boys, Williams and McQueen, he had no control at all.

GENEVA IN THE 1770's was at the peak of its fame for culture and learning. Many foreigners attended the Academy: nobles and princes of Germany, lords and gentlemen from England—even the Duke of Cambridge after he had completed his studies at Gottingen. "It was the Genevese society which they cultivated, aided by private teachers in every branch, with whom Geneva was abundantly supplied."[43] John Laurens summed up the scene for his uncle in December 1773: "You will think *Geneve* greatly in vogue, when I tell you that we count sixty English here at present—among whom are the Duke of Hamilton, Lords Stanhope, Mahon, Chesterfield, Lumley, etc. & so far are they from being an impediment to each other's Study by herding together and forming a variety of Parties

---

[41] *South-Carolina Gazette,* June 15, 1767. *Also see City Gazette,* June 30, 1800.
[42] Henry Laurens to James Laurens, May 13, 1772, *Laurens Letter-Book, 1771-1772,* SCHS.
[43] Albert Gallatin to Eben Dodge, January 21, 1847, *The Writings of Albert Gallatin,* ed. Henry Adams, Philadelphia, 1879, II, 649-650. For a letter in praise of the Genevan system, *see* Henry Laurens to James Laurens, June 4, 1773, *Laurens Letter-Book, 1773,* SCHS.

of Pleasure, that it is become quite the Fashion to take a great number of Lessons, and to make no visits but in the afternoon."[44] John Laurens lived in the house of M. Chais which fronted on a pleasant square overlooking the River Rhone.[45] He studied mathematics, modern history, philosophy, and civil law. In May 1773 he wrote his uncle that he had begun a course "of political Eloquence, in which I promise myself great Pleasure and Satisfaction—it was composed by a man of great ability for a young English Nobleman, and is particularly adapted to the English Constitution. I continue my riding and fencing both for exercise and as useful arts." Young Harry Laurens had been placed with the Chauvets, who lived a few miles from town on the banks of Lake Geneva. M. Chauvet undertook "to have a strict eye over the conduct of young Gentlemen" who studied with him and Madame Chauvet, "a notable woman," was "very careful in her Department." Chauvet himself taught Latin, French, and geography; for other subjects masters came in to give lessons. Harry, as his older brother reported, had begun Latin, spoke French very fluently, and was making progress in writing and arithmetic. John recommended the place to his uncle as one suitable for Petrie if he thought of transferring him from Clarke's.[46]

HENRY LAURENS was back in London by August 1772, safe in the assurance that his sons were properly settled and on the road to knowledge. Clarke's four remaining pupils, however, were not faring so well. Petrie's manners and address had certainly deteriorated; he was, in fact, Laurens wrote his brother, "not the Petrie you knew." One of the boys "by Mr. C.'s own account as well as by report of Petrie, ought not to be suffered to remain among boys— they live at table very well, the House rent is the same as if there were 12—and yet our young friend, among other things, justly complains that 3 of the 4 sleep in one room, and in a very odd sort of way." On taking Petrie with him one day to St. Martin's, Laurens discovered that Clarke had even been neglecting the Scriptures. Is it not strange, he asked his brother, that "our friend who used to impress the necessity for reading the Bible upon his particular friends as A Book containing the History of all Men and of All

[44] John Laurens to James Laurens, December 19, 1773, *Laurens Papers,* LIHS.
[45] John Laurens to James Laurens, August 27, 1772, *Laurens Papers,* LIHS.
[46] John Laurens to James Laurens, May 31, 1773, *Laurens Papers,* LIHS. *Also see* Gabriel Manigault, II, to Anne Manigault, October 24, 1775, *Manigault Papers,* SCL.

Nations, and even as a necessary part of a polite Education, should now totally neglect the reading of the sacred Book in his family and to his pupils and disallow or not encourage the reading it by them?"[47]

Once again Clarke promised to move his school, and once again Laurens went off on a visit to an old partner, George Appleby, at Aston in Shropshire.[48] On his return to London, Laurens kept Petrie (and perhaps Smith, too) while Clarke moved from Islington to Hackney (instead of to Chinkford as he had earlier planned), for naturally there could be no lessons during the moving.[49] After Clarke and the boys were settled in Hackney, Laurens took off for Geneva—this time taking John Grimké with him and traveling by way of the Low Countries and Germany.

Laurens was back in London for the winter of 1772-1773. After this second look at the Genevan system he was convinced of the wisdom of moving Smith and Petrie. He and John Nutt agreed that Smith should be taken from Clarke's but disagreed as to the place he should go. This indecision bore heavily on Laurens' heart. He wrote Thomas Smith: "I must confess to you that as often as I see Billy Smith and think of his Dear Father I am a good deal affected."[50] Meanwhile he did what he could for the boys—he took them in for Easter; he lent them books from John's library; he even got Hawkins to buy the *Spectator* for Petrie.[51]

Late in the spring of 1773 Laurens made a third trip to Geneva. He felt more than ever that the change to Geneva would be all for the good. Professors, tutors, and masters were punctual and constant in their duty. Temperance and sobriety in meats and drinks reigned there. The expense, however, was high. The cost for John in the upper class was as much as he would allow for Oxford or Cambridge.[52]

By January 1774 it had become absolutely apparent that Laurens must move the boys, even if he had to stretch his own authority.

[47] Henry Laurens to James Laurens, August 19, 1772, *Laurens Letter-Book, 1771-1772,* SCHS.

[48] Henry Laurens to Thomas Smith, September 24, 1772, *Laurens Letter-Book, 1772-1774,* SCHS.

[49] Henry Laurens to James Laurens, October 5, 1772, *Laurens Letter-Book, 1772-1774,* SCHS.

[50] Henry Laurens to Thomas Smith, April 12, 1773, *Laurens Letter-Book, 1772-1774, SCHS.*

[51] Henry Laurens to James Laurens, April 19, 1773, *Laurens Letter-Book, 1772-1774,* SCHS.

[52] Henry Laurens to James Laurens, June 4, 1773, *Laurens Letter-Book, 1773,* SCHS.

Clarke was intending to move once again and to give up his usher. Who would teach the boys French? It was only then that Laurens learned that the usher had run away from home in Switzerland at the age of sixteen or seventeen to enter the service of the French. After the evacuation of Corsica he had come to England and, with only three months' experience as a sub-teacher, joined Clarke. This young man of twenty-three was famous for his language, but not for his French! He had little more to offer than a few good campaign stories. When Laurens examined Petrie on Roman history, about the only subject on which he had read a book, Petrie knew neither how Julius Caesar came to rule the empire, nor when that empire declined, nor what was the cause of its fall. It was by then too late to train Petrie for the professions, although he still might make a respectable merchant! Clarke, quite oblivious to this world, was once again intent on calculating the arrival of the next. This time the great event was scheduled for 1777. Laurens, trying desperately to keep a level head, commented that "bankrupt prophets" might "enter into business again as well as bankrupt tradesmen."[53]

It was not only Clarke's, but also London, that was undermining the morals of the boys. William Hasell Gibbes, who was somewhat older, left a vivid account of one of his own escapades in London at this time with Jacob Read and Thomas Pinckney.

> We had supped at a fashionable place of resort in Covent Garden the rendezvous for Bucks and disorderly spirits and after being prepared for adventures, kicked the waiters down the stairs and sallied forth but the Landlord gave a signal for his spies (who were always at hand) for the Watchman at 2 O'Clock in the Morning who attempted to arrest us. We drew our swords (which were more for show than service[)], and defended ourselves heroically, but were overpowered, disarmed and taken prisoners, with broken swords, black eyes and bruises and conducted to the "Round House," a secure place or Cellar provided for such occasions which frequently occured. A Tavern of *genteel fame,* was attached to this Midnight asylum and we have a polite message from the keeper that we could be supplied with whatever refreshments we wished from Champagne or Tokay to humble Porter, but we were too much enraged at our past treatment to pay regard to his *friendly offer* for which we should have paid his own price. Early in the morning we were indulged with a hackney Coach being five in number and conducted amidst the shouts and scoffings of Chimney sweeps (with the music of their marrow bones etc.) and

[53] Henry Laurens to James Laurens, January 4, 20, 1774, *Laurens Letter-Book, 1772-1774,* SCHS.

other blackguards who mounted behind the Coach to Sir John
Fielding, the famous City Magistrate, for examination.
They were accused of beating up the watchman, but Thomas Pinckney and Jacob Read "produced their wounds and disheveled locks
all bloody" to prove that they were the abused party. They were
forced nevertheless to give bail and pay the fees. Then in order to
avoid prosecution by the Covent Garden landlord for rioting in
his house, they agreed to have a supper in his establishment at two
guineas each.[54]

The younger boys, of course, were not guilty of such frolicking.
Yet William Smith already knew of the Covent Garden world.
Among his pamphlets in the Charleston Library Society is a copy
of the April 1774 issue of *The Covent-Garden Magazine; or Amo-
rous Repository: Calculated solely for the Entertainment of the
Polite World* which, in fact, is full of suggestive stories and smutty
jokes.[55]

When Isaac Motte, Smith's brother-in-law, arrived in London, a
decision was made to send Smith off to Geneva. When Laurens and
Motte told Master Smith, he seemed to favor the scheme. Young
Petrie, as Henry Laurens told the story, looked up with great expectation, too. Yet there was no authority to send Petrie, and never
was there seen "so much dejection" in the face of so young a fellow.
Laurens recommended "bed and resignation," but Petrie came
downstairs the next morning with "the same cloudly downcast vis-
age." Laurens finally decided to stretch a point in his instructions
from his brother James, and he told Petrie he might accompany
Smith. "Figure to yourself—the most sudden and extraordinary transition that ever you beheld from gloom to cheerfulness and you will
see Jacky Petrie's new face." To the others in Laurens' household
Petrie must have opened his heart, for Mrs. Deane, the landlady,
told Laurens: "Oh, sir . . . you have made that boy happy."
"Ah!" added Mr. Deane, "He will love you forever."[56]

Once the decision was made Motte and Laurens lost no time in
sending the boys off. Laurens wrote James on February 17, 1774:

> Mr. Motte and myself put the two young gentlemen this morning
> into a post chais under the protection of Mons. De Jean a very
> careful sensible steady man who is to me as Kaltisen *was*, between
> Congrees and Charles Town—they set off with as grand an equip-

[54] "William Hasell Gibbes' Story of His Life," ed. Arney R. Childs, *SCHGM*,
L (1949), 61.
[55] See *William Loughton Smith Pamphlets*, CLS, V, number 9.
[56] Henry Laurens to James Laurens, February 17, 1774, *Laurens Letter-
Book, 1772-1774*, SCHS.

age as my Lord Clive an English post chais and four, and will probably be at Calais before tomorrow morning—thence they proceed by slower steps drawn by De Jeans horses and will be at Geneve a day sooner or later the 4th March—the whole expense from my door to their lodging House in Geneve twelve guineas each—except perhaps 4 or 5 shillings to the ladies of the bed chamber and waiters on the road and half a guinea to the coachman—this is travelling at upward of 600 mile at a cheap rate.[57]

Smith and Petrie settled down in the house of M. Chauvet. By July, Henry Laurens had enough information to write Thomas Smith: "I believe your nephew Mr. William Smith is now in as proper a place for obtaining a polite liberal and useful education and for cultivating at the same time a knowledge of mankind with as few incitements and temptations to vice and immorality as would have been found in Europe—he has all the means at hand, but much undoubtedly will depend upon his own diligence and a wise use of them."[58]

JOHN LAURENS, on the advice of Thomas Corbet, had studied civil law while in Geneva, and according to Corbet's plan, it was time in September 1774 for John to return to the Inns of Court to study the common law. John had long been entered at the Middle Temple and had done some reading in Blackstone, which Corbet had sent him, but for knowledge of the law he intended to practice it was necessary to study in England. John therefore returned to London and settled at Charles Bicknell's Carolina Coffee House in Chancery Lane near the law courts. Harry was also brought back to London and placed at Westminster, perhaps to be near his brother now that his father was sailing for home.[59]

Before the Laurens boys left Geneva their circle of Carolina, English, and Swiss friends had been somewhat extended by recent arrivals. Francis Kinloch had come from Eton. His family was of Scottish descent, rich Carolina merchants and planters, of whom three had sat at the royal Council board.[60] When his father died in

[57] *Ibid.* Kalteisen acted as a courier to the backcountry for Laurens.
[58] Henry Laurens to Thomas Smith, July 21, 1774, *Laurens Letter-Book, 1772-1774,* SCHS.
[59] Henry Laurens to John Laurens, October 8, 1773, "Letters from Hon. Henry Laurens to his son John, 1773-1776," *SCHGM,* III (1902), 89. *Also see* Henry Laurens to John Petrie, September 7, 1774, *Laurens Letter-Book, 1772-1774,* SCHS.
[60] His paternal grandfather James Kinloch, his maternal grandfather John Cleland, and his father Francis Kinloch were all members of the Council H. D. Bull, "Kinloch of South Carolina," *SCHGM,* XLVI (1945), 64-65. Alexander S. Salley, *Register of the National Society of the Colonial Dames of America in the State of South Carolina,* Charleston, 1945, p. 10.

1767, Francis had been placed under the guardianship of the ex-royal-Governor Thomas Boone, who had placed him at Eton, where he was remembered as the boy who had saved Lord North's son from drowning.[61] In Geneva, Kinloch lived in the country about a mile from the Chauvets. The Chauvets had welcomed to their little circle two English boys, John Manning, the son of William Manning, an important West Indian and Carolina merchant, and Morse Romilly, son of a prominent Huguenot family long resident in London.[62] L. de Vegobre, one of the masters who taught mathematics, was a familiar figure in the Chauvet circle.[63] If John Laurens had not moved to London, the picture of this Genevan group might have been lost.

M. Chauvet wrote him that because of young Manning's romantic temperament he had been upset by the reading of the letters of Clarissa, but Chauvet had brought him round with a severity which never relaxed yet never pushed too far. Billy Smith had broken his leg, but it was healing, and during the coming winter Chauvet expected him to make great progress, in fact he was already beginning to work very hard.[64] De Vegobre in a letter of December 24, 1774, revealed the pattern of friendship and of study.

> I thank you for the kind compliments you have sent to me in your letters to M. Kinloch and M. Petrie . . . how impossible should be to me to forget you! For (putting aside all friendship) you have been my first teacher in English tongue, at every progress I made in this language, at every delight (and many are) I feel both in books and in conversations of English men; I always remember that I am obliged to you for that. . . . Never, never in my life I have been so well entertained as I am when I read Milton; and why? First, for Poet's excellency, and secondly and chiefly because I read it with Kinloch. My beloved, my dearest friend is Kinloch, how happy am I, when I teach him some part of natural Philosophy, when I read with him both English and French poets, when

[61] Francis Kinloch to Thomas Boone, June 27, 1783, "Letters of Francis Kinloch to Thomas Boone," ed. Felix Gilbert, *Journal of Southern History*, VIII (1942), 96. Kinloch was sent to England in 1768. *South-Carolina Gazette*, May 16, 1768.

[62] William Manning was a West India merchant. He married in 1751 Elizabeth Ryan of St. Kitts, who owned two estates on that island. Edmund S. Purcell, *Life of Cardinal Manning*, New York, 1898, I, 6. William Manning to Henry Laurens, July 1775, *Emmet Collection*, NYPL. Morse Romilly was most probably of the well-known French Huguenot family established in London of whom Sir Samuel Romilly (1757-1818) was the most famous. J. M. Rigg, "Sir Samuel Romilly," *DNB*. M. Chauvet to John Laurens, November 1, 1774, *Laurens Papers*, LIHS.

[63] John Laurens to Gabriel Manigault, II, April 5, 1776, *Manigault Papers*, SCL.

[64] M. Chauvet to John Laurens, November 1, 1774, *Laurens Papers*, LIHS.

I talk with him about various matters plainly and heartily as with a friend! Let me say again: Kinloch is my beloved, my dearest friend.[65]

De Vegobre wrote that Morse Romilly had joined "our advocates." The English boys in Geneva had made it a practice to set up mock courts and mock parliaments to practice public speaking. In this way the English also taught their Swiss friends about their political institutions. Laurens and Kinloch had obviously taught something more; they had instilled in de Vegobre a deep affection for America. When the first rumblings reached Europe, de Vegobre wrote Laurens: "Poor America!—you cannot believe how much me heart is moved on its account; you, and after you Kinloch have raised in my mind such a concern for your native country! I am as much affected for what happens to it, as if I was an American. . . . English friends, I will, I will see you in your country, before I die!"[66]

News of Lexington and Concord had arrived and John was anxious to be off for home. He wrote his father on August 20, 1775: "Every intelligence I receive gives me fresh cause to wish that I were in America. I have written to you by the last two packets upon the subject of my return, and if conveyances were as swift as my wishes, should have been with you long before this time. What have I to do here in the present circumstances of my country: What have I not to do at home?"[67]

AT HOME IN CAROLINA the struggle between the royal governor and the royal officials on one side and the merchants, planters, and lawyers on the other had continued. Governor Lord Charles Montagu had tried to break the deadlock between King and Assembly, which had arisen over the gift to the Wilkes Fund, by calling the Assembly in October 1772 to meet at Beaufort, seventy miles from Charles Town. He hoped that the conservative Beaufort members would outvote those few who would take the trouble to journey to so remote a place. Thirty-seven representatives turned up on the first day—the ruse had failed. No act could have been more irritating to the sensible men of the colony.[68]

Royal officials in the colony were augmented at this time by the

[65] L. de Vegobre to John Laurens, December 24, 1774, *Laurens Papers,* LIHS.
[66] *Ibid.*
[67] John Laurens to Henry Laurens, August 20, 1775, *Miscellaneous Manuscripts,* NYPL. *See also* John Laurens to Henry Laurens, September 4, 1775, *Preston Davie Papers,* SHC.
[68] *South-Carolina Gazette,* October 8, 15, 1772.

arrival of the chief justice and three new assistant judges from England. When the colony was forced to reorganize its judicial system to meet the growing demands of the backcountry for justice, the King insisted that the judges be appointed to hold office during the pleasure of the Crown. Colonials refused to accept these positions due to the insecurity of tenure, even though these were now patent offices with salaries attached.[69] In 1772, when the last two assistant judges arrived, Montagu was forced to replace George Gabriel Powell and Rawlins Lowndes.[70]

Both Bull and Montagu tried to win the support of the moderate merchants and planters by offering them seats at the Council board, but these gentlemen still refused. Bull recommended Gabriel Manigault, John Savage, and David Deas, in October 1770.[71] Montagu in 1772 named Charles Pinckney, senior, Thomas Loughton Smith, and Benjamin Huger.[72] Bull in 1773 recommended Thomas Smith of Broad Street, Miles Brewton, and John Deas.[73] Their unwillingness to accept must have seemed extremely sensible after Lieutenant Governor Bull's dismissal of William Henry Drayton.

Drayton had been one of the two native-born South Carolinians to accept a Council seat in the 1770's.[74] Trouble began in 1774, however, when he criticized the Intolerable Acts, particularly objecting to the act that brought the Council of Massachusetts under the arbitrary sway of the British government. Drayton wrote that he was strongly opposed to having placemen sent out from England to be councilors, who "ought of right, to be called out of American families." Although he did not yet desire "dignities, lordships, and dukedoms," he made it clear that a second house, permanent and not subject to removal, either by the Crown, or by the people, was

[69] Edward McCrady, *The History of South Carolina under the Royal Government, 1719-1776*, New York, 1899, pp. 642-643. Thomas Knox Gordon, the chief justice, and Edward Savage, Charles Mathews Cosslett, and John Fewtrell, assistant judges, all came out from Britain in 1771-1772. Dr. John Murray, a local assistant judge, who had been highly recommended by Bull, had accepted. Bull to Hillsborough, March 7, 1770, *PRO*, XXXII, 205-208; Bull to Hillsborough, December 5, 1770, *PRO*, XXXII, 407; Hillsborough to Bull, February 11, April 1, 1771, *PRO*, XXXIII, 20-21, 40-41; Montagu to Hillsborough, January 25, 1772, *PRO*, XXXIII, 118.

[70] The assistant judges had formerly had no salary; they were now to receive £300 sterling annually. Montagu to Hillsborough, April 27, 1772, *PRO*, XXXIII, 141.

[71] Bull to Lords of Trade, October 16, 1770, *PRO*, XXXII, 337.

[72] Montagu to Hillsborough, August 2, 1772, *PRO*, XXXIII, 171.

[73] Bull to Dartmouth, April 9, 1773, *PRO*, XXXIII, 256.

[74] Drayton was sworn a councilor on April 3, 1772, *CJ*, XXXVI, part 2, 67. Barnard Elliott took his oath on September 26, 1772. *CJ*, XXXVI, part 2, 178.

desirable.[75] For his revolutionary activities Drayton was suspended by Bull on March 8, 1775.[76]

When Josiah Quincy, junior, visited Charles Town in 1773, he was informed that the judges, councilors, and other great officers were all appointed by mandamus from Great Britain. Several of the planters told Quincy that "we none of us, when we grow old, can expect the honours of the State—they are all given away to worthless poor rascals." The rich merchants and planters looked with contempt upon "the official grandee." "Thus," according to Quincy, "the rights and liberties of the State are in some measure safe—but from a very unstable cause." Quincy believed that the Crown could hold Carolina by a few simple measures: "Compose the Council of the first planters, fill all the Public offices with them, give them the honours of the State . . . introduce Baronies and Lordships—their enormous estates will bear it."[77] The Carolina aristocrats had been following a policy of prestige; they wanted to be respected; they wanted to rule. They began to see that this could only be achieved by independence. But was independence worth the risk?

A new crisis arose in Carolina with the arrival of East India tea consigned through the influence of John Nutt and William Greenwood to their friends and relatives in the colony, Roger Smith, William Greenwood, junior, and Peter Leger.[78] These three merchants were called before a meeting of the people held at the Exchange; there they promised not to receive the tea. Roger Smith said, to the accompaniment of loud shouts of approval and, as the *Gazette* commented, to "his lasting honour," that he had "determined some weeks before the tea arrived, not to have any concern

---

[75] [William Henry Drayton,] *Letter from Freeman of South Carolina, to the Deputies of North-America, Assembled in the High Court of Congress at Philadelphia*, Charles-Town, 1774, p. 32.

[76] Bull to Lords of Trade, March 8, 1775, *PRO*, XXXV, 32-34.

[77] "Journal of Josiah Quincy, Junior, 1773," *op. cit.*, p. 455.

[78] For the history of the firm of Leger and Greenwood, *see* the "Petition of Elizabeth Leger to the House of Representatives," 1782, William Greenwood folder, *Confiscated Estates*, SC Archives. The statement that John Nutt and William Greenwood, senior, had used their influence to gain the consignments of tea is based upon the following evidence: John Nutt had long been close to the Smith family. William Greenwood, senior, lived in London; his son in the colony. On November 24, 1775, John Nutt and William Greenwood appeared before the Board of Trade to plead for a continuation of trade with South Carolina and Georgia. Minutes of Board of Trade, November 24, 1775, *PRO*, XXXV, 2. Nutt and Greenwood may have been closely related, for William Smith on several occasions in 1781 and 1782 attended the theater with Mrs. Nutt and Miss Greenwood. *See* "Journals of William Smith, 1781 and 1782," *William Loughton Smith Papers*, SCHS.

in a business, which his countrymen conceived to have so fatal a tendency." Thereupon a committee composed of Christopher Gadsden, Colonel Charles Pinckney, Thomas Ferguson, Charles Cotesworth Pinckney, and Daniel Cannon waited upon all the merchants and asked them, each in turn, to sign an agreement not to receive the tea. The merchants could not have done otherwise.[79]

There was, of course, a threat to the lesser merchants in the way in which the tea was consigned, the danger that a few merchants would monopolize some of the principal imports. As the *Gazette* pointed out: "The establishing of Tea Ware-Houses in America, by the India Co., 'tis said is intended to pave the way for introducing large Factories for other goods at all principal ports and then to bring in an Hon. Board of Excise."[80] If patronage were extended to the point of granting monopolies to a favored few, the merchants would be moved to join the patriot cause.

The tug-of-war between moderates and radicals can be seen in the political events of 1774. A by-election in St. Michael's Parish was contested in April 1774 by David Deas, merchant, and Thomas Lynch, junior, a young planter, the son of the radical leader. David Deas was a Scottish merchant long settled in Charles Town. As a partner in the firm of Lennox and Deas he had made a fortune by the 1760's and like Gabriel Manigault and Thomas Smith had retired to a Goose Creek plantation. In the *Gazette* of April 4 "Craftsman" appealed to the friends of the "good old cause" to vote for Lynch. Some had urged that Deas, since he was acquainted with mercantile transactions, would be a useful man in the crisis, but "Craftsman" pointed out that Deas was a Scot and that most North Britons thought Parliament had a right to tax America. It was therefore imperative that they elect a man who had no connection with placemen, a man who had connection only with local people. These charges were unfair, as Deas's refusal of a Council seat indicated, and a majority of the voters knew they were unfair, for Deas won the election by a margin of six votes.[81] Deas, like moderates generally, was in essence a whig of 1688; Lynch, like the radicals, was much closer to the republicans of 1649.

[79] The story of "the tea party" is told in *South-Carolina Gazette*, December 6, 1773. *See also CJ*, XXXVIII, 8-9.
[80] *South-Carolina Gazette*, December 6, 1773.
[81] *Ibid*, April 4, 11, 1774. Deas was the candidate of the merchants who had formed the Charles Town Chamber of Commerce in December 1773. The officers were John Savage, president, Miles Brewton, vice-president, David Deas, treasurer, and John Hopton, secretary. *Ibid.*, December 28, 1773.

The news of the passing of the Intolerable Acts and the closing of the port of Boston redounded to the strength of the radical leaders. In the summer when it was time to elect five delegates to the First Continental Congress, radicals Thomas Lynch, Christopher Gadsden, and Edward Rutledge defeated Miles Brewton, Charles Pinckney, and Rawlins Lowndes. John Rutledge and Henry Middleton were agreeable to both groups.[82]

The division between radicals and moderates was mirrored in congressional debates. The radicals based their case on the rights of all men, the moderates on the rights of Englishmen. Patrick Henry declared in October: "Government is dissolved. Where are your landmarks, your boundaries of Colonies? We are in a state of nature, sir."[83] John Jay was quick to reply: "I can't yet think that all government is at an end."[84] John Rutledge added: "Our claims, I think, are well founded on the British constitution, and not on the law of nature."[85] James Duane was for "grounding our rights on the laws and constitution of the country from whence we sprung, and charters, without recurring to the law of nature; because this will be a feeble support."[86] And Galloway declared that he had looked for their rights "in the constitution of the English government, and there found them. We may draw them from this source securely."[87] According to John Adams, Patrick Henry had a "horrid opinion of Galloway, Jay, and the Rutledges. Their system, he says, would ruin the cause of America."[88] Radicals like Patrick Henry desired to rush into revolution without any thought of the consequences. The moderates did not wish to open up the seams of

---

[82] McCrady, *op. cit.*, p. 741.

[83] *The Works of John Adams,* ed. Charles Francis Adams, Boston, 1850, II, 366.

[84] *Ibid,* p. 368.

[85] *Ibid.,* p. 371.

[86] *Ibid.*

[87] *Ibid.,* p. 372.

[88] *Ibid.,* p. 396. Edward Rutledge, though elected as a radical leader, was ultimately drawn by the rapid approach of independence to the position of his brother and the moderates. He wrote John Jay on June 8, 1776, to tell him that "the sensible part of the House" opposed Richard Henry Lee's motion for independence. As late as June 29, 1776, Edward Rutledge wrote Jay urging him to return to Congress so that they might "effectually . . . oppose" the motion for independence. Concerning those who were foremost in the move for independence: "I dread their low Cunning, and those levelling Principles which Men without Character and without Fortune in general possess, which are so captivating to the lower class of Mankind, and which will occasion such a fluctuation of Property as to introduce the greatest disorder." *Letters of Members of the Continental Congress,* ed. Edmund C. Burnett, Washington, 1921, I, 476, 517-518.

society. They were horrified by the thought of being in a state of nature.

The First Continental Congress decided to back up their protests with non-importation, non-exportation, and non-consumption agreements. The fact that rice was excluded from the non-exportation agreement was symbolic of the exclusive, separate position of the rice nabobs, the Carolina aristocrats. In Carolina, the tyranny of the committee set up to enforce these agreements dragged the moderates against their will towards revolution. Bull saw in this situation one hope to halt the revolution—the hope that the planters and the merchants would return to their loyalty to the Crown. He wrote the Earl of Dartmouth on March 28, 1775:

> In the present situation of things, unless Massachusetts should change, any changes in the Democratical Plan which may be wished will most probably be effected by jealousies naturally arising from the variety of private interests in the Planter, the Merchant, and the Mechanic, and are more likely to be the work of chance than of design. The men of property begin at length to see that the many headed power the People, who have hitherto been obediently made use of by their numbers and occasional riots to support the claims set up in America, have discovered their own strength and importance, and are not now so easily governed by their former Leaders.[89]

After the news of Lexington and Concord reached Charles Town on May 8 there was little chance of staying the course of revolution. On June 3, the committee decreed that all Carolinians sign the non-importation agreement. When William Wragg, the most prominent of the Carolinians who refused to sign, was hailed before the committee on July 22 to give his reasons, he nobly stood on the right of conscience. For insisting on his right to judge for himself, he was banished to his plantation.[90] The royal placemen who refused to sign were confined to their houses in town. On September 1, the judges, attorney general, and clerk of common pleas informed the governor that they could no longer carry out the duties of their offices.[91] The end to royal government was sealed in September by the flight of Lord William Campbell to the British man-of-war *Tamar*, which was anchored in Rebellion Roads. The patriots assumed command and the way to independence was deep and clear.

[89] Bull to Dartmouth, March 28, 1775, *PRO*, XXXV, 79-80.
[90] For Wragg's answer, *see* "American Loyalists," *Southern Quarterly Review*, IV (1843), 142-145.
[91] Gordon, Savage, Cosslett, Fewtrell, Gregory, Simpson, and Trail to Lord William Campbell, September 1, 1775, *PRO*, XXXV, 217-228.

The descendants of these South Carolina patriots have looked upon them as of one mind and one purpose, but the common hostility to Britain only temporarily covered up the division within their own ranks that was bound to recur.

The dilemma was succinctly put by two young Carolinians studying abroad who in 1776 still had to make up their own minds. Francis Kinloch wrote John Laurens on April 28, 1776:

> For my part though I would rather not exist than be the slave of a despot, yet is the height of my wishes to live the subject of a monarch—In a democracy you are condemned to a hateful mediocrity, and the desire of excelling in any respect, though perhaps not really so is always looked upon as shocking the spirit of the constitution.—to be confounded in a heap of butchers, bakers, blacksmiths etc.—is dreadful for a man of any education, of feeling . . . in a Monarch every generous principle of the mind is developed,— Honour instils a warmth into the soul which pushes on to great actions, ambition becomes a virtue, and the hand of a King—but where am I running to?—For-give, dear Laurens, this length of letter, and a repetition of what you must have already often heard from others and from myself in point of politics, and principle.[92]

John Laurens replied on the 16th of June from London:

> My ambition Kinloch is to live under a Republican Government,— I hate the name of King—but this is returning you opinion for opinion, now let us examine the reasons upon which sentiments thus diametrically opposite, are founded—In a democracy say you a man is condemned to a hateful mediocrity and the desire of excelling shocks the spirit of the Constitution—to be confounded among Butchers etc. is dredful to men of education and feeling—If you mean by mediocrity, the government of a man's passions, the continual sacrifice of private interest to public good, from which kind of conduct, a happiness which riches cannot give, results to the individual and strength and grandeur are ensured to the state, I agree with you that it is required in the government to which I give the preference and am persuaded that no man who is governed by his reason will object to such mediocrity—if you mean . . . that ambition is closed by the government, and a man cannot make a figure by exerting laudable talents—that I must beg leave totally to deny—under a Republican government there is the fullest scope for ambition directed in its proper channel, in the only channel in which it ought to be allowed, I mean for the advancement of public good.[93]

Kinloch was filled with the fears of his generation; Laurens with the hopes.

[92] Francis Kinloch to John Laurens, April 28, 1776, *Miscellaneous Manuscripts*, NYPL.
[93] John Laurens to Francis Kinloch, June 16, 1776, *Chamberlain Collection*, BPL.

It was after the news of Lexington and Concord had reached Charles Town that James Laurens completed his plans for taking his family and his niece Martha Laurens, as well as young Gabriel Manigault, to England. The Laurenses went straight to Bath, but Gabriel Manigault traveled on to London to the home of Benjamin Stead, where his father, Peter, had died some two years before. Stead, an old friend of Benjamin Smith and Gabriel Manigault, I, made arrangements for Manigault to go on to Geneva.[94]

Manigault arrived in October and settled in the home of M. Chauvet, which he described as being "at a small distance from Geneva, which makes it very convenient for bathing."[95] There were then six others in the house: Billy Smith, three English boys, one of whom was John Manning, and two Genevans.[96] Kinloch and de Vegobre still lived nearby. De Vegobre in a letter of June 7, 1776, after thanking Laurens for "the pretty Swift," told of being charmed with Manigault, whom he taught geometry and who taught him French and English *belles-lettres*. They often walked together and on Saturday evenings would visit Kinloch, who lived one league in the country and there they might stay until Sunday or even Monday. Formal amusements there were none except the plays acted throughout the summer in theaters in the surrounding villages.[97] Manigault explained: "They are acted in the afternoon, that the people may have time to return home. There are two theatres one of them is patronized by Voltaire, and is at a large village where he lives, and to which he has always been a great friend. I find that going to the play is a means of my improvement in French besides the advantage of frequently seeing so celebrated an author, as Voltaire."[98]

In July 1776 Manigault, Smith, and a young Genevan went with M. Chauvet on a seventeen-day tour of the Alps. They marvelled at the romantic mountain scenery with peaks soaring through the

[94] Henry Laurens to John Laurens, May 15, 1775, *Myers Collection*, NYPL. Anne Manigault to Benjamin Stead, May 17, 1775, *Manigault Papers*, SCHS. "The Manigault Family of South Carolina," *Transactions of the Huguenot Society, of South Carolina*, IV (1897), 71-72, 80. Gabriel Manigault, II, to Benjamin Stead, October 24, 1775, *Manigault Papers*, SCL.

[95] Gabriel Manigault, II, to Anne Manigault, July 20, 1776, *Manigault Papers*, SCHS.

[96] Gabriel Manigault, II, to Anne Manigault, October 24, 1775, *Manigault Papers*, SCL. Petrie had already departed. Gabriel Manigault, II, to Anne Manigault, July 20, 1776; Gabriel Manigault, II, to Gabriel Manigault, I, October 1, 1776; Gabriel Manigault, II, to William Manning, October 1, 1776, *Manigault Papers*, SCHS.

[97] L. de Vegobre to John Laurens, June 7, 1776, *Laurens Papers*, LIHS.

[98] Gabriel Manigault, II, to Anne Manigault, July 20, 1776, *Manigault Papers*, SCHS.

clouds and at the long valleys of ice of the glaciers of Savoy, one of which was six leagues in length: "The ice was full of large cracks, which from the top of a mountain near it makes it appear like a sea which has been frozen all at once." They also went to the foot of the highest mountain in the Alps, Mt. Blanc, stood on a mountain from which they saw fourteen lakes, observed a number of cascades, and went a mile and a half into a salt mine through a passage seven feet high and only two and one-half wide.[99]

There was apparently little concern that summer for the war at home. In July 1776 John Laurens and Francis Kinloch were twenty-one, Gabriel Manigault was eighteen, and William Smith was seventeen[100]—all of military age, but only John Laurens was consumed with the desire to return and fight, and even he did not set sail from Europe until January 1777.[101]

Kinloch left Switzerland in the fall of 1776 to tour Italy, and after a leisurely progress across the continent paid a long visit to his Scottish cousin, Sir David Kinloch.[102] Manigault left Geneva in June 1777 to take up the study of law in London.[103] He stopped four days in Paris and visited all the palaces: Fontainebleau, Versailles, Marly, and St. Cloud. At Versailles he had the good fortune to see Louis XVI and Marie Antoinette. "The appearance of the Queen is very much in her favour," he reported, "but I cannot say so much for the King." He also stopped to see Chantilly, the seat of the Prince of Condé, which "pleased" him more than any of the palaces he had seen.[104]

In London, Manigault took lodgings at the Carolina Coffee House to be near the Inns of Court, but he got his news that summer at the home of his fellow Carolinian Ralph Izard, which was a bee-hive

[99] Gabriel Manigault, II, to Gabriel Manigault, I, October 1, 1776, *Manigault Papers*, SCHS.
[100] John Laurens was born October 28, 1754. Wallace, *op. cit.*, p. 502. Francis Kinloch: March 7, 1755. H. D. Bull, "Kinloch of South Carolina," *SCHGM*, XLVI (1945), 65. Gabriel Manigault, II: March 17, 1758, and William Smith: October 2, 1758. "Extracts from the Journal of Mrs. Ann Manigault, 1754-1781," ed. Mabel L. Webber, *SCHGM*, XX (1919), 131.
[101] John Laurens to Henry Laurens, August 20, 1775, *Miscellaneous Manuscripts*, NYPL. John Laurens to Francis Kinloch, May 1776, and September 30, 1776, *Emmet Collection*, NYPL. Wallace, *op. cit.*, p. 471.
[102] "Letters of Francis Kinloch to Thomas Boone," ed. Felix Gilbert, *Journal of Southern History*, VIII (1942), 93.
[103] Gabriel Manigault, II, to Gabriel Manigault, I, June 6, 1777, *Manigault Papers*, SCHS.
[104] Gabriel Manigault, II, to Anne Manigault, July 5, 1777, *Manigault Papers*, SCHS.

of comings and goings.¹⁰⁵ Some of the sojourners were patriots waiting for passage home. Daniel Blake and his wife were going to Spa with the daughter of Benjamin Stead to pass the time until the hurricane season was over, and then in November they would set sail for South Carolina with Walter Izard.¹⁰⁶ Others just arriving were loyalists, Carolinians who had refused to take the oath of allegiance to the new state and had, therefore, been banished. Robert Peronneau and Robert Cooper had made their way from America via Amsterdam; Mrs. Joseph Milligan and Mrs. John Watson came by way of Cork; and John Champneys had already arrived.¹⁰⁷ Lieutenant Governor and Mrs. Bull, just as they were entering a Dutch port, were taken by a man-of-war and brought to Gravesend.¹⁰⁸ William Wragg was shipwrecked that September off the coast of Holland and drowned, but his son was saved by a faithful slave and brought to London. Upon receiving news of Wragg's death, young Manigault and most of the Carolinians in London put on mourning.¹⁰⁹

Manigault began the study of law by keeping the Michaelmas term, but as soon as it was over he left London with Robert Williams, junior, to spend a month at Bath. There the two boys stayed with Robert Williams, senior, at Mrs. Heyward's in West Gate Street. Among the Carolina merchants who visited them at the spa were James Poyas, John Savage, Samuel Brailsford, and John Hopton.¹¹⁰

South Carolina had been quite generous to those who were banished for refusing to take the oaths. They were given a limited time to remove their property and were permitted to appoint attorneys

¹⁰⁵ *Ibid.* Ralph Izard to Lord George Germaine, March 27, 1777; Ralph Izard to George Livius, May 12, 1777; Ralph Izard to William Drayton, October 26, 1777, *Correspondence of Mr. Ralph Izard, of South Carolina, From the Year 1774 to 1804,* ed. Anne Izard Deas, New York, 1844, I, 272-274, 289, 365-369.
¹⁰⁶ Daniel Blake to Ralph Izard, November 7, 1777, *ibid.,* pp. 375-376.
¹⁰⁷ Robert W. Barnwell, Jr., "The Migration of Loyalists from South Carolina," *Proceedings of the South Carolina Historical Association, 1937,* ed. Robert L. Meriwether, Columbia, 1937, pp. 34-42. Sabine lists Robert Cooper, Joseph Milligan, Robert Peronneau, and John Watson as Carolina loyalists. Lorenzo Sabine, *The American Loyalists,* Boston, 1847, pp. 228, 469, 529, 676. John Champneys is listed by Josiah Smith, junior, as one banished at this time. "Josiah Smith's Diary, 1780-1781," *SCHGM,* XXXIV (1933), 198.
¹⁰⁸ Gabriel Manigault, II, to Gabriel Manigault, I, July 11, 1777, *Manigault Papers,* SCL.
¹⁰⁹ Manigault describes the drowning in a letter to his grandmother, October 8, 1777, *Manigault Papers,* SCL.
¹¹⁰ Gabriel Manigault, II, to Anne Manigault, December 15, 1777; Gabriel Manigault, II, "Bath in December 1777 & January 1778," *Manigault Papers,* SCL.

for that purpose.[111] The state did not look with favor, however, upon the Carolinians who had been abroad at the start of the conflict and had not returned. Gabriel Manigault sent off ominous news to Kinloch on March 12, 1778: "I am informed (but I do not know how true it is) that they have resolved in our Province to confiscate the Estate of every Carolinian who is above the age of twenty-one, and who does not return there; as they think that those who have any Property there, ought to help to defend it."[112] Kinloch answered on March 30 from Edinburgh that he would like to know "for certain, whether or no the South Carolina Assembly has entered into any resolution respecting the estates of absentees."[113] Spurred on by this rumor, Carolinians in England began feverish preparations to return to America. In May, Manigault wrote his grandfather that he would soon be the only Carolinian in London except for those who had been banished.[114] Although perfectly satisfied there, Manigault thought it necessary to consult his grandfather, and when Robert Pringle came down from his medical studies at Edinburgh on his way home, Manigault sent a note asking how far the law obliging absentees to return "may affect me, and whether it may be necessary for me to return."[115]

Kinloch sailed in the summer of 1778 with Robert Williams, senior, and Robert Williams, junior, for New York, which was then in British hands,[116] and proceeded overland to Carolina in a one-horse chair, stopping to visit John Laurens in camp. Laurens expressed some doubts about Kinloch's zeal for the cause in a letter

[111] See an "act establishing an oath of abjuration and allegiance," passed February 13, 1777, SC Statutes, I, 135-136.
[112] Gabriel Manigault, II, to Francis Kinloch, March 12, 1778, Manigault Papers, SCL.
[113] Francis Kinloch to Gabriel Manigault, II, March 30, 1778, Manigault Papers, SCL.
[114] Gabriel Manigault, II, to Gabriel Manigault, I, May 4, 1778, Manigault Papers, SCL.
[115] Gabriel Manigault, II, to Gabriel Manigault, I, June 2, 1778, Manigault Papers, SCL. Robert Pringle sailed from Nantes on July 28, 1778. Robert Pringle to John Pringle, July 28, 1778, "Letters and Will of Robert Pringle (1702-1776)," ed. Mary Pringle Fenhagen, SCHGM, L (1949), 151, n. 85. The laws of which the boys had heard were passed by the South Carolina legislature on March 28, 1778. An "act enforcing an assurance of allegiance and fidelity to the state" required all males in South Carolina over 16 and all absentees upon their return to take an oath. SC Statutes, I, 147-151. In section 2 of an "act for raising and paying into the public treasury of this state, the tax therein mentioned" all absentees were double-taxed, except minors and those not yet 22. Upon reaching the age of 21 the absentee was allowed one year in which to return. SC Statutes, IV, 413-422. The laws were not as harsh as the boys had feared.
[116] Robert Williams, junior, to Gabriel Manigault, II, September 18, 1778, Manigault Papers, SCHS.

to his father: "I am sorry that Kinloch did not return to America sooner. His former sentiments on the present contest give reason to suspect, if he is a convert, that success on our side has alone operated the change. Something may be drawn in palliation of his conduct from the education he received and the powerful influence which his guardian had over him."[117] By January 1779, Kinloch was acting as a confidential officer on the staff of General William Moultrie.[118]

The Williamses had slightly more trouble in resuming their former place in Carolina society. They, with John Hopton and the Georgia merchants, Telfair, Price, and Graham, obtained a flag of truce through the favor of the British commissioners then at New York and sailed for Charles Town. They were obliged, however, to remain on board ship under the guns of Sullivan's Island until they had petitioned the executive for permission to land. Even then both the elder Williams and Hopton had to undergo strict scrutiny by the president, Privy Council, and Assembly before they were admitted to the privileges of citizenship by taking and subscribing the oaths. Telfair and Price were permitted to land and proceed to Georgia, but Graham was forced to continue on his way, since he was a partner in a London house engaged in the Pensacola trade.[119]

William Smith seemed unconcerned by this flurry among the Carolinians in England. He finally left Geneva in November 1778, carrying a bust of Voltaire as a present for Manigault.[120] He stopped in Paris, where he resided "upwards of two months in the character of an American gentleman." After waiting on Doctor Franklin, John Adams, and Arthur Lee, he journeyed on to London in January 1779 to join Manigault.[121]

Smith and Manigault went to the Isle of Wight on one trip and to the Shakespeare country on another—the study of law in the

---

[117] John Laurens to Henry Laurens, September 24, 1778, *The Army Correspondence of Colonel John Laurens in the Years 1777-8*, ed. William Gilmore Simms, New York, 1867, p. 225.

[118] "Order Book of John Faucheraud Grimké," *SCHGM*, XIV (1913), 101.

[119] Josiah Smith, junior, to James Poyas, November 30, 1778, *Josiah Smith, junior, Letter-Book, 1771-1784*, SHC. They must have come on the ship which brought a special offer of peace to Carolina from the Carlisle Commission. David Ramsay, *The History of the Revolution of South-Carolina, from a British Province to an Independent State*, Trenton, 1785, I, 183-184.

[120] Richard Hammond to Gabriel Manigault, II, November 17, 1778, *Manigault Papers*, SCL.

[121] *Annals of the Congress of the United States*, Washington, 1834, I (1st cong., 1st sess.), 397-398.

eighteenth century left plenty of time for travel.[122] In the fall of 1779 Manigault crossed over to Holland for a short tour before taking passage via St. Eustatius for Carolina. Smith's letters to Manigault, the first that remain from his pen, reveal an uncontrolled, self-indulgent young man, a mocker of men of principles. Here was a man with a sense of realism that cut through men's pretences, a realism that was the stuff of wit and satire. He spoke of his second jaunt to the Isle of Wight, of his sightseeing at Goodwood, the Duke of Richmond's seat near Chichester, and of his plans for going to Bath at Christmas. In a bantering fashion he chided Manigault for going home by quoting the observations of Mrs. Bull: "I wonder he goes there for amongst them to have himself killed. I am sure if I was in his place I wouldn't have gone."[123] His irreverence and his ability to caricature came forth in his second letter describing the Bull household. He wrote on November 3, 1779:

> Governor Bull is now in Surry Street, and his wife is more dissatisfied than ever. I went to see them the day after their removal and asked her how she was accomodated: "Law, sir, very badly; I 'sure you Mr. Smith, there is not a room large enough to turn in; at our other house, we had at least a fine large parlour etc.—I think we should be better there again, for at least we knew before hand what we are to expect!" The poor Gentleman has been very deaf of late. He has however the satisfaction not to hear her discontents and nonsense. I dined there on Saturday with Colonel Howard or Howarth, Mrs. Simpson and Dr. Farquharson who said he had heard from you and whispered me that you were going to Boston.

Smith begged Manigault to write him "minutely and circumstantially" from Charles Town, yet warning him: "Pray don't mention in Carolina the company I keep."[124]

Manigault sailed from Holland to the neutral Dutch West Indian Island of St. Eustatius, the Switzerland of the American Revolution, through whose port passed much information and many supplies. From there Manigault made his way to Carolina, landing at Georgetown, and was in Charles Town by February 10, 1780. He was home in time to take part in the siege. Mrs. Anne Manigault made a

[122] William Smith to Gabriel Manigault, II, October 18, 1779; Gabriel Manigault, II, "Journey from London . . . to Birmingham," August 26 to 28, 1779, *Manigault Papers*, SCL.
[123] William Smith to Gabriel Manigault, II, October 18, 1779, *Manigault Papers*, SCL.
[124] William Smith to Gabriel Manigault, II, November 3, 1779, *Manigault Papers*, SCL.

simple notation in her diary for March 4: "My grandson G. went upon duty."[125]

WITH THE FALL of Charles Town in May 1780, the kaleidoscope of civil war took another violent turn, leaving each individual in new and strange relationships with his friends and enemies, with South Carolina and the King. Adjusting to the new circumstances was painful. Those who had been in Charles Town at the time of the surrender were prisoners-of-war on parole. They had given their word to live quietly and take no part against the King, but the British authorities soon put pressure upon them to take up arms against those Carolina patriots still in the field. In the summer of 1780 addresses were drawn up to congratulate Clinton and then Cornwallis. The prominent men of Charles Town who refused to sign and who failed to exchange their paroles as prisoners-of-war for the protection and privileges of British subjects were hustled off to St. Augustine.[126]

Others on parole had retired to their plantations, hoping to wait out the struggle. Most notable among these were the heads of the Goose Creek families. As Thomas Smith of Broad Street put it, they were "in the way of both parties," for Goose Creek lay between the British in Charles Town and the patriotic bands led by Marion and Sumter who sought refuge in the swamps.[127] Their property was in danger of being plundered by lawless bands on both sides, if not by the British authorities directly. Some of the outlying planters were therefore forced to take commissions in the militia raised by the British, in order to maintain law and order in their respective parishes. Others sought protection in order to defend their property before the authorities in town. Fathers also clearly understood the danger in which their sons were placed. Although the sons were pledged not to fight, they were often tempted to join the American cause. If captured, they could be executed—this was the fate of Colonel Isaac Hayne. Under the circumstances, some thought it best to retire to England, or at least to send their sons, to remove them from involvement in the strife at home.

[125] "Extracts from the Journal of Mrs. Ann Manigault, 1754-1781," ed. Mabel L. Webber, SCHGM, XXI (1920), 119. J. Franklin Jameson, "St. Eustatius in the American Revolution," AHR, VIII (1902-1903), 683-708.

[126] David Duncan Wallace, South Carolina, A Short History, 1520-1948, Chapel Hill, 1951, pp. 295-297, 304-306.

[127] Thomas Smith to Isaac Smith, August 19, 1783, Smith-Carter Papers, MHS. The story of these families has been told after reading the documents in Confiscated Estates, SC Archives.

Roger, Peter, Benjamin, and James, the four sons of Thomas Smith of Broad Street, had been in the lines at Charles Town, although Peter got sick and withdrew to Goose Creek before the surrender.[128] Their father had been at Goose Creek with the women of the family during the campaign and had been fortunate enough to lose only a few slaves.[129] Thomas Smith of Broad Street, being of the older generation, did not find it difficult to accept royal authority once again, and was soon listed by the military as a royal sympathizer. His primary concern was preserving the family property. With one foot in each camp the family would be able to take care of all eventualities, so the four sons were neatly spread over the tumult. Roger Smith, the eldest son, who stayed in Charles Town, was listed by the British as a rebel sympathizer.[130] Peter remained at Goose Creek and more nearly shared his father's views.[131] Benjamin, who had been entered at the Middle Temple in 1774 and had read law in the office of Edward Rutledge, might have been sent to England, but having married (in November 1777) Sarah Dry of Brunswick, North Carolina, he pursued his military career in that state, which eventually became his home.[132] James, the youngest, was shipped off to England in March 1781. As his father explained: "he could not accomplish himself in the Law here as we were then circumstanced and it was a pity he should be losing his time."[133] William Smith welcomed his cousin to London in June 1781, helped him enroll at the Middle Temple, and showed him the glories of Westminster Abbey on his first day in town. James also assisted William—by lending him £21 sterling.[134]

And James brought news of conditions at home. Only a William Smith could have looked upon the turmoil and heartache with amusement. He began a letter to his friend Manigault by chiding him for his failure to write. There could be no excuse, he said, since

---

[128] Thomas Bee to Isaac Smith, July 10, 1780, *Smith-Carter Papers*, MHS.
[129] Thomas Smith to Isaac Smith, August 19, 1783, *Smith-Carter Papers*, MHS.
[130] *See* the photostats of the "Lists of Loyalists and Rebels in South Carolina," from the *Clinton Collection*, WLCL in SCL.
[131] Edward Rutledge to Arthur Middleton, February 26, 1782, "Correspondence of Hon. Arthur Middleton," *SCHGM*, XXVII (1926), 8.
[132] John Pringle to William Tilghman, July 30, September 15, 1774, *Preston Davie Papers*, SHC. Barnwell Rhett Heyward, "The Descendants of Col. William Rhett, of South Carolina," *SCHGM*, IV (1903), 41.
[133] Thomas Smith to Isaac Smith, August 19, 1783, *Smith-Carter Papers*, MHS.
[134] "Journals of William Smith, 1781 and 1782," *William Loughton Smith Papers*, SCHS.

Manigault must be enjoying "idleness and a good fortune at Goose-creek."

> I both read and heard (from my cousin) of your great sufferings in the bloody field of Mars—you are in fact now another—what was that fellow's name who retired to his plough crowned with laurels? I don't immediately recollect it, but as you have trod in his steps, you are doubtless master of his history—Yours would I imagine make no contemptible figure in Bell's library under the denomination of the singular adventures of a young gentleman, shewing, *how* after having escaped the innumerable perils of the seas, he had scarce set his foot on dry land, before he was obliged to undergo the fatigues and horrid dangers of a bloody and desperate siege, *how* he escaped also from them, was taken prisoner of war, and tho' he had acquired immortal glory by his great actions, yet in the bloom of youth and in the height of bodily vigour, preferred like Cincinnatus (faith I believe that's his name) to retire from the shock of arms to cultivate his paternal acres.

This, of course, was not meant to be taken seriously, as Smith himself wrote, but he was serious when he explained that he did not intend to return to Carolina that summer. He had learned that his fortune had been lost by the depreciation of paper money and consequent inflation, and he declared he would not return until he could begin to recoup his fortune by the practice of law. "By telling me that it's not likely the courts will be opened for sometime to come, you make me fear that my return is still more distant than I thought it."[135]

When Gabriel Manigault, I, died on June 5, 1781, Gabriel Manigault, II, became the head of the family, and it was he who decided his brother Joseph should go to England.[136] Old Gabriel and Joseph had gone together into the lines in May 1779 when General Prevost had threatened the city, and young Gabriel himself had been in Charles Town at the surrender, but Goose Creek was not a safe place and Joseph was consequently shipped off in July 1781.[137] John Parker, who had been forced to defend his property at Goose Creek by shooting marauders, sent his son John with Joseph.[138] A third Goose Creek lad, William Allen Deas, may also have gone. He was

---

[135] William Smith to Gabriel Manigault, II, June 13, 1781, *Manigault Papers,* SCL.

[136] Mabel L. Webber, "Gabriel Manigault," *DAB.*

[137] For the grandfather's role, *see* Gabriel Manigault, II, to Joseph Manigault, September 13, 1808, *Manigault Papers,* SCL. For date of sailing *see* "Extracts from the Journal of Mrs. Ann Manigault, 1754-1781," ed. Mabel L. Webber, *SCHGM,* XXI (1920), 120.

[138] Joseph Johnson, *Traditions and Reminiscences chiefly of the American Revolution in the South,* Charleston, 1851, pp. 397-398.

the son of John Deas, who, although he had hired substitutes for the continental army and had lent large sums to the state, had taken protection after his house in town had been occupied by the British and the stock on his plantation at Goose Creek plundered.[139] The boys landed at Falmouth on August 5, and after a tour of Pendennis Castle set off for London.[140]

That fall there was a small community of Carolina boys in London, including Manigault, Parker, Deas, William Smith and his cousin James, and possibly others.[141] Their lodgings cost between twelve and fifteen shillings a week for bed and breakfast. In the evenings the boys dined together at one of their favorite coffee

---

[139] "Petition of John Deas to the Senate," 1783, *Confiscated Estates*, SC Archives. Joseph Manigault to Gabriel Manigault, II, October 1, 1781, *Louis Manigault Papers*, DUL.

[140] John Parker, junior, to Gabriel Manigault, II, August 7, 1781, *Manigault Papers*, SCL.

[141] William and Benjamin Smith had been entered at the Middle Temple in 1774, John Parker, junior, in 1775, Joseph Manigault and James Smith in 1781, and William Allen Deas in 1786. The boys were often entered several years before they took up their terms at the Temple. In the case of Benjamin Smith, as has been seen, he never reached London. J. G. de Roulhac Hamilton, "Southern Members of the Inns of Court," *North Carolina Historical Review*, X (1933), 279-280. Hamilton lists Gabriel Manigault, Middle, 1781, when he should have written Joseph Manigault, Middle, 1781. In July 1783 Joseph Manigault referred to six Carolinians as being at the Middle Temple. Joseph Manigault to Gabriel Manigault, II, July 5, 1783, *Manigault Papers*, SC Archives. The other South Carolinians listed at the Middle Temple during these years were Thomas Simons (1773), William Wragg (1775), Charles Lucas Pinckney Horry (1781), John and Theodore Gaillard and Peter Porcher (1782), and William Mazyck (1783). De Roulhac Hamilton, *op. cit.*, pp. 279-280. Thomas Simons, the son of Maurice Simons, who took protection, later attested to the fact that Aaron Loocock while in London in 1781 and 1782 consorted only with men of known whig principles. "Petition of Maurice Simons to the Senate," February 10, 1783, and John McCullogh to William Clarkson, February 5, 1783, Aaron Loocock folder, *Confiscated Estates*, SC Archives. William Wragg, junior, rescued from the sea in 1777, did not return to Carolina until 1788. Francis Kinloch to Thomas Boone, May 26, 1788, "Letters of Francis Kinloch to Thomas Boone," ed. Felix Gilbert, *Journal of Southern History*, VIII (1942), 103. Charles Lucas Pinckney Horry, was the son of Daniel Horry, who took protection, and Harriott Pinckney. He may have been abroad by 1781. He later married a niece of Lafayette and lived most of his life in Paris until his death in 1828. "The Thomas Pinckney Family of South Carolina," *SCHGM*, XXXIX (1938), 24. John and Theodore Gaillard were the sons of two brothers, John and Theodore Gaillard, planters in St. Stephen's Parish, who had taken protection and accepted commissions in the British militia. Theodore Gaillard took the boys to England and enrolled them in the Middle Temple. *See* the petitions in the John and Theodore Gaillard folders, *Confiscated Estates*, SC Archives. Peter Porcher was the son of Philip Porcher, a planter, who had been in much the same position as the Gaillards. Peter Porcher and his first cousin William Mazyck were both in England in 1782. "Petition of Philip Porcher to Governor Mathews," April 18, 1782, *Confiscated Estates*, SC Archives. S. Mazyck to Peter Porcher, June 14, 1783, *SCHGM*, XXXVIII (1937), 11-15.

houses, either the Oxford or the Carolina.[142] William Smith had
helped them get settled and had introduced them to his friends.
One of these, Dupan, an old Geneva acquaintance, amused the boys
by using his skill with the scissors to cut out their likenesses as well
as those of the great men of the day.[143] One of the first gifts that
Joseph sent home to his brother was "a Representation of the King
taken from one of Dupan's Decoupures" which Joseph thought
"very much like him." In November, Joseph Manigault went to
Geneva "to learn french, fencing, dancing," and a little music, planning to return later "to go on with the law."[144] He probably took
Deas with him, for the journals of William Smith refer principally
to John Parker and James Smith.

LEGAL EDUCATION in the eighteenth century, according to Holdsworth, was "a very melancholy topic." There was no effective teaching of the law. Since the Inns of Court had abandoned the collegiate
educational system, the law student was "obliged to get his knowledge of law by means of undirected reading and discussion, and
by attendance in chambers, in a law office, or in the courts." Read-
ings and moots formerly offered by the Inns had disappeared, and
by 1776 "at the Middle Temple the student's obligation to perform
exercises, and his obligation of residence, could all be commuted for
a money payment."[145] The one principal condition had been set
forth in 1762: "That for the future no person shall be called to the
Bar in this Society before the end of five years from ye time of his
admission, nor shall any person be called to the Bar who shall be
under the age of 21 years. That every person shall actually keep
commons in ye Hall twelve terms before he be called to the Bar. . . .
That no person be called to the Bar before the time prescribed on
account or pretense of his practising the law in Ireland or the Plantations."[146]

An examination of the letters, journals, and legal notebooks of
Gabriel Manigault and William Smith indicates that these boys followed the above pattern. Manigault, who had been entered at Lin-

[142] Joseph Manigault to Gabriel Manigault, II, October 1, 1781, *Louis Manigault Papers,* DUL. *Also see* "Journals of William Smith, 1781 and 1782,"
William Loughton Smith Papers, SCHS.
[143] William Smith to Gabriel Manigault, II, September 30, 1780, *Manigault
Papers,* SCL.
[144] Joseph Manigault to Gabriel Manigault, II, October 1, 1781, May 8, 1783,
Louis Manigault Papers, DUL.
[145] Sir William Holdsworth, *A History of English Law,* Boston, 1938, XII,
77-78.
[146] *Ibid.,* pp. 23-24.

coln's Inn, wrote his grandmother in December 1777 that he had already kept one term, "which is done by meeting five times in a large Hall, intended for that purpose, and making a certain number of what they call Exercises, which is no more than reading a few lines of law. When I shall have kept 12 terms and gone through 13 exercises I shall then be a Barister. But this cannot be done under three years, for there are only 4 terms in a year."[147] Manigault actually completed only eight terms.

Smith began two years later than Manigault, although he had been entered at the Middle Temple as early as 1774. In a long letter of September 30, 1780, he described for Gabriel the difficulties of his first year.

> I commenced my law campaign last November;—as ignorant of the technical part of the law, as any country clown, and provided with a most insignificant quantity of the theoretical part of it. I launched forth, resolved to seize upon all I could; but must say, (with truth), that for the first term I understood almost as little of what was going on, as the gaping crowd, who go to Westminster Hall for the sake of seeing two men in great wigs and black gowns abuse one another; not discouraged by my little success, and attributing it, not to the thickness of my head (as I should have done) but to the nature of the thing, I undertook a second course in which I perceived that attention was but of little service to me, and that I learnt as much by thinking of something else as by listening with all my ears. The third term, the divine light of the law began to shine upon me with its benign rays, and I thanked myself for having persevered long enough to get over the most perplexing part of it. By the attendance on the courts for four Terms, reading a great deal, conversing with lawyers, and being members of a law society, I have in the space of a twelve-month cleared away all the rubbish which stood in my way and made me stumble at every step: but all that I have learnt only serves to convince me that I still know but very little, particularly for a person who intends to make it a profession and not a matter of curiosity.[148]

There was always some levity in Smith's discussion of any subject, no matter how serious the subject, yet here he showed new determination, which was quite frankly due to the news "that my little fortune is frittered away to nothing." His future would depend on the law, and he was determined, as he wrote in September 1780, to stay in England and study as long as his funds held out.[149] Smith

---

[147] Gabriel Manigault, II, to Anne Manigault, December 15, 1777, *Manigault Papers*, SCL.
[148] William Smith to Gabriel Manigault, II, September 30, 1780, *Manigault Papers*, SCL.
[149] *Ibid.*

faithfully kept the terms of the courts and marked their dates in his journal. In 1781 Hilary Term ran from January 23 to February 12; Easter Term from May 2 to May 28; Trinity Term from June 15 to July 4; Michaelmas Term from November 6 to November 28. At the beginning of each there was always an entry in his journal of £1/2/3 for dining in commons and 10/6 for tips to the criers of the court. Smith kept six notebooks on the cases he listened to, and if the sixth, which is extant, is a good example, he took comprehensive and pertinent notes in a refined and elegant hand. Many of the decisions of Lord Mansfield and many of the arguments of the learned Dunning and Erskine were recorded. Smith attended some great trials. On February 5, 1781, he was present at Lord Gordon's trial, which lasted "all night." On the 9th he followed the appeal to the House of Lords. On March 10 he attended Alderman Kennedy's trial at Guildhall. Smith and the South Carolinians stood tests at the Temple: on November 7, 1781, Smith dined in commons at Parker's *recipiatur*; on November 23 and 24 Smith himself "made an exercise before the Reader."[150]

Between terms William Smith took advantage of his freedom to relax and to travel. He spent most of the summer of 1780 at a farmhouse in Buckinghamshire, making a side trip to the Isle of Wight with his friend Dupan.[151] In the summer of 1781 Smith toured the Lake Country and the Highlands of Scotland, and this, too, in the days before Wordsworth and Scott. The trip was planned in part by two of Smith's London friends, Mr. Morland and Lord Kinnaird. Mr. Morland was a partner in Ransom and Morland's bank and had a country seat in Yorkshire. Lord Kinnaird, a Scottish representative peer, had married Elizabeth, the only daughter of Griffin Ransom, the other partner in the bank, and had a country seat at Rossie Priory in Perthshire. Smith left London on July 6 by coach for Harrowgate, where he joined the Morlands on the 10th. They immediately set out for Penrith, going up Wensleydale and past the Duke of Bolton's castle.

The first day in the Lake Country was spent at Keswick, with a morning excursion to Bassenthwaite Water. The second took them by Thirlmere and Grasmere to Ambleside on Lake Windermere.

    [150] "Journals of William Smith, 1781 and 1782," *William Loughton Smith Papers*, SCHS. When footnotes are not given below, the material has been drawn from these two journals. *Also see* "Autograph Legal Note-book of William Smith, 1782-1805," *William Loughton Smith Papers*, RC.
    [151] William Smith to Gabriel Manigault, II, September 30, 1780, *Manigault Papers*, SCL.

The third began with an early morning visit to Coniston Water, and then after lunch at Ambleside, they rode to Penrith by Ullswater. The fourth day afforded a visit to Lowther Castle and Hawes Water. Undaunted by the rapid pace, the Morlands and Smith took a diligence from Carlisle to Glasgow and by traveling all night made the journey in twenty-four hours. Neither Glasgow nor Edinburgh seems to have been the main object of the tour, for less than two days was spent in each city. Six days, however, were devoted to the Highlands. They sailed on Loch Lomond; they drove to Inveraray, the seat of the Campbells; they went north of Loch Tay to the Earl of Breadalbane's; and they ended their tour at Rossie Priory, the home of Lord Kinnaird.

On the return to England, Smith left the Morlands, went back to the Lake Country, and spent August and September much in the manner of one of Jane Austen's country squires, making Carlisle his base with junkets hither and yon to the local notables. At Carlisle he dined with a Mr. Bird, accompanied a Miss Wilson to the assembly, and attended two balls and a public breakfast given by the sheriff. His longest side-trip was to Whitehaven, where he led a simple provincial existence: "at the Review," "company to tea," "a ride to Workington Hall," "to church." In vivid contrast to John Paul Jones's descent upon Whitehaven, Smith breakfasted, dined, and danced at the castle as the guest of Sir James Lowther.[152] One afternoon he sprained his ankle "in the whisky" and was laid up for over two weeks under the care of a surgeon. The bill was 12/2 but Smith generously offered a guinea. His activities were thereupon confined to "tea at the vicarage" or "cards." The sprain was a good excuse to proceed to Scarborough to indulge in the waters there.

Before returning to London, Smith paid a visit to Sir Thomas and Lady Sarah Frankland at Stockhold Hall in Yorkshire. Sir Thomas was an admiral in the English navy who had grown rich in the service in the West Indies and while on station in Carolina had married Sarah Rhett, a connection of William's aunt, Mrs. Thomas Smith.[153] Three idle days there, which always included "music in the evening," ended his summer tour. By October 24 Smith was back in London for breakfast with Parker and Manigault. The life

[152] Samuel Eliot Morison, *John Paul Jones*, Boston, 1959, pp. 138-142. Lowther, vastly rich, was a whig during the Revolution and introduced William Pitt, the younger, into the House of Commons in January 1781 by ordering his election for Appleby, Westmoreland. G. F. Russell Barker, "James Lowther," *DNB*.

[153] Barnwell Rhett Heyward, "The Descendants of Col. William Rhett, of South Carolina," *SCHGM*, IV (1903), 38.

of a law student was resumed. Smith's day on the 31st was: "break-fast with James," "at the Old Bailey," "dined at Oxford Coffee House," "to play with Parker."

During the winters Smith indulged in all of the pleasures of London: walking and riding in Hyde Park, cards, dances, concerts, plays, the opera, as well as frequent visits to the pleasure gardens at Vauxhall and Ranelagh. On occasion he might see some of the famous, as he once saw Dr. Johnson. Smith naturally kept in touch with the Carolina merchants of London. There were frequent notations in his journals of tea with the William Mannings and dinner with the John Savages. He often dined with John Nutt, who reluctantly doled out £10 at a time for his expenses. Twice Smith accompanied Mrs. Nutt and Miss Greenwood to the theater. He also visited the homes of the refugee Carolinians: William Drayton, Mrs. Peronneau, William Blake, Aaron Loocock, Miss Inglis.[154] Some of his acquaintances were women of "genteel fame," for a succession of Mollys, Phoebes, Dollys, and Sallys appear in Smith's accounts.

If the journals can be taken as evidence, Smith's interest in the Revolution was meagre; on only four occasions does he refer to the conflict. February 3, 1781: "St. Eustatia taken;" November 26, 1781: "received news of Lord Cornwallis capture;" December 31, 1781: "Mr. Laurens released from the Tower." These were facts recorded without comment; although the first cut him off from home, the second marked the end of the fighting, and the third involved a close family friend. In Smith's collection of pamphlets there are several magazines for the years 1780 and 1781 which indicate that he did, however, keep up with politics. *The Political Magazine and Parliamentary Naval, Military, and Literary Journal* for October 1780 contained letters from Cornwallis dated Charles Town, July 14 and 15, and August 6, as well as the "History and Character of Mr. Laurens, late President of the Rebel Congress, now a Prisoner in the

---

[154] William Drayton (1732-1790) formerly chief justice of East Florida, was in England from 1779 to 1783 as a refugee. *American Museum*, VIII (August 1790), 82-83. Mrs. Peronneau may have been the wife of Henry Peronneau. See "value of the office of public treasurer in 1776," *SCHGM*, XIII (1912), 229-230. William Blake (1739-1803) was a brother of Daniel Blake, royal councilor. He was a loyalist. "Blake of South Carolina," *SCHGM*, I (1900), 161-162. Aaron Loocock had submitted to the local authorities after the surrender of Charles Town to protect his property, but rather than be used against his friends had retired to England. According to Thomas Simons, one of the law students, he only associated with zealous whigs while abroad. *See* Aaron Loocock folder, *Confiscated Estates*, SC Archives. Miss Inglis (perhaps Catherine Inglis) was undoubtedly the sister of Thomas Loughton Smith's wife. *See* "Journal of Josiah Quincy, Junior, 1773," *op. cit.*, p. 443.

Tower of London."[155] The final reference to the war was a notation on March 5, 1782, that Lord North's government had fallen, and that he had attended the debates in Parliament that day.

JOHN RUTLEDGE had advised his brother Edward, when the latter was studying law in England before the Revolution, to take a short "circuit" before coming home, but he urged that it be to a place worth seeing, for the mode of doing business on the circuit was soon understood.[156] This was obviously a well-established tradition with the Carolina boys, for Peter Manigault, William Drayton, and Daniel Blake had traveled on the "northern circuit" in the summer of 1752, proceeding to York, Durham, Newcastle, Carlisle, Westmoreland, and Lancaster. They, however, had wasted little time in court, much preferring a jaunt to Castle Howard or a few days at Harrowgate.[157] Smith adopted the pattern in the summer of 1782 by combining a tour of South Wales and the Midlands with riding circuit on the Welsh border. He left London on June 29 and spent over a month with the Draytons of Birch Grove, near Neath in Glamorganshire.[158] The third week in August he rode the "western circuit." On five occasions he notes dining or supping with the judges and counsel. He left the circuit at Ludlow and toured Chester, Liverpool, Preston, and Manchester. The Duke of Bridgewater's canal made a deep impression on him as did the manufactories of Manchester.

The rest of September and October were devoted to visits to Buxton and Matlock, the famous spas of Derbyshire, and to a long stay at Serlby, the home of Lord Galway, for the Doncaster race meeting.[159] The running of the St. Leger had commenced in 1778, and on each day for three days there was a race, a concert, and an assembly. While staying with Lord Galway in October there was an excursion to dine with Lord Fitzwilliam at Wentworth House. On November 3, 1782, Smith was again in London.

SHORTLY after his 24th birthday, Smith finally decided to return to America. On November 12 he paid out £31/10/0 sterling for

[155] See William Loughton Smith Pamphlets, CLS, V, numbers 2, 7, 8.
[156] John Rutledge to Edward Rutledge, July 30, 1769, O'Neall, op. cit., II, 122.
[157] Peter Manigault, "Northern Circuit," summer of 1752, Louis Manigault Papers, SHC.
[158] This is either the John Drayton or the William Drayton family.
[159] Robert Monckton Arundell (1758-1810), Fourth Viscount Galway (Irish Peerage), was member of Parliament from York and Pontefract. Burke's Peerage, Baronetage & Knightage, London, 1959, p. 917.

passage to St. Kitts. As he explained later on the floor of the American Congress, he planned to go from St. Kitts to a Danish island and thence to some American port in North Carolina or Georgia and thus finally make his way to the American camp.[160] The week before he left London, Smith spent £106, which included £24/16/0 for books, £16/5/0 for clothes, £5/19/0 for shoes, and £4/13/0 for wine and rum. This ran his expenses for 1782 to £331/16/0 (not including £40/0/6 for his passage, bedding, etc.), which was more than double the £143/5/10 that he had spent in 1781. The preparations for departure had obviously run up his bills, but after receiving more funds from home late in 1781 and in 1782 he had raised his standard of living. Visiting cards, a lady's hat, silver buckles, lawn and linen for shirts, and a weekly visit to the hairdresser had been added to his regular expenditures.

On November 19 Smith crossed from Dover to Calais on his way to Brussels, where he saw much of William Lee before going on to Ostend. Contrary winds kept his ship from leaving until after the New Year. In February Smith was shipwrecked on the coast of England and was forced to return to London.[161] New plans were made to come out with the William Draytons early in the summer, yet again he delayed.[162] His family and friends could only wonder why. His brother-in-law James Ladson wrote Gabriel Manigault on September 10, 1783, that Billy Smith had postponed his return and gone to Ireland, from where he meant to take his passage—"the Lord knows when."[163] Manigault, who was certainly less free to criticize than Ladson, replied: "I was very much inclined to wonder at Billy Smith when I read in your letter of his being gone to Ireland, but checked myself and reflecting that I did not like to have my own actions wondered at, and that it was but charitable to suppose every man to have reasons for his conduct though I might not be acquainted with them—I hope it will not prevent our having the pleasure of seeing him in Carolina the approaching winter: when he will explain to us the propriety of his movements."[164]

[160] *Annals of the Congress of the United States,* Washington, 1834, I (1st cong., 1st sess.), 398.
[161] *Ibid.*
[162] Joseph Manigault to Gabriel Manigault, II, June 21, 1783, *Manigault Papers,* SCL. Joseph Manigault to Gabriel Manigault, II, July 5, 1783, *Manigault Papers,* SC Archives.
[163] James Ladson to Gabriel Manigault, II, September 10, 1783, *Manigault Papers,* SCL.
[164] Gabriel Manigault, II, to James Ladson, September 22, 1783, *Manigault Papers,* SCL.

VI

THE RETURN OF THE BRITISH MERCHANTS

WILLIAM SMITH came back to Charles Town with the British merchants; he prospered during the turmoil of the 1780's with the local lawyers; and he entered politics with the support of the Goose Creek planters. On first glance it is strange that a young man who had been away for thirteen years should be elected to the state legislature after being home less than one year. Yet, if one examines the importance of the three groups—British merchants, Charles Town lawyers, and Goose Creek planters—and understands William Smith's close connections with each, the strangeness dissolves and a natural sequence of events comes to light.

After the British evacuated Charles Town on December 14, 1782, merchants swarmed in to mend the fabric of commerce in this area that had long stagnated under the interruptions and devastations of war. Pierce Butler described the scene in the spring of 1783: "The effect of peace is very sensibly felt here already—Not one day passes without two or three and often more, topsail vessels arriving—Produce in consequence very high—All imports low—Our harbour has a respectable appearance; and we have certain information of many vessels being on the point of sailing from England and Jamaica for this place—The injury this country experienced from the enemy has given a new spring to industry—All ranks of men think of little else than repairing their losses—Our wharfs present a scene of bustle and activity that I have not seen for many years."[1]

The native-born Carolina merchants were among the first to return. A number of the important merchants had been seized by the British after the fall of Charles Town and shipped off to St. Augustine. After a year of confinement they were permitted to proceed to Philadelphia where they joined their banished families and marked time at makeshift jobs until the news of the evacuation of Charles Town permitted their return. Among those going back in 1783 were Edward Darrell, Josiah Smith, junior, and Daniel DeSaussure.[2]

---

[1] Pierce Butler to Thomas Fitzsimons, May 18, 1783, *Gratz Collection*, PHS.
[2] "Josiah Smith's Diary, 1780-1781," *SCHGM*, XXXIII (1932), 2-4, 100; XXXIV (1933), 31-32, 39, 68-69. DeSaussure had worked six months as a teller in the Bank of North America in Philadelphia before being appointed a commissioner to settle the continental accounts of the state of Maryland. John Wilson to Joseph Pemberton, July 25, 1782, *Pemberton Papers*, PHS.

Darrell arrived by land from Philadelphia shortly after the evacuation of Charles Town. Josiah Smith sailed home in April with Darrell's family and his own "in a vessel too much crowded" for comfort.[3] The DeSaussures came in by land after Christmas 1783. Before the Revolution, Smith and Darrell, who were brothers-in-law, had been partners in a Charles Town house in close touch with that of Poyas and DeSaussure in Beaufort. They now faced competition from a swarm of Dutch, English, Irish, and Scottish factors, so many, in fact, that store and house rents had risen fully three hundred per cent since before the Revolution. Encouraged by planters who were desirous of seeing some of the old merchants again in trade, Smith, Darrell, and DeSaussure joined with Smith's cousin, George Smith, to form a new house: Smiths, DeSaussure, and Darrell.[4] This house emerged in the post-Revolutionary period as the strongest mercantile establishment controlled by local capital.

Josiah Smith immediately sent off letters to all of his former commercial correspondents. He first wrote to thank the great Philadelphia merchant, James Pemberton, for his kindnesses to the Smith family while they were in exile, but he carefully added: "I have lately commenced mercantile business in a house of four partners under the firm of Smiths DeSaussure and Darrell. We shall be much obliged for your interest among Friends with you. Our concerns will be chiefly in the commission way, and hope to render our Employers due satisfaction."[5] To George Appleby he explained that three of the partners were natives and the fourth had long been a resident, so that all members of the firm knew the local needs. With most of his capital locked up in the state treasury (he estimated that he had loaned the state £100,000), Smith asked Appleby to use his influence in England to help the new firm establish its credit.[6] To William Manning, Smith wrote that due to his absence of two years and seven months from Charles Town his losses had been great and that he must resume his commercial activities in order to make some provision for his family.[7] To James Poyas, who

[3] Josiah Smith to James Pemberton, May 15, 1783, *Pemberton Papers*, PHS.
[4] Josiah Smith to James Poyas, January 31, 1784, *Josiah Smith, junior, Letter-Book, 1771-1784*, SHC. *South-Carolina Weekly Gazette*, May 10, 1783.
[5] Josiah Smith to James Pemberton, May 15, 1783, *Pemberton Papers*, PHS.
[6] Josiah Smith to George Appleby, June 5, 1783, *Josiah Smith, junior, Letter-Book, 1771-1784*, SHC. Smith and Appleby were both administrators of the estate of George Austin. Smith wrote that Austin's estate had been saved from confiscation at Jacksonborough through the influence of Christopher Gadsden.
[7] Josiah Smith to William Manning, May 20, 1783, *Josiah Smith, junior, Letter-Book, 1771-1784*, SHC.

had been the absentee partner of DeSaussure at Beaufort, he wrote to explain why the new firm was not using him as their London agent. Poyas had evidently ridiculed Smith's loyalty to Carolina and criticized him for his handling of Poyas's funds. Smith was therefore unwilling to resume the old commercial connection. In pointing out to Poyas the scope of the new firm's activities—Smiths, DeSaussure, and Darrell would have two country stores, one at Georgetown run by John Cogdell and one at Beaufort run by J. M. Verdier—he emphasized that the new firm would order their goods from Bird, Savage, and Bird.[8]

Bird, Savage, and Bird represented a new generation of Carolina merchants in London. The partners in this concern were the brothers Henry M. and Robert Bird and Benjamin Savage.[9] Henry M. Bird had married Betsey Manning in the spring of 1778 and had received his commercial training under the guidance of his father-in-law William Manning.[10] Benjamin Savage was the son of John Savage, who for thirty years had been an eminent merchant of Charles Town. John Savage had been recommended by Bull in 1770 for a seat on the royal Council and in December 1773 had been elected the first president of the Charles Town Chamber of Commerce.[11] He had, however, taken the King's side, removed to London, and in 1778, after his first wife's death, married the sister of William Manning. At that time he placed his only son Benjamin with Manning.[12] This new firm was therefore well suited for the Carolina trade, being launched under the protective eyes of William Manning and John Savage, old friends of the former colony. Smiths, DeSaussure, and Darrell was destined to do business with Bird, Savage, and Bird for twenty years. It was a connection of immense influence on both sides of the ocean and is the best example of the immediate re-establishment of commercial ties after the Revolution.

THE LARGER and more important group of merchants in post-Revolutionary Charles Town was British. Some had stayed on in Charles Town after the evacuation of the British troops, having gained per-

[8] Josiah Smith to James Poyas, January 31, 1784, *Josiah Smith, junior, Letter-Book, 1771-1784*, SHC.

[9] *South Carolina Circuit Court Records, 1790-1809*, FRC Georgia, pp. 290, 326.

[10] William Manning to John Laurens, April 11, 1778, *Laurens Papers*, LIHS.

[11] *South-Carolina Gazette*, April 24, 1749, December 28, 1773. "Diary of William Dillwyn During a Visit to Charles Town in 1772-1773," ed. A. S. Salley, *SCHGM*, XXXVI (1935), 108.

[12] Gabriel Manigault, II, to Gabriel Manigault, I, May 4, 1778, *Manigault Papers*, SCL.

mission from Governor Mathews to stay six months in order to dispose of their goods and collect monies due them.[13] As soon as the House of Representatives met in Charles Town, they petitioned for an extension of the time limit. They had not been able to collect all that was due them, nor had they found cargo space sufficient to ship off all that they had been paid in produce. Since some of the merchants had expressed their intention to become citizens of the state, the House found their requests reasonable and granted the extension on March 11, 1783.[14] Among the fifty signatures to this memorial were the names of men who contributed much to the later life of the city. Henry Shoolbred and Benjamin Moodie headed an important commercial house and in the 1790's served in turn as British consul in Charleston. William Tunno was of an influential London-Charleston merchant family. Jonathan and William Simpson, Thomas Stewart, James Miller, and David O'Hara were leading merchants, while John M'Iver became a successful printer.[15]

There were at the time of General Greene's entry other British merchants in town who had not made their peace with the governor. These were seized and paroled, yet the House also granted them an extension on March 11. Among these were George Tunno, John Geyer, James Gregorie, Laurence Campbell, William Blacklock, James La Motte, and Alexander Bethune, merchants; John Elihu Bay, lawyer; Joseph Purcell, surveyor; and Joel Poinsett, apothecary.[16]

The British community was composed not only of those who had remained after the evacuation but also of those who came out from England to take advantage of the new opportunities. During the summer of 1783 the newspapers were filled with announcements of those who had just arrived. Hary Grant, who disembarked on July 4, advertised on the 12th "a general and handsome assortment of European goods" to be sold at 3 Tradd Street. Grant begged leave "to inform all persons who are concerned in Insurance done in Lloyd's Coffee House, that he is appointed agent for the underwriters for

---

[13] "Memorial of the undersigned British Merchants residing in Charleston . . . to the Senate," n.d., citizenship folders, *Legislative Papers*, SC Archives.

[14] *JHR*, XLIII, 295-297.

[15] *The Charleston Directory for 1785. The Charleston Directory for 1790.*

[16] "Reports of Senate committee on petitions of several persons British subjects found in said town when General Greene took possession of it and then paroled and who have severally petitioned to become subjects of this state," n.d., citizenship folders, *Legislative Papers*, SC Archives. *JHR*, XLIII, 295-297. *The Charleston Directory for 1785. The Charleston Directory for 1790.*

this state." The same issue of the 12th gave a passenger list which included David Price and Samuel Midwood, merchants.[17] On September 6, Blacklock and Tunno advertised that they had just imported from London an assortment of goods in the *Roman Emperor* which were offered for sale at 87 Church Street, corner of St. Michael's Alley.[18] On September 9, Dr. David Ramsay, who regretted the rapid change from the noble purposes of the Revolution to the mercenary motives of peacetime, described for Dr. Benjamin Rush of Philadelphia the burgeoning commercial activity: "The genius of our people is entirely turned from war to commerce. Schemes of business & partnerships for extending commerce are daily forming. The infamous African trade which you so justly abhor will among other branches of business be resumed. . . . I firmly lament the renewal of this trade & shall for my own part have no concern in it."[19]

THE MERCHANTS who had the greatest difficulty in regaining a foothold were the loyalists, those who had traded in South Carolina prior to the war and had openly taken the side of England. They had been banished and their estates confiscated by the Jacksonborough legislature which met in January and February 1782. As soon as peace was announced, they exerted every effort to return to the colony and regain their property. The cases of Aaron Loocock, Alexander Inglis, and John Tunno represent their plight.

Ancrum, Lance, and Loocock had been an important Charles Town house in the 1760's. The firm had employed Joseph and Eli Kershaw and John Chesnut as country factors, principally resident at Camden on the Wateree.[20] Loocock had contributed to the defense of Charles Town in 1776,[21] and at the time of the town's surrender in 1780 he had retired to his plantation "at the Waterees." Once back in Charles Town he discovered that he had been plundered by British officers, and in order to call the plunderers to account he had accepted protection. To avoid being used against his friends, he planned to go to England, but in order to leave he

[17] *South-Carolina Weekly Gazette*, July 5, 12, 1783.
[18] *Ibid.*, September 6, 1783.
[19] David Ramsay to Benjamin Rush, September 9, 1783, *Ramsay Letters*, LCP.
[20] Lelia Sellers, *Charleston Business on the Eve of the American Revolution*, Chapel Hill, 1934, p. 91.
[21] Barnard Elliott to Henry Laurens, December 2, 1775, *Emmet Collection*, NYPL.

had to sign the congratulations to Cornwallis.[22] While in England he associated only with zealous whigs and contributed to the relief fund for the American prisoners at Portsmouth.[23] This, however, was not known at home, and in 1782 the estates of Loocock and his old partner William Ancrum were confiscated and the men banished.[24] In an effort to recover his estate Loocock sent a petition to the Senate and sailed for New York to be nearer at hand.[25] In March 1783 the legislature amended the confiscation act to permit those who had been banished and who had petitioned the legislature to return to South Carolina.[26] With this news, Loocock sailed for Charles Town, only to be confined "in the Provost." According to the modification of the confiscation act, he could remain in South Carolina only if he put up bail. Loocock decided "to go to New York and Philadelphia for a Month or two" and return in October, by which time he expected to be "at full Liberty."[27] It was not until March 1784, however, that Loocock's name was removed from all lists and he was free to take his former place in Carolina society.[28]

Alexander Inglis, who had lived in South Carolina and Georgia for twenty years prior to the Revolution, had definitely taken the King's side, even going so far as to petition the British commandant of Charles Town for permission to be armed as one of the loyal militia. As a consequence, the Jacksonborough legislature confiscated his estate and banished him. His wife Mary Deas Inglis, who had remained in town when the British evacuated the city, petitioned the Senate in his behalf in 1783. Not denying that her husband had taken the King's side, she pointed out that he had refused a seat on the police board during the occupation and that he was the principal guardian of several minor and orphan children, "those of his Uncle George Inglis & those of his late worthy partner Mr. Thomas Loughton Smith."[29] When Inglis arrived in Charleston,

[22] "Petition of Aaron Loocock to Senate," 1783, Confiscated Estates, SC Archives.

[23] John McCullogh to William Clarkson, February 5, 1783, Aaron Loocock folder, Confiscated Estates, SC Archives.

[24] SC Statutes, VI, 630.

[25] S. Mazyck to Peter Porcher, June 14, 1783, SCHGM, XXXVIII (1937), 11-15.

[26] SC Statutes, IV, 553-554.

[27] S. Mazyck to Peter Porcher, June 14, 1783, SCHGM, XXXVIII (1937), 11-15.

[28] SC Statutes, VI, 635. William Ancrum was taken off confiscation list but was amerced 12%. SC Statutes, VI, p. 634. Mrs. Loocock arrived from the Downs in December 1783; Loocock arrived from Philadelphia in March 1784. South-Carolina Weekly Gazette, December 26, 1783, March 24, 1784.

[29] "Petition of Mary Inglis to Senate," 1783, Confiscated Estates, SC Archives.

he was not permitted to land and had to seek refuge in Georgia. While on board the *Rebecca* at Cockspur, Inglis wrote John Houston in Savannah: "I have letters from Mr. Lowndes and Mr. Lloyd as well as others, who have no doubt of my being permitted to remain in Georgia, until the meeting of the Assembly in South Carolina—could this indulgence be granted to me—I shall readily conform to any restrictions that the laws may lay me under."[30] The South Carolina legislature finally in March 1784 placed his name on the twelve per cent amercement list and removed the disability of banishment, thus permitting Inglis to rejoin his family.[31]

John Tunno, merchant, had refused to take the state oath in 1777 and had been banished.[32] He must have returned during the British occupation, for he, too, had petitioned the commandant to be armed as one of the loyal militia. His name was on the confiscation list, and when the city was evacuated he sailed with the fleet.[33] He attempted to return to Carolina in 1783 with Alexander Inglis and was refused permission to land.[34] But in 1784 the legislature made no concession in his favor. John Tunno apparently retired to London, where he engaged in the Carolina trade through his brother Adam, as agent, who then came out to Charles Town and shortly became a citizen.[35]

Another merchant with an interesting story was Nathaniel Russell. He came from Rhode Island in 1765 as the agent of the Browns of Providence, followed an equivocal course during the Revolution, and although not banished by the law of 1782, was barred by an ordinance of March 17, 1783.[36] When he arrived in Charleston on

[30] See S. Mazyck to Peter Porcher, June 14, 1783, *SCHGM*, XXXVIII (1937), 11-15. Alexander Inglis to John Houston, n.d., *Miscellaneous Manuscripts*, NYPL.
[31] *SC Statutes*, VI, 635. Inglis must have withdrawn to England, as he arrived from London in the *Britannia* in December 1784. *South-Carolina Weekly Gazette*, December 8, 1784.
[32] "Josiah Smith's Diary, 1780-1781," *SCHGM*, XXXIV (1933), 198.
[33] *SC Statutes*, VI, 631.
[34] S. Mazyck to Peter Porcher, June 14, 1783, *SCHGM*, XXXVIII (1937), 11-15.
[35] John Tunno married in 1781 the daughter of John Rose, who was also banished. John's brother, Adam Tunno, was trying as late as 1796 to straighten out his brother's affairs. See "Petition of Adam Tunno to the Senate," December 8, 1796, John Rose folder, *Confiscated Estates*, SC Archives. Adam Tunno became a citizen on April 17, 1784. *Miscellaneous Records*, SC Archives, book Q, p. 1.
[36] Nathaniel Russell advertised good horses from Rhode Island, northward rum, candles, apples, onions at his store on Colonel Beale's wharf in February 1765. *South-Carolina Gazette*, February 2, 1765. As "consignee of Mr. Brown" see *Men and Times of the Revolution: or, Memoirs of Elkanah Watson*, ed. Winslow C. Watson, New York, 1857, pp. 53-54. For the ordinances see *SC Statutes*, IV, 568-570.

September 19, 1783, from London, he was not permitted to land, but was forced to spend four months afloat in Charleston harbor. During this period he managed his affairs from shipboard with the aid of Samuel Legare.[37] When the legislature convened in 1784, Russell's petition was the first presented, and by act of March 26, 1784, he was expressly exempted from the ordinance of March 17, 1783.[38]

WITH THIS RETURNING FLOOD of merchants and loyalists came William Smith. He arrived on November 21, 1783, in the ship *Britannia*, Captain Ball, after a nine-week voyage from London. With him came the families of two former members of the royal Council, Mrs. Blake, the widow of Daniel Blake; and John Drayton, his wife, and five children; also Thomas Simons, who had been at the Middle Temple; James and Thomas Gadsden, sons of the deceased Thomas Gadsden; as well as the Messrs. Bayley, Stephens, Blackford, Gourdine, Moncreef, Kingsley, and others.[39] Smith had spent the last thirteen of his twenty-five years abroad—is there any wonder that his right to land was challenged! For ten days he was not permitted to come ashore. He wrote his sister: "How cruel is my situation. . . . After so long an absence, such a variety of disappointments and I may add, after being on my voyage above a Twelve-month, this unexpected Restraint was wanting to complete the singularity and the hardship of my Fate." This enforced idleness was made bearable only by "the kind sollicitude" of "friends in town" and by "the beauty of the weather." Smith had an easier time than did Nathaniel Russell in getting permission to land. He was not banned by law, and he did have powerful family connections. His Uncle Thomas must have helped, for it was to his uncle's house that he went when finally permitted to go ashore.[40]

What did the local people think of this great influx of British merchants and loyalists? John Sandford Dart wrote Ralph Izard on July 11, 1783: "The old inhabitants of the town are becoming very uneasy, respecting the admission of such a number of British

[37] *South-Carolina Weekly Gazette*, September 20, 1783. Nathaniel Russell to Caleb Davis and Co., February 28, 1784; Samuel Legare to Caleb Davis and Co., June 17, 1784, *Caleb Davis Papers*, MHS.
[38] *SC Statutes*, IV, 626.
[39] *South-Carolina Weekly Gazette*, November 21, 1783.
[40] William Smith to Mrs. Carnes, n.d., *Miscellaneous Manuscripts*, SCHS. Susannah Smith had married first Barnard Elliott and then Captain Patrick Carnes of the continental line. A. S. Salley, Jr., "William Smith and Some of His Descendants," *SCHGM*, IV (1903), 249-250.

merchants etc. subjects to the state—riots have already happened in consequence thereof—last evening six Caledonians were severely pumped in the streets for making use of their favoriate word *Rebel*, amongst them a son of James Simpson—it is reported a town meeting will be called in consequence."[41] Dr. David Ramsay wrote a similar letter on the same day to Dr. Benjamin Rush:

> A spirit has gone forth among the lower class of people to drive away certain persons whom they are pleased to call Tories. It is opposed by the leading men, but, a few firebrands have lately taken up some supposed Tories & maltreated them with a design of recommending to them a peaceable departure from the state. This revolution has introduced so much anarchy that it will take half a century to eradicate the licentiousness of the people. I wish for the honor of human nature that in these last ages of the world it may appear that mankind are capable of enjoying the blessings of freedom without the extravagancies that usually accompany it.[42]

The "leading men" were willing to welcome the returning merchants and loyalists, but "the lower class of people" was not.

At a meeting of the people on July 14 two committees were appointed. One was to sit each afternoon from six to eight at the Charles Town Tavern to hear grievances; the other was to state these grievances in a memorial which would be presented to the legislature urging the expulsion of British merchants and a bar against their future entry.[43] In spite of this pressure, the legislature resolved on August 9 that no further compact was needed with the British merchants, since the treaty of peace had guaranteed their right to return.[44] Instead of moving against the merchants, the legislature strengthened local regulations for maintaining public peace by incorporating Charles Town as the City of Charleston.

The city was divided into thirteen wards, each of which had a warden elected by those who paid three shillings a year in taxes. These thirteen wardens selected one of their number to be the intendant. In the event of a riot, any city officer who refused to obey the intendant could be fined £10 sterling, and any inhabitant who refused to obey him could be fined £5 sterling. The wardens would, as justices of the peace, hear and fine. This was the legislature's answer to the people's petition.[45]

The leading men in 1783 did not consider the feelings of the

[41] John Sandford Dart to Ralph Izard, July 11, 1783, *Miscellaneous Manuscripts*, NYPL.
[42] David Ramsay to Benjamin Rush, July 11, 1783, *Ramsay Letters*, LCP.
[43] *South-Carolina Weekly Gazette*, July 19, 26, 1783.
[44] *JHR*, XLIII, 48 (second pagination).
[45] *SC Statutes*, VII, 97-101.

people, but they were earnest in their desire to re-establish law and order as quickly as possible. Thomas Smith of Broad Street wrote to his cousin in Boston about the dangers of peace in August 1783: "God grant that all of us may make a proper use of it and that religion and piety, love and charity may be the happy consequences of it, for however it may have been with you, it was in a manner banished from us and is generally the consequences especially of a Civil War."[46] Francis Kinloch wrote on September 1, 1783, to the ex-royal-Governor Thomas Boone of "the torrents of illiberal party rage, which has borne down everything before it in Carolina." He commented:

> It is not the determined resolution of men bearing up against the calamities of war, this spirit has fled, and given way to a passion which I can compare to nothing but to that, which animates a child to torment some helpless insect, that falls within its reach. . . . I wish we in Carolina may make good use of our newly acquired sovereignty, but I much doubt it, and am much afraid, that our civil dissensions, and they are natural, you know, to our form of government, will end in blood, the precedent of proceeding by bill of attainder at Jacksonborough will fall heavy upon the head of some; if not, there is no faith to be put in history.[47]

These anxieties could only be abated by strengthening conservative forces within the state. This was why at the next session of the legislature in February and March 1784 most of the restrictions that had been placed on the loyalists were removed, and the way was cleared for the merchants to become citizens. On March 26 an act was passed to restore to certain persons their estates and permit them to reside in Carolina.[48] On March 26 the alien act was also passed; this made it possible for British merchants to become citizens of South Carolina.[49] South Carolina was trying to live up to the terms of the treaty of peace. As Governor Guerard well knew, all South Carolinians were not pleased. So, for the big celebration on March 17, when the Definitive Treaty of Peace was proclaimed, he banned all illuminations, fearful that they might become an excuse for disorders.[50]

During the summer of 1784 a new crisis arose when the mer-

[46] Thomas Smith to Isaac Smith, August 19, 1783, *Smith-Carter Papers*, MHS.

[47] Francis Kinloch to Thomas Boone, September 1, 1783, "Letters of Francis Kinloch to Thomas Boone, 1782-1788," ed. Felix Gilbert, *Journal of Southern History*, VIII (1942), 97-98.

[48] *SC Statutes*, IV, 624-626. Among those who particularly benefited by this act was John Savage, whose name was taken off all lists. *SC Statutes*, VI, 635.

[49] *SC Statutes*, VI, 600-601.

[50] *JHR*, XLIV, 311.

chants began to press the debtors and the sheriff's sales came on.[51] There were threats of violence if the lesser folk should lose the annual wardens election.[52] Yet when the election was held, Intendant Richard Hutson and his ticket were returned to power.[53] One member of the defeated party wrote:

> As to the boasted majority of which we have so much said, perhaps a short time will discover in what manner it was obtained; and therefore shall observe at present, that the good citizens of Charleston ought to be very careful about admitting British merchants and refugees, who the other day were in arms against us, so early to interfere in matters of government, and have the privilege of voting at elections, when so many of our old citizens who have fought for us, and lost their all in the way, are not admitted to vote, because they are unable to pay three shillings tax.[54]

The battle between the new city government and the mob raged on into 1785. Benjamin Waller pointed out that corporations rarely existed except "under *Royal* or *Aristocratical* Governments," and charged Intendant Hutson with being no more than the tool of the twenty families, perhaps as few as five, who ran the state.[55] There must have been much truth in these charges, for in the place of Thomas Heyward on September 14, 1785, young William Smith, home less than two years, was elected warden for Ward Six.[56]

DURING THE NEXT TWENTY YEARS there remained in Charleston a community of British merchants. Many of the great pre-war Charleston merchants had died; those who were left had retired to plantations. Their sons had either become planters or professional men, so that there was room for new merchants. These new merchants, so many of whom were British, seemed to be set slightly apart, although, in a society still fluid, the dividing lines were blurred. The British merchants tended to live in Charleston, as they did in foreign ports all over the world, in a "factory"—that is, in a business and social world which was distinct from that of the natives. Robert Hunter, junior, "a young merchant of London," visited Charleston for a few days in June 1786 and fortunately recorded enough in his

---

[51] *South-Carolina Gazette and Public Advertiser*, July 22, 1784, and subsequent issues.

[52] *See* letters by "Aristides," *ibid.*, July 22, 27, 1784.

[53] The forces of Alexander Gillon were defeated. *Ibid.*, September 11, 1784. Charles Gregg Singer, *South Carolina in the Confederation*, Philadelphia, 1941, p. 29.

[54] *South-Carolina Gazette and Public Advertiser*, September 25, 1784.

[55] *Ibid.*, July 9, 12, August 13, 1785.

[56] *Ibid.*, September 17, 1785. He was elected a warden for the second time on October 8, 1788, in the place of Rawlins Lowndes, elected intendant. *City Gazette, or the Daily Advertiser*, October 11, 1788.

diary to paint a picture of this community. Hunter was the son of a Scottish merchant dwelling in Coleman Street, London, who had considerable debts due him in America and who had sent his son to America for the double purpose of laying siege to these debtors and of traveling. This twenty-year-old lad acted as a personal messenger from his father to business associates along the Atlantic Coast and was, therefore, provided with introductions to the leading British merchants of Charleston.[57]

Young Hunter stayed at a coffee house opened the previous winter by John Williams at the corner of Tradd and the Bay, a place where "gentlemen and captains of vessels may be accommodated with Board and Lodging on easy Terms." More than an inn, it was something of a club. Williams subscribed to "the London, Liverpool, Bristol, West India, and Continental newspapers, reviews and magazines," which were filed and preserved. Coffee was ready every morning at seven, soups at noon, and an ordinary at two o'clock. Membership was one guinea per annum. Williams' Carolina Coffee-House and Tavern was the hub of the British community.[58] Hunter's journal reveals the inner society of British merchants:

> (June 22, 1786) After getting my hair dressed at Williams' coffee-house, where we stay, I immediately called upon Mr. Auldjo in Broad Street to know the fate of my letters. . . . I took a walk with him (Auldjo) to the bay where he introduced me to a genteel Frenchman, and Mr. Bize, brother to the person of that name in London. We then called upon Mr. Penman, where I left my letters about business. We then called upon the merchant, Hary Grant. His lady is at Newport, where he also means to spend the summer. We found him at the coffeehouse which resembles Lloyd's in miniature. We ordered supper at ten. Mr. Grant was exceedingly polite and very sorry he was under the necessity of going away so shortly. I was again introduced to several gentlemen who supped with us— Mr. Price, Mr. Tunno are the only two names I recollect. They were all very jovial and merry.
>
> (June 23, 1786) I was surprised to see Charleston so well lighted up. We returned to Williams', where I played two rubbers at whist with Mr. Bize and two other gentlemen and won four dollars.
>
> (June 24, 1786) We afterwards paid a visit to Mr. Penman, who politely asked me to dine with him tomorrow. I was much hurt to

---

[57] *Quebec to Carolina in 1785-1786, Being the Travel Diary and Observations of Robert Hunter, Jr., a Young Merchant of London,* eds. Louis B. Wright and Marion Tinling, San Marino, 1943, pp. 3-4.

[58] *Columbian Herald,* January 4, December 12, 1786. An Evening Club was formed in 1786 of which the officers in 1792 were Hary Grant, president, William Price, vice-president, and Laurence Campbell, secretary and treasurer. William Waring, *The South-Carolina and Georgia Almanac, For the Year of Our Lord 1793,* Charleston, [1792].

hear his opinion of the trade and people of this state in particular. . . . At three I went to dine with Mr. La Motte, Mr. Miller, and Mr. Auldjo. In the evening we intended taking a ride but were obliged to defer it till tomorrow morning, as one of the horses was out. I called in Church Street and drank tea with Mr. Shoolbred and Mr. Moodie and afterwards took a walk with them on the bay. At night I retired to Williams'. Mr. Tunno invited me to the club, where I played at whist with Mr. Jennings, Mr. Ogilvie, and another gentleman and exactly lost my winning of last night.

(June 25, 1786—Sunday) Dr. Miller read the prayers extremely well and Dr. Purcell preached a most excellent sermon upon the vices and immorality, want of honor, honesty, and everything that is virtuous, of South Carolina. I thought some of the audience held down their heads. . . . In the evening we went to drink tea at Dr. Turnbull's, where we had the pleasure of finding a large circle of ladies. I had the honor of being introduced to the two Miss Turnbulls, Miss Smith (a beautiful girl), Miss Bay, Miss Mutrui and Mrs. Mutrui from Smyrna and St. Augustine. . . .[59]

Hunter apparently met few planters or native-born merchants. Tunno, La Motte, Miller, Shoolbred, and Moodie were British merchants who had remained after the evacuation of Charleston. Grant and Price had come out in 1783. Edward Penman, Andrew Turnbull, and John Elihu Bay had been forced by the British evacuation of Florida to find a refuge in Charleston.[60] Hunter's account is evidence of a distinct British community in the city.

PENMAN'S REMARKS and Purcell's sermon undoubtedly referred to the recent eruption in Camden where debtors had refused to pay their creditors and to the condition of the state in general, for the government could hardly enforce decisions of the court of common pleas more than twenty miles outside the gates of Charleston. South Carolina in 1786 was close to a Shaysite rebellion. A pamphlet published in Charleston in 1786 (four months after the affair at Camden) gave the history of the troubles: *A Few Salutary Hints, Pointing out the Policy and Consequences of Admitting British Subjects to Engross our trade and become our Citizens. Addressed to those who either risqued or lost their all in bringing about the Revolution.* The history of the 1780's began, according to the author, with

---

[59] *Quebec to Carolina in 1785-1786, Being the Travel Diary and Observations of Robert Hunter, Jr., a Young Merchant of London,* eds. Louis B. Wright and Marion Tinling, San Marino, 1943, pp. 290-294.

[60] For Penman see "Josiah Smith's Diary, 1780-1781," *SCHGM,* XXXIII (1932), 103. Wilbur H. Siebert, "Andrew Turnbull," *DAB.* Elihu Hall Bay had been judge of vice-admiralty, and secretary of West Florida, by deputation. Cecil Johnson, *British West Florida, 1763-1783,* New Haven, 1943, p. 99.

the evacuation of Charleston, after which the city split into two factions—one contending to keep the British merchants, the other to ship them off. After that matter was decided, the British sent forth "shoals" or rather planted in Carolina "a standing army of merchants, factors, clerks, agents, and emissaries, who out-manoeuvre, undersell, and frighten away the French and Dutch who came here, monopolized our trade, speculated on our necessities, and holding out every object of temptation, plunged us into a debt which their depredations a little before, and our wants and distresses joined to their subtilty now, seduced us to contract."[61] They raked in the circulating coin, shipped it off, and when crops failed sold the Carolinians out. "This must be the consequence, if sales of property go on, at this time that crops have failed us, and no money in the country."[62]

The clannish social life that centered around Williams' Coffee House had raised suspicions: "Is it true, that your meetings in this city, are not so much social parties, as conspiracies against the government, as far as your power goes? Can you deny, that you are not more merchants, than members and heads of a British faction, to sow discontent and promote the views of your ministry?"[63] This threat seemed greater than any posed by Clinton or Cornwallis, for "there is a much surer way for the British regaining influence in America, than by fleets and armies. It is only employing a few millions in linens, woolens, silks, and haberdashery, feasting men in power, and tampering with men without, and by holding out every object to tempt and corrupt, involve in debt all orders of men, from the wealthy rice planter to the wagoner."[64] Without the possession of capital there were no blessings of independence, for the British "superiority of capitals will enable them to ruin our own merchants, to undersell and drive away, as they have already done, those of other nations. . . . As well might a pigmy be compared to a giant, as the impoverished miserable funds of an American merchant, who lost his fortune in the war, to the immense capitals of British traders."[65] They were expected to "shortly raise a power among us, as

---

[61] *A Few Salutary Hints, Pointing out the Policy and Consequences of admitting British Subjects to Engross our trade and become our Citizens. Addressed to those who either risqued or lost their all in bringing about the Revolution*, Charleston, Printed, New York, Re-printed, 1786, p. 4.
[62] *Ibid.*, p. 5.
[63] *Ibid.*, p. 6.
[64] *Ibid.*, p. 7.
[65] *Ibid.*, p. 9.

formidable as the tyranny we suffered by their armies."[66] There was no need to struggle against the inevitable. "Mingling together of British and Americans in the present generation, will be like a mixture of oil and water; agitation will seemingly incorporate them, but after standing for a while, the fatter and richer part will get uppermost."[67]

[66] *Ibid.*, p. 8.
[67] *Ibid.*, p. 11.

VII

THE RISE OF THE CHARLESTON LAWYERS

LAWYERS HAD PLAYED a prominent part in the colonial Assembly, but as a group they had never wielded the power that they were to wield in the immediate post-Revolutionary period. The merchants had been the most powerful group in colonial Carolina, but the most successful merchants had steered their sons into the legal profession. It was only on the eve of the Revolution that Carolinians formed the largest group of Americans studying at the Inns of Court. Young men who had studied in England during the 1760's and 1770's came of age in South Carolina after the Revolution, and they dominated the scene. The new merchant class was largely alien in origin, while the lawyers were native-born, although educated abroad. These lawyers, therefore, provided a link between the new merchants and the old planters.

The most famous Charleston lawyer was John Rutledge (Middle Temple, 1754)—a strange mixture of ability and pride.[1] Rutledge was, as William Pierce put it, "one of those characters who was highly mounted at the commencement of the late revolution."[2] As he was leaving Charleston to attend the First Continental Congress, John Pringle, who was then reading law in his office, described him as a man "of quick apprehension, sound judgment, much sagacity, and ready eloquence; tho he may not perhaps have had that extensive education and reading requisite to compleat the orator."[3] The Revolution provided him with an opportunity to sharpen his talents, first in the Continental Congress, then as governor, and later as virtual dictator of the state.

In March 1784 Captain William Thompson was sent to the common jail for daring to insult the magnificent, marmoreal John Rutledge.[4] The same year Rutledge was selected as the first chancellor

---

[1] For all references to South Carolinians at the Inns of Court in this chapter see J. G. de Roulhac Hamilton, "Southern Members of the Inns of Court," *North Carolina Historical Review*, X (1933), 279-280.

[2] William Pierce, "Character Sketches of Delegates to the Federal Convention," *Records of the Federal Convention of 1787*, ed. Max Farrand, New Haven, 1927, III, 96.

[3] John Pringle to William Tilghman, July 30, 1774, *Preston Davie Papers*, SHC.

[4] David Duncan Wallace, *South Carolina, A Short History, 1520-1948*, Chapel Hill, 1951, pp. 335-336.

of the court of equity.[5] By 1787, when he attended the Constitutional Convention, he was, according to a French sketch: "*L'homme
le plus eloquent, mais le plus fier et le plus imperieux des Etats-
Unis.*"[6]

Next to John Rutledge in ability and pride was William Drayton
(Middle Temple, 1750). William Drayton had been chief justice of
East Florida, but after differences with the governor, he had withdrawn to England in 1779.[7] During the next four years he was im-
mersed in the same Anglo-Carolina circles in which the young William Smith had moved. Smith and Drayton had planned to return
together in the summer of 1783, but Smith at the last moment delayed, and the William Draytons came out by themselves. In March
1784, shortly after Drayton's return from England, the legislature
elected him judge of the admiralty court.[8] In 1789, two vacancies
occurred on the state bench; Thomas Waties was elected to the first
vacancy and William Drayton to the second; Drayton refused to
accept until Waties should yield to him "that precedency on the
bench to which his years maturity of experience and legal knowledge" so justly entitled him.[9]

Of those who had studied at the Inns of Court in the 1760's five
presided over the state courts. Thomas Bee (Lincoln's Inn, 1762)
and John Mathews (Middle Temple, 1764) were elected judges in
1776. Thomas Heyward, junior (Middle Temple, 1765), and John
Faucheraud Grimké (Middle Temple, 1769) were elected in 1779.
In 1784 when the court of equity was established, Mathews was
made a chancellor. In 1791, Hugh Rutledge (Middle Temple, 1765)
was also named a chancellor. The lawyers held other high positions
in the post-war decade. John Mathews was governor at the time
of the evacuation of Charleston, and he was succeeded by Benjamin
Guerard (Lincoln's Inn, 1756). Alexander Moultrie (Middle
Temple, 1768) was attorney general of the state, and William Hasell

[5] John Belton O'Neall, *Biographical Sketches of the Bench and Bar of South
Carolina*, Charleston, 1858, II, 597.
[6] "*Liste des Membres et Officiers du Congrés*," *Records of the Federal Convention of 1787*, ed. Max Farrand, New Haven, 1927, III, 238.
[7] *American Museum*, VIII (August 1790), 82-83.
[8] The House resolved on March 22 "that William Drayton Esq. being a
native of this state, but having been absent for some years, that he be admitted
to all the rights and priviledges of a free citizen of this state." *JHR*, XLIV,
360. For his election as judge *see JHR*, XLIV, 400.
[9] John Brown Cutting to John Rutledge, junior, February 21, 1789, *John
Rutledge, junior, Papers*, SHC. O'Neall, *op. cit.*, II, 597.

Gibbes (Inner Temple, 1771) was both master in chancery and recorder of the city court of Charleston.[10]

Francisco de Miranda, the famous South American patriot who visited Charleston in the fall of 1783, had his own opinion of the men locally considered the most brilliant at the bar, Edward Rutledge (Middle Temple, 1767), Charles Cotesworth Pinckney (Middle Temple, 1764), Alexander Moultrie, and Thomas Pinckney (Middle Temple, 1768):

> *El primero pose un conosimiento mediano de las Leyes, brillante y facil explicacion, con un modo bastante agradable, recomendable persona; el segundo es hombre de buen juicio, profundos conosimientos en su profesion, y fuerza en el argumento, aunque su eloquencia ni es tan brillante, ni tan sonora como la del primero. Moultry tiene solidez, juicio, y mui buena locuzion; el ultimo en nada es completo aun, sin embargo de que muchos le creen un prodigio en todo: ha logrado una buena educacion en Europa, es joven aun, y da mui buenas esperanzas, sin que sus progresos manifesten todavia nada de extraordinario.[11]*

Moultrie went on to ruin his promising career by embezzling £60,000 of state funds.[12] Thomas Pinckney, as Miranda suspected, never developed his full talents as a lawyer.

Among those who practiced law in Charleston during the next twenty years Edward Rutledge and Charles Cotesworth Pinckney were undoubtedly the leaders. Pinckney returned from England in 1769 and Rutledge in 1773, and both established their reputation at the bar before the Revolution. They were drawn together by their marriages to the daughters of Henry Middleton (Pinckney to Sarah Middleton in 1773 and Rutledge to Henrietta Middleton in 1774), and until the death of Edward Rutledge in 1800 they worked

[10] The date given for Thomas Bee by de Roulhac Hamilton is 1782 which is obviously a mistake. Perhaps it should be 1762. De Roulhac Hamilton, *op. cit.*, p. 279. O'Neall, *op. cit.*, II, 213-214, 597-598. Wallace, *op. cit.*, p. 704.

[11] *The Diary of Francisco de Miranda, Tour of the United States, 1783-1784*, ed. William Spence Robertson, New York, 1928, pp. 22-23. Translation: "The first has an average knowledge of law, a brilliant and effortless discourse, with a very agreeable manner, a worthy person; the second is a man of good judgment, profound knowledge in his profession, and strength in his arguments, although his eloquence is neither as brilliant nor as sonorous as that of the first. Moultrie is solid, has good judgment, and expresses himself very well: the last is not yet complete in anything, although many believe him to be a prodigy in everything: he has obtained a good education in Europe, is still young, and shows great promise, although his accomplishments have not yet shown anything extraordinary." Translated from the Spanish by Carroll E. Mace, assistant professor, Department of Foreign Languages, University of South Carolina.

[12] Moultrie was impeached by the House in December 1792 and convicted by the Senate in December 1793. *JHR*, LI, 220, 226-227, 242-244, 446-447. *Also see* Charles Cotesworth Pinckney to Thomas Pinckney, February 4, 1794, *Pinckney Papers*, LC.

as a team. Both fought with distinction during the Revolution, and Rutledge suffered banishment to St. Augustine.[13] They were therefore among the lawyers the most staunchly patriotic—indeed, of the Carolina patriots they were the noblest of them all, the least tarnished by equivocation, the ones whose historic profiles need little revision by contemporary historians. In the post-war decade they were devoted to the practice of law and the accumulation of wealth. According to the Duke de la Rochefoucauld-Liancourt, they earned from £3,500 to £4,500 sterling a year.[14] They invested jointly in two confiscated plantations, which they struggled to improve as the basis of their new estates.[15] It was around these two—the most powerful and influential in the entire state—and their two brothers, John Rutledge and Thomas Pinckney, that the political history of the state was made.

John Julius Pringle and Jacob Read came close to challenging the predominant place of Edward Rutledge and Charles Cotesworth Pinckney at the bar. John Julius Pringle was the son of Robert Pringle, a Scottish merchant often associated in commercial ventures with Benjamin Smith and for many years an assistant judge. John was entered at the Middle Temple in 1773, but read law in John Rutledge's office for three years before sailing for England in December 1774.[16] He was another Carolina boy who heard the news of Lexington and Concord and Bunker Hill in London.[17] After completing his twelve terms at the Temple he served a year as secretary to Ralph Izard before coming home in the summer of 1779 via Amsterdam and St. Eustatius.[18] In the 1780's and 1790's Pringle's income from the practice of law equaled that of Rutledge and of Pinckney.[19]

Jacob Read (Gray's Inn, 1773) was the son of James Reid (later

[13] J. G. de Roulhac Hamilton, "Charles Cotesworth Pinckney"; Robert L. Meriwether, "Edward Rutledge," *DAB*. After the death of his first wife, Pinckney married a daughter of Benjamin Stead. *Charleston Morning Post, and Daily Advertiser*, July 24, 1786.

[14] Duke de la Rochefoucauld-Liancourt, *Travels through the United States of North America*, London, 1800, II, 389.

[15] The two estates were known as Tippicutlaw and Charleywood. Edward Rutledge to Henry Middleton Rutledge, July 21, 1796, *Rutledge Papers, Dreer Collection*, PHS.

[16] John Pringle to William Tilghman, July 30, December 13, 1774, April 22, 1775, *Preston Davie Papers*, SHC.

[17] John Pringle to William Tilghman, May 1, August 7, 1775, *Preston Davie Papers*, SHC.

[18] J. Harold Easterby, "John Julius Pringle," *DAB*. John Pringle to Ralph Izard, April 26, 1778, *Miscellaneous Manuscripts,* NYHS. John Pringle to [William Lee], June 20, 1779, *Preston Davie Papers*, SHC.

[19] Rochefoucauld-Liancourt, *op. cit.*, II, 389.

spelled Read), a Charles Town merchant as early as 1735, owner of a rope walk, and powder receiver after 1760.[20] In the years before the Revolution he was more closely connected with Savannah. Although the father was a reluctant supporter of the Revolution, the son had returned to fight for the patriot cause.[21] In 1780 he was exiled by the British to St. Augustine. After the war he took the occasion of service in the Continental Congress (1783-1785) to introduce himself to the commercial communities of Philadelphia and New York. In 1785 he married the daughter of David Van Horn, a rich New York merchant.[22] After his terms in Congress, he became a leading lawyer in Charleston, particularly ardent in behalf of the interests of British merchants.[23] Both Pringle and Read were speakers of the House of Representatives of South Carolina: Pringle in 1787 and 1788; Read from 1789 to 1794.

Another lawyer, younger than the rest, but with talents even more promising, was Charles Pinckney, first cousin once removed of Charles Cotesworth and Thomas Pinckney, being the son of Colonel Charles Pinckney, who had been the acknowledged leader of the pre-Revolutionary Charles Town bar.[24] Although he was entered at the Middle Temple in 1773, he apparently did not go to England. He was present at the siege of Savannah and was captured at the surrender of Charles Town. His father, however, resumed his allegiance to the Crown, and the family estate suffered an amercement of twelve per cent at the hands of the Jacksonborough legislature. Charles Pinckney nevertheless inherited a great fortune. Eschewing the profits of the bar, he served in Congress from 1784 to 1787 and

[20] De Roulhac Hamilton does not record Jacob Read in either the South Carolina or Georgia lists, although he mentions a James Read, Gray's Inn, 1773, from Georgia. Since James Reid (or Read) the father lived in Savannah, the James Read of Gray's Inn may be Jacob Read. De Roulhac Hamilton, *op. cit.*, p. 280. "Petition of James Reid," recorded under date of January 9, 1755, *JC*, XXIV, 1-2. W. Roy Smith, *South Carolina as a Royal Province, 1719-1776*, New York, 1903, p. 411.

[21] Anne King Gregorie, "Jacob Read," *DAB*. James Read wrote in May 1775: "May Heaven avert the threatening storm and send us once more a happy meeting." James Read to Jacob Read, May 16, 1775, *Miscellaneous Manuscripts*, NYPL.

[22] Francis Marvin, *The Van Horn Family History*, East Stroudsburg, [1929,] p. 114. Pierce Butler thought this connection an important influence in the life of Read. Pierce Butler to James Monroe, January 19, 1795, *Monroe Papers*, LC.

[23] After Read became a United States senator, he was still retained by the British consul in Charleston. Benjamin Moodie to Jacob Read, December 29, 1795, October 14, 1796, *Miscellaneous Manuscripts*, NYPL.

[24] Col. Charles Pinckney (1732-1782) was a first cousin of Charles Cotesworth and Thomas Pinckney. "The Thomas Pinckney Family of South Carolina," *SCHGM*, XXXIX (1938), 15-35. J. Harold Easterby, "Charles Pinckney," *DAB*.

at the age of twenty-nine represented the state in the Constitutional Convention. William Pierce praised him above the other Carolinians:

> Mr. Charles Pinckney is a young Gentleman of the most promising talents. He is . . . in possession of a very great variety of knowledge. Government, Law, History and Phylosophy are his favorite studies, but he is intimately acquainted with every species of polite learning, and has a spirit of application and industry beyond most Men. He speaks with great neatness and perspicuity, and treats every subject as fully, without running into prolixity, as it requires. He has been a Member of Congress, and served in that Body with ability and eclat.[25]

It was amid this talented group that William Smith had to find a place.

WILLIAM SMITH's first task was to reorganize his little fortune so that it would begin once again to produce an income. The £15,000 currency which he had inherited from his father had been placed out at interest—eight per cent until 1777, when seven per cent became the legal rate of interest.[26] When Thomas Loughton Smith died in 1773 his property had been sold and the proceeds also placed out at interest.[27] During the Revolution, debtors were able to pay their creditors with cheap money; consequently the fortunes of both William and his brother had been considerably diminished. Thomas Smith of Broad Street wrote in 1783: "My Brother's and Nephew's Estates are lessened much by it [the depreciation of money] and I am afraid there is little satisfaction to be expected from those who paid off their Bonds at a shilling, 9d, or 6d, in the pound. It had made at least a difference of £20,000 sterling to my estate."[28]

Smith, however, was not in the unhappy position that many Charleston commission merchants found themselves. At the beginning of the war they had owed sums to London merchants which were at that time counterbalanced by sums due them locally. During the war the local debts had been paid off at a fraction of their true value, while those due London merchants remained outstanding. Then under the terms of the treaty of peace, Charleston com-

---

[25] Pierce wrote that Pinckney was 24 years old, but his birth date was October 26, 1757. Pierce, *op. cit.*, III, 96.

[26] By an act of January 2, 1777. *SC Statutes*, IV, 363-365.

[27] *Will Book, 1771-1774, Charleston County, S.C.*, SC Archives, p. 365.

[28] Thomas Smith to Isaac Smith, August 19, 1783, *Smith-Carter Papers*, MHS.

mission merchants found themselves pressed by the British to pay the old debts in sterling.

One of them, writing under the pseudonym of "Plain Truth," told the sad story in a letter to the *South-Carolina Weekly Gazette* in June 1783. At the beginning of the war he had had large amounts due him locally, but the courts early in the contest had been closed, so he was not able to recover them. Then a resolution forbade remittances to Great Britain. Finally, the interest rate had been lowered and paper currency made legal tender for all payments. He had been paid off at the rate of twenty, thirty, forty, and fifty to one. How could he now be expected to repay the British merchant as the treaty of peace demanded? A man in this position was in danger of being sold out, and "Plain Truth" called urgently for a meeting of those who had been paid in depreciated money.

Smith was faced with only half of this dilemma because he owed no one in Great Britain. The difference between him and these commission merchants was essentially the difference between a man of independent capital and men who operated on borrowed capital. The latter group was in danger of being swept away, and many of them were. Those who never recovered remained a discontented group in Charleston.[29] The phenomenon by which many of the native-born merchants were ruined helps explain the distinctly British character of Charleston commercial life in the two decades after the Revolution. Because of this experience, William Smith would have adopted the attitudes of a creditor towards paper money, but not necessarily any antipathy towards British merchants.

That part of Smith's fortune not borrowed by individuals had been used by South Carolina during the Revolution. The Smith family, like all the rich patriot families, lent large sums to the state between 1776 and 1780. William Smith acknowledged publicly in 1788 that his family had lent £20- to £30,000 sterling.[30] Other important creditors of the state were Gabriel Manigault, I, (whose grandson said in 1808 that he had lent $170,000) and Josiah Smith (£100,000).[31] During the 1780's the state did nothing more than issue indents in lieu of interest on these loans.[32] This portion of

[29] *South-Carolina Weekly Gazette*, June 28, 1783.
[30] William Smith to the Electors of the Parish of St. Bartholomew, November 22, 1788, *Personal Papers, Miscellaneous*, LC.
[31] Gabriel Manigault to Joseph Manigault, September 13, 1808, *Manigault Papers*, SCL. Josiah Smith to James Poyas, January 31, 1784, *Josiah Smith, junior, Letter-Book, 1771-1784*, SHC.
[32] *Annals of the Congress of the United States*, Washington, 1834, II (1st cong., 2nd sess.), 1322-1324, 1356-1360, 1517-1519.

Smith's fortune, therefore, could not be touched. It was locked-up capital which could only be released by public action.

In the attempt to recover his fortune it was an advantage to Smith to be a lawyer. Smith was admitted to the roll of attorneys on January 6, 1784, less than two months after his return.[33] Before the Revolution the qualifications for admission to the bar were framed by the chief justice and his brother judges. On the eve of the Revolution the rule forbade anyone to be admitted who had not studied five years in Carolina, or three years in Carolina plus two at one of the law colleges abroad.[34] Judges Burke, Heyward, and Grimké drew up new rules for the new state. In order to qualify in 1784 a man had to be a citizen of the state, to have studied law in a law office within the state for four years, or to have studied law "in any foreign nation as to qualify . . . to follow the profession of the law" there, to give proof of being a person "of Fair Character & Competent Abilities," and to take the oath of allegiance to the state.[35]

Smith was first concerned with litigation involving his own estate. In June 1784 the chancery court handed down a decision in the case of *Legatees Smith* v. *Executors Smith*. Benjamin Smith had devised his estate to be divided equally among his children, share and share alike, and in case any of them should die before the time of receiving his share, that share should go to Benjamin Smith's surviving children. Thomas Loughton and Anne had received their legacies and subsequently died. Benjamin Wragg Smith had then died before he attained his majority. The question the court had to decide was whether Benjamin Wragg Smith's share should be divided among the testator's surviving children to the exclusion of the children of Thomas Loughton and Anne, or whether the said children *in loco parentis* should come in for their respective parent's proportion. The court determined that it could never have been the intention of the testator to exclude his grandchildren and they should therefore have their respective parent's proportion of Benjamin

---

[33] O'Neall, *op. cit.*, II, 603.

[34] John Pringle to William Tilghman, November 1, 1774, *Preston Davie Papers*, SHC.

[35] Aedanus Burke, Thomas Heyward, junior, J. F. Grimké, "Qualifications for admission to practice as attornies," n.d., *Autographs of the Signers of the Declaration of Independence*, PML. The legislature passed an "act to regulate the admission of attornies at law" on March 17, 1785. This law required a clerkship of four years at home or study for three years abroad at a law college. *SC Statutes*, IV, 668-669.

Wragg Smith's share. The court limited the survivorship to the death of the testator and not to the death of any of his children.[36]

Benjamin Smith, William's father, had made a great deal of money as administrator for the estates of friends. This was also one of Smith's chief sources of income in the 1780's. As head of the family after the death of his elder brother, Smith came naturally to these duties. Even if he had handled only the property of the descendants of his father and done nothing for his uncle's branch of the family, he would have been quite busy. Within his own immediate family group he managed the fortunes of his nieces, the daughters of Thomas Loughton Smith, of his half-brother Joseph Allen Smith, and of his nephew Barnard Elliott.[37]

Thomas Loughton Smith's widow and her four beautiful daughters had been decidedly pro-British. The widow had married, in 1775, Dr. James Clitherall, who after the surrender of Charles Town was appointed surgeon to the South Carolina royalist troops.[38] Ann Loughton, the second daughter, married, on November 7, 1782, Major Thomas Fraser of the South Carolina royalist troops, who had been present in many of the sanguinary actions in the state.[39] In May 1784, Elizabeth, the eldest daughter, married Lieutenant David Campbell, formerly of the 63rd British Regiment.[40] Maria, the youngest, married John Deas, junior, in October 1788 and lived at Thorogood until the death of her husband two years later.[41] Her subsequent marriage to Dr. John Ramsay vastly complicated the settlement of the Deas estate.[42] Claudia, the third daughter, was reputed to be the most beautiful girl in Charleston, but like many great beauties she took a long time in making up her mind to marry.

[36] "Autograph Legal Notebook of William Smith, 1782-1805," *William Loughton Smith Papers,* RC, pp. 145-146.

[37] "Memorandum of agreement between Col. William Thompson of the one part and William Smith, Executor to the estate of Barnard Elliott, Esq. of the other," May 16, 1786, *Dreer Collection,* PHS. *Also see* "Papers relating to the estate of Barnard Elliott," *William Loughton Smith Papers,* SCHS. In 1788 William Smith was trying to collect interest on indents in behalf of Joseph Allen Smith (who held £916/15/10), the estate of Barnard Elliott (£5,001/ 8/3), and the estate of Thomas Loughton Smith (£412/17/9). *See* "list of indents," July 1788, *William Loughton Smith Papers,* SCHS.

[38] "Journal of Alexander Chesney, a South Carolina Loyalist in the Revolution and After," ed. E. Alfred Jones, *Ohio State University Bulletin,* XXVI (1921), number 4, 98, 111-112.

[39] *Ibid.,* pp. 111-112.

[40] A. S. Salley, Jr., "William Smith and Some of His Descendants," *SCHGM,* IV (1903), 252.

[41] *State Gazette of South-Carolina,* October 9, 1788. *City Gazette, or the Daily Advertiser,* October 26, 1790.

[42] *See Ramsay* v. *Deas* in "Autograph Legal Notebook of William Smith, 1782-1805," *William Loughton Smith Papers,* RC, pp. 165-176, 235-236.

One of those enthralled by her beauty wrote John Rutledge, junior,
in February 1789: "Your favourite Miss Claudia Smith is a charming
little creature—full of fire and fancy—with sparkling demeanour and
a face crowded with vivacity. I was introduced to her on the race
ground—in the chariot of her sister the wife of Mr. John Deas
Junr."[43] Claudia found it difficult to exchange such universal admiration for marriage. In 1791 she was to have the highest honor
of sitting at George Washington's right hand at the ball given
during the President's visit to Charleston. Very late in life she became the second wife of Henry Izard, Ralph Izard's eldest son.[44]
It was William Smith who managed the estates of these charming
and beautiful ladies. He qualified on December 24, 1783, as an
executor of his brother's will.[45] He also worked diligently to make
it easier for Dr. Clitherall, the step-father, to pay off the amercement of twelve per cent on his estate.[46] Ultimately when Smith went
to Congress, he turned over a good many of these matters to David
Campbell, the husband of his niece Elizabeth.[47]

Besides this, William Smith was retained by British merchants
to recover their debts. The most important of these was John Nutt,
the great London merchant who had watched over him during his
student days. John Nutt was trying to collect debts totaling over
£ 100,000 sterling;[48] one of the debtors was Gideon Dupont who
had received vast quantities of goods from Nutt before the war.
According to Cornelius Dupont, Nutt had persuaded his brother
Gideon to remain loyal to the Crown,[49] and as a consequence the
Jacksonborough legislature had confiscated his estate. The state
admitted claims against the estates confiscated, so in order to meet
the legitimate claims against Dupont's estate, it had appropriated all
the bonds and indents to satisfy the creditors. William Smith, whose

[43] John Brown Cutting to John Rutledge, junior, February 17, 1789, *John
Rutledge, junior, Papers*, SHC.
[44] "Izard of South Carolina," *SCHGM*, II (1901), 218-219.
[45] *Will Book, 1771-1774, Charleston County, S.C.*, SC Archives, pp. 487-489.
[46] Dr. Clitherall's name was removed from the confiscation list in 1784 and
placed on the list of amercements. *See* petitions, James Clitherall folder, *Confiscated Estates*, SC Archives. William Smith probably presented his petition
of February 18, 1786. *JHR*, XLVI, 75, 138, 151.
[47] *See* "Papers relating to the affairs of David Campbell and William Smith,"
William Loughton Smith Papers, SCHS. In 1792 Campbell married Nancy
Motte, the daughter of Colonel Isaac Motte and Anne Smith. Charles Cotesworth Pinckney to Thomas Pinckney, October 13, 1792, *Pinckney Papers*, LC.
[48] John Nutt was down for £ 103,680 sterling in "List of debts due by the
citizens of the United States of America to the merchants and traders of Great
Britain, contracted previous to the year 1776, with interest on the same to the
1st of January, 1790," *FO*, VIII, 1-2.
[49] Cornelius Dupont to Jacob Read, December 27, 1790, *Read Papers*, DUL.

client John Nutt was the principal creditor, called all the creditors
to meet at ten o'clock on the morning of Monday, January 7, 1788,
at the City Tavern to divide the bonds and indents.[50] Smith was
obviously successful, for in July 1788 he held £5,171/3/8 in indents
for the creditors of Gideon Dupont's estate.[51] William Smith and
Samuel Legare, as attorneys to the assignee of the estate, advertised
in the *State Gazette of South Carolina* for July 24, 1788, that all
persons indebted to the estate of Gideon Dupont who had not
settled by September 1 would be sued.

One of the little ironies in this story was that Cornelius Dupont,
American patriot, was being squeezed to pay John Nutt, Englishman. He was obliged to pay a bond for which he had become security for his brother, while having at the same time some of his
own demands against his brother Gideon's estate set aside. In 1790
he petitioned the state legislature for relief: "Have I not in justice
a wright to expect that my country will not let me be so great a
sufferer as to loose, not only what it justly owes me, but to be also
obliged to pay a large debt for which I never had the least benefit,
nor ever shall, and what I still think hardest of, is that Mr. Nut
should come in equal with the creditors in this country, especially
as I believe he was an enemy to the cause of America."[52]

The remainder of Smith's income must have come from ordinary
litigation. In the case of *Perry* v. *Cantey* he secured payment of a
hundred guinea note. His charge was £6/4/6 of which 24/6 was
the sheriff's fee. The ordinary nature of his legal business can be
seen from the items in the debt of £95/10/0 which Benjamin Singleton owed to Smith: for entering twenty appearances (at 30/-
each), £30; for drawing several titles, bonds, etc., £7/10/0; fee,
in cause of *Singleton* v. *Oliphant*, if successful, £30. The last item
was a note for £26, with interest, £28.[53] In February 1786 he
helped the state's attorney general, Alexander Moultrie, prosecute
Major William Clay Snipes for the murder of Maurice Simons.
Snipes retained William Drayton, John Julius Pringle, Jacob Read,
and John Parker, junior (his first case), to defend him. This was

[50] William Smith to Cornelius Dupont, December 19, 1787, *William Loughton Smith Papers*, SCL. Smith signed the letter as "Attorney for John Nutt
Principal Creditor." On February 18, 1786, Smith had presented a petition of
John Nutt, London merchant, with demands against the estate of Gideon
Dupont. *JHR*, XLVI, 85.
[51] "List of indents," July 1788, *William Loughton Smith Papers*, SCHS.
[52] Cornelius Dupont to Jacob Read, December 27, 1790, *Read Papers*, DUL.
[53] "Bonds and Notes of William Loughton Smith, before 1790," *William
Loughton Smith Papers*, SCHS.

a celebrated trial with leading lawyers on both sides. Major Snipes was convicted of manslaughter but obtained a full pardon.[54]

It is almost impossible to estimate Smith's income at the bar. Since he started out with very little and had by his own account a fortune of £19,000 sterling in September 1789, he must have done exceedingly well.[55] The leading lawyers during these years were known to have made from £3,500 to £4,500 sterling annually, so Smith must have been doing as well as any of them to accumulate such a sum. Thomas Smith of Broad Street perhaps understated it when he wrote on February 8, 1786, that his nephew William "promises to be eminent in his Profession, the law."[56]

Although Smith was able and successful, he was not considered a leader in his profession. In all that he did, he just missed the top rung. This may have been due to some defect in his character. Perhaps it resulted from the lack of restraint in his early training, the loose hand of the Reverend Richard Clarke. Smith certainly lacked the seriousness, dedication, and integrity which character-ized the leader of the Charleston bar, Charles Cotesworth Pinckney. Once, an action was brought in the court of common pleas by five musicians against Milligan, master of the City Tavern, to recover damages for a beating the five had received from Milligan. General Pinckney, defending Milligan, observed that the plaintiffs had been aggressors by abusing Milligan in his own house, which was his castle. Smith, the lawyer for the musicians, ridiculed Pinckney as undoubtedly the first person since Don Quixote to mistake an inn for a castle![57] In the course of his career Smith often let his wit outrun his discretion. The result was a collection of unnecessary enemies.

In a satire on the young men of Charleston written in 1785, Smith's character was pinned down in these words:

> Now rise my Muse, exert your utmost skill,
> To paint the Charms of priggish little Will.
> Great at the Bar the Senate and the Balls,
> He charms our ears and every sense enthralls;
> 'Tis Dunning's self We now must all declare,
> But like him only in his vacant *stare*.[58]

[54] See "Simons-Snipes Duel," *SCHGM*, XII (1911), 160-162.

[55] "State of the Honble. W. Smith's affairs, in the hands of D. Campbell, 1st Sept. 1789," *William Loughton Smith Papers*, SCHS.

[56] Thomas Smith to Isaac Smith, February 6, 1786, *Smith-Carter Papers*, MHS.

[57] "Newspaper clippings," *William Loughton Smith Papers*, RC.

[58] "Satire upon the Young Men of Charleston," summer 1785, *State Boxes (South Carolina)*, NYPL. A marginal note says that these lines refer to "Will. Smith."

VIII

THE RE-EMERGENCE OF THE
GOOSE CREEK PLANTERS

A T THE TIME of the calling of the Jacksonborough legislature the lower part of the parish of St. James Goose Creek was within the sphere of British influence. The leading men were sitting tight, waiting for the last swing of the war pendulum. Of the six delegates representing the parish at Jacksonborough only Ralph Izard was of the old ruling group. The others were Alexander Broughton of St. John's Berkeley, Thomas Elliott of St. Andrew's, Dr. George Flagg and William Johnson of Charleston, and Colonel John Baddeley of Goose Creek.[1] The letters of Edward Rutledge written at the time of the Jacksonborough meeting indicate how close the Goose Creek men came to ruin. Rutledge, who spoke of them as the "protection gentry," was quite willing to see his own father-in-law Henry Middleton, who "keeps constantly at Goosecreek," suffer.[2] He noted that his brother-in-law Peter Smith had escaped confiscation "from his insignificance, tho' I believe he is still with the Enemy, or at Goosecreek, which is nearly the same Thing." The name of Thomas Smith of Broad Street had been mentioned "but struck off. . . . However, it is not clear to me that he will get off altogether: it is said & believed that he subscribed to raising the Horse: if so, he will be amerced 30 per cent, & justly too." According to Rutledge, Gabriel Manigault was fortunate to escape with an amercement of only ten per cent.[3] There must have been much haggling over who should be included and who excluded. When the final lists were drawn up, the Goose Creek gentlemen could consider themselves quite lucky; the names of Henry Middleton, Peter Smith, Thomas Smith of Broad Street, and Gabriel Manigault were nowhere to be found. Of the men who had sent their sons abroad to study, only

[1] *Journal of the House of Representatives of South Carolina, January 8, 1782-February 26, 1782,* ed. A. S. Salley, Jr., Columbia, 1916, p. 131. For Broughton *see SCHGM,* XXII (1921), 23. For Baddeley *see SCHGM,* XX (1919), 144.

[2] Edward Rutledge to Arthur Middleton, February 14, 1782, "Correspondence of Hon. Arthur Middleton," *SCHGM,* XXVII (1926), 5.

[3] Edward Rutledge to Arthur Middleton, February 26, 1782, *ibid.,* pp. 8-9. For the divisions in prominent families *see* Edward McCrady, *The History of South Carolina under the Royal Government, 1719-1776,* New York, 1899, pp. 557-558.

Dr. Alexander Garden suffered the confiscation of his estate and John Deas an amercement of twelve per cent.[4]

Once free from the threat of confiscation or amercement, these families began to reassert their influence. Early in 1784 they were able to save the Alexander Garden estate from confiscation,[5] and by the November 1784 election the parish was definitely again in the hands of the old ruling families: Ralph Izard, Gabriel Manigault, William Smith, Alexander Garden, junior, John Parker, junior, and William Johnson won seats in the House of Representatives.[6] To the men of Goose Creek it mattered not that Smith had been away for thirteen years; Parker was still in England (not to return for another year) when he was elected![7]

To label William Smith's Goose Creek support as planter support, even though the Goose Creek men lived on plantations, might be misleading. The plantations along Goose Creek were not as productive as those on the Santee or to the south of Charleston; they were principally country retreats for retired merchants or home plantations for the wealthiest planters. These, the richest Carolinians, had diversified economic interests. Many before the Revolution had lived off the interest from funds out on loan. This group, despite its lack of enthusiasm for the patriot cause, had lent the state large sums during the Revolution and after the war were its most important domestic creditors. They might be called entrepreneurs, for it was largely from them that capital was obtained for developing the country.

Who were these Goose Creek capitalists? Peter Smith lived at Broom Hall;[8] John Deas at Thorogood.[9] Gabriel Manigault, busy ornamenting the grounds with temples and Chinese bridges, resided at The Oaks.[10] Joseph Manigault was at Wilson's;[11] Alexander Gar-

---

[4] *SC Statutes,* VI, 630-635.

[5] *See* petitions, Alexander Garden folder, *Confiscated Estates* SC Archives. *SC Statutes,* VI, 634. Alexander Garden, junior, Smith, and Manigault had been a "sociable trio" in London; Garden returned late in 1780. William Smith to Gabriel Manigault, II, September 30, 1780, June 13, 1781, *Manigault Papers,* SCL.

[6] *South-Carolina Gazette and Public Advertiser,* December 4, 1784. William Johnson had been tied with Peter Bacot in the election, but Johnson took his seat early in the session. *JHR,* XLV, 7.

[7] For Parker's return *see* Joseph Manigault to Gabriel Manigault, II, August 4, 24, 1785, *Manigault Papers,* SC Archives.

[8] Henry A. M. Smith, "Goose Creek," *SCHGM,* XXIX (1928), 274-277.

[9] *Ibid.,* p. 271.

[10] *Ibid.,* pp. 16-18. Joseph Manigault to Gabriel Manigault, II, October 24, 1783, *Manigault Papers,* SC Archives.

[11] Henry A. M. Smith, *op. cit.,* pp. 16-18.

den, junior, at Otranto.[12] John Splatt Cripps, a native-born merchant of immense influence in post-war Charleston, had a three hundred ninety acre plantation on the creek. After William Smith's departure for Congress in 1789, Cripps managed the Barnard Elliott estate for him.[13] Dr. Charles Drayton, son of the former royal councilor John Drayton, had a four hundred forty-six acre plantation next to Cripps, but lived at Drayton Hall on the Ashley.[14] Governor Benjamin Guerard, son of another royal councilor John Guerard, bought the 1,474-acre estate, Fontainbleu, in 1784.[15] John Parker, whose two sons were close friends of William Smith, had two plantations: John Parker, junior, who married Susannah, a daughter of Henry Middleton, received Hayes in 1793; Thomas who married Mary, a daughter of William Henry Drayton, received Woodlands in 1800.[16] Nearby was the retreat of Mrs. Richard Shubrick, who in 1786 became the third wife of Thomas Bee.[17] Another family with whom William Smith was to be closely associated was that of Peter Bacot, who resided at Cherry Hill. His estate passed in 1787 to Thomas Wright Bacot and Henry Bacot.[18] Crowfield, perhaps the most magnificent of them all, was bought on March 16, 1784, by John Middleton, who had recently come out from England. He was the son of a former owner of Crowfield, William Middleton, who had resigned as royal councilor and withdrawn to England in 1755.[19]

The constituency of St. James Goose Creek, once the old families had reasserted themselves, was something of a "pocket borough." In November 1786 the parish returned Ralph Izard, William Smith, Gabriel Manigault, Peter Smith, John Deas, junior, and John Parker, junior.[20] In 1788 they elected the same gentlemen plus Benjamin Smith delegates to the ratification convention.[21] In November 1788

[12] Ibid., p. 23.

[13] Ibid., pp. 5-6. See letters of John Splatt Cripps to William Smith, 1789-1794, in folder on Barnard Elliott estate, William Loughton Smith Papers, SCHS.

[14] Henry A. M. Smith, op. cit., pp. 13-14.

[15] Ibid., pp. 74-75.

[16] Ibid., pp. 76-81. Notes of Mr. William Henry Parker in the hands of the author.

[17] Charleston Morning Post, and Daily Advertiser, June 3, 1786. Henry A. M. Smith, op. cit., p. 89.

[18] Ibid., p. 185.

[19] Ibid., pp. 270-272.

[20] Charleston Morning Post, and Daily Advertiser, December 1, 1786.

[21] Debates in the Several State Conventions on the Adoption of the Federal Constitution, ed. Jonathan Elliot, Philadelphia, 1941, IV, 339. Benjamin Smith was a descendant of William Smith and Elizabeth Schenckingh Smith. A. S. Salley, Jr., "William Smith and Some of His Descendants," SCHGM, IV (1903), 240-241, n. 11. He married the daughter of George Smith, partner in Smiths, DeSaussure, and Darrell, SCHGM, XIX (1918), 172.

the parish returned Peter Smith, Ralph Izard, John Deas, junior, Gabriel Manigault, William Smith, and Peter Gray.[22] The delegates to the state constitutional convention of 1790 were John Deas, junior, Peter Gray, Nathaniel McCants, William Allen Deas, James Smith, and Aaron Loocock.[23] In 1790, after the parish was allotted one senator and three representatives under the new state constitution, it sent Peter Smith to the Senate and Gabriel Manigault, William Allen Deas, and Aaron Loocock to the House of Representatives.[24] In 1792 the delegation consisted of Peter Smith, senator, and Gabriel Manigault, Thomas Rhett Smith, and Major Thornly, representatives.[25] The parish of St. James Goose Creek was in the pocket of five families: Izard, Smith, Manigault, Deas, and Parker.

THE MAN who was proclaimed by all to be the leader of this Goose Creek world was Ralph Izard. He resided at The Elms, at the head of Goose Creek, to which estate he continually added properties until in 1801 it encompassed 2,353 acres.[26] He was the richest planter of his day, owning five plantations totaling 4,319 acres on which he kept five hundred slaves at work.[27] Nor did anyone surpass him in pretensions. Izard spent a fortune on The Elms trying to make it a seat befitting his rank. A vast pleasure ground was laid out with lawns and clumps of trees artfully arranged. The walks, lined with Lombardy poplars, were used to divide the grounds and were kept raked by "Old Moses and the two boys." From the piazza in one direction there was a view down an avenue of mulberry trees and in another, a glimpse of a well-stocked fish pond. There was a grape arbor. There were peach trees and pear trees and apple trees. There were fine Antwerp raspberries and strawberries transplanted from the Congarees. Tubbed lemon and sweet orange trees could be housed in the winter and moved outside in the summer. Izard must have had a vision of Versailles or of Chantilly. Those were estates of which an Izard could be proud! Did not a neighbor have his Fontainbleu![28]

[22] *State Gazette of South-Carolina*, December 1, 1788.
[23] *Journal of the Constitutional Convention of South Carolina, May 10, 1790-June 3, 1790*, ed. Francis M. Hutson, Columbia, 1946, p. 4.
[24] *State Gazette of South-Carolina*, October 18, 1790.
[25] *Ibid.*, October 13, 1792. Thomas Rhett Smith was the eldest son of Roger Smith. Major Thornly was one of Izard's lieutenants. Mathias Hutchinson to Ralph Izard, October 22, 1794, *Izard Papers*, SCL.
[26] Henry A. M. Smith, *op. cit.*, pp. 168-171.
[27] *Heads of Families at the First Census of the United States Taken in the Year 1790*, Baltimore, 1952, pp. 33, 34, 37.
[28] This picture is drawn from an interesting series of letters exchanged between Ralph Izard and his gardener, James Mills. James Mills to Ralph Izard,

Ralph Izard was as influential in the neighboring parish of St. George Dorchester on the upper reaches of the Ashley River as he was in St. James Goose Creek. According to Henry A. M. Smith, the Izards late in the century owned sixteen plantations of approximately 20,000 acres on the upper Ashley.[29] Ralph Izard, junior, who had married a daughter of Benjamin Stead, lived at Skieveling; Walter Izard was at Cedar Grove.[30]

In December 1786 Ralph Izard used his political influence to prevent the election of Dr. Thomas Tudor Tucker, a young Virginian who was practicing medicine in South Carolina. In a public harangue at Dorchester he warned the voters not to support Dr. Tucker and then sent "one of his overseers to engage as many votes as he could for another party." Tucker had not been present at the harangue, but after his defeat he called on Izard at The Elms and expressed sentiments which provoked a duel in which Tucker was shot through his left thigh and incapacitated for months. Tucker, in spite of his defeat and his wound, admired the ruthless self-assurance of Izard. When charged with making uncomplimentary remarks about certain people, Izard "did not scruple to acknowledge what he had said, to insist on the right of saying it, and to wish every man in the parish had been present to hear it."

Tucker had his revenge, for while he was ill the death of one of the Dorchester representatives made possible another election, and, in this contest, Tucker defeated Ralph Izard, junior, even after Ralph Izard himself had campaigned in behalf of his cousin. This defeat, however, did not nullify the power and artfulness of Ralph Izard as a planter-boss of the lowcountry.[31]

After Charleston District, containing several parishes, was set up in 1788 to send a representative to the national Congress, Izard's overseers still campaigned for Izard's friends. In 1794, Prior, one of them, exerted himself in St. James Goose Creek and the two neighboring parishes in behalf of William Smith, while his son made a trip through the upper part of Charleston District.[32] Ralph Izard

March 7 (two letters of this date), July 2, 1794; Ralph Izard to John Owen (with information for James Mills), July 10, 15, 1794; Ralph Izard to James Mills, August 10, 1794, *Izard Papers*, LC. *Also see* E. T. H. Shaffer, *Carolina Gardens*, New York, 1937, pp. 38-40.

[29] Henry A. M. Smith, "The Upper Ashley; and the Mutations of Families," *SCHGM*, XX (1919), 195.

[30] Shaffer, *op. cit.*, pp. 30-31.

[31] Thomas Tudor Tucker to St. George Tucker, April 8, 1787, *Coleman-Tucker Papers*, CW.

[32] Mathias Hutchinson to Ralph Izard, October 22, 1794, *Izard Papers*, SCL.

was not a lovable man, but he was rich and he did have political influence.

In 1785 Gabriel Manigault married Margaret Izard, one of Ralph Izard's daughters.[33] William Smith proposed at the same time to Charlotte, a younger sister—"so animated, so lovely a woman."[34] She was only sixteen, and the wedding did not take place until May 1786.[35] Izard wrote Jefferson that his new son-in-law was "a very sensible, and worthy young Gentleman."[36] Through marriage Ralph Izard had gained two powerful lieutenants. Political power in the parish of St. James Goose Creek was henceforth concentrated in the hands of the triumvirate of Izard-Manigault-Smith.[37]

RALPH IZARD not only improved his own plantations, but also looked beyond these to the development of the state. In order to develop the state, lines of communication with the backcountry had to be opened up. The accepted mode of improvement was canals—canals meant capital and capital meant corporations. Here was an area of public effort which would naturally link the men of money with the men of law. Two new types of businessmen emerged to play roles more advanced than that of the merchant in the capitalistic economy: entrepreneurs and corporation lawyers. Ralph Izard might be called South Carolina's first entrepreneur and William Smith her first corporation lawyer.

The corporation was not unknown in colonial history, although it was something of a rarity. According to English common law there were two types of private corporations—"corporation sole" consisting of a single person and his successors and "corporation aggregate" consisting of several persons and their successors. In South Carolina each minister of the Established Church was recognized after 1706 as a "corporation sole," the legal device by which glebe lands and church property were held and protected in the courts.[38]

---

[33] "Izard of South Carolina," *SCHGM*, II (1901), 216.

[34] Alice Izard to Margaret Manigault, December 18, 1808, *Manigault Papers*, SC Archives.

[35] Smith married exactly one year after Manigault. "Izards of South Carolina," *SCHGM*, II (1901), 217.

[36] Ralph Izard to Thomas Jefferson, July 1, 1786, *The Papers of Thomas Jefferson*, ed. Julian P. Boyd, Princeton, 1954, X, 83-84.

[37] In July 1785, after Ralph Izard had declined, William Smith was elected to the Privy Council by a vote of three to two over Dr. Thomas Tudor Tucker. *CJ*, XL, 43.

[38] Joseph Stancliffe Davis, "Corporations in the American Colonies," *Harvard Economic Studies*, Cambridge, 1917, XVI, 75.

Although there were a number of associations for erecting bridges, building or repairing roads, and improving the navigation of small rivers and streams, there were no business corporations. There were only four private corporations—"corporations aggregate"—and these were founded for educational or charitable purposes. These were a reflection of the eighteenth-century charity-school movement which had taken over the joint-stock device for philanthropic purposes. The South Carolina Society (1751) and the Winyaw Indico Society (1757) were established for the support of charitable schools. The Charlestown Library Society was incorporated in 1754, and the Fellowship Society, for the purpose of erecting a convenient infirmary or hospital for distressed persons, in 1769.[39]

There were two reasons for the great increase in private corporations after the Revolution.[40] The disestablishment of the Anglican Church by the Constitution of 1778 put all Protestant congregations on equal footing; Episcopal churches were permitted to retain their property by acts of incorporation, and other Protestant churches could exercise equal religious and civil rights by being incorporated.[41] The need for an improved network of transportation provided the other reason for incorporation. Roads and canals had to be built, and the navigation of rivers, improved; since the state provided only token assistance, these had to be done by private capital. At first, ordinances were passed for roads and bridges; acts of incorporation, for canals.[42]

William Smith was the first South Carolina lawyer to devote his skill to drawing up acts of incorporation. Smith took his seat in the House for the first time on January 3, 1785, but a quorum was not present until the 20th. On the 31st he reported his first bill: an ordinance to establish a fair and markets in the town of Greenville at Long Bluff on the Peedee River. By the 8th of February he had five additional bills ready: one for an ordinance to permit a bridge to be built across Thompson's Creek in Cheraw District, two for

[39] *SC Statutes*, VIII, 106-113.

[40] The public corporations chartered were: Charleston, 1783; Camden, 1791; Beaufort, 1803; Georgetown, 1805; and Columbia, 1805. *Ibid.*, pp. 165, 218, 227, 235.

[41] "Constitution of South Carolina, 1778," Francis Newton Thorpe, *The Federal and State Constitutions, Colonial Charters, and other organic laws of the states, territories and colonies now or heretofore forming the United States of America*, Washington, 1909, VI, 3248-3257.

[42] Joseph Stancliffe Davis, "American Charters to Business Corporations, 1781-1800," *Harvard Economic Studies*, Cambridge, 1917, XVII, 332-345.

roads in the same district, and the other two for bills of incorporation for two Baptist churches on the Peedee River at Welsh Neck
and on Cheraw Hill. Henceforth in the journals, petitions for establishing roads and ferries and for incorporating churches were referred to the committee of which Smith was the most active member. Smith spoke for the committee in the House with the authority
of one well-versed in the subject. On March 1 he was instructed to
consider the petition of the Kershaws and Chesnut requesting the
incorporation of the town of Chatham. On the 18th he reported
the ordinance to incorporate the Master Taylor's Society of Charleston. During the fall session Smith reported a bill to explain and
amend the "acts of Incorporating the City of Charleston and en-
larging the powers of the City Council," the most complicated piece
of legislation in this field. The greatest number of incorporations
were those involving church congregations, and Smith handled a
majority of these during his four years in the House.[43]

THE FIRST CORPORATION of a speculative nature involving large sums
of money was the Santee Canal Company. Ralph Izard was a prime
mover in the project. He envisioned joining by canal the Santee
River and the Cooper River, of which Goose Creek was a tributary,
so that the produce of the backcountry could flow down to Charleston rather than to Georgetown. If the upper tributaries of the Santee
could then be improved, there would be one vast system of river
and canal highways making the state one great economic unit. At
the Santee end of the canal Izard planned to build "Izardtown" on
land that he owned, which, if the scheme worked, would obviously
become a great emporium.[44]

On November 10, 1785, a number of men petitioned the legislature for a charter. The Company for the Inland Navigation, from
Santee to Cooper River, was established by law on March 22, 1786,
with license to build a canal and fix and collect tolls "not exceeding
at any time £.25 per cent. per annum, on the money which they
shall have expended in making and keeping in repair the said canal
and locks." It was given not only the right of eminent domain, but

[43] *JHR*, XLV, 1, 55, 97, 235, 360 (first pagination), and 11 (second pagination). In 1787 when Commodore Gillon urged a repeal of the law establishing the city corporation, Smith stood forth as the champion of that body. *See*
the speeches quoted in the *Charleston Morning Post and Daily Advertiser*,
February 12, 1787.
[44] For Izard's influence *see* remarks in Henry Savage, Jr., *River of the Carolinas: The Santee*, New York, 1956, pp. 244-246. For "Izardtown" *see* end-map
in Prof. F. A. Porcher, *The History of the Santee Canal*, Moncks Corner, 1950.

also all lands within seven miles of the canal not then vested in any-one, as well as the power to command the use of materials for build-ing the canal. Damaging the banks or other works for navigation was considered a felony, the penalty for which was death. In addi-tion to these concessions the shares of the company were to be exempt from any tax and were transferable. At a meeting on March 23 it was decided to issue initially 1,000 shares of stock at £100 per share.[45]

Merchants, planters, and professional men bought shares. Mer-chants like Nathaniel Russell and Samuel Midwood understood that the port of Charleston would gain by the shorter route to the back-country. Planters like Harry Laurens at Mepkin on the Cooper and Aaron Loocock at the Waterees could see the necessity of improv-ing the highways to market. Doctors like Peter Fayssoux and John Budd might be looking for investments for surplus funds. Edward Rutledge and Charles Cotesworth Pinckney had already invested their profits from the practice of law in one of the confiscated estates, Tippicutlaw, through which the proposed canal was to run, and therefore had a direct interest in the project.[46]

Christian Senf, an engineer in the American army during the Revolution, was chosen to supervise the construction of the canal.[47] During the summer of 1786 Senf spent four days with George Wash-ington to observe the work on the canal which was to bypass the falls of the Potomac.[48] Senf's talents must be questioned, for the work on the Santee Canal proceeded at a tedious pace. Skilled workers were hard to find; they were sought both in the North and in England. Thomas Pinckney, while minister to Great Britain, sent out artisans and information on the latest achievements of English canal engineering.[49] Throughout the 1790's more and more money

[45] *South-Carolina Gazette and Public Advertiser,* October 29, November 12, 1785. *Rules of the Company for Opening the Inland Navigation, between the Santee and Cooper Rivers, Agreed to on March the 23rd, 1786,* Charleston, 1786. *SC Statutes,* VII, 541-543.

[46] For Tippicutlaw *see* Porcher, *op. cit.,* end-map.

[47] *Ibid.,* [p. 2].

[48] Christian Senf to an unidentified general, September 15, 1786, *Gratz Col-lection,* PHS. In 1789 Senf suggested to Washington that an inland waterway between New York and East Florida be built at federal expense. Christian Senf to the President of the United States, May 1789, *Knox Papers,* MHS. The Pres-ident replied that Congress was too busy to take up such a scheme. George Washington to Christian Senf, October 12, 1789, *Miscellaneous Letters, De-partment of State,* National Archives.

[49] David Ramsay to Thomas Pinckney, May 31, July 14, 1792, *Pinckney Papers,* LC. Thomas Pinckney to Edward Rutledge, September 7, 1793, *Rut-ledge Papers, Dreer Collection,* PHS.

was poured into the venture, and it was not until 1799 that the canal was put into operation. David Ramsay wrote Jedediah Morse, the American geographer, on July 20, 1799, that the canal had cost more than £400,000 sterling and that he himself had sunk £6,000 in it, which was double the sum he had intended to invest.[50]

William Smith invested more money in canals than did any other Carolinian of his day. By 1808 he had poured more than £14,000 sterling into the Santee Canal Company alone. He had held ten shares originally and had added sixty-seven more in 1792. On these seventy-seven shares he paid year after year the semi-annual requisitions made to complete the work on the canal. No one would have held on so long unless he had had faith in the efficacy of canals; Smith had seen the Duke of Bridgewater's canal near Manchester and knew of the great profits that were realized from it.[51] Smith and Izard also hoped for political profits. They realized that the political power of the lowcountry would eventually be doomed unless men of property and education could be distributed through all parts of the state. As Izard tried to explain several times during the 1790's to Edward Rutledge and Charles Cotesworth Pinckney, this evil could be avoided by an efficient system of inland navigation.[52]

The second biggest canal project in South Carolina was the Catawba Canal, planned in 1787. This canal was designed to open up the navigation of the Catawba River from Camden to the North Carolina line, thus being a project subordinate to, but tied in with, the Santee project. A few of the biggest of the upcountry men had joined with Charleston and Goose Creek capitalists, but the financial resources of the upcountry men were soon drained. Eventually William Smith gained control of the company with the help of his father-in-law Ralph Izard and his brother-in-law Gabriel Manigault. Thomas Sumter sold his share to Smith and Izard on April 28, 1792, provided they would repay him all he had advanced plus ten per cent interest on that amount. This share eventually cost Izard and Smith £710/14/5. At the same time Smith and Manigault bought a share from Daniel Bourdeau for £580/4/8. It was then reckoned

---

[50] David Ramsay to Jedediah Morse, July 20, 1799, copy in *Morse Papers*, YL.
[51] William Smith to [Herman LeRoy], June 21, 1792, *Gratz Collection*, PHS. *Also see* "Papers relating to the Santee Canal Co.," *William Loughton Smith Papers*, SCHS.
[52] Ralph Izard to Edward Rutledge, November 9, 1791; Ralph Izard to Charles Cotesworth Pinckney, January 18, 1795, *Izard Papers*, SCL.

that it would cost £16,000 to improve the eighty miles from Camden to the North Carolina line. The work proceeded with Smith and his friends meeting the constant requisitions.[53] By 1804 Smith and Gabriel Manigault controlled two hundred eighty shares of the four hundred twenty on which requisitions were still being paid.[54] In 1811 Smith estimated that he had spent $15,554.07 on this company.[55]

The Santee and Catawba canals were parts of one gigantic scheme to open up the interior of the state. Upcountry promoters like Thomas Sumter joined originally, but they were unable to bear the continuing financial burden and sold out to the capitalists of the lowcountry, particularly the Goose Creek promoters. In 1791, when the Santee Company was reorganized, it was Smith and Izard who talked with the moneyed men of Philadelphia and New York. Izard reported to Edward Rutledge that the northern men would be willing to take two-fifths of the shares, but they were, of course, only interested in profits, while as Izard put it, the southern men were as equally interested in the happiness of the state.[56] With the prospect of small profits, the southerners were forced to continue on their own. Izard, Manigault, and Smith, the triumvirate that ruled St. James Goose Creek Parish, were the principal entrepreneurs in the state, men with surplus capital willing to risk their fortunes on the future of their country. William Smith, the lawyer-politician, spoke, therefore, not only for the British merchants and returning Tories, but also for the entrepreneurs of Goose Creek.

[53] The story of the sale of these two shares, the costs of construction, and the requisitions can be found in "Papers relating to the Catawba Canal Company," *William Loughton Smith Papers*, SCHS.

[54] See "list of stockholders," 1803, *William Loughton Smith Papers*, SCHS.

[55] "Statement of Monies laid out and advanced by W. L. Smith for his shares in Catawba Co. with interest to 30 September 1811," *William Loughton Smith Papers*, SCHS.

[56] Ralph Izard to Edward Rutledge, November 9, 1791, *Izard Papers*, SCL.

IX

THE NEW FEDERAL CONSTITUTION

THERE WAS AN ECONOMIC CRISIS in South Carolina in 1785. British merchants who had appeared after the evacuation of Charleston in December 1782, remembering the prosperous pre-war years, had given extensive credit on slaves and goods. Farmers and planters contracted large debts which, with the failure of two successive crops in 1784 and 1785, they were unable to honor.[1] The backcountry farmer was willing to go to great lengths to avoid being sold out, even to the point of preventing the courts from sitting, but the low-country planter, being a man of property and thereby a respecter of creditors, faced a cruel dilemma. The planter's credit was his honor and the mainspring of the system that supported him. Timothy Ford, a Yankee lawyer just settling in Charleston, wrote:

> . . . this habit of giving & obtaining long & extensive credit implied or begot a great deal of honor & punctuality in dealing—'twas the merchants interest to cultivate it because he received a proportional profit on his goods—it was the planters interest to support it because he got goods at his pleasure & paid at his leisure. . . . His credit of consequence became a very delicate & important part of his interest; & in a degree little inferior to that of the merchant himself. Perhaps the principle of commerce has seldom if ever entered more into the genius of the planting interest.[2]

Planters, though hard-pressed, could not afford to act like typical debtors.

The South Carolina crisis was set within an international system of arrangements. The merchants had to make remittances to Europe, and the pressure from abroad during 1785 was severe and mounting. An Amsterdam house wrote to its Charleston correspondent "of another victim of American connections"; merchants of real capital in Amsterdam had decided to withhold credits "until they shall be justified in renewing them, by the experience of punctuality and ability in the merchants of your continent to fulfill their engagements."[3] An eminent house in London had taken alarm at the talk

---

[1] Timothy Ford, born 1762 at Morristown, N. J., educated at Princeton, came to South Carolina in 1785 after the marriage of his sister to Henry William DeSaussure, son of Daniel DeSaussure. Ford and young DeSaussure practiced law together. "Diary of Timothy Ford, 1785-1786," *SCHGM*, XIII (1912), 132-133, 193.

[2] *Ibid.*, pp. 201-202.

[3] *South-Carolina Gazette and Public Advertiser*, September 29, 1785.

of emitting paper money and wanted its agent in Charleston to diminish orders upon England.[4] Faith and confidence, the rocks upon which the international commercial community rested, were being undermined by the news from America.

The flow of specie to England caused a great drain upon the specie within the state. During the colonial period this drain had been drastically reduced from time to time by cutting off the importation of slaves, the most expensive articles imported. William Smith led the attempt in the House in March 1785 to prohibit the importation of slaves, but the plan was defeated by votes from the upcountry, which was developing rapidly and needed slaves. Upcountrymen suspected that non-importation was a ruse of the lowcountry to retain power and wealth in its own hands. The lowcountry representatives, however, managed to push through an additional duty of twenty shillings sterling per head on imported slaves.[5]

One most important reason for the specie crisis was the fact that Britain had shut off trade in American vessels to the British West Indies. This trade had always been a source of specie or bills of exchange on England which could be used to balance payments. Lord Sheffield in his *Observations on the Commerce of the American States* had presented an argument, ruthless in its logic, for excluding American vessels. This exclusion would ensure to Britain a large carrying trade, which was the nursery of the navy, which in turn was the lifeline of the nation. The remaining British North American colonies could supply the West Indies with provisions and lumber. America could not afford to retaliate, for her trade was based on British credit; neither the French nor the Dutch could supply it. If she did attempt to retaliate, any system devised would break down because there was no strength at the center of the confederation to enforce it. England had nothing to fear and everything to gain by excluding the Americans from the British West Indies. This was the official British policy until the Jay Treaty (1795).[6]

The situation within the state deteriorated rapidly in the late summer of 1785 as news of the poor crop came in from the country and threats rumbled across the Atlantic. Merchants and planters of American birth, no matter how much they desired to see the

[4] *Ibid.*, September 22, 1785.
[5] *JHR*, XLV, 290, 302.
[6] John, Lord Sheffield, *Observations on the Commerce of the American States,* London, 1784.

courts stay open and the interests of the creditors respected, could not look idly on while their compatriots were sold out to the former enemy. Both the native-born merchants and the planters offered suggestions in August 1785 for dissolving the crisis.

THE CHARLESTON Chamber of Commerce was the voice of the native-born merchants. On August 4, Edward Darrell, the vice-president, called a meeting of the people to consider letters received from Boston and New York calling for common action in the national crisis.[7] This meeting, presided over by Daniel DeSaussure, protested British trade policies, particularly the exclusion of American vessels from the British West Indies and the loosing of the Algerines against American vessels, no longer protected by British treaties with the Barbary states. It was suggested that closer commercial ties should be established with the French and the Dutch.[8]

The planters, in an effort to find a solution, organized the Agricultural Society of South Carolina on August 24, 1785.[9] They were thinking in terms of the diversification of agriculture which would enable them to look for new markets.[10] The letters exchanged by William Drayton, chairman of the committee for promoting and improving agriculture, and Thomas Jefferson are eloquent testimony of this attempt.[11] For the next five years, South Carolinians tried desperately to escape the stranglehold that Britain had on Carolina commerce, but all attempts failed. Their failure attests to the great strength of the British position in the Carolina commercial community. New trade connections with France, Holland, and other

[7] *South-Carolina Gazette and Public Advertiser*, August 4, 1785.

[8] *Ibid.*, August 13, 1785. *Also see* "A Memorial . . . from sundry Persons Citizens of this state, praying that Congress might be vested for a limited time with full powers to regulate trade with Foreign Nations, with whom no commercial treaties have been formed," *JHR*, XLV, 3 (second pagination).

[9] *South-Carolina Gazette and Public Advertiser*, August 25, 1785.

[10] *See* the address of the new society printed in *ibid.*, August 27, 1785. This important point is hardly mentioned in the history of the society. Chalmers S. Murray, *This Our Land, The Story of the Agricultural Society of South Carolina*, Charleston, 1949, pp. 29-48.

[11] William Drayton to Thomas Jefferson, November 23, 1785; Thomas Jefferson to William Drayton, May 6, 1786, *The Papers of Thomas Jefferson*, ed. Julian P. Boyd, Princeton, 1954, IX, 53, 461-462. Thomas Jefferson to William Drayton, February 6, 1787; William Drayton to Thomas Jefferson, May 22, 1787; Thomas Jefferson to William Drayton, July 30, 1787, *ibid.*, XI, 119-120, 374-375, 644-650. William Drayton to Thomas Jefferson, November 25, 1787; Thomas Jefferson to William Drayton, January 13, 1788, February 6, 1788, *ibid.*, XII, 380-382, 507-508, 567. Thomas Jefferson to William Drayton, May 7, 1789, May 1, 1791, *Jefferson Papers*, LC.

countries were at any rate a long-range solution and would not have solved the immediate problem of debts.[12]

Governor William Moultrie, unable to resist the storm, called a special session of the legislature and on September 26, "in the language of a frightened man," clearly asked for "an interposition of the Legislature in private contracts." Such drastic action was necessitated by the scarcity of circulating medium, destruction of several crops, and total lack of confidence. Because of these conditions the courts had been insulted and the laws defied, and civil process was then confined to a small part of the state. These were the "melancholy truths." If the law had continued to operate as it stood, a large part of the property of Carolina citizens would have been transferred to aliens.[13] The legislature therefore passed an "act for regulating sales under executions." This law was designed to prevent property under execution from being sold below its true value. Land might be tendered in the payment of debts, but it could not be sold for less than three-fourths of its appraised value. This was known as the "pine barren act" by the merchants who much preferred payment in specie to payment in land lying in remote corners of the state.[14]

The government was authorized at the same time to emit £100,000 in bills of credit which were to be loaned on land of triple the value or on a deposit of gold or silver plate of double the value of the sums loaned. The sums borrowed were to be paid back at the end of five years with interest annually computed at seven per cent. No person could take more than £250, nor less than £30. The new paper money, which was to be issued for the first time on May 1, 1786, was to be received for all public taxes and duties at the treasury, but was not made legal tender in private contracts. In this fashion, paper money would be put into circulation, but it was more from the top down than from the bottom up. As Singer has explained, it was a compromise measure. The upcountry radicals wanted to issue as much as £400,000, while the lowcountry conservatives would have been satisfied with as little as £83,000.[15]

[12] For the most important series of letters on these points see "Letters of Morris & Brailsford to Thomas Jefferson," ed. Richard Walsh, SCHGM, LVII (1957), 129-144.
[13] "Diary of Timothy Ford, 1785-1786," SCHGM, XIII (1912), 194. The address was printed in the South-Carolina Gazette and Public Advertiser, September 26, 1785.
[14] SC Statutes, IV, 710-712. Also see Charles Gregg Singer, South Carolina in the Confederation, Philadelphia, 1941, pp. 16, 22.
[15] SC Statutes, IV, 712-716. Also see Singer, op. cit., pp. 21-22. For an excellent description of how the law was to work see Gervais & Owen to Messrs.

Charleston merchants made a vain attempt to prevent the paper money's depreciating in value. At a meeting on May 1, 1786, at Williams' Coffee House, they agreed to accept the paper at face value and not to purchase produce from any factor who offered an abatement. This agreement was written down and left at the counting house of Smiths, DeSaussure, and Darrell for all to sign.[16] By September the promises of the spring had been broken. John Splatt Cripps wrote to a Boston merchant in September that rice was expected to break at 12/- to 13/- "owing principally to the fluctuating state of our paper money, which are in such discredit that the merchants are afraid to let any sum of it remain in their hands— that they now exchange it for specie at 30% discount. It has been a most unfortunate circumstance to the merchants of this country, that there has been any paper money made. The good sense and virtue of your legislature in not going into a measure of this kind will be commended by all the world."[17]

Merchants found themselves in difficulty at another point. During the winter of 1785-1786 the state's attorney general sued many merchants for back customs duties even though they themselves were barred from the recovery of debts due them. Pierce Butler took up their cause in February 1786; he asked relief for them on the basis that suits were then pending for £25,000 sterling, yet the paper money would not be issued for four months. Butler said: "We divided our conduct, we said you shall gain nothing from us, but we will order our Attorney General to prosecute, or rather persecute you!"

William Smith also pointed out the injustice to the merchants. He spoke of a house that owed £6,000 for duties, "which the Sheriff's sales bill effectually prevented them from paying." This house was "determined in case they were sued to bring their case before a jury, and he sincerely believed a jury would determine against the state." Smith tried to ridicule the opposition by proposing that a clause "be inserted, empowering keepers of stores to sort up all the old goods that now lay in dust on their shelves, calculate which commodity was useless or could be best spared, and send them into the Treasury. The house would at once see the propriety

John de Neufville & Son, April 25, 1786, *Miscellaneous Manuscripts*, NC Archives.
[16] The lists of those who signed were published in *Charleston Morning Post and Daily Advertiser*, May 3, 5, 1786.
[17] John Splatt Cripps to Caleb Davis, September 30, 1786, *Caleb Davis Papers*, MHS.

of this motion, because it tended to give effectual relief to all parties, and do away all complaints; for the Treasurers might sort the goods into parcels, and when any person came with a claim for money, they might present them with old bales of oznaburgs, or a piece of moth-eaten negro cloth." Patrick Calhoun, however, expressed the hostility of the upcountry to the British merchants in sharp words devoid of any sympathy: "Who sent for them to come among us?—Nobody."[18]

South Carolina was not alone in her economic and financial distress. These conditions were prevalent throughout the thirteen states. Pierce Butler, who had made a trip to England and to Holland in 1784-1785 ostensibly to find new trade connections for Carolina and to secure credits for himself, had heard the complaints of European merchants trading to America. He wrote to Thomas Fitzsimons, a Philadelphia merchant, in this vein: "If I am rightly informed, trade, and all money transactions are on a disagreeable footing throughout America. If I am to judge of the situation of things in the other states by our own, nothing can be much worse. [We must acknowledge that the British merchants] have too much cause, from what they have seen with respect to American connections in general, to be guarded—It requires time to bring things to their proper channel."[19]

Since South Carolina suffered as did her sister states, why did she not send a delegation to the Annapolis convention in 1786? Pierce Butler answered this question in a letter of May 30, 1786, to Fitzsimons:

> Our legislature at their last sitting declined appointing commissioners to the Commercial Congress; assigning for a reason, that as they had given powers to Congress to regulate all matters respecting trade, it would be inconsistent and have an appearance of either revoking or infringing on those powers—much good I think will result from the meeting, provided you, that is the states, confine your choice of delegates to men, who are not only conversant in the nature and principles of the trade of America in general, of their own states in particular; but who also went through the different scenes and vicissitudes of fortune, in some line or other, with the country during the contest; these are the men, the sincerity of whose professions you can best depend on—If you admit among you men of yesterday, if you will allow me the expression, they will rather confound your councils; they will intrigue, with a view of

[18] *Charleston Morning Post and Daily Advertiser*, February 20, March 16, 1786.
[19] Pierce Butler to Thomas Fitzsimons, February 26, 1786, *Gratz Collection*, PHS.

dividing you—I am in my own mind pretty clear, that most of the merchants who have come to, and settled in America since the peace, are no more than the factors or tools of greater merchants in Europe; of course then in all their sentiments and opinions they will be guided by the Interest of their employers; that interest, in many instances, militates with the true interest of the general trade of the United States.[20]

Butler made a clear distinction in this letter between the native-born merchants who had been through the vicissitudes of the war and those merchants who had recently come among the people. He felt that only the former could be trusted to work for the good of the new nation.

Although South Carolina did not send a delegation to Annapolis, many of her most important citizens made a trip to the North during the summer of 1786. This was the first great exodus of vacationers since the war. On June 17 the brig *Mercury*, Captain Tinker, left for New York with Mrs. Ralph Izard, William Smith "and lady," Francis Kinloch "and lady," George Smith "and lady," Dr. Henry C. Flagg, and others.[21] On June 23 the ship *Charleston*, Captain Allibone, sailed for Philadelphia with William Hasell Gibbes "and lady," Colonel Lewis Morris "and lady," Walter Izard, John Rutledge, junior, Mr. Hary Grant, Mrs. Heyward, and others.[22] On June 28 the sloop *Dane*, Captain Phillips, departed for Newport with Edward Rutledge "and lady," Thomas Pinckney "and lady," Mrs. Motte, Mrs. Middleton, and Mrs. Hort as passengers.[23] There was much local criticism of these "health-hunting parties" of planters and merchants for carrying with them "upwards of 5000 guineas" which, of course, depleted the specie resources of the state. A correspondent of July 6 wrote: "It would not be amiss to grant additional powers to Dr. Logan, by virtue of which he might lay an interdict on those who wish to leave the state on SUPPOSITION of being indisposed."[24] A correspondent on July 15 suggested that these citizens instead of flocking to Philadelphia, New York, and Newport with large sums of hard money might stay at home and visit Pacolet Springs—which, in consequence, might become the Bath or Montpelier of the Southern states.[25] The outflow of summer

[20] Pierce Butler to Thomas Fitzsimons (by internal evidence), May 30, 1786, *Miscellaneous Manuscripts*, SCHS. The act giving Congress the power to regulate trade was passed on March 11, 1786. *SC Statutes*, IV, 720.

[21] *Charleston Morning Post and Daily Advertiser*, June 17, 1786.

[22] *Ibid.*, June 23, 1786.

[23] *Ibid.*, June 28, 1786.

[24] *Ibid.*, July 6, 1786.

[25] *Ibid.*, July 15, 1786.

visitors continued, however, for as soon as the courts closed, judges and lawyers proceeded to the North. Judge William Drayton sailed on August 10, and Judge Thomas Bee, on the 19th.[26]

Already in New York when the summer began were the South Carolina delegates to Congress. David Ramsay had withdrawn from Congress on May 12, but John Bull, John Kean, John Parker, junior, Daniel Huger, and Charles Pinckney were in attendance that summer.[27] Surely men such as William Smith, Francis Kinloch, Lewis Morris, Edward Rutledge, Thomas Pinckney, William Drayton, and Thomas Bee talked with their own representatives in Congress and with the principal men in the North about the state of the nation. Americans of the first rank in the eighteenth century would not have gotten together in the summer of 1786 without discussing the Articles of Confederation and the Annapolis Convention. Among the southerners there were many who could unlock northern doors. Mrs. Alice DeLancey Izard and Colonel Lewis Morris belonged to great New York families.[28] The home of John Jay, then secretary for foreign affairs, was the very center of society that summer, and John and Edward Rutledge, who had worked closely with Jay in 1776, introduced their families to Mr. and Mrs. Jay, who were full of gracious attentions. Jay, when he had searched in vain for horses correct in size and color for Edward Rutledge's "very high English built coach," sent his own carriage horses to South Carolina.[29] At the end of the summer he wrote a letter to Count O'Reiley, captain general of Andalusia, to pave the way for the visit of John Rutledge, junior, to Spain.[30] But the Rutledges were not the only South Carolinians received by Mrs. Jay; these names also were on her "invitation list": Butler, Huger, Izard, Kean, Mathews, Parker, Pinckney, and Read.[31]

[26] *Ibid.*, August 10, 19, 1786.

[27] *Letters of Members of the Continental Congress,* ed. Edmund C. Burnett, Washington, 1936, VIII, xcvi-xcvii.

[28] Ralph Izard had married Alice DeLancey of New York in 1767. Mabel L. Webber, "Ralph Izard," *DAB.* Colonel Lewis Morris while serving under General Nathanael Greene met and married an Elliott heiress. "Letters from Col. Lewis Morris to Miss Ann Elliott," *SCHGM,* XL (1939), 122-136; XLI (1940), 1-14.

[29] Edward Rutledge to John Jay, January 16, 1787, *Correspondence and Public Papers of John Jay,* ed. Henry P. Johnston, New York, 1892, III, 229-231. John Jay to Edward Rutledge, February 25, 1787, *Miscellaneous Manuscripts,* SCHS.

[30] John Jay to Count O'Reiley, October 12, 1787, photostat in *John Rutledge, junior, Papers,* SHC.

[31] Rufus Wilmot Griswold, *The Republican Court or American Society in the Days of Washington,* New York, 1855, pp. 98-99. *Also see* Frank Monaghan, *John Jay,* New York, 1935, pp. 273-277.

Over in Rhode Island the South Carolinians were equally alert in assessing the scene. John Mathews took the occasion to make a study of New England shipping.[32] Francis Kinloch, who had recently married a daughter of John Rutledge, attended a session of the Rhode Island legislature. He wrote his former guardian Thomas Boone:

> I was present at the debate of the lower house the other day, & for the first time conceiv'd some idea of what had carried the inhabitants of this state, & Connecticut so headlong into the war. A little reflection might have told them, that they would infallibly be ruined as merchants, if they succeeded in their politics; that G. Britain would encourage the fisheries, & oil manufactory of its own subjects, & that the want of a naval protection would prevent their going into the Mediterranean; but they are descended, as their looks, their language, the cut of their clothes, their wigs, & their religion prove, from those men who first raised the flame of rebellion in England in the last century, & who glories in suffering for the good old cause—like their ancestors they are uneasy under any form of government, & tyrannical to excess when possessed of power: do but cast your eye over the enclosed copy of an act passed at the last session.[33]

This was undoubtedly the act which subjected any person who refused to receive paper money to a penalty of £100 and the loss of the rights of a freeman. The famous case of *Trevett* v. *Weeden* was tried in Newport in the September term of the superior court in 1786. A pamphlet written by James Varnum describing the Rhode Island paper money war is in the papers of William Smith.[34]

Nor did the disturbances in western Massachusetts that led to Shays' Rebellion go unnoticed. Thomas Pinckney wrote his sister after spending a week in Boston: "They are at present in some confusion on account of an opposition to their government. Something similar to our Camden business tho rather more violent."[35]

The men who went north in 1786 certainly came home with a greater determination to support the movement for a stronger central government. They had obviously been urged to do so by their northern friends. Edward Rutledge wrote in November to John Jay:

[32] *See* speech of John Mathews, January 1788, in the Carolina legislature. *The Debates in the Several State Conventions on the Adoption of the Federal Constitution*, ed. Jonathan Elliot, Philadelphia, 1941, IV, 298.

[33] Francis Kinloch to Thomas Boone, July 8, 1786, "Letters of Francis Kinloch to Thomas Boone, 1782-1788," ed. Felix Gilbert, *Journal of Southern History*, VIII (1942), 101-102.

[34] *William Loughton Smith Pamphlets*, CLS, II, number 1.

[35] Thomas Pinckney to Harriott Pinckney Horry, September 16, 1786, *Pinckney Papers*, LC.

"On my return home, I found several of my compatriots, so highly disgusted with the artifices of some unworthy characters, that they had determined to withdraw from the theatre of public action, to scenes of retirement and ease. But I have the pleasure to think that I have prevailed on them to change their resolutions and to continue in responsible stations."[36] John Jay wrote Jacob Read in December urging him to call forth the best men: "If the best men should be prevailed upon to come forward, and take the lead in our legislatures as well as in Congress, and would unite their endeavours to rescue their country from its present condition, our affairs, both at home and abroad, would soon wear a more pleasing aspect."[37]

The news of the Annapolis Convention was brought back to Charleston by the returning summer visitors. The ship *Charleston*, Captain Allibone, arrived Saturday afternoon, October 21, from Philadelphia. Among the passengers were William Smith "and lady," Thomas Bee "and lady," Cleland Kinloch "and lady," Major John Edwards and family, and John Rutledge. On Sunday in the ship *Philadelphia*, Captain Strong, came Francis Kinloch "and lady," Mr. Midwood, Mrs. Lushington, and others. The Monday morning newspaper published the news from Annapolis with the recommendation that a general convention meet in Philadelphia on the second Monday of May next.[38]

The election of representatives to the new legislature was hotly contested. Aedanus Burke charged that he was defeated by the machinations of the intendant, the wardens, and the British residents in Charleston. The intendant had made out lists of desirable candidates, which the wardens had distributed throughout the city. The managers of the election had been told which persons ought to vote and ought not to vote. Burke, who had dared to attack the Society of the Cincinnati, once again spoke out. The cabal, he said, was "formed and composed of foreign merchants, combined with a party of our own citizens, to bring it about."[39]

This legislature selected Henry Laurens, John Rutledge, Charles Cotesworth Pinckney, Charles Pinckney, and Pierce Butler to represent South Carolina in the Constitutional Convention.[40] Laurens

[36] Edward Rutledge to John Jay, November 12, 1786, *Correspondence and Public Papers of John Jay*, ed. Henry P. Johnston, New York, 1892, III, 216-219.
[37] John Jay to Jacob Read, December 12, 1786, *ibid.*, pp. 221-222.
[38] *Charleston Morning Post and Daily Advertiser*, October 23, 1786.
[39] See "Memorial of Aedanus Burke, citizen of Charleston," February 4, 1787, *ibid.*, February 7, 1787.
[40] They were elected on March 8, 1787. *The Records of the Federal Convention of 1787*, ed. Max Farrand, New Haven, 1927, III, 581-584.

was ill with gout and could not attend.[41] Of the others, three were lawyers and one (Butler) was a planter. There was no upcountry-man on the delegation, nor was there any merchant, although Butler had engaged in some commercial ventures during the 1780's. This delegation is in sharp contrast to those sent to the national House of Representatives after 1789. In those delegations the upcountry was always strongly represented because the representatives were selected by districts. Rutledge, who understood the local situation, advocated at Philadelphia that representatives to the new lower house be elected by the state legislatures. He pointed out that "if this convention had been chosen by the people in districts it is not to be supposed that such proper characters would have been preferred."[42] Charleston and the surrounding parishes were represented at Philadelphia; South Carolina was not.

THE FOUR SOUTH CAROLINIANS were in favor of an aristocratic republic, but not a monarchy. They were unanimous in their desire for a single executive, yet not quite sure what characteristics this executive should have.[43]

They favored a bicameral legislature, with both houses reflecting the property interests of the states. In the lower house this could be done by basing representation on the quotas of contributions made by each state to the national treasury. These representatives should be elected by the state legislatures. rather than by the people. The representatives in the upper house should also be chosen by the state legislatures, but for a longer term than members of the lower house. Although the South Carolinians wanted an aristocratic republic, they did not think of the upper house as a replica of the House of Lords. They would not consider an hereditary upper house, yet senators were not to receive a salary, so only men of wealth could have accepted.[44]

All agreed that there should be a supreme judicial tribunal with judges appointed for life; high salaries were to attract the finest talent. Yet they were against their appointment by the national executive for fear, as Rutledge said, that "the people will think we are leaning too much towards Monarchy."[45]

[41] Ramsay was prescribing cold baths for his father-in-law. David Ramsay to Henry Laurens, March 16 (date received), 26, 1787, Society Collection, PHS.
[42] The Records of the Federal Convention of 1787, ed. Max Farrand, New York, 1927, I, 359.
[43] Ibid., I, 64-65, 68-69, 88-89, 91; II, 30, 57, 511.
[44] Ibid., I, 147, 155, 192-193, 219, 233, 359, 397-404, 410-412, 426, 510-511, 534; II, 5.
[45] Ibid., I, 116, 119, 124; II, 45, 429.

After the structure of government was agreed upon, there was a discussion of the powers to be granted to the new government. They supported the government's power to tax and the prohibitions upon the states which denied the states the right to emit bills of credit, to make anything but gold and silver legal tender, and to impair the obligations of contracts. In fact, they were against having paper money issued as legal tender by the central government.[46]

Rutledge wanted to make sure that funds appropriated to pay public creditors would not be diverted to other purposes.[47] Although the four South Carolinians favored paying the public debts, they wanted a discrimination made favoring original creditors over speculators. Charles Pinckney and John Rutledge also wanted state debts to be assumed by the new government. Pinckney considered them federal expenditures; Rutledge thought the assumption just, since these debts had been contracted in the common defense.[48]

No one doubted that the federal government should regulate commerce. Rutledge said: "We need to secure the West India trade to this country. That was the great object, and a navigation act was necessary for obtaining it."[49] However, there were dangers for the South in vesting supreme control over commerce in the new government, since the South was a staple-producing region and the New England states were a shipping region. Navigation acts might easily be passed which would benefit one region at the expense of another. As an added protection, the South wanted a two-thirds vote for the passage of any navigation act. Charles Pinckney was the staunchest supporter of this provision. He pointed out that there were five major economic interests in the United States and each needed protection: the fisheries and West Indian trade of New England, the interests of the free port of New York, the wheat and flour trade of Pennsylvania and New Jersey, the tobacco of Maryland and Virginia, and the rice and indigo of the Carolinas and Georgia. As a protection for these diverse interests Pinckney suggested even a three-fourths vote for navigation acts.[50] This apparently was a point of major disagreement with his three colleagues, for after the North had made concessions on slavery, Butler, Rutledge, and General C. C. Pinckney were willing to accept the principle of a simple majority vote. Rutledge thought a navigation act would bear hard

[46] *Ibid.*, I, 53, 137, 309-310.
[47] *Ibid.*, II, 326.
[48] *Ibid.*, II, 327.
[49] *Ibid.*, II, 452.
[50] *Ibid.*, II, 449.

for only a little while on the southern states and that the South
ought to take a permanent view of the situation.[51] General Pinckney
summed up his position by saying that

> it was the true interest of the S. States to have no regulation of
> commerce; but considering the loss brought on the commerce of
> the Eastern States by the revolution, their liberal conduct towards
> the views [on slavery] of South Carolina, and the interest the
> weak Southn. States had in being united with the strong Eastern
> States, he thought it proper that no fetters should be imposed on
> the power of making commercial regulations; and that his con-
> stituents though prejudiced against the Eastern States, would be
> reconciled to this liberality—He had himself, he said, prejudices
> against the Eastern States before he came here, but would acknowl-
> edge that he had found them as liberal and candid as any men
> whatever.[52]

Charles Pinckney's proposal of a three-fourths vote is close to
Calhoun's ideas on nullification, and the line from Pinckney to Calhoun is straight. This was the particular point at which Charles
Pinckney was beaten by his colleagues, and the defeat, since he
could later think he had been right, would rankle in his heart.

Connected closely to the power over commerce was the power to
make and enforce treaties. No American commercial policy was
possible unless the new government could be sure that agreements
made with foreign countries would be honored by each state. The
South Carolinians supported the provision by which treaties would
be ratified by a two-thirds vote of the Senate.[53] It was Rutledge
who then worked hardest to see that the treaties as well as the
Constitution and the laws passed under it would be the supreme
law of the land and that the judges in the states would be bound
by their oaths to enforce them.[54] Federal courts backed by a federal
army would make the federal will effective.

The South had succeeded in getting representation in the lower
house based partly on property in slaves. The South wanted something more—the right to import slaves and to apprehend those who
ran away. General Pinckney led the fight for the right to import.
"S. Carolina & Georgia cannot do without slaves. As to Virginia she
will gain by stopping the importations. Her slaves will rise in value,
& she has more than she wants. . . . He contended that the importation of slaves would be for the interest of the whole Union.

[51] Ibid., II, 452.
[52] Ibid., II, 449-450.
[53] Ibid., II, 549.
[54] Ibid., II, 389, 431.

The more slaves, the more produce to employ the carrying trade: The more consumption also, and the more of this, the more of revenue for the common treasury."[55] He would accept an import duty, but no abandonment of importation. When the convention was willing only to allow importation to the year 1800, Pinckney asked for and got an extension to the year 1808.[56] Both Butler and Charles Pinckney worked to insert a fugitive slave clause.[57]

This is what the South Carolina delegation wanted, not necessarily what it got. All four favored an aristocratic republic, not a monarchy, which would be based quite securely upon property interests. In this they were no different from the vast majority of their colleagues. The new government was to be strong enough to pay off the public debt and set forth a sound financial policy for the nation. It was also to establish an American commercial policy that would counter English policy and permit all sections of the new nation to flourish. Although the four South Carolinians were willing to sign the completed document and support it in all of its sections at home, there were indications that they could be alienated from the new government, once it was established, if certain tendencies should appear. If the new institutions should be perverted to monarchical or pro-British ends, these four gentlemen would protest. If the executive branch should adopt the trappings of royalty or assume the prerogatives of the crown, they might sound an alarm. If public office should be used to perpetuate a group that should grow stronger year by year, they would begin to perceive the old British system. If the debts should be paid off without discrimination among the holders, jealousy of the speculators would be added to their suspicions. Finally, if the South should discover that slavery was being attacked or the interests of the staple-producing region were being sacrificed to the financial and commercial interests of the North, distaste for the document might grow to even greater lengths.

THE BRITISH COMMUNITY in Charleston was not represented in the state government, nor in the delegation to the Constitutional Convention, but it did have influence in the city, and this influence was used in favor of ratification. Since the new government was designed to counter British commercial policy, it might seem strange

[55] *Ibid.*, II, 371-372.
[56] *Ibid.*, II, 415.
[57] *Ibid.*, II, 443, 453.

that the British favored ratification. The commercial policy of the new government might have been, of course, a danger in the long run, but at that moment the merchants' chief desire was to be rid of paper money, stay laws, and installment acts, and here the new government seemed designed to serve their interests.

The passage of the pine barren act in 1785 had moved the Carolina merchants of London to ask the Marquis of Carmarthen, secretary of state for the foreign department, to appoint a consul to South Carolina.[58] George Miller, who arrived as consul in 1787, was sent out to prevent the state legislature's passing any more stay-law legislation.[59] Upon his arrival he found that the new federal Constitution, a copy of which he immediately sent to Carmarthen, might make his work easier. "If it is approved of, and should be adopted, it promises I think, to rescue Congress from that inefficient situation in which they have long stood, as it grants sufficient powers to comply with, and enforce their treaties and other national engagements, without submitting to the controul of state legislatures, who, on most occasions, have paid no farther regard to the recommendations of Congress, than as the same did not operate against their own particular and local interests."[60] Yet, Miller confessed, he still had to work carefully, for "the exclusion of vessels under American colours from the trade to the free ports lately established in the West Indies and the Bahama Islands, has given umbrage to some of the leading men of this state."[61]

Miller moved quietly behind the scenes and was happy to report on April 15, 1788, that the legislature had adjourned "without having passed any new Laws contrary to the commercial Interest of Great Britain." They had tried to extend the operation of the installment law from three to seven years, to pass a valuation law forcing creditors to take property at a scheduled value, and to emit paper money to the amount of £200,000 sterling. Miller wrote: "To the Members of both Houses individually, I was not negligent in pointing out, the manifest injustice of carrying such measures into effect, as well as the mortal wound they would inflict on the Credit and national Faith of the State,—both already too much shaken by

[58] "Memorial of the Committee of Merchants trading to North America," June 20, 1786, FO, IV, 417-420.
[59] Marquis of Carmarthen to George Miller, April 1787, FO, V, 203-208.
[60] Miller arrived in Charleston on July 8, 1787. George Miller to Carmarthen, July 10, 1787, FO, V, 441-444. The letter enclosing the Constitution with comments was dated November 17, 1787, FO, V, 717-720.
[61] George Miller to Carmarthen, December 24, 1787, FO, V, 791-793.

former Laws.—What influence this reasoning had upon their minds, I do not pretend to judge, but I would flatter myself some were convinced by it."[62] Thus from the time of the meeting of the Constitutional Convention in Philadelphia until the assembling of the ratification convention in Charleston, a British consul was at work in the city rallying the British interest.

There were two debates in South Carolina on the Constitution. One was in January 1788 in the state legislature, where the decision was made to call the ratification convention; the other, in May in that convention itself. A complete record of these debates does not exist, but enough of the speeches remain to indicate definitely the drift of the arguments. Speaking in favor of ratification were the Charleston lawyers, led by the members of the delegation that had gone to Philadelphia. Rawlins Lowndes, the most important opponent of the Constitution, described "his antagonists" as "mostly gentlemen of the law, who were capable of giving ingenious explanation to such points as they wished to have adopted."[63] Against this array of legal talent stood only Lowndes and a few hesitant speakers from the upcountry. James Lincoln (who spoke after Patrick Calhoun!) declared "that if ever any person rose in a public assembly with diffidence, he then did; if ever any person felt himself deeply interested in what he thought a good cause, and at the same time lamented the want of abilities to support it, it was he."[64] Alexander Tweed, another of the upcountry men, said "a man of my circumscribed scale of talents is not adequate to the task of contending with . . . members of this respectable convention, whose profound oratory and elocution would, on the journals of a British House of Commons, stand as lasting monuments of their great abilities."[65] Patrick Dollard arose "with the greatest diffidence, to speak on this occasion, not only knowing myself unequal to the task, but believing this to be the most important question that ever the good people of this state were called together to deliberate upon."[66] The spokesmen for the lowcountry never prefaced their speeches with such apologetic remarks. Talent and social position were a heavy weight on the scales for ratification.

Those who spoke for ratification gave two important reasons for

[62] George Miller to Carmarthen, April 15, 1788, FO, VI, 243-246.
[63] Debates in the Several State Conventions on the Adoption of the Federal Constitution, ed. Jonathan Elliot, Philadelphia, 1941, IV, 271.
[64] Ibid., p. 312.
[65] Ibid., p. 333.
[66] Ibid., p. 336.

setting up a strong central government. The united strength of thirteen states was needed to deal with foreign nations and with local factions. The power to regulate commerce, to make and enforce treaties, and to raise and support a navy would solve the first problem; the denial to the states of the power to emit paper currency and to impair the obligation of contracts, enforced by a system of federal courts, would solve the second. It is noteworthy that the American merchants could support both of the above solutions while the British merchants could approve only of the second. This split in mercantile thinking explains how the opponents of the Constitution could charge the proponents with being tools of British influence. It also explains how the proponents could look upon themselves as the truest patriots. There was much truth in both arguments.

Charles Pinckney, who bore the major burden of explaining the work done at Philadelphia, introduced his remarks with a reference to the commercial question:

> It must be recollected that, upon the conclusion of the definitive treaty, great inconveniences were experienced, as resulting from the inefficacy of the Confederation. The one first and most sensibly felt was the destruction of our commerce, occasioned by the restrictions of other nations, whose policy it was not in the power of the general government to counteract. The loss of credit, the inability in our citizens to pay taxes, and languor of government, were, as they ever must be, the certain consequences of the decay of commerce. Frequent and unsuccessful attempts were made by Congress to obtain the necessary powers. The states, too, individually attempted, by navigation acts and other commercial provisions, to remedy the evils. These, instead of correcting, served but to increase it; their regulations interfered not only with each other, but, in almost every instance with treaties existing under the authority of the Union. Hence arose the necessity of some general and permanent system, which should at once embrace all interests, and, by placing the states upon firm and united ground, enable them effectually to assert their commercial rights.[67]

Charles Cotesworth Pinckney backed up this argument with a rhetorical flourish: "Ask the crews of our vessels captured by the Algerines if respect for our government hath softened the rigors of their captivity. Inquire of our delegates to congress if all the despatches from your public ministers are not filled with lamentations of the imbecility of Congress; and whether foreign nations do not declare they can have no confidence in our government, because

[67] *Ibid.*, pp. 253-254.

it has not power to enforce obedience to treaties."[68] Edward Rutledge spoke in the same vein: ". . . we must hold our country by courtesy, unless we have a navy."[69]

This argument was an admission that England's mercantile system had been valuable and had worked. America's own system, and this was always understood, had to fit into England's paramount system as best as it could, all cutting and fitting being as far as possible to the advantage of the Americans. This was the sensible, realistic program of American commercial interests. In order to establish such a system and to win respect for it, the American states had to be strong, and therefore a united nation. It was this impulse, flowing from different sources—from the Charleston Chamber of Commerce and the South Carolina Agricultural Society, from the patriot merchants and planters—that emptied into the Constitutional Convention.

The other side of the argument, and the second big force behind the Constitution, was the need to restore faith and confidence in the international community of trade. Charles Pinckney was against the emission of paper money, for "while it remains, all of the foreign merchants, trading in America, must suffer and lose by it; therefore, that it must ever be a discouragement to commerce."[70] For Pinckney "the soul of the Constitution"[71] was the tenth section of Article I:

> . . . how much will this section tend to restore your credit with foreigners—to rescue your national character from that contempt which must ever follow the most flagrant violations of public faith and private honesty! No more shall paper money, no more shall tender-laws, drive their commerce from our shores, and darken the American name in every country where it is known. No more shall our citizens conceal in their coffers those treasures which the weakness and dishonesty of our government have long hidden from the public eye. The firmness of a just and even system shall bring them into circulation, and honor and virtue shall be again known and countenanced among us. . . . Public as well as private confidence shall again be established; industry shall return among us; and the blessings of our government shall verify that old, but useful maxim, that with states, as well as individuals, honesty is the best policy.[72]

To Rawlins Lowndes's question, "What harm had paper money done?" Charles Cotesworth Pinckney rang the changes on the same

[68] Ibid., p. 282.
[69] Ibid., p. 299.
[70] Ibid., p. 334.
[71] Ibid., p. 333.
[72] Ibid., p. 336.

theme as his cousin when he replied, "It had corrupted the morals of the people; it had diverted them from the paths of honest industry to the ways of ruinous speculation; it had destroyed both public and private credit, and had brought total ruin on numberless widows and orphans."[73]

Rawlins Lowndes was the ablest opponent of ratification. He did not object to a government's reflecting the interests of the rich. Nor did he criticize the system of checks and balances, those mechanisms for checking the passions of the people and ensuring that the words of wise men would still be heard in the land. He did not believe, as Patrick Dollard did, that "the general voice of the people is the voice of God."[74] Lowndes had joined the Revolutionary movement to secure for his own group the power to rule. In this sense he was a conservative, and he did not differ much in this respect from the Rutledges and the Pinckneys. His chief objection was that southern interests were not sufficiently protected against invasion by northern interests. The New England states were to become the carriers and the southern states would be the consumers. Lowndes saw the logic of the period from Jefferson's embargo to the Civil War. Could the South protect itself under the new Constitution? Lowndes thought not.[75] Although the South Carolina delegation had fought hard in the convention to protect southern interests where they directly opposed northern interests, they did not reveal at home that there had been any such differences. They had taken Franklin's advice to accept at the end the work of the convention as a whole and to go home to defend it without revealing the dissensions in the convention.[76] This was a legitimate strategic move, but it covered a weakness that was left to grow and haunt the South for years to come.

Since Lowndes had revealed his hostility towards the Constitution in the legislature, his constituents failed to elect him to the ratification convention. The leaders of the opposition in that body were, therefore, from the upcountry, and their chief objection was that the Constitution had no bill of rights. After a few amendments were

---

[73] *Ibid.*, p. 306.
[74] *Ibid.*, p. 338.
[75] *Ibid.*, pp. 271-274. For the role of Lowndes in the legislature *see* Henry William DeSaussure to Jedediah Morse, February 11, 1788, *Miscellaneous Manuscripts*, NYHS.
[76] Charles Pinckney endorsed Franklin's admonition in an open letter, dated May 2, 1788, published in the *State Gazette of South-Carolina*. *Records of the Federal Convention of 1787*, ed. Max Farrand, New Haven, 1927, III, 300-301.

recommended, the Constitution was adopted by a vote of one hundred forty-nine to seventy-three.[77]

The city of Charleston and the six surrounding parishes voted unanimously in favor of ratification, supplying seventy-three votes for and not one against. St. Helena and Prince William's, the two parishes surrounding Beaufort, cast fourteen votes for and not one against. Prince George Winyaw, All Saints, and St. James Santee, the three parishes around Georgetown, cast twelve votes for and only one (John Bowman) against. Therefore, in the three coastal centers there were ninety-nine votes for and only one against. John Bowman stands out as the one prominent lowcountry opponent of ratification in the convention. In the six parishes that fill out the lowcountry area, there was a vote of twenty-two for and fifteen against. So the complete count for the lowcountry was one hundred twenty-one for and only sixteen against, leaving the backcountry with twenty-eight votes for ratification and fifty-seven against. The lowcountry unquestionably carried the ratification of the Constitution in South Carolina.[78]

Other leaders of the movement for ratification, besides the Charleston lawyers, were the merchants and Goose Creek planters. Every lawyer who had ever been entered at the Inns of Court voted for the ratification of the federal Constitution. This group was led by three Pinckneys and three Rutledges, although Thomas Pinckney, who presided over the convention, did not cast a vote. Josiah Smith, Daniel DeSaussure, and Edward Darrell were the most prominent merchants in the ratification convention. None of the naturalized British had been elected, and only Nathaniel Russell among the returning tory merchants. The Goose Creek planters had been represented by Ralph Izard, Peter Smith, Benjamin Smith, Gabriel Manigault, William Smith, John Parker, junior, and John Deas, junior, who cast seven votes in favor of ratification.

It is interesting to note that of the South Carolinians who can positively be identified as having been in the North during the summer of 1786, fourteen were members of the convention and all

[77] Debates in the Several State Conventions on the Adoption of the Federal Constitution, ed. Jonathan Elliot, Philadelphia, 1941, IV, 338-340.
[78] According to Libby's analysis the lowcountry voted 88% for and 12% against; the middle country 49% for and 51% against; the upcountry 20% for and 80% against. Orin Grant Libby, Geographical Distribution of the Vote of the Thirteen States on the Federal Constitution, 1787-8, Madison, 1894, pp. 43-44.

fourteen were in favor of the Constitution.[79] It is also interesting to point out that William Smith and his schoolboy friends represented an important element in the victory. Smith, Harry Laurens, Gabriel and Joseph Manigault, Francis and Cleland Kinloch, and John Parker, junior, had spent part of the Revolutionary years studying abroad.[80] Finally, it should be recognized that William Smith was at the center of a large family group that supported ratification. William Smith's father-in-law (Ralph Izard), his three brothers-in-law (Gabriel Manigault, Isaac Motte, and James Ladson), his nephew by marriage (John Deas, junior), his first cousin (Peter Smith), and his more distant cousins (Josiah and Benjamin Smith) were all members who cast yea votes. Thus all the groups with which William Smith had been associated supported the movement for a stronger central government: Charleston lawyers, native-born merchants, Goose Creek planters, summer vacationers, and his schoolboy chums and family. Looming up behind all of these, silently but powerfully, were the British merchants residing in Charleston.

Those who favored ratification were not only closely connected locally, but were also organized nationally; those who opposed were not only out of touch locally, not having acted together before in any united effort, but also completely out of touch with those in other states who thought as they did. John Lamb of New York tried to set up a nation-wide network of opposition, but this attempt came too late. Rawlins Lowndes wrote Lamb on June 21, 1788: "Had your plan been proposed in time I doubt not it might have produced very good effect in this country: A strong systematic opposition wherein the opinions and sentiments of the different states were concenter'd, and directed to the same specific objects, would have had a weight, which the advocates for the Constitution must have submitted to, and have removed the force of an objection, strongly insisted upon, arising from this seeming diversity and dissimilarity of the several amendments contended for."[81]

The whole story of ratification in South Carolina, told from the point of view of the opposition, is contained in a most remarkable

---

[79] W. Smith, F. Kinloch, L. Morris, E. Rutledge, T. Pinckney, T. Bee, C. Pinckney, J. Kean, J. Parker, D. Ramsay, J. Mathews, J. Edwards, C. Kinloch, and J. Rutledge.

[80] Cleland Kinloch's estate had been amerced 12%. See "Petition of Francis Kinloch to the Senate in behalf of his brother Cleland," 1783, *Confiscated Estates*, SC Archives.

[81] Rawlins Lowndes to John Lamb, June 21, 1788, *Lamb Papers*, NYHS.

letter written on June 23 by the undauntable Irishman, Aedanus
Burke, to John Lamb:

> Your favour of the 19th of May I received the 1st of June inst.
> That it came not to hand sooner, I cannot account for; however, it
> came too late; for our convention had acceded to the new Consti-
> tution on the 24th of May by a Majority of 149 the minority con-
> sisting of 73.
>
> It is now unnecessary perhaps to state to you the different causes,
> whereby the new plan has been carried in South Carolina, notwith-
> standing 4/5 of the people do, from their souls detest it. I am con-
> vinced, from my knowledge of the country, that I am rather under,
> than over, that proportion. In the first place, we in the opposition,
> had not, previous to our meeting, either wrote, or spoke, hardly a
> word against it, nor took any one step in the matter. We had no
> principle of concert or union, while its friends and abettors left no
> expedient untried to push it forward. All the rich, leading men,
> along the seacoast, and rice settlements; with few exceptions,
> lawyers, physicians and divines, the merchants, mechanicks, the
> populace, and mob of Charleston. I think it worthy of observation
> that not a single instance in So. Carolina of a man formerly a Tory,
> or British adherent, who is not loud and zealous for the new Con-
> stitution. From the British Consul (who is the most violent man
> I know for it) down to the British scavenger, all are boisterous to
> drive it down. Add to this, the whole weight and influence of the
> press was in that scale. Not a printing press, in Carolina, out of the
> city. The printers are, in general, British journeymen, or poor citi-
> zens, who are afraid to offend the great men, or merchants, who
> could work their ruin. Thus, with us, the press is in the hands of a
> junto, and the printers, with most servile insolence discouraged
> opposition, and pushed forward publications in its favour; for no
> one wrote against it.
>
> But the principle cause was holding the Convention in the City,
> where there are not fifty inhabitants who are not friendly to it.
> The merchants and leading men kept open houses for the back and
> low country members during the whole time the Convention sat.
> The sixth day after we sat, despatches arrived, bringing an account
> that Maryland had acceded to the scheme. This was a severe blow
> to us; for next day, one of our best speakers in the opposition,
> Doctor Fousseaux, gave notice he would quit that ground, as
> Maryland had acceded to it. Upon which we were every day after-
> wards losing ground and numbers going over to the enemy, on an
> idea that further opposition was useless. But notwithstanding these
> misfortunes, the few of us who spoke, General Sumpter, Mr. John
> Bowman, a gentleman of fortune and fine talents, of the low-
> country; myself and a few of the back country men, found it neces-
> sary, in supporting the opposition, to exert the greater spirit and
> resolution, as our difficulties increased. Our minority is a respect-
> able one, and I can with great truth assure you, that it represents

by far a greater number of citizens than the majority—The minority are chiefly from the back country where the strength and numbers of our republick lie—and although the vote of the Convention has carried it, that has not changed the opinion of the great body of people respecting its evil tendency. In the interiour country, all is disgust, sorrow, and vindictive reproaches against the system, and those who voted for it. It is true, the ratification of it was solemnized in our city, with splendid procession and shew. We hear from the back country, however, that in some places the people had a coffin painted black, which, borne in funeral procession, was solemnly buried, as an emblem of the dissolution and interment of publick liberty. You may rely upon it if a fair opportunity offers itself to our back country men they will join heart and hand to bring ruin on the new plan unless it be materially altered. They declare so publickly: they feel that they are the very men who, as mere militia, half-armed and half-clothed have fought and defeated the British regulars in sundry encounters. They think that after having disputed and gained the laurel under the banners of liberty, now, that they are likely to be robbed both of the honour and the fruits of it, by a Revolution purposely contrived for it. I know some able men among us, or such as are thought so, affect to despise the general opinion of the multitude: For my own part I think that that government rests on a very sandy foundation, the subjects whereof are convinced that it is a bad one. Time alone will convince us.

This is the first time that I ever put pen to paper on the subject *(to another)* and it is not for want of inclination to do it. Nobody views this matter from the point of light and view in which I see it; or if any one did, he must be crazy, if he told his mind. The true, open, rising ground, no one has dared to take, or will dare to do it, till the business is all over. If you live two or three years, you will find the world will ascribe to the right author, this whole affair, and put the saddle on the right horse, as we say. I find myself approaching too near to forbidden ground, and must desist. I am sorry it hath been my lot not to be able to serve the Repub. on the present business, Virginia and New York adopting it (and of which I have no doubt) they will proceed to put it into motion, and then you, and I, and all of us, will be obliged to take it, as we take our wives, "for better, for worse."[82]

In contrast to Burke's fears were Francis Kinloch's rising hopes. Kinloch had interrupted a vacation in Virginia to hurry home and

---

[82] Aedanus Burke to John Lamb, June 23, 1788, *Lamb Papers*, NYHS. The "right author" undoubtedly refers to Washington. Washington as the evil genius of the times is a recurring theme in Burke's letters. *See* remarks on the "Popular Citizen" in Aedanus Burke to Citizen Genêt, February 16, 1794, *Genêt Papers*, LC.

cast a vote for ratification.[83] He was obviously quite pleased with the results. In a letter written on May 26, 1788 (just two days after he had cast his vote for ratification), to thank Thomas Boone for sending him the Kinloch coat of arms, he commented: "As our steps towards monarchy are very obvious, I would wish my Children to have all the Rights to rank, & distinction, which is to be claimed from Ancestry." It was quite appropriate that young William Wragg, who was returning to his native land for the first time since the Revolution, should have been the bearer of this precious coat of arms. Kinloch's expectations were clearly revealed in his description of the powers of the new government:

> We are to have an elective President, who is eligible at the end of every four years for life; he will have a qualified negative on the laws of the new Congress, & will enjoy somewhat more power than the Statholder of the united Provinces, though the Statholder's influence in consequence of many different circumstances is much greater. A Senate, chosen by the different Legislatures of the States, who share the Executive power with the President, & the Legislature with the house of representatives,—(this body unites the powers of your privy council & House of Lords, but has no judicial capacity except in cases of impeachment)—& A House of Representatives chosen by the *People* of the different states, which has no right of interference with the Executive, but enjoys the peculiar privileges of your house of Commons. The regulation of Commercial affairs,—the right of imports, of excise, of ordering out & commanding the Militia with many etc. are given up by the individual States to the Federal Government, & *we are getting back fast to the system we destroyed some years ago.*[84]

[83] Edward Rutledge (brother of John Rutledge, junior) to John Rutledge, junior, April 8, 1788, *John Rutledge, junior, Papers,* SHC.

[84] Italics are the author's. Francis Kinloch to Thomas Boone, May 26, 1788, "Letters of Francis Kinloch to Thomas Boone, 1782-1788," ed. Felix Gilbert, *Journal of Southern History,* VIII (1942), 103-105.

X

THE NEW FEDERAL GOVERNMENT

AFTER A SUFFICIENT NUMBER of states had ratified the Constitution, Congress adopted a set of resolutions calling for elections to be held in the winter. Governor Thomas Pinckney called the state legislature into session in October and presented these resolutions along with the journals of the ratification convention. The procedures for holding the first federal elections in the state were then adopted. South Carolina was divided into five Congressional districts (Charleston, Beaufort and Orangeburg, Georgetown and Cheraw, Camden, and Ninety Six), and the elections scheduled for November 24 and 25.[1]

The major concern of this short session was with petitions from the backcountry asking the legislature for help for debtors.[2] These petitions were referred to a large committee of which William Smith was a member.[3] The committee reported unanimously "that there is an indispensable necessity for the further interposition of the legislature between creditors and their debtors." However, it reserved the right to report any plan that might offer a solution. Three plans were reported: one suggested a law to set a value on all property seized in execution; another, to extend the installment law to five years; a third, to emit more paper money.[4]

The valuation bill was first brought forward on October 16 and was ordered to be read a second time on the 21st. As George Miller, the British consul, wrote to the Marquis of Carmarthen, "this bill was so strongly characteristic of the Sheriff's sale bill, passed in 1785, well known by the name of 'the pine barren Law,'—leaving nothing optional with the creditor respecting choice of property, and being expressly contrary to the 4th Article of the Treaty of Peace, and to the interests of the British Creditors, by that Article

---

[1] *JHR*, XLVIII, 312. *SC Statutes*, V, 84-86.
[2] *JHR*, XLVIII, 324, 329, 330, 332, 337, 341, 343.
[3] *JHR*, XLVIII, 324, 325.
[4] *JHR*, XLVIII, 345. George Miller to Carmarthen, November 30, 1788, *FO*, VI, 693-699. The basic laws in each category were: "an act for regulating sales under executions," passed October 12, 1785, to run to the end of the next ensuing session, *SC Statutes*, IV, 710-712; "an ordinance respecting suits for the recovery of debts," passed March 26, 1784, allowing suits in four installments beginning January 1, 1786, for debts contracted before February 26, 1782, *SC Statutes*, IV, 640-641; "an act to establish a medium of circulation by way of loan," passed October 12, 1785, *SC Statutes*, IV, 712-716.

secured, that I conceived myself called upon by every principle of duty to make representations against it."⁵ Therefore, on the day before the second reading, Miller summed up his objections in a letter which he asked Governor Pinckney to communicate to the legislature. Miller objected to the fact that land rather than sterling money would be offered to the creditor and that the creditor would have to wait twelve months after obtaining a judgment before he could recover. Miller hoped his representations would "be deemed of sufficient weight, to prevent *any farther interference* between British creditors, claiming under the Fourth Article of the Treaty of Peace, and their debtors in this state."⁶ This strong statement was transmitted to the legislature by Governor Pinckney on the morning of the 21st. Pierce Butler, who had brought in the valuation bill, opposed the reading of the letter on the ground that no commercial treaty existed between Great Britain and the United States and that the British consul consequently did not have sufficient standing to make representations. The letter was not read, but was left to lie upon the table. Even so, after two days of debate the valuation bill was defeated by a vote of eighty-eight to forty-four.⁷

Thereupon, on the 24th, a motion was made and seconded that a committee be appointed to bring in a new installment bill. Smith, Gillon, Barnwell, Waties, Sumter, and Butler were named. Smith reported the new bill for the first time that very day, giving it the earmarks of a counter move to obtain the least evil among the three bills.⁸

George Miller wrote home: "Both houses considering themselves pledged, by their having agreed to the report of the committee, to adopt one of the modes of redress above mentioned, and *the members possessed of the best principles conceiving, that an extension*

⁵ *JHR*, XLVIII, 331. George Miller to Carmarthen, November 30, 1788, *FO*, VI, 693-699.
⁶ George Miller to Thomas Pinckney, October 20, 1788, *FO*, VI, 625-628. George Miller upon his arrival had hoped to be recognized as consul and commissary for commercial affairs. The latter role would have permitted him to deal officially with the state government on matters affecting trade, such as stay laws, which ordinarily would have been handled by the highest diplomatic authorities. Governor Pinckney urged Miller to seek recognition of his position by Congress. As Congress had only recognized Phineas Bond at Philadelphia as consul, Congress could only confirm Miller as consul, which they did on October 20, 1787. Miller had himself proclaimed as consul in South Carolina, North Carolina, and Georgia. Even though he thought he lacked power he proceeded to act in October 1788. George Miller to Carmarthen, July 10, November 17, and December 24, 1787, *FO*, V, 441-444, 717-720, 791-793.
⁷ George Miller to Carmarthen, November 30, 1788, *FO*, VI, 693-699. *JHR*, XLVIII, 351-353.
⁸ *JHR*, XLVIII, 355-356.

of the Installment law would be attended with the least distress to the creditors, that plan was preferred to a farther emission of paper medium. . . ."⁹

On the 25th the installment bill was read a second time. It was intended to prolong the period for the payment and recovery of debts and was to extend the prohibition on importing slaves. A seven-year extension was voted down, but a five-year extension passed by a vote of seventy-three to forty-seven.¹⁰

The author of the valuation bill, seeing his bill by-passed and being aware of foreign influence, offered on the 30th a resolution "that no Consul residing in this state, has any power or authority to represent to this House, upon any bill depending or passed the Legislature thereof." A long debate ensued, with the principal speakers defending the right of the consul to present his views. The resolution was defeated with only eight voting for and a hundred against.¹¹

On November 2, Smith and Edward Rutledge managed to push through by a vote of sixty-nine to forty-one, a bill to extend the ban on slave importation to January 1, 1793.¹² The non-importation of slaves, in effect since March 28, 1787, was looked upon as a means of reducing the drain on specie within the state and therefore as a substitute for the emission of more paper money.¹³ This non-importation bill plus the installment bill, which was adopted on November 4, represented a moderate course, and Smith's name was the most prominent in the records of those favoring such a course.¹⁴ Smith was not a friend of debtors; but something had to be done to alleviate their distress and prevent commotions, and he thought the installment law was the answer. It was the least evil of the three proposals being considered by the legislature, and might prove to be only an empty shell. Extending installments from three to five years would bring the fewest immediate results, whereas a valuation or an emission-of-paper-money law would have had immediate practical significance. Miller, who was hired to penetrate to the

⁹ George Miller to Carmarthen, November 30, 1788, *FO,* VI, 693-699.
¹⁰ *JHR,* XLVIII, 357-360.
¹¹ George Miller to Carmarthen, November 30, 1788, *FO,* VI, 693-699. In 1790 the capital was moved to Columbia in order (among other things) to get the legislature beyond British influence. *See* Charles Pinckney to Thomas Jefferson, October 16, 1800, quoted in John Harold Wolfe, *Jeffersonian Democracy in South Carolina,* Chapel Hill, 1940, pp. 155-156.
¹² *JHR,* XLVIII, 388.
¹³ *SC Statutes,* V, 36-38.
¹⁴ *JHR,* XLVIII, 410.

heart of politics, made all of these points in a letter to the Marquis of Carmarthen on November 30:

> Every legislative interference in contracts between individuals, is a disgraceful method of alleviating the real or supposed distress, of a people at large, and in the present instance bears exceedingly hard on British creditors, yet I cannot help being of opinion, that of the three evils suggested, the one received will be the mildest in its effects, were it for no other reason than that, whenever the new Government is set in motion, and a federal judicature is appointed, the Treaty of Peace being declared by the Constitution paramount to the Law of the land, the judges will be constrained to admit and hear all causes brought under the 4th Article of the Treaty, notwithstanding any partial state laws to the contrary, as the establishment of these courts will operate as a repeal to such laws, as far as suitors under the Treaty are concerned.
>
> How long it may be before the Government of this country shall have acquired a degree of efficacy sufficient to carry its constitution into force, I cannot pretend to judge, but until that is the case, much is the British creditor to be pitied, whether claiming for debts secured by the Treaty, or contracted since, for little is to be expected from the integrity of individuals, and the present Government is too lax and feeble to carry the laws into execution, even to the extent they are suffered to operate, which I have little doubt was one reason with many, for acceding to the extension of the Installment Law, as the probable means of preventing serious commotions in the country.[15]

When this statement is placed beside the record in the journals, it is obvious that Smith had played a skillful game.

EARLY IN NOVEMBER, Smith announced that he was a candidate for election to the national House of Representatives from Charleston District.[16] He was opposed by Alexander Gillon and David Ramsay—Gillon being the more formidable of the two. He had been born in Amsterdam and apprenticed to trade in London. Soon after he came to Charles Town in 1766 he married a widow, Mrs. Mary Cripps, and with his step-son John Splatt Cripps he engaged in trade, acquiring a large fortune by the eve of the Revolution. During the war Gillon had tried to augment his fortune by privateering, but only succeeded in squandering most of it in what was popularly called a "balloon expedition"—the voyages of the frigate South Caro-

---

[15] George Miller to Carmarthen, November 30, 1788, *FO*, VI, 693-699. For similar views subscribed to by five South Carolinians *see* "Dissentient," signed by Daniel DeSaussure, John Bull, Arnoldus Vanderhorst, Benjamin Smith, and William Allston, November 4, 1788, *Gratz Collection*, PHS.

[16] William Smith to Citizens of Charleston District, November 22, 1788, *State Gazette of South-Carolina*, November 24, 1788.

lina. There was more sound than substance in his title of Commodore of the South Carolina Navy. As the "hero" of the patriot sailors of Charleston, he had become the leader of the lower elements in the city, but his forces had been crushed by the incorporation of Charleston in 1783 and by his own defeat in September 1784 when he ran against Richard Hutson for the office of intendant. With his fortune abated and his political following crushed, Gillon had retired to the banks of the Congaree where he built Gillon's Retreat. From this vantage point he returned to battle against the corporation in 1787; William Smith, upholding the city's charter, was his chief opponent.[17]

David Ramsay was a unique figure on the Carolina scene. He had come from Pennsylvania before the Revolution to practice medicine. He was ambitious and had been successful, for through his profession and by three judicious marriages he had amassed a moderate fortune.[18] Although he had won an eminent position in the community, his mind was alien to the Carolina climate of opinion. He himself recognized that there were local prejudices which worked against him. He wrote on September 29, 1788, to Dr. Benjamin Rush: "Our narrow minded politicians say that the Southern States will be made tributary to the northern by the new constitution. Some may and probably will object to the impolicy of trusting the legislative part of that business in the hands of a northern man by birth."[19]

Ramsay was very religious, devoted to the principles of Congregationalism. The Reverends William Hollinshead and Isaac Stockton Keith had no more devoted parishioner than he;[20] nor did the New England divines, John Eliot and Jedediah Morse, have a more faith-

---

[17] Allan Westcott, "Alexander Gillon," *DAB*. Charles Gregg Singer, *South Carolina in the Confederation*, Philadelphia, 1941, pp. 27, 29.

[18] R. L. Meriwether, "David Ramsay," *DAB*.

[19] David Ramsay to Benjamin Rush, September 29, 1788, *Ramsay Letters*, LCP.

[20] Charleston, of course, was not solidly Anglican. At this period the Congregational, or Independent, Church was perhaps the strongest and most active congregation in the city. Important figures like Daniel DeSaussure, Josiah Smith, Edward Darrell, and Nathaniel Russell were members. There were two Congregational churches in Charleston. The Meeting Street Church was reopened in December 1783 by Hollinshead, who came from Philadelphia with returning exiles, and the Archdale Street Church was reopened on October 25, 1787, by Hollinshead. In 1788 Keith settled as co-pastor. After this the two ministers interchanged pulpits each week. Samuel Gilman, *Farewell to the Old Church: a historical discourse, delivered in the Unitarian Church, in Archdale-Street, Charleston, S. C.*, Charleston, 1854, pp. 11-13. The church on Archdale became the Unitarian Church in 1819.

ful correspondent in the South.[21] Ramsay told Eliot that he wrote
his histories more in spite of his surroundings than with any help
from them.[22] His third wife, Martha Laurens the beloved daughter
of Henry Laurens, was a pietist with a deeply embedded evan-
gelical strain. In 1775 when Martha Laurens visited England she
met the Countess of Huntingdon, the patroness of John Wesley, who
gave her a book of hymns from which she read every day until she
died.[23] At Vigan in France she had taken part of a gift of five hundred guineas to provide Bibles for the community, and then used
the rest to endow a school for the local inhabitants.[24] If broad
humanitarian impulses flowed through any Carolinians in the years
that followed the Revolution they certainly flowed through David
and Martha Ramsay.

Ramsay took the Declaration of Independence literally. He gave
the first Fourth-of-July oration in 1778 and urged that the festival
be continued as an annual celebration.[25] Throughout the Revolution
he hoped that the struggle might end in freeing the slaves.[26] Similar
thoughts were rarely found in the letters of Carolinians, a notable
exception being the letter of John Laurens to his friend Kinloch in
1776.[27] David Ramsay and John Laurens had been foremost in
urging the arming of the slaves at the Jacksonborough legislature,
but the Rutledges had led the overwhelming opposition.[28] John
and Martha Laurens were remarkable offspring, their characters
stamped with the will and courage of their heroic parent. David
Ramsay was the perfect husband for Martha Laurens.

Smith had two formidable opponents. Both Gillon and Ramsay
represented forces unleashed by the Revolution, while Smith repre-

[21] In 1794 Ramsay introduced I. S. Keith to Eliot not only as his pastor but
also as an "intimate friend." David Ramsay to John Eliot, July 2, 1794,
Andrews-Eliot Papers, MHS. There are many Ramsay-Eliot letters in the *Andrews-Eliot Papers* covering the years 1782 to 1798. There are Ramsay-Morse
letters in the *Gratz Collection,* PHS, and in the *Morse Papers,* YL.

[22] David Ramsay to John Eliot, April 20, 1787, *Andrews-Eliot Papers,* MHS.

[23] David Duncan Wallace, *The Life of Henry Laurens,* New York, 1915,
pp. 390-391. David Ramsay, *Memoirs of the Life of Martha Laurens Ramsay,*
Boston, 1814, pp. 45-47.

[24] *Ibid.,* p. 20.

[25] David Ramsay, *An Oration on the Advantages of American Independence:
spoken before a publick assembly of the inhabitants of Charleston in South-
Carolina, on the second anniversary of that glorious aera,* Charlestown, 1778.

[26] David Ramsay to Benjamin Rush, June 3, 1779, August 22, 1783, *Ramsay
Letters,* LCP.

[27] John Laurens to Francis Kinloch, May 1776, *Emmet Collection,* NYPL.

[28] Edward Rutledge to Arthur Middleton, February 8, 1782, "Correspondence of Hon. Arthur Middleton," *SCHGM,* XXVII (1926), 4. *See also* Benjamin
Quarles, *The Negro in the American Revolution,* Chapel Hill, 1961, pp. 60-67.

sented the conservatism of the moderate patriots. Gillon appealed
to the new elements in society, the mechanics of Charleston and the
farmers of the backcountry. Ramsay appealed not only to those who
admired his character and favored his religion, but also to those
who had caught some of the spirit of equality. Little is known of this
campaign other than that Ramsay ran far behind the other two.
In an effort to catch up, he charged in the *Morning Post* of November 22 that Smith was ineligible to sit in Congress under the constitutional requirement that a representative shall have been for
seven years a citizen of the United States. Smith's absence from the
country for thirteen years, especially during the fighting years, was
thereby vividly called to the attention of the voters. Smith's immediate reaction was to pen a reply to the newspapers, address letters
to the leading men in each of the country parishes, and circulate
a broadside in Charleston entitled "A Dose for the Doctor."[29]

These documents were typical of Smith's style of attack. Ramsay,
Smith charged, having failed to win the attention of the public, had
stooped to spurious methods: "May not the Dr. with propriety be
compared to a certain cunning animal, who when hard run, and
all his windings, artifices and tricks have availed him nothing, steeps
his tail in an unsavory liquor, and endeavors to whisk it in the eyes
of his pursuers."[30] Smith defended himself against what Ramsay
had called the evils of a foreign education. He pointed out that his
father had sent him abroad, that his English guardian had refused
him passage money in 1779, and that after the fall of Charles Town
his American guardians had advised him to stay with his studies.
Although he had been abroad, most of his fortune had been placed
in the state treasury. His family had in fact loaned some £20,000
to £30,000 sterling to the state.

Smith turned the tables on Ramsay by pointing out that if there
were any disadvantages to having a foreign education, Ramsay's
own schooling in the North should act as a disbarment. He, Smith,
was a Carolinian born and bred; Ramsay was not. Ramsay was "an
enemy to slavery." He was "principled" against the institution, and
therefore a man tinctured with alien ideas. Ramsay in "A short

[29] William Smith to the Citizens of Charleston District, November 22, 1788,
State Gazette of South-Carolina, November 24, 1788. William Smith to the
Electors of the Parish of St. Bartholomew, November 22, 1788, William
Smith folder, *Personal Papers, Miscellaneous*, LC. William Smith, "A Dose for
the Doctor," November 25, 1788, *Broadsides*, LC. "A Dose for the Doctor" was
also printed in the *State Gazette of South-Carolina*, December 1, 1788.
[30] William Smith, "A Dose for the Doctor," November 25, 1788, *Broadsides*,
LC.

REPLY to a long Piece" reiterated his principal charge: the state had required an oath of all men over sixteen, but Smith had never taken this oath and had returned in 1783 at the age of twenty-five,[31] so he had not been a citizen for seven years. Each had found the other's vulnerable spot, but Ramsay must have been more vulnerable than Smith. It was better to have been slightly tory than slightly abolitionist.

The votes for this Congressional election are almost complete:

	Smith	Gillon	Ramsay
Charleston	349	169	146
St. James Goose Creek	34	3	4
Christ Church	17	6	18
St. Andrew's	28	24	8
St. John's Berkeley	12	11	10
St. John's Colleton	32	4	5
St. Bartholomew	70	150	0
St. Thomas & St. Dennis	28	0	0
St. Paul's	30	19	0
	600	386	191[32]

Smith had more votes than his two competitors combined. The low-country combination that had pushed through the ratification of the Constitution was behind Smith: the native-born merchants, the lawyers (the Rutledges and the Pinckneys were particularly strong in Charleston),[33] and the Goose Creek planters. Gillon had more support in the city than did Ramsay, as well as a large measure of support in the more inland parishes, particularly St. Bartholomew. It was rather ironical that William Smith should have defeated both the "hero" of the anti-tory mob in Charleston and the man who more than any other Carolinian cherished the principles of the Declaration of Independence.[34]

---

[31] "A short REPLY to a long Piece signed William Smith," November 24, 1788, *State Gazette of South-Carolina*, November 27, 1788.

[32] *State Gazette of South-Carolina*, December 1, 1788.

[33] Thomas and Charles Cotesworth Pinckney and Edward Rutledge led the poll in Charleston for members of the state legislature. *Ibid.*, December 4, 1788.

[34] Ramsay wrote Eliot on November 26: "I was a candidate and lost my election on two grounds. One was that I was a northward man and the other that I was represented as favoring the abolition of slavery. Such is the temper of our people here that it is unpopular to be unfriendly to the further importation of slaves." David Ramsay to John Eliot, November 26, 1788, *Andrews-Eliot Papers*, MHS. George Miller thought that "the choice of the people has generally fallen upon the most deserving men who offered to serve them." George Miller to Carmarthen, November 30, 1788, *FO*, VI, 693-699.

Smith was also elected in November to the next session of the state legislature, which he attended from January to March 1789.[35] In January the legislature elected Pierce Butler and Ralph Izard to the United States Senate.[36] This session successfully opposed any further change in the installment law and prevented the issuance of any paper money. George Miller reported that the legislature had adjourned "without having passed any act or ordinance, that affected, the commerce of Great Britain." As for the future, he added, with the lawyers meeting "under the new Constitution . . . there is the less danger to be apprehended of any evils proceeding from the state legislatures."[37] The battle was shifting to the national front.

WILLIAM SMITH, Aedanus Burke, Daniel Huger, Thomas Tudor Tucker, and Thomas Sumter were the South Carolina representatives in the First Congress. Smith represented Charleston District; Burke, Beaufort and Orangeburg; Huger, Georgetown and Cheraw; Tucker, Ninety Six; and Sumter, Camden.[38]

Burke was the Irish judge who had made a name in America and Europe by incisively attacking the Society of the Cincinnati as being a citadel of privilege; nor was he afraid to debunk the pompous heroes of the Revolution—a Knox or even Washington.[39] He was a Carolinian imbued with the history of the English Civil War, looking for his heroes not among the trimmers of 1688 but among the regicides of 1649. (He once wrote Ezra Stiles urging a monument to the glorious memory of Whalley, Goffe, and Dixwell.[40]) As his letter to John Lamb revealed, he had not been satisfied with the Constitution. But Burke was too jovial a person, too full of the joys of life, to be considered an inveterate enemy. Even Smith warmed to him. "Your Brother Burke," Smith wrote to Judge Grimké, "is become very pleasant—a great Speaker, and often entertains us with humorous strokes of fancy."[41]

[35] State Gazette of South-Carolina, December 1, 1788.
[36] JHR, XLIX, 75-76.
[37] George Miller to Carmarthen, May 20, 1789, FO, VII, 197-200.
[38] State Gazette of South-Carolina, December 8, 1788, November 11, 1790.
[39] [Aedanus Burke], Considerations on the Society or Order of Cincinnati; lately instituted by the Major-Generals, Brigadier-Generals, and other Officers of the American Army, Proving that it creates a Race of Hereditary Patricians, or Nobility, Philadelphia, 1783. For interesting comments on the pamphlet see Henry Knox to George Washington, February 21, 1784; Henry Knox to General Greene, February 15, 1784, Knox Papers, MHS.
[40] Aedanus Burke to Ezra Stiles, September 17, 1792, printed in American Museum, XII (1792), 259-260.
[41] William Smith to Judge Grimké, March 3, 1790, Emmet Collection, NYPL.

Daniel Huger, leader of an important group of families in the Georgetown area, was the only lowcountry planter in the delegation. He had already served in Congress and had his northern contacts. He might have been a great help to Smith, but he was sick most of the time and consequently a cipher in the House.[42]

Thomas Tudor Tucker was the most active member, next to Smith, of the delegation, but Tucker had been a rival of Smith and the Izards. Smith had defeated him in 1785 for a place on the Privy Council; Izard tried to prevent Tucker's election in St. George Dorchester, and as a result they had fought a duel, in which Tucker was wounded. In this session of Congress he was to present Ramsay's petition challenging Smith's right to a seat. The relations between Smith and Tucker must have been quite cool.

Thomas Sumter, ashamed of his origins and wracked by greed, could never have been a happy man.[43] He arrived in South Carolina as an escapee from a Virginia debtor's prison, and though he lived to be ninety-eight he was never free from creditors—in spite of that fact, he was one of the largest landholders in South Carolina. He set up a country store, married a woman seven years his elder for her fortune, and took out grants for 2,450 acres; yet even in the years before the Revolution he was constantly in debt to Charleston merchants.[44] During the war, in spite of his magnificent sorties, his record was tarnished by charges of plundering which brought a warning from Greene and a proclamation from Rutledge. The tradition, according to Anne King Gregorie, was that Sumter always got his share.[45] If one considers Sumter's "over-sensitive pride," the failure of Congress to promote him, his resignation from the Continental line, his subsequent election as general by his men, which Rutledge delayed four months in confirming, and finally Greene's placing Morgan over Sumter, his hatred of the "Congress heroes" is fully explained.[46] He was never a member of the Cincinnati, and like Burke and the Jeffersonians, he remained a strong supporter of the militia, always hostile to the regular army. By 1789 he had tried and failed to get the state capital located at Stateburg,[47] and the

[42] Biographical Directory of the American Congress, 1774-1949, Washington, 1950, p. 1344. Daniel Huger was the brother-in-law of Col. Lewis Morris. "Letters from Col. Lewis Morris to Miss Ann Elliott," SCHGM, XL (1939), 125, n. 5.
[43] Anne King Gregorie, Thomas Sumter, Columbia, 1931, pp. 4, 23.
[44] Ibid., pp. 22, 25, 30, 31, 35, 217.
[45] Ibid., p. 183.
[46] Ibid., pp. 35, 62, 69, 73, 80, 109, 128.
[47] Ibid., pp. 212-213.

South Carolina Senate had refused to grant him rank and honor.[48] He could not have been in good humor as he joined the new Congress.

THE HOUSE of Representatives assembled in New York on March 4, 1789, but a quorum was not present for business until April 1. Tucker attended from the first day, but Burke, Huger, and Smith did not arrive until April 13, having traveled together by sea from Charleston.[49] Sumter put in his appearance on May 25. He traveled overland, perhaps to avoid sailing from Charleston, a city he always despised, and during the last thirty-five years of his life never entered.[50]

The committee on elections, which was responsible for scanning members' credentials had as its first duty the scrutiny of Ramsay's petition (presented by Tucker on April 15) asserting that Smith had been ineligible at the time of his election because he came within the disqualification of the third paragraph of Article I of the Constitution, that is, not having been a citizen of the United States for seven years.[51] The report of the committee was read on the 18th and ordered to be laid on the table. On the 29th the committee was instructed to take such proofs as could be obtained in New York. Smith was permitted to attend the committee to examine witnesses and offer counter-proofs.

When the House itself took up the matter on May 22 (devoting the entire day to the subject) Smith was permitted to speak in his own behalf. He emphasized the early age at which he was sent abroad, his position as a student, and his sincere but unavailing efforts to return from 1779 on. Ramsay had implied that residence was necessary for citizenship. Smith pointed out that some of America's leading figures were abroad before the Revolution and stayed abroad after the Declaration of Independence. Congress employed these gentlemen abroad, so they must be considered American citizens by virtue of the Revolution. Surely a student would be considered in the same light. He acknowledged that his father had died,

[48] *Ibid.*, pp. 222-223.
[49] *Annals of the Congress of the United States*, Washington, 1834, I (1st cong., 1st sess.), 95, 121.
[50] *Ibid.*, p. 408. Gregorie, *op. cit.*, pp. 224, 278. Burke, Huger, and Tucker lived at Mr. Huck's, Wall Street; Sumter by himself at 40 Wall Street; Smith on Broadway, next to the Spanish minister's. Rufus Wilmot Griswold, *The Republican Court or American Society in the Days of Washington*, New York, 1855, p. 167, n.
[51] *Annals of the Congress of the United States*, Washington, 1834, I (1st cong., 1st sess.), 143.

but his guardians, "who were *in loco parentis*," were residents of Carolina at the time of the Declaration. His property was in Carolina, and his money in her treasury, assisting the war effort. South Carolina had never recalled her young men from abroad, but had given them permission to remain until twenty-two; if they stayed longer, they were taxed double.

To the charge that he had never taken an oath under the act of March 1778, he showed that it applied to the inhabitants of South Carolina at that time and no consequences of not having taken the oath had ever befallen him. Since the Jacksonborough legislature of February 1782 had not placed his name on the confiscation list, he must have had their permission to be abroad. "If the Legislature in 1782 recognized as citizens some of those persons whose estates were confiscated for adhering to Great Britain, and for being disaffected to America, *a fortiori*, did it not recognize as a citizen one whose estate was not forfeited, who had not been deemed worthy of punishment, and who had been absent under the sanction of the law?" Furthermore, by the constitution of the state, no person was eligible for a seat in the state legislature unless he had been three years a resident, or for a seat in the Privy Council unless five years a resident, yet he had obtained a seat in both before he had resided two years in South Carolina, and no objection had been made. An act of March 26, 1784, had conferred the right of citizenship on aliens, but he had never qualified for the benefits of that law considering himself already a citizen. When he took his seat in the legislature in January 1785 and in the Privy Council in October 1785 he had not been challenged. Ramsay had even cast a vote for him for privy councilor![52]

James Madison, soon to be Smith's chief antagonist in the House, made a strong statement in his behalf. He conceived Ramsay's position to be based on the theory that the Revolution threw all into a state of nature, which would imply that each individual had to take a positive step to affirm his position in the new society. Madison held to a contrary theory that the American society separated from Great Britain as a unit and that Smith's allegiance was transferred from King to Carolina automatically, without any need for a positive affirmation on his part since he was a minor. Elias Boudinot of New Jersey and James Jackson of Georgia rejected Madison's theory fearing that it would permit the return of far too many loyalists. However, they were willing to vote in favor of Smith on the peculiar

[52] *Ibid.*, pp. 168, 231, 397-402.

nature of his position: that South Carolina had given him leave and had not objected to his return. The vote was thirty-six to one to seat Smith. This was the first contested election to be brought before Congress.[53]

THE TASK of Congress in 1789 was to erect the three great branches of government: legislative, executive, and judicial. After the Congress was sure that it had been properly assembled, it turned to the establishment of the executive branch. Here there were fears that English institutions might creep in—particularly the high prerogatives of the Crown. When the Senate, under the leadership of Vice-President John Adams, began to toy with titles, even Izard tried to stifle the nonsense by suggesting that the Vice-President might be addressed as "His Rotundity."[54] The House was even more cautious. Burke later objected to the style of "Chief Justice" until it was pointed out that it was a provision of the Constitution itself.[55]

In establishing the executive departments the chief debate was over whether the President could remove the head of a department at will. Those who feared executive power demanded that the Senate concur in removals since it was to be consulted in appointments. Oddly enough, in the light of their later positions, Madison argued for the strong executive and Smith against. It was not always easy in the beginning to see the consequences of one's position. There were often counter-arguments in mind, and one could not see clearly which was the more important principle to follow. What confused Smith at this point was his belief (and it was an accepted eighteenth-century idea) that a man's office was his property. No man could be deprived of his property, "but by a fair and impartial trial"—in this case, by impeachment.[56] Later, when he had come to recognize

[53] *Ibid.*, pp. 403-408. Ramsay had sent a dissertation on American citizenship to Elias Boudinot with the request that it be printed and a copy sent to each member of Congress. David Ramsay to Elias Boudinot, March 31, 1789, *Gratz Collection*, PHS. There was a delay, and the dissertation was not printed until after Smith had won his case. David Ramsay, *Observations on the Decision of the House of Representatives of the United States, on the 22nd Day of May, 1789; Respecting the Eligibility of the Hon. William Smith, of South-Carolina, to a Seat in that House*, New York, 1789.

[54] *Journal of William Maclay*, ed. Edgar S. Maclay, New York, 1890, pp. 30, 65. On the other hand Izard did not want too much "contemptible affectation of ROMAN SIMPLICITY." Ralph Izard to Edward Rutledge, May 16, 1789, *Izard Papers*, SCL.

[55] *Annals of the Congress of the United States*, Washington, 1834, I (1st cong., 1st sess.), 783.

[56] *Ibid.*, p. 458.

the need for energy in the executive, he admitted that he had been wrong.[57]

Smith had another argument against conferring the removal power upon the President. If the power had been given by the Constitution, there would be no need to give it by law; if it were not given, it would be "nugatory also to attempt to vest the power." The question of right in the last instance would be left to the judiciary. "It will be time enough to determine the question when the President shall remove an officer in this way. I conceive it can properly be brought before that tribunal; the officer will have a right to a mandamus to be restored to his office, and the judges would determine whether the President exercised a Constitutional authority or not." When someone who was unable to see how such a case could come into the courts challenged Smith, he replied: "Wherever a man has a right, he has a remedy; if he suffers a wrong he can have a redress; he would be entitled to damages for being deprived of his property in his office."[58] The situation that Smith envisaged was remarkably like that in *Marbury* v. *Madison*. Although fundamentally wrong on the President's power of removal, Smith had a vision of the federal structure with its smoothly working parts. He became an authority on the Constitution and later wrote a constitutional-history textbook that was used at Princeton.[59]

Once the structure of the executive branch had been hammered out, Congress turned to a discussion of policy. The new government's need to raise funds by levying duties brought forth Smith's concern for Charleston's commercial interests. The South Carolina delegation as a whole acted as defenders of a staple-producing region, but Smith fought harder against tonnage duties, while Burke and Tucker worked eagerly for exemption of articles consumed by their constituents. Tucker had spoken as early as April 9 on the subject of duties, urging his colleagues to postpone a serious discussion until other Southern members had arrived. He was willing to support a five per cent ad valorem tax on all imports (suggested by

[57] William Smith to James McHenry, October 9, 1797, *McHenry Papers*, WLCL.
[58] *Annals of the Congress of the United States*, Washington, 1834, I (1st cong., 1st sess.), 459, 507-510.
[59] William Smith, *A Comparative View of the Constitutions of the Several States with each other, and with that of the United States: Exhibiting in Tables the Prominent Features of each Constitution, and Classing together their most important Provisions under the Several Heads of Administration; with Notes and Observations*, Philadelphia, 1796. At the end of this debate Smith and Madison voted together to strike out the clause granting the power of removal. *Annals of the Congress of the United States*, Washington, 1834, I (1st cong., 1st sess.), 585.

the Congress in 1781) and additional duties on certain enumerated items.[60] It was the prospect of those additional duties that aroused the greed of the manufacturers of New England and the Middle States. Tucker was against extra duties on candles, unwrought steel, and nails.[61] Burke was for a duty on hemp to encourage its cultivation in the upcountry.[62] Both Tucker and Burke spoke against the duty on salt as falling on the poor and the upcountrymen.[63] Smith was also against the salt duty: "The inhabitants of the interior part of South Carolina are opposed to the new Government," and it would have been dangerous to tempt them to further opposition.[64]

It was the question of tonnage, introduced by gentlemen from New York, that was ominous to the Carolinians, for a high tonnage rate on foreign vessels would hurt South Carolina, a non-carrying state. A scale had been proposed to favor United States vessels, then the vessels of nations in commercial alliance with the United States, and finally the vessels of nations without any treaties of commerce with the United States. Madison posed the problem succinctly on May 4: "How far it is expedient, at this time, to make a discrimination between foreign nations and the United States, for the purpose of promoting and accelerating the improvement of the American navigation? And how far it is expedient to make such a discrimination between foreigners, as may induce them to permit us to extend our own navigation on principles of reciprocity?"[65] There would be discrimination against foreign vessels, but even more discrimination against the vessels of Great Britain, who had no commercial treaty with the United States.

Smith was the chief spokesman for those who did not wish to discriminate against the vessels of Great Britain. In this he worked against one economic interest in Charleston, for the shipwrights had given Smith a petition to present to Congress requesting a navigation act which would relieve their distresses and those of their fellow shipwrights in America.[66] But Smith spoke for the merchants of Charleston, not the mechanics. The South had already shown enough favor to the manufacturing states by the import duties agreed on; these might cut down on the goods which the South took

[60] Ibid., pp. 107-109.
[61] Ibid., pp. 146, 147, 157.
[62] Ibid., p. 155.
[63] Ibid., pp. 158-159.
[64] Ibid., p. 160.
[65] Ibid., pp. 236-237.
[66] Ibid., p. 123.

from England. The English could not be expected to send their vessels to South Carolina in ballast; and perhaps if a great tax were placed on their tonnage, they would send no vessels at all. South Carolina was completely dependent on English ships.[67] As Burke, who was certainly no friend of British interests, said, New England could not supply the South with sufficient ships.[68] Until she could, the South should have low tonnage rates.

Smith made his strongest statement on May 7 in defense of South Carolina's close economic ties with Great Britain, which, of course, the tonnage duties would tend to sever. He said he would as soon throw himself out of a two-story window as believe a high tonnage duty favorable to South Carolina. His state might like to support New England manufacturing and marine, but it could not, for it was tied to Britain. "Our connections are kept up with them by the vast debts due to her merchants and factors; it is their policy to continue us in these commercial fetters. . . . The course of the stream in which our navigation has so long flowed, cannot be altered in a day. The debts due from the merchants of the country to the British, will be an insuperable bar." The New Englanders did not have sufficient connections abroad to dispose of southern crops; they could not secure the best prices; they did not have goods to bring back; above all, the British had capital; they gave credit. Smith said: "It is the custom of British merchants to send out their goods upon credit; they establish agents and houses to deal them out to planters as they are wanted, and take their crops in return. . . . It is well known, that we have not ready money there to pay down for the articles we want, credit being the established medium of trade in that country. Gentlemen must see that it would take much time and the strongest efforts to alter it, though I am sensible that we pay severely for the indulgence; yet the habit, being established, is hard to be broken."[69]

This is a clear indication that the economic ties between Great Britain and South Carolina, broken during the Revolution, had now been reforged. Smith also admitted the existence of a British interest in Charleston for which he assuredly spoke. But it was in the interest of South Carolina that he did so. The removal of the British interest after 1808 was only to mean the eventual substitution of the Yankee for the Englishman—a result which was clearly foreshad-

[67] *Ibid.*, pp. 259-261.
[68] *Ibid.*, pp. 256-257.
[69] *Ibid.*, pp. 286-287.

owed in this debate, especially since New England won. The scale of tonnage duties adopted was six cents and nine cents per ton on American owned vessels, thirty cents per ton on foreign vessels of any allies, and fifty cents per ton on all others. The Senate ultimately prevented any special discrimination against Britain.[70]

The two most momentous questions to be settled in the first session involved a bill of rights and the judiciary; they were intimately connected and eventually decided together. Madison moved on June 8 to take up the amendments to the Constitution. Smith objected: "It must appear extremely impolitic to go into the consideration of amending the Government, before it is organized, before it has begun to operate."[71] Burke and Sumter, unlike Smith, were keen on amending the Constitution, but favored temporary postponement. Sumter, in his first speech, was so ardently for amendments that he did not care how they came before the House as long as they were fully discussed.[72]

On August 13, Smith once again tried to get the judiciary established before going on with a discussion of amendments: "The Constitution establishes three branches to constitute a whole; the Legislative and Executive are now in existence, but the Judicial is uncreated. While we remain in this state, not a single part of the revenue system can operate; no breach of your laws can be punished; illicit trade cannot be prevented."[73] In spite of his sound reasoning, Smith lost, and the amendments were taken up. In the discussion that followed, there appeared the first clear signs of the division between Smith, the future Hamiltonian, and Burke, Tucker, and Sumter, future Jeffersonians.

Tucker wanted to add to the first amendment the Wilkite principle of the right of the people to instruct their representatives.[74] Sumter agreed that the people should bind the vote of their representatives.[75] Smith very naturally opposed, although he did not use

[70] *Ibid.*, p. 290. In May 1790 when there was a move to raise the tonnage to $1 a ton on foreign ships, Smith once again explained the difficulties a Boston merchant would have in the carrying trade between Charleston and Amsterdam. Capital and connections were needed. The British had them; the New Englanders did not. "The only mode of supplanting these foreign merchants is to imitate their conduct. . . ." Smith's basic position was that the United States ought not to condemn Britain for following "her usual policy in her navigation laws; they are not particularly aimed at us; her navigation act was originally aimed at the Dutch." *Ibid.*, II (1st cong., 2nd sess.), 1559, 1574.
[71] *Ibid.*, I (1st cong., 1st sess.), 424.
[72] *Ibid.*, pp. 426, 448.
[73] *Ibid.*, p. 705.
[74] *Ibid.*, p. 733.
[75] *Ibid.*, pp. 744-745.

the argument that a representative should be free to follow his conscience (the position of Edmund Burke). Instead, Smith argued that representatives of distant states would be placed at a disadvantage, and such a provision might belie the necessity of a numerous representation, for one person voting in this manner might then represent an entire state.[76] Tucker's amendment was voted down, forty-one to ten.[77]

Burke and Sumter cautioned against haste. The amendments had come out of a committee of eleven, of whom five had been members of the Constitutional Convention. Burke asked if one could expect "solid and substantial amendments" from such a group. To him the amendments reported were "little better than whip-syllabub, frothy and full of wind, formed only to please the palate." They were like "a tub thrown out to a whale, to secure the freight of the ship and its peaceable voyage."[78]

Smith, however, was one of those in a hurry. Fisher Ames of Massachusetts moved (and Smith seconded) that the committee of the whole house be discharged; this would automatically have referred the amendments to the floor of the House. Only a simple majority was needed in the committee of the whole, but in the House a two-thirds vote was necessary to pass an amendment. When Burke and Tucker opposed the motion on the grounds that it was designed to cut off debate, Smith and Ames quickly retreated.[79]

Elbridge Gerry of Massachusetts moved to bring up for discussion all those amendments proposed by states that had not been reported by the committee of eleven.[80] Tucker voiced the threat that failure to discuss all of the amendments suggested by states might cause them to demand a new constitutional convention, a fear that haunted the Federalists for a decade.[81] In spite of this, Gerry's motion was defeated thirty-four to sixteen, Smith voting with the majority, and Burke, Sumter, and Tucker with the minority.[82]

After the militia amendment was agreed to, Burke proposed the following: "A standing army of regular troops in time of peace is dangerous to public liberty, and such shall not be raised or kept up

[76] *Ibid.*, p. 739.
[77] *Ibid.*, p. 747.
[78] *Ibid.*, p. 745.
[79] *Ibid.*, pp. 747-749.
[80] *Ibid.*, p. 757.
[81] *Ibid.*, pp. 757-759.
[82] *Ibid.*, p. 759.

in time of peace, but from necessity, and for the security of the people, nor then without the consent of two-thirds of the members present of both houses; and in all cases the military shall be subordinate to the civil authority." This was voted down by a majority of thirteen.[83] Then Sumter tried to alter the quartering clause to make the prohibition effective in war as well as in peace, but he lost by sixteen votes.[84]

Smith objected to the phrase, "nor cruel and unusual punishments" as being too indefinite. Samuel Livermore of New Hampshire objected that this might rule out whipping, ear clipping, or even hanging—punishments which both Smith and Livermore undoubtedly considered desirable.[85]

The only suggested amendment change that all the members of the South Carolina delegation could agree on was Burke's motion to prevent Congress from interfering in state elections. Livermore, speaking in favor of Burke's motion, used the Smith election case as an example of how election disputes should be handled. "Was not his qualification as a member of the Federal Legislature determined upon the laws of South Carolina?" Yet this was defeated by a vote of twenty-eight to twenty-three.[86]

Tucker's motion to prevent the levying of a direct tax except as a final resort, and only then after requisitions had been tried, was defeated by a vote of thirty-nine to nine; Smith voted with the majority against his three compatriots.[87]

Nothing better revealed the gulf that separated Smith from his colleagues than the debate on the judiciary bill. Tucker, seconded by Sumter, moved that inferior federal courts not be set up, since state courts "were fully competent to the purposes for which these courts were to be created, and that they would be a burdensome and useless expense."[88] Smith, on the other hand, had no doubt that federal district courts should be established. All agreed that courts with admiralty jurisdiction were needed. But should these courts be given additional jurisdiction? Should the jurisdiction of the district courts be confined to admiralty causes, or should they take cognizance "of all causes of seizure on land, all breaches of impost laws, or offenses committed on the high seas, and causes in which for-

[83] *Ibid.*, pp. 751-752.
[84] *Ibid.*, p. 752.
[85] *Ibid.*, p. 754.
[86] *Ibid.*, pp. 768-772.
[87] *Ibid.*, pp. 773, 777.
[88] *Ibid.*, p. 783.

eigners or citizens of other States are parties?" Smith was in favor of the latter course. In fact, he felt that, if anything, the jurisdiction of the districts courts in the bill as it came from the Senate was too narrow. These courts were not taking jurisdiction away from state courts, because they were to try offenses against the United States. "Every nation upon earth punishes by its own courts offenses against its own laws." Otherwise, the revenue due the national government could not be collected. If there were no lower federal courts, the state courts would have to handle these causes but with a right of appeal to the federal Supreme Court. Consequently, there would be countless overrulings which would undermine the prestige of the state courts with their own people. It was therefore essential to draw a clear line between the two court systems and thus prevent, as far as possible, "a clashing or interference between them." To meet the criticism of added expense, Smith pointed out that admiralty courts would in any case exist, and with only a little added expense these courts could handle other federal cases. Some had objected "that there must be court-houses, judges, marshals, clerk constables, jails, and gibbets," but would there not be need for these with the admiralty courts?[89] This defense of a strong national court system earned for Smith the praise of the emerging Federalist leaders. Both Theodore Sedgwick of Massachusetts and Ames, when they arose to speak in behalf of the new court system, confined themselves to details, since "the honorable gentleman from South Carolina" had covered the major points so completely.[90]

Burke expressed the despair of those who opposed the larger jurisdiction when he said that the people "never had an idea that by this revolution they were to be put in a worse situation than they were under the former government." He thought the new courts would harass the people in a number of ways, and that the sitting of the federal court would conflict with the sitting of the state courts. Even worse, he feared, "the place might be at the most distant part of the State, where a man might be dragged three or four hundred miles from his home, and tried by men who know nothing of him, or he of them." The freemen of America would never submit, but, search as he would, Burke could find no way out: ". . . which ever way he turned, the Constitution stared him in the face." He determined therefore, to be a silent spectator while the bill passed.[91]

[89] *Ibid.*, pp. 797-801.
[90] *Ibid.*, pp. 805-807.
[91] *Ibid.*, pp. 812-813.

Jackson of Georgia agreed with Burke that "a resident on Lake Erie might be dragged to New York for trial, or one on the Oconee to Savannah."[92] Burke had feared that someone as far away as the Alleghany Mountains might be carried to Charleston, "far from the aid of his friends, far from his witnesses; and if, in times of civil troubles, he be obnoxious to those in power, to be tried for his life in the fangs of his enemies."[93] The Whiskey Rebels were to suffer such a fate.

Smith replied to Burke and Jackson that the objections to district courts arose from establishing the Government itself. ". . . these objections come too late, a National Government is established. . . . If we have a Government pervading the Union, we must have a Judicial power of similar magnitude; we must establish courts in different parts of the Union." As the legislative power had been divided between the states and the federal government, so must the judicial power be. It had been facetiously asked if the marshal of the district court and the sheriff of the state court happened to seize the same debtor were they to cut him in halves? That sort of problem would have to be worked out by sensible men. At the moment the question was one of principle: whether there should or should not be such federal courts.[94]

Another critic was concerned about the great number of appeals from state courts to the Supreme Court through the district and circuit courts. Smith showed his command of the details of the system by replying: "There is no appeal from the State to the District courts; and only a power of removal in certain cases of a Federal jurisdiction, from the State to the Circuit court; neither is there any appeal of fact from the District to the Circuit court, and only a power of removal in certain cases of a Federal jurisdiction from the State to the Circuit court; neither is there any appeal of fact from the District to the Circuit courts, but in admiralty cases; and these cannot be afterwards carried up to the Supreme Court, but when the value exceeds two thousand dollars."[95]

Smith's final stand in behalf of a strong judiciary was in defense of adequate salaries for judges. High salaries had to be held out to induce men of ability to accept appointments and ensure their independence. The judicial department was the "sheet anchor" of the

[92] *Ibid.*, p. 815.
[93] *Ibid.*, pp. 833-834.
[94] *Ibid.*, p. 816.
[95] *Ibid.*, p. 818.

Constitution; a department of consequence to the Union; a department which, in all civilized countries, was placed in an independent situation. Smith's position was upheld—the bill passed, and the future rested with the new institution.[96]

The South Carolina delegation in this first session had voted together whenever the manufacturing and mercantile interests of the North threatened the interests of a southern staple-producing economy. Yet within the delegation there was a division between Smith and his colleagues along lines that' heralded the division between Hamilton and Jefferson. Smith fought hardest for low tonnage duties and a strong federal judicial system. Burke, Tucker, and Sumter were more concerned about democratic institutions, individual rights, and a policy of taxation that would bear lightly upon "the little man." Smith was concerned with erecting a strong, sturdy national government; the others worried about the individual caught amid these new and greater government powers. Neither was absolutely right; both were necessary. Out of this struggle would arise the American nation.

AFTER THE STRUCTURE of government was outlined, the offices had to be filled. Patronage was to be the cement of the new government. In each state, President Washington had a few favored correspondents upon whom he relied for the suggestion and clearance of names for public office. In South Carolina, Edward Rutledge and Charles Cotesworth Pinckney were his links. They suggested names either directly to Washington and his secretaries or indirectly through Senator Ralph Izard and Representative William Smith. Although Rutledge and Pinckney themselves preferred to stay in South Carolina, to run things from the state legislature, they were vitally interested in high positions in government for their relatives and close friends. The Rutledges and the Pinckneys looked to the judiciary, the diplomatic corps, the cabinet, and ultimately the vice-presidency and presidency.

The federal judicial system was established by act of September 24, 1789. Washington named John Rutledge as one of the original associate justices of the Supreme Court, but Rutledge resigned in March 1791 to become the first chief justice of the State of South Carolina.[97] In 1791 the federal office seemed less important. There

---

[96] *Ibid.*, p. 902.

[97] George Washington to John Rutledge, September 29, 1789; John Rutledge to George Washington, March 5, 1791; *Miscellaneous Letters, Department of State,* National Archives.

must have been some doubt in the minds of the Rutledges and the Pinckneys, as there was in the minds of many of the public figures during the first years of the new government, as to where the true center of power was to rest—in the federal government or in the state governments. By 1795, however, when the prestige of the central government and of the federal courts had grown, John Rutledge was willing to ask Washington to appoint him Chief Justice, when Jay stepped down to run for the governorship of New York. Washington promptly honored Rutledge with the appointment.[98]

The Rutledges and the Pinckneys could have had two federal judgeships in the beginning, since Thomas Pinckney was offered the position of federal district judge. He refused, however, and the place was then offered to William Drayton on the strong recommendation of Edward Rutledge. Rutledge wrote Washington, "[If Drayton] is exceeded by any man in this State, in legal Knowledge, it is only by General Pinckney who cannot accept, and by my brother who has already accepted an appointment."[99] Washington replied to Rutledge that he had appointed Drayton "in consequence of your warm recommendation of him, and the concurrent testimony of his abilities and integrity by those gentlemen who are acquainted with him, and who have spoken to me on the subject."[100] When Drayton died the following year, Thomas Bee was chosen to take his place.[101]

Thomas Bee, although trained at the Inns of Court, had been a prime mover in the Revolutionary struggle as early as the Stamp Act crisis and had been a state judge since 1776. He was a man of great personal charm who got on well with all factions, but he owed his appointment in great measure to the influence of William Smith. Bee's second wife had been a daughter of Thomas Smith of Broad Street. His third wife, the widow of Richard Shubrick, who had a plantation at Goose Creek, had brought him even more into the circle of Izards, Manigaults, and Smiths. Thomas Bee held the position of federal judge until his death, in 1812.

[98] Quoted in Charles Warren, *The Supreme Court in United States History*, Boston, 1923, I, 127-128. Washington's answer, dated July 1, 1795, is also quoted in *ibid.*, p. 128.

[99] Edward Rutledge to George Washington, October 31, 1789, *Miscellaneous Manuscripts*, SCHS.

[100] George Washington to Edward Rutledge, November 23, 1789. The President enclosed Drayton's commission in George Washington to William Drayton, November 18, 1789, *Miscellaneous Letters, Department of State*, National Archives.

[101] Bee's commission, dated June 14, 1790, was enclosed in Thomas Jefferson to Thomas Bee, June 15, 1790, *Bee Papers*, LC. He accepted in Thomas Bee to Thomas Jefferson, July 15, 1790, *Miscellaneous Letters, Department of State*, National Archives.

The district court had four offices: judge, attorney, marshal, and clerk. John Julius Pringle was the first federal district attorney, but he resigned after three years because of the pressure of personal affairs. In his letter of resignation Pringle recommended Thomas Parker as his successor.[102] Rutledge and Pinckney wrote Izard that they approved of Parker, and Izard sent this information with his own endorsement to Washington by William Smith, who was at that time on his way to pay a visit to Mount Vernon.[103] William Smith was undoubtedly pleased to speak to the President in behalf of Thomas Parker, since John and Thomas Parker were his friends and, since his departure for Congress, his attorneys.[104] Thomas Parker was district attorney until 1812, when he succeeded Bee as judge. Although the higher judicial posts went to the Rutledge-Pinckney faction, the federal courthouse in South Carolina was somewhat more closely tied to William Smith since Bee and Parker were both family intimates. At the time of the Jay Treaty discussions, when the Rutledges and the Pinckneys were critical of the national administration, Parker was found firmly on the government side. William Read wrote in October 1795, "Thomas Parker is a strong supporter of Federal measures." Parker had confided to Read "that it was high time that men who were determined to support government were known to each other. . . ."[105]

The position of federal marshal was awarded to a Huger to keep that important family group in the Georgetown area allied to the federal cause. General Isaac Huger, a brother of Representative Daniel Huger, was the first federal marshal.[106] As marshal he was responsible for the first federal census in South Carolina. When he was late turning in his figures, due to the fact that one of his assistants had run off to St. Augustine taking some of the returns with him and making it necessary to do part of the work again, Smith had to ask Congress to give South Carolina extra time to file her

[102] John Julius Pringle to George Washington, September 3, 1792, *Miscellaneous Letters, Department of State,* National Archives.

[103] Ralph Izard to Edward Rutledge, September 28, 1792, *Dreer Collection,* PHS.

[104] *See* William Smith to Messrs. Parker, March 14, 1789, *William Loughton Smith Papers,* SCHS.

[105] William Read to Jacob Read, October 27, 1795, *Miscellaneous Manuscripts,* NYPL.

[106] Daniel Huger, who died in 1755, had four sons: Daniel, Isaac, John, and Benjamin. "South Carolina Gleanings in England," *SCHGM,* XV (1914), 92-94. In 1794, John Hart was elected sheriff of Charleston District "by General Huger's interest." John Brown Cutting to Thomas Pinckney, December 19, 1794, *Pinckney Papers,* LC.

returns.[107] This census was especially important because representation in the House of Representatives was to be altered in 1790, based on these returns. When General Huger stepped down, his place was taken by his son Daniel Lionel Huger, who was appointed with the approval of Ralph Izard.[108]

The clerk of court throughout the period was Thomas Hall. Jacob Read discussed his qualifications and his loyalty to the administration in a letter of October 10, 1799. Thomas Hall, he wrote, "was a captain in the first So. Carolina Regt. in the Cont. estab. & toward the close of the war was acting adjutant Genl. of the Southern Army. He is now clerk of the federal dist. & circuit court of S. C. dist.—& a respectable man—tho *lately* unfortunately tinctured with Judge Burke's Politics—he is however recovering from that folly."[109]

The diplomatic corps was small during the first decade of the nation's history. In 1801 the United States still had only five ministers abroad: in London, Paris, Madrid, Lisbon, and The Hague. There was one consul general (in Algiers), plus forty-seven consuls, four vice-consuls, and eleven commercial agents.[110] Thomas Pinckney was minister to England and then minister extraordinary to Spain; Charles Cotesworth Pinckney was minister to France and then one of three commissioners selected to negotiate with the Directory in 1797. Each appointed a young man from Carolina to act as his secretary: Thomas Pinckney took William Allen Deas, and Charles Cotesworth Pinckney employed his nephew Henry Middleton Rutledge.[111] William Smith was never able to secure anything more than the lesser post at Lisbon. The pattern of South Carolina diplomatic appointments under the new government parallels appointments to the federal judiciary—the Rutledges and the Pinckneys secured the choice spots.[112]

[107] Thomas Bee to George Washington, October 2, 1791, *Miscellaneous Letters, Department of State,* National Archives. *Annals of the Congress of the United States,* Washington, 1849, III (2nd cong., 1st sess.), 148.

[108] Edmund Randolph to Ralph Izard, December 11, 1794, *Izard Papers,* SCL.

[109] Jacob Read to Timothy Pickering, October 10, 1799, *Pickering Papers,* MHS.

[110] Leonard D. White, *The Federalists,* New York, 1959, p. 128.

[111] Charles Cotesworth Pinckney to Thomas Pinckney, July 1, 1792, *Pinckney Papers,* LC. Edward Rutledge to Henry Middleton Rutledge, September 1796, *Rutledge Papers, Dreer Collection,* PHS.

[112] Two South Carolinians served as consuls: Elias Vanderhorst at Bristol and Joseph Fenwick at Bordeaux. *See* the letters of Elias Vanderhorst to Rufus King, *King Papers,* NYHS. Fenwick was responsible for shipping olive plants from Marseilles to Charleston. Joseph Fenwick to Thomas Pinckney, January 25, 1793, *Pinckney Papers,* LC. *Also see* Charles Cotesworth Pinckney to James Monroe, November 16, 1796, *Monroe Papers,* NYPL.

This stranglehold on jobs helps to explain the alienation of two important figures from the administration. Charles Pinckney was certainly disappointed by the appointment of his cousin Thomas Pinckney to the Court of St. James', and Pierce Butler was equally disappointed by the special appointment of Thomas Pinckney to the Court at Madrid.[113] Charles Pinckney and Pierce Butler have long been enigmatic figures, whose careers were marked by inconsistencies. Historians have found them very difficult to categorize. The chief ambiguity comes from the fact that they both represented the state in the Constitutional Convention and both fought—Charles Pinckney fought hard—for ratification. And yet, almost as soon as the 1790's opened, they began to take the Jeffersonian course. There were obviously many motives working within their complex personalities, but one undoubtedly was chagrin due to the fact that they were ignored. Charles Pinckney may have been alienated from his cousins as early as the Jacksonborough legislature, in which Edward Rutledge and Charles Cotesworth Pinckney played such a prominent part, when his father's estate was amerced twelve per cent.[114] When Colonel Charles Pinckney died late in 1782, his Revolutionary fame was under a cloud. These shadows on the family reputation may have darkened the brow of the son and moved him to jealousy of the branch of the family that won all the laurels.

Butler may also have had personal reasons for opposing the Rutledges and the Pinckneys. In 1792 when Mrs. Daniel Blake died, she left some important property to the children of Pierce Butler, but she stated in her will that the property must be managed by her executors, Edward Rutledge, Charles Cotesworth and Thomas Pinckney, and Ralph Izard, junior, and that the father was not to be permitted to touch the property.[115] General Pinckney wrote his brother that "Major Butler is very much discontented with her will, and has thrown off his mourning."[116] It was bad enough that Butler could not touch property that belonged to his own children, but worse than that, it was to be managed by his political foes. A combination of pettinesses may have helped to dislodge both Charles Pinckney and Pierce Butler from the Federalist fold before Jeffer-

[113] J. Harold Easterby, "Charles Pinckney," *DAB*. Samuel Flagg Bemis, *Pinckney's Treaty*, New Haven, 1960, p. 208, n. 10.
[114] *SC Statutes*, VI, 633.
[115] *Will Book, 1786-1793, Charleston County, S.C.*, SC Archives, pp. 1113-1122.
[116] Charles Cotesworth Pinckney to Thomas Pinckney, July 14, 1792, *Pinckney Papers*, LC. *Also see* Ralph Izard to Edward Rutledge, September 28, 1792, *Dreer Collection*, PHS.

sonian principles surrounded them and carried them full speed into the enemy camp.

The customs service, established on July 31, 1789, was the most important of the field services that came under the direction of the secretary of the treasury. The government's income during the first decade, 1789-1799, came from the following sources:

duties on merchandise and tonnage	$50,321,525.77
internal revenues (excise)	3,632,769.93
postage	280,808.84
sales of public lands	100,339.84
fines, penalties, and forfeitures	17,078.81[117]

Since nearly all these funds came from the collection of duties, a large force of officials was needed to man the customs service. In 1800 there were eighty-two collectors, thirteen naval officers, and fifty-five surveyors in the United States.[118] In addition there was a host of petty officials. Each large port had all three important officials. The collector "assessed customs and tonnage dues and employed 'proper persons' as weighers, gaugers, measurers, and inspectors as well as seamen to man boats in the revenue service." The naval officer "countersigned all orders of the collector, received copies of manifests, and in general acted as check upon the collector." The surveyor, "who superintended the weighers and measurers, was under the joint control of the collector and the naval officer."[119]

The customs collector was the most important local federal official. George Abbott Hall, who had been collector for the state, was recommended to Washington by no less than seven of the most important local gentlemen.[120] He had the support of all groups. Isaac Motte, the brother-in-law of William Smith, was the first naval officer.[121]

The second collector was Isaac Holmes, who served from 1791 until 1797. Holmes was removed from office because of his ineffi-

[117] White, op. cit., p. 336.

[118] Ibid. White points out that the secretary of the treasury could make more appointments than any other cabinet member. Ibid., pp. 117-118.

[119] Ibid., p. 200.

[120] See letters of George Washington to W. Moultrie, E. Rutledge, C. C. Pinckney, J. Mathews, J. Rutledge, T. Bee, and C. Pinckney, May 5, 1789, Miscellaneous Letters, Department of State, National Archives.

[121] Smith wrote urging Motte as the successor to Hall, but the President replied that Holmes had been appointed before Smith's letter had been received. Tobias Lear to William Smith, September 9, 1791, Miscellaneous Letters, Department of State, National Archives.

ciency in collecting the backlog of debts owed to the government by the merchants.[122]

The third collector was James Simons who quite blatantly supported the Federalist party. Like Hall and Holmes, Simons was an important merchant; during the 1780's, he had been a partner of Hary Grant and had run the Beaufort branch of Grant and Simons.[123] James Simons' nephew Thomas Simons had married the sister of Jacob Read, and the fortunes of James Simons rose with those of Jacob Read.[124] After Read's elevation to the Senate in 1795, Simons was appointed to succeed Colonel Isaac Motte as naval officer.[125] Simons thanked Read profusely: "As long as I live, I shall entertain an affectionate and grateful sense of your affectionate attention and conduct towards me; and I shall endeavor, by a friendly and polite deportment, to give satisfaction to the Mercantile Gentlemen. . . ."[126]

The naval officer was intended to be a check upon the collector, so it was natural, when the collector faltered, for the naval officer to step into his place. In a letter of June 22, 1797, when Holmes was in trouble, Simons delicately skirted that business and then told Read "that I sincerely believe I could give Satisfaction to Mr. Wolcott [secretary of the treasury]. He may be assured of one thing, that is, that I will obey him and execute his instructions punctually; and he may be assured of another, and that is, that I will make those under me do their duty."[127] There can be no doubt that Simons was an able, efficient officer of the government; neither can there be any doubt that he ran the customs house in the interests of the Federalist party. Charles Pinckney strongly urged his removal in 1801 when the Jeffersonians had won their victory.[128]

Edward Weyman was the first surveyor of the customs, but when illness forced him to give up the office in 1790, there was a flurry of

---

[122] *Year Book, 1883, City of Charleston*, p. 458.

[123] The partnership of Hary Grant and James Simons was set up in January 1784. *South-Carolina Weekly Gazette*, January 16, 1784. This partnership along with that of James Simons and Co. of Beaufort was dissolved in May 1786. *Charleston Morning Post, and Public Advertiser*, May 6, 1786.

[124] Robert Bentham Simons, *Thomas Grange Simons III, His Forebears and Relations*, Charleston, 1954, pp. 10-11, 26.

[125] William Read to Jacob Read, July 10, 1795, *Miscellaneous Manuscripts*, NYPL.

[126] James Simons to Jacob Read, August 21, 1795, *Miscellaneous Manuscripts*, NC Archives.

[127] James Simons to Jacob Read, June 22, 1797, *Miscellaneous Manuscripts*, NYPL.

[128] Charles Pinckney to Thomas Jefferson, May 26, 1801, *Jefferson Papers*, LC.

interest among the merchants in behalf of their candidate Colonel John Mitchell. Stephen Drayton's friends had written Izard to use his influence for Drayton, but, as Izard wrote Manigault, the principal merchants wanted Colonel Mitchell and he would conform with their wishes.[129] William Smith was one of Mitchell's supporters. He wrote on March 3, 1790, to Judge Grimké (Grimké had written in behalf of Colonel Mitchell) that his recommendations would add weight "to those of the merchants which have been sent to me & which I have laid before the President. I believe the impressions on the President's mind are not the most favorable from a recollection of the Colonel's conduct some years ago at Philadelphia upon his abandonment of his wife, a measure which a man so uxorious and domestic as the President does not approve of." Smith had tried to remove these impressions "by assurances that the Col. was considerably reformed . . . & stated that the most reputable merchants approved of the appointment."[130] All this activity was for nothing, however, for Weyman recovered in 1790, and Mitchell did not get the job. When Weyman died in 1793, his son received the appointment.[131]

Although Smith had some influence in the customs service through his brother-in-law Colonel Motte, the naval officer, he had more over the excise service. The customs service was set up at the very beginning of Washington's administration, before William Smith had "learned the ropes" of the new federal government. The excise service was set up by an act of 1791.[132] Customs duties were collected only at ports of entry, while the excise was collected through the length and breadth of the land. The excise service was, therefore, more numerous than the customs service and permitted an extension of governmental influence into the backcountry, but it was not as well paid. In 1800 there were sixteen supervisors of the excise, twenty-two inspectors of surveys, three hundred twenty-one collectors of revenue, and one hundred auxiliary officers in the United States.[133] South Carolina had a supervisor, three inspectors of the surveys, and a host of collectors and auxiliary officers.

Daniel Stevens was the first supervisor. Smith's interest in Stevens

[129] Ralph Izard to Gabriel Manigault, February 19, 20, 1790, *Izard Papers*, SCL.
[130] William Smith to Judge Grimké, March 3, 1790, *Emmet Collection*, NYPL.
[131] *City Gazette and Daily Advertiser*, January 9, 1793.
[132] White, *op. cit.*, pp. 200-201.
[133] *Ibid.*, p. 336.

can be seen in the following letter to Treasury Secretary Oliver Wolcott, which he wrote in behalf of Stevens, who wanted to succeed Captain Blake as superintendent of the lighthouse: "The trouble and attention to it will not be great and the emoluments may in some small measure assist in making up the deficiency of his present compensation, as Supervisor. As I have a great regard for Mr. Stevens and know him to be an excellent officer and good federal citizen, I request you will recommend him to the President."[134] Stevens not only got this job, but was soon asking to be paid for a third. As inspector of survey number one, he thought he was clearly entitled to receive—in addition to his salary as supervisor—the same emolument as the inspectors of surveys two and three. He explained that he was the officer "who had carried the Excise Law fully into effect notwithstanding the difficulties I have had in Organizing that System, and encountering the prejudices of the people against it, and in bringing order out of confusion by a firm and steady conduct—in which I may with truth say, I have borne the heat and burden of the day."[135] Daniel Stevens served William Smith, as James Simons later served Jacob Read.

The post office was the most far-flung of the federal field services. In 1790 there were seventy-five post offices; in 1800 there were nine hundred three.[136] Leonard White has written that there was "little evidence of political affiliation" in the appointments of postmasters, yet he emphasizes that the merchants were always considered.[137] Timothy Pickering, United States postmaster from 1791 to 1795, certainly took into consideration the recommendations of merchants when making appointments. Pickering removed the postmaster of Salem, Massachusetts, when the merchants objected to him. In the letter of dismissal Pickering said: "You cannot be uninformed of the prevailing wishes of the merchants in Salem to have a person appointed to succeed you in the P. Office. The merchants support the Department: because all correspondence yielding postage is chiefly amongst them. The merchants therefore must be accommo-

---

[134] William Smith to Oliver Wolcott, September 8, 1795, *Wolcott Papers,* CHS. Stevens had been appointed supervisor of the excise in 1791. *See* Daniel Stevens to Thomas Jefferson, April 1791, *Miscellaneous Letters, Department of State,* National Archives.

[135] Daniel Stevens to Oliver Wolcott, January 21, 1797, *Wolcott Papers,* CHS. In 1796 Stevens introduced Benjamin Cudworth, inspector of revenue for survey no. 2, as "a steady supporter of the Federal Government." Daniel Stevens to George Washington, August 27, 1796, *Miscellaneous Letters, Department of State,* National Archives.

[136] White, *op. cit.,* p. 178.

[137] *Ibid.,* p. 179.

dated."[138] Thomas Hall, who had been postmaster since July 1783, was reappointed on February 16, 1790, but when Hall resigned in 1794 the Charleston appointment went to Thomas Wright Bacot, whose father lived at Cherry Hill on Goose Creek.[139] In his letter of appointment, Pickering wrote: "The warm recommendation of my nephews—the perfect concurrence of Mr. Izard with their opinion of your merit, and the very respectable testimony of the Merchants of the first eminence in Charles town in your favor, determine me to offer you the post office in that city."[140] In 1796 when Bacot petitioned Congress for increased financial help, he indicated that his chief duty was to serve the merchants. "Your Petitioner begs to observe, that Charleston being a considerable commercial city, where an extensive trade is carried on and regular attendance obliged to be given at the office: and that two persons are absolutely necessary to conduct the business, with the occasional assistance of a third. And that your petitioner is obliged to keep his office in the mercantile part of city, where rents are extraordinarily dear, and are constantly encreasing. . . ." Therefore he wanted provision for an assistant, office rent, or other compensation.[141]

There was one other important group in Charleston that had considerable claims upon the federal government to patronage—the partners in the house of Smiths, DeSaussure, and Darrell. And they were not forgotten. When the national bank was established by Hamilton, the Charleston branch was firmly in the hands of this house. Daniel DeSaussure was the first president of the Charleston branch, Josiah Smith, its first and only cashier, and Edward Darrell, a director. Since William Smith was the only South Carolinian among the first directors of the parent bank in Philadelphia, he was obviously the channel through which bank patronage flowed. This group of native-born merchants reaped further rewards, when the son of Daniel DeSaussure was made director of the mint.

The mint was an institution that fell halfway between Jefferson's department and Hamilton's, and its history reveals the differences in Jeffersonian and Hamiltonian appointments.[142] Jefferson's first

[138] Quoted in *ibid.*, p. 181.

[139] *Year Book, 1883, City of Charleston*, p. 458. William Smith practiced law with H. H. Bacot, the brother of Thomas Wright Bacot, after Smith's return from Europe in 1803. *See* David Campbell to Smith and Bacot, June 29, 1805, *William Loughton Smith Papers*, SCHS.

[140] Quoted in White, *op. cit.*, p. 179.

[141] "Petition of Thomas Wright Bacot to the United States Senate," November 1796, *Various, Senate Papers*, National Archives.

[142] White, *op. cit.*, pp. 140-142.

director of the mint was David Rittenhouse, despite the fact that he had once written Rittenhouse that there was "an order of geniusses" above the obligation to be employed in civil government, and that "no body can conceive that nature ever intended to throw away a Newton upon the occupations of a crown."[143] Jefferson did just that, for the philosophic talents of Rittenhouse were lost on government service and he failed as an administrator. Both Hamilton and William Smith were to agree that the philosopher had no place in government.[144]

When Washington looked for a successor to Rittenhouse in 1795, he selected Henry William DeSaussure.[145] The change from the philosopher to the son of a merchant augured well for the mint. DeSaussure at once drew up a memorandum of suggestions for improving the output: copper might be bought more economically if the mint were permitted to import sheet copper, and since the workmen engaged in melting and refining the metal worked in too small an area, a small lot adjacent to the mint might be purchased so that the work area could be expanded and efficiency increased.[146] DeSaussure had been in office only four months when domestic and personal reasons forced him to return to Charleston. Yet much had been done. He wrote Senator Jacob Read: "I have the pleasure of leaving it pretty well organized—and after demonstrating that much may be done in it—as much has been coined within the last 4 months as in all the preceding period of its establishment." DeSaussure charitably expressed the opinion that it was the poor health of "the able Mr. Rittenhouse," that had kept him from acting with energy.[147] Washington sent DeSaussure a final letter assuring him

[143] Thomas Jefferson to David Rittenhouse, July 19, 1778, *The Papers of Thomas Jefferson*, ed. Julian P. Boyd, Princeton, 1950, II, 202-203.

[144] Alexander Hamilton to George Washington, January 31, 1795, *The Works of Alexander Hamilton*, ed. John C. Hamilton, New York, 1851, V, 70-72. [William Smith], *The Pretensions of Thomas Jefferson to the Presidency Examined; and the Charges against John Adams Refuted. Addressed to the Citizens of America in general; and particularly to the Electors of the President*, n. p., 1796, pp. 1, 14, 16.

[145] Henry William DeSaussure (1763-1839) was an important figure in the Federalist party from this date. Leonard White was unaware that he was a director of the mint. James H. Easterby, "Henry William DeSaussure," *DAB*. Another South Carolinian, Nicholas Everleigh, a merchant, was comptroller of the mint. He died in 1791 and his widow married Edward Rutledge. *City Gazette*, April 29, 1791, October 30, 1792.

[146] Henry William DeSaussure to Edmund Randolph, July 14, 1795, *Miscellaneous Letters, Department of State*, National Archives.

[147] Henry William DeSaussure to Jacob Read, October 24, 1795, *Miscellaneous Manuscripts*, NYPL. Henry William DeSaussure to George Washington, September 7, 1795, *Miscellaneous Letters, Department of State*, National Archives.

"that your conduct therein gave entire satisfaction. . . ."[148] The mint was then turned over to Elias Boudinot, the staunch Federalist merchant and manufacturer from New Jersey.

The story of federal patronage in South Carolina in the 1790's reveals four important factions: Rutledge-Pinckney, Izard-Manigault-Smith, Read-Simons, and Smith-DeSaussure-Darrell. The Rutledge-Pinckney faction was initially the most important, and it always won the highest positions in the gift of the government; as judges and ambassadors, however, the Rutledges and the Pinckneys could not build up an army of underlings. In the beginning, the Izard-Manigault-Smith faction worked with Edward Rutledge and Charles Cotesworth Pinckney, but a split occurred in 1794 which left the former faction in the stronger position. Izard and Smith were much closer to Hamilton and his friends, who dominated the central government after Jefferson's retirement at the end of 1793. Rutledge and Pinckney refused to support Smith in the election of 1794, charging him with seeking to aggrandize his own interests. Mrs. Ralph Izard, who was very fond of her son-in-law, wrote her husband in Smith's defense:

> I think the opponents of Mr. S. might have given a more worthy reason for deserting him. It is natural for every one to wish to agrandize their own families, & friends, & those who resist such feelings must be superiorly virtuous, or very unfeeling. The first is to be desired in public life yet there are few who can attain it. Fortunately your connexions, & Mr. Smiths, & Mr. Manigaults, if united, as I hope they always will be, are sufficient to withstand any opposition.[149]

In 1794 the Izard-Manigault-Smith faction still had the support of the Charleston commercial community.

In 1795 Jacob Read entered the patronage scene. He was so avid for office that he begged Washington in a secret communication of 1791 to appoint him to John Rutledge's place on the bench of the Supreme Court.[150] His ambition often made him ridiculous. When Washington visited Charleston in 1791, Read wore his "Speaker's Gown over his Regimental Coat, when he accompanied the President to Church."[151] Once in power, Read drew his friends into

[148] George Washington to Henry William DeSaussure, November 1, 1795, *Writings of George Washington*, ed. John C. Fitzpatrick, Washington, 1940, XXXIV, 354-355.
[149] Alice Izard to Ralph Izard, December 6, 1794, *Izard Papers*, SCL.
[150] Jacob Read to George Washington, February 16, 1791, *Miscellaneous Letters, Department of State*, National Archives.
[151] Ralph Izard to Charles Cotesworth Pinckney, January 18, 1795, *Izard Papers*, SCL.

office, and the Read-Simons combination became the most powerful in the state, especially after the Izard-Manigault-Smith faction broke up, following Izard's stroke and Smith's departure for Europe in 1797. Read replaced Smith as a director of the national bank and as the confidant of Pickering, Wolcott, and James McHenry. In 1801 he himself became one of the "midnight judges."[152]

The members of the fourth faction, Smith-DeSaussure-Darrell, were not so much interested in holding political office as in marshaling the support of native-born merchants for the administration, or more specifically first for Izard and Smith and then for Read and Simons.

The agencies of the federal government, such as the judiciary, the foreign service, the customs service, the excise service, the post office, the mint, and the bank, were designed primarily to serve the mercantile community. By the middle of the 1790's the two most successful politicians, William Smith and Jacob Read, had used their patronage to staff most of these positions with their friends. Smith's and Read's positions locally were bolstered by their friendship with Hamilton, Pickering, Wolcott, and McHenry.

The Rutledge-Pinckney faction by 1793 and 1794 found themselves much in the same position as Jefferson. They were uneasy in their alliance with the administration. This was due to the fact that the Rutledges and the Pinckneys were less tinctured with the commercial-financial spirit and were more truly patriotic, in the sense that they were somewhat anti-British. As the Federalist party nationally tended to break into two groups (arch-Federalists and moderate Federalists) in the middle of the decade, so it did in South Carolina. William Smith and Jacob Read were arch-Federalists; the Rutledges and the Pinckneys were moderates.

[152] Jacob Read to George Simpson, January 12, 1801, *Etting Papers*, PHS. Anne King Gregorie, "Jacob Read," *DAB*.

XI

WILLIAM SMITH, CONGRESSMAN, 1790-1793

THE SOUTH CAROLINA delegation, with the exception of Thomas Sumter, was present on the first day of the second session, January 4, 1790. On January 9 Hamilton was ready to present in person his first report on the public credit, but Congress denied him the floor, requiring that he present it in writing. As the House began to consider Hamilton's report, Smith offered five resolutions to promote orderly discussion:

> Resolved, That Congress ought not to adjourn, until they have adopted such measures as will make an adequate provision for the public debt.
>
> Resolved, That in making such provision, no discrimination shall be made between the original holders of the evidences, and the assignees thereof.
>
> Resolved, That such of the debts of the individual States, as have been incurred by them, during the late war, ought to be assumed by the General Government, and like funds provided for them.
>
> Resolved, That the arrearages of interest on the Continental and State debts, ought to be funded, and consolidated with the principal.
>
> Resolved, That the interest to be paid thereon does not exceed _____ per cent. per annum, for the present.[1]

Although this set of resolutions was not adopted for discussion—a set of eight offered by Thomas Fitzsimons of Pennsylvania replaced them—these represent the major points that were to be taken up in turn by the House.[2]

The first question was whether to fund the debt or pay it off entirely. Smith favored funding as a temporary measure. Others feared that funding would saddle the people with a permanent debt, and therefore they favored paying it off as quickly as possible. Jackson of Georgia marshaled Blackstone and Adam Smith as authorities opposed to a standing debt, but Smith rebutted that those authorities had made a distinction between large and small debts and said that "funding a small debt" was "beneficial."[3] Blackstone had been "writing of an enormous public debt when he mentions it as injurious, because he expressly says, that 'a certain proportion of debt

---

[1] *Annals of the Congress of the United States,* Washington, 1834, I (1st cong., 2nd sess.), 1131.
[2] *Ibid.,* p. 1139.
[3] *Ibid.,* p. 1143.

seems to be highly useful to a trading people; but what proportion that is, it is not for me to determine.' To be sure he adds, afterwards, 'that the present magnitude of our national incumbrances very far exceeds all calculations of commercial benefit, and is productive of the greatest inconveniences.' And here I agree with him: but our public debt is not of such enormous magnitude as to counterbalance the good effects of throwing out such a quantity of a stable paper as will answer all the purposes of a circulating medium."[4] According to Smith, a small debt properly funded would aid the commercial community, and the House agreed with him.

After the decision to fund the debt had been reached, Madison introduced the idea of discriminating between the original holders of securities and the assignees thereof. Smith had disapproved of discrimination in his resolutions, but both Burke and Tucker favored Madison's suggestion.[5]

On February 15 Hamilton's supporters unleashed their heavy artillery. Speeches by Sedgwick, John Laurance of New York, Smith, and Ames took up the entire day. The Senate adjourned early in order to attend the debates, and even Maclay, the ardent republican, said that "they seemed to aim all at one point, to make Madison ridiculous."[6] Smith would not argue the feasibility of the measure, but insisted on arguing the principle. Whatever might be the merits of the original holders (war-time service) or the sins of the present holders (speculation), it was not the business of government to interpose. These were contracts that must be paid as far as the public resources would extend. "The purchaser bought under the act of Congress, making the securities transferable; and having given the market price, without fraud or imposition, he was, by virtue of such purchase, vested with the complete and absolute ownership of the certificate, as fully as the original holder; and had as much right to demand full payment as the original holder would have had, had the security been still in his hands." Discrimination would be a violation of a sacred contract and would check the negotiability of public securities in the future; it would enhance the terms of future loans and would thereby injure public credit. "Who would purchase, when he had before his eyes the terror of a discrimination?" The entire argument was buttressed by the fundamental belief that

---

[4] *Ibid.*, II (1st cong., 2nd sess.), 1175.
[5] *Ibid.*, pp. 1179-1182.
[6] *Journal of William Maclay*, ed. Edgar S. Maclay, New York, 1890, p. 197.

"the right of property is a sacred right."[7] Smith's argument persuaded Burke to cast his vote against discrimination even though he knew that pilot boats were secretly being sent from New York to Charleston by speculators, "while the people there were asleep, as it were."[8] The vote was thirty-six to thirteen against Madison's motion for discrimination.[9]

On the next question, whether the federal government should assume state debts, Smith and Burke worked hand in hand. South Carolina and Massachusetts were the two states with the largest debts, and their delegates led the crusade for assumption. When states pointed out as Virginia did that they had paid off a great part of their own debt, implying thereby that assumption would be unfair, Smith replied: "The states which made the greatest exertions during the war, were unequal to great exertions after the return of peace; while those states that had exerted themselves least during that dreadful conflict, were best able to exert themselves after its termination; so that, at the present moment, it is fairly presumable the exertion has equalized itself throughout the United States."[10]

South Carolina had imposed taxes from 1784 to 1789 totalling "above 300,000 dollars annually" to pay interest on the debt contracted by the war. The state issued indents in payment of the interest, and made them receivable in payment of duties. This gave them circulation and kept up their value. They depreciated only twelve or thirteen per cent in 1784 and 1785, but the state's distress since that time—caused by the expense and ruin of war, the great load of private debts, and the crop failures—had caused an amazing depreciation in these securities. At the last session of the legislature, no provision was made for them. During the same period $1,500,000 of the principal of the debt had been sunk by sales of land and the collection of taxes. Smith intimated that the state could have paid off her debt by using the confiscated estates but at the request of Congress she had returned most of these. Congress had precluded her paying; it was Congress's duty to assist South Carolina now. Actually the debt had been contracted to assist the weak Confederacy, and Carolinians felt that the strong Union should help by reassuming the burden.[11] When some suggested cutting down the

[7] *Annals of the Congress of the United States,* Washington, 1834, II (1st cong., 2nd sess.), 1211-1216.
[8] *Ibid.,* p. 1294.
[9] *Ibid.,* p. 1298.
[10] *Ibid.,* pp. 1356-1357.
[11] *Ibid.,* pp. 1322-1324, 1356-1360, 1517-1519.

size of the sum assumed for South Carolina, especially by referring to the voyages of the frigate *South Carolina* as "a balloon expedition," Burke came to Smith's aid with his version of the frigate episode. He told how indigo shipped abroad to pay for building the frigate had fallen into British hands and how Gillon and Izard had then been forced to pledge their private fortunes to build it.[12] Ames, also coming to the defense of South Carolina, pointed out that Carolina had had little cause for complaint against Great Britain, yet had come into the Revolution anyway. Many considered this a remarkable admission for a Yankee.[13] When the vote was taken on assumption on April 15, Smith and Burke were in the minority of twenty-three, with Tucker and Sumter in the majority of thirty-three, opposed to assumption.[14] The question of assumption was not taken up again in the House until the Senate returned the bill with an amendment recommending assumption.

In the meantime, there was much discussion on where the permanent seat of government should be located. The discussion on this question went back to the previous session when a resolution had been passed asserting that the permanent seat should be near the center of wealth, population, and territory, as far as this would be consistent with convenience of navigation of the Atlantic Ocean and with due regard for the approaches to the western country. At that time the four South Carolinians preferred the north bank of the Potomac to the east bank of the Susquehannah, the two major alternatives.[15] A new consideration was introduced in the second session when the Quakers of Philadelphia, through their society for promoting the abolition of slavery, presented a petition against the slave trade. It was signed by Benjamin Franklin, "a man who ought to have known the Constitution better," as Tucker said.[16] The South Carolina delegation, shoulder to shoulder, fought this threat and in doing so became suspicious of Philadelphia as the home of the new government.[17] Burke charged the Quakers with being spies, profiteers, and tories—and was called to order.[18]

[12] *Ibid.*, pp. 1484-1486.

[13] *Ibid.*, p. 1368.

[14] *Ibid.*, p. 1530. Thomas Sumter had taken his seat on March 1. *Ibid.*, p. 1377. Smith warmed to Burke during the course of this debate. William Smith to Judge Grimké, March 3, 1790, *Emmet Collection*, NYPL.

[15] *Annals of the Congress of the United States*, Washington, 1834, I (1st cong., 1st sess.), 786, 851, 881.

[16] *Ibid.*, II (1st cong., 2nd sess.), 1198.

[17] Burke, Huger, Smith, and Tucker all voted against referring the memorials. *Ibid.*, p. 1205.

[18] *Ibid.*, pp. 1662-1663.

Smith also launched into a long and vitriolic harangue. He queried: "Why did not they leave that, which they call God's work, to be managed by Himself?" He threw out that oft-repeated question: "Had any of them ever married a negro?" He was very caustic: "We took each other, with our mutual bad habits and respective evils, for better, for worse; the Northern States adopted us with our slaves, and we adopted them with their Quakers." He was realistic: his state needed slaves. Had not Great Britain failed in her attempt to settle Georgia by whites alone? He was mercenary: New England benefited from South Carolina's 140,000 slaves; she stood to gain $350,000 by supplying five yards of cloth for each at fifty cents a yard. He was historical: the French and the Spaniards, the Romans and the Greeks, had all had slaves and yet had been civilized nations. Smith certainly did not wish to see the government lodged amid a band of Quakers.[19]

Smith, by conferring with Izard constantly, had kept track of the assumption scheme as it passed through the Senate. Robert Morris of Pennsylvania, Philip Schuyler of New York, and Rufus King of New York ("members who are said to be deeply interested") would not consent to assumption unless the continental debt was funded at six per cent, instead of four per cent. Oliver Ellsworth of Connecticut, Caleb Strong of Massachusetts, and others would not agree to assumption if more than four per cent were given to the continental lenders. Butler, who was at first completely opposed to funding, threw his support to the extremists. Izard was neutral, willing to go for any group that would favor assumption. This was the gloomy state of things on July 13.[20]

On the morning of the 14th, Smith and Izard walked to Federal Hall together and on meeting Hamilton learned of a compromise that he had just achieved. The principal of the public debt was to be funded at six per cent (that is, two-thirds funded at six per cent and the remainder at the end of seven years); the arrears of interest including the indents on the said domestic debt would be funded at three per cent. The amount assumed from the states would be assumed on the basis of two-thirds as contained in the alternative above and one-third at three per cent.[21] This finally passed the Senate on July 21 by a vote of fourteen to twelve.[22]

[19] *Ibid.*, pp. 1453-1464.
[20] William Smith to Edward Rutledge, July 14, 17, 1790, *Pinckney Papers,* LC.
[21] *Ibid.*
[22] Both Butler and Izard were in the majority. *Annals of the Congress of the United States,* Washington, 1834, I (1st cong., 2nd sess.), 1016.

On the 24th, a House resolution to disagree with the Senate's scheme was defeated by a vote.of thirty-two to twenty-nine, with Smith, Burke, and Tucker in the majority and Sumter in the minority.[23] Jefferson then agreed to let the assumption go through in return for the promise that after a ten-year interval in Philadelphia the national capital would be permanently located on the banks of the Potomac. Smith, who ardently opposed leaving New York for Philadelphia, felt that the bait of the Potomac had taken in a few.[24]

DID WILLIAM SMITH, in voting for funding and assumption, act in his own interest, or in behalf of his friends, or of his mercantile supporters, or of the state and nation? These are questions that have been relevant to any discussion of the Federalist party ever since Beard published his famous work in 1913.[25] The answer can never be unequivocal. A man can act solely in his own interest and good can flow to the nation; a man can also act for the best interests of his state and nation and thereby indirectly benefit himself. This is a matter of degree. Undoubtedly the funding scheme established the public credit and was therefore beneficial to the nation; it also very definitely enriched speculators. How did Smith fit into the picture?

Was there speculation in the domestic national debt held by South Carolinians? Was there speculation in the state debt of South Carolina that was later assumed by the nation? The answer is yes in both instances, although there was relatively more speculation in the latter than in the former. South Carolina and Massachusetts had the largest outstanding state debts in 1790, so there was bound to be more speculation there than in other states. South Carolina's location, away from the center of decision and information, afforded more opportunity for unscrupulous speculators to exploit the ignorance and poverty of her average citizen.

The two great speculators of the day were William Duer and Andrew Craigie, whose tangled operations can be unraveled by studying the Duer Papers in the New York Historical Society and the Craigie Papers in the American Antiquarian Society.[26] In 1788 Duer and Craigie tried to set up an international pool to exploit the

[23] *Ibid.*, II (1st cong., 2nd sess.), 1710-1711.
[24] William Smith to Edward Rutledge, July 14, 17, 1790, *Pinckney Papers*, LC.
[25] Charles A. Beard, *An Economic Interpretation of the Constitution of the United States*, New York, 1954.
[26] *Duer Papers*, NYHS. *Craigie Papers*, AAS.

American debts. Dutch, Swiss, and French bankers were to supply specie to be used by Duer and Craigie and their agents in buying up the most likely debts. Duer in 1788 promised Brissot de Warville, emissary of the continental bankers, to find out the amount of the domestic national debt, by whom it was held, the current price, the manner in which interest on it would be paid, whether the states would ratify the new Constitution, and the size of the state debts. Duer and Craigie definitely bought large quantities of the American national debt in 1788, 1789, and 1790 for themselves and their foreign connections. Herman LeRoy, a New York merchant-banker with close Dutch connections, was equally busy. This activity established a market in New York for securities—the beginning, in fact, of the New York Stock Exchange—which drew into America large amounts of specie, which, as the supporters of funding argued, was at last helping to counter the constant drain of specie to Europe. Funding acted as a magnet for European capital vitally needed to spark the infant American economy.[27]

Did any of this specie find its way to South Carolina, a state in great need of it? The answer is again yes, and the evidence is found in the Duer and Craigie Papers. Agents did go south in pilot-boats and sent large sums of continental and state paper back to those for whom they acted. William Steele, sent by Duer to Charleston in March 1788, found that others had arrived before him. Adam Gilchrist, formerly a partner in New York of his brother Robert Gilchrist, was constantly purchasing continental securities, as long as New York prices justified such purchases. South Carolina debt certificates were scarce in 1788; the legislature had agreed once more to pay interest on state notes granted to soldiers and officers: "This has greatly enhanced their value and determined the holders of them to keep them."[28]

In 1789 Duer sent George Reid to Charleston with twelve hogsheads of rum and ten pipes of Teneriffe wine which Reid was unable to sell immediately because of a temporary glut. Instead of storing the spirits in a warehouse, he rented a shop and opened for business, explaining to Duer that this would give him a better chance to speculate, for the store would serve as a blind.[29]

Andrew Craigie sent Leonard Bleecker to Charleston in Decem-

---

[27] Joseph Stancliffe Davis, "William Duer, Entrepreneur, 1747-99," *Harvard Economic Studies*, Cambridge, 1917, XVI, 151-173.

[28] William Steele to William Duer, March 13, 1788, *Duer Papers*, NYHS.

[29] George Reid to William Duer, April 27, 1789, *Duer Papers*, NYHS.

ber 1789. Bleecker "providentially" bunked in the same stateroom
with a Mr. Pomeroy who, he discovered, was on a similar mission to
Charleston. After a bit of pumping, Bleecker found out that Pomeroy would have the assistance of "two respectable houses" in
Charleston. Neither would tell the other for whom he was acting,
but they did decide it would be better to cooperate than to
work against each other and thereby drive up prices. Both men
carried drafts on the collector of customs in Charleston. Bleecker's
draft was collected by Robert Hazlehurst, who after charging a
commission of two and a half per cent made the sums (about
$5,000) available to Bleecker. Bleecker also had bills of exchange
drawn by Wm. Constable and Co. of New York on London, which
could only be converted into funds in Charleston if endorsed by a
reputable merchant. Hazlehurst endorsed the bills for Bleecker,
once again charging a two and a half per cent commission. On
consulting Hazlehurst about the local market, Bleecker and Pomeroy
were urged to work through the house of Colcock and Graham.
Meanwhile, Pomeroy went off to Savannah to see what he could
do there.[30]

Bleecker in his first analysis for Craigie certainly underestimated
the extent of speculation in Charleston. "There are no persons here
who make a business in the certificate line, and in general they seem
possessed of as little knowledge of the state of their funds, and of
less enterprise in speculation, than any people that I am acquainted
with." The atmosphere was different from New York, but, as
Bleecker soon learned, much went on behind the scenes. The price
at that time for continental debt was 6/- on the principal and 3/3
to 3/6 on the interest, in Carolina currency, which was at a twelve
and a half per cent discount, but none was available. The local
people seemed ignorant of Pickering's notes, new emission money,
and treasury warrants, types of continental debt then being bought
and sold in New York.[31]

The South Carolina debt fell under two heads: principal indents
issued for various services and supplies, and special indents issued
for interest on them. The principal was then selling at ten to one;
the special indents had been issued annually and, except for the
current year, had been made receivable for taxes and were then

[30] Leonard Bleecker to Andrew Craigie, December 15, 1789, *Craigie Papers*,
AAS.
[31] *Ibid.* For an explanation of why there was little of the continental debt in
South Carolina *see* E. James Ferguson, *The Power of the Purse*, Chapel Hill.
1961, pp. 182-187.

selling at one-third the nominal value. Bleecker was not happy with his prospects, for he wrote on December 21, 1789: "I must confess sir, I feel almost discouraged at appearances here, and unless you think proper for me, to enter upon the purchase of the state debt, I think it will not pay expences to continue here; and in that case beg to suggest to you the propriety of returning the next voyage with Capt. Snell, unless Mr. Pomeroy is very successful at Savannah."[32]

With the return of Snell (whose craft must have been the pilot boat so often referred to in the accounts of the day) Bleecker was instructed to buy the state debt. Had the New Yorkers gotten word of assumption? The price was suddenly up—from eleven and fourteen to one on principal indents when he had arrived, to ten to one when he last wrote, to eight or seven to one in mid-January. When he asked Colcock and Graham to purchase $5,000, he found that they were commissioned to purchase £30- to £40,000 at nine to one with a five per cent commission for their trouble. With fine rice crops flowing to market, the local people were in funds and holding on to their paper.[33] On January 23, after having received more instructions to buy the state debt, Bleecker wrote: "It was a very unfavorable circumstance that you had not sooner concluded to purchase the state debt. The holders in town, generally keep it up with the expectation that Congress will assume the payment of it, and fund it as the United States debt: what foundation there is for such an opinion; you, as being at the seat of government, may best determine. The result of this general sentiment is, that persons are here from N. York and Philadelphia not only, but four persons citizens in this place, are also engaged in purchasing it, and at present there is great demand for it at about one ninth in specie." In spite of the competition, Bleecker reported that he had bought $7,000. He said he would continue to purchase through a person in the country and another in town. Although the legislature had refused to issue special indents that year, the price still kept up, which could only mean that people expected Congress to assume the debts of the states. As for continental paper, there was little activity. He had thought of trying Wilmington, but understood from a man who had just arrived that $150 could not be laid out there.[34] North Carolina was also being combed by speculators.

[32] Leonard Bleecker to Andrew Craigie, December 21, 1789, *Craigie Papers,* AAS.
[33] Leonard Bleecker to Andrew Craigie, January 8, 1790, *Craigie Papers,* AAS.
[34] Leonard Bleecker to Andrew Craigie, January 23, 1790, *Craigie Papers,* AAS.

The market for South Carolina state debt had its ups and downs during the first six months of 1790. This fluctuation was caused by the changing votes in Congress. In February there was a possibility of assumption; in April defeat; yet in the summer hopes rose again. In March, Andrew Craigie got scared and wrote his agent to sell $40,000 worth of South Carolina debt at one-fifth, if he could.[35] Théophile Cazenove, acting for his Dutch backers, bought $100,000 worth of South Carolina debt in April.[36] These sums may well have been purchased from men like Craigie. William Duer apparently continued to buy.[37] A Major Haskell left England in the spring of 1790 with £10,000 sterling, reached South Carolina in June, and speculated heavily in state debt.[38] In July, tension mounted as each day brought a new rumor concerning Congress's intentions. Should one buy or should one sell? At the very last moment Craigie unloaded more of his holdings. Théophile Cazenove, who continued to buy through the agency of Herman LeRoy, was the lucky man.[39]

When the books were opened for the subscribers to the new national debt, the names of South Carolinians did not figure largely. The story was quite different for the state debt of South Carolina. The subscribers of sums over $10,000.00 were as follows:

LeRoy and Bayard of New York	$395,386.01
Abijah Hammond of New York	131,794.79
John Edwards and Co. of Charleston	114,325.20
George Lewis of New York	105,545.93
H. M. Bird of London	103,027.83
Richard Puller of London	100,084.26
Daniel Badcock of New York	99,182.32
George Service of New York	96,141.78
Gustavus Calhoun of Charleston	85,892.60
Andrew Craigie of Boston	82,034.03
Henry Laurens of Charleston	79,291.37
Nicholas Low of New York	54,037.41
Robert Gilchrist of New York	49,510.77
Adam Gilchrist of Charleston	47,026.32
John Splatt Cripps of Charleston	43,466.91
Edwards, Fisher and Co. of Charleston	43,211.06
Nathaniel Russell of Charleston	39,565.81
Gabriel Manigault of Charleston	36,610.86

[35] Andrew Craigie to Horace Johnson, March 3, 1790, *Craigie Papers*, AAS.
[36] Davis, *op. cit.*, p. 193.
[37] William Duer to George Reid, April 4, 1790; George Reid to Walter Livingston, May 28, 1790, *Duer Papers*, NYHS.
[38] Andrew Craigie to Horace Johnson, April 17, 1790, *Craigie Papers*, AAS. *Also see* Andrew Craigie to Major Haskell, June 30, 1790, *Craigie Papers*, AAS.
[39] Andrew Craigie to Samuel Rogers, August 18, 1790, *Craigie Papers*, AAS.

William Rogers of New York	36,121,96
Rawlins Lowndes of Charleston	35,805.31
Horace and Seth Johnson of New York	34,313.29
Josiah Smith of Charleston	31,926.61
John Moultrie, junior, of London	30,861.28
Edward Darrell of Charleston	25,310.99
John Champneys of Charleston	23,303.41
Joseph Barrall of Boston	19,899.18
Philip Guillaume Chion of Charleston	18,480.90
Ralph Izard of Charleston	18,159.13
James Poyas of London	15,185.47
Nicholas Brown of Providence	14,972.01
Ebenezer Thayer, junior, of Charleston	14,812.16
Isaac Motte of Charleston	12,787.86
William Smith of Charleston	11,910.70
Charles Cotesworth Pinckney of Charleston	10,865.30
Benjamin Savage of London	10,473.26
Thayer, Bartlett and Co. of Charleston	10,163.30[40]

This list can be broken down into two general categories: the northern and English speculators, who were the most important group, and the Charlestonians. Not one South Carolinian living outside Charleston subscribed as much as $10,000.

First among the Charlestonians were the members of the house of Smiths, DeSaussure, and Darrell. Josiah Smith was down for $31,926, Edward Darrell for $25,310, and Daniel DeSaussure for $3,427. It should be noted, however, that this firm acted as attorneys for London men. H. M. Bird and Benjamin' Savage, partners in Bird, Savage, and Bird, were down for $103,027 and $10,473 respectively. John Savage, Benjamin's father, held $8,629.[41] Furthermore, Josiah Smith had long acted as attorney for John Moultrie, junior, and James Poyas. Moultrie was a grandson of George Austin, a large part of whose estate had been locked up in the state funds. Josiah Smith had also placed a large portion of Poyas's funds in the state treasury during the Revolution.[42]

Another group directly interested in the assumption of the state debt was the Izard-Manigault-Smith faction. Izard was down for

[40] *Ledger for Assumed Debt*, National Archives, vol. 1258, *passim*.
[41] *See* John Savage's power of attorney in *Miscellaneous Records*, SC Archives, XVIII, 350-351. Bird was in Charleston in January 1790. H. M. Bird to George Washington, January 23, 1790, *Miscellaneous Letters, Department of State*, National Archives.
[42] Moultrie lived at Aston Hall in Shropshire, the old home of George Austin. "The Moultries of South Carolina," *SCHGM*, V (1904), 247-249. Josiah Smith, junior, to George Appleby, June 5, 1783, March 30, 1784; Josiah Smith, junior, to James Poyas, January 31, 1784, *Josiah Smith, junior, Letter-Book, 1771-1784*, SHC.

$18,159, Manigault for $36,610, and Smith for $11,910. Closely linked with these gentlemen were Smith's brother-in-law Colonel Isaac Motte, who held $12,787, and John Splatt Cripps, to whom Smith had turned over the management of the Barnard Elliott estate, who held $43,466.

None of these Charlestonians was necessarily a speculator. Josiah Smith, Gabriel Manigault, and William Smith had themselves loaned, or their guardians had loaned, large sums to the state during the Revolution. They were merely getting back, therefore, what they had loaned with interest. Even Londoners Moultrie and Poyas were not speculators. However, there were some Charlestonians connected with northern speculators. Nathaniel Russell and Thayer, Bartlett and Co. kept their Rhode Island friends informed.[43] The brothers Robert and Adam Gilchrist spanned the New York-Charleston financial communities.[44] John Edwards and Co., Edwards, Fisher, and Co., and Gustavus Calhoun had important Philadelphia connections.[45] Among the other Charlestonians listed were John Champneys, a former loyalist, and Philip Guillaume Chion, who had come from Holland.[46] Henry Laurens and Rawlins Lowndes simply represented themselves or the local firms for which they had acted.[47]

It should be noted that the Rutledge-Pinckney coalition had very little capital invested in the state debt. Charles Cotesworth Pinckney was listed for $10,865 and Edward Rutledge for $1,331. Both John Rutledge and Charles Cotesworth Pinckney had favored the assumption of state debts at the time of the Constitutional Convention, but both had also explicitly stated that they favored discriminating

[43] See letters referred to by George Rogers Taylor, "Wholesale Commodity Prices at Charleston, South Carolina, 1732-1791," *Journal of Economic and Business History*, IV (1931-1932), 368-369, n. 3.

[44] Adam Gilchrist, for thirty years a Charleston merchant, married a daughter of Dr. John Budd in 1784. "Marriage and Death Notices from the *South-Carolina Weekly Gazette*," *SCHGM*, XIX (1918), 77. He died in Charleston in 1816. "Inscriptions from the Independent or Congregational (Circular) Church Yard," *SCHGM*, XXXVIII (1937), 144.

[45] Edwards, Fisher and Company was the firm of John Edwards, I, who died in Philadelphia in 1781. John Edwards and Co. was undoubtedly the firm of John Edwards, II (1760-1798). Mary Pringle Fenhagen, "John Edwards and Some of His Descendants," *SCHGM*, LV (1954), 15-22. For Calhoun see *Letter Book of Nalbro' Frazier, 1783-1799*, NYPL, *passim*.

[46] Champneys received a special exemption from the act of confiscation and banishment in 1789. *SC Statutes*, V, 94. Champneys became a citizen on March 25, 1789. John Francis Chion, the son of Philip Guillaume Chion, "late of the United Province of Holland," became a citizen on June 15, 1789. *Miscellaneous Records*, S. C. Archives, book Q, pp. 54, 56.

[47] Laurens held $10,000 for himself and the rest for the creditors of Hawkins, Petrie and Co. and for the estate of James Laurens.

between the original holders and speculators. On this point Smith was at odds with the Rutledges and the Pinckneys. It is quite obvious that the factions of Izard-Manigault-Smith 'and Smith-DeSaussure-Darrell, although the members themselves were original holders and therefore not speculators, were more closely linked in interest to northern and English moneyed men than were the Rutledges and the Pinckneys. This is another important distinction which sets off the arch-Federalists in South Carolina from the moderate Federalists.

In discussing the role of William Smith in the funding scheme there is one other angle that must be considered. Although Smith was an original holder, he might also have engaged in undercover speculation through New York agents, perhaps through LeRoy and Bayard. Did William Smith ever use his official position in Congress to secure information which would have permitted him to speculate successfully? Of the three factions, the Izard-Manigault-Smith faction was the best situated to take advantage of prior knowledge obtained at the center of government. With Izard in the Senate, Smith in the House, and Manigault in the state legislature, the team was in an enviable position. Charges were made, most specifically against Smith. Jefferson in his letters as well as in the *Anas* made allusions to Smith's interests.[48] John Taylor named him in 1794 as one of "a faction of monarchic speculators."[49] James T. Callender made the most direct accusation in a pamphlet of 1798: "By purchasing certificates with one hand, and making laws with the other they could accumulate, as William Smith actually did, an enormous fortune."[50]

There can be no doubt that the Izard-Manigault-Smith team worked for assumption. Izard wrote Manigault on December 19, 1789, urging him to work for a vote in the state legislature approving assumption of the state debts.[51] During the time of the funding discussion in Congress both Izard and Smith kept Manigault informed of the votes; as Izard said in one letter: "I know it is of

[48] With reference to the assumption, Jefferson wrote: "The eastern members particularly, who, with Smith from South Carolina, were the principal gamblers in these scenes, threatened a secession and dissolution." "The Anas," *The Writings of Thomas Jefferson,* ed. H. A. Washington, Washington, 1854, IX, 93. *Also see* a list of "paper men" communicated to Jefferson by Beckley, dated March 23, 1793, *Jefferson Papers,* LC.

[49] [John Taylor,] *An Examination of the Late Proceedings in Congress, Respecting the Official Conduct of the Secretary of Treasury,* [1793,] p. 11.

[50] James Thomson Callender, *Sedgwick & Co. or a Key to the Six Per Cent Cabinet,* Philadelphia, 1798, p. 13.

[51] Ralph Izard to Gabriel Manigault, December 19, 1789, *Izard Papers,* SCL.

considerable importance to you."[52] When the battle was over and the victory won, Smith wrote: "I have pleasure in congratulating you on the Assumption, a measure not only beneficial to the U.S. and to So. Car. particularly, but to yourself personally, a circumstance which adds much to the satisfaction I have felt."[53] Smith was also in touch during these months with Edward Darrell, Edward Rutledge, Colonel Isaac Motte, and very closely so with David Campbell, his agent in Charleston.[54] He later defended himself against charges of speculation by pointing out that he had kept the local people informed of the votes. However, as one critic pointed out, he might have told the public rather than a few choice agents.[55] The letters to Edward Rutledge must have been a shrewd move, for they kept the Rutledges and the Pinckneys silent for four years.

No one ever denied, not even Smith himself, that he had a direct interest in assumption. He gave warning in 1788, when he was running for the House, that he was interested and that his family had invested £20,000 to £30,000 sterling in the state debt. According to David Campbell, Smith funded £2,500, his share of the family investment, plus £180 which he had received in payment on a bond, the indents having been taken at 7/6 on the pound.[56] This was presumably all that Smith had funded. If this was all, then Smith did not speculate in 1790.

Yet there is still the possibility that Smith might have speculated through northern agents. It is important to note that the largest holders of state debt were LeRoy and Bayard. They held the enormous sum of $395,386. It was known that this firm was speculating for others, particularly the Dutch, and more specifically for Theophile Cazenove.[57] They might well have been speculating for the

[52] Ralph Izard to Gabriel Manigault, February 19, 1790, *Izard Papers*, SCL. *Also see* Ralph Izard to Gabriel Manigault, October 28, 1790, *Izard Papers*, SCL.

[53] William Smith to Gabriel Manigault, August 3, 1790, "South Carolina Federalist Correspondence, 1789-1797," ed. Ulrich B. Phillips, *AHR* (1908-1909), 778-779. *Also see* William Smith to Gabriel Manigault, March 26, 1790, *ibid.*, p. 778.

[54] *See* David Campbell's letter printed in *City Gazette and Daily Advertiser*, February 2, 1793. There were two explicit warnings in William Smith to Edward Rutledge, July 14, 1790, *Pinckney Papers*, LC. The fact that this letter is found in the *Pinckney Papers* may indicate that Rutledge had passed it on to General Pinckney.

[55] *See* letter of "A Voter" in *City Gazette and Daily Advertiser*, February 1, 1793.

[56] "Sworn statement of David Campbell," January 23, 1793, printed in *ibid.*

[57] Brissot de Warville introduced Cazenove to Duer as follows: "The bearer of this letter is Mr. Casenove of Amsterdam who I mentioned to you very often—he is to settle himself in America, and I believe to make some specula-

triumvirate of Izard-Manigault-Smith. There is proof that Herman LeRoy did buy and sell stock for Smith in the years 1792 through 1796.[58] Izard did business with LeRoy during the same period.[59] Further evidence can be obtained by a close scrutiny of Gabriel Manigault's journals for his tours to the North in 1789, 1791, and 1793-1794. On the last two trips Manigault was often in the company of LeRoy, Bayard, and Cazenove. He was acquainted with all three by 1791. In 1793 and 1794, when Manigault was constantly "at the North," the connections increased until such intimacies as the following could be recorded in his journal: "We dined at Mr. Bayard's, it being his birthday. 33 yrs.—Mr. LeRoy is 2 months older than I am." The date was June 11, 1794. Not only were the connections with the New York moneyed men close, but when Smith and Manigault visited Massachusetts in the summer of 1793 they dined with Andrew Craigie at Cambridge and with Joseph Barrall at Boston; Craigie and Barrall were the two Massachusetts men most heavily involved in South Carolina debt.[60] This is circumstantial evidence. It does not prove any speculation at the time of the assumption, but it does prove that Izard and Manigault and Smith were friends of the most important northern moneyed men; they did see eye to eye with their friends on the subject of investments; and they were certainly the Charlestonians in closest touch with the northern capitalists.

The evidence points to the conclusion that in 1790 the Izard-Manigault-Smith faction did nothing more than work to redeem the state debt. No one would have considered this improper. They did not then speculate—that is, take advantage of the ignorance of others to buy up securities. However, by watching their northern friends they must have gained an appreciation of the possibilities,

---

tions in your funds. I am sure . . . you'll give him good information about his speculations." Brissot de Warville, to Col. Duer, November 27, 1789, *Duer Papers*, NYHS. William Smith referred to Cazenove as a friend in 1792. William Smith to [Herman LeRoy], June 21, 1792, *Gratz Collection*, PHS.

[58] William Smith to [Herman LeRoy], June 21, 1792, *Gratz Collection*, PHS. William Smith to Herman LeRoy, August 2, 1792, *William Loughton Smith Papers*, LC. William Smith to Herman LeRoy, February 1, 1793, *Chamberlain Collection*, BPL. William Smith to Herman LeRoy, July 15, 1796, *William Loughton Smith Papers*, DUL.

[59] Ralph Izard to Herman LeRoy, January 22, 1794, *Miscellaneous Manuscripts*, SCHS. Ralph Izard to Messrs. LeRoy and Bayard, September 18, 1794, *Gratz Collection*, PHS. Ralph Izard to Messrs. LeRoy, Bayard, and McEvers, April 28, 1796, *Izard Papers*, SCL.

[60] Gabriel Manigault, "Tour to the Northward, 1783, and again in 1789 and 1791" and "Tour to the North in 1793, & 4, and 1801 by my Father & family," *Manigault Papers*, SCL.

and the story changes in 1791 and 1792. There was certainly speculation in those years, as the facts prove. The later speculations were
read back upon the known speculations of the northern and English
moneyed men in 1790. Those who were moving into opposition to
the government in 1791 and 1792 could easily blur the picture and
believe the charges against Smith. Some of the hatred focused on
speculators in general certainly enveloped Smith.

One side of the speculation picture usually ignored is the fact
that speculation worked to the great advantage of America and
South Carolina. South Carolina had always needed specie. Edward
Rutledge and William Smith had cut off the importation of slaves
to reduce the drain. Now speculation meant an influx of specie. Did
not Major Haskell sail from London for Carolina with £10,000 in
specie which he laid out in South Carolina certificates!

WILLIAM SMITH, by the summer of 1790, had become a figure of
national prominence. He had been unknown on entering Congress,
but within a year he was a companion of Washington and the confidant of northern Federalist leaders. He was often at the President's
home: the levees on Tuesday afternoons, the dinners on Thursdays,
Mrs. Washington's "at homes" on Fridays. When the Manigaults
visited the Izards and Smiths in New York in the summer of 1789,
they all dined with the President and Mrs. Washington. Manigault
recorded the occasion:

> We dined at the President's of the United States. There were 18
> persons at Table, Ladies and Gentlemen. The President and Mrs.
> Washington sat at the middle of the table, opposite to each other,
> and the two ends were occupied by his secretary, Mr. Lear, and
> Major Jackson—The dinner was a very elegant one, of one course
> of meat, a desert, and a course of fruit, which last remained on the
> table as long as we continued at it, the cloth not being removed.
> In the middle of the Table was a surtout, according to the French
> fashion. Five servants waited, besides a Butler, all of whom gave
> the best attendance. The wines were champagne, claret, madeira,
> and frontignac. The President was very attentive, and drank wine
> with every guest at table.[61]

The young congressman and the President must have found themselves on easy and congenial terms, for Smith was on at least two
occasions a guest at Mount Vernon, the second time just after the

---

[61] Gabriel Manigault, "Tour to the Northward, 1783, and again in 1789 and
1791," *Manigault Papers*, SCL. There is an invitation to dine from Washington
in the *William Loughton Smith Papers*, RC.

death of his wife.[62] Smith was also invited to accompany Washington to Rhode Island in August 1790.

As Congress had adjourned, Smith had planned to tour New England and New York. When Washington resolved to pay a visit to Rhode Island in recognition of the state's accession to the Union and invited Smith to be of the party, he could not decline "so acceptable an invitation" and therefore merged the two expeditions.[63] The voyage was an easy one by Rhode Island packet, the *Hancock*, Captain Brown, "an agreable passage" of two days on the Sound. The visits to Newport and to Providence were in the manner of the day, as near a royal progression as America could afford. The President's suite was carefully composed to represent the various branches of government: Governor George Clinton of New York, Secretary of State Thomas Jefferson, Senator Theodore Foster of Rhode Island, Associate Justice John Blair of the Supreme Court, Congressmen William Smith and Nicholas Gilman, and the President's personal aides: Colonel David Humphreys, Major William Jackson, and Thomas Nelson, junior.[64]

The packet arrived in Newport harbor at ten A.M. on Tuesday, August 17. When she heaved into sight, the standard of the state was hoisted at Fort Washington, the bells rang, and all ships displayed their colors. Thirteen cannons were fired as the ship passed the fort and thirteen more at the President's landing. The President and his entourage were received on the wharf by the principal inhabitants of the town and by the clergy, all of whom then formed a procession and escorted the President through a considerable concourse of citizens to lodgings which had been prepared for him. There Judge Henry Marchant introduced some of the most respected inhabitants and then issued to the President and his friends an invitation to a public dinner. The President took a walk about the town and the heights above it accompanied by a large number of those present.

At four o'clock a committee of citizens waited upon the President and escorted him to the State House, where in the council chamber

[62] *See* William Smith to George Washington, May 9, 1790, and William Smith, "Journey to Charleston from Philadelphia, 1791," *William Loughton Smith Papers*, RC. *Also* Ralph Izard to Edward Rutledge, September 28, 1792, *Dreer Collection*, PHS.
[63] William Smith, "Journey to Rhode Island—Connecticut, Massachusetts, Vermont, August 1790," *William Loughton Smith Papers*, RC. All facts not otherwise footnoted concerning this tour are to be found in this journal. No pagination.
[64] *Newport Herald*, August 19, 1790.

he again met with the clergy and other leading citizens. At five they
were conducted into the representative chamber which had been
emblematically decorated, and there about eighty persons partook
of a dinner which "was well dressed and conducted with great
regularity and decency."

After dinner there were thirteen toasts. Thirteen cannons were
discharged at the first and thirteenth toasts and one cannon at each
of the others. The first toast was to the United States; then the President gave: "The State we are in, and Prosperity to it." Smith thought
the eighth ("may the last be first") particularly fitting, since it
alluded to Rhode Island's recent admission. He also noted that
after the twelfth toast the President withdrew and Judge Marchant
gave "the man we love," which the company drank standing. After
the dinner the President once again walked in several parts of the
town to the great satisfaction of the people, who according to the
Newport *Herald* looked with "increasing pleasure on THE MAN."[65]
A stop at Judge Marchant's for a glass of wine closed the day. Smith
slept in the room with Governor Clinton—proof perhaps that this
was a bipartisan affair!

Immediately after breakfast on Wednesday, the 18th, addresses
were presented from the town of Newport, the clergy, and the
Society of Free Masons. Marchant read the first, but became so
agitated that he had to resign the task to Colonel Henry Sherburne.
By nine A.M. the President was on board the packet, having been
escorted to the wharf in the same manner as at his landing. The
procession had been interrupted, however, by Washington's desire
to purchase a pair of gloves. Smith had a chance, therefore, to
record an authentic Washington story.

> On our way thro the main Street in Newport the President desired
> Mr. Nelson, one of the gentlemen of his family (a relation of
> Mrs. Washington's) to step into a store & buy a pair of gloves for
> him; Mr. N. in vain applied to the mistress of the Store, who would
> not stir from the window, where she stood with her eyes rivetted
> on the President, after having first hastily thrown a bundle of gloves
> on the Counter; the delay occasioned by the Lady's refusal to assist
> in finding a proper pair of gloves induced the President to enter the
> shop where he provided himself with gloves to the great gratifica-
> tion of the above Lady, who had little idea that the gloves were
> wanted for him.

The passage to Providence took seven tedious hours, and the
reception and visit there followed closely the Newport pattern.

---

[65] *Ibid.*

BENJAMIN SMITH

by John Wollaston

William's father was a "shopkeeper, Indian trader, slave trader, share-holder in several vessels, and banker . . . in fact, the greatest of the native-born Charles Town merchants."

FEDERALIST LEADERS

RALPH IZARD
by John Trumbull

JACOB READ
by John Trumbull

WILLIAM LOUGHTON SMITH
by John Trumbull

GABRIEL MANIGAULT, II
by Walter Robertson

Yale Art Gallery

JOHN RUTLEDGE
by John Trumbull

Frick Art Library

EDWARD RUTLEDGE
by James Earl

Gibbes Art Gallery

THOMAS PINCKNEY
by Charles Fraser

Gibbes Art Gallery

CHARLES C. PINCKNEY
by Charles Fraser

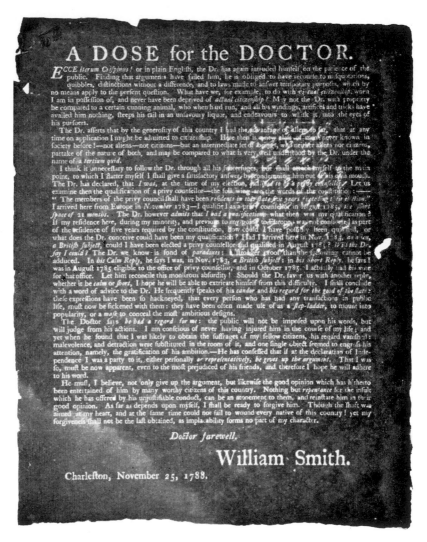

"DOCTOR FAREWELL"

In his first bid for Congress, Smith used this broadside to answer the charge that he was ineligible to serve because of his 13-year absence for study abroad. Smith easily defeated both Dr. David Ramsay, who made the charge, and Alexander Gillon and was seated in the First Congress.

(Broadside from the files of the Library of Congress.)

The *Hancock's* arrival at the harbor entrance was announced by a cannon on Federal Hill. As soon as the packet touched the wharf, the Governor of Rhode Island "so zealous in his respect . . . jumped aboard." As the President went ashore, cannon and bells proclaimed the local joy. The procession from the wharf to the lodgings at Mr. Daggett's Tavern was however "more solemn and conducted with much greater formality" than that at Newport "having Troops and music." *The Providence Gazette and Country Journal* printed the order of the procession:

The United Company of the Train of Artillery, in Uniform,
commanded by Col. Tillinghast
The Constables of the Town, with their Wands
The Deputy-Sheriffs
The Town-Clerk
The Town Council
Committee of Arrangements
High Sheriff of the County
Marshal of Rhode Island District
Council of the State
Secretary of the State
His Excellency Governor Fenner
The PRESIDENT of the United States
His Suite
Governor Clinton
Mr. Jefferson, Secretary of State
Theodore Foster, Esq. and Judge Blair
Mr. Smith, of South-Carolina, and Mr. Gilman, of New-Hampshire
Members of the General Assembly of the State
Town Treasurer
Justices of the Peace
The Corporation of the College
The Reverend Clergy
Physicians
Lawyers
Merchants and Shopkeepers
. . . .
The Providence Association of Mechanics and Manufacturers,
etc.[66]

This was a very good example of eighteenth-century society on parade. On reaching the door of Daggett's Tavern the President stood for a moment, acknowledged the cheers of the people, and withdrew. "After Tea, just as the President was taking leave to go to bed, he was informed by Col. Peck, (Marshal of the District, who had sailed with us from N. York) that the Students of the Col-

[66] *Providence Gazette and Country Journal*, August 21, 1790.

lege had illuminated it & would be highly flattered at the President's
going to see it, which he politely agreed to do, tho he never goes
out at night & it then rained a little & was a disagreeable night."
However, the President and those with him made "a nocturnal procession to the College, which indeed was worth seeing, being very
splendidly illuminated." That night Smith slept at the handsome
home of Mr. Clarke, a prosperous merchant, who with much civility had offered him a bed "immediately on my arrival, tho I had
never seen him before."

"Thursday morning began with heavy rain and cold easterly
wind," but it cleared by nine when the President, accompanied as
before, "began a walk which continued till one OClock" and which
"completely fatigued the company which formed his Escort." He
walked through the principal streets to view the town, was escorted
to the college by the students and shown all the apartments of the
college by Dr. Manning, including the college library and museum,
as well as the roof of the college whence there was a "beautiful
and extensive prospect." Afterwards he went on board an Indiaman
of nine hundred tons on the stocks, belonging to Messrs. Brown and
Francis. On the return they stopped and drank wine and punch at
Mr. Clarke's, Mr. Brown's, Mr. Bowen's, and Governor Arthur
Fenner's.

"As soon as he was dressed, he received the addresses of the Cincinnati, the Rhode Island College and the Town of Providence,"
delivered by their respective leaders Colonel Olney, James Manning, and Jabez Bowen. "At three o'clock an elegant entertainment
was served in the Court-House for 200 persons." Again thirteen
toasts were given, each one accompanied by the firing of cannon.
First, to the Congress of the United States; second, to the President
of the United States ("at which the whole company within and
without gave three Huzzas and a long clapping of hands"); next, to
the Governor and State of Rhode Island; and then, to the King and
National Assembly of France (this in honor of several French gentlemen who "then rose and bowed"). Of those that followed, Smith
thought it fitting to recall the toasts to "faithfulness in the collection
and economy in the expenditure of the public revenue" and "the
establishment of public credit and private faith." These he no doubt
felt were proper reminders for the Rhode Islanders of the significance of the occasion. At the conclusion of the toasts the President
raised his glass to "the Town of Providence" and then immediately
took his departure, accompanied by the governor, who saw him on

board the packet. Smith did not return to New York with the President, but "took chaise at the same moment for Norwich."

The Rhode Islanders mentioned in Smith's narrative were those who had worked for union and who were no doubt happy to use the President's prestige to cap their recent success and to fix themselves in the seats of power. Federal appointments had already helped in this process of consolidation. It was Federal District Judge Marchant who welcomed Washington to Newport. Federal Marshal Peck had attended on the voyage and looked after details in Providence. Senator Theodore Foster was at all times placed near the President. These officials and solid Newport and Providence merchants like Sherburne, Clarke, Brown, Fenner, Francis, and Moses Seixas had sponsored the two celebrations. The dignity and reserve of each visit was a mark of good taste, broken only by the cheers of the populace, which, however, must have been sweet music to these not-always-popular gentlemen. Only the presence of Jefferson and the toasts to France marred the Federalist scene, but this was 1790 and division lines had not yet been sharply drawn. Jefferson commented briefly on the tour to his daughter: "a very pleasant sail" through the Sound and visits to Newport and Providence "where the President was received with great cordiality."[67]

SMITH'S JOURNEY of 1790 can be compared to Jefferson's and Madison's more famous "botanizing expedition" of 1791.[68] Both undoubtedly had political results, although with Smith there was no chance of pulling the veil of science over his activities. His view of nature was the same as Wordsworth's:

> Sweet is the lore which Nature brings;
> Our meddling intellect
> Misshapes the beauteous forms of things,—
> We murder to dissect.

> Enough of science and of art;
> Close up those barren leaves;
> Come forth, and bring with you a heart
> That watches and receives.[69]

[67] Thomas Jefferson to Mrs. Randolph, August 22, 1790, *Edgehill-Randolph Papers*, UVL.

[68] For the mixed nature of the Jefferson-Madison jaunt in 1791 *see* Irving Brant, *James Madison, Father of the Constitution, 1787-1800*, Indianapolis, 1950, pp. 336-340.

[69] *The Complete Poetical Works of William Wordsworth*, London, 1909, p. 85.

Smith recorded his view of the countryside in simple phrases. The Connecticut Valley was "a rich plain containing beautiful meadows & woods." Rivers meandered, distant hills rose, delightful prospects followed one after the other. The unique person, the quaint custom, the unusual episode attracted his attention. The landlord of the Manchester Tavern who complained of taxes; the Saturday night beans and bacon of Norwich; the two smart girls who kept wigs handy, as was the custom of lower class females of New England, to spruce up their appearance by becoming "well frized and powdered." Of especial interest was Mr. Willis of Hartford who had lived upwards of eighty years, sixty of them as secretary of state for Connecticut. This was proof for Smith of the good sense of these eastern inhabitants "who continue their old Servants in office, as long as they behave well."

Smith observed the lesser elements of society, but his time and talk were reserved for the men of wealth, men who were seizing the opportunities the new land afforded—the Huntingtons of Norwich, the Trumbulls of Lebanon, the Wadsworths of Hartford, the Worthingtons of Springfield, the Sedgwicks of Stockbridge. Benjamin Huntington was a member of Congress and the father of a large family, whose eldest son was a coachmaker.[70] Smith thought Huntington's enterprise exceeded his manners when he discovered that the one-horse chaise he had asked Huntington to procure for him to go to Lebanon from Norwich was Huntington's own, although he never said so and let Smith pay for it. Smith spent a night at Jonathan Trumbull's house at Lebanon, "a valuable township," the produce of whose fertile fields found a mart through Norwich-landing and New London.[71]

Jeremiah Wadsworth was most attentive.[72] Smith went with the family to church on Sunday (the singing impressed him more than the preaching), rode to Middletown and to Wethersfield on Monday, where the colonel climbed the steeple with him, and on Tues-

---

[70] Benjamin Huntington (1736-1800) was congressman from Connecticut, March 4, 1789, to March 3, 1791. *Biographical Directory of the American Congress, 1774-1949*, Washington, 1950, p. 1352.

[71] Jonathan Trumbull (1740-1809) was congressman from Connecticut, March 4, 1789, to March 3, 1795, and served as speaker during the 2nd Congress; elected to U. S. Senate and served March 4, 1795, to June 10, 1796, when he resigned. *Ibid.*, p. 1934.

[72] Jeremiah Wadsworth (1743-1804) was congressman from Connecticut, March 4, 1789, to March 3, 1795; declined to be a candidate for re-election in 1794. *Ibid.*, p. 1961. Wadsworth acted as banker for Smith on this trip. William Smith to Col. Wadsworth, August 29, 1790, *Wadsworth Papers*, CHS.

day "a party was made by Col. Wadsworth to the mountain west
of Hartford. . . ."

> We set off a party of about a dozen after breakfast & rode 7 or 8
> miles to the foot of the mountain—we ascended some time a rugged
> steep road; from the summit is a commanding view of a level well
> cultivated country on each side the river, with Hartford & Weath-
> ersfield & Suffield—from the other side of the mountain looking
> West is a very grand view; just under our feet was an immense
> thick forest, the tops of which resembled the waves of the ocean &
> appeared a considerable distance below us,—a very extensive range
> of country lay before us to the right & left, the whole highly culti-
> vated & interspersed with settlements; the town of Farmington is
> seen at a distance & the whole is extremely picturesque. At the top
> of this mountain is a curious pond surrounded with woods & rocks
> in a very romantick situation; upon my observing that the piece of
> water was disgraced by calling it a Pond & that it well merited
> the name of Lake, it was resolved by the company that it should in
> future be denominated a Lake & as I was the first person who had
> dignified it with that appellation, it should be termed thereafter
> Lake Smith. We sat down to a rustick dinner (which we had car-
> ried with us) on the verdant moss in a beautiful spot, encircled
> with rocks & groves, with the Lake just below us.—In the afternoon
> we returned to Hartford & was made acquainted with Mr. John
> Trumbull the celebrated author of the Poem McFingal, who supped
> with us at Col. Wadsworth.

A few years later this would have been called the Federalist tour,
for on Wednesday the journey continued with breakfast at Windsor
in the "neat house" on Senator Oliver Ellsworth's "pleasant little
farm" and with tea in Springfield with the Misses Worthington,
daughters of Colonel Worthington, "one of the most respectable
characters" of that part of the country, whose eldest daughter was
about to be married to Fisher Ames.[73]

The Massachusetts turnpike which now leaps with deerlike ease
across the Berkshires provides a startling contrast to Smith's rugged
way. He headed for New Lebanon, just over the New York-Massa-
chusetts line, to meet his family. The road was almost impassable;
his four-wheeled carriage at times could advance only at the rate
of one mile per hour, and even then Smith "trembled every step
of the way."

New Lebanon (also occasionally called "the Pool" or "the Springs"

[73] Oliver Ellsworth (1745-1807) was senator from Connecticut, March 4,
1789, to March 8, 1796, when he resigned to become chief justice of the U. S.
Biographical Directory of the American Congress, 1774-1949, Washington,
1950, p. 1129. Fisher Ames (1758-1808) was congressman from Massachusetts,
March 4, 1789, to March 3, 1797; declined to be a candidate for re-election
in 1796. *Ibid.*, p. 779.

or "Lebanon Springs") was renowned for its waters, which were then reckoned "serviceable in a variety of disorders." Here in the summer the ill and the idle gathered to drink and bathe. The spa was an eighteenth-century rendezvous of the rich, in America as well as in Europe, now that America had its leisure class. The "soft, moderately cool" waters of New Lebanon recalled the waters at Matlock in Derbyshire which Smith as a young law student had taken. Indeed, the surrounding country had an English tilt, rolling hills and comfortable vales, some cultivated, some "still beautifully cloathed with wood." The rude state of taverns and dwelling houses could be overlooked in such surroundings, for the zest of life was restored, if not by the waters, at least by the regularity of diet and of exercise. "The Pool" was the center of an easy summer life.

Just as Smith had made excursions in the English Lake Country or from Serlby, Lord Galway's seat, he and his friends made leisurely excursions in the neighborhood of New Lebanon. With Colonel Bull he went on a two-day ride to Bennington.[74] Cantering up the enchanting "Housack" Valley, they caught a glimpse of the handsome brick college built with Mr. Williams's donation. Bennington was "a very neat pretty town at the foot of a high hill in the shape of a cone, which is entirely covered with maple trees." Tea with Isaac Tichenor, "a polite reception" at Governor Robinson's, a lodging in the "large & good Tavern" kept by Captain Isaac Dewey meant that in the space of a few hours Smith had met the solid Federalists who were to bring Vermont into the Union the following year.[75] And a glance at his journal confirms that Smith returned with his head full of their lengthy squabbles over land.

Another excursion was made with Henry Izard, his brother-in-law, and Joseph Allen Smith, his half-brother, to see Theodore Sedgwick at Stockbridge. The friendship of Sedgwick and Smith began in the First Congress and continued through the years of Federalist ascendancy in Philadelphia before the capital was moved to what Smith was wont to call the "New Jerusalem" on the

---

[74] This was either William Bull (1749-1805), a nephew of Lieutenant Governor William Bull, junior, or John Bull (1740-1802) who had recently served in Congress. "The Bull Family of South Carolina," *SCHGM*, I (1900), 82, 89. *Also see* William Smith to Col. Wadsworth, August 29, 1790, *Wadsworth Papers*, CHS.

[75] Isaac Tichenor (1754-1838) served as Federalist senator from Vermont from October 18, 1796, to October 17, 1797. *Biographical Directory of the American Congress, 1774-1949*, Washington, 1950, p. 1920. Moses Robinson was governor of Vermont in 1789 and 1790. Elected as a Democrat to the Senate he served from October 17, 1791, to October 15, 1796. *Ibid.*, p. 1750.

Potomac.[76] This was a friendly call, a ride south past the iron works at Richmond to spend a night in Mr. Sedgwick's handsome house. The final jaunt took him to New York City by the Hudson Valley. The Smiths and Izards visited Albany and then stopped at General Schuyler's. They made a side-trip to the vast estate ("3200 tenants" and a rental of "£12,000 per annum York currency") of Stephen Van Rensselaer, then only twenty-five but who is known today as the last patroon. Mrs. Ralph Izard was a De Lancey, and the Southern families were as at home on the Hudson as they were on Goose Creek. By easy stages the two families descended the river.[77]

Of all the South Carolina Federalist leaders, none was more at home among the northern Federalists than William Smith and Ralph Izard. Rufus King and Oliver Ellsworth in a secret meeting with John Taylor of Caroline in May 1794 said that when Smith and Izard were gone there would be no one left from the South to prevent the Union splitting into two completely opposite factions.[78] The South Carolina delegates in 1787 had opposed long terms for senators and representatives, fearing that long sojourns in the North might wean their public leaders away from southern interests. Smith and Izard were in some danger of becoming expatriates. Smith did not even return to South Carolina in 1790 to campaign for re-election. This matter was managed by others.[79] Smith spent the fall with the Izards in New York City, both families being kept busy by the arrangements to move their furniture and servants to Philadelphia.[80]

WHEN THE THIRD SESSION of the First Congress convened, Hamilton presented two reports: one advocated new excise taxes and the other

[76] Theodore Sedgwick (1746-1813) was a congressman from Massachusetts, March 4, 1789, until his resignation in June 1796; elected to U. S. Senate to fill the vacancy caused by the resignation of Caleb Strong and served from June 11, 1796, to March 3, 1799; elected to 6th Congress, March 4, 1799–March 3, 1801, and served as speaker. *Ibid.*, p. 1792. William Smith to Theodore Sedgwick, August 17, 1800, *Sedgwick Papers*, MHS.

[77] Jefferson and Madison were to visit Clinton, Burr, and Chancellor Livingston; Smith and Izard visited Philip Schuyler and Stephen Van Rensselaer. George Dangerfield, *Chancellor Robert R. Livingston of New York, 1746-1813*, New York, 1960, pp. 251-255.

[78] *Disunion Sentiment in Congress in 1794—A Confidential Memorandum Hitherto Unpublished Written by John Taylor of Caroline Senator from Virginia for James Madison*, ed. Gaillard Hunt, Washington, 1905.

[79] Smith apparently had no opposition. See *City Gazette and Daily Advertiser*, October 13, 15, 18, 1790.

[80] William Smith to Edward Rutledge, October 23, 1790, *Pinckney Papers*, LC.

a national bank.[81] It was in this session's debates on these two issues that a clearer line of demarcation between the Hamiltonians and the Jeffersonians became visible.

When the North Carolinians, newly arrived in Congress, appeared reluctant to accept an excise, Smith blasted them with a volley of sharp words. North Carolina, he said, knew that the government had the power to levy an excise. The secretary of the treasury had said that funds were needed to meet the cost of the funding system. "The opposition," Smith suspected, "was against the object to which the money is to be appropriated."[82] In the vote on the excise Smith was in the majority of thirty-five, with Burke and Tucker in the minority of twenty-one. Of the thirty-five, twenty were hard-core Hamiltonians, having voted against limiting the excise to two years. Among those twenty were Smith and several of his northern friends: Ames, Benson, Fitzsimons, Foster, Goodhue, Huntington, Laurance, and Trumbull.[83]

Smith was against the bank bill as it was first presented to the House. He had three objections: that those who were obliged to receive the subscriptions were not obliged by the bill to give security for their fidelity; that the clause which excluded foreigners from voting by proxy was exceptionable; and that the time in which subscriptions were to be received was too short.[84] Holding these views, certainly alone in that he wished foreigners to vote by proxy, Smith voted with Madison, Burke, and Tucker to have the bill recommitted, but they lost by a vote of thirty-four to twenty-three.[85] In the great debate that followed, Smith, since he was fundamentally in favor of the bank, supported the bill.

Madison opened the debate on February 2 with the argument that the Constitution had not granted to Congress the power to incorporate a bank, neither could this power be inferred from any of the general phrases in that document.[86] The booming of the Federal artillery began on the 3rd with Ames, continued on the 4th with Sedgwick, Laurance, and Boudinot, and on the 5th with Smith. Smith attacked Madison's constitutional arguments by pointing out that Madison had spoken in favor of implied powers in the

[81] "Report on Public Credit," December 13, 1790; "Report on a National Bank," December 13, 1790, *Annals of the Congress of the United States*, Washington, 1834, II (1st cong., 3rd sess.), 2023-2059.
[82] *Ibid.*, II (1st cong., 3rd sess.), 1851.
[83] *Ibid.*, pp. 1884, 1966.
[84] *Ibid.*, p. 1891.
[85] *Ibid.*, p. 1894.
[86] *Ibid.*, pp. 1894-1902.

debate over the President's power to remove men from public office.[87] When Madison charged Smith with stretching the federal power too far, to the extent that whatever the legislature thought expedient was constitutional, Smith replied:

> He [Smith] had only argued that, in cases where the question was, whether a law was necessary and proper to carry a given power into effect, the members of the Legislature had no other guide but their own judgment, from which alone they were to determine whether the measure proposed was necessary and proper to carry the powers vested in Congress into full effect. If, in such cases, it appeared to them, on solemn deliberation, that the measure was not a violation of the rights of any State or individual, and was peculiarly necessary and proper to carry into operation certain essential powers of the Government, it was then not only justifiable on the part of Congress, but it was even their duty to adopt such measure. That, nevertheless, it was still within the province of the Judiciary to annul the law, if it should be by them deemed not to result by fair construction from the powers vested by the Constitution.[88]

Madison and Smith had set forth the narrow and broad interpretations of the Constitution before Jefferson and Hamilton wrote their famous papers. Madison was already the Jeffersonian spokesman in the House as Smith was already the Hamiltonian.

The bank bill was passed by a vote of thirty-nine to twenty. The twenty men in the minority represented the hard core of Jeffersonian opposition, men like Madison and William Branch Giles of Virginia, James Jackson and Abraham Baldwin of Georgia, Burke and Tucker of South Carolina.[89] Henceforth the battle in the House was for the votes of the moderates in the middle, about eleven to nineteen representatives. These were the men whom the circumstances of the day influenced. The Whiskey Rebellion might swing them to the Hamiltonians, the Jay Treaty to the Jeffersonians, and the XYZ Affair back again to the Hamiltonians.

Before the session ended, Smith won two concessions: subscriptions for the bank were not to be opened until the first Monday in July, and the first payment for bank stock "in the six per cents of the United States may be deferred till the first Monday in January next."[90] These changes favored those in South Carolina who might want to put up some of their funded debt as a subscription for the new bank stock.

[87] *Ibid.*, p. 1929.
[88] *Ibid.*, p. 1937.
[89] *Ibid.*, p. 1960.
[90] *Ibid.*, p. 1968.

THE USUAL MODE of transportation between Philadelphia and Charleston was by Captain Allibone's or Captain Garman's packet.[91] Smith, however, at the end of the session in the spring of 1791 decided to go home by land in order to sample public opinion. Smith traveled by stage from Philadelphia to Richmond, where he was met by his own sulky, which he had sent by water. His family did not accompany him; he traveled with only "his Man."[92] He left Philadelphia on Wednesday, April 20, and arrived in Richmond during the afternoon of Wednesday, the 27th, having rested one full day, Sunday, at Mount Vernon. This was a leisurely journey, proceeding by intervals which afforded time for observing the growing country. His notes reflect a greater interest in commerce and industry than in agriculture.

The way led through "the most barren part" of Maryland, and he saw "a good many old fields and deserted plantations and fences in ruins" along the road from Wilmington to Baltimore. In Virginia he commented on the decay of tobacco and the rise of wheat. The only farm or plantation that he described was Mount Vernon and here, interestingly enough, the notation described those varied interests of Washington, which later economic historians used to explain Washington's federalism in a land of tobacco planters. "A great fishery of herrings" was carried on, these fish being sold to the country people who "salt it for provisions." "Upwards of 100,000 bricks" were made annually. Washington had recently sold his tramontane lands of 30,000 acres; yet there were "other estates tenanted in Loudon and other counties." Washington was the gentleman-developer who lived magnificently on income from varied sources.

> The House at *Mount Vernon* is most magnificently situated; I hardly remember to have been ever so struck with a prospect. It stands on a small plain near the River which is 200 feet below—the view extends up & down the River a considerable distance; the river is about 2 miles wide & the opposite shore is beautiful, as is the country along the river—there is a verdant Lawn between the house & the river & a rapid descent, wooded, down to the river— from the grand portico which fronts the river, the assemblage of

[91] Captain Allibone sailed the ship *Charleston*. *Charleston Morning Post and Daily Advertiser*, June 23, 1786. Captain Garman is mentioned in many of the letters of the day. Manigault's family sailed "in Garman" in July 1789 and June 1791. "Tour to the Northward, 1783, and again in 1789 and 1791," *Manigault Papers*, SCL.

[92] William Smith, "Journey to Charleston from Philadelphia, 1791," *William Loughton Smith Papers*, RC. All facts not otherwise footnoted concerning this tour are to be found in this journal. No pagination.

objects is grand beyond description embracing the magnificence of the river, with the Vessels sailing about & the verdant fields, woods & parks. The Mansion is large & commodious—the portico 96 feet long & lofty—the grand Salloon 32 by 28 & very high ceiling, handsomely ornamented with a representation of implements of husbandry—the chimney piece is of marble, richly wrought & representing rustic scenes—the hath [hearth] inlaid—the Stable for 40 horses—2 pretty gardens separated by a gravel serpentine walk, edged with willows & other Trees—a lawn circular back of the house—the grounds well cultivated & improved—There is a Jack Ass upwards of 15 hands high sent by the King of Spain—another from Malta upwards of 14—fine animals both—The Estate extends down the river about 3 miles & up the river about 6—and is about 3 or 4 miles back from the River, containing from 9 to 10,000 acres one half under cultivation, the remainder woods.

Smith was interested in all the towns. Before entering Wilmington he stopped to inspect the Brandywine Mills, conveniently placed on the banks of Christiana Creek, which was navigable for sloops and offered a place for "loading and unloading the Wheat and flour from the Vessels into the Mill by cranes." The bustle of Baltimore was due to the enterprise of "several thriving & wealthy merchants" who had triumphed over many obstacles. Baltimore had "thriven most astonishingly" in spite of the fact that it had been "a very inconsiderable place" twenty-five or thirty years before. Large vessels could not yet come within a mile of the town; goods had to be loaded and unloaded by lighters, which was "a great inconvenience to trade." The exports of wheat and flour, however, were increasing rapidly and almost equalled Philadelphia's. Looking for an explanation of this rapid growth, Smith found it in conditions existing under the Confederation when high duties in Virginia had driven trade to Maryland, where duties had been low. This initial thrust towards prosperity had been sustained under the new government, for Baltimore was easily accessible to interior farms. Baltimore stood as a great contrast to Georgetown.

George Town is said to have risen to some importance in the commercial world from the same cause as Baltimore, viz. the impolitic revenue Laws of Virginia which carried her produce to George T. & sent the Imports from Europe, which otherwise would have gone to Alexandria. The Navigation is certainly not equal to that of Alex. for there are some rocks opposite Georgetown, the channel is narrow & bad & no Vessel can withstand the Ice, which comes down the Potowmac. For which reasons Insurance on Vessels can't be made till they have got to Eastern Branch. The situation of Georgetown is likewise inconvenient for trade, the land being very uneven & full of steep declivities & hollows & lofty eminences,

which tho beautiful to the Eye of the traveller & afford delightful
prospects, are certainly ill calculated for a place of trade.

Smith's was not the eye of the ordinary traveler; his was the measur-
ing eye of the entrepreneur.

Smith, of course, traveled with more than ordinary advantages.
Major L'Enfant himself explained to him the plans for the new
"federal city," and together they rode over most of the ground that
skirted the Potomac between Rock Creek and the Eastern Branch.

> The Major pointed out to me all the eminences, plains, command-
> ing spots, projects of canals by means of rock creek, eastern branch,
> & a fine creek, called Goose Creek, which intersects the plan of the
> City; the place intended for the Presidents palace, States House for
> Congress, public buildings, mercantile part of the City along the
> Eastern branch, Quays, bridges, etc. magnificent public walks &
> various other projects, but he never once mentioned a convenient
> spot for a Church, & what is more surprising I never once thought
> of asking him where he proposed placing them.—The ground
> pleased me much; the Major is enraptured with it; nothing he says,
> can be more admirably calculated for the purpose; Nature has
> done much for the place, & with the aid of art it will become the
> wonder of the World. I propose calling this new Seat of Empire
> Washingtonople.

For Smith, who feared that the capital might long continue in the
land of the Quakers, this prospect was indeed pleasing. Naturally,
he did not fail to note the effect of the government's decision upon
land values. Speculation had been great "since the President has
fixed on the Spot." Land had quintupled in value.

The only other "considerable place of Trade" before reaching
Richmond was Alexandria, which had recovered from what it had
suffered "under the old Constitution." About Richmond itself Smith
was most enthusiastic, being captivated by its commanding natural
position on a high eminence overlooking the James. The capitol,
towering above the town, with "its antique appearance, resembling
at a distance a Roman Structure amidst rocks and woods," was a
striking building. The governor, "a plain looking man" living "in a
plain House," politely invited Smith to dine and showed him the
plaster of Paris replica of the temple at Nîmes that Jefferson had
sent home as a model for the Virginia capitol.[93] The capitol—secure
from fire, with its commodious public offices, its "grand Portico" and
imposing pillars—and Mount Vernon were the only two buildings
that caught his eye and diverted his pen from material concerns.

[93] The governor was Beverley Randolph (1755-1797), *Appleton's Cyclo-
paedia of American Biography,* eds. James Grant Wilson and John Fiske, New
York, 1900, V, 172.

Smith was part eighteenth-century gentleman and part nineteenth-century entrepreneur, and Richmond touched both sides of his nature. The capitol appealed to his appreciation of elegance and form, and the new canal to his interest in profit and progress.

A company had been formed to build a canal to extend the navigation of the James, which was blocked above Richmond by rocks and shoals. This was to be a valuable communication with the interior and had then already been brought within two miles of the town. Smith rode out to the spot where the canal ended, and there he found a "curious and pleasing" scene. The roaring of the water was enhanced by the noise of Negroes hammering on the rocks and increased at intervals by the explosions set off to blow them up; the din of progress drowned out the music of nature.[94]

As Smith proceeded southward from Richmond, riding now in his own sulky, the atmosphere changed. The tempo of life slowed down, and Smith found himself in a world that to this staunch Federalist seemed strange, alien, hostile—the world of Jeffersonianism. He was often greeted with the title of colonel: "This happened to me more than once and I could scarce keep my countenance at hearing myself addressed as Col. Smith, when I have so little of a martial appearance and such small pretensions to the Title." Since these people could gain a livelihood easily from the land ("cultivated in many parts altogether by their Negroes"), they had a great deal of leisure, which they spent on the "Piazzas" of the taverns, gossiping about their neighbours and comparing the merits of their horses. Even the dwellings of men of property had a lounging, run-down look which was due, Smith thought, to being "remote from Cities and mechanics." "If a pane of glass be broken, or some of the paper loose; or the wall pealed off, or the lock of a door deranged, they will continue so for years, for there is no remedy at hand." The story of a night "at one Pridie's, a sorry Tavern," completed the altered picture. "I had for company an Idiot, my Landlords brother, who was himself but one remove from it, & I was waited on by an ugly broken back'd old negro woman. My fare was indifferent & I was kept awake a great part of the night by bugs & fleas & the united grunting & snoaring of the hogs under the window & my man Ben in the chamber with me; all this agreable music was enlivened by perpetual peals of thunder & the rattling of heavy rain on the shingles over my head, which continued nearly

[94] Smith made a sketch of this canal. *William Loughton Smith Papers,* SCHS.

the whole night, & began just as I entered the Tavern." This journey imbued Smith with distaste for the rough and rude American of the frontier.

In this rural world Smith heard strong criticism of the federal government. The chief grievance was the excise tax which in 1794 was to bring on the Whiskey Rebellion in western Pennsylvania, a region not unlike the parts of Virginia and North Carolina through which Smith was then traveling. Smith often kept his identity hidden and listened attentively to the conversations in the taverns to get a true picture of popular thinking. On one such occasion, he was recognized, and the speakers hastily apologized for the sharp opinions they had expressed before they knew who he was. He inquired of them whether or not the state certificates of Virginia had been raised in value and was informed they had doubled. He asked whether the excise was as odious in Virginia as had been represented and was informed that when all stills (particularly domestic ones) had been made liable to a duty the gentlemen had been satisfied.[95] One gentleman expressed the fear that lands belonging to individuals within the ten-mile-square Washington District would be at the disposal of Congress; Smith "assured him not & acquainted him with the meaning of the Constitution as generally explained." Smith was finding out what the opposition was like, but one gets the impression from the journal that he felt that any well-informed gentleman could answer all objections in a few sentences, as he thought that he himself had done. Undoubtedly he overestimated his powers of persuasion. On many occasions he must have mistaken politeness and hospitality for signs of being convinced, for Smith had that sort of self-assurance.

The one oasis on his journey was the Moravian settlement at Salem, North Carolina. "After travelling thro woods for many days, the sight of this little Settlement of Moravians is highly curious & interesting. Between 2 & 300 persons of that Sect here assembled live in brotherly love & set a laudable example of industry, unfortunately too little observed & followed in this part of the Country. Every man follows some occupation; every woman is engaged in some feminine work: a Tanner, Shoemaker, Carpenter, Potter, Sad-

[95] Smith must have conveyed his findings to Hamilton, for later in the summer Hamilton wrote General Pinckney urging him to assist the supervisor of the excise in finding "proper characters to serve as inspectors to carry out the law." Hamilton was not in favor "of deputing persons from Charleston." He wanted supporters in the backcountry. Alexander Hamilton to General Pinckney, August 3, 1791, *Charles Cotesworth Pinckney Papers*, SCL.

ler, Tinner, Brewer, Distiller, Weaver, &c is here seen at work: from their labours they not only supply themselves, but the country all around them. . . . The Brewery & Distillery are considerable—the Beer is very good, & a Cordial made out of Whiskey excellent." The antique appearance of the Houses, "built in the German stile," lent an old world charm. "The whole resembles a beautiful village & forms a pastoral scene, truly & peculiarly agreable to the Sight. . . . The Church Yard is on a hill above the Town surrounded with shady groves . . . it is also astonishing to find the small number of·Deaths . . . a surprizing proof of the good effects of industry, sobriety temperance & a good situation."

In traveling through Virginia and North Carolina Smith lacked, as was not the case in New England, friends with whom to stay. Colonel George Mason was the only gentleman of "eminence" with whom he stopped overnight in Virginia. There were others who put him up for the night, a Colonel Meade, a Colonel Coles, but only once on the trip from Philadelphia to Charleston did he visit a Federalist politician. This was John Steele of North Carolina, who showed Smith around Salisbury, an unimpressive place with "but little business."[96]

After leaving Mr. Steele, Smith wrote that he passed through Charlotte ("this place does not deserve the name of a Town"), Camden (where he visited the battlefield and left letters for Washington), Stateburg ("a delightful situation"),·and the Eutaws. On May 12 he reached Goose Creek; he dined with Peter Smith and spent the night with the Izards at The Elms.

WILLIAM SMITH spent May and June of 1791 in Charleston, endeavoring to stimulate interest in subscriptions to stock in the new national bank. The Chamber of Commerce adopted resolutions urging the people to subscribe and also instituted steps to secure a branch of the new bank in Charleston. On June 2, certain public-spirited citizens of Charleston announced in the papers that they would receive and transmit subscriptions to Philadelphia, but they urged haste, as subscriptions were pouring in so fast in the North that Charlestonians might be left out unless they acted at once.

[96] Steele wrote Hamilton in 1792 that the people were beginning to accept the excise. Hamilton replied: "The late symptoms of acquiescence in the duty on distilled spirits, which you announce in your quarter, are particularly satisfactory. If the people will but make trial of the thing, their good-will towards it will increase." Alexander Hamilton to John Steele, October 15, 1792, *The Works of Alexander Hamilton*, ed. Henry Cabot Lodge, New York, 1904, X, 25-28.

Annual profits on the stock were forecast at eight to ten per cent.[97] After Smith had marshaled support for the bank in Charleston, he set sail for Philadelphia on the 19th with the Izards and the Manigaults. He was so eager to be about his business that he left the vessel as soon as she reached the Philadelphia wharf on June 25.[98]

On the Fourth of July the lists were opened in Philadelphia. In less than an hour there was an oversubscription of 4,000 shares. Each request for stocks was scaled down so that all who had applied might participate. The bank stock could be bought by putting up a fraction of the cost in specie and pledging funded debt for the rest. For those who held funded debt the terms were advantageous, for the funded debt would be accepted at par, and the return on the bank stock would be much higher than six per cent. Those who subscribed received scrip.[99] If South Carolinians shared in the management and profits of this great institution, Smith certainly deserved the credit. He had secured a delay in the opening of the lists, he had gone home to raise support, and he had returned to Philadelphia to enter the subscriptions for himself and his friends. If he had not acted decisively and quickly, the bank would have been entirely in the hands of the easterners. With all of his exertions, the southern share was relatively small. Izard wrote Edward Rutledge on July 18 that New York and the other eastern states so dominated the subscriptions that they would be able to put in what directors they chose, but Izard added: "I am desirous Mr. Smith will be one of them."[100]

The demand for bank stock had been high and the expectation of profits great, and in the speculation in scrip during July and early August, fortunes were made. More and more money was lured into speculation; the price of scrip went up and up, until the bubble burst in mid-August. On August 25 Jefferson described for Edward Rutledge a somewhat different view of the Philadelphia scene than Izard had sent:

> What do you think of this scrip-pomany? Ships are lying idle at the wharfs, buildings are stopped, capitals withdrawn from com-

[97] John Thom Holdsworth, *The First Bank of the United States* [Philadelphia, 1910], pp. 22-23.

[98] Gabriel Manigault, "Tour to the Northward, 1783, and again in 1789 and 1791," *Manigault Papers*, SCL.

[99] The best descriptions of events in Philadelphia forwarded to Charleston are in the letters of Nalbro' Frazier. *See* Nalbro' Frazier to Presstman and Calhoun, July 11, 1791; Nalbro' Frazier to Horace Johnson, August 15, 1791; Nalbro' Frazier to Robert Hazlehurst and Co., August 15, 1791, *Letter Book of Nalbro' Frazier, 1783-1799*, NYPL.

[100] Ralph Izard to Edward Rutledge, July 18, 1791, *Izard Papers*, SCL.

merce, manufactures, arts & agriculture, to be employed in gambling, and the tide of public prosperity almost unparalleled in any country, is arrested in it's course, and suppressed by the rage of getting rich in a day, no mortal can tell where this will stop for the spirit of gaming, once it has seized a subject, is incurable. The taylor who has made thousands in one day, tho he has lost them the next, can never again be content with the slow & moderate earnings of his needle.

Jefferson, knowing that Edward Rutledge and the Pinckneys were opposed to the speculative spirit, bringing in its train—they felt—a debasement of public virtues, tried to rally them to the opposition: "Would to god yourself, General Pinckney, Maj. Pinckney would come forward and aid us with your efforts. You are all known, respected, wished for: but you refuse yourselves to every thing. What is to become of us, my dear friend, if the vine and the figtree withdraw, & leave us to the bramble & thorn?"[101]

According to Jefferson's definition, Smith and his friends were certainly brambles and thorns. The men who had exchanged state indents for a part of the funded debt had a golden opportunity now to subscribe to bank stock. It was this type of South Carolinian that became the subscribers to the new bank stock. Josiah Smith led the way with a huge subscription.[102] Gabriel and Joseph Manigault were subscribers, the former to a large extent.[103] According to David Campbell in 1793, Smith subscribed all of his funded debt, £2,500. John Taylor of Caroline charged him later with holding from three to four hundred shares of bank stock, but Smith wrote in the margin of Taylor's pamphlet that he never held more than thirty shares.[104] The Izard-Manigault-Smith and Smith-DeSaussure-Darrell factions were certainly more directly concerned in the bank than were the Rutledges and the Pinckneys.

[101] Thomas Jefferson to Edward Rutledge, August 25, 1791, *Jefferson Papers,* LC.

[102] Josiah Smith transferred $55,000 in May and June 1792 to the president and directors of the bank in payment for his stock purchases. *Ledger of Assumed Debt,* National Archives, vol. 1258, f. 43.

[103] Joseph Manigault to Gabriel Manigault, August 6, September 2, 1791, *Manigault Papers,* SC Archives.

[104] *See* David Campbell's letter printed in *City Gazette and Daily Advertiser,* February 2, 1793. Taylor wrote: "Mr. S.—, it is well known, holds between three and four hundred shares in the bank, of the United States, and has obtained discounts, *ad libitum.*" Smith on his personal copy wrote: "Mr. Smith never held more than *Thirty* Shares in the Bank." On the title page Smith wrote: "This pamphlet teems with falsehoods." [John Taylor,] *An Examination of the Late Proceedings in Congress, Respecting the Official Conduct of the Secretary of the Treasury,* [1793,] a copy of which is in *William Loughton Smith Pamphlets,* CLS, VI, number 15.

JEFFERSON'S EFFORTS to detach the Rutledges and the Pinckneys from the administration were aided by a number of pressures in 1791 that were pushing them in Jefferson's direction. These gentlemen, first of all, were not in an easy financial position. John Rutledge's fortune had largely disappeared.[105] Throughout the 1790's he drifted close to the shoals of bankruptcy, and this fact contributed to his mental instability. By 1791 the federal courts were in operation, and the northern and British capitalists were beginning their suits to recover debts. Edward Rutledge and Charles Cotesworth Pinckney, as lawyers for debtors, were aware of these new developments.[106]

Rutledge and Pinckney themselves had borrowed money to develop their plantations and were being pressed for payment in 1791. Nalbro' Frazier wrote from Philadelphia on August 15, 1791: "I trust I am addressing Gentlemen who will feel for the very unpleasant situation in which I am placed by having so much property detained from me, and who having the ability will do all in their power, so far as it regards the payments they have to make, to grant that relief I so much stand in need of."[107] The following spring Christopher Gadsden, another old patriot, wrote Thomas Pinckney: "the Northern lads generally act systematically. Get one to begin and then the rest like sheep soon follow."[108] It was with a sense of frustration that Edward Rutledge answered Jefferson's letter of August 25, 1791:

> Ah! my dear friend, if the sentiments which are now current had prevailed in the years 1775, 6, & 7—the lovers of liberty would have died on a gibbet, or perished in a wilderness—and the rest of our fellow citizens would have been hewers of wood, and drawers of water for the most insolent set of beings that today inhabit the earth—My Friend Izard for whom I have a very great esteem, says

[105] Joseph Manigault to Gabriel Manigault, September 2, 1791, *Manigault Papers,* SC Archives. "Memorandum of John Rutledge, junior," October 30, 1795, *John Rutledge, junior, Papers,* SHC.
[106] The great case of *Higginson* v. *Greenwood* began in the October term of the federal circuit court, held in Charleston, 1791. *South Carolina Circuit Court Records, 1790-1809,* FRC Georgia, p. 15.
[107] Nalbro' Frazier to Charles Cotesworth Pinckney and Edward Rutledge, August 15, 1791. Frazier wrote in March 1792 complaining that Pinckney and Rutledge had not even answered his last letter. Nalbro' Frazier to Charles Cotesworth Pinckney and Edward Rutledge, March 19, 1792. Gen. Mordecai Gist was also being pressed by Frazier. Nalbro' Frazier to Gen. Mordecai Gist, August 15, 1791, December 23, 1791, August 4, 1792, *Letter Book of Nalbro' Frazier, 1783-1799,* NYPL.
[108] Gadsden was being forced to "sacrifice" his plantation and Negroes on Black River. Christopher Gadsden to Thomas Pinckney, April 17, 1792, *Chamberlain Collection,* BPL.

that on this subject, I am 'Mad'—I wish to god, he, & his colleague had a little of my madness; the more especially as they must all admit, that there is method in it.[109]

Edward Rutledge was a most mercurial man. Historians have never understood him. They have generally labeled him a Jeffersonian when they have not in despair merely called him inconsistent or found him filled with Rutledge instability. Actually, Edward Rutledge oscillated between the two opposing camps, moved first by one deep conviction and then by another. The two strong desires in Rutledge were to be a gentleman and to be a patriot, and the two were not always compatible.[110] As a gentleman he was against all leveling influences; he believed in the rule of the wise and the intelligent, particularly in the rule of the Rutledges and the Pinckneys. As a patriot he was always vehemently anti-British. He wrote Jefferson in May 1792: "We are melting down, too fast I fear, into the people, I speak of the Americans and the British.—I fear that the latter, will attain an ascendancy in this country; and that those who have Right to the first Rank, will scarcely reap the second. . . . I have infused into the mind of my son the propriety of considering his own country as a distinct nation, and of considering the British, as aliens, under every circumstance."[111] As a gentleman Rutledge had supported the work of the Constitutional Convention, but as a patriot he regretted what he felt was the growing influence of the British. And did not the funding system and the bank play into the hands of the British?

SMITH, HEEDLESS of these murmurs of discontent, was busily preparing with the northern moneyed men for the birth of the Bank of the United States. The Smiths and Manigaults left Philadelphia on July 25 for a holiday at Amboy. On August 13 they dined with Mr. Cazenove at Florida, three miles from Amboy. In September they were in New York supping with Bayard, or visiting the British consul Sir John Temple, or dashing off notes to Jeremiah Wadsworth. By

[109] Edward Rutledge to Thomas Jefferson, October 7, 1791, *Jefferson Papers*, LC.

[110] Edward Rutledge was South Carolina's counterpart of Elbridge Gerry. The inconsistency in both men can be explained on the basis of a struggle within each between the gentleman and the democrat. *See* the essay on Gerry in Samuel Eliot Morison, *By Land and by Sea, Essays and Addresses*, New York, 1954, pp. 181-199.

[111] Rutledge was inveighing against the Alien Act by which so many British merchants had become citizens of South Carolina. Edward Rutledge to Thomas Jefferson, May 26, 1792, *Jefferson Papers*, LC. Rutledge included in this letter a number of cases in which the British had won claims for pre-war debts in state courts.

early October they had all moved back to Philadelphia, where they moved in the circle of the Binghams and the LeRoys. On October 10 Smith gave a dance. Plans for the new bank were obviously discussed at these social functions, and Smith, by his activity and presence, had assured himself of a directorship in the new institution.[112]

The first meeting of the stockholders was held on October 21. Among the twenty-five directors chosen, only four were southerners: Charles Carroll of Maryland, Dr. James McClurg of Virginia, Samuel Johnston of North Carolina, and William Smith of South Carolina. The other twenty-one represented the moneyed class of Boston, New York, and Philadelphia.[113] Among them were Smith's stockbroker Herman LeRoy, his friend Jeremiah Wadsworth, his fellow congressman Fisher Ames, as well as George Cabot, who was to fear the effects of Smith's loss from Congress in 1792, and Rufus King, who was to hope for his victory in 1794.[114] Two had been speculators in South Carolina debt—Nicholas Low of New York and Joseph Barrall of Boston. Of all the South Carolinians who might have been chosen, Smith seemed to fit in best with this northern moneyed group.

On October 25 the directors chose Thomas Willing of Philadelphia as the first president and John Kean as cashier.[115] John Kean was a former merchant of Beaufort, who had represented South Carolina in Congress (1785-1787) and while in New York in 1786 had married Susan Livingston. Although he had served in the South Carolina ratification convention of 1788 and had voted yea, he had after that taken up residence in New York City, where he was closely associated with the firm of LeRoy, Bayard and Company, the partners of which he was connected with by marriage.[116] On October 28 at a general meeting of the stockholders, a committee of seven was appointed to draft bylaws and regulations for the bank.

---

[112] William Smith to Jeremiah Wadsworth, September 5, 1791, *Wadsworth Papers*, CHS. Gabriel Manigault, "Tour to the Northward, 1783, and again in 1789 and 1791," *Manigault Papers*, SCL.
[113] *Philadelphia Daily Advertiser*, October 24, 1791.
[114] *Disunion Sentiment in Congress in 1794—A Confidential Memorandum Hitherto Unpublished Written by John Taylor of Caroline Senator from Virginia for James Madison*, ed. Gaillard Hunt, Washington, 1905, no pagination. George Cabot to Theophilus Parsons, October 3, 1792, Henry Cabot Lodge, *Life and Letters of George Cabot*, Boston, 1877, p. 57.
[115] Holdsworth, *op. cit.*, pp. 25-26.
[116] *Debates in the Several State Conventions on the Adoption of the Federal Constitution*, ed. Jonathan Elliot, Philadelphia, 1941, IV, 339. *Also see* John Kean to Herman LeRoy, July 1, 1792, *Gratz Collection*, PHS.

This committee reported a month later when the bylaws and regulations were adopted. Although there was a lot of slackness in the paying up of subscriptions, the methods adopted were most favorable to the subscribers. The bank opened on December 12, 1791, for business.[117]

The important question of whether there should be branches or not had to be settled by the stockholders. They decided to open branches (the one great departure from their model, the Bank of England) in New York, Boston, Baltimore, and Charleston.[118] The directors of the parent bank were to appoint annually in February not less than nine directors for each branch, a majority of whom would constitute a board. Not more than three-fourths of them, exclusive of the president, would be eligible for the next year. The directors of the main bank would appoint the cashiers of branch banks; the directors of the branches would elect their own president, tellers, etc., but the sureties of the latter officials were subject to the approval of the directors of the Bank of the United States.[119]

At a meeting of the national directors on January 12, 1792, thirteen directors were elected for each of the branches at New York, Boston, and Charleston. Those for Baltimore were chosen a month later.[120] The Charleston directors were Daniel DeSaussure, Nathaniel Russell, Edward Rutledge, Arnoldus Vanderhorst, Adam Tunno, John F. Grimké, Edward Blake, Robert Hazlehurst, William Thayer, Adam Gilchrist, David Ramsay, Daniel Jennings, and Thomas Morris.[121] William Smith, the only South Carolinian on the national board, obviously had great influence in the selection of the above individuals.

An analysis of the list indicates that the house of Smiths, DeSaussure, and Darrell was in a position to run the institution. Daniel DeSaussure was elected to serve as the first president, and Josiah Smith as the first cashier. Edward Darrell was put on the board the following year.[122] Nathaniel Russell, Robert Hazlehurst, Wil-

[117] Holdsworth, op. cit., pp. 27-29.
[118] On November 9, 1791, Izard wrote Rutledge to tell him that there would be a branch bank in Charleston, Izard Papers, SCL.
[119] Holdsworth, op. cit., pp. 36-37.
[120] Ibid., p. 38.
[121] William Waring, The South-Carolina and Georgia Almanac, for the Year of our Lord, 1793, Charleston, [1792]. Henry Laurens and Rawlins Lowndes, who must have also subscribed their funded debt for bank shares, were originally elected directors but refused to serve. Daniel DeSaussure to John Kean, March 9, 1792, Gratz Collection, PHS.
[122] Both Kean and DeSaussure had been Beaufort merchants. See Daniel DeSaussure to John Kean, March 9, April 18, 1792, Gratz Collection, PHS.

liam Thayer, and Adam Gilchrist were Charleston merchants with important northern connections.[123] Adam Tunno and Daniel Jennings were rich Charleston merchants with British connections.[124] Arnoldus Vanderhorst, Edward Blake, and Thomas Morris represented the smaller commission merchants.[125] Judge Grimké, married to a daughter of Thomas Smith of Broad Street, was a consistent supporter of William Smith. The selection of Rutledge and Ramsay appears to have been a gesture made by Smith to win the support of two individuals who might stand in his way. No planter had a seat on the board.

The Office of Discount and Deposit, as the branch was called, was set up immediately in Charleston. By March 9, 1792, a house had been rented, a vault obtained, and the officials were merely awaiting the books, specie, paper, and necessary directions from Philadelphia.[126] The founding of the branch bank stimulated other local men to set up another bank.[127] The establishment of these two banks marked a new era in the business life of Charleston, sparking the boom of the mid-1790's. As James Shoolbred explained to his father in London: "The existing Banks give a facility to the operations of merchants which without them could not possibly be carried into effect in the present instance." James Shoolbred was describing the process by which he took the bonds held in his father's

Aaron Loocock, Edward Darrell, and John Woddrop took the places of Edward Blake, William Thayer, and Daniel Jennings. *The South-Carolina and Georgia Almanac, for the Year of our Lord, 1794*, Charleston, [1793].

[123] Russell and Thayer had Rhode Island connections; Gilchrist, New York connections. For Hazlehurst, *see* Robert Hazlehurst and Co. to William Duer, February 3, July 16, 1785, *Duer Papers*, NYHS; Leonard Bleecker to Andrew Craigie, December 15, 1789, *Craigie Papers*, AAS. DeSaussure indicated that he, Russell, and Gilchrist were particularly interested in the establishment of the bank. Daniel DeSaussure to John Kean, March 9, 1792, *Gratz Collection*, PHS.

[124] Jennings and Woddrop was an important mercantile house. Its activities are described in almost every issue of *South-Carolina Weekly Museum*, I (January-June 1797), II (July-December 1797).

[125] Captain Edward Blake was also superintendent of the lighthouse. He died in August 1795. *SCHGM*, XX (1919), 149. William Smith to Oliver Wolcott, September 8, 1795, *Wolcott Papers*, CHS.

[126] Daniel DeSaussure to John Kean, March 9, 1792, *Gratz Collection*, PHS.

[127] The Bank of South Carolina was organized in the spring of 1792 but was not chartered until 1801. *SC Statutes*, VIII, 1-6. Smith tried to crush the Bank of South Carolina before it got started. Smith wrote Kean: "The Tontine or So. Car. Bank begins to totter; their script is under par; but they say they are resolved to carry it through—I wish the Bank of the U. S. would send on a further aid to the specie capital of the Branch here immediately and authority to discount at 60 days; if such an arrangement could be made by the 15th July (the day on which the last payment to the So. Car Bank is to be made) it would completely crush it." William Smith to John Kean, June 20, 1792, *Etting Papers*, PHS.

name against Carolinians to the bank, where they could be discounted and ready cash obtained. These funds were then used to purchase the "*Rosina's* cargo," without resorting to bills of exchange drawn on London.[128] The new banking system permitted the merchants to free funds tied up in debts for commercial ventures. This stimulated trade. The banks were soon flourishing; the Bank of the United States regularly paid a dividend of eight to nine per cent while the local bank paid up to fifteen per cent.[129]

By 1792, CHARLESTON had recovered from the decay and destruction of the Revolutionary period. The wharves with their warehouses extended into Cooper River from Granville Bastion on the south to Market Street on the north. The Exchange, at the foot of Broad Street in the center of the commercial district, dominated the waterfront. The city did not yet extend south of Granville Bastion, High Battery being an early nineteenth-century improvement. On the Ashley River only an occasional wharf protruded as William Gibbes's, but many creeks pierced the side of the city that sprawled up the neck. The fortifications had run along Boundary Street, but these were gradually being torn down to make way for important new buildings. Harmony Hall (1786), the College of Charleston (*c.* 1790), and the Orphan House (1792) rose on the site, or made use, of the old fortifications. The parade grounds were still open but took on new names: Federal Green, Marion Green, College Green. The rice mills did not yet dot the edges of the city, but with new affluence and mechanical improvements were not long in coming. From the heart of the city the spires of St. Michael's and St. Philip's shot up to provide a skyline and landmarks for the surrounding sea and countryside.[130]

The city was soon to give outward evidence of prosperity and federal rule. The State House had burned in 1788 and was being replaced by a new building, designed by Judge William Drayton. However, Columbia was made the capital in 1790; this building was converted to a courthouse with rooms set aside for the federal district and circuit courts. Judge Bee had these rooms furnished at

[128] James Shoolbred to John Shoolbred, May 31, 1796, *Shoolbred Business Letter Book, 1793-1796,* CLS, p. 407.

[129] James O. Wettereau, "New Light on the First Bank of the United States," *Pennsylvania Magazine of History and Biography,* LXI (1937), 284. John Rutledge, junior, mentioned 15% in 1797. *Annals of the Congress of the United States,* Washington, 1851, VII (5th cong., 1st sess.), 396-397.

[130] *See* map of Charleston, 1788, in *Charleston, South Carolina,* eds. Albert Simons and Samuel Lapham, New York, 1927, p. 101.

federal expense.[131] The Custom House was the largest building built during the decade. It was placed on the south side of Market Creek, evidence that commercial activity was moving up the Cooper River waterfront. William Read wrote his brother the senator on January 11, 1798: "The new Custom House is a most stupendous erection, particularly on its inside view—it argues the vast increase of the trade and revenue of this city, and much taste and method in the Collector."[132] Jacob Read, after seeing for himself, wrote the secretary of the treasury: " 'Tis by far the best arranged and hand-somest public office I ever saw in the United States. . . . I wish every public officer of his grade in the Union . . . could take a lesson from my friend Major Simons."[133] The branch bank had opened for business in a private home on Church Street, but with the great increase in business a special bank building was needed. Gabriel Manigault, the most important local architect though an amateur, designed a handsome building which was erected in 1800 on the corner of Meeting and Broad streets opposite the court-house.[134] These fine public buildings gave evidence of federal rule, but the multitude of magnificent private dwellings erected after 1792 attested to the unparalleled prosperity of the period. The city ever since has worn a Federal air.

IN 1792, CHARLESTON was actually on the threshold of great com-mercial expansion brought on by the French Revolution and the wars of Napoleon. Smith sensed that this was the eve of a new golden age for the city, the state, and the nation. He wrote Herman LeRoy on June 21, 1792:

> From the approaching general war in Europe there is every pros-pect of a considerable rise shortly in our funds; the great demand which will be excited for our provisions of all kinds, lumber &c, the advantages which will result to our shipping from being neutral whereby they will become the carriers of the belligerent powers, the emigrations & the increased desire to risk their property in our funds which will take place in those who find their own countries perpetually harassed with tumults & wars, all these are circum-stances which can hardly fail to give a powerful stimulus to the prosperity & growing importance of our country & of course to the rapid rise of our funds: that a general war is on the eve of breaking

[131] Beatrice St. Julien Ravenel, *Architects of Charleston,* Charleston, [1945,] pp. 69-71, 73. Thomas Bee to John Julius Pringle, January 2, 1796, *Dreer Col-lection,* PHS.
[132] William Read to Jacob Read, January 11, 1798, *Miscellaneous Manu-scripts,* NYPL.
[133] Jacob Read to Oliver Wolcott, April 18, 1799, *Wolcott Papers,* CHS.
[134] Simons and Lapham, *op. cit.,* pp. 103, 110.

out is pretty evident from the late accounts, & that it will have the effects I have mentioned is as clear.[135]

The Hamiltonians had organized the country for the benefit of the commercial interests, and now, as a gift from Europe, was to come the golden opportunity. Smith was eager to take advantage of the situation. He planned to retire in 1792 and devote his efforts to the accumulation of a fortune, a fortune to befit the rank that he had attained in the political world. When the widow of Daniel Blake died in 1792, Smith bought her "large Dwelling house & Lot" for £4,000 sterling. Although he got the house at a bargain by taking over some of the debts of the Blake estate, he still had to borrow money from LeRoy to conclude the deal.[136]

It was in the summer of that year that Smith plunged heavily into speculation. He added sixty-seven shares of Santee Canal stock to the ten he already held. He bought twelve shares in the Dismal Swamp Canal Co., two shares in the Susquehanna Canal Co., and a half-share in the Catawba Canal Co. In addition to the shares in the Bank of the United States that he had purchased the previous year, he bought a hundred scrips in the "Univers Tontine" and forty scrips in the Boston Tontine.[137] These were largely long-term investments, although Smith was willing to sell some of his Santee Canal stock in New York or Boston if a profit could be made.[138]

The more speculative side of his operations in 1792 involved the unassumed portion of the South Carolina debt. Congress was still considering the possibility of assuming South Carolina surplus indents, after-date indents, and Gillon indents.[139] By the summer of 1792, Smith had acquired indents to the value of £684, which were held by George Service, and £873/12/0, held by LeRoy, as well as £1,232/11/0, held by David Campbell, his agent in Charleston. Campbell bought rather heavily in September for their joint account. Smith was obviously speculating, since rather than sell these indents to pay for his canal and bank stocks, he tried to borrow from LeRoy. "Besides my bank-shares, I have in your hands & Mr. Serv-

[135] William Smith to [Herman LeRoy], June 21, 1792, *Gratz Collection*, PHS.
[136] *Ibid.* "A Voter" charged that it would take £3,000 more to furnish. *City Gazette and Daily Advertiser*, February 1, 1793. David Campbell wrote that Smith had bought it on a credit of five years. *Ibid.*, February 2, 1793.
[137] *See* statement respecting speculations, August 29, 1792, *William Loughton Smith Papers*, SCHS.
[138] William Smith to [Herman LeRoy], June 21, 1792, *Gratz Collection*, PHS. William Smith to Herman LeRoy, August 2, 1792, *William Loughton Smith Papers*, LC.
[139] "Statement F, joint concerns of William Smith and David Campbell," *William Loughton Smith Papers*, SCHS.

ice's a considerable number of indents, which will in November next (at the meeting of Congress) bring a good price & which I shall then sell, but in the meantime I should be very glad to have the command of a few thousand Dollars." He wanted five thousand dollars and was willing to give seven per cent interest. LeRoy was told that if he could not lend the sum, he was to try to obtain it "from Mr. Casenove or any other friend."[140] Smith eventually borrowed $6,000 from the Bank of the United States. He estimated his profits from speculation in 1792 at $8,960.[141]

In the light of these facts the picture of Smith with regard to speculation must be altered. It is true that in 1790 Smith did not speculate; it is equally true that in 1792 he did. Had he been tempted by the possibilities? Certainly his very close connection with Herman LeRoy and Théophile Cazenove, the men who had made the greatest profits from the assumption of the state debt in 1790, put him in the way of temptation. Speculation, of course, is no crime. It need only be condemned when a man takes advantage of his official position to profit. Smith was in this awkward position. The one extenuating circumstance was that he intended in the summer of 1792 to give up his political career, and it was only against his wishes that he was drawn back into politics. The death of his wife was the first reason for a change in plans; the persuasions of his friends and the criticisms of his enemies provided other reasons.

CHARLOTTE IZARD SMITH had been ill for months when doctors recommended a sea voyage to restore her to health. Smith took his wife to Philadelphia in July, and there she died early in September.[142]

Even after his wife's death it was still his intention to abandon politics. George Cabot, in Boston, had heard the news and lamented Smith's departure from the political scene.[143] Washington very considerately invited Smith to Mount Vernon and may have helped to

[140] William Smith to [Herman LeRoy], June 21, 1792, *Gratz Collection*, PHS.
[141] Statement respecting speculations, August 29, 1792, *William Loughton Smith Papers*, SCHS. In 1793 John Taylor wrote that Smith had "obtained discounts, *ad libitum*," from the U. S. Bank. [John Taylor,] *An Examination of the Late Proceedings in Congress, respecting the Official Conduct of the Secretary of the Treasury*, [1793,] p. 11.
[142] Mrs. William Smith had been very ill from early spring. John Brown Cutting to Gabriel Manigault, March 26, 1792, *Manigault Papers*, SCHS. Charles Cotesworth Pinckney to Thomas Pinckney, May 25, July 1, 14, 1792, *Pinckney Papers*, LC. For her death *see* Alice Izard to Gabriel Manigault, September 8, 1792, *Izard Papers*, SCL.
[143] George Cabot to Theophilus Parsons, October 3, 1792, Cabot, *op. cit.*, p. 57.

change his mind at that time.[144] Alexander Hamilton wrote General
Pinckney in October 1792 urging support for Smith's re-election.
Hamilton, too, had feared that Smith might not run again, but he
wrote, "I believe his present intention is rather to continue to serve.
I trust there can be no doubt of his success, and I wish means to be
used to determine his acquiescence. He is truly an excellent member—a ready, clear speaker, of a sound analytic head, and the justest
views. I know no man whose loss from the House would be more
severely felt by the good cause."[145]

It was the charge that Smith had profited from the assumption
of the state debt that stung him into action. He wrote to Edward
Rutledge in an attempt to clear the air of "a cruel report which
I have been informed some ill intentioned persons have propagated
about me." He urged Rutledge to recall "some of my letters to you
while the assumption was depending" which would certainly refute
the present calumnies.

> Sensible as I am that the Man who embarks on the boisterous
> element of public life must expect these things & ought therefore
> to submit with patient resignation. Yet I confess I have not brought
> my mind to that callous state of political perfection. . . . To you,
> my dear Sir, I feel myself particularly accountable; to your friend-
> ship I owe much—it will always be a pledge for an honorable con-
> duct in my present station. . . . were there no other ties, that
> alone would hold me steady to the maxims of political rectitude.

Smith was ready to support his reputation with an oath until he
could personally return to refute all charges. Meanwhile he hoped
"my character & the zeal of my friends will make amends for my
absence." In a last effort to convince Rutledge, he tried to prove
that calumnies and libels were becoming the customary weapons
of the opposition. Had not John Adams been made to appear as
"the greatest rascal in the continent" while Clinton "who offered to
draw his sword against the new Constitution" had been called "the
most virtuous patriot!"[146]

Smith was undoubtedly hurt and aggrieved, for he took his pen
and lashed out viciously at the opposition—descending to the level
of his critics. *The Politicks and Views of a Certain Party, Displayed,*
an analysis of the rise of the opposition of Madison and Jefferson to

[144] Ralph Izard to Edward Rutledge, September 28, 1792, *Dreer Collection,*
PHS.
[145] Alexander Hamilton to Charles Cotesworth Pinckney, October 10, 1792,
The Works of Alexander Hamilton, ed. Henry Cabot Lodge, New York, 1904,
X, 22-25.
[146] William Smith to [Edward Rutledge], November 30, 1792, *Pinckney
Papers,* LC.

the Federalists, was his first political pamphlet. Before the adoption of the Constitution there had been "the languid state of commerce, navigation and manufactures, the general want of confidence and credit at home and abroad, the inability of the government to support itself, and the alarming prospect of a speedy dissolution of the Union. . . ."[147] Knowing these things, Madison had worked in 1789 for a strong government, had even chaired the committee which recommended that the secretary of the treasury prepare a report on the national credit. The first sign of Madison's change of heart came in the debate over the assumption. Even after Burke, who had introduced the idea of discrimination, had seen the folly of it and "with an honest candor as honorable to his head as to his heart" had withdrawn his motion, Madison continued to support it.[148] All of this happened "previous to the arrival in this Country of a certain Personage [Jefferson]," who came back in the spring of 1790 but who "did not get warm in his office" for some months.[149] It was with the residence bill that faction began to rear its ugly head. This bill "was the offspring of a political cohabitation (for it cannot be called a marriage) between Pennsylvania and Virginia. . . . Pennsylvania was to have in it an estate for years with remainder over to Virginia."[150] The system of attack "was not matured and completed till about the fall of 1791."[151] By that time criticism came from one quarter (Jefferson) and one gazette (Freneau's *National Gazette*).

With Washington ill and Adams' decline in popularity, Hamilton alone stood in the way of the Republicans. For Smith, Hamilton was soldier, statesman, and financier. But what had Jefferson to offer?

> The Merit of being Chairman of the Committee who drew up the Declaration of Independence, the title of quondam Governor and quondam Minister Plenipotentiary, some knowledge of Natural Philosophy, and a knack at Mechanics. Such was the Medley of heterogeneous qualities with which he was to enter the lists against his supposed competitor. Had an inquisitive mind in those days sought for evidence of his abilities as a Statesman, he would have been referred to the confusions in France, the offspring of certain political dogmas fostered by the American Minister, and to certain theoretical principles only fit for Utopia: As a Warrior, to his Exploits at Montecelli; as a Philosopher, to his discovery of the

[147] [William Smith,] *The Politicks and Views of a Certain Party, Displayed*, n.p , 1792, p. 4.
[148] *Ibid.*, p. 7.
[149] *Ibid.*, pp. 3, 21.
[150] *Ibid.*, pp. 13, 16.
[151] *Ibid.*, p. 22.

inferiority of Blacks to Whites, because they were more unsavory and secrete more by the kidnies; as a Mathematician, to his own whirligig chair.[152]
Jefferson was the author of a system of detraction which his press had sparked. He was determined to prove that he was a Republican and then convince all that they were miserable and that Hamilton had made them so. He was the undoubted author of those attacks, though he lurked behind the press "like a certain tall and aukward Bird which hides its head behind a tree and supposes itself unseen tho' its posteriors are publickly displayed."[153] What had Jefferson done as secretary of state? He had produced, according to Smith, a report on fisheries and a "pedantic and plagiary compilation respecting weights and measures," nothing more than "a dreary waste."[154] Smith's pamphlet was a measure of his hurt pride. It was not fair, but it was politics.

The election of representatives to Congress was not to be held until February 4 and 5, 1793. The delay was due to the fact that the state had to be redistricted after the census of 1790, and the legislature did not attend to this business until December 21, 1792. There would now be six districts in South Carolina, Washington and Pinckney District having been added to the original five.[155] In Charleston District, Smith was opposed by Thomas Tudor Tucker and Jacob Read.[156]

Smith was on the defensive against the charge that he had taken advantage of his public position to speculate. He decided to assemble what he thought were the relevant documents and put them in a public place where all who were interested might examine them. The key document was a sworn statement by David Campbell, who had been acting as Smith's agent in South Carolina, that Smith had not purchased any indents during the period that the assumption law was under debate. One voter pointed out that Campbell's statement lacked two denials: first, that Smith had not speculated since the assumption bill had passed, and second, that Smith had not speculated through northern agents. Certainly Smith must have speculated in order to be able to purchase in 1792 a house for £4,000 sterling.[157] Campbell was forced to answer these

---

[152] *Ibid.*, pp. 28-29.
[153] *Ibid.*, pp. 32-33.
[154] *Ibid.*, p. 35.
[155] *SC Statutes*, V, 212-214.
[156] When David Ramsay was announced as a candidate, he withdrew his name. *State Gazette of South-Carolina*, January 17, 29, 1793.
[157] *City Gazette and Daily Advertiser*, February 1, 1793.

additional charges. This time he gave a full history of Smith's fortune from the moment he entered Congress, but once again he was cautious and only said that Smith did not speculate from the time he went to Congress "until every man in the United States knew that the assumption law had passed and been published and books of commissioners opened to receive subscriptions."[158] In the light of the fact that Campbell himself had been buying for Philadelphia connections and that Smith was certainly speculating in 1792, Campbell's statements consist of half-truths. Yet his answers were sufficient for most of the voters. So honest a man as Christopher Gadsden wrote a letter to the paper accepting Campbell's statements and dismissing the charges against Smith as "flimsy insinuations." Gadsden particularly admired the fact that Smith had acted with spirit in the interest of the state.[159]

Smith won handily against formidable opponents. The poll in Charleston gave him three hundred eight votes, Tucker one hundred eighteen, and Read fifty-four.[160] In the country parishes Smith did proportionately as well.[161] He actually did much better in Charleston in 1793 than he had done in 1788. With the Rutledges and the Pinckneys supporting him Smith was unbeatable.

SMITH HAD NOT even been home for the election. He was quite busy in Philadelphia at the lame duck session of Congress. Those qualities for which he was rightly praised shine through the records of the House; he was the workhorse of the party and Hamilton's chief lieutenant in the House. Smith was indefatigable, and he was able. He was always present on the first day of a session and at the end was frequently called upon to tidy up the loose ends of legislation. He was often consulted concerning the date for the next session. When the House had to wait upon the President, Smith was a member of the committee. In February 1793, Smith, Madison, and John Laurance of New York were the House committee to meet with the Senate committee to examine the votes for President and Vice-President. Smith reported that on the 13th they would count the votes, and on that day he was a teller. After delivering the results of the voting, he asked the House to appoint a committee to wait upon the President with the news. He, Madison, and Laurance were

[158] Ibid., February 2, 1793.
[159] Ibid., February 4, 1793.
[160] State Gazette of South-Carolina, February 8, 1793.
[161] Ibid., February 18, 20, 1793.

thereupon appointed.[162] Other signs of approval and recognition from his colleagues were the frequent appointments of Smith as chairman when they sat as a committee of the whole house and the way in which they often called upon him for his constitutional views. Smith had emerged as one of the principal parliamentarians.

His most superb victory over Giles and Madison came toward the conclusion of the session, when Giles introduced resolutions censuring Hamilton.[163] Smith took the nine resolutions, cut them down one by one, and finally had them thrown out in one of the most amazing performances of parliamentary maneuvering that the House has ever witnessed.[164] After this there was no doubt that Smith was a leader. He battled Madison in the House as Hamilton battled Jefferson in the cabinet.

[162] *Annals of the Congress of the United States,* Washington, 1849, III (2nd cong., 2nd sess.), 861, 873, 875-877.

[163] *Ibid.,* p. 900.

[164] *Ibid.,* pp. 900-963. It was Taylor who recognized Smith as Hamilton's chief lieutenant. Taylor first refers to this debate: "And in all inquiries relative to the conduct of the office, in the management of the public monies, these members of Congress, *bank directors,* and the bank itself, give him [Hamilton] their firm and uniform support. In *their eyes,* his conduct will appear *immaculate, angelic,* and partaking perhaps of something still more divine." At this point Taylor adds a footnote: "See the speech of William Smith, of South Carolina, on the late proceedings, where he says, 'That the Secretary would in the issue rise above every calumny, as fair as the purest angel in heaven.'" [John Taylor,] *An Examination of the Late Proceedings in Congress, respecting the Official Conduct of the Secretary of the Treasury,* [1793,] p. 11.

XII

WILLIAM SMITH, CONGRESSMAN, 1793-1797

SMITH'S FIRST FOUR YEARS in Congress had been devoted to domestic problems; the next four were to be devoted to foreign problems. However, returning to Charleston late in March 1793, he was not yet aware that a profound shift in the nature of national political problems was about to take place. He merely wished to test his own public actions against local public opinion and then canvass the newly elected Congressional representatives in the hope that some of them might be won to the support of the administration. With reference to local public opinion, he found, as he wrote Hamilton, "a very general satisfaction pervading the city on the triumph we had recently obtained over the Sons of Faction in Philadelphia. I received congratulations from all quarters & particularly from the respectable part of the mercantile interest, who considered your cause as their own."[1] Having found his own actions so much approved in Charleston, Smith turned his attention to the members from the backcountry.

Smith and Izard had long been concerned by the fact that the backcountry did not send Federalist representatives to Congress. In the Second Congress, Georgetown had been represented by Huger, Charleston by Smith, and Beaufort by Robert Barnwell, all good Federalists, but Camden and Ninety Six had sent Sumter and Tucker, who refused to support the administration. The situation, as Smith and Izard saw it, could only be corrected by the rise of a group of wealthy gentlemen in the backcountry who would see that it was to their interest to use their influence in behalf of government. The inland navigation scheme had been pushed by Smith and Izard to make it possible for backcountry farmers to produce for export. Surely under such conditions a few would rise above the others to dominate their local areas. The excise service fitted into their plans by providing federal officials in the backcountry who could be used as rallying points.[2] In the February 1793 elections, only Charleston returned an incumbent, which meant that five gentlemen from the backcountry were to go to Phila-

[1] William Smith to Alexander Hamilton, April 24, 1793, *Hamilton Papers*, LC.
[2] Alexander Hamilton to Charles Cotesworth Pinckney, August 3, 1791, *Charles Cotesworth Pinckney Papers*, SCL.

delphia for the first time.[3] Since Burke, Tucker, and Sumter had been swept aside, there was the chance to win new adherents, and Smith lost no time in setting off for the backcountry to note the state of its material progress, inspect the excise service, and meet the new representatives.

He headed first for Georgia, in search of men in that area who would support the government. Smith left Charleston on April 5 and arrived in Augusta on the 10th, having spent one day with his sister Mrs. Carnes and one evening at the Edisto Saw Mills.[4] At Augusta he visited Macartan Campbell, whose father had engaged in the Indian trade in the 1750's with Benjamin Smith,[5] and then rode about a mile out of town to, see Governor Edward Telfair, who exercised great caution in speaking to such a known Federalist as Smith.[6] At Washington, in Wilkes County, the center of the fastest growing region in Georgia, Smith breakfasted with a Revolutionary hero, Colonel John Graves, before attending the county court, where he mingled with "the strangest mixture of emigrants from other countries" that he had ever seen.[7] "Bad as they are," Smith wrote, "I am told they are considerably ameliorated, & that a few years ago they were such a set of banditti that it was less safe for a gentleman to be among them than in the middle of the Wabash tribes."[8] These backcountry Georgians were equally unable to understand what had brought Smith among them. They could not believe "that a gentleman or a member of Congress should travel so far from home, merely to see a country," so they set him down as a "*Land-Speculator.*"

[3] After the redistricting of December 1792, the state had six districts. Andrew Pickens was elected from Washington and Pinckney District, Richard Winn from Camden, Lemuel Benton from Georgetown and Cheraw, John Hunter from Ninety Six, and Alexander Gillon from Beaufort and Orangeburg. *State Gazette of South-Carolina*, March 15, 1793.

[4] William Smith, "Journey in the Back Country of South Carolina & Georgia, 1793," *William Loughton Smith Papers*, RC. All facts not otherwise footnoted concerning this tour are found in this journal. No pagination. David Campbell purchased these sawmills and Smith endorsed his notes, which venture proved disastrous for Campbell and endangered Smith's entire fortune. *See infra* Chapter XIV.

[5] *JCHA*, XXXII, part 1, 214. Macartan Campbell, a son of the Indian trader, had married Sarah Fenwick in 1777. He died late in 1793 in Augusta. D. E. Huger Smith, "An Account of the Tattnall and Fenwick Families in South Carolina," *SCHGM*, XIV (1913), 10.

[6] Edward Telfair (1735-1807) was a Scottish factor in Virginia before the Revolution. He was governor of Georgia in 1786 and from 1790 to 1793. *Biographical Directory of the American Congress, 1774-1949*, Washington, 1950, p. 1903.

[7] Eliza A. Bowen, *Story of Wilkes County*, n p., n.d., pp. 1-28.

[8] William Smith to Alexander Hamilton, April 24, 1793, *Hamilton Papers*, LC. The descriptions of individuals that follow are from this letter.

He stayed overnight with Colonel Hendricks, one of the county court judges who was "a very good & respectable man & (to give the Devil his due) a Virginian." On the mantel were regularly filed copies of the *National Gazette*, the only newspaper Smith had seen since he had left Charleston, and about which Smith made the following comment:

> I took occasion to remark that I was surprised at his countenancing such a party paper; he was no less surprised at my giving it that epithet, assuring me that he had been informed it was the most *liberal* paper printed at Philadelphia & that *Fenno's* was the party paper; on my entering into an historical explanation of the business, he said he was sorry to find that such a paper should be introduced by a member of Congress; I explained to him Baldwin's conduct & assured him that the National Gazette was stuffed with lies & propagated by a malicious party. . . . I am in hopes my stay at his House will have not been without some benefit.[9]

Smith crossed the Savannah River into South Carolina at Petersburg on the 13th and stayed with a Colonel Baird in Abbeville County that night. At this stop Smith had to defend the excise. Colonel Baird said that the people of Ninety Six District had been violently opposed, but they were beginning to be reconciled to it. However, he thought some of the collectors would turn the people against it again. He mentioned an instance of rough and menacing conduct on the part of one Wright, an inspector, and Smith promised to see Daniel Stevens, the supervisor, who Smith was sure would ask his officers to execute the laws with mildness.

On the 16th Smith visited with General Andrew Pickens, the old Indian fighter and Revolutionary hero, who had been elected to represent Washington and Pinckney District in Congress. His home stood on a promontory above a large and beautiful tract of fertile low ground where Pickens had negotiated the Treaty of Hopewell with the Cherokees. Since the Revolution, Pickens had been living comfortably in his two-story house with its "decent" but "not elegant" furniture and its "well-furnished" table. Smith passed the day with the general, went over the whole treasury debate with him, and "from his conversation" reported to Hamilton that he had hopes that Pickens would "do well."[10]

[9] Abraham Baldwin (1754-1807) was born in Connecticut and moved to Augusta, Georgia, in 1784. Member of Congress from March 4, 1789, to March 3, 1799; then elected senator and served until his death. *Biographical Directory of the American Congress, 1774-1949,* Washington, 1950, p. 808.

[10] Andrew Pickens (1739-1817) was born in Pennsylvania and moved to South Carolina in 1752. Member of Congress from March 4, 1793, to March 3, 1795. *Ibid.,* p. 1679.

On the 17th he left the general's, passed by Pendleton Court House, dined at Washington Court House, and proceeded to Greenville Court House. He forded the Saluda River, crossed the Enoree on a bridge, and arrived at Union Court House on the 19th.

> At Union Court House I found a smart young county court lawyer, who had been reading (in the National Gazette) a part of the debates—he was desirous of understanding the business well in order to explain it to the people, with whom he is a kind of oracle, and as I found in him very good dispositions (for he is a New England-man) I left with him a duplicate of the speeches, which I had carried with me & a pamphlet; before I left him, he was quite one of us. He told me the people in that part were much prejudiced against the Secretary of the Treasury but that he saw it was all party-work & he would do away the impressions.

This was without doubt Abraham Nott, who one day would be a Federalist member of Congress from the backcountry of South Carolina.[11]

At Winnsboro, Smith stayed with Mr. Evans, the inspector of the excise for that part of the state, who reported that the excise "goes on very well."[12] Smith passed a day with Colonel Winn and part of another with his brother, "my new colleague," General Richard Winn. They were influential men in that part of the state, and both favored the excise. General Winn told Smith that he had been reading the debates on the secretary's conduct and that it appeared to him Hamilton's opponents had been censuring him for only having done his duty. Smith reported: "I have great hopes he will go right."[13]

While in Winnsboro, Smith received word of the reception being planned at Camden for Citizen Genêt, who had arrived in Charleston during Smith's absence. Smith wrote Hamilton on the 24th: "Monsieur Genêt is expected at Camden today on his way to Philadelphia—a gentleman arrived from that place this morning tells me they mean to compliment him with a public dinner, a foolish thing *entre nous*."

[11] Abraham Nott (1768-1830) was born in Connecticut, graduated from Yale, and practiced law in Union, S. C. Member of Congress from March 4, 1799, to March 3, 1801. *Ibid.*, p. 1623.

[12] Smith much later employed Evans (probably David Reid Evans) as solicitor for the Catawba Canal Co. Judge Grimké to William Loughton Smith, October 11, 1809, *William Loughton Smith Papers*, SCHS.

[13] Richard Winn (1750-1818) was born in Virginia, grew up in Georgia, and later moved to what is now Fairfield County in South Carolina in 1768. Member of Congress from March 4, 1793, to March 3, 1797, and later served from January 24, 1803, to March 3, 1813. He died on his plantation in Tennessee. *Biographical Directory of the American Congress, 1774-1949*, Washington, 1950, p. 2033.

News of Genêt's activities may have persuaded Smith to cut short his tour of the backcountry. At any rate he did not get a chance to visit Lemuel Benton and John Hunter, two of the other newly elected members of Congress.[14] Perhaps Smith felt sure of them, since they had both voted for ratification in 1788.[15] Smith did visit Alexander Gillon, the fifth new member, on his way to Charleston,[16] even though he had run against Smith in 1788 and was, therefore, something of an old enemy. Gillon told Smith that he understood there were two parties in Congress and that he would judge for himself in Philadelphia. After leaving Gillon's Retreat, Smith tarried long enough to inspect the operations on the Santee Canal with Governor Moultrie, and the two gentlemen dined with Colonel Senf at his camp. On the 30th Smith dined with Harry Laurens at Mepkin and spent the night with the Izards at The Elms. On May 1 he was in Charleston in time for breakfast.

GENÊT'S ARRIVAL in South Carolina in April 1793, while Smith was in the backcountry, brought the issues of the French Revolution to the local scene. Two political groups had emerged in the United States during Washington's first administration as Americans took differing views of Hamilton's domestic program. In 1793 the impact of foreign issues, stemming from the French Revolution, crystallized these factions into two political parties. The South Carolina leaders, as well as the national leaders, were forced by events in 1793 to line up either for or against the French Revolution. Those who had supported Hamilton's program were largely opposed; those, on the other hand, who had opposed Hamilton's schemes looked with sympathy upon the aspirations of the revolutionaries. This sorting out of individual positions and strengthening of party lines was, of course, a very gradual process.

In 1789 almost all Americans received the first news of the revo-

---

[14] Lemuel Benton (1754-1818) as a young man moved to that section of Cheraw District which is now Darlington County, where he lived until his death. Member of Congress from March 4, 1793, to March 3, 1799; unsuccessful candidate for re-election in 1798. *Ibid.*, p. 842. John Hunter (1732-1802) was born in the state and cultivated a plantation near Newberry. Member of Congress from March 4, 1793, to March 3, 1795; elected to Senate to fill vacancy caused by the resignation of Pierce Butler and served from December 8, 1796, to November 26, 1798, when he resigned. *Ibid.*, p. 1351.

[15] Benton had represented St. David's and Hunter, Little River. *Debates in the Several State Conventions on the Adoption of the Federal Constitution*, ed. Jonathan Elliot, Philadelphia, 1941, IV, 340.

[16] Gillon (1741-1794) was a member from March 4, 1793, until his death on October 6, 1794. *Biographical Directory of the American Congress, 1774-1949*, Washington, 1950, p. 1212.

lution in France with great joy. The abolition of feudal privileges and the Declaration of the Rights of Man brought back memories of the American Revolution. In August 1790, John Rutledge, junior, sailed into New York harbor bringing the key to the Bastille as a gift for the immortal Washington from the illustrious Lafayette.[17] Louis XVI acquiesced in a constitution in September 1791, which was another good omen. The popular toasts of the day were to the King, the National Assembly, and Lafayette. When the revolution took another turn and a republic was proclaimed on September 22, 1792, most Americans anticipated a still brighter future for France.

When Citizen Genêt, the first emissary from the French Republic, arrived in Charleston in April 1793, he was heartily welcomed, and almost every important person in town paid his respects to the Frenchman.[18] Genêt dined with Charles Cotesworth Pinckney on the 15th and with Ralph Izard on the 17th.[19] Everyone offered him assistance. Gillon mapped out his route northward; Pinckney supplied horses.[20] Genêt sent word home that the English in town were furious because of his great success.[21]

Genêt was received in the backcountry with even greater enthusiasm. At Camden he met Aedanus Burke, whom he described as an "intrepid Republican, author of a work against the Soc. of Cincinnati and consequently very opposed to Washington. *C'est un homme ardent, instruit et ne manquant pas d'esprit. Il est ami de la France, et admirateur de ses nouveaux principes de Gouvernement.*"[22] Burke led the people of Camden in expressing their "gratitude for services rendered to us whilst we struggled to emancipate ourselves from Tyranny."[23] The gentlemen of Stateburg, with Thomas Sumter at their head, had drawn up an address to Genêt which they sent to him in Camden. They regretted that he could

[17] *Providence Gazette and Country Journal,* August 21, 1790. In 1790 John Rutledge, junior, was a friend of Thomas Paine. *See* Thomas Paine to John Rutledge, junior, June 2, 3, 1790, *John Rutledge, junior, Papers,* SHC.

[18] "List of Visits made to Genêt in Charleston," *Genêt Papers,* LC. This list is not wholly accurate; it includes the name of William Smith, who was not in town.

[19] Charles Cotesworth Pinckney to Thomas Pinckney, April 16, 1793, *Pinckney Papers,* LC. Ralph Izard to _____, April 17, 1793, photostat from BPL in *Izard Papers,* SCL.

[20] Alexander Gillon to Genêt, April 14, 1793, *Genêt Papers,* LC. Genêt bought four horses from Mrs. Horry, Pinckney's sister. Genêt to General Pinckney, April 15, 1793, *Genêt Papers,* LC.

[21] Genêt to minister of foreign affairs, April 16, 1793, *Genêt Papers,* LC.

[22] Translated from the French of M. Genêt, filed under December 1793, *Genêt Papers,* LC.

[23] Citizens of Camden to Citizen Genêt, April 25, 1793, *Genêt Papers,* LC.

not stop with them, but praised the dedication to duty which urged him on to Philadelphia. They wished that they might "retribute the favors of your martyr'd nation with more affectionate means than gratitude."[24]

William Smith was one of the few who was not eager to compliment Genêt. As a conservative, he was quick to disabuse his mind of any sympathy for the French Revolution. He no doubt would have agreed with his cousin Thomas Rhett Smith, who wrote John Rutledge, junior, from London, on December 26, 1790:

> There is very little resemblance between our revolution and that of the French, either in their effects, or in the motives and principles which were the causes of them. We did not say, as the French did, whatever is, is not right, and set about levelling all that had been raised. We acknowledged that part of what we possessed was worthy to be retained and only put up a bank against the encroachments of tyranny. But the French made an indiscriminate destruction of everything good or evil.[25]

Genêt's popularity was far too great at the time for Smith and the pro-British element to overcome. Smith and Izard adopted a subtle answer for those who urged that America go to the aid of France; they simply told their friends: "Our poverty is too great in everything."[26] National weakness was for the moment the counter to radical enthusiasm for helping France.

The attitude of William Smith towards the French Revolution was quite clearly one of hostility from the very beginning. It is much more interesting to watch the moderate Federalists, like men of the Rutledge-Pinckney faction, who started out with warm sympathy for the revolution, but found themselves in 1798 distinctly hostile to France.

AMONG THE THINGS that began to push moderate men into the arms of the William Smiths were the excesses of the revolution. A vivid example of its horrors was brought quite early to the attention of the Carolina leaders. By 1791 the Negro slaves in the French island of Santo Domingo were terrorizing the planters, and Governor Charles Pinckney received a letter from the General Assembly of

---

[24] Citizens of Stateburg to Citizen Genêt, April 1793, *Genêt Papers*, LC. Thomas J. Kirkland and Robert M. Kennedy, *Historic Camden*, Columbia, 1905, I, 314-320.

[25] Thomas Rhett Smith to John Rutledge, junior, December 26, 1790, *John Rutledge, junior, Papers*, SHC.

[26] James Ladson to Thomas Pinckney, shortly after June 17, 1793, *Pinckney Papers*, LC.

Santo Domingo requesting armed assistance. The letter described a civilization "gone with the wind."

> The miseries of St. Domingue are at their highest pitch—This superb country will soon be nothing more than a heap of ashes— the planters have already bathed with their blood the ground that their hard labour had rendered fertile—fire is in this moment consuming those productions which made the splendour of the french Empire—Principles destructive of our properties have brought flames into our cities and armed our very slaves against us—Philosophy in general the comfort of men brings to us despair. . . .[27]

Pinckney forwarded the letter to Washington with the warning that if the situation in Santo Domingo were not checked in time it would become "a flame which will extend to all the neighbouring islands, and may eventually prove not a very pleasing or agreeable example to the Southern States."[28] To Santo Domingo, Pinckney wrote with sympathy and understanding, but he refused to send aid, explaining that the new United States Constitution had made foreign policy a federal matter.[29]

Refugees flocked to Charleston with their tales of horror. Charles Cotesworth Pinckney described some of these "unfortunate people" for his brother:

> There are some very genteel but unfortunate people here from St. Domingo—Among others General Casadeux, & his sister & niece—a Mr. and Madame Remoupin & Miss Pierre—a Mr. la Gorgue & his wife & sister—The Remoupins are a very musical family. Madame sings admirable & Miss Pierre her daughter by a former marriage plays very well on the pedal harp—Mrs. Middleton has a private concert every Wednesday Evening, which is attended by the best Company in Town; on Wednesday sen'night above fifty persons were present—great attention & hospitality is shewn to the unfortunate French Families abovementioned.[30]

The presence of these refugees in Charleston meant that henceforth no South Carolinian who owned slaves could view the French Revolution with impassivity. The tales from Santo Domingo, long before the uprisings of Denmark Vesey and Nat Turner, engraved fear upon the southern mind.

General Pinckney, although disturbed by the events in the West Indies, still admired France. On January 7, 1793, he wrote his

[27] A copy of this letter is enclosed in Charles Pinckney to George Washington, September 20, 1791, *Miscellaneous Letters, Department of State,* National Archives.

[28] *Ibid.*

[29] A copy of this letter, dated September 12, 1791, is enclosed in *ibid.*

[30] Charles Cotesworth Pinckney to Thomas Pinckney, August 27, 1792, *Gratz Collection,* PHS.

brother: "I am glad my nephew has been so long in France, as I trust he will return a good republican; at least he will find that the French have been much misrepresented when viewed through a British medium, and, that they are not the people the British say they are. . . . I trust they will continue to be so."[31] The doubt expressed in that last sentence began to grow with the news that the King had been guillotined. Pinckney wrote on April 16, 1793: "We have heard of the decapitation of Louis, & altho every feeling mind must lament his death considering all circumstances yet we are too far from the scene of action, & our information is not sufficiently authentic to determine whether the measure was positively wrong, or excusable, or justifiable."[32] As the Reign of Terror mounted in France during 1793 and 1794, the enthusiasm of many Americans for the French Revolution waned.

ALTHOUGH ENTHUSIASM for France might be waning, it was impossible to stir up any enthusiasm for Great Britain. In 1793 there were, in fact, many good reasons for hating the British. British merchants had long been trying to collect their pre-war debts, and in 1793 they at last won important decisions in the new federal courts. The crucial case was that of William Higginson, surviving partner of Greenwood and Higginson, versus William Greenwood, surviving partner of Leger and Greenwood. Greenwood and Higginson claimed in 1790 that they were due £295,891 sterling from United States citizens.[33] William Higginson was suing for a portion of that sum. The case was begun in the October term, 1791, of the federal circuit court, sitting in Charleston. At the May term, 1792, when the court sat in Columbia, Jacob Read was the lawyer for the plaintiff and Charles Cotesworth Pinckney, for the defendant. The case was continued over to the October term, which was always held in Charleston. At that time John Julius Pringle joined Read, and Edward Rutledge and John Bee Holmes joined Pinckney. The problem was whether interest should be allowed on debts during the years of the Revolution as well as for those since 1783. The court could reach no decision.[34] James Shoolbred wrote his father, a London mer-

[31] Charles Cotesworth Pinckney to Thomas Pinckney, January 7, 1793, *Pinckney Papers*, LC.
[32] Charles Cotesworth Pinckney to Thomas Pinckney, April 16, 1793, *Pinckney Papers*, LC.
[33] "List of debts due by the citizens of the United States of America to the merchants and traders of Great Britain, contracted previous to the year 1776, with interest on the same to the 1st of January, 1790," *FO*, VIII, 1-2.
[34] *South Carolina Circuit Court Records, 1790-1809*, FRC Georgia, pp. 15, 21.

chant, that "the question of Interest on open accounts during the war appears too momentous for the Judiciary to determine, I imagine either the legislative branch will decide in what manner it is to be disposed of, or the Executive of Great Britain & America take it into consideration as a proper subject for national negociation."[35] John Nutt, who also had a large sum outstanding, had written to Lord Grenville on August 29, 1792: "With respect to opening the Law Courts of America at this distant, period of time, . . . we have but too much reason to fear it will now avail us but little, such has been the devastation and change of property occasioned by deaths, insolvencies, removals and other attendant circumstances of delay."[36]

In May 1793, the case was re-argued in Columbia with the full array of legal talent, but the court divided, and the case was held over for the October term in Charleston. In October each side put up a list of eighteen special jurors, and a jury was then drawn from these names. The jury was composed of men prominent in the mercantile and banking community of Charleston: Daniel DeSaussure (foreman), David Alexander, Edward Darrell, Joshua Hargraves, Edward North, Robert Henry, James McCall, Robert Harvey, William Somersall, John Black, Joseph Vesey, James Bulgin. The jury decided for Higginson with two awards, one for $87,918.60 and the other for $53,902.58. The jury did, however, disallow interest during the war on the debits and credits and merely allowed simple interest of five per cent since the peace. This compromise was not completely satisfactory to either side.[37]

William Higginson had had many cases pending. During the October term, 1792, he had won, with the legal assistance of Jacob Read, a case against William Clarkson, administrator of the estate of William Loocock, for $2,971.50, as well as a case against the executors of John Ward for $13,311.80. During the October term, 1793, besides the major case discussed above, Higginson won awards for $6,967.30, $6,538.82, and $57,258.11. The decisions were rendered during the meeting of the court in Charleston; the awards

[35] James Shoolbred to John Shoolbred, January 30, 1793, *Shoolbred Business Letter Book, 1793-1796*, CLS, pp. 10-11.

[36] John Nutt to Lord Grenville, August 29, 1792, *FO*, XVI, part 2, no pagination.

[37] *South Carolina Circuit Court Records, 1790-1809*, FRC Georgia, pp. 35-41. General Pinckney wrote on October 28 that the case was "referred to a jury to liquidate the account and assess the damages, by which means the question of interest during the war will be determined, as it ought to be, by a jury." Charles Cotesworth Pinckney to Thomas Pinckney, October 28, 1793, *Pinckney Papers*, LC.

were therefore made by Charleston juries. In all of the above cases Jacob Read argued for the British merchants against Pinckney and Rutledge, who represented the defendants.[38]

Two petitions presented to Congress during this period give evidence of the pressure upon the debtors. On December 23, 1791, sundry merchants who had been engaged in commerce in Carolina prior to the Revolution petitioned Congress for relief, saying that they had had to accept payment during the Revolution on local debts in depreciated money but were then prevented from paying their British creditors. Now these creditors, their former enemies, were demanding payment in specie.[39] On December 3, 1792, one hundred forty-eight names of local citizens were placed on a petition requesting a federal bankruptcy law.[40]

The British creditors, after winning in the courts, still found it difficult to have the decisions carried out. This was particularly true where state courts were involved. The sheriffs, even when they collected the debts, would often not turn the money over to the merchants. The merchants petitioned the state legislature to have the bonds of the sheriffs increased, but the backcountry voted it down. James Shoolbred wrote his father on April 4, 1794: "Since I have known Carolina I never witnessed a similar year to the present for collections—political prejudices run so strong that Judges, Lawyers and even the most subordinate officers of the courts discover a partiality in all cases concerning the British merchants infinitely to the prejudice of this class of the Society." Shoolbred wrote that collection of Wade Hampton's debt was dubious, since "as sheriff of a district he could not be arrested." The possibility of General Thomas Sumter's paying his debt was equally remote, for "as a Representative of the state in Congress his person and property have been equally protected." The whole question of debt collections was made more difficult by the threat of war between England and America; no debtor wanted to pay when there was a prospect that his creditor's property might be confiscated at the outbreak of war.[41]

[38] *South Carolina Circuit Court Records, 1790-1809,* FRC Georgia, pp. 23, 35, 43-44.
[39] "The memorial and petition of sundry merchants engaged in commerce previous to the late revolution," *Various Subjects, 1791, Senate Papers,* National Archives.
[40] "Petition of a number of merchants and others formerly in trade in South Carolina who want a bankruptcy law for their relief," *Various Subjects, 1792-1793, Senate Papers,* National Archives.
[41] James Shoolbred to John Shoolbred, April 4, 1794, *Shoolbred Business Letter Book,* CLS, p. 132.

In spite of all the difficulties placed in the way of British creditors, many families were ruined by these suits. What seemed to
make them so unfair was that many men had become involved
quite innocently by lending their names to friends as security. John
Rutledge, junior, who had been a cosignatory for his father, was
quite bitter on this subject. He wrote his father-in-law: "This
securityship is a dredful business in all countries, but more mischievous, I believe, in ours than any other." He was appalled to
review "the history of our community since the revolutionary war,
and contemplate the number of wretched and beggered remnants
of opulent and respectable families, whose fortunes stood founded,
as it seemed on a rock, and, which have crumbled away and van-
ished by means of securityship."[42]

In the light of the concerted effort in 1793 of the British merchants to recover their debts, the moderate men in the state, like
the Pinckneys and the Rutledges, might have taken an anti-British
stand. They were about to when they discovered that the radical
enthusiasts for the cause of France—mechanics in town and the
farmers in the backcountry—had organized Democratic-Republican
societies and were on the verge of supporting their stand with violent action. These gentlemen recoiled at the thought of being pup-
pets of the mob. Moderate men of means were caught between
Scylla and Charybdis.

ON THE FRINGES of Carolina society were a number of malcontents,
who were always ready to take advantage of a crisis to recover their
lost prominence. Among these were army officers who had served
with the militia during the Revolution. The rivalry that originated
in the days of Nathanael Greene and Thomas Sumter between the
officers of the continental line and those who had served in the
militia establishment had simmered ever since. Some of Greene's
officers had remained in the state and exercised great influence:
General William Washington and Colonel Lewis Morris had both
married heiresses, voted yea in the ratification convention, and
become pillars of the Federalist party.[43] Continental officers formed

---

[42] John Rutledge, junior, to Bishop Smith, February 9, 1800, *John Rutledge,*
junior, Papers, SHC.
[43] Washington married Jane Elliott on April 21, 1782. "Records from the
Elliott-Rowand Bible," ed. Mabel L. Webber, *SCHGM,* XI (1910), 61. For
the votes of Morris and Washington, *see Debates in the Several State Conven-*
tions on the Adoption of the Federal Constitution, ed. Jonathan Elliot, Philadelphia, 1941, IV, 339.

the Society of the Cincinnati, which Judge Burke had once so savagely attacked for its aristocratic pretensions, with George Washington as the national head. The Pinckney brothers and General William Washington were the dominant figures in the local chapter.[44] The rivalry had been sharpened after 1789 by the favoritism shown by Washington and Hamilton in dispensing public offices to former continental officers and by the speculation in the state debt at the time of assumption.[45]

Stephen Drayton was a drifter and an opportunist who wanted the position of surveyor of the customs in 1790, but got no federal office.[46] He petitioned the United States Senate in January 1791 for compensation for Negroes lost during the war, but got no action.[47] He was the original secretary of the Santee Canal Company.[48] William Moultrie, although governor of the state, was not a happy man. He was aware that the patriot Moultries had suffered financial reverses, while the loyalist Moultries had made money out of the funding of the state debt. He petitioned Congress in behalf of himself and others for further compensation for military services during the war, explaining that many who had fought had been forced to give up their indents, from which the speculators had profited, but General Moultrie also got no action.[49] Alexander Moultrie, William's half-brother, who had been attorney general of the state since 1776, was impeached in 1792 "and found guilty of being a defaulter of the public money to the amount of £60,000."[50] His place in public life was taken by John Julius Pringle.[51] William Tate and his brothers, all of whom had fought under General Andrew Pickens, had been deeply involved in the South Carolina Yazoo Company, as was Alexander Moultrie, but this company

[44] The Original Institution of the General Society of the Cincinnati, as formed by the Officers of the Army of the United States, at the conclusion of the Revolutionary War, which gave Independence to America, Charleston, 1808, pp. 33, 44, 45-50.
[45] See Burke's speech in Congress, February 19, 1790, Annals of the Congress of the United States, Washington, 1834, II (1st cong., 2nd sess.), 1294.
[46] Ralph Izard to Gabriel Manigault, February 19, 1790, Izard Papers, SCL.
[47] "Petition of Stephen Drayton to the United States Senate," January 7, 1791, Claims, Senate Papers, National Archives.
[48] Prof. F. A. Porcher, The History of the Santee Canal, Moncks Corner, 1950, p. 14.
[49] "Petition of William Moultrie in behalf of himself and others for further compensation for military services during the war," January 19, 1793, Claims, Senate Papers, National Archives.
[50] Charles Cotesworth Pinckney to Thomas Pinckney, February 4, 1794, Pinckney Papers, LC.
[51] John Benton O'Neall, Biographical Sketches of the Bench and Bar of South Carolina, Charleston, 1859, II, 598.

failing to secure a princely domain on the Mississippi River, succeeded only in bringing its officials into touch with some of the most infamous conspirators in the western country.[52] Here was a group of disgruntled men ready to listen to the blandishments of a Citizen Genêt.

GENÊT WAS EAGER to exploit local discontents. Spain was at war with France, and Genêt was eager for Americans to attack Spanish Florida and Louisiana. Genêt discussed his plans in the backcountry, exciting backcountry leaders and discontented officers with the interesting possibility of uniting the sturdy yeomen of America with republican France to defeat not only Spain and England, but the effete aristocrats of the coastal areas. Ironically, out of such plotting arose a new vision of America.

Alexander Moultrie painted for Genêt a glowing and prophetic picture of the westward possibilities. The Mississippi Valley would become "the great nursery of the growing strength and future athletic power of America—here will be her riches, here her population and here her weight in the great scale of political influence. . . . On the mouth of the Mississippi will arise the great Emporium of the new age." The mouths of the Mobile and the Mississippi were likened to "two keys of locks which open the doors of a new and great world." On the Atlantic coast "we find the soil degenerating fast, the country depopulating and mostly a foreign interest & mercantile aristocracy of the most poisonous kind prevailing there." Moultrie urged that they look to the new states soon to come into the union and outvote the older ones on the coast, for France would find her supporters in the central valley, men who would set the British influence in the east at defiance.[53] Stephen Drayton and Alexander Moultrie took the lead in forming societies to carry out Genêt's projects.

La Société Républicaine de la Caroline du Sud was formed in August 1793 in Charleston. Stephen Drayton was its first presi-

---

[52] William, Robert, and James Tate were the owners of the largest upcountry ironworks. John Drayton, *A View of South Carolina, As Respects Her Natural and Civil Concerns,* Charleston, 1802, pp. 151-152. James Ripley Jacobs, *Tarnished Warrior, Major-General James Wilkinson,* New York, 1938, pp. 104-105. There are a number of Alexander Moultrie letters for 1791 and 1792 in the *Emmet Collection* and *Miscellaneous Manuscripts,* NYPL, and in the *Dreer* and *Gratz Collections,* PHS. Many of them are in code. Moultrie had embezzled state funds to finance the Yazoo speculation. *JHR,* LI, 242-244.

[53] Alexander Moultrie to Citizen Genêt, January 9, 1794, *Genêt Papers,* LC.

dent.[54] According to Eugene Perry Link, "an analysis of an incomplete list of members of the Republican Society of South Carolina shows that the largest proportion of the membership is made up of mechanics and tradesmen, with seamen (captains, shipwrights, harbor officials, etc.) next, then, in order merchants, lawyers, teachers, planters, doctors, and printers."[55] Mangourit, the French consul, wrote that the society was composed mostly of shipowners and captains of privateers, together with old soldiers who had been ruined by Hamilton's policies.[56] Among the leading members were William Tate, Alexander Moultrie, and the printers, Peter Freneau, John Markland, and Thomas Bowen.[57] The address of this group to Citizen Genêt was a history of their thoughts. In essence it was a warning to Frenchmen to profit from America's mistakes and not let the fruits of revolution slip through their hands.

> We too, have fought the battles of our country and by the assistance of your nation were successful. We are therefore your brethren, and in that capacity take the liberty of giving to your countrymen, through you their Ambassader, a caution against supiniss and negligence in respect to public affairs. After your army has bestowed peace, and perhaps liberty to the world, you then by inattention to public affairs, may see a Junto arrise among you, who may have the address, under cover of law, to rob the French Soldier of the price of his blood shed for the liberty of his country, and the honest citizen of the fruits of his labour applied for the same purpose. Probably some neighbouring nation groaning under the shackles of tyranny, (perhaps your only ally,) may break their chains form a Republic and send to you an Ambassador. By the criminal negligence of your citizens you may have among you even Judges and Senators, who unmindfull of the dignity conferred on them by their country, will descend so low as to become the vile instruments (perhaps, by a foreign influence) for sowing the seeds of dissention between the greatest of your countrymen and this ambassador. It might also happen that the same Judges will so far disgrace the Sacred Bench of Justice as to pronounce from thence in a solemn mood that a Frenchman has no right to expatriate himself, and they will found their authority on a few garbled maxims out of a wretched compendium called the Law of Nations, which is nothing more than the History of the mutual accomodations of a great number of little Tyrants among each other, and the Liberty of your country will be lost, if there is no jury to say

[54] See announcement to Citizens of Charleston, August 20, 1793, *Genêt Papers,* LC.

[55] Eugene Perry Link, "The Democratic Societies of the Carolinas," *North Carolina Historical Review,* XVIII (1941), 262.

[56] *Ibid.,* p. 262, n. 16.

[57] *Ibid.,* pp. 262, 265.

that the sentence upon such authority is not the law which governs the country of the Franks. We also entreat your countrymen, to set their faces against the pernicious system of funds, and Banks, for by political management, through such a medium a man may be divested of substantial wealth and have left to him a phantom in exchange, and the hard earnings of a long life of industry will be in a moment convey'd into the pockets of some worthless minion of administration, without labour or other honest equivalent. By inattention of the people, the officers of your government may learn the mystery as such as the act of carrying on warr, as such as negotiations for peace without ever coming to any conclusion and in the mean time your wives and children will be massacred by a ruthless enemy.[58]

Fortunately for the Federalists, Genêt ruined a good cause by overplaying his hand. When Genêt let a privateer slip out of the port of Philadelphia and then attempted to appeal over the head of Washington to the American people, even Jefferson recoiled in dismay. Jefferson, like his friends the Rutledges and the Pinckneys, was partial to France, but never at the expense of law, order, honor, and dignity. Governor William Moultrie, who had been drawn into an awkward position by his sympathy for Genêt, wrote him for an explanation:

Through the medium of the Northern News Papers, we in this state, have been informed, that a dispute had taken place between the President of the United States and yourself, on some point relating to a prize, and upon your differing thereon, you said with a degree of warmth, *that you would appeal to the people.*—Viewing it as here represented, many real friends to the Republic of France have taken great offence, as it conveys insult to a character highly respected by his country, independent of the station which he fills—from hence much conversation and warm altercations arises.

My regard for you personally as well as being the representative of a Nation I really esteem induces me to request from you, an exact relation of what did happen in your dispute, if any you have had, and that you would, in favoring me in my request mention the time, the place, and the manner: because, opinions lead people more often astray for want of the knowledge of particulars—for my part be assured my regard for you leads me to suppose, that your good sense could not permit you to behave with the least impropriety to the President.[59]

[58] "The address of the undersigned Citizens of the State of So. Carolina to the Citizen Edmond Charles Genêt Minister Plenipotentiary from the French Republic to the United States of America," August 1793, *Genêt Papers*, LC.
[59] William Moultrie to Citizen Genêt, September 5, 1793, *Genêt Papers*, LC. Governor Moultrie had given his confidence to Genêt from the start. Genêt to the minister of foreign affairs, April 16, 1793, *Genêt Papers*, LC.

The Federalists in South Carolina seized this opportunity to crush their foes. Mangourit, the French consul in Charleston, was busy in the fall of 1793 arranging for three expeditions to descend upon Spanish Florida and Louisiana: Colonel Samuel Hammond of Georgia was to advance with Georgia and Carolina frontiersmen upon St. Augustine, Elijah Clark of western Georgia was to collect men for an advance upon West Florida, and William Tate of South Carolina was to descend the Tennessee River and co-operate with an expedition led by George Rogers Clark in an attack against Louisiana. In December the South Carolina legislature was enough aware of the fact that Tate and Drayton were receiving funds from the French consul to appoint a committee to investigate a report that an armed force was being levied within the state by persons under a foreign authority without the permission of the state or federal authorities.[60] Colonel Robert Anderson was chairman and the members were Henry William DeSaussure, John Rutledge, junior, Timothy Ford, John Drayton, Captain William Butler, and James Green Hunt. The committee had power to send for persons, papers, and records. They ordered the apprehension of Drayton, Hamilton, Brown, Speake, and two of the Tate brothers, all of whom were members of Democratic-Republican societies.[61]

"Citizen" Stephen Drayton wrote immediately to Genêt of his persecution and warned him that "the genius of Britain overawes that of America and Freedom. Let France continue to benefit from lessons she receives from us—the first which she learnt, was to have a proper and just knowledge of the inherent rights of man—her second will be to avoid introducing a general government which is organized upon the basis of a monarchical one."[62] When Genêt was recalled to France, the investigation was dropped, but not soon enough to avoid damaging the cause of France and giving heart to British sympathizers.[63] Aedanus Burke summed up the lesson for Genêt:

[60] See Mangourit to Genêt, October 19, 1793, "The Mangourit Correspondence in Respect to Genêt's Projected attack upon the Floridas, 1793-94," ed. Frederick J Turner, Annual Report of the American Historical Association for the Year 1897, Washington, 1898, pp. 601-602.

[61] Charles Cotesworth Pinckney to Thomas Pinckney, February 4, 1794, Pinckney Papers, LC.

[62] Citizen Stephen Drayton to Citizen Genêt, December 9, 1793, Genêt Papers, LC.

[63] JHR, LI, 349, 377-378, 381-386, 491-496, 621-625. Moultrie wrote to express his "great concern" at Genêt's recall. "Your stay among us, Citizen, is the desire of much the greater part of the people of America (the trading towns excepted) who are most under British influence; nay, should your recall

The newspapers from Philadelphia have announced to us that the arts made use of by our administration against you both in America and France, have been but too successful. We have in Charleston one thing in common with her sister cities of Philadelphia and N. York; that is, a Ministerial party, toned to perfect unison with a strong British party, both together celebrating at this moment, a sort of jubilee or triumph for the victory supposed to be obtained over you: while the few Republicans in Town, and the mass of the Inhabitants of the Country, are sincerely afflicted for it: still hoping however, that your countrymen will not pass to any measures of disapprobation respecting your conduct, without first giving you an opportunity to defend yourself. . . . As for yourself, be assured, that as a Patriotic Republican . . . you have in South Carolina, the veneration and affections of that great body of men who, in our late conflict for overturning Royalty, have on many honorable and hard trials, given good proof how warm was their love for Republican Liberty. Nor have they, like some whom you and I know, changed their old tenets with their recent good fortune. They do not see, with the half-way Republican, Mr. Jefferson, the great criminality in your landing in South Carolina. On the contrary they view in it a great deal of good to both countries. For had you gone directly to Philadelphia, you would very naturally have judged of the patriotism of the *many* by the sample of a *few.* You would never have known how congenial is the Republicanism of Frenchmen to that of Americans in general. . . . The popular enthusiasm for liberty which bore us thro the war, lay buried since the peace; owing partly to that weariness and repose which naturally succeed great exertion; but principally to that lethargy and stupefaction, that always has in every republic, and ever will creep on, when idolatry for a Popular Citizen becomes a general disease. Out of this we were happily awakened by your tour from Charleston. Altho your progress was rapid, yet bearing as you did, not only the public character of your nation, but also that of its Republicanism, this, together with the energy of your own spirit, by a sort of electrical transmission of kindred impulse, rekindled in us the honest, ardent feelings of our leading men, yet a little time and better information will develop to the patriots of your Republic, how much you merit tributes of praise, and not persecution for your services in America.[64]

WHEN THE THIRD CONGRESS assembled in December 1793, it was faced with an entirely new international situation. England and

take place, let the French Republic send whom they may, he must expect to combat the same difficulties which you have encountered; unless he shall quit the interest of his Country, and tamely submit to what may be dictated to him. Adieu. This letter's not for publication on any account." William Moultrie to Citizen Genêt, February 11, 1794, *Genêt Papers,* LC.

[64] Aedanus Burke to Citizen Minister Genêt, February 16, 1794, *Genêt Papers,* LC.

France had gone to war on February 1, 1793. Washington had issued a proclamation of neutrality on April 22, 1793. Both England and France had begun, however, to interfere with American shipping. Britain, adhering to the doctrine that "free or neutral bottoms do not make free goods" began to search American vessels.[65] Besides the searching of American vessels in European waters, the British by an order in council of November 6, 1793, began to seize all American vessels in West Indian waters that might be loaded with the produce of French islands, on the basis that trade not open in time of peace (the direct trade between the French Islands and France) could not be considered open in time of war. This order resulted in many seizures and was of prime consideration during this session of Congress.

When Congress convened, two basic views on foreign policy emerged. One group was ready to resent any slight upon the national honor. These men were impatient of diplomacy, of carrying on negotiations "without ever coming to any conclusion." They were ready to act, to fight if necessary. The mechanics of Charleston, who represented so well this first group, had had no faith in "a few garbled maxims out of a wretched compendium called the Law of Nations."[66] Lawyers, on the other hand, understood that this was a set of fundamental rules designed to preserve the fabric of international society and that the doctrines of international law could and should be debated. William Smith was the only member of the South Carolina delegation who spoke in the latter spirit.

On January 13, 1794, Smith delivered a great speech, in which he asked that debate on the crisis be strictly confined to the subject of commerce.[67] He wanted to exclude such peripheral subjects as Indians, Algerines, and western forts, which were issues that could only inflame and divert the House from deciding commercial matters purely on commercial principles. He first embarked on a full

[65] Charles Cotesworth Pinckney to William Allen Deas, July 21, 1793, *Pinckney Papers*, LC.

[66] "The address of the undersigned Citizens of the State of So. Carolina to the Citizen Edmond Charles Genêt Minister Plenipotentiary from the French Republic to the United States of America," August 1793, *Genêt Papers*, LC.

[67] *The Speeches of Mr. Smith, of South-Carolina, Delivered in the House of Representatives of the United States, in January, 1794, on the subject of certain Commercial Regulations, proposed by Mr. Madison, in the Committee of the Whole, on the Report of the Secretary of State*, Philadelphia, [1794]. *Speech, in the House of Representatives of the Congress of the United States, Delivered January 14, 1794, by James Madison, of Virginia, in support of his Propositions for the Promotion of the Commerce of the United States, and in Reply to William Smith, of South-Carolina*, New York, 1794.

scale analysis of the English and French systems of commerce, explaining that they were designed to protect the commerce of their respective countries. One had to expect each country to act in its own self-interest. If America wanted to break through the English trade restrictions, the attempt "ought to be pursued with moderation, not under the instigation of a sense of injury, but on the ground of temperate negotiation and reasonable equivalent." There was a certain "Quixotism" in any attempt "by violence, on the part of this young country to break through the fetters which the universal policy of nations imposes on their intercourse with each other."[68] Portugal and Spain, as well as Great Britain, had failed to make commercial treaties with the United States. "Why, then, is Great Britain selected, but that it is most in unison with our passions to enter into collisions with her?" Enmity should never be the basis of policy, for "commercial regulations ought to be bottomed on commercial motives."[69] This would be the policy of wise men uninfluenced by the passions of the crowd. It would not be popular, but it would be in the best interests of the country.

One had to recognize the inequality of the contest. Although America was making progress, England was more powerful. Therefore, "wisdom admonishes us to be patient." A temporary defeat might be suffered for a long-run gain, for the country did not have to be one hundred per cent successful each time it acted. "Why should this young country throw down the gauntlet in favor of free trade against the world? There may be spirit in it, but there will certainly not be prudence."[70] Here was Federalist prudence placed against Jeffersonian spirit.

Smith wished to negotiate from a position of strength, for idle threats were useless. His program was to build a navy (six frigates were suggested), fortify the ports, expand the army, and obtain new revenue from a land or stamp tax.[71] Public credit had to be maintained, so there could be no sequestration of debts. A temporary embargo to show that America meant business might also help.

Smith's position was liable to misinterpretation. In fact one mem-

[68] *Annals of the Congress of the United States,* Washington, 1849, IV (3rd cong., 1st sess.), 196.
[69] *Ibid.,* p. 198.
[70] *Ibid,* p. 208.
[71] Smith was secretary of a meeting in 1794 attended by Senators Izard, Morris, and Ellsworth and Representatives Ames, Sedgwick, and Dayton, as well as Hamilton and Knox, at which plans were made for a national navy. It was decided that six frigates should be built. *See* notes taken by Smith, "origin of the navy, 1794," in *Manuscript Collection,* CLS.

ber of the House got up and said that if a stranger had appeared in
the House during the debate he might have thought Smith a British
agent.[72] Among the letters Smith received in Congress in 1794 was
the following anonymous one:

> William Smith—
>
> Your aristocratical behaviour in Congress (has induced us to form
> a conspiracy against you) and for that toryism you shall fall by the
> hands of private murder and nobody shall know who commited it—
> for all America son's are crying out against you—you rascal—we
> again repeat by the hand of private murder you shall fall—and so
> beware of your life—for we are determined to mangle your body
> at a most horid rate.
>
> 15 Republicans
> and boys of Liberty to exterpate torys[73]

Although this letter was obviously from the lunatic fringe, there
were others from more sober citizens expressing disapproval of his
speeches. Smith, therefore, sat down at the end of the session and
wrote a letter to his constituents. It was a frank statement of what
he had said, and it shone with his own conception of what a representative ought to be.[74] He was in Congress not to seek popularity
with the people, but to do what he thought was best for them. If
they disapproved, they were free to vote him out of office the following fall. A public man must either follow his conscience or seek
popularity; William Smith was determined to do the former.

It was Smith's opinion, "that the *commercial system* of Great-
Britain was, on the whole, more favorable to the United States than
the *permanent commercial system* of France."[75] France's deviation
from that permanent system in favor of America (by permitting
neutrals to take part in the carrying-trade between France and her
colonies) was due only to the necessity of the moment. He was
therefore against any restrictions on British trade, for they would
"beget counter-restrictions on the part of Britain and would terminate in a commercial warfare" which would only injure South
Carolina—"depending so much on foreign supplies and requiring
a great quantity of shipping for the export of bulky products. Both
of these opinions were sanctioned by the authority of all the mer-

---

[72] *Annals of the Congress of the United States,* Washington, 1849, IV (3rd
cong., 1st sess.), 425-427.

[73] "Anonymous letter received in Congress in 1794," *William Loughton
Smith Papers,* LC.

[74] *An Address from William Smith, of South-Carolina, to his Constituents,*
Philadelphia, 1794. (*Also* printed in *South-Carolina State Gazette,* May 30,
1794.)

[75] *Ibid.,* p. 7.

cantile members of the House of Representatives and by a considerable number of other enlightened and respectable statesmen."[76]

Smith had wanted the debate to be solely on the relative merits of the two commercial systems and had therefore refrained from mentioning the political wrongs inflicted by England on America. The debate therefore, continued on commercial points only until the opposition saw that they were losing ground; then they brought out their "*corps de reserve*—the Indians, Algerines, western posts, and violations of neutral rights."[77] As Smith pointed out, there was no proof that the British had stirred up the Indians or the Algerines. The other two matters were then being negotiated. Such was the debate until the arrival of news of the November 6 instructions and the resulting depredations. It was then that Smith advocated building up national defenses and giving the President the discretionary power to institute a limited embargo. He emphasized the fact that his speeches had been made before the November 6 instructions were known. Even with this news, he cautioned that public men must act in a different way from private individuals: "The private individual speaks from the impulse of the moment; his American pride is hurt by injury, he cries aloud for war; the public man, no less stung and feeling as keenly the injury, speaks not as from the impulse of the moment nor until he has seriously reflected on the tendency of his conduct."[78] It would have been easy, Smith admitted, to clamor for liberty, equality, and war instead of speaking in behalf of negotiation, moderation, and peace. But for himself "the stings of conscience" were more demanding than the charms of popularity.[79] He had never wished to please all men. He knew that "the citizen who takes an active part on the stage of government must become obnoxious to one party or the other."[80] He was, therefore, addressing the sober, second-thinking men who had been misled by slander and who could be appealed to on the basis of reason: the Edward Rutledges and the Charles Cotesworth Pinckneys. He, therefore, advocated supporting the President's move to send an emissary to England.

Ironically, John Jay's mission did more than anything else to undermine Smith's arguments with the Rutledge-Pinckney faction. Having Jay chosen to speak for the United States on this matter

[76] *Ibid.*, pp. 7-8.
[77] *Ibid.*, p. 10.
[78] *Ibid.*, p. 18.
[79] *Ibid.*, p. 29.
[80] *Ibid.*, p. 19.

was a blow to the pride of Thomas Pinckney, then minister in London. Ralph Izard had tried to soothe the Pinckneys by writing General Pinckney that the President "in his public & private conversations uniformly declares that Mr. Jay is sent, not on account of any diminution of confidence in you, but merely because he thinks the situation of America is such with regard to Great Britain, that an envoy should be sent who is acquainted with the present temper & disposition of the people from being himself a witness of them & whose remonstrances will give additional weight by their being made by an envoy sent for that express purpose & no other." Charles Cotesworth Pinckney commented to his brother Thomas: "I dare say the President is sincere in his declarations; but the appointment of a Judge to that office has been generally deemed inconsistent with the spirit of our Constitution."[81] Thomas's reply was: "With respect to Mr. Jay's Mission as it personally concerns me, if I were to say that I had no unpleasant feelings on the occasion, I should not be sincere." He did add, however, that if it were for the good of the country, he would accept it.[82]

BY 1794, SMITH REPRESENTED all that the Rutledges and the Pinckneys had come to fear. In 1789 he had protected the interests of the John Nutts and William Higginsons by fighting for the establishment of lower federal courts; in 1790 he had played into the hands of the northern speculators by putting his political strength behind the assumption of state debts without any discrimination in favor of the original holders; and in 1791 he had worked ardently for the local moneyed interests by securing a branch of the new national bank for Charleston. Although Smith had speculated in 1791 and 1792, he had been able to dodge the charges made against him in his campaign for re-election in 1793. Had the Rutledges and the Pinckneys been hoodwinked at that election? Had more evidence of Smith's speculations come to their attention since then? Was not Smith's open disapproval of the French and warm support of British commercial policies further proof that he had sold out to the British merchants? The last straw was Smith's support of the Jay mission. On top of all this, Smith had been in office for six

[81] Quoted in Charles Cotesworth Pinckney to Thomas Pinckney, May 29, 1794, *Pinckney Papers*, LC. By October General Pinckney seemed to be convinced of the President's sincerity. Charles Cotesworth Pinckney to Thomas Pinckney, October 5, 1794, *Pinckney Papers*, LC.

[82] Thomas Pinckney to Charles Cotesworth Pinckney, July 8, 1794, *Pinckney Papers*, LC.

years and had seldom come home. Could such a man be trusted any longer? With these thoughts in mind, the Rutledges and General Pinckney sponsored John Rutledge, junior, as Smith's opponent in the fall of 1794. As the pro-French forces pushed forward Dr. Peter Fayssoux and Dr. Thomas Tudor Tucker, this was to be the hardest fought of all Smith's campaigns for re-election.

David Campbell, his campaign manager, announced Smith's candidacy on September 20 in a letter to the "Electors of Charleston District." Campbell admitted that "some part" of Smith's political conduct had given offense, but he thought Smith's address to his constituents had been a sufficient explanation and contented himself with printing extracts from the address in the *City Gazette*. Campbell was much more worried about a rumor that Smith intended to live permanently in the North and that he had disposed of his estate in South Carolina. The fact that Smith was not returning to South Carolina for the election was damaging. Campbell tried to explain that "the fatigues of a long session, and the shortness of the recess of congress" stood in the way of Smith's having "a personal interview with his constituents." He also implied that Smith's health had been impaired by his constant attendance. Smith had "never been absent from his seat a single day between the 2d of December and the 9th of June, besides being constantly upon committees of importance." To counter the story that he was disposing of his estate, Campbell stated that Smith had £20,000 sterling in bonds and lands in South Carolina, with only one vacant lot sold since 1789.[83]

On October 2 an "elector" raised the old question of speculation by asking for further information about Smith's investments: how much did he have in the funds, when did he buy indents, and was he a member of Congress at the time of the purchases? Campbell replied on the 3rd by reminding his readers that "A Voter" had made similar charges in 1793, but that *the* voters had re-elected Smith by an overwhelming majority. Campbell did not say that Smith had never speculated, but simply stated that he did not speculate "until every man in the United States knew of the assumption law." If South Carolinians had not received information concerning the progress of the assumption law in Congress, it had not been Smith's fault. At this point, with a neat twist of fact, Campbell put the blame on Edward Rutledge. Smith, according to Campbell,

[83] *City Gazette and Daily Advertiser*, September 20, 26, October 2, 3, 1794.

had given intelligence of the possible passing of the assumption law to those he was accustomed to correspond with on public matters, and they (principally Edward Rutledge and General Pinckney) should have informed the public.[84]

At this point Charles Cotesworth Pinckney summed up the campaign for his brother:

> A great deal of electioneering business is now going on for a member of Congress for this district—I think Wm. Smith has shewn too great a bias to Britain & British politics for me to wish him to be reelected; & the British merchants & old Tories are doing all they can to get him in once more; Drs. Tucker & Fayssoux are also candidates but I do not think their sentiments are sufficiently federal, for me to wish to see either of them elected—John Rutledge Junior is also a candidate, & I think there is so much in his favour that I sincerely desire that he may be our representative—He has lately shewn considerable abilities in our legislature & at our public meetings—He is by no means partial to Britain, & tho he wishes well to the French & their cause, he prefers America to every foreign interest, he is also a decided Federalist & a promoter of federal measures.[85]

The Republican Society of Charleston entered the political battle with an address printed in the *City Gazette* of October 8. There were hints of "doubtful characters" whose "connections and most intimate friends" were "in Europe," but the most damaging thing they could think to do was to publish the resolutions of the Democratic Society of Pennsylvania (drawn up the previous May 8), which roundly condemned the Jay mission.[86]

In the election, held on October 13 and 14, Smith, Rutledge, and Tucker (Fayssoux must have withdrawn) received the following votes:

	Smith	Rutledge	Tucker
Charleston	332	256	85
St. James Goose Creek	18	4	6
St. Bartholomew	80	151	8
St. Paul's	27	11	9
St. Andrew's	5	22	2
St. John's Berkeley	26	4	3
St. John's Colleton	50	0	0
St. Thomas and St. Dennis	16	9	----

[84] *Ibid.*, October 2, 3, 1794.

[85] Charles Cotesworth Pinckney to Thomas Pinckney, October 5, 1794, *Pinckney Papers*, LC.

[86] *City Gazette and Daily Advertiser*, October 8, 1794.

St. James Santee	28	38	18
Christ Church	30	5	5
St. George Dorchester	81	2	13
St. Stephen's	5	2	----
	698	504	149[87]

For the first time, Smith did better in the country parishes than in Charleston. The strength of the Rutledges and the Pinckneys undoubtedly cut into his support in the city. It might be noted, however, that Smith had done exceedingly well in St. James Goose Creek and in St. George Dorchester—Izard's overseers had worked hard and with good results.[88] Markland and M'Iver, the editors of the *City Gazette,* must have been pleased, for they noted that Smith, "the real patriot and friend of this country," had been re-elected, even though traduced by others as a person under "a foreign, a British interest."[89]

Whether Smith was traduced or not, he certainly had the support of the British merchants in Charleston and old tories in the country. This election is the most positive proof that a British faction did exist and that it was for Smith. He could not have won over the Rutledges and the Pinckneys, as well as the pro-French faction, without their help. It was an amazing victory, as Pierce Butler noted in a letter to James Monroe: "Mr. Wm. Smith, tho' openly opposed by Messrs. Rutledges and Pinckney, has been re-elected."[90] Smith had won a handsome victory, but Mrs. Izard wrote her husband to warn Smith not to stretch his luck too far. She wrote on December 6: "I am glad Mr. Smith is rechosen; but I think after the expiration of this term, he would do well to live a few years at home."[91] On December 25 she added advice for both Izard and Smith: "Six, & eight years are too long terms for gentlemen to be absent from their country."[92]

THE DECEMBER 1794 session of the South Carolina legislature was the most important of the decade. The backcountry, urged on by the Representative Reform Association and the writings of "Appius," was making a concerted effort to change the basis of representation

[87] *Ibid.,* October 15, 20, 28, 29, November 20, 1794.
[88] Mathias Hutchinson to Ralph Izard, October 22, 1794; Ralph Izard to Mathias Hutchinson, November 20, 1794, *Izard Papers,* SCL.
[89] *City Gazette and Daily Advertiser,* November 20, 1794.
[90] Pierce Butler to James Monroe, January 19, 1795, *Monroe Papers,* LC.
[91] Alice Izard to Ralph Izard, December 6, 1794, *Izard Papers,* SCL.
[92] Alice Izard to Ralph Izard, December 25, 1794, *Izard Papers,* SCL.

in the state legislature to get a voice equal to that of the low-country. This move was defeated, but only barely, and the back-country did succeed in trimming the salaries of state officials.[93] (This might be the reason why John Rutledge decided to give up his position as chief justice of the state.) Although forestalled in 1794, the pressure from the backcountry for some sort of reform in representation was bound to grow. Both Ralph Izard and Henry William DeSaussure, who addressed themselves to this problem in 1795, hoped that the inevitable day could be postponed until the backcountry was producing numerous rich and well-educated citizens as leaders.[94]

The legislature had to select a governor and also a senator, for Izard had decided to step down. These contests reveal a three-fold division within the state. There were the arch-Federalists, the Rutledge-Pinckney faction, and the backcountry leaders. For governor the Charleston merchants supported Jacob Read; the Rutledges and the Pinckneys put forward Arnoldus Vanderhorst; and the back-country voted for Colonel Thomas Taylor. Vanderhorst came within seven votes of having a majority on the first ballot; more than enough of Read's supporters shifted to Vanderhorst on the second, giving him the election. "Mr. Read's chagrin was conspicuous." By way of compensation, many of Read's original supporters then urged him to stand for United States senator. In this contest the candidates were Jacob Read for the Charleston merchants, David Ramsay for the Pinckneys and the Rutledges, and John Hunter for the up-country. There was some question about Ramsay's views on slavery; Generals Pinckney and Washington supported him, but only after they had quizzed him on the subject of Negroes and received "unequivocal assurances" that he would vote against emancipation in Congress. On the first ballot Read got fifty-one, Hunter forty-nine, and Ramsay forty-five. A few planters not being sure of Ramsay had voted for Read, and the Ramsay men then saw that unless they supported Read, a candidate "wholly in the interest of the upper country" would be chosen. They persuaded Ramsay to withdraw, and then voted for Read, who won triumphantly. This was to "the

---

[93] Mrs. Pinckney called these "Appian measures." Alice Izard to Ralph Izard, December 25, 1794, *Izard Papers*, SCL.

[94] Ralph Izard to Charles Cotesworth Pinckney, January 18, 1795, *Izard Papers*, SCL. Henry William DeSaussure to Richard Bland Lee, February 14, 1795, *Richard Bland Lee Papers*, LC.

surprize and very great gratification of the new Senator and all his drooping friends."[95]

Jacob Read's victory was undoubtedly due to an unexpected stroke of luck. His views were held by only a small minority in the state. He was in fact more of an arch-Federalist than Smith. Pierce Butler summed up the situation for Monroe:

> The Legislature of this state have chosen Mr. Reid to succeed Mr. Izard—You may possibly know something of the general character of this gentleman. He married a Miss Van Horn of New York—there is as little prospect of his drawing with me as of Mr. Izard's—He is decidedly anti-Gallican and I think, not much of a Republican—He is said to have tried to be chosen Governor of this state; he failed in that attempt, and in order to prevent mortification, they made him a Senator.[96]

This was indeed a strange reason for electing to the Senate a man who had made a fortune representing British creditors and who was at that time retained by the British consul in Charleston to argue cases in the federal courts.[97] Even Izard was doubtful, as his letter to Charles Cotesworth Pinckney, dated January 18, proves:

> Mr. Read is certainly a man of sense, I believe a friend to the government, & I think will in general vote right. But when I recollect his vanity, pomposity, & above all the Speaker's Gown over his Regimental Coat, when he accompanied the President to church, I fear that something, not perfectly respectable either to himself, or the State, may now & then escape from him. You say he has anti-gallican prejudices. If so, I am sorry for it, would advise him to leave them behind him when he embarks for this place. To divest himself of all national prejudices is the duty of every man who has anything to do with public affairs.[98]

It was ironical that Ramsay's softness on the slavery question helped both Smith and Read get into Congress.

THE POLITICAL FUTURE of William Smith and Jacob Read in South Carolina depended upon the success of Jay's mission to England. If the negotiations were broken off, it would mean war with England, with the accompanying cessation of commerce, decline in revenues, and rise in strength of the friends of France. If negotiations were

[95] John Brown Cutting to Thomas Pinckney, December 19, 1794, *Pinckney Papers*, LC. *Also see* Charles Cotesworth Pinckney to Ralph Izard, December 20, 1794, a copy in *Charles Cotesworth Pinckney Papers*, DUL.
[96] Pierce Butler to James Monroe, January 19, 1795, *Monroe Papers*, LC.
[97] The British consul even complained of Read's fees. Benjamin Moodie to Jacob Read, December 29, 1795, October 14, 1796, *Miscellaneous Manuscripts*, NYPL.
[98] Ralph Izard to Charles Cotesworth Pinckney, January 18, 1795, *Izard Papers*, SCL.

concluded successfully, commerce would flourish, government revenues would rise, and there would be a chance to destroy the pro-
French forces in America. Most importantly there would be a
chance to crush the Democratic-Republican societies.

Smith and Izard used all their influence at home and abroad to
marshal support for the Jay negotiations.[99] Ralph Izard wrote H. M.
Bird in October 1794 to urge the British government to make haste
in their negotiations, for delays played into the hands of the "anarchists" in America. The delays gave added importance to the
Democratic societies—"those children of Mr. Genet"—and these
societies, Izard thought, were behind the insurrection in western
Pennsylvania as well as the move for additional representation in
western South Carolina. Izard said that the British government
could not hope to benefit from these insurrections, since they weak-
ened the only friends England had in America.[100] In November,
Izard wrote again, indicating the real need that the friends of
Britain in America felt for ensuring the success of the Jay negotiations.[101]

Actually, instead of weakening the Federalist position, the Whiskey Rebellion strengthened it. The episode was used by Hamilton
to prove that the new government could impose its will directly
upon the individual, which it had never been able to do with success
under the old government. Aedanus Burke, whose sympathies were
entirely with the western Pennsylvanians, pointed this out in a very
perceptive letter written to James Monroe: "The insurrection in the
four Western counties of Pennsylvania against the Excise, is a most
unfortunate business. To quell it by arms became necessary; and
this has given, at one stroke, to the administration, more energy
and decisive power, than any government of the old world have
obtained in a whole century. . . . The consequences are important;
but what did the silly, mischievous Yahoos over the Allegeny think,
or care, about consequences."[102]

The Whiskey Rebellion offered a grand opportunity to strike at
the Democratic-Republican societies. Washington led the attack

[99] Smith was writing to London in May 1794. *See* Samuel Flagg Bemis, *Jay's
Treaty,* New York, 1923, p. 190, n. 9.
[100] Ralph Izard to H. M. Bird, October 22, 1794, *Izard Papers,* LC. *Also see*
Ralph Izard to Charles Cotesworth Pinckney, November 21, 1794, *Izard Papers,*
SCL.
[101] Ralph Izard to H. M. Bird, November 10, 1794, *Izard Papers,* LC.
[102] Aedanus Burke to James Monroe, December 26, 1794, *Gratz Collection,*
PHS.

by scoring these "self-created" societies in his annual address. He charged them with fomenting civil strife. In the debate on the President's address Smith followed Washington's lead. He advised keeping in service a portion of the militia used in western Pennsylvania, compensating those individuals who had suffered damage to property because they had stood loyally by the national government, and censuring the societies. The first was agreed to unanimously; Smith had little success with the second; the third required the greatest effort and all Smith's parliamentary skill. Smith wanted the committee appointed to reply to the President's speech to condemn these societies in a positive fashion, for Congress's silence "would be an avowed desertion of the Executive." He asked: "Would any one compare a regular town meeting where deliberations were cool and unruffled, to these societies, to the nocturnal meetings of individuals, after they have dined, where they shut their doors, pass votes in secret, and admit no members into their societies, but those of their own choosing?" These societies had grown amazingly during 1793 and 1794.[103] Smith reminded the members of a set of resolutions adopted by the Democratic Society of Philadelphia the previous May condemning the appointment of John Jay; they had objected to him as a judge and as one willing to give up the western posts to the British. These resolutions had been published and circulated to similar societies in the country, including the Republican Society of South Carolina, which had used them in the campaign against Smith. Smith won his point, for by a vote of forty-seven to forty-five the words "self-created societies" were included in the answer to the President. This was a solid Federalist vote, with Smith the only South Carolinian in favor. The opposition moved to limit the effect of the statement by adding "in the four western counties of Pennsylvania," which was agreed to. Smith, hoping to extend the censure further, moved to insert the words, "countenanced by self-created societies else where." But this was defeated by a vote of fifty to forty-two. Smith had fought more brilliantly

---

[103] Forty-two Democratic-Republican societies were organized between March 1793 and the election of Jefferson in 1800. Eleven were formed in 1793, twenty-four in 1794, three in 1795, none in 1796, one in 1797, and three in 1798. Five of these were in South Carolina: Republican Society of South Carolina (1793), Democratic Society of Pinckney District (1793), Madisonian Society of Greenville (1794), Franklin or Republican Society of Pendleton (1794), and Republican Society of St. Bartholomew's Parish (1795). Eugene Perry Link, *Democratic-Republican Societies, 1790-1800*, New York, 1942, p. 10.

than any other member of the House to uphold Washington's condemnation of the Democratic-Republican societies.[104]

A minor debate in this Congress over one aspect of the naturalization bill illustrates the drift of sentiment in both parties. The Jeffersonians still feared that the Federalists aimed at aristocracy and monarchy and wanted to be sure that French royalist emigrés did not add to the strength of the monarchical party in America. Giles warned of the possible arrival of 20,000 members of the French nobility! He demanded that foreigners be required to renounce their titles before becoming American citizens. Smith, entirely unmoved by such petty fears, saw this as a delicious chance to turn the whole debate into a farce. His wit was never sharper. As for titles, he had known a woman commonly referred to as "the Duchess," and no one had thought her harmful; in fact, her charms were well-known. If one pursued the opposition's train of thought one would reach the absurdity of the French themselves, who had gone around changing place-names, as Havre de Grace to Havre de Marat. Perhaps New Yorkers would change King Street to Liberty Street, and where then would such nonsense end? Was not the Marquis de Lafayette a brilliant example of a nobleman with republican sympathies? Soon a man would not be able to wear a cape for being thought possessed of an aristocratical cloak. If badges were to be forbidden: "Why not forbid the wearing of certain badges of distinction used by Jacobins?" Such petty actions, asserted Smith, came from little minds, more concerned with *amour propre* than with world realities. However, the Giles amendment won, fifty-nine to thirty-two, with Benton, Hunter, Pickens, and Winn all voting against Smith.[105]

IT IS DIFFICULT to explain how William Smith kept his political footing in South Carolina in 1794 and 1795 when he was so outspoken on the major issues of the day. He warmly supported the sending of John Jay to England. He rejoiced at the quick suppression of the Whiskey Rebellion, and he used the occasion to try to censure the Democratic-Republican societies. These views certainly ran counter to those held by a vast majority of the people of his state,

---

[104] *Annals of the Congress of the United States,* Washington, 1849, IV (3rd cong., 2nd sess.), 892-894, 896, 899, 901-902, 942-944. The final text of the statement to the President did not contain any of the above phrases. *Ibid.,* pp. 947-948.

[105] *Ibid.,* pp. 1030-1034, 1049-1050, 1057. For a strong condemnation of France's abolition of titles *see* Thomas Rhett Smith to John Rutledge, junior, December 26, 1790, *John Rutledge, junior, Papers,* SHC.

yet Smith was re-elected in 1794 and again in 1796. The only explanation is that the administration's policy was congenial to the Charleston commercial community. Smith was fighting to hold the Anglo-American commercial community together. It held—commerce flourished and the merchants grew rich. Proof of this can be found in the mercantile correspondence of Bird, Savage, and Bird with Smiths, DeSaussure, and Darrell.

These letters show that what held the British and American merchants together in 1793 and afterwards were the rising prospects for trade as the war developed in Europe.[106] In 1793, rice had been in little demand because of vast crops in Europe. In May 1794, the market was still dull, as shown by the fact that rice brought only 17/- per hundredweight, but Bird, Savage, and Bird believed that the demand created by large armies in the field would force the price up in the autumn.[107] In October they wrote that if Holland were flooded, the price would continue to mount.[108] By January 1795, it was known that the previous year's crop of grain in England "yielded, so indifferently, that we must look to America for importations, the rest of Europe being similarly situated with ourselves."[109] By the end of February, rice was selling at from 34/6 to 42/-, and the British Parliament in order to meet the shortage of foodstuffs removed duties from the importation of grains (including rice) and other provisions. During the next few months, Bird, Savage, and Bird were frantically urging Smiths, DeSaussure, and Darrell to ship rice to Cowes in any way possible. If American vessels were not available, they were to charter "Danish, Swedish, and Hamburghers" since rice could temporarily be imported in the vessels of any nation.[110]

War between England and America would have ruined these prospects, so these men worked diligently to prevent a break. Henry M. Bird, senior partner in the principal London house in the Caro

---

[106] This important series of letters addressed to Messrs. Edward Darrell and Company (but containing much information about Smiths, DeSaussure, and Darrell) begins in April 1793 and runs through 1795. *Josiah Edward Smith Letters*, DUL.

[107] Bird, Savage, and Bird to Messrs. Edward Darrell and Company, May 9, June 7, 1794, *Josiah Edward Smith Letters*, DUL.

[108] Bird, Savage, and Bird to Messrs. Edward Darrell and Company, October 21, 1794, *Josiah Edward Smith Letters*, DUL.

[109] Bird, Savage, and Bird to Messrs. Edward Darrell and Company, January 27, 1795, *Josiah Edward Smith Letters*, DUL.

[110] Bird, Savage, and Bird to Messrs. Edward Darrell and Company, January 27, February 23, April 2, June 3, 1795, *Josiah Edward Smith Letters*, DUL. Also see James Shoolbred to John Shoolbred, April 29, October 8, 1795, *Shoolbred Business Letter Book, 1793-1796*, CLS, pp. 255-262, 331-333.

lina rice trade, was a key figure. Through the influence of Izard and Smith, he had secured from Hamilton the agency for servicing the national debt abroad and had thereby set up a European market in American debt and stocks. His firm held this agency until bankruptcy dragged them under in 1803, and they were superseded by the Barings, who in turn gave way to the Rothschilds. This was, therefore, no ordinary firm.[111] In May 1794, Bird published a pamphlet to explain to the British government what the "principal American merchants" in London thought about the ministry's measures, which were driving the Americans into the arms of France.[112] Bird's chief point, and it was good advice for the ministry, was that Sheffield's *Observations*—the basis of England's commercial policy towards America—should now be superseded. Circumstances had shown that the two countries had much in common. America had been patient under the seizure of her ships, so why not withdraw the orders in council and open to America trade with the British West Indies? He concluded that the "most experienced and enlightened merchants" agreed with him.[113] No wonder Bird, Savage, and Bird wrote, July 5: "We hope with you that Mr. Jay's mission will be attended with success and be the means of establishing a lasting friendship between our two countries."[114] On November 21, they sent news of the signing of the treaty and though details were unknown wrote that "both Mr. Jay & the Duke of Portland have declared them to be so liberal that they have no doubts they will give general satisfaction."[115] And on December 30, they added, "We agree with you that your government have much credit for

---

[111] Bird wrote Washington from Charleston to ask for the agency either for Bird, Savage, and Bird or for Mannings and Vaughan: "I trust that on enquiry of the most honorable Ralph Izard Esquire or the honorable William Smith Esquire the competency of one or both these houses will be found equal to the undertaking." H. M. Bird to George Washington, January 23, 1790, *Miscellaneous Letters, Department of State*, National Archives. For bankruptcy see *South Carolina Circuit Court Records, 1790-1809*, FRC Georgia, p. 327.

[112] [Henry M. Bird], *A View of the Relative Situation of Great Britain and the United States of North America*, London, 1794, pp. 1-2. Smith's copy is in *William Loughton Smith Pamphlets*, CLS, I, number 5. Smith has written the name of Henry M. Bird on the title page under "By a Merchant."

[113] *Ibid.*, pp. 6, 11, 24.

[114] Bird, Savage, and Bird to Messrs. Edward Darrell and Company, July 5, 1794, *Josiah Edward Smith Letters*, DUL. James Shoolbred wrote that he was glad to hear of the good reception of John Jay. James Shoolbred to John Shoolbred, October 2, 1794, *Shoolbred Business Letter Book, 1793-1796*, CLS, p. 200.

[115] Bird, Savage, and Bird to Messrs. Edward Darrell and Company, November 21, 1794, *Josiah Edward Smith Letters*, DUL.

their moderation in trying the effects of a special mission."[116] Josiah Smith, Daniel DeSaussure, and Edward Darrell were, of course, working in America for the success of the Jay mission.

It is this commercial picture that explains why, when Smith returned to Charleston in the spring of 1795, after an interval of two years, he was received with great acclaim. Charleston, like the rest of commercial America, was reaping the harvest of the neutral trade. The policy of the national government had paid off. On May 5, 1795, Smith wrote Jedediah Morse from Charleston: "Our state, and particularly this city, is increasing rapidly in prosperity; rice now sells for 20/- whereas the current price was generally from 10/- to 12/-." Who would complain amidst such unparalleled prosperity? "My reception here has been very flattering—My Constituents are . . . satisfied, that my conduct was justified by policy and those who opposed me, have been among the foremost to pay me respect. Many of them are now enjoying that wealth, which our neutrality has been instrumental in procuring them. A society of the most remarkable merchants had it in contemplation, to give me on my arrival a public dinner; but were restrained by a fear of wounding the feelings of some respectable citizens; who in a moment of delusion took part against me."[117]

IN JUNE, South Carolinians were waiting for news of the terms of the Jay Treaty. Thomas Sumter, junior, wrote to Fulwar Skipwith, who was in Paris: "We know nothing of its shape as yet—and as usual—mystery breeds some discontents which you know are the actual off spring of suspense and secrecy."[118] Aedanus Burke wrote to Monroe, also in Paris: "What the terms or articles are, is a profound secret to the people, as yet."[119] Both Sumter and Burke were quite sure, however, that the terms would have to be acceptable to the moneyed, mercantile interest or they would not be approved. Sumter noted that "the war in Europe has been of infinite advantage to the money interest of America."[120] When Burke heard that Jay

---

[116] Bird, Savage, and Bird to Messrs. Edward Darrell and Company, December 20, 1794, *Josiah Edward Smith Letters*, DUL.

[117] William Smith to Jedediah Morse, May 5, 1795, a copy in *Morse Papers*, YL. David Ramsay wrote on the day the treaty was ratified: "Our state is in a more flourishing condition than it ever was." David Ramsay to John Eliot, June 24, 1795, *Andrews-Eliot Papers*, MHS.

[118] Thomas Sumter, junior, to Fulwar Skipwith, June 8, 1795, *Miscellaneous Manuscripts*, NYHS.

[119] Aedanus Burke to James Monroe, June 14, 1795, *Gratz Collection*, PHS.

[120] Thomas Sumter, junior, to Fulwar Skipwith, June 8, 1795, *Miscellaneous Manuscripts*, NYHS.

had been elected governor of New York, he remarked: "How thick his honors grow upon him." Yet there had been a challenge to the count and Jay would be in trouble unless "the terms of the treaty be acceptable to the mercantile interest of New York, and that immense mass of influence which they are masters of, thro every part of that extensive state."[121]

The terms of the treaty were known in Charleston by July 11, being brought in seven days from Philadelphia.[122] By the Jay Treaty, America gained the cession of the northwest posts and the right to trade with India and the British West Indies, but in the latter case only with ships of seventy tons displacement or less. Mixed commissions were to be created to settle the dispute over the northeast boundary of the United States and the spoliation claims. In return, Jay agreed to a mixed commission to settle the pre-war debts owed to British merchants. The United States accepted the British interpretation of maritime rights, which meant giving up the principle that "free ships make free goods" for the duration of the war. No privateers were to be fitted out in American ports, and no prizes were to be brought in and sold. There was no mention of compensation to southerners for slaves lost during the war of independence, nor did the British agree to terminate the impressment of American seamen by the British navy. Neither Washington nor Hamilton liked the treaty, but the United States needed peace and could afford to bide her time. Hamilton had urged ratification with the omission of Article Twelve, which limited United States trade to the British West Indies to vessels of seventy tons. On this basis the Senate had ratified the treaty by a vote of twenty to ten. Jacob Read was for the treaty; Pierce Butler against. Read's vote was crucial, for the change of one vote from the majority would have defeated the treaty.[123]

Charlestonians reacted to the news of the Jay Treaty in much the same manner as they had greeted the news of the Stamp Act. Gentlemen protested by words; the mob by deeds. Christopher Gadsden presided over a preliminary meeting of citizens in front of the Exchange, but a more select body assembled later in St. Michael's with John Mathews presiding.[124] John Rutledge made the principal speech, a tirade marked by quibbles and digressions—

[121] Aedanus Burke to James Monroe, June 14, 1795, *Gratz Collection*, PHS.
[122] *City Gazette Extraordinary*, July 12, 1795.
[123] Samuel Flagg Bemis, *Jay's Treaty*, New York, 1923, pp. 321-345.
[124] *Philadelphia Aurora*, July 29, 1795.

a speech radiating more heat than light.[125] Afterwards, a committee of fifteen was selected by vote to draw up a statement of the views of those assembled. The committee members and the number of votes each received were recorded as follows:

C. Gadsden	792	J. Mathews	440
J. Rutledge	792	Tho. Norris	429
D. Ramsay	775	Tho. Jones	411
E. Rutledge	757	Wm. Johnson	379
C. C. Pinckney	571	John Bee Holmes	372
T. T. Tucker	566	J. Rutledge, junior	345
Aedanus Burke	545	J. J. Pringle	295[126]
W. Washington	480		

The Rutledges, with General Pinckney, had become further detached from the other Federalist leaders, being willing now to work with Tucker and Burke. Not one prominent merchant nor any federal officeholder except John Rutledge was appointed to the committee. No member of the Izard-Manigault-Smith clan, nor of the Smith-DeSaussure-Darrell faction, was selected. It looked as though the South Carolina Federalist party had been irrevocably split and that the most important wing of the Rutledges and Pinckneys had fluttered into the Jeffersonian camp.

Once again, however, the Rutledges and the Pinckneys had to walk carefully. "The excitement was tremendous." The mob had been aroused. A gallows was "erected in front of the Exchange, in Broad-Street, on which were suspended six effigies, designed to represent the prominent advocates of . . . the treaty"—John Jay, John Adams, Timothy Pickering, Jacob Read, William Smith, and "his satanic majesty." "They remained the whole day, polluted by every mark of indignity, and, in the evening, were carried off to Federal Green, where they were burnt." Jacob Read's house was threatened just as Henry Laurens's had been in 1765.[127] The spirit of the American Revolution was abroad again. Even Christopher Gadsden was brought out of his long retirement to preside over the preliminary meeting. The Rutledges, disgruntled and peevish, must have caught some of this spirit, for they had never been more mercurial and unstable. Edward Rutledge was teaching his son to

[125] Henry Flanders, *The Lives and Times of the Chief Justices of the Supreme Court of the United States*, Philadelphia, 1858, I, 633-636.
[126] *Philadelphia Aurora*, August 11, 1795.
[127] Charles Fraser, *Reminiscences of Charleston*, Charleston, 1854, p. 45.

sing the Marseillaise, "if not with as much harmony, at least with as much animation" as it would be heard in Paris.[128]

Smith, who was in Charleston during the crisis, refused to be daunted by this apparently overwhelming opposition to the treaty. He dared to stand up for the treaty, relying on the expectation of continuing prosperity to secure the support of the entire mercantile community. On July 17, he analyzed for Jedediah Morse the opposition as being composed of four groups: one would have been opposed to any treaty with Britain no matter how good it was, the second had "personal objections to Mr. Jay," the third was the French faction, and the fourth was the war faction. These had united to condemn the treaty. The clamor they had raised had prevented many men from expressing their sentiments, lest "they should be held up, as wishing to place the U. S. again under British Subjugation; for this is the color they give it to influence the ignorant." Smith thought that when the ferment subsided, sensible men would discuss the treaty dispassionately and see that "as the price of peace, the sacrifices we have made, ought not so much to be regretted." No piece had yet appeared in the papers in vindication of the treaty; Smith felt that at that time no piece would do any good and that perhaps when tempers cooled, a straightforward account of the facts could be presented.[129]

The "Address of the Citizens of Charleston to the President," which was ready on the 19th, advised a suspension of the ratification of the treaty for a short time until the effects could be fully comprehended.[130] On July 22 Charles Pinckney made a long speech on the treaty, but Izard wrote Read that Pinckney was "so well known," and held in such "universal abhorrence, and contempt" that "nothing from him could produce much effect."[131] Yet as the news spread inland, the rest of the state was aroused. On the 25th the citizens of Camden District adopted resolutions which were far

---

[128] Mary Rutledge (Mrs. Edward Rutledge) to her step-daughter Sally, July 15, 1795, *Pinckney Papers*, LC.

[129] William Smith to Jedediah Morse, July 17, 1795, *William Loughton Smith Papers*, SCL.

[130] "Address of the Citizens of Charleston (South Carolina) to the President of the United States, transmitted by Thomas Lowndes, one of the Members of the House of Representatives of that State," *American Remembrancer*, Philadelphia, 1795, II, 51-52.

[131] "Speech of Mr. Charles Pinckney, late Governor of South Carolina, at a very numerous Meeting of the Citizens of Charleston, the 22d July, 1795, to hear the Report of their Committee on the Treaty between Great-Britain and the United States of America," *ibid.*, I, 5-20. Ralph Izard to Jacob Read, October 12, 1795, *Izard Papers*, SCL.

stronger than those adopted by the citizens of Charleston. They praised Butler and damned Read.[132]

Izard and Smith were not entirely pleased with the treaty, but they were determined to rally support. Izard wrote Read on July 30 that he himself had been "mortified" and "disappointed" upon reading the treaty, for he had flattered himself "that G. Britain, whose interest it certainly is to be well with this country would by conciliatory measures have disappointed those turbulent spirits, who are continually on the watch to find fault, & to do mischief." Although admitting this, Izard still could not approve of the proceedings in Charleston and felt that "those gentlemen who have been engaged in them have done no honor to themselves."[133] Izard disliked Article Twelve, the omission of the principle that free ships make free goods, the failure to exclude provisions from the list of contraband, and the fact that nothing had been done about slaves. With reference to the last matter, Izard, although one of the greatest sufferers, did not blame Jay.[134]

In this general situation, it took courage for Smith to defend the treaty, which he did in a well reasoned pamphlet published in Charleston in August. It was later republished in New York and won for Smith renown as a good and loyal Federalist, especially when there seemed to be so few in South Carolina.[135] Read reported in September from New York that Smith's pamphlet had been published there with great applause. The author, he said, "had infinite merit" to write so well on such short notice and without documents.[136]

The Pinckneys were of a different temperament from the Rutledges. Charles Cotesworth Pinckney obviously practiced great self-restraint during the summer and fall of 1795, although he wrote Jacob Read, "The coolest men . . . may sometimes unguardedly express their sentiments." He did not attend the meeting of the citizens in Charleston; furthermore, he posted a notice that he

---

[132] "Resolutions of a meeting of the Citizens of Camden Town and District, (South Carolina) held at the Court-house, on Saturday the 25th Day of July, assembled for the purpose of considering the Treaty, lately agreed upon between the United States of America and the King of Great Britain," *American Remembrancer,* Philadelphia, 1795, II, 54-56.

[133] Ralph Izard to Jacob Read, July 30, 1795, *Izard Papers,* LC.

[134] Ralph Izard to Jacob Read, October 12, 1795, *Izard Papers,* SCL.

[135] *A candid Examination of the Objections to the Treaty of Amity, Commerce, and Navigation, Between the United States and Great Britain, as stated in the Report of the Committee, appointed by the Citizens of the United States in Charleston, South-Carolina,* Charleston, 1795.

[136] Jacob Read to Ralph Izard, September 14, 1795, *Izard Papers,* SCL.

would not serve if elected to the committee of fifteen. When he was elected anyway, he would not attend. He even resolved not to read the treaty so as not to have to give any opinion at all. He explained to Read that he had done this because, if he had not approved, everyone would have said, "I was piqued because my brother had been superseded by Mr. Jay." If he had approved, then it would have been because "my brother had acknowledged the terms were more favourable than the British would have conceded before Mr. Jay's arrival." Either way his intentions would have been misconstrued. His concluding remarks show that he had been hurt, was slightly bitter, and had retreated as only a Pinckney or a Washington could—to his own Olympian heights.

> I exceedingly lament the schism it has made among the federalists; and you may be assured that a great many who are averse to war, and have been among the strongest supporters of the federal government, and are now warmly attached to it, disapprove the treaty; while the anti-federalists chuckle and are delighted at the division; more particularly as expressions are made use of in the controversy not warrantable in argument, and which can only tend to excite personal enmities—However true federalists may differ with regard to the treaty; if they have a real regard for their country; they should so conduct the controversy as to conciliate each other if possible by argument, and not widen the breach by invective.[137]

The administration could ill afford to lose the support of Pinckney, the most incorruptible of men. Washington offered him, in August, the position of secretary of state, but Pinckney refused.[138]

While Charles Cotesworth Pinckney was explaining to Jacob Read and George Washington his aloofness, Edward Rutledge sought out Jefferson in his retirement to confide that the treaty was "a most wretched affair" and the surmise that if the war continued and the treaty went into operation its evils would "multiply daily."[139] Jefferson replied that the treaty was an "execrable thing. . . . Nothing more than a treaty of alliance between England and the Anglomen of this country against the legislature & people of the United States." Jefferson's only hope was that the House of Representatives would negate the treaty by refusing to supply the necessary funds.[140]

[137] Charles Cotesworth Pinckney to Jacob Read, September 26, 1795, *Emmet Collection*, NYPL.
[138] George Washington to Charles Cotesworth Pinckney, August 24, 1795; Charles Cotesworth Pinckney to George Washington, September 16, 1795, *Writings of George Washington*, ed. John C. Fitzpatrick, Washington, 1940, XXXIV, 285-286.
[139] Edward Rutledge to Thomas Jefferson, October 12, 1795, *Jefferson Papers*, LC.
[140] Thomas Jefferson to Edward Rutledge, November 30, 1795, *Rutledge Papers, Dreer Collection*, PHS.

THE DANGER that the Rutledges and the Pinckneys would end up in the camp of the opposition grew. There was one way, however, by which the division in the local party could be healed, and that was by confirming Rutledge's appointment as chief justice. The Senate was to vote in December, but rumors had begun to fly that the northern chieftains would block the appointment because of Rutledge's July speech. Izard saw the dangers in such a policy and warned Jacob Read on November 17 that the enemies of the government "are in hopes that the Senate will not confirm the appointment of Mr. Rutledge as Chief Justice; and if so, will immediately raise a clamor, & endeavour to ascribe the rejection to party. I most sincerely hope that the Senate will agree to the nomination, & that the Anarchists may be disappointed. No man could be more afflicted than I was at the part Mr. Rutledge took in opposition to the Treaty. I am sure he is now very sorry for it himself." Izard blamed the unwise speech on the great strain that Rutledge was under after his wife's death. These considerations were to be passed on by Read to Izard's friends in the Senate, Cabot, Strong, Ellsworth, and Frederick Frelinghuysen of New Jersey, with a final warning that "the minds of the people in this State begin to be calmed, & I wish that everything may be avoided which will be likely to rekindle the flame, which has already given us too much trouble."[141]

John Rutledge and Jacob Read were bitter enemies. At some time in the past Rutledge had been "exceedingly cruel" to Read. However, Read wrote Izard that he would not take his revenge at this time. He and Smith had shown Izard's letter to George Cabot, but Cabot had said that he would not cooperate.[142] The vote, taken on December 15, was fourteen to ten—not sufficient to confirm Rutledge.[143] Although Read himself had voted for Rutledge, he tried to explain for Izard's benefit that New Englanders could not vote for a man who had headed a town meeting and excited the citizens in the manner of a demagogue. Full reports of Rutledge's pecuniary embarrassments had circulated, but these excited only minor objections. Read, of course, wanted it known in South Carolina that he had fought hard for Rutledge. He wrote that he had told his

[141] Ralph Izard to Jacob Read, November 17, 1795, *Emmet Collection*, NYPL.
[142] Jacob Read to Ralph Izard, December 8, 1795, *Izard Papers*, SCL. Also see William Read to Jacob Read, December 16, 29, 1795, *Read Papers*, SCL.
[143] George S. McCowen, Jr., "Chief Justice John Rutledge and the Jay Treaty," *SCHGM*, LXII (1961), 21.

Federalist friends about Rutledge's connections, the state of the party in South Carolina, his great legal knowledge, his resigning an equally respectable position, but none of these arguments had been effective. He concluded: "I would not have done more for my father. Do tell all of this to Mr. Rutledge's friends."[144]

In spite of the fact that John Rutledge's appointment was not confirmed, the Federalists made an amazing recovery. The Rutledges themselves, of course, knew by December that John Rutledge was not fit to be chief justice of the United States. William Read wrote his brother on the 16th: "I believe the Rutledges have been at their wits end how to conduct themselves in the delicate state of old Johns affairs, his pending appointment &c."[145] By this time, too, those who had been against the treaty were scrambling to regain a footing against the turning tide of public opinion. Judge Grimké, Henry William DeSaussure, and William Read all noted the "most striking change of sentiment" among those who had opposed the treaty. Edward Rutledge, after a great deal of "hedging about," permitted the tide to engulf him. When there was a move in the state legislature to censure the President of the United States, Edward Rutledge led the opposition. His speech was his recantation.[146]

For the Rutledges the year 1795 ended on a note of tragedy. At the time of John Rutledge's rejection by the Senate, there were rumors that he was at times out of his mind. John Rutledge had gone to Philadelphia to preside as chief justice over the August term of the Supreme Court, and in the fall he rode circuit.[147] William R. Davie wrote Judge James Iredell on September 4, 1795: "I will be obliged to you to let me know what Judge rides the So. Circuit. If your Chief Justice raves on the bench as he does at a town meeting, we shall be highly edified."[148] Did the rumors of his insanity stem from such random remarks? It was said that at Camden he had attempted to drown himself. But again this was only a rumor. The one concrete fact is that Rutledge did attempt to commit suicide in Charleston after Christmas. William Read has left us the full story:

> The unfortunate Judge Rutledge has been much Housed, said to be indisposed, ever since his return from a half finish'd circuit—on

[144] Jacob Read to Ralph Izard, December 19, 1795, *Izard Papers,* SCL.
[145] William Read to Jacob Read, December 16, 1795, *Read Papers,* SCL.
[146] William Read to Jacob Read, December 29, 1795, *Read Papers,* SCL. Judge Grimké to Jacob Read, December 18, 1795, *Gratz Collection,* PHS.
[147] Rutledge asked Iredell to help him get a gown. John Rutledge to James Iredell, August 11, 1795, *Emmet Collection,* NYPL.
[148] William R. Davie to James Iredell, September 4, 1795, copy in *Davie Papers,* NC Archives.

Sunday Morning that miserable old man attempted to put an end to his life by drowning himself—They say he is mad—Tho' on this occasion there appear'd much consistent arrangement—He left his House by stealth early in the morning, & went down to Gibbes's Bridge—there, with his clothes on he went deliberately into the water—It was just day light—A negro child was near, & struck with the uncommonness of the sight she call'd to some negroes on the Deck of a Vessell—he had now gone beyond his depth & had sunk, but struggleing sometimes rose—The fellows had the presence of mind to run with a Boat hook & catch hold of his arm—he made violent opposition to them but they draged him out & detain'd him by force, they calling out for assistance, while he cursed & abused them, & would drive them away. The noise brought out Jack Blake's House-keeper who he also scold'd, & drove her away, she gave Mr. Blake the alarm, he ran out & secured the miserable old man, brought him to his House where he attempted to reason him out of such design—He is related to have had a Razor in his pocket—He was prodigiously agitated, & shook with cold & perhaps shame—He persisted in his intention said he had a right to dispose of his own life as he pleased—"he had long been a Judge & he knew no law that forbid a man to take away his own life." "That if he had not been prevented he would by this time have been happy." Mr. B. reason'd with him on a regard for reputation, on the disgrace such an end would bring on his children— He reply'd that his life was his own that he cared not a Button for his children. Thus spoke this unfortunate wise old man—his conduct to most people is unaccountable as 'tis extraordinary—some suppose it arrising from his reflections on his late political conduct—I hear that he was reasonable & calm today—It has been said that he made an attempt to drown himself at Camden—Every Body appears to pity and lament Mr. Rutledge's situation—Young Ned has been severely shook with fever—This will almost kill him. . . .[149]

A series of unfortunate circumstances could certainly have driven John Rutledge to the point of suicide: the death of his wife, financial reverses, rejection by the Senate.[150] On December 28, he wrote President Washington that after "a fair experiment" of the strength of his constitution he must resign.[151] Ever afterwards young John

[149] William Read to Jacob Read, December 29, 1795, *Read Papers*, SCL. December 29 was a Tuesday; the attempt at suicide was, therefore, made on Sunday, December 27.

[150] Rutledge's wife died in 1792. Robert L. Meriwether, "John Rutledge," *DAB.* For his financial difficulties see "Memo of John Rutledge, junior," October 30, 1795, *John Rutledge, junior, Papers*, SHC. *Also see* Benjamin Moodie to Jacob Read, December 29, 1795, *Miscellaneous Manuscripts*, NYPL. The author has been unable to ascertain when Rutledge learned of his rejection by the Senate.

[151] John Rutledge to George Washington, December 28, 1795, *Miscellaneous Letters, Department of State*, National Archives. This would have been the day after the attempt at suicide.

Rutledge referred to his father as "my unfortunate Parent."[152] Robert Lindsay wrote Samuel Johnston on January 13, 1796, that the late chief justice had "attempted, about ten days ago, to drown himself in Ashley River, but was taken out, by some Negroes, before he finished the end of his career in this world. The Treaty is very seldom mentioned."[153]

THE FINAL BATTLE in the great debate over the Jay Treaty was waged in the House of Representatives. The Jeffersonians attempted to undermine the treaty by withholding the necessary financial arrangements. In this the first session of the Fourth Congress, Smith had three new colleagues: Samuel Earle, Wade Hampton, and Robert Goodloe Harper.[154] Of these, Harper was to become an important Federalist figure, the first produced by the backcountry of South Carolina. He had actually entered Congress in the lame-duck session of the Third Congress (taking his seat on February 5, 1795), having been elected to take Alexander Gillon's seat in a by-election.[155] He had also defeated John Hunter in the fall of 1794 to represent Ninety Six District in the Fourth Congress.[156]

At first glance he seemed to be another radical from the backcountry—in 1794, as "Appius," he had written in behalf of greater representation for the backcountry.[157] Both Edward Rutledge in a letter of introduction to Jefferson in 1791 and Pierce Butler in another to Madison in 1795 emphasized the fact that Harper was ambitious, and events confirmed that he was obviously willing to

[152] John Rutledge, junior, to Bishop Smith, February 27, 1799, *John Rutledge, junior, Papers,* SHC.
[153] Robert Lindsay to Samuel Johnston, January 13, 1796, microfilm, reel 5, *Hayes Collection,* SHC. (Original in the possession of Mr. John G. Wood, Edenton, North Carolina.)
[154] Samuel Earle (1760-1833) moved from Virginia to South Carolina in 1774. Member of Congress from March 4, 1795, to March 3, 1797. Wade Hampton (1752-1835) moved from Virginia to South Carolina before the Revolution. Member of Congress from March 4, 1795, to March 3, 1797, and later served from March 4, 1803, to March 3, 1805. Hampton was an unsuccessful candidate for re-election in 1796 and in 1804. Robert Goodloe Harper (1765-1825) was born in Virginia, grew up in North Carolina, and after studying at Princeton practiced law in the Ninety Six District of South Carolina. Member of Congress from February 5, 1795, to March 3, 1801; unsuccessful candidate for re-election in 1800. *Biographical Directory of the American Congress, 1774-1949,* Washington, 1950, pp. 1114, 1261, 1270.
[155] *City Gazette and Daily Advertiser,* November 18, 1794.
[156] *Ibid.,* October 28, 1794.
[157] [Robert Goodloe Harper,] *An Address to the People of South-Carolina, By the General Committee of the Representative Reform Association, at Columbia,* Columbia, 1794.

be seduced by the flattery and admiration of great men.[158] By June 1795, Butler was sorry he had introduced Harper to Madison.[159] But this man certainly had talent, and he soon put it to good use for the Federalist cause by writing the most famous defense of the Jay Treaty, a pamphlet which warranted fifteen editions at home and abroad.[160] John Jay himself wrote Harper: "Had all the publications on that subject been written with equal knowledge and attention, or with equal candour and decorum, more truth would have been disseminated, and less irritation excited."[161] However, if Harper had changed from one side to another merely for ambition's sake, he would never have been re-elected, and he was—twice. There was a sizeable covey of Federalists in Ninety Six District by this time; in fact, "the Harperian Federalists" were to be notorious.[162] Smith at last had an able lieutenant from the backcountry.

Livingston's motion in March, which called upon the President to send all papers concerning the treaty to the House, opened the debate. The Jeffersonians refused to appropriate funds to establish the three commissions before they had examined each step in the negotiations. Smith opposed the motion by expounding upon the principle of the separation of powers. The treaty-making power properly belonged to the executive, for secrecy was needed. The only possible interpretation of a request for papers was that the opposition intended to impeach the President.[163] Smith had asked for an adjournment of the House for half an hour on Washington's birthday so that the members might pay their respects to the President; the defeat of this motion by a vote of fifty to thirty-eight can be taken as an indication that the House was not overawed by the

[158] Edward Rutledge to Thomas Jefferson, August 7, 1791, *Jefferson Papers*, LC.

[159] See John Harold Wolfe, *Jeffersonian Democracy in South Carolina*, Chapel Hill, 1940, pp. 87-88, n. 75.

[160] Robert Goodloe Harper, *An Address from Robert Goodloe Harper, of South-Carolina, to His Constituents. Containing His Reasons for Approving of the Treaty of Amity, Commerce, and Navigation, with Great-Britain*, Philadelphia, 1795.

[161] John Jay to Robert Goodloe Harper, January 19, 1796, *Correspondence and Public Papers of John Jay*, ed. Henry P. Johnston, New York, 1933, IV, 198-203.

[162] "Diary of Edward Hooker, 1805-1808," ed. J. Franklin Jameson, *Annual Report of the American Historical Association for the Year 1896*, Washington, 1897, p. 889.

[163] *Annals of the Congress of the United States*, Washington, 1849, V (4th cong., 1st sess.), 438-444. Smith was receiving constitutional arguments from Hamilton. See Alexander Hamilton to William Smith, March 10, 1796, *The Works of Alexander Hamilton*, ed. Henry Cabot Lodge, New York, 1904, X, 147-148.

mighty Washington.[164] The great debate that followed pitted Smith
and Harper against the Jeffersonian phalanx of Edward Livingston
of New York, Giles, John Nicholas of Virginia, and Madison.[165] In
the final vote on Livingston's motion, Benton, Earle, Hampton, and
Winn voted with the majority of sixty-two, while Smith and Harper
were in the minority of thirty-seven.[166] Washington, however, refused to send the papers; he charged that the only interest the
House could have in such documents would be for the consideration
of an impeachment. He had accepted the line laid down for him
by Hamilton and Smith. When the House then took up the subject
of appropriations, the supporters of the administration were able
to win by only the smallest of margins.[167]

SMITH SAILED for Charleston as soon as the session was over, for he
had been asked to make the Fourth-of-July oration. This celebration
marked the summit of his career. His greatest parliamentary battle
was in behalf of the treaty, and in this he had been successful. That
treaty brought ten years of friendly cooperation between England
and America, a period aptly designated by Bradford Perkins as the
"First Rapprochement."[168]

Smith arrived in Charleston on July 1 after "a very tedious pas-
sage" from Philadelphia, just in time to prepare his address.[169]
William Read has left us an account of the celebration on the 4th.
"Mr. Smith's oration was spoken in the Old Church (St. Philip's).
A very crowd'd & elegant assembly attended—It was an eloquent
thing & spoken with neat oratory—It was no doubt a studied piece—
The exordium was fine but painfully long, his allegories stupendous
& elegantly contriv'd."[170]

The oration was in fact a defense of Washington, the administration, the policy of neutrality, and the glorious consequences for
commerce.[171] But to Read there was a jarring note—"that the fine

[164] *Annals of the Congress of the United States,* Washington, 1849, V (4th
cong., 1st sess.), 355.
[165] *Ibid.,* pp. 438-760.
[166] *Ibid.,* pp. 759-760.
[167] *See* vote on April 22 which was 50 to 49 and then a bit later that day a
vote of 51 to 48, which carried the appropriation with Smith and Harper in
the majority. *Ibid.,* pp. 1289, 1291.
[168] Bradford Perkins, *The First Rapprochement, England and the United
States, 1795-1805,* Philadelphia, 1955.
[169] William Smith to Oliver Wolcott, July 9, 1796, *Wolcott Papers,* CHS.
[170] William Read to Jacob Read, July 8, 1796, *C. E. French Collection,* MHS.
[171] William Smith, *An Oration, Delivered in St. Philip's Church, Before the
Inhabitants of Charleston, South-Carolina, on the Fourth of July, 1796, in Commemoration of American Independence,* Charleston, 1796.

picture Mr. Smith drew of our happiness & flourishing commerce" was not at that hour "a true one." Many then were experiencing "a painful reverse," and the thoughtful felt that American commerce would be "a mutilated bone of contention" for some time to come, at least as long as Britain and France continued to oppose each other.[172]

A number of merchants found themselves short of funds. They had suffered from British spoliations in the West Indies, and though the Jay Treaty promised compensation, it was just that, a promise for the future, not a present actuality. Men like William Crafts, Nathaniel Russell, Hary Grant, John Geyer, Adam Gilchrist, and William Somersall could not hold on much longer. Smith had presented to Congress on April 18 a memorial from thirty-six Charleston merchants asking for a loan of money, or other help, until they received compensation from the British government.[173] Added to this local situation was the collapse of the price of rice in England. Many bills for great amounts had come back protested. Thayer and Sturgis were thought to be ruined. The losses of one house equalled its profits of the year before.[174] Except for the banks' continuing to discount their notes, many more firms might have gone under.[175]

Some of the largest planters had also been hurt—those who tried to bypass local factors and merchants to secure greater profits. Izard stood to lose £3,000 sterling because of his gamble.[176] As William Read remarked, there was general gloom among the Cincinnati on the 4th due to the change in affairs in England. General Pinckney was not himself that afternoon; he had just heard from England of the fall of the price of rice, and he had already remitted rice to his brother and on his own account. The whole commercial community was reeling. Even William Read wondered if it were any longer fitting to work with England. "But alas! What could we have done? It would appear madness to adopt France after their avowed principles."[177]

[172] William Read to Jacob Read, July 8, 1796, *C. E. French Collection*, MHS.
[173] "Memorial of sundry merchants of Charleston in respect to losses by British spoliations," April 18, 1796, *Claims, Senate Papers*, National Archives. *Annals of the Congress of the United States*, Washington, 1849, V (4th cong., 1st sess.), 1025.
[174] William Read to Jacob Read, July 8, 1796, *C. E. French Collection*, MHS.
[175] James Shoolbred to John Shoolbred, May 31, 1796, *Shoolbred Business Letter Book, 1793-1796*, CLS, p. 407.
[176] Smith wrote Wolcott: "Mr. Izard will probably lose near 3000 £ sterling by having refused to sell his rice here at 30/- sterling which he was offered, and having shipped it to London." William Smith to Oliver Wolcott, July 9, 1796, *Wolcott Papers*, CHS.
[177] William Read to Jacob Read, July 8, 1796. *C. E. French Collection*, MHS.

Smith's policies were long-run policies, and this was, after all, only a temporary fluctuation. The committee that sponsored Smith's oration asked for permission to print it.[178] An advertisement in the newspaper said "that the works which have lately had the greatest run in town, are Paine's Age of Reason & Smith's Oration." Smith sent a copy to Rufus King, commenting, "You will smile at seeing any work of mine associated with Paine's & the heroic actions of the French." He concluded: "The Treaty phobia is completely cured here, and federal politics, when they engage the attention, excite generally approbation. Those who made such a ridiculous clamor last summer, seem ashamed of themselves and are glad to throw a veil over what has passed.—Mr. Rutledge, the late C. J., lives quite retired & avoids being seen; his health is said to be mended."[179]

SMITH WAS SURE of his own re-election in 1796. In July he wrote Herman LeRoy: "As to politics, everybody seems contented with the treaty and the government."[180] To him this meant, too, that they were content with William Smith.[181] The dangers of 1794 had been successfully circumvented by the completion of the Jay negotiations. The Democratic-Republican societies had consequently fallen into the background. With his own seat safe, Smith sailed in August with General Pinckney for Philadelphia, the breach between Smith and the Rutledge-Pinckney faction apparently healed.[182] John Rutledge, junior, instead of opposing Smith in 1796, successfully canvassed Beaufort and Orangeburg District. Smith had only minor opposition from Robert Simons in Charleston District and won easily in the October elections.[183] Harper's tremen-

---

[178] The request was made by the American Revolution Society and the South-Carolina State Society of the Cincinnati. *See* title page of William Smith, *An Oration, Delivered in St. Philip's Church, Before the Inhabitants of Charleston, South-Carolina, on the Fourth of July, 1796, in Commemoration of American Independence*, Charleston, 1796.

[179] William Smith to Rufus King, July 23, 1796, *King Papers*, NYHS.

[180] William Smith to Herman LeRoy, July 15, 1796, *William Loughton Smith Papers*, DUL.

[181] Smith wrote Wolcott that there was no objection to his own re-election except on the ground that he ought "not to monopolize, but make room for others." William Smith to Oliver Wolcott, July 9, 1796, *Wolcott Papers*, CHS.

[182] Pinckney sailed in August; Smith returned to the North at the same time. Whether they sailed on the same vessel is not known. Edward Rutledge to Henry Rutledge, August 13, 1796, *Emmet Collection*, NYPL. On September 28 Smith received an honorary doctor of laws degree from Princeton, along with Fisher Ames. *Minerva*, October 1, 1796. *Gazette of the United States*, October 3, 1796.

[183] *City Gazette and Daily Advertiser*, October 29, 1796. *South-Carolina State Gazette*, October 12, November 1, 1796. Robert Simons (1758-1807) was a brother of James Simons, the collector. Robert Bentham Simons, *Thomas Grange Simons III, His Forebears and Relations*, Charleston, 1954, pp. 11, 61.

dous victory in Ninety Six District gave the Federalist party three representatives from South Carolina in the Fifth Congress.[184]

Interest that fall centered on the presidential contest. Washington did not announce his retirement until September, but the leaders on both sides had understood that he would not be a candidate. Washington had inspired unanimous support; consequently, his decision to retire made possible for the first time a national political campaign. It was obvious that the Federalists had to run Adams, and the Republicans, Jefferson. However, there was much less agreement in each party on who should be the second man. Smith wrote Izard in May that the Republicans were "at a stand" on the second man: "The persons in nomination are Burr, Langdon, Butler and Chancellor Livingston; the latter is said to stand highest. . . . Butler, they say, they have no objection to except being a Southern man and as Jefferson is to be President, it won't do:—Burr, they think unsettled in his politics and are afraid he will go over to the other side: Langdon has no influence." Smith confessed that "our side are also unsettled."[185]

The northern Federalists needed votes in the South in 1796, and South Carolina was the most likely state in which to find them. Smith wrote Izard that Adams would get the unanimous vote of New England, New York, New Jersey, Delaware, and a few in Maryland. One or two votes in South Carolina would, therefore, make Adams's election certain.[186] Within South Carolina the Rutledges and the Pinckneys held the balance of power, so the national Federalist leaders set to work to woo the Pinckneys, who seemed more sober and conservative than the Rutledges. If the Pinckneys could be won, the Rutledges and South Carolina would surely go along. George Washington wrote Charles Cotesworth Pinckney on July 8, inviting him to become the new American minister to France. Washington said that he was looking for "a man whose abilities, and celebrity of character are well known to the people of this country; and who ought, as far as the nature of the case will admit, be acceptable to all parties."[187] Pinckney, who up to this time had

---

[184] Harper defeated General Butler by a vote of 1618 to 774. *City Gazette and Daily Advertiser*, October 25, 1796.

[185] William Smith to Ralph Izard, May 18, 1796, "South Carolina Federalist Correspondence, 1789-1797," ed. Ulrich B. Phillips, *AHR*, XIV (1909), 780.

[186] William Smith to Ralph Izard, November 3, 1796, *ibid.*, p. 781.

[187] George Washington to Charles Cotesworth Pinckney, July 8, 1796, *Writings of George Washington*, ed. John C. Fitzpatrick, Washington, 1940, XXXV, 129-131.

refused all national offices, accepted on the 27th.[188] An even higher honor was reserved for Thomas Pinckney. William Smith had been asked by the northern Federalists, when he returned to South Carolina in July, to sound out Thomas Pinckney's friends about placing his name on the Federalist ticket with John Adams. Smith canvassed the local leaders and summed up his findings for Wolcott on July 9: "They will not undertake to promise that he will be a candidate, as he is expected here soon . . . in the mean time, I think his name ought to be circulated among our friends to the Eastward. Should he positively decline, I don't know whom we could recommend from this quarter; I believe both General Pinckney and Mr. Izard would be unwilling to run."[189] Since General Pinckney had already accepted the mission to France and Izard had retired from public life, the name of Thomas Pinckney was left before the public. It was thought that Thomas Pinckney, being a southerner, would complement the Yankee Adams, and that the popularity of the Pinckney Treaty would make him strong in the West.[190] The team of Adams and Pinckney was an excellent one.

The hitch in the constitutional system for electing a president was the unforeseen possibility of a tie in the electoral college. The eastern leaders, in order to avoid a tie, considered dropping a few votes for Pinckney in New England so that Adams could come in first. Among some of the South Carolinians, there popped up the similar idea of dropping some of the votes for Adams and bringing Pinckney the victory. This latter idea was particularly congenial to the lukewarm South Carolina Federalists, especially to Edward Rutledge.

Rather ironically, both Pinckneys were out of the country during the crucial election period. Charles Cotesworth sailed for Philadelphia in August and for France in November.[191] Thomas did not return to Charleston from England until December 17.[192] In between, their affairs, both private and public, were managed by Edward Rutledge (John Rutledge was in retirement and John Rutledge, junior, was just making his first successful bid for Congress), whose one aim was to make sure that the arch-Federalists did not use his friends the Pinckneys for their own ulterior purposes.

[188] Charles Cotesworth Pinckney to George Washington, July 27, 1796, *ibid.*, p. 131, n. 61.
[189] William Smith to Oliver Wolcott, July 9, 1796, *Wolcott Papers*, CHS.
[190] Samuel Flagg Bemis, *Pinckney's Treaty*, New Haven, 1960, p. 294.
[191] Harper wrote that "General Pinckney's absence is a great loss." Robert Goodloe Harper to Ralph Izard, November 4, 1796, "South Carolina Federalist Correspondence," *op. cit.*, p. 783.
[192] *South-Carolina State Gazette*, December 19, 1796.

Edward Rutledge was well aware of his responsibilities. After obtaining for his son Henry the position as secretary to his Uncle Charles Cotesworth Pinckney at £300 per annum, he offered this parting advice:

> Altho I am fully convinced you are neither anxious, or desirous of entering on Public Duties, yet if at certain times & in certain Seasons it is so absolutely incumbent on Men of Talents, & Independence & Virtue to participate in the affairs of the Republic, that I consider your Chance for retirement to be small indeed—The family, my Son, from which you have descended,—the Style of your Education;—the long & steady attachment of your Uncle Pinckney towards you;—the early acquaintance which you have formed with Public Men;—the Habits to which they themselves are accustomed of considering your nearest Connections as the property of their Country, form such a Combination of Circumstances as forbid the Idea of private Life—[193]

Edward Rutledge had cast himself and his children in a heroic mold. When he urged Henry to write home sketches of the leading characters of France, he suggested the plan that Algernon Sydney used in writing to his father of the characters of the cardinals.[194] This yearning for a great role, comparable to those played by the Hampdens and the Sydneys, imbued Rutledge with the idea of being a president-maker. He thought that New England would vote for Adams and Pinckney and the southern states would vote for Pinckney and Jefferson. Thomas Pinckney would therefore be at the top of the poll. On October 20, Rutledge wrote: "I believe he will fill the Presidential chair."[195] On November 1, he was definitely of that opinion. The important thing was to hold Carolina for Pinckney and Jefferson. Rutledge knew that great exertions would be made for Adams, but if the members of the backcountry attended the legislature in large numbers he was sure the Adams men would fail.[196]

Edward Rutledge was also using his influence in North Carolina. He had written Benjamin Smith, William Smith's first cousin, who was an influential North Carolina politician of the Wilmington area, and urged him not to support Adams. Benjamin Smith conveyed the news to William Smith. William Smith, who was sure of his cousin

[193] Edward Rutledge to Henry Rutledge, September 1796, *Rutledge Papers, Dreer Collection*, PHS.
[194] Edward Rutledge to Henry Rutledge, September 5, 1796, *Rutledge Papers, Dreer Collection*, PHS.
[195] Edward Rutledge to Henry Rutledge, October 20, 1796, *Rutledge Papers, Dreer Collection*, PHS.
[196] Edward Rutledge to Henry Rutledge, November 1, 1796, *Rutledge Papers, Dreer Collection*, PHS.

and increasingly suspicious of Rutledge, wrote Izard: "I suspect he is tampering with my cousin, but he won't succeed with him."[197]

Smith had already taken up his pen to crush Jefferson. He had been greatly irritated by an argument of "Hampden" in a Richmond paper of October 1 that Jefferson would make a good President because he was a philosopher. The result of Smith's irritation had been a savage satire called *The Pretensions of Thomas Jefferson*.[198] This was published first as a series of articles in the *Gazette of the United States* under the signature of "Phocion." Smith, when he learned of Edward Rutledge's moves to push Jefferson rather than Adams, must have been furious and decided to ship his articles off to South Carolina. These ran in the *South-Carolina State Gazette* from November 8 to December 15.[199] Nothing brought out Smith's satiric qualities more quickly than Jefferson.

Did "Hampden" mean moral or natural philosopher? If moral philosopher, had Jefferson ever condemned the cruelties of France? If only a natural philosopher, why should this qualify any man for President? One might as well have the great bridge-builder Cox or the famous equestrian Ricketts as President. A natural philosopher would make the worst of politicians. Imagine an important official of the government coming to see the President only to find him busy impaling butterflies or working in his whirligig chair, "which had the miraculous quality of allowing the person seated in it to turn his head, without moving his tail."[200] But a philosopher would never do for President. The great Locke was employed to frame a constitution for Carolina, but it was "so full of *theoretic whimsies* . . . inapplicable to the state of things for which it was designed [that] it was soon thrown aside."[201]

Yet even if Jefferson were a philosopher, he was far from consistent. Compare his *Notes on Virginia* to a letter written to Benjamin Banneker, a Negro. In the first he said that the blacks were inferior to whites; in the second, that they were equal. Either Jefferson had discovered his error or "he was so influenced by a

[197] William Smith to Ralph Izard, November 3, 1796, "South Carolina Federalist Correspondence," *op. cit.*, p. 784. Adams got one vote in North Carolina, Benjamin Smith's.
[198] [William Smith,] *The Pretensions of Thomas Jefferson to the Presidency Examined; and the Charges against John Adams Refuted. Addressed to the Citizens of America in general; and particularly to the Electors of the President,* n.p., 1796, p. 1.
[199] *South-Carolina State Gazette,* November 8, 9, 11, 12, 14, 15, 16, 17, 19, 21, 22, 23, 24, 26, 28, December 3, 5, 6, 7, 8, 15, 1796.
[200] [Smith], *The Pretensions of Thomas Jefferson . . .,* p. 16.
[201] *Ibid.,* p. 14.

ridiculous vanity, so tickled by a silly compliment from 'an un-savoury animal of an inferior race,' " that he had changed his mind. "What shall we think of a *secretary of state* thus *fraternizing* with negroes, writing them complimentary epistles, stiling them *his black bretheren,* congratulating them on the evidences of their *genius,* and assuring them of his good wishes for their speedy emancipation."[202] This change in mind could only be explained by Jefferson's residence in France. Should a philosopher who wished to emancipate the slaves be trusted? Recall the words of Condorcet: "Perish all the colonists, rather than that we should deviate one tittle from our principles."[203] If southerners voted for such a man as Jefferson, who had been a friend of Condorcet, they would deserve their fate. Smith could sink to such depths, because he had a prejudiced heart and a witty mind, and he wanted very much to win.

It was clear to all the readers of the *South-Carolina State Gazette* that "Phocion" was William Smith. This attempt to chop Jefferson down to size was naturally resented by the Republicans, and they replied in kind with the same sharp invective aimed at Smith. Aedanus Burke felt that the people of South Carolina were too wise to be gulled by Smith's "keen sarcasms or ingenious ridicule."[204] "Bob the Weaver's" explanation was that "Phocion" had become hysterical by the knowledge that he would not be able to favor the British as much under Jefferson as he would under Adams.[205] The final darts were contained in a piece entitled, "The Similarity between Phocion and the Ass in the Fable."[206] The entire debate remained at a very low level on both sides.

When the legislature of South Carolina finally chose electors, the Jeffersonians overwhelmed the Adams men:

Jefferson electors		*Adams electors*	
Edward Rutledge	113	Arnoldus Vanderhorst	31
Andrew Pickens	112	H. W. DeSaussure	29
John Mathews	112	Robert Barnwell	28
Thomas Taylor	110	William Washington	28
Arthur Simkins	110	David Ramsay	28
John Rutledge, junior	109	Gen. John Barnwell	28
John Chesnut	109	Nathaniel Russell	28
William Thomas	109	John Bull	24[207]

[202] *Ibid.,* pp. 8, 10.
[203] *Ibid.,* p. 16.
[204] *South-Carolina State Gazette,* November 14, 1796.
[205] *Ibid.,* November 16, 1796.
[206] *Ibid.,* December 12, 1796.
[207] John Harold Wolfe, *Jeffersonian Democracy in South Carolina,* Chapel Hill, 1940, p. 98.

Only the two Rutledges and John Mathews appear out of place, having left their former friends to work with Pickens, Taylor, Simkins, and Chesnut from the upcountry.[208] It was the shift of the Rutledge group that made it impossible for Adams to receive a single vote in South Carolina, and, quite ironically, also seemed to make it impossible for Pinckney to win the second place.

Smith received "the disagreeable intelligence of the election" on December 22. He wrote immediately to Gabriel Manigault:

> Tho fortunately it cannot prevent Mr. Adams's election, yet it endangers Mr. Pinckney's & is disgraceful to the State. If there could be any consolation in the reflection that Mr. Pinckney will thus be disgraced by the shameful conduct of his own friends, we should now enjoy it, as it is nearly certain that the 8 votes for Jefferson in S. C. will prevent the election of Major P. to the Vice Presidency: had 3 votes been thrown away for Jefferson Maj. P'y's election would have been certain. By the returns we have heard of, Mr. Adams has already 71 votes, one more than a majority, Mr. Jefferson can have only 68. Mr. Pinckney has (including N. Hampshire, about which there has been some doubt, but now removed) 65; unless he has 3 votes in Georgia, Kentucky or Tennessee, his election is lost, & Jefferson will be V.P. It is very uncertain whether Pinckney will get them; if he does, there will be a tie & the Senate will undoubtedly elect him.—S. C. might have settled this point; if Maj. P. is thrown out, it will be owing entirely to the ridiculous & wicked conduct of his own State & particular friends. It will be a very mortifying thing, when to have been held up even as President, to be handsomely supported by the Eastern people & yet to lose his Election even as V.P. by the folly & mismanagement of his friend, E. R.!!

In the final count, Adams got every vote of New England, New York, New Jersey, Delaware, and seven out of eleven in Maryland. He also picked up one each in Pennsylvania, Virginia, and North Carolina to make seventy-one. Jefferson got all of his votes in the South and West plus four in Maryland and fourteen in Pennsylvania for a total of sixty-eight. Pinckney got only fifty-nine (Smith was counting six from New Hampshire which eventually went to Oliver Ellsworth). Pinckney's votes came from the states that Adams swept, plus two in Pennsylvania, four in Maryland, one each in Virginia and North Carolina, and eight in South Carolina.

---

[208] Mathews, like the Rutledges, was in financial difficulties. John Mathews had been security for George Abbot Hall, former collector, and the U. S. Treasury was pressing him for payments. Smith wrote Wolcott: "As Mr. Mathews situation is a hard one, being a security only, and having the burden of a large family of Mr. Hall's to assist in supporting, I would recommend the allowance of the equitable reductions." William Smith to Oliver Wolcott, July 9, 1796, *Wolcott Papers*, CHS.

What will E. R. say to *his* Virginia friends, when he knows that Jefferson's party would not give a single vote for Pinckney in any part of the Union? When he knows that the federal party, the Adams party, have given (except in S. C.) every vote which Pinckney has got? for in this State, the two votes for Pinckney were given by the two men in the federal ticket, one of whom voted for Pinckney & Jefferson—in V. & N. C. the votes for P. were given by the Adams electors. Will not E. R. feel resentment at being betrayed by the antifederal party & remorse at having separated from the federal party? disgust with his new friends & contrition for injuring his old ones?

Another interesting fact to be drawn from these votes was that Aaron Burr got only one of his thirty votes from Virginia, for Virginia threw away fifteen votes ón Samuel Adams. "Burr's friends have betrayed him in Virginia—he had been so duped by them, that he has not yet showed his face here; tho his lodgings were engaged for him the first instant. They have made a complete catspaw of him; Langdon chuckles, rubs his hands & laments the ill success of Brother Burr."[209] Virginia had failed to support both Burr and Pinckney. Undoubtedly Burr's supporters in the North and Pinckney's supporters in the South harbored a great deal of bitterness as a result of this election. Four years later, when Burr tied Jefferson and the House had to decide the election, a deadlock for thirty-five votes ensued. One reason for the deadlock was that the South Carolinians consistently supported Burr, even against the known wishes of their state. More importantly, the South Carolina delegation at that time was dominated by Thomas Pinckney and John Rutledge, junior. Sometime during the next four years the Pinckneys and the Rutledges came to hate Jefferson. With John Rutledge, junior, the transformation from friend to foe would be complete.[210]

ONE OF THE CHIEF GLORIES of the American Constitution is that it provides for an orderly transfer of power. Neither Cromwell nor Napoleon, great as their own powers and abilities were, ever solved this problem. Smith described the transfer of power in a letter to Rufus King:

[209] William Smith to [Gabriel Manigault], December 22, 1796, *Manigault Papers*, SCHS. To check on electoral votes, *see* Stephen G. Kurtz, *The Presidency of John Adams*, Philadelphia, 1957, pp. 412-414.

[210] In 1796 young Rutledge voted for Jefferson; yet by 1800 he was violently opposed to him. His letters of June and July 1797 indicate a change in attitude. John Rutledge, junior, to Edward Rutledge, June 27, July 4, 7, 1797, *Rutledge Papers, Dreer Collection*, PHS.

The change of the Executive here has been wrought with a facility
and a calm which has astonished even those of us who always
augured well of the government and the general good sense of our
citizens. The machine has worked without a creak. On the 4th of
March John Adams was quietly sworn into office, George Washington attending as a private citizen. A few days after he went quietly
home to Mt. Vernon; his successor as quietly took his place, and in
sword, bag &c. at his first levee, which was a very crowded one.
The Jacobins are flattering him and trying to cajole him to admit
the V. P. into the Council. Jefferson lodged at Francis' hotel (with
Adams) while here, attended the Philosophical Society of which
he is President, made a dissertation about a Lion's claw, and soon
after returned to Monticello.[211]

William Smith was now even closer to the throne. Abigail Adams
was born a Smith of Boston, and William Smith of Charleston was
often "at Court." In June, Smith wrote Izard: "I dined yesterday
with the President; he was easy and cheerful; sufficiently familiar
without loosing his dignity; Mrs. Adams conducted herself with
the greatest propriety. The dinner was genteel, without profusion;
the wine rather mediocre."[212]

Smith had been ready to return to Charleston when news of
General Pinckney's rejection by the French arrived. The successes
of Bonaparte in Italy permitted the Directory to take "a still more
haughty tone." The President had been compelled to call a special
session of Congress for May 15. For the Federalists this seemed like
the long-awaited opportunity to break with the French. Did this
mean even closer ties with England?

Much has been said about Smith's pro-British sympathies. Perhaps it is time to pause and indicate that, in spite of these undoubted sympathies, Smith was always steadily working for what
he thought were the best interests of America. The letter to Rufus
King of April 3 reveals his fundamental attitude.

It has been so much a fashion of late years to call parties here by
foreign names, that many conceive we cannot be alienated from the
French without throwing ourselves *a corps perdue* into the arms
of the English; and unfortunately many of the *ci-devant* English
merchants here, yielding without due reflection to an habitual impulse, encourage this degrading idea; it is important that it should
be banished from our sight and that we should forcibly inculcate
the sentiment, that if we are alienated from the French, it is because we cherish our independence and have determined to form

[211] William Smith to Rufus King, April 3, 1797, *King Papers*, NYHS.
[212] William Smith to Ralph Izard, June 2, 1797, "South Carolina Federalist
Correspondence," *op. cit.*, p. 790.

no connexions but those which unite independent nations for their common interest.

It was the "haughty conduct of France" that was forcing many Americans to become aware of France's real views. The public mind in the United States was, therefore, ready to receive favorable impressions of England. Smith continued, "Nothing will be so conducive to the complete establishment of our independence, as a conduct on the part of G. Britain at this crisis, marked with sincere good will to this country." Since Rufus King was the American minister in London and Robert Liston, who was "much liked," was the new British minister in Philadelphia, and since the northwest posts had been given up in good order, the scene was set for Britain and the United States to become firm friends and cooperate.[213]

In the special session, William Smith again sat for Charleston, Robert Goodloe Harper for Ninety Six, and Lemuel Benton for Georgetown and Cheraw. Thomas Sumter resumed his old seat from Camden District, replacing Richard Winn. The two new members were John Rutledge, junior, for Beaufort and Orangeburg District, and another William Smith for Pinckney and Washington District.[214] The new session promised to be an important one, and since the opposing parties were almost equal, the new members were ardently courted by both sides. The speaker had honored Rutledge by placing him on the select committee to prepare an answer to the President's address. According to Smith, "every manoeuvre" had been "practised to seduce Rutledge" to follow the friends of France, "but he stood out and was decidedly for a high-toned report" in support of the President. Rutledge spoke twice on the floor of the House against any alterations that would weaken the draft. "His last speech yesterday was a very good one; it is argumentative, ingenious and sarcastic and had much effect; he delivered himself with ease, fluency and grace: he has very much the manner of his Uncle Edward; the federal party and the audience were highly pleased and the french faction prodigiously mortified, except at one part of his speech (which might as well have been omitted) respecting the British treaty."[215] Rutledge leaned in the Federalist

[213] William Smith to Rufus King, April 3, 1797, *King Papers*, NYHS. Thomas Pinckney had introduced Liston to Smith "in warm terms." *See* William Smith to Ralph Izard, May 18, 1796, "South Carolina Federalist Correspondence," *op. cit.*, p. 780.

[214] Rutledge had defeated Wade Hampton, and William Smith had defeated Samuel Earle. *Biographical Directory of the American Congress, 1774-1949*, Washington, 1950, pp. 63, 68, 1114, 1261.

[215] William Smith to Ralph Izard, May 23, 1797, "South Carolina Federalist Correspondence," *op. cit.*, p. 786.

direction, but he would be difficult to manage, for he had not forgotten his father's rejection by the Senate.

Edward Rutledge wrote on June 9 to warn his nephew to beware of Smith's blandishments: "I have not as yet seen your speech. I am told it is a very good one; it is spoken of, as such, particularly by a Gentleman, who is a decided party man, & attached, I think, to the Interest of Great Britain. You know who I mean—He is subtle, & specious, & will be attentive. But don't trust him. His heart is too cold for fidelity, or friendship, and he resolves everything, into 'self'—you can't mistake my _____."[216] Young Rutledge replied on the 27th: "Many thanks my dear friend for your cautionary hints—I do assure you they are quite unnecessary—the flattery & artful caresses of S & H can make no more impressions upon me than the pressure of my little Daughters little finger would upon the Pillars of Saint Philip's church—I regard the one as a cold-hearted selfish little anglo-american & the other as a pompous thick-headed Prater."[217] Smith and Harper, of course, only wanted Rutledge's vote, not his admiration.

Smith and Harper also worked on William Smith of Washington and Pinckney District, the other new South Carolina delegate. Smith described the new member in uncomplimentary terms: "He looks like a thin puritanical Methodist, is rather an elderly man and appears to be a great simpleton." Yet he, too, had a vote. Although he lodged with Rutledge, Sumter had got him seated in the House between himself and John Milledge of Georgia "and they together with Baldwin have been debauching him." Twice Harper invited him to dinner with Rutledge, Smith, James A. Bayard of Delaware, and Harrison Gray Otis of Massachusetts. As Smith wrote: "We tried to infuse good opinions into him, but he appears to be composed of materials very unpromising."[218] A week later Smith wrote that "my colleague and namesake voted against us, which I attribute in some measure to a visit he received yesterday from that rascal Bache; Rutherford tried to keep him right, but I fear he is gone."[219] There was, of course, no hope for Sumter. He lodged

[216] Edward Rutledge to John Rutledge, junior, June 9, 1797, *John Rutledge, junior, Papers*, DUL.
[217] John Rutledge, junior, to Edward Rutledge, June 27, 1797, *Rutledge Papers, Dreer Collection*, PHS.
[218] William Smith to Ralph Izard, May 23, 1797, "South Carolina Federalist Correspondence," *op. cit.*, p. 787.
[219] William Smith to Ralph Izard, May 29, 1797, *ibid.*, p. 789. Benjamin Franklin Bache was the grandson of Benjamin Franklin and editor of the *Aurora*, a pro-Jefferson, Philadelphia newspaper. Edmund Kimball Alden, "Benjamin Franklin Bache," *DAB*.

at Francis's hotel with Jefferson and "a knot of Jacobins."[220] Of the six South Carolinians in the House, three were Federalists (Smith, Harper, and Rutledge) and three were Jeffersonians (Sumter, Smith of Washington and Pinckney District, and Benton), although on closer analysis Rutledge took an independent position, somewhere in the middle.[221]

The President decided to send two new envoys to join Pinckney. Hamilton had been in favor of an extraordinary mission of three, which was to include Madison and "some strong man from the North, Jay, Cabot, and two of the three should rule."[222] Smith was against sending either Jefferson or Madison, for neither would go "unless as Senior Commissioner & this would be harsh to Pinckney, who has conducted himself well." Smith's idea was to send Pinckney a new commission as envoy extraordinary. He was "unexceptionable to all parties, the French have no personal objection to him, the Jacobins of most of the Southern States have great confidence in him, & he has made great sacrifice to go on a mission which has hitherto been attended with nothing but mortification." More important was the warning Smith sent Hamilton: "It is not improbable too that any thing like slight to him may alienate more friends than would be acquired by adding to the mission one of the other party."[223] Until May 28, Smith still thought Pinckney should be the "*sole Envoy*."[224] On that date he heard that a commission of three was definitely planned, with Chief Justice Francis Dana of Massachusetts and General John Marshall ("the celebrated lawyer") joining Pinckney. Smith registered his strong objection with the President, and the nominations were held up two days; but Smith wrote Izard on June 2: "It is done. I immediately took measures to satisfy Rutledge and he is perfectly satisfied: _____ has shown much ill humor and endeavored to prejudice Rut. but I was before hand. General Pinckney is at the head of the commission and will I hope be pleased with the arrangement."[225]

It was on this issue, of Pinckney's reappointment to the commis-

[220] William Smith to Ralph Izard, May 23, 1797, "South Carolina Federalist Correspondence," *op. cit.,* p. 787.

[221] Benton did not arrive until June 26. *Annals of the Congress of the United States,* Washington, 1851, VII (5th cong., 1st sess.), 386.

[222] Alexander Hamilton to William Smith, April 5, 1797, *The Works of Alexander Hamilton,* ed. Henry Cabot Lodge, New York, 1904, X, 253-254.

[223] William Smith to Alexander Hamilton, May 1, 1797, *Hamilton Papers,* LC.

[224] William Smith to Ralph Izard, May 29, 1797, "South Carolina Federalist Correspondence," *op. cit.,* p. 788.

[225] William Smith to Ralph Izard, June 2, 1797, *ibid.*

sion, that Rutledge broke with the Jeffersonians and joined the Federalists. The Virginia and North Carolina senators had voted against Pinckney's appointment. "They said the appointment of Gen. Pinckney was calculated to irritate the french & urged his incompetency to protect & advance our Interests because his anger & resentment must have been excited by the personal Insults rec'd from the french." Rutledge told his uncle Edward about the conduct of the Virginians. He pointed out that Nicholas was the brother-in-law of "poor Randolph," and Giles was closely connected with Monroe. Since Pinckney had been picked out in each instance to succeed these men, the resentment of Virginia was aimed at Washington and Pinckney. Young John Rutledge had been so disturbed by this course of events that he had sought out Jefferson (still "our friend Mr. Jefferson") and had had a long conversation with him. Rutledge had explained that the votes of the Virginia and North Carolina senators would "excite great disgust in our State & that the citizens of it would believe there was much truth in what they had often heard from the Eastward—viz. *that the Virginians oppose everything emanating from the Executive.*" This news gave Jefferson some "uneasiness," and he promised to write and explain everything for the benefit of Edward Rutledge. John Rutledge concluded his account by saying that Jefferson was "a wonderfully great & good man but I really believe that the severe persecution he has lately undergone (& which continues) had occasioned a little french bias." From this point on, Rutledge listened more to the easterners than to the Virginians.[226]

Once the decision to send the three envoys had been made, the next task was to ready the country to defend itself. Here Smith, as chairman of the ways and means committee, took the lead. He had sponsored the navy in 1794 and had struggled since that time to keep the naval program underway. In the lame-duck session of 1796 he got funds to finish the three frigates then under construction: the *United States*, the *Constitution*, and the *Constellation*.[227] Harper had also urged the government to buy up liveoak lands in Georgia and South Carolina and establish a navy yard at Charleston.[228] Smith had desperately sought funds to fortify Charleston

[226] John Rutledge, junior, to Edward Rutledge, June 27, 1797, *Rutledge Papers, Dreer Collection*, PHS.
[227] *Annals of the Congress of the United States*, Washington, 1849, VI (4th cong., 2nd sess.), 2339, 2342, 2349.
[228] *Ibid.*, pp. 2126-2128, 2150.

harbor,[229] and as part of a ten-point program he urged that appropriations be made to outfit completely the three frigates and fortify all American ports. He also wanted to add a number of new frigates and sloops to the navy, which could then be given convoy duty. He urged that merchant vessels be armed, the military establishment increased, a provisional army raised, and the export of arms forbidden.[230]

New expenses demanded new revenues. Smith had actually advised in the previous Congress a complete overhaul of the tax program, since the government had long been dependent on the collection of import duties for its income, and these in time of war would be naturally reduced. Smith had, therefore, suggested a shift from import duties to excise taxes and to direct taxes on land and slaves. He also proposed that the President be given authority to borrow money to accomplish the preparedness program and that new taxes be levied to pay off the loans over a period of years.[231]

On June 17, Smith brought before the House a stamp bill and was supported in this measure by Rutledge.[232] Thirty-two years after Benjamin Smith and John Rutledge, senior, had opposed the English Stamp Act, their sons found it necessary to introduce the same sort of measure in the American Congress. The difference, of course, was that they were now taxing themselves, but for the opposition it was easy to equate federal rule with royal tyranny. Rutledge felt it was to South Carolina's advantage to have a tax on stamped papers rather than on lands and slaves. He wrote his uncle on July 4: "I have endeavoured to make Sumpter Smith & Benton think so, but it would be as difficult to make them jump into a fiery gulph as to get them, on any occasion, to vote differently from Monsieur Gallatin."[233]

Although Rutledge supported the stamp tax, he differed with Smith on which items should be taxed. Smith was in favor of excluding bank notes from the tax, while Rutledge thought them a proper object of taxation. They were taxed in Great Britain, which had a thriving banking system.

> Mr. R. asked, where would be the propriety of taxing notes issued by fifty individuals in their individual capacity, and exempting those issued by them when they associated, called themselves a

[229] *Ibid.*, pp. 2211-2212, 2216-2217, 2220, 2222.
[230] *Ibid.*, VII (5th cong., 1st sess.), 239.
[231] *Ibid.*
[232] *Ibid.*, pp. 331-332.
[233] John Rutledge, junior, to Edward Rutledge, July 4, 1797, *Rutledge Papers, Dreer Collection*, PHS.

Banking Company, and issued notes to three times the amount of their capital? The measure seemed to him unwise, and he was sure it would be unpopular. He could not conceive why people who had no other property than stock, which, in many instances, yielded an interest of fifteen per cent., should not contribute to the support of Government. A vast proportion of stockholders are foreigners, persons who do not contribute in any way to the support of Government, not even by personal services. He never would consent to exempt them from taxation, when we were burdening the active enterprising merchant and the industrious and hardworking farmer.[234]

Smith thought that Rutledge had confused bank notes with individual notes. Most of the latter were large, but most bank notes were for only five dollars. To impose a duty on the notes issued by the Bank of the United States would be to violate its charter. Furthermore, the tax already bore heavily on commercial men. In order to make their custom-house payments, they were obliged to renew their notes every sixty days; having to pay a fresh tax for every renewal would constitute a real burden. Harper stood by Smith, arguing that the proprietors of banks already paid taxes imposed on individuals.[235] Rutledge had taken an independent position which re-emphasized the division in South Carolina between the Smith Federalists and the Rutledge Federalists; the former always supported funding, banks, and commercial interests, while the latter exhibited strong distaste for moneyed men. The bill passed the House on July 3, 1797.[236]

Before the session was over, James Monroe, who had been recalled from his position as minister to France, returned to America, and a grand dinner was given in his honor by the Republicans. Rutledge's description of that affair is the best indication of his frame of mind at the end of the session.

'Twas given out publickly (at the Coffeehouse & City Tavern) that a grand Dinner was to be given to Citizen Munroe, & the friends of that Republican & of republicanism were invited to come & partake. This general invitation was very generally accepted & (it is with much sorrow I mention it) our friend the vice President was of the Party. It was a complete medley. Perhaps there never was a company in any country (in the most democratic times) which was more completely mosaic. Here you saw an american disorganiser & there a blundering wild Irishman—in one corner a banished Genevan & in another a french Spye—on one side a greasy

---

[234] *Annals of the Congress of the United States*, Washington, 1851, VII (5th cong., 1st sess.), 396-397.
[235] *Ibid.*, pp. 397-399.
[236] *Ibid.*, p. 434.

Butcher & on the other a dirty Cobler—'twas infinitely more mixed than Bouteilles Parties used to be at Citizen Harris's—you may figure to yourself some idea of the heterogeneous mixture when I tell you the Group was brought together by a general invitation— Butler, with all his pretensions to Democracy, could not be prevailed upon to be of this party—'twas so vulgar that our little Senator Hunter resisted the solicitations of Tazewell & would not go to it.[237]

[237] John Rutledge, junior, to Edward Rutledge, July 4, 1797, *Rutledge Papers, Dreer Collection*, PHS.

XIII

WILLIAM SMITH, MINISTER TO PORTUGAL, 1797-1801

BY THE SUMMER of 1797, William Smith could afford to retire from politics. He had been elected five successive times to represent Charleston District and had served eight full years in the House. He had successfully led the Federalist forces in a long fight for the *rapprochement* with Great Britain, which would endure for a decade. In South Carolina, he had helped to draw out of the backcountry a Federalist figure of the stature of Robert Goodloe Harper, who was quite capable of leading the South Carolina delegation and taking Smith's place among the party chieftains. In Charleston, the Rutledges and the Pinckneys had been drawn back into the party. Had not John Rutledge, junior, even in his initial term in Congress, exhibited the correct view of public policy? In the light of these successes, Smith decided to withdraw from the forum, relinquish his seat to Thomas Pinckney, and accept a diplomatic post.[1]

As early as May 30, 1795, Smith had written "in confidence" to Oliver Wolcott, the new secretary of the treasury, asking him to intimate to the President—"in the most delicate manner"—that he was ready to accept a post in the diplomatic service. His reason was personal yet garnished with a zeal for public service: "Having it now in my power to go abroad with more convenience than at a future period, I am desirous of making one more visit to Europe before my final establishment at home; in that case it would be my wish to visit it invested with some public trust that I might thereby enjoy every advantage of acquiring information and rendering myself useful to my country on my return." Smith was eager to be one of the commissioners provided for in the Jay Treaty. He knew through Hamilton that Washington had been considering him for other appointments and therefore would not have felt that he was remiss in suggesting this. His knowledge of French, as well as of a little Spanish and Italian, plus his longtime interest in diplomatic studies, were in his favor.[2]

[1] William Smith to Thomas Pinckney, July 18, 1797, *Dreer Collection*, PHS.
[2] William Smith to Oliver Wolcott, May 30, 1795. Hamilton had recommended Smith as a foreign agent for the treasury. Alexander Hamilton to Oliver Wolcott, April 10, 1795, *Wolcott Papers*, CHS.

Washington had considered Smith for the position of secretary of state in October 1795 but had been worried about his unpopularity. Hamilton had summed up Smith's qualifications for the President:

> But for a Secretary of State, I know not what to say. Smith, though not of full size, is very respectable for talent, and has pretty various information. I think he has more *real talent* than the last incumbent of the office. But there are strong objections to his appointment. I fear he is of an uncomfortable temper. He is popular with no description of men, from a certain *hardness* of character; and he, more than most other men, is considered as tinctured with prejudices towards the British. In this particular his ground is somewhat peculiar. It may suit party views to say much of other men, but more in this respect is *believed* with regard to Smith. I speak merely as to *bias* and *prejudice*. There are things, and important things, for which I would recommend Smith—thinking well of his abilities, information, industry, and integrity; but, at the present juncture, I believe his appointment to the office in question would be unadvisable. Besides, it is very important that he should not now be removed from the House of Representatives.[3]

This unpopularity with all but the leaders of his party kept Smith out of the great offices of state, although he remained a powerful figure beyond the public gaze, a fact which explains why historians have left him in relative obscurity. He was a Federalist's Federalist; a workhorse, rather than a public idol.

When Washington was forced to recall Monroe from France, Smith was considered as a replacement. Pickering, Wolcott, and McHenry had recommended for presidential consideration Patrick Henry, John Marshall, Charles Cotesworth Pinckney, and William Smith.[4] Washington had answered that he felt sure neither Henry nor Marshall would accept, that the chances against Pinckney's doing so were strong, and that "with respect to Mr. Smith, altho' it would be a very agreeable choice to me, I am sure it would not concenter those opinions which policy would require."[5] Smith had

[3] Alexander Hamilton to George Washington, November 5, 1795, *The Works of Alexander Hamilton*, ed. Henry Cabot Lodge, New York, 1904, X, 130. *Also see* George Washington to Alexander Hamilton, October 29, 1795, *Writings of George Washington*, ed. John C. Fitzpatrick, Washington, 1940, XXXIV, 349.

[4] Pickering, Wolcott, McHenry to George Washington, July 2, 1796, *Writings of George Washington*, ed. Worthington Chauncey Ford, New York, 1893, XIII, 216-217. Hamilton did not recommend Smith but suggested either General Pinckney, John Marshall, Henry William DeSaussure, Bushrod Washington, James McHenry, or Judge Peters. Alexander Hamilton to Oliver Wolcott, June 15, 1796, *Wolcott Papers*, CHS.

[5] George Washington to Timothy Pickering, July 8, 1796, *Writings of George Washington*, ed. John C. Fitzpatrick, Washington, 1940, XXXV, 127-128.

the firm support of Pickering, Wolcott, and McHenry, but Washington and Hamilton, though they appreciated his talents, realized that he would never be a popular choice. Smith's true place in the party was in the second rank, among those "not of full size." He belonged with the Pickerings, Wolcotts, and McHenrys, not with the Washingtons, Hamiltons, and Pinckneys.

The approval of John Quincy Adams's mission to Berlin made available a post at Lisbon. John Adams nominated Smith as "Minister Plenipotentiary of the United States at the Court of Portugal" on July 6, 1797, and he was confirmed by the Senate on the 10th. With Adams in Berlin, Smith in Lisbon, William Vans Murray in The Hague, David Humphreys in Madrid, Rufus King in London, and Pinckney in Paris, every important diplomatic post was filled by an outstanding Federalist. Two of the six posts were held by South Carolinians.[6]

As each minister received $9,000 for an outfit, in addition to his first year's salary of $9,000, Smith spared no expense in preparing for his departure.[7] He ordered a new $1,300 coach and arranged for McHenry to supervise its casing and shipping.[8] He wrote David Campbell in Charleston to pack six dozen bottles of his best Madeira in six barrels of rice and turn the whole lot over to Adam Tunno for shipment to Lisbon.[9] To be his secretary he engaged young John Pickering, who not only was fluent in French and Spanish, but was also the son of the secretary of state.[10] In the bustle of departure he did not forget his children, who lived with their grandmother at The Elms in South Carolina. In a hurried note to Mrs. Izard, Smith explained that although he could not come to South Carolina before his departure he would return in the spring to arrange a plan for Tom's education.[11] On the 18th he sent off two letters to South Carolina by John Rutledge, junior. One, ad-

[6] *Journal of the Executive Proceedings of the Senate*, Washington, 1828, I, 248-249. Murray had sailed to Amsterdam in 1797 carrying a copy of Smith's new book on the constitution. William Smith to Rufus King, April 3, 25, 1797, *King Papers*, NYHS.

[7] William Smith to Thomas Jefferson, March 18, 1793; Thomas Jefferson to William Smith, March 18, 1793, *Jefferson Papers*, LC. "The emoluments of Mr. Smith as minister to the court of Portugal will be 18,000 dollars for the first year." *South-Carolina Weekly Museum*, II (July 29, 1797), 128.

[8] James McHenry to William Smith, December 3, 1797, *William Loughton Smith Papers*, LC.

[9] David Campbell to William Smith, February 28, 1798, *William Loughton Smith Papers*, SCHS.

[10] Mary Orne Pickering, *Life of John Pickering*, Boston, 1887, p. 95.

[11] William Smith to Alice Izard, July 12, 1797, *Izard Papers*, SCL. Tom and Caroline were to live at The Elms until Smith returned in 1804.

dressed to the "Electors of Charleston District," was written for publication in the Charleston papers to announce his resignation from Congress. The other was written to Thomas Pinckney to urge Pinckney to run for his seat in the House.[12] With these matters attended to, early on the morning of the 19th Smith set off for New Castle, Delaware, riding down from Philadelphia accompanied by John and Timothy Pickering.[13] Passengers for Europe boarded ship at New Castle to save the time it took to go down the river from Philadelphia; that way they could go on board at the last moment, when all was in readiness for departure. Thomas Pinckney had sailed from New Castle for England in 1792; Charles Cotesworth Pinckney, for France in 1796.[14] In those days extra provisions were carried aboard for the important guests. John Vaughan had supplied Thomas Pinckney with four barrels of flour to make fresh bread every morning, as well as livestock for fresh meat and milk. Yams, two dozen pineapples, some limes, and "almonds and raisins as a compliment to the young ladies" were also stocked.[15] Secretary Pickering saw his son John and William Smith off on the *Dominick Terry* that afternoon. However, "four tedious days" passed before the vessel reached the Capes due to "light winds and warm weather."[16]

This ship belonged to the house of Dominick Terry and Company of Cadiz, American merchants engaged in trade between Spain and the United States. Peter Walsh, of that firm, had long supplied information to the government concerning American seamen imprisoned in Algiers or impressed by the British. This house was engaged in the provision trade: flour from Philadelphia and rice from Charleston in return for the fruits and wines of the Iberian Peninsula.[17] Since the chief responsibility of the American minister at Lisbon was to protect and foster this trade, Smith in his new post would continue in his old role as defender of American commerce.

[12] William Smith to Thomas Pinckney, July 18, 1797, *Dreer Collection*, PHS. "To the Electors of Charleston District," July 18, 1797, *City Gazette*, August 3, 1797.

[13] Pickering, *op. cit.*, p. 95.

[14] John Vaughan to Thomas Pinckney, June 26, 1792, *Pinckney Papers*, LC. "Letter-Book of Mary Stead Pinckney, November 14, 1796, to August 24, 1797," *Pinckney Papers*, LC.

[15] John Vaughan to Thomas Pinckney, June 26, 1792, *Pinckney Papers*, LC.

[16] John Pickering to Timothy Pickering, August 23, 1797, *Pickering Papers*, EI.

[17] See letters of Peter Walsh to the secretary of state, October 17, November 20, 1793, September 20, 1794, *Naval Documents Related to the United States Wars with the Barbary Powers*, Washington, 1939, I (1785-1801), 51, 54-55, 82.

Captain DeHart sailed his vessel across the Atlantic in record time. The ship left the Capes on July 23; it was lying at anchor in Lisbon harbor on August 20. According to John Pickering, they had "a remarkably fine passage" with "rough weather only about two days." Other than a little sea-sickness and unusually cool evenings for July, the voyage was uneventful. The great danger was from privateers, but they met only a small French squadron of three vessels. After a brief, polite examination, they were given a passport to show to any other French privateer and allowed to pass. John Pickering, and presumably Smith, too, read a Portuguese grammar and translated newspapers to help pass the time. Landfall was on the 19th; on the 20th they drew near Lisbon. The Rock of Lisbon did not come into view until between seven and eight in the morning, "partly owing to the dazzling reflection of the sun on the water."[18]

Lisbon was to be Smith's home for four years. It was an admirable door to Europe, and as he approached, his expectations must have been caught and enhanced by what he saw. Robert Southey, whose uncle was an English doctor in Lisbon, vividly related an experience that must have been similar to Smith's. Arriving from the stormy Bay of Biscay, he wrote, "We were near enough the shore to see the silver dust of the breakers, and the sea-birds sporting over them in flocks. A pilot-boat came off to us: its great sail seemed to be as unmanageable as an umbrella in a storm; sometimes it was dipped half over in the water, and it flapped all ways, like a woman's petticoat in a high wind." The entrance to the Tagus presented a magnificent scene. Numerous windmills stood "in regiments upon all the hills," which in turn were studded with convents and quintas and checked with "gray olive-yards, green orange-groves, and greener vineyards." "The river bright as the blue sky which illuminated it," swarmed "with boats of every size and shape, with sails of every imaginable variety"—so cheerful did "every thing look under a southern sun."

The travelers were struck by the rapid transition from the clean smell of the sea to the rank odor of the town, where everything unwanted was thrown in the street—"all refuse of the kitchen and dead animals are exposed to these scorching suns." Nor did the rains perform an agreeable service, for in wet weather "if you walk under

[18] John Pickering to Timothy Pickering, August 23, 1797, *Pickering Papers,* EI. William Smith to Oliver Wolcott, August 24, 1797, *Wolcott Papers,* CHS. Pickering, *op. cit.,* pp. 95-97.

the houses you are drenched by the water-spouts; if you attempt the middle, there is a torrent; would you go between the two, there is the dunghill." Lisbon, according to Southey, had only been clean twice, once when washed by Noah's flood and once when purified by fire after the great earthquake. Lisbon boldly presented the European extremes of unsurpassed beauty and abject ugliness which have charmed and appalled countless American and English travelers.[19]

SMITH AND PICKERING were met by John Bulkeley, an English merchant, and his son Thomas Bulkeley, the American consul. The English merchants, as they had done all over the world from Charleston to Calcutta, had established a factory, a social and commercial world of their own within that of the Portuguese. John Bulkeley was "one of the wealthiest Merchants of the Factory," having made the greater part of his fortune in the American trade. His daughter Anne Frances had married Colonel David Humphreys, Smith's predecessor, just before he was transferred to Madrid. Humphreys described his father-in-law for Washington as "a good Englishman and a true Merchant in heart."[20] The trade of Portugal had been dominated by the English ever since the Methuen Treaty of 1703. Although the pre-eminent position of the English merchants was then being challenged by the rising Portuguese middle class, many of whom had been trained in the English counting houses, the Bulkeleys were invaluable to the newly arrived American minister.[21]

The English lived in the Lisbon suburb called Buenos Ayres, which commanded "a fine prospect of the Tagus, shipping and ocean."[22] Smith rented the same house there that Humphreys had occupied, about a mile from the Bulkeleys'. John Pickering described the new surroundings:

> It is a neat house and in a very pleasant situation; and our street is almost the only clean one in the city. From a balcony on the

[19] *The Life and Correspondence of Robert Southey*, ed. Rev. Charles Cuthbert Southey, New York, 1851, pp. 122-124. Robert Southey, *Letters Written During a Short Residence in Spain and Portugal*, Bristol, 1799, p. 213. Smith sent to London for a copy of Southey's *Travels in Spain and Portugal in 1796*. William Smith to Rufus King, June 20, 1798, *William Loughton Smith Papers*, HEHL.
[20] David Humphreys to George Washington, May 12, 1791, Frank Landon Humphreys, *Life and Times of David Humphreys*, New York, 1917, II, 107-108.
[21] David Humphreys to George Washington, July 23, 1792, *ibid.*, p. 146.
[22] William Smith to James McHenry, October 9, 1797, *McHenry Papers*, LC.

back of the house we have a very good prospect of the sea, the mouth of the Tagus, the remains of a palace which was partly destroyed by fire a few years ago, and some handsome gardens. From the front windows we have a view of the river and shipping, and the opposite banks, which are not very beautiful at present, for there is not the least verdure upon them. Besides all these beautiful objects which are at a distance, we have one at home, which is a small garden, that with a little (perhaps I should come nearer the truth if I say much) labor will be a pleasant retreat in summer. It contains lemon trees, and some other kinds which I am not acquainted with. In addition to all this I am told we have good neighbours, of whom I have yet seen only two,—a Mr. Hill, an English clergyman, and a Dr. Moore (or More), an English physician.[23]

The house itself was less satisfactory. Because of its lofty position, it was very bleak in winter, and extraordinary precautions had to be taken to guard against the cold. Although few houses had fireplaces except in the kitchens, Smith wrote, "I have two in my house, but one is stopped up, & the other smokes dreadfully; unless I can remedy this evil, I must follow the custom of the country which is to smother under enormous cloaks."[24]

It was the custom of the English to spend part of the late summer at Cintra, a village about eighteen miles from Lisbon. Smith, who quickly adopted the English pattern of life, paid annual visits to this Portuguese resort.[25] In spite of a certain Puritan reluctance to engage wholeheartedly in amusements, John Pickering found the spot a "romantic place." Orange and lemon trees ornamented the gardens, "the Rooms" were open every evening for gaming or dancing, and many pleasant evenings were spent in the company of ladies and officers who came over from the English and French (royalist emigré) camps, which were about five miles distant. Sunday nights were the most festive, with more dancing than any

[23] Pickering, *op. cit.*, p. 103.

[24] William Smith to James McHenry, October 9, 1797, "Correspondence of William Smith, American Minister to Portugal," ed. Bernard C. Steiner, *Sewanee Review*, XIV (1906), 86.

[25] Smith and Pickering spent four weeks in September and October 1797 at Cintra. They spent six weeks there in 1798. In July 1799, Smith spent a few days there alone since he had not taken a house for the season. When Pickering left in November 1799, Smith set off for eight days at Cintra to escape the dullness of his empty house. In the late summer of 1800, Smith was at Collares, near Cintra, for over five weeks. John Pickering to Timothy Pickering, September 8, 24, 1797, October 29, 1798, July 13, 1799; William Smith to John Pickering, August 18, 1800, quoted in Pickering, *op. cit.*, pp. 99-103, 132-133, 143-145, 176-177. William Smith to James McHenry, October 9, 1797, *McHenry Papers*, LC. William Smith to Timothy Pickering, November 2, 1799, *Pickering Papers*, MHS.

other night in the week—a fact which struck the young New England as quite curious.[26]

AFTER CALLING ON Foreign Minister Luis Pinto de Sousa Coutinho, Smith's first duty as a new minister was to arrange to be presented to the sovereign.[27] Maria I was Queen, but she had gone mad under the triple blows of the death of her husband, who was also her uncle, the death of her eldest son, and the outbreak of the French Revolution. It was, therefore, to the Queen's second son, the Prince of Brazil, that Smith was to pay his respects.[28] The court was at Queluz about eight miles from Lisbon. The road was circuitous and badly paved, but Smith and the new Prussian minister "borrowed the Danish Minister's chariot & four servants & having hired six Mules . . . proceeded in great state." Smith sent home the following account:

> He was first presented; I was then Introduced, made the proper reverences at the proper distances & delivered to the Prince of Brazil, who represents the Sovereign, the President's Letter, making him a very concise address in French to which he replied in terms as laconic in French that he was very glad to See me & would acquaint his Mother of my arrival: I then made my bows retreating with my face to the Prince & withdrew; had I not rehearsed this Ceremony with my friend the Dane, a very good natured friendly man, I should have probably committed some fauxpas as I did afterwards at my audience of the Princess, respecting which (there having been some doubt whether I should See her Highness) I had not been so particular in my inquiries; being suddenly ushered into a large room where I beheld a splendid sight of Ladies in large hoops, arranged along the wainscot in Solemn Silence, as cold and awful as the Wax-work; I was a little discomposed at first, but recovering myself approached the Princess, whom I discovered by her Jewels, & told her in French how happy I should be if I should be honored with her favor & protection during my residence at this court, to which she made some very gracious reply, which I didn't understand not having heard it; I then, wishing to be abundantly polite, & to bow to the Ladies who were paraded along the wall on my way out, unfortunately was so indecent as actually to turn my Side to the Princess & indeed very nearly turned my back; when I approached the door, I recollected my crime & to expiate it suddenly faced about & made her Highness a most profound reverence & withdrew. But when we got into the antechamber, I found that I had omitted a very essential part of the Ceremony, which was,

---

[26] Pickering, *op. cit.*, pp. 101-103.
[27] William Smith to Timothy Pickering, August 24, 1797, *William Loughton Smith Papers*, HEHL.
[28] H. S. Livermore, *A History of Portugal*, Cambridge, 1947, p. 386.

making a complimentary Speech to the Prince's sister and his daughter, a child of four years, a circumstance I had not been apprised of: I was however consoled on learning from the Prussian Minister that he had committed the same blunder.[29]

That evening the Danish minister gave a dinner for his new colleagues, the American and Prussian ministers, at which the errors and absurdities of the day were related; their blunders thereby became a common bond, drawing the ministers of the smaller powers together in friendship.

Smith, in order to place the dignity of his own country on a high plane, gave a dinner on October 19 in honor of the President's birthday. Smith thought his party a great success and composed a social note for McHenry to have inserted in Fenno's paper.

Thursday the 19th October, being the Anniversary of the President's Birth, was celebrated at Lisbon by Mr. Smith, the Minister of the United States at that Court, who gave on the Occasion an Entertainment at his Hotel at Buenos-Ayres to a numerous and respectable company of American Captains and Citizens. After sixteen patriotic Toasts intermixed with convivial songs, the Company, having spent the day with great good humour and festivity, broke up at nine o'clock, much pleased with the occasion, which had collected together so many Americans at such a distance from home. All the American vessels in the Harbour were gayly decorated during the day and at twelve o'clock a federal salute of sixteen guns was fired by some of them in honor of the day, and at five in the afternoon the salute was repeated. This Anniversary occurring on a day, highly distinguished in the Annals of the American Revolution by the Surrender of York-town, recollection of so auspicious an event could not fail to increase the happiness of the Company.

Even the presence of two or three Jacobins, according to Smith, had not marred the success of the occasion, for they had "all behaved extremely well," joining in the toasts "with great zeal" and singing "when I began to sing."[30]

DURING THE EIGHTEENTH century, Portugal was continually caught amid the jealousies of England, France, and Spain. The situation had been quite clear from March 1793 to July 1795, when England, Spain, and Portugal had been at war with France, but this picture changed when Spain first made peace with France (July 1795)

---

[29] William Smith to James McHenry, September 9, 1797, "Correspondence of William Smith, American Minister to Portugal," ed. Bernard C. Steiner, *Sewanee Review*, XIV (1906), 83-84.

[30] William Smith to James McHenry, October 21, 1797, *McHenry Papers*, LC.

and then declared war on England (October 1796). When Smith arrived in the summer of 1797, Portugal was apprehensive of a war with Spain. The dominant influence in Portugal was still British. Although the Portuguese army defended the frontier, Sir Charles Stuart commanded a force near Lisbon which included 6,000 English troops and which was paid for by Britain; and the English fleet under Lord St. Vincent, who as Admiral Jervis had won a great victory over the Spanish fleet off Cape St. Vincent on February 14, 1797, patrolled the coast.[31]

Smith, after surveying the domestic and international scene, thought that if Spain and France invaded Portugal, Portugal would be revolutionized. The clergy and the students of the universities were already ardent Jacobins. In the event of a revolution, the Portuguese fleet would join the British, who would then seize Madeira and Brazil; and the royal family would probably, although Smith was not sure of this, flee to Brazil.[32] Portugal hung in this awkward position between the three great powers until Spain declared war on her in March 1801. The war lasted only a few months; the Portuguese sued for peace before the French troops could arrive. Smith wrote Mrs. Izard that the Spanish were demanding the removal of the British from Portugal, $4,000,000, a part of Brazil, and a slice of Portugal.[33] These were close to the actual terms worked out at Badajos in the summer of 1801.[34]

Smith felt great sympathy for all of the smaller European countries, buffeted by the rivalries of the great powers, but he was far more concerned about the interferences of the French than of the English. He felt that England should have given Portugal more support in 1801.[35] Smith was most friendly with the Danish, Swedish, and Prussian ministers, who had to defend interests similar to those of America, yet he was not interested in the Dane's proposed alliance of neutral powers to defend neutral commerce.[36] Such an

[31] Livermore, op. cit., pp. 387-390. Also see William Smith to James McHenry, August 24, 1797, William Loughton Smith Papers, HEHL.

[32] William Smith to Rufus King, February 17, June 20, 1798, William Loughton Smith Papers, HEHL.

[33] Alice Izard to Margaret Manigault, August 31, 1801, Manigault Papers, SC Archives.

[34] Livermore, op. cit., p. 391.

[35] Alice Izard to Margaret Manigault, August 31, 1801, Manigault Papers, SC Archives. Also see William Smith to Rufus King, June 13, 20, 29, July 13, 27, 1801, William Loughton Smith Papers, HEHL.

[36] William Smith to Timothy Pickering, August 24, 1797, "Correspondence of William Smith, American Minister to Portugal," ed. Bernard C. Steiner, Sewanee Review, XIV (1906), 79-80.

armed neutrality would have been aimed at the British; it was not the English navy, however, that Smith feared, but the French "fifth column." Smith was influenced by the memory of the Genêt projects, which he saw as one part of a general pattern of French subversion.

The French had begun with Switzerland, "exciting rebellion in the Valais and then marching troops to assist the friends of liberty."[37] After Switzerland, they had subverted Holland. Smith wrote McHenry in February 1798: "The F. Directory finding that the Dutch were very much divided about a Constitution have made one for them and finding that a majority of the Batavian Convention did not relish it, they have caused the arrest of the six members of the Committee of foreign affairs (or public safety) and twenty one other members of the Convention who are all to be transported to Cayenne; the Constitution will now meet no further difficulty from the Dutch aristocrats."[38] Smith was afraid that America might also succumb.

America's danger stemmed from the influx of European revolutionaries, particularly the Irish and the French, and on November 2, 1798, Smith wrote Rufus King: "For God's sake, use your influence with Lord Grenville to prevent the U. Irishmen going to America."[39] His first suspicions when he heard of the Kentucky and Virginia Resolutions were of French influence. He wrote McHenry: "I see you are likely to have some trouble with Kentucky and Virginia, which the agents of the Directory wish to convert into an American La Vendée and when schemes are ripe to make the medium of their attack on our liberties."[40] By 1800 what Smith feared most from an agreement with France was "the pestilential influence of their fraternizing Agents in every part of the U. States."[41] Smith's suspicions of France were shared by Rufus King, William Vans Murray, and young John Quincy Adams.[42]

[37] William Smith to James McHenry, February 2, 1799, ibid., p. 101.
[38] William Smith to James McHenry, February 18, 1798, ibid., p. 91.
[39] William Smith to Rufus King, November 2, 1798, William Loughton Smith Papers, HEHL.
[40] William Smith to James McHenry, February 2, 1799, "Correspondence of William Smith, American Minister to Portugal," ed. Bernard C. Steiner, Sewanee Review, XIV (1906), 101.
[41] William Smith to Rufus King, March 15, 1800, William Loughton Smith Papers, HEHL.
[42] See particularly, Rufus King to William Smith, November 20, 1797, King Papers, NYHS; William Vans Murray to William Smith, November 28, 1797, William Vans Murray Correspondence, PML; John Quincy Adams to William Smith, January 10, 1798, William Loughton Smith Papers, LC.

In the fall of 1797, the eyes of the American ministers in Lisbon, London, The Hague, and Berlin had focused on the three American envoys in Paris. Would the new mission of Pinckney, Marshall, and Gerry be received by France's new foreign minister, Talleyrand? Smith took advantage of an earlier acquaintance with Talleyrand in Philadelphia to write and congratulate him on his appointment and to disabuse him of the idea that America was gravitating towards England. Smith assured him that America's sole object was neutrality: "I have read with pleasure in the public papers that our Envoys had arrived at Paris & had been introduced to you, and from my knowledge of those gentlemen & the opinion I have indulged of your friendly disposition to my country, I anticipate the most agreeable consequences." This was the language of diplomacy, for Smith had a low opinion of Talleyrand, expected the mission to fail, and was actually much more interested in the education of General Pinckney.[43]

Pinckney had written Smith from The Hague after he had been forced to retire the first time from France, revealing that his attitude towards the French was changing. Although all Frenchmen had held up the British Treaty as an abandonment by the United States of French friendship, Pinckney was convinced that this was more a pretext than the real quarrel. The essential point was that France was as bent on "Universal Empire" as she had been "in the time of Louis the 14th." Yet Pinckney's old admiration for the French seeped through. "If every American was as much attached to America, as every Frenchman is to France, we need not be under any apprehensions from all Europe united, & a Crusade against us (I speak my sincere opinion both as a Citizen & a Soldier) would be as unsuccessful, as the chivalrous Crusade of old." He felt that if America put herself in a posture of defense and closed ranks behind the President, all would be well. "For God's sake banish party as much as possible, say & write nothing to irritate each other, but all unite in a resolution to think and act as Americans. We should not find the business with the French so difficult, if they did not rely on our divisions."[44]

Smith, King, Murray, and Adams all hoped that the three envoys in Paris would adopt an attitude like their own towards France.

[43] William Smith to Talleyrand, November 8, 1797, ibid. See Smith's description of diplomacy as a game of "Blindman's Buff" in William Smith to Rufus King, December 22, 1798, *William Loughton Smith Papers*, HEHL.

[44] Charles Cotesworth Pinckney to William Smith, July 16, 1797, *William Loughton Smith Papers*, RC.

Murray, when he wrote of the arrival of Marshall and Gerry, inti-mated that he expected that little would be achieved by the new negotiations.[45] King wrote from London on November 20 that the American envoys were still at Paris but accomplishing little.[46] A few days later, Murray sent word that the commissioners had not been received. He added: "I would give much to see General P. and Mr. G. our fellow-member, to know how they like Paris repub-licanism, now; though, both almost gave up their predilection be-fore they left this. Marshall thought as we did, I believe entirely."[47] John Quincy Adams wrote his father in the same spirit, preparing him for the change of heart which would soon throw the President, at least temporarily, into the arms of the arch-Federalists.[48] In Feb-ruary 1798, Smith wrote McHenry that he thought the situation of the American envoys in Paris was "a very degrading one."[49]

SMITH WAS EAGER to go to Spain and looked for a good excuse to leave Lisbon. He found it in the news that an American ship with funds to finance the Barbary affairs had arrived at Gibraltar on the way to Algiers. Smith made a hurried departure on March 2, 1798, on the British ship *Swiftsure*, embarking at one o'clock after only three hours' notice.[50] After a tedious ten-day passage, he landed at Gibraltar under "a federal salute." He was met by Governor Gen-eral O'Hara, who personally conducted him over the fortifications. He embarked after a fortnight on the *Swiftsure* to return to Lisbon, but on its way out of the bay the ship was involved in "a fierce en-gagement" with Spanish gunboats and received "two shots in the hull, five in the sails and had four men wounded." The *Swiftsure* was thereupon ordered to join the fleet off Cadiz; Smith went in under a flag of truce and spent three weeks in Cadiz.[51]

There he stayed with an old acquaintance, American Consul

[45] William Vans Murray to William Smith, September 24, 1797, *William Vans Murray Correspondence*, PML.
[46] Rufus King to William Smith, November 20, 1797, *King Papers*, NYHS.
[47] William Vans Murray to William Smith, November 28, 1797, *William Vans Murray Correspondence*, PML.
[48] *See* particularly John Quincy Adams to William Smith, July 18, 1798, *William Loughton Smith Papers*, LC. *Also see* John Quincy Adams to John Adams, April 15, 1798, *Writings of John Quincy Adams*, ed. Worthington Chauncey Ford, New York, 1913, II, 275-278.
[49] William Smith to James McHenry, February 15, 1798, *McHenry Papers*, WLCL.
[50] John Pickering to Timothy Pickering, March 3, 1798, typed copy in *Pickering Papers*, EI.
[51] Pickering, *op. cit.*, pp. 110-111. William Smith to James McHenry, June 23, 1798, *McHenry Papers*, LC.

Joseph M. Yznardi, long a prominent merchant in the American trade, who had been with the Smiths and Izards in Philadelphia in 1794.[52] American wheat and rice were in great demand in Spain, and a large number of American traders were resident in Cadiz, the most important port of entry.[53] They gave Smith "a handsome dinner."[54]

Having been offered a seat in the carriage of an English-speaking Spanish gentleman, Smith left Cadiz on April 24 for Xeres. They arrived in time for dinner in this town "where the sherry wine is made" and lingered two days. From Xeres they traveled by way of Seville to Aranjuez where the Spanish Court then sat. At Aranjuez, Smith stayed in the home of his traveling companion, a man so charming and intelligent that Smith urged him to seek the position of Spanish minister to the United States.

Aranjuez in early May was "in all its beauty"—"a curious melange of Court magnificence and rural beauty." Humphreys presented him to the royal family, to the French minister Truguet, to the members of the *corps diplomatique,* and—at Smith's insistence—to Saavedra, the foreign minister, to whom Smith suggested the appointment of his Spanish friend. Smith also took time to explain to Saavedra that the United States was carrying out the terms of the Pinckney Treaty. Smith had intended to stay only a week, but he enjoyed himself so much in this "very charming place" that he had time for only a short visit to Madrid and to see "a multitude of fine things" in the Escorial. He returned to Lisbon by way of Toledo, where he observed the manufacture of sword blades as well as a grand religious procession on Corpus Christi Day. On crossing the border, he was impressed by the change in accents, and he found he much preferred the Spanish to the Portuguese sounds. All in all it was a wonderful trip; he felt refreshed and was full of thoughts that he would one day divulge, as he wrote his good friend McHenry, on a "cool walk to the Skuylkill."[55]

BACK IN LISBON Smith received a letter from Pinckney, written on June 1 from Lyons, in which he described the last episodes in the

[52] Timothy Pickering to Oliver Ellsworth and William R. Davie, October 21, 1799, copy in *Davie Papers,* NC Archives. Joseph M. Yznardi to Ralph Izard, July 12, 1794, *Izard Papers,* LC.

[53] *See* "Extract of a letter from a respectable Mercantile house in Cadiz to their correspondent in Boston," September 28, 1796, reprinted in *South-Carolina Weekly Museum,* I (February 18, 1797), 224-226.

[54] William Smith to James McHenry, June 23, 1798, *McHenry Papers,* LC.

[55] Pickering, *op. cit.,* pp. 117-119. William Smith to James McHenry, June 23, 1798, *McHenry Papers,* LC.

negotiations at Paris: "After my Colleagues & myself had been near seven Months in Paris General Marshall & myself received without our having demanded them (Mr. Gerry having refused to join us in such demand) our passports to depart. But they were not sent us before Mr. G. had promised the Minister of foreign affairs to remain. This promise was made without the approbation of his Colleagues, & he had for some time previous to it carried on *solely* an intercourse with the *Minister*, under injunctions from *him* not to communicate the purport to them—Which injunctions he faithfully observed."[56] Talleyrand's refusal to negotiate, combined with Gerry's behavior, crushed Pinckney's last doubts about France and the Jeffersonians. From this point on, Pinckney was an arch-Federalist. As early as January 25, 1798, Pinckney had written to Edward Rutledge in rather decisive terms: "There is not the least hope of an accomodation with this government—we sue in vain to be heard—we shall therefore very shortly depart—You shall be immediately informed what our destination is. In the meantime take care of your coasts—guard against emissaries and prepare for every event."[57] The supersession of Thomas Pinckney by Jay had been a slight, the rejection of John Rutledge by the Senate a blow, but neither episode left as broad a scar upon the Rutledge-Pinckney faction as Charles Cotesworth Pinckney's being twice thrown out of France, especially when a shuffling Jeffersonian had been permitted to remain. This insult to the Pinckneys was an insult to the nation. "Millions for Defense but not a cent for Tribute" expresses the thoughts of a proud man.[58]

America was now willing to build up her armed might. John Adams's new popularity and the administration's newly acquired strength from the shift in public opinion made it possible to push a preparedness program through Congress. The army was expanded, the navy finally established, and the alien and sedition acts passed. New taxes were levied to finance the war program. Smith was overjoyed, for these "most excellent and wise measures" were the same as those he had urged upon Congress in the special session of 1797.

[56] Charles Cotesworth Pinckney to William Smith, June 1, 1798, *William Loughton Smith Papers*, RC.
[57] Charles Cotesworth Pinckney to Edward Rutledge, January 25, 1798, *John Rutledge, junior, Papers*, SHC.
[58] Pinckney's actual words were, "Not a sixpence, sir." Apparently, however, General Pinckney acquiesced in the use of the more famous phrase which was coined in a toast by Robert Goodloe Harper at a banquet in honor of John Marshall on June 18, 1798. *SCHGM*, I (1900), 100-103. *Also see* Albert J. Beveridge, *The Life of John Marshall*, Boston, 1916, II, 348-350.

He wrote James McHenry: "These are grand specimens of real American spirit . . . had they been adopted at the extraordinary session . . . we should now have secured our object with France." What had been needed was "energy in our government and unanimity in the citizens."[59] In his bantering style Smith asked McHenry whether he would continue as secretary of war or become secretary of the navy: "Are you to be Mars or Neptune? Are you to wield the Truncheon or the Trident?"[60] The alien and sedition acts were, of course, pleasing to Smith, who had feared the Irish and French agents in America, but he still thought that there was too "much french nonsense" lurking in America. "Can't the *suaviter in modo* be maintained by decent and mild language without this everlasting cant about our sensibilities and our love and our ardour and all this lovesick nonsense & why perpetually confessing our dread of war and our deprecation of its calamities and that we are ready to agree to anything to avert its horrors, short of a sacrifice of our independence—do these people see no horrors no calamities in french rule and tyranny—the question lies in a nut shell—it is war, or misery under french oppression."[61] He confessed to Oliver Wolcott his feeling that America was like "a weak dupe, who finds himself compelled to turn an unfaithful wench out of doors, stopping her at the threshold to whine over their former loves, and to remind her of past joys?"[62]

THERE IS SOME DOUBT among historians as to whether Federalist leaders wanted war with France in 1798 or not.[63] William Smith was certainly one arch-Federalist who wanted war. He explained his position in a letter of February 1799 to Oliver Wolcott: "It has occurred to me, in contemplating the subject that we should be placed, by a declaration of war, in a much more eligible situation than we are now in; 1st the government would carry into full operation the Act concerning Alien Enemies, 2nd the measure of defence would be more vigorous, concentrated and united and the national spirit more directed to one great object, abandoning domestic dissentions, 3rdly the commerce of the U. S. would be more protected." The war would assist the merchants, for in a state of war their ves-

---

[59] William Smith to James McHenry, August 4, 1798, *McHenry Papers*, LC.
[60] William Smith to James McHenry, June 23, 1798, *McHenry Papers*, WLCL.
[61] William Smith to James McHenry, August 4, 1798, *McHenry Papers*, LC.
[62] William Smith to Oliver Wolcott, August 14, 1798, *Wolcott Papers*, CHS.
[63] William Smith to James McHenry, February 2, 1799, *McHenry Papers*, LC.

sels would be well-armed or sail under convoy, knowing that if they
were captured they would be condemned. Now "our merchants,
captains, and underwriters . . . are deluded by every report of
negotiations; every amicable profession; every idle paragraph, or
scrap of fabricated letter." Our captains have no guide as to what
papers are necessary. "Multitudes, relying on the goodness of their
papers, rush into the jaws of the devouring monster, which respects
no papers, but cartridge papers, the only proper ones now for our
protection. There is no prospect of a repeal of their plundering
decrees; on the contrary they now talk of extending them to the
goods of Turkey, Russia, Portugal, and Naples, so that a bit of
Naples shaving soap will be a cause of condemnation."[64] The arch-
Federalists of the Smith mold never got their war with France because of the innate good sense of John Adams. Wolcott wrote Smith
on November 29, 1798, that the President was determined to adhere
to the existing system. He stated, "We shall not declare war,
against France nor shall we send any new ministers—we shall prepare for defence *at home* and fight Frenchmen when we meet them
armed, abroad."[65]

EVEN THOUGH there was to be no war with France, there was at
least to be closer cooperation with the British navy. Both Smith and
John Pickering had been favorably impressed by the exploits of
Lord St. Vincent. Soon after their arrival in Lisbon the English
admiral had escorted the Americans over one of the Spanish ships
taken in the great battle off Cape St. Vincent. John Pickering wrote
that the British "showed us the place where Admiral Nelson entered with two men by the quarter-gallery, described to us the
situation of the Spanish commander, who was found dreadfully
mangled,—in short, gave us a very particular account of every
principal event which happened during the engagement." Before
they visited the Spanish ship, they had been guests on the *Britannia,*
"an English first-rate." Pickering "was amazed at almost everything;
it seemed like an empire itself. We saw about eight hundred men,
which is nearly her complement. Seeing these two ships has been
a greater gratification to me than anything I have met with in this
country."[66]

[64] William Smith to Oliver Wolcott, February 3, 1799, *Wolcott Papers,* CHS.
Also see William Smith to Rufus King, March 9, 1799, *William Loughton
Smith Papers,* HEHL.
[65] Oliver Wolcott to William Smith, November 29, 1798, *William Loughton
Smith Papers,* LC.
[66] Pickering, *op. cit.,* pp. 99-101.

Smith saw a great deal of the admiral and the British captains, and through them he kept up with the war in the Mediterranean. When Napoleon was in Egypt, Smith hoped that Nelson and the English fleet might "derange his projects."[67] Since the Portuguese fleet was helping the British in the Mediterranean, Smith was against having any accommodations reached between the Portuguese and the French. The Russians were also helping the British in the North Sea, and Smith undoubtedly thought the new American navy might help the British in the Atlantic. He wrote: "I am happy to find that at length the American navy begins to be known; the present crisis is very favourable to its establishment."[68]

IN THE SPRING of 1799 Smith took Pickering on a tour of the northern provinces of Portugal.[69] They left Lisbon on April 10 for Coimbra, making use of the stagecoach line lately established under Her Majesty's patronage and the only thing of its kind in Portugal. On the afternoon of the 11th they arrived at Coimbra, which presented "a beautiful appearance" as they approached from the South. The bridge, as they entered, was lined with university students, who interrupted their evening walk to stop and stare at Smith and Pickering, "as we at them." The students wore no hats, but each had a black cloak thrown over his left shoulder. Their mode of saluting was to throw open their cloaks and bow at the same time. In this gracious way, the travelers were literally swept into the old university town.

Before the reforms of Pombal (1772) there had been between 7,000 and 8,000 students, but in 1799 their number had shrunk to 1,200 or 1,300, and these were obliged to take their studies very seriously. Smith and Pickering had half a day to see the university, which they did in the company of two professors who warmed to young Pickering for his interest in and knowledge of the classics. They saw the new observatory with its many excellent instruments. The library lacked Roman and Greek manuscripts (John Pickering

---

[67] William Smith to Oliver Wolcott, August 14, 1798, *Wolcott Papers,* CHS.

[68] A Portuguese squadron patrolled the Strait of Gibraltar to bottle up the Algerines in the Mediterranean Sea. Another squadron was with Admiral Nelson in Egyptian waters. William Smith to Oliver Wolcott, August 14, 1798, *Wolcott Papers,* CHS.

[69] This account has been drawn from a description of the journey written by John Pickering, *Pickering Papers,* MHS. *Also see* John Pickering to Timothy Pickering, April 5, 30, 1799, Pickering, *op. cit.,* pp. 139-140; John Pickering to Timothy Pickering, June 3, 1799; John Pickering to Henry Pickering, June 28, 1799, copies in *Pickering Papers,* EI.

had asked to see some), for the Philips of Spain had carried them off. The museum was noteworthy for its Brazilian specimens.

The party progressed towards Oporto on the afternoon of the 13th. That night was spent at the quinta, or country-house, of Peter de Clamouse Brown, the American consul in Oporto who was also the son of a British merchant.[70] Brown put on for his visitors an evening of folk-singing and folk-dancing. The singing was in competition *(cantar so desafio)*.

> A country lad & lass, accompanied by a guitar, sing an *extempore* song in praise of their respective lovers, & in ridicule of each other's; just in the manner, related by the ancient poets, of the shepherds & shepherdesses of those days. The verses, you will suppose, were not the most elegant; but much better than our country-people would be able to make; for the Portuguese language admits of versification (I mean *rhime*) much more easily than ours.

The most common dance was the *chula* (a word meaning vulgar). It was entirely destitute of grace, danced in large wooden shoes with three steps only, to right and left alternately—more of a march than a dance. The *lundu* had been brought from Brazil and partook, in Pickering's words, "of all the lasciviousness of warm climates."

The next day, accompanied by Brown, they arrived in Oporto, on the north side of the "over muddy Douro River." Oporto was more compact than Lisbon; there were about 80,000 inhabitants, but the houses were three to six stories high. The principal buildings were the prison, the courthouse, the new hospital, and the English factory's house.

In Oporto the English community was proportionately larger than in Lisbon, consequently there was greater association between the Portuguese and the English. Everything had the "English *ton*." Smith and Pickering "passed for Englishmen," but Pickering wondered whether this "was of great advantage" to them, at least among the Portuguese. Pickering noted that English officers were frequent visitors and never found anything to admire. "Some of our Portuguese friends were therefore very much amazed when we allowed anything, that was Portuguese, to be good." As Brown's guests, their entertainment was largely among the English colony, who showered "the greatest attentions" upon them, both in town and at the country-houses around Oporto. Even though it rained incessantly, they took a number of pleasant excursions. On the south

---

[70] Timothy Pickering to Oliver Ellsworth and William R. Davie, October 21, 1799, copy in *Davie Papers*, NC Archives.

side of the river was the Villa-Nova where the merchants had their wine cellars (some of seven to eight thousand pipes). On the sea-coast north of the river was Matazinhos, famous for a church with a miraculous image of the Saviour. At the time of their visit, several persons were going around the church on their bare knees and others knelt inside amidst hanging wax arms and legs.

On May 1, they proceeded to the provinces of Beira and Entre Douro e Minho. They stayed at the home of General Calder, a Scotsman by birth, who commanded the northern department. Barcellos was an ancient fortified town. At Braga, the seat of an archbishopric, they observed the manufacture of hats and cutlery. On the 10th they proceeded to Guimaraeus ("an idea of an old city in its ancient state") which manufactured cutlery and thread. They rode back to Oporto in sedan chairs strapped to mules. The sedan chairs had no cushions, and their coats were almost cut through in the back. Bad roads could not be avoided, but they escaped bad inns by staying in private homes.

On leaving Oporto for Lisbon they went to the head of the Bay of Aveiro (Ovar) and were rowed twenty-eight miles to Vagos on the southern side. At Vagos they had to wait an hour while the muleteers had a mass said for them. The villages (Toche and Mira) they passed were filled with miserable mud huts with thatched roofs. The poor people still talked of the Marquis de Pombal, who had tried to restrain the rapacity of the hidalgos. Although there was respect for the royal family, there was none for the hidalgos.

At Marinha Grande they visited a famous glass manufactory belonging to an Englishman, Mr. Stephens. He had established a model factory town, with even a theater in which the workmen acted, putting on a play once a month. Smith and Pickering heard the band play Haydn and Pleyel with such perfect execution and taste that they were astonished. Mr. Stephens had also taught the workmen country dances and minuets as a substitute for the indecent national dances. Mr. Stephens had no real monopoly from the Crown, but the prohibitive duties on glass and his privi-lege of cutting wood in a royal forest nearby gave him a great advantage. Consequently some years before, he had given an enter-tainment for the royal family which lasted three days and cost him £2,000 sterling. Smith and Pickering made one digression on the return to see the Convent of Batalha, the wonder of Portugal and a most remarkable specimen of Gothic architecture.

DIPLOMACY AND TRAVEL did not take up all of Smith's time; he spent many hours in Portuguese society. The same pattern of parties and balls was followed week after week. Every Sunday, Mrs. Pinto, the wife of the foreign minister, had "a rout." "After all the preliminaries of Bows, Curtsies, Compliments & Inquiries, which generally last three hours," there were cards and dancing. Monday was opera night, "but as they generally continue the same opera for two months together, none but an enthusiast in music would think of going very often." On Tuesday and Wednesday there were evening parties "at the Houses of Two Noble Persons, much in the same stile as at Mrs. Pinto's." Every Thursday there was an English ball. "The room is very elegant, the music excellent, & the company numerous and genteel; there are a number of pretty English women, who dress extremely well. This is undoubtedly the most agreeable entertainment of the week." Friday was opera night again. On Saturday, the week ended with a ball at the Prince of Waldeck's. The prince was an officer in the service of the Emperor, who had been lent to the Queen to reorganize her forces. He had a very handsome establishment at the public expense. Besides these regular entertainments there were often private dances, a Portuguese play twice a week, and many religious festivals and "bull feasts." In spite of the fact that Smith had mastered Portuguese and had many parties to attend, he was bored and lonely. He longed for the company of his friends in his "frequent solitary walks in the beautiful environs of Lisbon." As he wrote McHenry: "I often wish for the society of our friend Murray who writes me that his Spirits have been at times depressed by the gloomy fogs of Holland." Nevertheless he was forced to accept the "insipid and tranquil scene." It was "a quiet, easy life—enough of the *otium*, I will not add, *cum dignitate*."[71]

Smith devoted some of his energy and time to maintaining his dignity. When his carriage arrived from Philadelphia, Smith gave detailed instructions to his secretary on how it should be fitted out. A new footman had to be engaged, which meant a new hat. The hats of the other footmen were to be brushed up. The coats of the new liveries were to be lined with orange, and the waistcoats and breeches were also to be orange. If not orange, then yellow. The tailor knew what lace to use. Additional plated harness had to be obtained for the leaders, and the mules were to be frequently exer-

[71] William Smith to James McHenry, October 31, 1797, *McHenry Papers*, LC.

cised in the new chariot so that there would be no miscue when it was used for the first time on the prince's birthday.[72]

Yet it is the *otium* not the *dignitate* which must be emphasized in the story of these Portuguese years. One of the amusements of genteel company was making verses. In Smith's papers are fragments of many poems in his own hand in Portuguese, French, and English, which date from this period.[73] The following is one of his frivolous verses which can be read across or down, giving two opposing views:

Single Life and Matrimony Contrasted

The matrimonial state—	All prudent men approve,
The wise sincerely hate—	A cause of changling love;
True happiness we find—	In Hymen's silken chain,
With those who are unjoin'd—	There's naught but fear & pain;
I'll therefore wisely dare—	To have a constant wife;
To change from fair to fair—	Is but a wretched Life.[74]

Smith was also laying up a store of musical knowledge. He wrote Mrs. Izard that he had promised himself much pleasure in accompanying Caroline upon his return. In the meantime he looked upon music "as the best sweetner of sorrow, and companion in sickness and old age."[75]

SMITH TRIED HARD to escape the boredom of Portugal by finding a more important post. As he wrote in 1799: "My little talent is fast rusting in the scabbard."[76] Smith sought, in turn, missions to Spain, Austria, the Ottoman Empire, the Kingdom of the Two Sicilies, and France. He had broached the idea of a mission to Spain to Pickering and McHenry before he left America. From Lisbon he wrote that Colonel Humphreys would welcome Smith's assistance. "A third would not be necessary."[77] When Austria acquired Venice from Napoleon and thereby became a naval power, Smith urged a mission to make a commercial treaty with the Emperor.[78] He came closer, however, to his mission to Turkey than he did to any of the

[72] Pickering, *op. cit.*, pp. 117-118.
[73] *William Loughton Smith Papers*, RC. *William Loughton Smith Papers*, SCHS.
[74] *William Loughton Smith Papers*, RC.
[75] Alice Izard to Margaret Manigault, August 31, 1801, *Manigault Papers*, SC Archives.
[76] William Smith to James McHenry, December 26, 1799, *McHenry Papers*, LC.
[77] William Smith to James McHenry, October 9, 1797, *McHenry Papers*, WLCL.
[78] William Smith to James McHenry, February 15, 1798, *McHenry Papers*, WLCL.

others. It was his idea that he could negotiate with the King of the Two Sicilies on his return from Constantinople.[79]

In February 1799, John Adams nominated Smith as ambassador to the Sublime Porte and Rufus King as ambassador to Russia, both to negotiate commercial treaties. The Senate approved the appointments.[80] King knew nothing of the President's nomination and the Senate's approval until he read the news in the papers. As the Turkish and Russian ambassadors in London were equally ignorant of these developments, an omission which in European diplomacy was an insult, King had to approach the ambassadors with cautious explanations. He wrote Smith that he thought the move "a little premature. . . . I still think that it will require some management in order to give to it a turn that may not embarrass us." King had told the Turkish ambassador that the American Senate had to approve appointments; that it often only met in the winter; that it was therefore often necessary to make an appointment a long time ahead; and that "notwithstanding the news that you were appointed . . . still all the customary measures would be observed whether it would be agreeable to him to receive our Ambasador." When the Turkish ambassador wanted to know something about Smith, King replied:

> I answered that you were 38 or 40 (too young a man would not do) a Gentleman of fortune, a man of letters, always employed in great affairs, and a distinguished member of Congress, answering to Parliament, lately come abroad and for the first time, a pronounced friend of order, and an enemy of the Philosophy, and Politicks of France.—The answer shewed that all this pleased.

King finally asked the Turkish ambassador to send an account of the conversation home, which he promised to do. King thought that his own nomination "had been made on the supposition that the treaty with Russia would be negotiated" in London. "This cannot be done, and I presume the business will pass into other hands."[81]

Smith first heard of his appointment from King through letters received in Oporto while he was on his northern tour. Secretary Pickering's dispatches, which arrived shortly after King's letters, suggested that Smith might take passage in an American frigate, but if none were available he might try a British man-of-war. Smith was concerned about Pickering's saying nothing about waiting for

[79] William Smith to Rufus King, June 21, 1799, *William Loughton Smith Papers*, HEHL.
[80] *Journal of the Executive Proceedings of the Senate*, Washington, 1828, I, 311-312.
[81] Rufus King to William Smith, March 26, 1799, *King Papers*, NYHS.

the Sultan's approval and until proper presents could be procured. Smith wanted King to get him a letter of introduction to the British ambassador in Constantinople, who might serve as an avenue of introduction to the Sultan.[82] He was obviously eager to go, for he began to read Eton's *Turkish Empire* and Dalloway's *Constantinople, Antient and Modern.* He wrote King again to ask what "furniture, servants, carriages, liquors, dress etc. to carry." He also inquired about fireplaces in Constantinople, for he had found Portugal quite cold.[83] These preparations were all to no avail, for both King's mission to Russia and Smith's to the Sublime Porte proved abortive. Pickering wrote that because of French advances in Italy and the Mediterranean, the mission to Turkey had been suspended.[84]

AT THE SAME TIME that Adams had nominated Smith and King as envoys to Turkey and Russia, he had asked the Senate to approve another mission to France. The President selected Oliver Ellsworth of Connecticut and William R. Davie of North Carolina to join Murray on the commission. Although appointed in February, Ellsworth and Davie did not sail from America until November 3. As McHenry said, the mission was "an apple of discord";[85] it undermined the hopes of the arch-Federalists for war and led to their break with Adams. Smith believed that it was French policy to fluctuate between harshness and kindness in order to keep America stirred up and at a distance. He dreaded more "their Smiles than their Blows."[86] In November 1798, he was afraid that the French proposal to renew negotiations would be a weapon in the hands of the French party in America.[87] By June 1799, he was sure that "our Executive is taken in."[88]

Pickering was quite slow in getting the mission off. On October 21, he instructed the envoys that "if you put into Lisbon, you will

---

[82] William Smith to Rufus King, May 18, 1799, *William Loughton Smith Papers,* WLCL.
[83] William Smith to Rufus King, June 5, 1799, *William Loughton Smith Papers,* WLCL. John Pickering had begun to study Arabic "as a foundation" for Turkish. Pickering, *op. cit.,* p. 140.
[84] William Smith to Rufus King, June 21, 1799, *William Loughton Smith Papers,* WLCL.
[85] James McHenry to William Smith, October 22, 1799, *William Loughton Smith Papers,* LC.
[86] William Smith to Rufus King, August 14, 1798, *William Loughton Smith Papers,* HEHL.
[87] William Smith to Rufus King, November 2, 1798, *William Loughton Smith Papers,* HEHL.
[88] William Smith to Rufus King, June 21, 1799, *William Loughton Smith Papers,* HEHL.

of course call on our Minister Mr. Smith, from whom you will receive correct information of whatever shall be most interesting for you to know." If they needed money before they could draw on the Dutch bankers, the Bulkeleys could be counted on to supply them.[89] Smith was not the best person to advise the envoys. Although he had not favored the mission, he would most likely have been pleased to be a member of the commission, so he was peeved for a number of reasons. Smith wrote King on December 7: "A suspension of my Journey to the East is the natural consequence of the French mission, an opposition being apprehended from England and Russia."[90] On the 26th, he wrote McHenry that "my friend Murray's trip to Paris is to knock up mine to Constantinople."[91]

The envoys arrived on November 27 on the *United States,* under the command of Captain John Barry, having put in to Lisbon to learn the state of affairs in Europe and to avoid the hazards of a Dutch port at that time of the year.[92] The new revolution in France—Napoleon's rise to power by the *coup d'état* of the 18th *Brumaire*—did not alter their plans. Smith himself thought that it would be "impolitic" to abandon the mission at this stage, but he expected no good from it; in fact, he thought it would bring about "much mischief." Bonaparte was the question mark. Would he restore the throne? Would he end his career as a Caesar, a Cromwell, a Monk, or a Robespierre?[93] To McHenry, Smith wrote: "Some think Bonaparte will prove in the end a General Monk, others that he will act the part of Oliver Cromwell—time will discover; at any rate, as far as relates to us, I trust that our Connect. Oliver aided by his colleagues will be more than a match for the Corsican Oliver." After the envoys had sailed on, he added: "Opposition to or condemnation of it can certainly now render no benefit to our country: I therefore presume our friends by this time acquiesce in it."[94]

[89] Timothy Pickering to Oliver Ellsworth and William R. Davie, October 21, 1799, copy in *Davie Papers,* NC Archives.
[90] William Smith to Rufus King, December 7, 1799, *William Loughton Smith Papers,* HEHL. The war of the Second Coalition was underway, in which England, Russia, and the Ottoman Empire were allies against France.
[91] William Smith to James McHenry, December 26, 1799, *McHenry Papers,* LC.
[92] Blackwell P. Robinson, *William R. Davie,* Chapel Hill, 1957, pp. 332-336.
[93] William Smith to Rufus King, December 7, 1799, *William Loughton Smith Papers,* HEHL.
[94] William Smith to James McHenry, December 26, 1799, *McHenry Papers,* LC.

While the envoys tarried in Lisbon, Smith honored them with a dinner and a ball. The guest list included one hundred thirty-two people, forty-one ladies and ninety-one gentlemen. Each group was carefully counted. Ellsworth, Davie, Swift, Littlejohn, and Ellsworth, junior, were five.[95] Captains Barry, Decatur, and two officers were four. Captains Williamson, Dehon, and Russell were three. Smith was accustomed to tally up on a list of guests the number of ladies dancing and not dancing, the gentlemen dancing and not dancing.[96] His planning was always quite careful, yet Captain Barry complained to Pickering that Smith's treatment of the American officers and envoys had been "marked with singular inattention & disrespect." At the dinner, Ellsworth and Davie had been placed below a British officer and the Chevalier de Freire. At the ball they were slightly noticed, and the American officers were quite neglected, none being introduced nor asked to dance. Barry wrote that Smith was "the damndest Englishman he had met with." As Pickering explained, this news had pained Smith's friends.[97]

Smith, in order to exonerate himself, wrote Oliver Ellsworth for a statement. Ellsworth sent one on August 2, 1800, from Paris:

> I was perfectly satisfied with your politeness & attention to me while at Lisbon. General Davie also assures me that your treatment of him was perfectly satisfactory; tho he frankly adds, that the circumstances of placing at the table, a brigadier, tho of a foreign nation, above a Ch: Justice of your own did strike him as an improper arrangement.—Whether the officers of the frigate had or had not an opportunity to dance did not fall under our notice as we retired soon after the dancing commenced. I heard indeed afterwards on shipboard, that none of them had been invited to dance, but made no remarks upon it nor ever intimated that I thought you had been deficient in attention to any person.[98]

In spite of this letter, there remains the stain of ungraciousness. Smith was too precise in his planning to have been guilty of an oversight. He had not liked the mission, and he showed it. Smith was indeed only amused by Davie's objections. He wrote King on November 25, 1800: "I have had a very humourous letter from Murray concerning the respective rights of Brigadier and Chief Justice, written in his pleasant stile of Badinage, which his resi-

[95] Swift and Littlejohn were the secretaries to Ellsworth and Davie respectively. Robinson, *op. cit.*, p. 336.

[96] Lists of guests among the *William Loughton Smith Papers*, RC.

[97] Timothy Pickering to William Smith, May 7, 1800, *William Loughton Smith Papers*, LC.

[98] Oliver Ellsworth to William Smith, August 2, 1800, *William Loughton Smith Papers*, LC.

dence in Paris has I think improved." Smith added as a postscript: "I wish I had an opportunity of quieting Gov. Davie's scruples, by informing him that the Brigadier was a *Lieut. General.*"[99]

There was a great deal of dissension on board the *United States* concerning the best way to proceed. Ellsworth, who had suffered greatly from sea-sickness, wanted to proceed by land but thought that the journey would take too long. They were on board the ship in the Tagus for over a week waiting for favorable weather and did not sail until December 21. At the last moment, Swift and Gibbes of Newport left the ship and went by way of Madrid.[100] On February 28, Smith wrote John Rutledge, junior, that the envoys had finally been put ashore at Corunna and had met Swift and Gibbes at Burgos. "There is no doubt that they will be well received at Paris and will commence a negotiation but how it will end, or if in a treaty, how long it can be maintained, are questions of much consideration."[101] The envoys did not arrive at Bayonne until mid-February. They had broken their carriage and had to finish that part of the journey on horseback and muleback—"a melancholy procession." They did not reach Paris until March 2. When Smith conveyed this news to King, he still expected the envoys to make a treaty with France, but with the French privateers scouring the ocean and independent governments still remaining in the West Indies, he saw no advantages to be gained from such a treaty.[102]

On September 30, 1800, Napoleon agreed on a compromise. America was released from her promise made in the Treaty of 1778 to defend the French West Indies "forever." In return, the American government agreed to assume the responsibility for meeting the claims that American shippers had against France.[103] Smith wrote King on November 25 that he was pleased with the convention and that the Danish and Swedish ministers had congratulated him on it (Talleyrand had included very liberal provisions on neutral rights):

> All the great points concerning navigation are settled to our advantage; they are extremely liberal and contain all we could require:

[99] William Smith to Rufus King, November 25, 1800, *William Loughton Smith Papers,* HEHL.

[100] William Smith to Rufus King, December 7, 18, 21, 1799, *William Loughton Smith Papers,* HEHL.

[101] William Smith to John Rutledge, junior, February 28, 1800, *John Rutledge, junior, Papers,* SHC.

[102] William Smith to Rufus King, March 15, 1800, *William Loughton Smith Papers,* HEHL.

[103] For the negotiations, *see* E. Wilson Lyon, "The Franco-American Convention of 1800," *Journal of Modern History,* XII (1940), 305-333.

as to the compensation, all we could have expected would be a commission, which would only create useless expence and end in disappointment—it is as well to give it up with a good grace; tho I think the relinquishment on the other side of the guarantee article, the Consular privileges and other points of the old Treaties a very full Indemnity for our pecunairy loss—indeed in the article of treaties, a few millions of dollars more or less ought never to determine their merits or demerits—what judicious American would not have willingly paid these few millions to change our former Treaties for this Convention?[104]

The Convention of 1800 with France was comparable to the Jay Treaty of 1795 with England. Smith only hoped that it would not alienate England as the Jay Treaty had once alienated France. He would have liked to have been the new ambassador to France but felt that the place was reserved for the President's son or for Murray. Murray did go to Paris to make the final arrangements after the Senate had excluded Article Two of the Convention.[105]

SMITH HIMSELF was involved in one important area of late eighteenth-century American diplomacy. The American minister at Lisbon was responsible for American interests in the Mediterranean. Before the Revolution, about one-sixth of the wheat and flour exported from the thirteen colonies, and about one-fourth of the dried and pickled fish, and some rice had found markets in the Mediterranean ports. This loaded annually eighty to a hundred ships of approximately 20,000 tons, which had a complement of 1,200 seamen. Great Britain had protected this commerce by paying tribute to the four Barbary powers: Morocco, Algiers, Tunis, and Tripoli. After 1776, America was no longer protected by British treaties, and in 1785 two American vessels, one from Boston and one from Philadelphia, were taken off the coast of Portugal. The British were suspected of urging the Algerines to seize American vessels, but under the confederation government the United States was too weak to protest.

Jefferson, in a report to the President of December 28, 1790, sketched two broad alternatives: one involved ransom and tribute, the other, war. It was suggested that the United States might pay an annual tribute as did the Dutch, Danes, Swedes, and Venetians, who paid about $24,000 to $30,000 a year. The Dutch and Danes

---

[104] William Smith to Rufus King, November 25, 1800, *William Loughton Smith Papers*, HEHL.

[105] For the controversy over Article Two, *see* Lyon, *op. cit.*, pp. 329-333. William Smith to William Eaton, June 11, 1801, *William Loughton Smith Papers*, HEHL.

paid in naval stores; the Swedes and Venetians in money. Force, as an alternative, might succeed, for the Algerine vessels were hard to maneuver, since they attacked by boarding and were, therefore, usually crowded with men. Temporarily, as Jefferson reported, the problem was partly solved by the fact that the Portuguese had a squadron patrolling the Strait of Gibraltar to keep the pirates out of the Atlantic.[106]

The Washington government decided upon tribute. Money was to be borrowed in Amsterdam or London and channeled through the American minister in Lisbon to the consuls in North Africa.[107] Before this system could function, the Portuguese had withdrawn their squadron; and in October and November 1793, the pirates seized four ships, five brigs, and two schooners belonging to Americans.[108] Edward Church, the American consul in Lisbon, called the Portuguese withdrawal a "hellish plot" of the British. "The conduct of the british in this business leaves no room to doubt, or mistake their object, which was evidently aimed at us, and proves that their envy, jealousy, and hatred, will never be appeased, and that they will leave nothing unattempted to effect our ruin."[109]

Congress's answer to this new outburst was to call for a navy but at the same time to make available $800,000 for negotiation. If the negotiations were successful, work on the frigates was to be halted. David Humphreys, the minister in Lisbon, was to be the link between Amsterdam funds and American agents. When the loan could not be negotiated in Amsterdam, the American government had to turn to British bankers. American stock was shipped to the Barings of London who were to sell it (without depressing the market for American securities) and make the proceeds available to Humphreys through their Lisbon agents, John Bulkeley and Sons.[110] Anglophobe Edward Church was removed, and Thomas Bulkeley was appointed consul in an effort to make the system run more smoothly.[111]

[106] *Naval Documents Related to the United States Wars with the Barbary Powers,* Washington, 1939, I (1785-1801), 19, 22-26.
[107] Secretary of state to Thomas Barclay, May 13, 1791, *ibid.,* pp. 30-31.
[108] "List of American vessels captured by the Algerines in October and November 1793," *ibid.,* p. 56.
[109] Edward Church to the secretary of state, October 12, 1793, *ibid.,* pp. 47-50.
[110] Secretary of state to David Humphreys, August 25, 1794; message of Washington to Congress, February 28, 1795; secretary of state to David Humphreys, March 28, 1795, *ibid.,* pp 80-81, 93, 95-96.
[111] Church admitted to Madison in 1801 that he had been removed for undertaking a mission for the French in Portugal, but that it had been humil-

Colonel Humphreys left America in April 1795 accompanied by Joseph Donaldson, consul for Tunis and Tripoli. They reached Gibraltar, where James Simpson, the American consul, was instructed to make a treaty with Morocco, which he did on August 18, 1795.[112] Donaldson then continued to Algiers and arranged a treaty on September 5, 1795, which finally freed the sailors captured in 1785,[113] and Humphreys went on to Lisbon, where his chief problem was to see that the funds promised by Simpson and Donaldson reached the Barbary rulers. The delivery of the money was so slow that in March 1796 Donaldson offered the Dey of Algiers a frigate in an effort to quiet his impatience. The American government backed Donaldson's offer, and the frigate was ordered to be built at Portsmouth, New Hampshire.[114] Humphreys finally received funds from the Barings in August 1796 and dispatched them immediately. However, when nothing conclusive had been heard in America by February 1797, William Smith moved a debate in Congress, and a new grant was made.[115]

It was then that Smith was named minister to Lisbon, responsible for servicing the arrangements already made. Humphreys' assignment had been changed to Madrid, and he left Lisbon early in August 1797.[116] Richard O'Brien, the former captive, was to be consul general in Algiers, with James Leander Cathcart in Tripoli, William Eaton in Tunis, and James Simpson in Gibraltar. The consuls and American naval commanders were, to keep in touch by corresponding with Smith.

When the frigate *Crescente* was finally launched (on the Fourth of July!), O'Brien was ordered to take it to Algiers. According to instructions from Pickering, O'Brien was to stop at Gibraltar to ascertain if the Dey of Algiers had been paid. If the payments had not been made, he was to continue direct. If they had been, he was

---

iating to be replaced by "a young Englishman." He had added that he had not expected any redress "during the late administration." Edward Church to secretary of state, June 23, 1801, *Consular Dispatches from Lisbon I (1791-1802), Department of State*, National Archives.

[112] James Simpson to secretary of state, August 18, 1795, *Naval Documents Related to the United States Wars with the Barbary Powers*, Washington, 1939, I (1785-1801), 106-107.

[113] *See* treaty and list of captives released, *ibid.*, pp. 107-117.

[114] David Humphreys to secretary of state, April 26, 1796, *ibid.*, pp. 151-152.

[115] *Annals of the Congress of the United States*, Washington, 1849, VI (4th cong., 2nd sess.), 2235-2446.

[116] William Smith to Timothy Pickering, August 24, 1797, *William Loughton Smith Papers*, HEHL.

to deposit the money at Gibraltar and inform Smith of that fact. Smith could then draw on the money to repay the Barings.[117]

O'Brien stopped briefly at Gibraltar in February 1798, but sailed on before Smith arrived there; he had carried the funds with him to Algiers, since the governor of Gibraltar was unwilling to accept a deposit. When the Dey of Algiers died, on May 15, all of the arrangements had to be renegotiated. Fortunately, the new Dey consented to receive O'Brien and to renew the treaty with the United States, and to guarantee one with Tripoli. O'Brien promised three corsairs and presents worth $5,000.[118]

The three corsairs, which were fitted out in Philadelphia, arrived in the Mediterranean in the winter of 1798-1799, bringing out both Cathcart and Eaton for the Tripoli and Tunis consular posts. Cathcart had some trouble in getting settled in Tripoli, although he carried a strong letter of recommendation from the Dey of Algiers to the Bashaw of Tripoli. O'Brien thought that America would have to send stores or a cash payment before the Bashaw would be pacified; otherwise, the twenty-one United States vessels at Leghorn (as of April 1799) would be in danger of seizure.[119]

In May 1799, O'Brien wrote Smith requesting additional presents for Algiers. The general of the marine wanted a sextant, two "best night and day glasses," four sheets of the colours of all nations, two books of the best English draughts of the Mediterranean on a large scale; the Dey wanted twenty brass cannons (twenty-four pounders) with their carriages, which would cost approximately $20,000.[120] Smith passed these requests on to King, with the information that O'Brien had used up the funds at Algiers. Smith explained that the expenses of maintaining consular staffs in the three regencies had gone up, due to the change of consuls in Tunis

[117] Secretary of state to Joel Barlow, May 13, 1797, *Naval Documents Related to the United States Wars with the Barbary Powers*, Washington, 1939, I (1785-1801), 202-203. Secretary of state to Richard O'Brien, December 29, 1797, *ibid.*, pp. 231-234.

[118] Richard O'Brien to William Smith, April 30, 1798; Richard O'Brien to David Humphreys, May 21, 1798, *ibid.*, pp. 247-248, 250. William Smith to Rufus King, June 20, 1798, *William Loughton Smith Papers*, HEHL.

[119] Secretary of state to Richard O'Brien, December 21, 1798; Richard O'Brien to secretary of state, [January 23 to March 1799], *Naval Documents Related to the United States Wars with the Barbary Powers*, Washington, 1939, I (1785-1801), 280-283, 290-295. Richard O'Brien to William Smith, April 23, 1799, *William Loughton Smith Papers*, HEHL.

[120] Richard O'Brien to William Smith, May 27, 1799, copy in *William Loughton Smith Papers*, HEHL.

and Tripoli, the accession of a new Dey in Algiers, and the delay in transmitting stores to Tripoli.[121]

Neither Smith nor the American consuls in North Africa were pleased with this state of affairs in the Mediterranean. They wanted to have a strong American naval force cruising the sea in order to keep the Barbary powers in check. After giving the system much thought, Smith wrote the secretary of state on July 1, 1799, to suggest a new approach to the problem. First, he recommended that the superintendency of Barbary affairs should be vested in the minister at Madrid rather than in the minister at Lisbon, since most of the letters from Algiers came via Alicante and Madrid. Communication between North Africa and Lisbon was most uncertain. He then suggested a major overhaul in the existing system:

> To fix at Gibraltar an intelligent, active, and confidential American citizen, under the denomination of Consul, or Superintendent of Barbary Affairs, or Agent for Mediterranean Commerce, or Consul General for the Mediterranean, with such a salary as will induce a very respectable character to undertake it; the emoluments of trade may be an additional inducement: To vest this officer with enlarged powers, and an ample credit on Leghorne, Madrid, Lisbon, and London, and to station at Gibraltar one or more armed packets, for purpose of prompt communication with the Regencies and the United States.

Smith did not think that James Simpson, the consul then in Gibraltar, would do since he was a foreigner; but with a salary of $4,000 or $5,000, a worthy American citizen could be secured for the position.[122]

In the fall of 1799, Tunis represented the immediate danger. She had made peace with Naples and Portugal, and with Venice protected by the Porte, the Tunisians would have a hundred corsairs unemployed. Eaton wrote that Tunis was merely waiting for a pretext to strike against American commerce. Under these circumstances, when the Bey of Tunis demanded that the United States have his sword and scabbard mounted with numerous diamonds, there was nothing else for Eaton and Smith to do. During 1800, the Bey of Tunis was kept quiet with promises concerning his regalia.[123]

[121] William Smith to Rufus King, June 21, 1799, *William Loughton Smith Papers,* HEHL.

[122] William Smith to Timothy Pickering, July 1, 1799, *William Loughton Smith Papers,* HEHL.

[123] Richard O'Brien to William Smith, September 13, 1799; William Smith to William Eaton, November 2, 1799; William Smith to Rufus King, April 7, June 27, 1800; William Eaton to William Smith, September 10, 1800; William Smith to Rufus King, December 13, 1800, *William Loughton Smith Papers,* HEHL.

The irritation of the Dey of Algiers was assuaged in 1800 by the arrival of the *Sophia* with stores and presents.[124] In the fall, he was mollified by O'Brien's permitting Captain Bainbridge to sail the *George Washington* to Constantinople with the Dey's envoy—a signal favor to Algiers. Meanwhile the Bashaw of Tripoli was getting out of hand, and O'Brien tried to get the Dey to keep him in line. Even though O'Brien reminded the Dey that the treaty with Tripoli had been made under his auspices, he refused to interfere, and the Bashaw continued his threats of war unless he got an extraordinary present.[125]

When Captain Bainbridge returned from Turkey in February 1801, he wrote Smith that "now is a propitious time for you to go [to Constantinople] in a fine ship of war."[126] Bainbridge carried a special letter of invitation from the captain bashaw to Smith. As Smith explained to King, the captain bashaw although third in rank was first in power at Constantinople.[127] There was, however, no chance to revive Smith's mission to Turkey. Tripoli declared war on the United States on May 14, 1801.[128] There was obviously only one thing to do, and that was to use the new American navy. Smith hoped that Madison as secretary of state would be more energetic than Adams had let Pickering be. He wrote Eaton that he thought Madison "a very able man" who would "I am confident pay great attention to Mediterranean commerce."[129] Smith was absolutely correct in his estimation of the new secretary of state; a fleet commanded by Commodore Richard Dale arrived at Gibraltar on July 1 and sailed on July 3 against the Tripolitans. Commodore Dale wrote Smith on July 2 that he had with him three frigates, the *President* (forty-four guns), the *Philadelphia* (forty guns), and the *Essex* (thirty-two guns), as well as the schooner *Enterprise* (twelve guns). His orders were to protect American commerce.[130]

[124] William Smith to Rufus King, April 7, 1800, *William Loughton Smith Papers*, HEHL.
[125] Richard O'Brien to William Smith, December 23, 1800, *William Loughton Smith Papers*, HEHL.
[126] William Bainbridge to William Smith, February 4, 1801, *William Loughton Smith Papers*, RC.
[127] William Smith to Rufus King, February 18, 1801, *William Loughton Smith Papers*, HEHL.
[128] William Smith to Rufus King, July 27, 1801, *William Loughton Smith Papers*, HEHL.
[129] William Smith to William Eaton, June 11, 1801, *William Loughton Smith Papers*. HEHL.
[130] Richard Dale to William Smith, July 2, 1801; William Bainbridge to William Smith, July 29, 1801, *William Loughton Smith Papers*, RC. Irving Brant, *James Madison, Secretary of State, 1800-1809*, Indianapolis, 1953, p. 60.

Smith was not in office long enough to see the eventual triumph of the policy that he had urged.

SMITH WAS NOT a great diplomat. Most of his time had been spent on routine matters: forged American sea-letters, French privateering, English impressment of American seamen, decisions of the admiralty courts.[131] But since he was not in a key spot, there was little scope for greatness. He is best described as a Federalist diplomat who worked for greater cooperation with Britain—one of those who had made the *rapprochement* work. In this role he was of real service to his country. If he was not an outstanding diplomat, he was at least the traveler *par excellence*. Once relieved of his official duties, he spent two years touring western Europe.

HARPER HAD WARNED Smith that Jefferson and Madison planned to remove him.[132] Smith was, therefore, not surprised when he received his letter of dismissal, dated June 1, on July 25, 1801. For reasons of economy, Jefferson had decided to abolish the post of American minister to Portugal, and Smith's last duty was to try to explain to the Portuguese that this did not imply any slight. As Smith wrote King, Bezerra, who had been appointed to succeed the Chevalier de Freire as Portuguese minister to the United States, was deeply disappointed at the cancellation of his own assignment.[133]

Smith made plans to visit England, France, Holland, and Italy before returning to America. He, as always, wanted to travel as an official person (the important doors being thereby more easily opened), and he was presumptuous enough to write King suggesting that he might take over the London post for three or four months, if King should by chance be leaving before his successor arrived. King, of course, was in a position to be of immense help. During August and September, Smith transferred to King's hands the £920/2/7 sterling he had collected as a fund for traveling and upon which he intended to draw.[134]

---

[131] William Smith to Timothy Pickering, August 24, 1797; William Smith to Rufus King, January 7, July 29, 1799, February 18, 1801, *William Loughton Smith Papers*, HEHL.

[132] William Smith to Rufus King, June 13, 1801, *William Loughton Smith Papers*, HEHL.

[133] William Smith to Rufus King, July 27, August 4, 1801, *William Loughton Smith Papers*, HEHL. Thomas Bulkeley to James Madison, August 5, 1801, *Consular Dispatches from Lisbon, I (1791-1801), Department of State*, National Archives.

[134] William Smith to Rufus King, July 27, August 4, 15, September 3, October 21, 1801, *William Loughton Smith Papers*, HEHL.

On September 14, he sailed for Falmouth in the packet. He arrived on the 26th with a lame leg, having suffered a bruise at sea, which kept him confined there for a fortnight. Fortunately William Vans Murray was in Falmouth on his way to America, so the time was passed most pleasantly. Smith then spent ten days in the neighborhood of Plymouth and on October 21 was in Exeter en route to meet his brother in Bath.[135]

Joseph Allen Smith had come abroad in 1793 for his health. He had had a short sojourn in Portugal, but London became his home base.[136] He had asked Thomas Pinckney in July 1793 to present him at court, saying that this "will not only facilitate an introduction abroad, without which, I am told, it is impossible to get into any good company, but also enable me thro' the medium of some friend, to procure letters, as an American gentleman, to the British ministers at Vienna, Turin, and Naples. . . . The anxious desire I have of travelling with every advantage I can procure and the information I have received from those who are acquainted with the Punctilios of foreign countries have led me to give you this trouble."[137] Joseph Allen traveled extensively, using the contacts supplied by Thomas Pinckney and Rufus King, the American ministers in London. On a tour of Ireland he was accompanied by Lord Wycombe, the son of Lord Shelburne, America's great friend. Wycombe must have been in sympathy with the Irish revolutionaries, for William Smith heartily disapproved of Joseph Allen's views on Irish events, which he attributed to the influence of Lord Wycombe.[138]

The brothers must have met in Bath and then, when they heard that England and France intended to conclude a peace, hurried to Paris, arriving there on November 7, having passed Lord Cornwallis, the British envoy sent to negotiate with the French, on the road from Calais. Smith, who wrote fascinating letters (Mrs. Izard thought him the most "agreeable" of correspondents), captured the mood of Paris in an anecdote about Bonaparte. He described the illuminations and fireworks of November 9 as grand, but the weather had not been good. Yet when Bonaparte appeared at the

[135] William Smith to Rufus King, September 26, October 21, 1801, *William Loughton Smith Papers,* HEHL.
[136] David Humphreys to Thomas Pinckney, June 10, 1793, *Pinckney Papers,* LC.
[137] Joseph Allen Smith to Thomas Pinckney, July 18, 1793, *Pinckney Papers,* LC.
[138] Joseph Allen Smith to Rufus King, August 22, 1797, June 1, August 15, 1798, *King Papers,* NYHS. William Smith to Rufus King, June 20, 1798, *William Loughton Smith Papers,* HEHL.

windows of the Palace of the Tuileries, the clouds suddenly dispersed, and a person in the crowd shouted: "*Voilà la bonne fortune qui accompagne Bonaparte.*" The brothers' eagerness to be at the center of these festivities prompted them to write King for a letter of introduction to Lord Cornwallis, once the ravager of South Carolina and now the pacifier of France. King duly sent a letter, but it arrived the day after Cornwallis had departed for Amiens.[139]

Smith did not find Paris quite as charming as his fancy had anticipated. Yet "the movement, the variety, and the bustle" prevented "ennui." The people, he wrote King, cared less "for a violation of the new constitution than they do for a riot at the theatre over a new piece or a ball to be given tonight by a pretty woman."[140] William and Joseph Allen Smith mixed with the frivolous and the fabulous and on occasion dabbled in diplomacy. William had known Talleyrand in Philadelphia; Joseph Allen had met Joseph Bonaparte the previous year, and the two Josephs had discussed the future of Louisiana.[141] That winter they dined with Talleyrand, were present at the receptions of the First Consul, and were honored by invitations from Madame Récamier, the reigning beauty and society wit.[142]

After the Peace of Amiens (March 27, 1802), the brothers returned to London. That spring Smith lived at No. 2 Wimpole Street. Ransom and Morland, his old friends, were his bankers. He dined with Shelburne, now Lord Lansdowne, on April 18. On May 29, he was entertained at Cleveland Square by Lord Castlereagh. On June 4, General Willetes, whom he had known in Lisbon, invited him to the King's birthday celebration, and Lord Hawkesbury had him to dinner afterwards. As Smith wrote Mrs. Izard, he had had a full view of English public life from the servile acts of men on hustings seeking a seat in Parliament to the King himself.[143]

[139] William Smith to Rufus King, November 10, 1801, *William Loughton Smith Papers*, HEHL. Alice Izard to Margaret Manigault, October 2, 1802, *Manigault Papers*, SC Archives. Henry Morse Stephens, "Charles Cornwallis, first Marquis and second Earl Cornwallis," *DNB*.

[140] William Smith to Rufus King, January 26, 1802, *William Loughton Smith Papers*, HEHL.

[141] Joseph Allen Smith to *Citoyen* Joseph Bonaparte, 30 *ventose*, copy enclosed in Joseph Allen Smith to Rufus King, received by King, May 26, 1801, *King Papers*, NYHS. Joseph Allen Smith to Thomas Jefferson, March 22, 1801, *Jefferson Papers*, LC.

[142] Invitations in *William Loughton Smith Papers*, RC. *Also see* Joseph Allen Smith to Rufus King, April 13, 1802, *King Papers*, NYHS.

[143] London invitations and Lisbon party lists in *William Loughton Smith Papers*, RC.

In July 1802, the brothers crossed to Holland, but in Amsterdam they parted company.[144] Joseph Allen went off to Russia on what was perhaps the most extensive tour any American had yet made of that distant land. He visited Count Bernstorff in Copenhagen, dined with the Czar in Moscow, ventured into the Caucasian Mountains, was entertained by the captain bashaw at Constantinople, and viewed the antiquities of Greece, before returning to England in 1805. He had quite frankly hoped to be the first American minister to Russia, just as William had hoped to be the first American minister to Turkey.[145]

William traveled in Switzerland and Italy with all the advantages of a man of his station.[146] He revisited Geneva, the scene of his school-days, and in Turin he met Bossi, the Italian dramatist, who presented him with a copy of his play *Kotzbue in Siberia*.[147] In Genoa, which had been the capital of the Ligurian Republic since 1797, he studied a copy of the new *Constituzione della Repubblica Ligure*.[148] In Pisa he talked with Philip Mazzei, the friend of revolutionary Virginia, a correspondent of Jefferson, and the author of an accurate work on the United States.[149] In Naples he met his old friend Lord Elgin, who was returning from a four-year mission to the Ottoman Porte, and who now arranged for Smith's presentation to the King of the Two Sicilies.[150]

Smith and two Neapolitan princes sailed with the American squadron under Commodore Richard V. Morris from Naples to Leghorn. Commodore Morris, who had been sent to the Mediterranean to crush the Tripolitans, was overly cautious and somewhat doubtful as to whether his fleet could anchor at the Etrurian port. Smith accompanied Morris to Florence to ascertain whether or not Leghorn was a French port and therefore subject to French decrees concerning British goods on neutral vessels. Leghorn was under the jurisdiction of a French general, and the squadron soon sailed

[144] Joseph Allen Smith to Rufus King, July 15, 1802, *King Papers*, NYHS.
[145] See "Letters from Russia, 1802-1805," ed. George C. Rogers, Jr., *SCHGM*, LX (1959), 94-105, 154-163, 221-227.
[146] Alice Izard to Margaret Manigault, October 12, 1802, *Manigault Papers*, SC Archives. Passport and other papers in *William Loughton Smith Papers*, RC.
[147] *William Loughton Smith Pamphlets*, CLS, III, number 1.
[148] *Ibid.*, XVI, number 14.
[149] Mazzei's *Recherches historiques et politiques sur les Etats-Unis de l'Amérique septentrionale* had come out in four volumes in 1788. Richard Cecil Garlick, Jr., "Philip Mazzei," *DAB*.
[150] William Smith to Timothy Pickering, September 22, 1799, *Pickering Papers*, MHS.

for Tangier.[151] There Morris learned that he had been suspended from his command due to a lack of initiative in carrying out his orders. In Tangier Bay, Smith, then on his way home, met two young midshipmen from Charleston, Ralph Izard and Christopher Gadsden, who had just arrived in the Mediterranean on board the *Constitution*.[152] Smith finally sailed from Gibraltar for America on October 18 on either the *John Adams* or the *New York*.[153] After a fifty-day passage, the two frigates reached the navy yard of the city of Washington, where they were met by the President and all the heads of the departments, as well as most of the members of both houses of Congress.[154] Smith therefore had a chance to try the air of the new capital before taking passage from Philadelphia for home.[155]

[151] James Leander Cathcart to secretary of state, August 30, 1803, *Naval Documents Related to the United States Wars with the Barbary Powers*, Washingon, 1940, II (January 1802-August 1803), 523-525.

[152] Ralph Izard to Alice Izard, October 11, 1803, *Naval Documents Related to the United States Wars with the Barbary Powers*, Washington, 1941, III (September 1803-March 1804), 126-127.

[153] "Extract from journal of midshipman F. Cornelius de Krafft," October 18, 1803, *ibid.*, p. 154.

[154] William Henry Allen to Gen. William Allen, December 12, 1803, *ibid.*, p. 263.

[155] Pickering, *op. cit.*, p. 219.

XIV

THE FIRST SOLID SOUTH CAROLINA

WHEN WILLIAM SMITH left the United States in 1797, the Federalist party was approaching the zenith of its power; when he returned in 1803, it had reached its nadir. It is difficult to explain its rapid decline in the nation, but it is even more difficult to explain its demise in South Carolina in view of the fact that the Rutledge-Pinckney faction had in this period quite definitely returned to the fold. Charles Cotesworth Pinckney upon his return from France had picked up his new commission as major general, and with Washington and Hamilton he had worked to transform the American army into a fighting machine, one that would be absolutely loyal to the government and to the Federalist party.[1] General Pinckney's firm decision, after his second repulse by the French, was to support the arch-Federalists in their war program. This decision was known and respected by his friends in South Carolina.

In the fall of 1798, South Carolina returned five Federalists and one Republican to Congress, a feat that neither William Smith nor even Robert Goodloe Harper had ever considered to be within the realm of possibility. Harper had sent the joyous news to Smith, and Smith had passed on to Rufus King the good tidings that Thomas Pinckney had been returned from Charleston, John Rutledge, junior, had defeated Major Pierce Butler, and Harper had beaten William Butler, "a general of the militia from the backcountry." Smith ventured the opinion that Benjamin Huger, a nephew of Daniel Huger, who had defeated Lemuel Benton in the Georgetown District, would be "right." William Smith of Pinckney District had been succeeded by Abraham Nott, "a young lawyer from N. England of good principles." Thomas Sumter was the only Republican returned.[2]

Even more pleasing was the news that Edward Rutledge had been elected governor of the state in December 1798 to succeed

---

[1] He was commissioned July 19, 1798. J. G. de Roulhac Hamilton, "Charles Cotesworth Pinckney," *DAB*.

[2] William Smith to Rufus King, January 22, 1799, *William Loughton Smith Papers*, HEHL. DeSaussure considered Pinckney, Rutledge, Harper, and Huger as "decidedly federal." Nott was "a good man and attached to the government; not however I believe so decidedly as the other gentlemen—But he is not to be led by a party formed to destroy the government." Henry William DeSaussure to Timothy Pickering, November 10, 1798, *Pickering Papers*, MHS.

Charles Pinckney. Edward Rutledge, the most reluctant of the Rutledges and the Pinckneys to espouse the Federalist cause, had been brought around by the fact of General Pinckney's humiliation at the hands of the French. His son, who had been General Pinckney's secretary, had kept him informed during negotiations.[3] After the election, DeSaussure wrote Jacob Read to assure him that Rutledge would act "in perfect harmony with General P. and the General government."[4] A little later, DeSaussure assured Pickering, when forwarding a packet to William Smith via the secretary of state, that Rutledge was not a Jacobin:

> Permit me to say that notwithstanding some prepossessions with respect to our present governor, he is a man of ardent patriotism and high worth, and may be relied upon implicitly, for an entire cooperation in all the great measures of preparation and defence planned by the government. I hope it will be deemed neither officious nor arrogant to express myself in this manner—my sole motive is to give just impressions of a man whom I know well and love much, and against whom I know some misconceptions have been entertained—a cordial union of hearts and of hands is necessary at this all important crisis.[5]

Rutledge obviously wished to close the Federalist ranks, for on becoming governor he wrote "a handsome letter" to Smith enclosing a commission for Smith as the governor's aide-de-camp with the rank of lieutenant colonel. Smith was quite pleased—"a very acceptable thing in a country like this where dress is so much attended to and where a military dress saves an immense expense."[6]

The year 1799 marked the height of the power of the Federalist party in South Carolina and of the Rutledge-Pinckney faction, every member of which was in public service then. Charles Cotesworth Pinckney was a major general; Thomas Pinckney and John Rutledge, junior, were representatives in Congress, with young Rutledge being seriously considered for speaker in December;[7] and Edward Rutledge was governor of the state. Yet so changeable are

[3] Henry M. Rutledge to Edward Rutledge, August 10, October 2, 1797, *Rutledge Papers, Dreer Collection*, PHS. *Also see* Henry M. Rutledge to William Vans Murray, July 19, 1798, *Gratz Collection*, PHS.

[4] Henry William DeSaussure to Jacob Read, January 1, 1799, *Miscellaneous Manuscripts*, NYPL. Rutledge was really much closer to the Federalist leaders at this time than Wolfe has indicated. John Harold Wolfe, *Jeffersonian Democracy in South Carolina*, Chapel Hill, 1940, pp. 123-124.

[5] Henry William DeSaussure to Timothy Pickering, February 5, 1799, *Pickering Papers*, MHS.

[6] William Smith to Rufus King, June 5, 1799, *William Loughton Smith Papers*, HEHL.

[7] John Rutledge, junior, to Bishop Smith, December 3, 1799, *John Rutledge, junior, Papers*, SHC.

the fortunes of life and politics that no sooner had their strength been built up than it began to ebb.

There were two important reasons for the nationwide collapse of the party. First, John Adams brought the crisis of 1798 to an end by his second peace mission, which, in September 1800, arranged with Napoleon for the United States to be released from the entangling alliance with France and to iron out the outstanding grievances between the two countries on the high seas. Secondly, the Federalists, while enjoying their unaccustomed popularity, had extended their system too far. They had greatly increased the number of federal offices and had staffed all available offices with good party members. They also levied new taxes to pay for the war effort. They made many of the same mistakes that the English had made prior to 1776. The machinery of government became top-heavy, and instead of tying the party together, it crushed the movement. The revolt in 1776 was against placemen, monopoly, and taxes; in 1800, it was against public officeholders, moneyed men, and taxes.

The extent of the increase in public offices can be seen in South Carolina. Under James Simons the customs service had greatly expanded, so that by 1798, there was a deputy collector, a deputy naval officer, and a deputy surveyor as well as a cashier, a boarding officer, five inspectors of exports, twenty-four inspectors of imports, a gauger, a weigher, and a measurer. There was also a cutter in service whose captain's pay was comparable to that of an army captain, and a crew of mariners who got $10.00 a month. This was a little army of faithful officials.[8] The growth of the service was symbolized by the new Custom House.

The Federalist gentleman like the English aristocrat had come to look upon the government as a support for the family. Ralph Izard had fitted his son George for the army by sending him at an early age to Marburg, Germany, for military training.[9] Izard actually had his son commissioned a lieutenant in the United States Army before George had returned from Europe.[10] In 1798 at the request of his mother-in-law, William Smith wrote McHenry urging George Izard's promotion to captain:

[8] *The South-Carolina and Georgia Almanac, For the Year of our Lord, 1796,* Charleston, [1795]. *The South-Carolina and Georgia Almanac, For the Year of our Lord, 1799,* Charleston, [1798].
[9] George Izard to Thomas Pinckney, May 3, 1793; Ralph Izard to Thomas Pinckney, August 12, 1793, *Pinckney Papers,* LC.
[10] Timothy Pickering to George Izard, November 4, 1795, *Myers Collection,* NYPL.

I am persuaded you see the policy of encouraging respectable men to give good military educations to their children, which can be most effectively done by rapid promotions of those who have been well educated. Mr. Izard, in educating his son for a military life, was influenced by patriotic motives (which the late President approved by then facilitating his son's absence), and a desire to obviate a recurrence in case of war to foreigners; our worthy and good President, who has always the public good in view must applaud such motives and his friendship for Mr. I. whose worth he well knows must stimulate his inclination to promote the son of an honorable and patriotic citizen now lingering under a most dreadful disorder.[11]

Then, after John Pickering had gone to London, Smith tried to secure the appointment of Captain George Izard as his own secretary.[12]

The navy was an even more desirable field in 1798, as it was undergoing rapid expansion—from three frigates to thirty-three war vessels in the space of three years. John Rutledge, junior, was eager to have the secretary of the navy appoint his brother States as a midshipman on board the *United States* under Captain Barry.[13] Stoddert replied: "It is very much the President's wish, that such young gentlemen as your brother, should enter into the navy." States was to report to Captain Barry when the *United St tes* arrived in Newport in November 1798.[14] The next year Rutledge secured a midshipman's commission for John Smith, who, :s Rutledge wrote Bishop Smith, would be "the youngest officer in the navy."[15] So eager were the gentlemen of Charleston for their sons to be midshipmen that Stoddert told Harper that if he desired he could fill the fleet with midshipmen from Charleston alone.[16]

The establishment of the Charleston navy yard with its marine

---

[11] William Smith to James McHenry, August 4, 1798, *McHenry Papers*, LC. *Also see* William Smith to James McHenry, December 26, 1799, *McHenry Papers*, LC. In 1797, Izard suffered "a stroke of paralysis [which] made him an invalid for the rest of his days." Mabel L. Webber, "Ralph Izard," *DAB*.

[12] William Smith to Rufus King, March 15, April 7, 1800, *William Loughton Smith Papers*, HEHL. For the efforts of Lewis Morris in behalf of his brothers Staats and William, *see* Lewis Morris to James Morris, March 15, 1791, February 15, 1800, *Miscellaneous Manuscripts*, NYHS.

[13] John Rutledge, junior, to Bishop Smith, September 3, 1798, *John Rutledge, junior, Papers*, SHC.

[14] Benjamin Stoddert to John Rutledge, junior, October 12, 1798, *John Rutledge, junior, Papers*, SHC.

[15] John Rutledge, junior, to Bishop Smith, December 23, 1799, *John Rutledge, junior, Papers*, SHC.

[16] Secretary of the navy to Robert Goodloe Harper, August 22, 1799, *Naval Documents Related to the Quasi-War Between the United States and France, Naval Operations from August 1799 to December 1799*, Washington, 1936, p. 112.

hospital gave doctors a chance to serve the government. Dr. William Read, the senator's brother, volunteered his services at the marine hospital during the crisis, but by January 1800 he felt the need for remuneration, for he wrote his brother: "I confess that altho' I set out with motives purely disinterested and patriotic, the labour became so continued and arduous that it required some hopes of reward to support me under the fatigues." He had had to appoint Dr. Robert Wilson to act as "prescriber" while he was out of town and wanted to know how he could pay him.[17]

With the army and navy in need of supplies, merchants also had their opportunities. William Crafts, a leading Federalist merchant, secured the agency for supplying the navy. Daniel Stevens, who already held three public offices, acquired a fourth, the agency for supplying the army.[18] John Tunno, one of the British merchants banished from Charleston, heard in London that America was fitting out "a respectable Naval force" and wrote Senator Jacob Read on October 10, 1798:

> The preparation throughout the United States for warlike operations must require a considerable supply of naval and military stores indeed I have seen orders to houses here already to a handsome amount for such articles, and as such business is fully understood by me it would be pleasing to come in for a share if it could be procur'd *without* using any uncommon influence which is what I could not desire; however I shall not enlarge further well knowing that you would not miss any opportunity of being useful to me.[19]

John Tunno, a brother of Adam Tunno, the prominent Charleston merchant, understood the system of naval and military procurement.

New taxes also meant new tax officials, but it was difficult to find men to take these jobs. The Stamp Act—"an ominous symbol"—called for a stamp office with an issuing officer and a stamping officer, and the two men named for South Carolina were James Swinton and William Primrose Harrison.[20] The new direct tax which provided for an assessment on lands; dwelling houses, and slaves would have been under any circumstances a difficult tax to administer, but, since it was not to anyone's liking, it was difficult to get

---

[17] William Read to Jacob Read, January 17, 1800, *Emmet Collection*, NYPL. Mrs. Ralph Izard wrote Jacob Read on July 31, 1798, to recommend Dr. James Moultrie, nephew of General William Moultrie, for the position of assistant physician with the army, *Izard Papers*, SCL.

[18] *The South-Carolina and Georgia Almanac, For the Year of our Lord, 1799*, Charleston, [1798].

[19] John Tunno to Jacob Read, October 10, 1798, *Read Letters*, DUL.

[20] *The South-Carolina and Georgia Almanac, For the Year of our Lord, 1799*, Charleston, [1798].

anyone to take a commissionership. Wolcott was shocked when Daniel Stevens wrote that it had been almost impossible to find suitable men for the new jobs. Wolcott answered, "It was expected, that men of talents, property, and public spirit could be found who were willing to devote a few months to aid an important arrangement of the government."[21] Wolcott actually had more trouble finding direct-tax commissioners than Hamilton had had finding inspectors of the excise.

The opposition saw a monolithic federal structure growing before their eyes, staffed by a new elite of public office-holders. "Appius" had pointed out in 1794, when arguing for increased representation in the backcountry, that unless a change took place soon, an aristocracy would arise in the lowcountry, and then two separate worlds would flourish.[22] William A. Schaper has written that the backcountry feared that an inequality in wealth would lead to an inequality in condition, "which is the parent and nurse of aristocracy; for superior wealth is not only apt to beget and cherish a love of power and privilege, but has a strong tendency to bestow them." An aristocratic tradition had been rising in the lowcountry which, it was feared, if not stopped, would root out liberty, for it "favored numerous offices, large salaries, and great expenditures in the government."[23]

Perched on top of this federal structure was the pompous figure of Senator Jacob Read. His wife was from New York, and they spent most of their time in Newport when Congress was not in session, so he was looked upon as something of an alien.[24] He had succeeded to William Smith's seat on the board of directors of the Bank of the United States;[25] through James Simons he controlled the customs service; through Daniel Stevens he had influence in the excise service; and through Thomas Simons he had his voice in the Charleston branch of the Bank of the United States.[26] Behind

[21] Oliver Wolcott to Daniel Stevens, September 21, 1798, *Wolcott Papers*, CHS.

[22] [Robert Goodloe Harper], *An Address to the People of South-Carolina, By the General Committee of the Representative Reform Association, at Columbia*, Columbia, 1794, pp. 30-31.

[23] William A. Schaper, "Sectionalism and Representation in South Carolina,' *Annual Report of the American Historical Association for the Year 1900*, Washington, 1901, I, 411.

[24] Jacob Read to George Simpson, June 18, October 31, 1803, *Gratz Collection*, PHS.

[25] Jacob Read to George Simpson, January 12, 1801, *Etting Papers*, PHS.

[26] By 1802, Thomas Simons was the most important Carolina-born member of the local board. *South-Carolina Weekly Museum*, III (1798), 224. W. A. Clark, *The History of the Banking Institutions Organized in South Carolina Prior to 1860*, Columbia, 1922, p. 46.

this visible structure was Read's firm support from representatives of northern and British merchants in Charleston. It was this system, suddenly grown larger, that the Jeffersonians wanted to topple in 1800.

THE FEDERALIST PARTY in South Carolina suffered in 1800 from the effects of time. Its leaders were the older men of the community. The opposition, on the other hand, represented the new generation just beginning to spread its political wings. The Rutledge-Pinckney faction had already been hit by illness and death: Thomas Pinckney had suffered a critical illness early in 1798 and had been forced to withdraw from Congress in May to seek relief on Sullivan's Island.[27] Edward Rutledge died on January 23, 1800, having been struck down "with apoplexy," from which he never recovered, upon hearing of Washington's death.[28] Edward Rutledge's death was a serious blow to the faction in the state, for as Timothy Ford wrote Jacob Read, Rutledge was "an important spoke in the political wheel."[29] The Federalist party in 1800 had decided to nominate John Adams for President and Charles Cotesworth Pinckney for Vice-President, an apparently strong ticket since it united the northern and southern wings of the party, but in 1800 the Rutledges and the Pinckneys had much less to offer the party than they had had in former years.

For the state to be carried by Adams and Pinckney, the state legislature would have had to be dominated by Federalists. The prominent men in each locality were urged to run for the legislature. Henry William DeSaussure wrote John Rutledge, junior: "All the elderly men, of high character, whose health will allow them . . . will come out efficiently at the election, and many of them will be candidates. Mr. Russell, Mr. Jones, Mr. Corbett, and others of that stamp will offer to go—we shall put up General Pinckney himself [as state senator], and we shall prevail on others, who do not like the legislature but who feel the importance of the occasion to go." DeSaussure had written to Hunter, Colhoun, Anderson, and others in the backcountry who were definitely for the government but did not see the danger from the opposition. General William Washington had been "a good deal indisposed," but

[27] Rutledge described Pinckney's illness as "premonitions of an apoplexy." John Rutledge, junior, to Bishop Smith, February 8, 1798; Thomas Pinckney to John Rutledge, junior, June 25, 1798, *John Rutledge, junior, Papers,* SHC.
[28] William Read to Jacob Read, January 17, 1800, *Emmet Collection,* NYPL.
[29] Timothy Ford to Jacob Read, January 29, 1800, *Miscellaneous Manuscripts,* NYPL.

he was to be urged to campaign. In Beaufort, Rutledge's own constituency, General John McPherson and the Barnwells could be counted on to add their influence for Rutledge. However, General John Barnwell was in very poor health, with scarcely a hope for recovery. This was indeed a party of ailing old men.[30]

Charles Pinckney, the leader of the opposition, was working with "the most astonishing zeal and industry."[31] It was he who tried to drive a wedge between the supporters of John Adams and General Pinckney. He tried to exploit the split that had occurred on the national level between Adams and the arch-Federalists by circulating the news of the dismissal of the secretaries of state and of war by Adams, as well as copies of Hamilton's pamphlet criticizing the President.[32] In spite of these efforts, DeSaussure was able to write John Rutledge, junior, in October that the vote in South Carolina would be "a fair and joint one for Mr. Adams and General Pinckney."[33] DeSaussure explained at greater length to Jedediah Morse:

> General Hamilton's pamphlet has been received and read here. It is lamented as an indiscreet ill-timed publication, likely to produce division among ourselves but utterly incapable of producing any good. I do not perceive that it has produced any effect upon the minds of the leading men here, in relation to Mr. Adams. Most of them knew before that he had committed some indiscretions in his speech and in his letter, and many were not satisfied with some of the later measures of his administration—but they know and reverence his virtue and his talents and they will not put to hazard the great cause by dividing themselves from the great federal party.[34]

General Washington was clearly of the opinion "that Mr. A. and General P. ought to be run fairly together."[35] General Pinckney

[30] Henry William DeSaussure to John Rutledge, junior, August 14, 1800, *John Rutledge, junior, Papers*, SHC. *Also see* Robert Goodloe Harper to John Rutledge, junior, September 4, 1800; Thomas Pinckney to John Rutledge, junior, September 23, 1800, *John Rutledge, junior, Papers*, SHC.

[31] Henry William DeSaussure to John Rutledge, junior, December 2, 1800, copy enclosed in James Hillhouse to Jonathan Trumbull, junior, December 15, 1800, *Trumbull Papers*, CHS.

[32] Henry William DeSaussure to Timothy Pickering, August 12, 1800, *Pickering Papers*, MHS. Henry William DeSaussure to Jedediah Morse, November 3, 1800, copy in *Morse Papers*, YL.

[33] Henry William DeSaussure to John Rutledge, junior, October 22, 1800, *Miscellaneous Manuscripts*, NYPL.

[34] Henry William DeSaussure to Jedediah Morse, November 3, 1800, copy in *Morse Papers*, YL.

[35] Henry William DeSaussure to John Rutledge, junior, August 14, 1800, *John Rutledge, junior, Papers*, SHC.

himself refused all offers to organize a group in support of a Jefferson-Pinckney ticket.[36]

Unable to undermine Adams's support among the leading men, Charles Pinckney turned to the building of a Jeffersonian organization in the lowcountry, concentrating on securing some Republican representatives from Charleston in the state legislature, so that the state might be carried for Jefferson and Burr. A Republican ticket and a Federalist ticket were placed before the voters of Charleston for the crucial contest on October 13 and 14. General Pinckney easily defeated Colonel Thomas Lee for state senator, and fourteen of the fifteen Charleston representatives were selected from the Federalist ticket.[37] The Republicans made immediate plans to contest the election of the last eight on the list. Charles Pinckney described the struggle for Jefferson on October 16, 1800:

> I never before this knew the full extent of the federal interest connected with the British and the aid of the Banks and the federal Treasury and all their officers—they have endeavoured to shake Republicanism in S. C. to its foundations—but we have resisted it firmly and I trust successfully—our country interest out of the reach of banks and custom houses and federal officers is I think as pure as ever—I rejoice our legislature meets 130 or 140 miles from the sea—as much as I have been accustomed to politics and to study mankind this election in Charleston has opened to me a new view of things never certainly was such an election in America—we mean to contest it for 8 or 9 of the 15—it is said several hundred more voted than paid taxes—the lame crippled deseased and blind were either led lifted or brought in Carriages to the poll. The sacred right of ballot was struck at (for at a late hour when too late to counteract it) in order to know how men, who were supposed to be under the influence of banks and federal officers and English merchants, voted, and that they might be watched to know whether they voted as they were directed—the novel and unwarrantable measure was used of voting with tickets printed on green and blue and red and yellow paper and men stationed to watch the votes—[38]

Although the Republicans were not able to unseat eight or nine of the Charleston delegation, they still dominated the state legisla-

---

[36] Henry William DeSaussure to John Rutledge, junior, December 2, 1800, copy enclosed in James Hillhouse to Jonathan Trumbull, junior, December 15, 1800, *Trumbull Papers,* CHS. *Also see* Christopher Gadsden to John Adams, March 11, 1801, *The Works of John Adams,* ed. Charles Francis Adams, Boston, 1854, IX, 578-580.

[37] Pinckney received 623 votes; Lee, 387. *City Gazette and Daily Advertiser,* October 13, 14, 15, 1800. For a sketch of Lee, *see* John Belton O'Neall, *Biographical Sketches of the Bench and Bar of South Carolina,* Charleston, 1859, I, 83-101.

[38] Charles Pinckney to Thomas Jefferson, October 16, 1800, quoted in Wolfe, *op. cit.,* pp. 155-156.

ture.[39] When the legislature was polled, the Jefferson-Burr electors had won with the following votes:

John Hunter	87	William Washington	69
Paul Hamilton	87	John Ward	69
Robert Anderson	85	Thomas Roper	67
Theodore Gaillard	85	James Postell	66
Arthur Simkins	84	John Blossingame	66
Wade Hampton	82	William McPherson	66
Andrew Love	82	William Falconer	64
Joseph Blyth	82	Henry Dana Ward	63[40]

As the election in South Carolina determined the outcome in the nation, DeSaussure was correct in writing: "Thus ends our hopes and I fear the hopes of the federal party in America for from all I can learn the election decides the matter."[41] William Smith, far off in Lisbon, commented for the benefit of Rufus King that "such was the bitterness of party spirit that one of the most distinguished citizens of America had not one vote in his own state."[42]

In the race for seats in Congress in 1800 the Republicans had also done quite well. Thomas Lowndes managed to hold Thomas Pinckney's old seat for the Federalists. Benjamin Huger and John Rutledge, junior, thanks to their support in Georgetown and Beaufort, were able to hold their seats, but in the upcountry Harper lost his to William Butler. Thomas Sumter defeated General Richard Winn, and Thomas Moore defeated William Smith. The Federalists were thus reduced to three seats in the next Congress.[43]

The magnitude of the Republican victory in 1800 stunned the Federalists. DeSaussure attributed the success of the Jeffersonians to the energy of Charles Pinckney and his ability in building up a party in the lowcountry. Charles Pinckney was able to exploit the hostility that many felt towards the administration, especially those who, like himself, were not of the inner group. Once again, as in 1776, the revolt was led by men who wanted a share in power. The irony was that those who had won the fruits of the first revolution had begun to wax aristocratic, to solidify as a ruling group—the patriots of 1776 had become the conservatives of 1800. Christopher

[39] The Republicans announced that they would make such an attempt. *City Gazette and Daily Advertiser*, November 19, 1800. They failed, however, in their attempt. *JHR, November 28-December 20*, 1800, pp. 27, 71, 175.

[40] *City Gazette and Daily Advertiser*, December 6, 1800.

[41] Henry William DeSaussure to John Rutledge, junior, December 2, 1800, copy enclosed in James Hillhouse to Jonathan Trumbull, junior, December 15, 1800, *Trumbull Papers*, CHS.

[42] William Smith to Rufus King, February 14, 1801, *William Loughton Smith Papers*, HEHL.

[43] *City Gazette and Daily Advertiser*, October 29, November 5, 1800.

Gadsden and John Adams could not quite understand what had happened. Gadsden wrote Adams: "Our old-standers and independent men of long well-tried patriotism, sound understanding, and good property, have now in general very little influence in our public matters."[44] Adams replied with a rhetorical question: "What is the reason that so many of our 'old standbys' are infected with Jacobinism? The principles of this infernal tribe were surely no part of our ancient political creed."[45] The difference was twenty-five years. Gadsden had not been inconsistent, he had not changed, but he had grown old in times that had grown more democratic. The battle between aristocracy and democracy has been fought by each generation, but each new skirmish is fought with the preceding victory as a legacy which both contestants accept *ipso facto*. Perhaps the most important element in history is not perennial issues but the inevitability of new generations. Democracy and equality have been the victors each time.

THE FEDERALIST PARTY in South Carolina sealed its doom by the role its leaders took in deciding the tie in the electoral college between Jefferson and Burr. Jefferson and Burr had each received seventy-three electoral votes, and according to the Constitution the House of Representatives was to decide which man was to be President. Each state cast one vote with a simple majority necessary for election. South Carolina's vote was cast by the lame-duck delegation of Pinckney, Rutledge, Harper, Huger, Nott, and Sumter; not by the recently elected delegation of Lowndes, Rutledge, Huger, Butler, Sumter, and Moore. That lame-duck delegation was decidedly Federalist and cast its vote for Burr. Eight states voted for Jefferson, six for Burr, and two abstained on the first ballot; Jefferson needed one more vote. For thirty-five roll calls there was a deadlock in the House.[46]

Since South Carolina had cast eight votes for Jefferson and Burr, the South Carolina representatives thought that they had the freedom, according to a strict interpretation of the Constitution, to

[44] Christopher Gadsden to John Adams, March 11, 1801, *The Works of John Adams*, ed. Charles Francis Adams, Boston, 1854, IX, 578-580. DeSaussure wrote Rutledge after the death of Bishop Smith that it was "painful to see the pillars of the revolution tumbling down, one after the other." Henry William DeSaussure to John Rutledge, junior, November 2, 1801, *John Rutledge, junior, Papers*, SHC.
[45] John Adams to Christopher Gadsden, April 16, 1801, *The Works of John Adams*, ed. Charles Francis Adams, Boston, 1854, IX, 584-585.
[46] *Annals of the Congress of the United States*, Washington, 1851, X (6th cong., 2nd sess.), 1028-1033.

weigh carefully the merits of both candidates and vote for the best man.[47] General Pinckney was known to be deeply disturbed by the prospect of Jefferson as President, so Burr was given close scrutiny.[48] Harper and Rutledge were his most active proponents;[49] Rutledge was apparently an admirer of his "bold, daring, revolutionary character," but others were not. DeSaussure wrote from Charleston: "I go with you in your preference; yet not on the ground of Col. Burr's supposed character—for if those traits are faithful delineations of his mind, I should dred him far more than Mr. Jefferson."[50] So arch a Federalist as Fisher Ames warned Rutledge of Burr's character. Ames suggested that "if Jefferson would promise or only encourage you to expect that he would not countenance democratic amendments—dependence on France—a wrangle or war with G. Britain—plunder of the Banks and Funds or Madison's empiricism in regard to trade and navy, would it not be safest to take him?"[51] These views must have eventually predominated in the South Carolina delegation, for on the thirty-sixth ballot they abstained. This was the ballot on which Jefferson obtained ten votes and the election.

This was the last important public action taken by Pinckney and Harper in Congress. Thomas Pinckney had refused to stand for re-election in 1800. Harper had begun the practice of law in Maryland and soon after this married the daughter of Charles Carroll of Carrollton, and he thereafter showed no interest in Carolina politics.[52] Huger, who had apparently been willing to vote for Jefferson, remained in Congress, as did Rutledge.[53] Abraham Nott, however, had ended his political career "by voting for Burr."[54] It is rather easy to understand how Harper, an arch-Federalist, could vote for Burr, but it is more difficult to explain the votes of Thomas

[47] Henry William DeSaussure to John Rutledge, junior, January 12, 1801, *John Rutledge, junior, Papers*, SHC.
[48] Henry William DeSaussure to John Rutledge, junior, February 1801, *John Rutledge, junior, Papers*, SHC.
[49] Morton Borden, *The Federalism of James A. Bayard*, New York, 1955, p. 87.
[50] Henry William DeSaussure to John Rutledge, junior, February 1801, *John Rutledge, junior, Papers*, SHC.
[51] Fisher Ames to John Rutledge, junior, January 26, 1801, *John Rutledge, junior, Papers*, SHC.
[52] William Smith to Rufus King, June 13, 1801, *William Loughton Smith Papers*, HEHL.
[53] Henry S. Randall, *The Life of Thomas Jefferson*, New York, 1858, II, 596.
[54] "Diary of Edward Hooker, 1805-1808," ed. J. Franklin Jameson, *Annual Report of the American Historical Association for the Year 1896*, Washington, 1897, I, 863.

Pinckney and John Rutledge, junior. Both had once been close to Jefferson, but in 1796, the Pinckneys and the Rutledges began to suspect the sincerity of Jefferson and his Virginia supporters. Virginia had given only one vote to Thomas Pinckney in 1796, and her senators had voted against Charles Cotesworth Pinckney's being appointed envoy to France in 1797. Jefferson's pro-French views in the intervening period must have completely alienated them. They had made the decision to vote against Jefferson in 1801, and they had to bear the burden of having done so, for this vote seemed to be contrary to the wishes of most of the people in the state. The Pinckneys and the Rutledges thus lost forever any support they might formerly have had among the Jeffersonians.

THE REPUBLICANS, in order to strengthen their control over the delegation in Congress, tried to change the mode of the election of representatives to one general ticket which would be run throughout the state.[55] DeSaussure had hoped that Congress itself would frustrate the local Republicans by calling for the election of all members of the House of Representatives by districts.[56] Fortunately for the Federalists, this move of the Republicans was defeated in the state legislature, but the Republicans then turned to gerrymandering.[57] After the census of 1800 South Carolina was given two additional seats in the House; by an act of December 18, 1802, the following districts were outlined: Charleston; Beaufort, Barnwell, and Edgefield; Georgetown, Horry, Marion, Darlington, and Marlborough; Orangeburg, Colleton, and Richland; Sumter, Kershaw, Lancaster, Fairfield, and Chesterfield; Abbeville, Laurens, and Newberry; Chester, Spartanburg, Union, and York; Pendleton and Greenville. The first elections in the new districts were scheduled for February 7 and 8, 1803.[58] According to both General Pinckney and DeSaussure the sole consideration in redesigning the districts was to undermine the Federalist influence on the coast. Rutledge's supporters in Beaufort and Huger's in Georgetown were meant to be overwhelmed by backcountry votes. DeSaussure explained to Rutledge that "the association of Edgefield (General Butler's own district), with Barnwell and Beaufort, was done ex-

[55] Henry William DeSaussure to John Rutledge, junior, September 11, 1800, *John Rutledge, junior, Papers,* SHC.
[56] Henry William DeSaussure to John Rutledge, junior, November 2, 1801, *John Rutledge, junior, Papers,* SHC.
[57] Henry William DeSaussure to John Rutledge, junior, December 19, 1801, *John Rutledge, junior, Papers,* SHC.
[58] *SC Statutes,* V, 430-432.

pressly to destroy the federal vote in the two latter." He, therefore, advised Rutledge not to run again.[59] Rutledge announced his retirement from politics on February 4 in the *City Gazette*, and General William Butler was elected to succeed him. Benjamin Huger, however, was able to retain his seat.[60]

Charleston District had been cut off and left to itself, perhaps as the one safe Federalist seat. Yet the Republicans in 1803 ran Robert Marion, the nephew of the "Swamp Fox," in the hope "that the name will have a tendency to procure success."[61] They hoped in vain; Thomas Lowndes beat Marion. This election sent six Republicans to Congress: William Butler (Beaufort), Wade Hampton (Orangeburg), Richard Winn (Sumter), Levi Casey (Abbeville), Thomas Moore (Chester), and John B. Earle (Pendleton).[62] The South Carolina Federalists were at a new low ebb, down to two seats in the House of Representatives.

WILLIAM SMITH returned to Charleston just twenty years after he had returned the first time from Europe. His goals in 1804 were quite similar to those of 1784: to gather up his fortune, to establish himself in the law, to marry and found a new family, to find a place in politics. In the 1780's these steps had led to fame and fortune, but by two decades later his generation had had its day.

Smith did not now come home in a flood of returning British merchants and old tories. In fact, many of the old ties with England and with the London merchants were beginning to snap (Bird, Savage, and Bird, for example, had gone bankrupt after the Peace of Amiens).[63] There were, however, old friends such as the Izards at The Elms on Goose Creek and the Manigaults in their new mansion on Meeting Street to welcome him home. Mrs. Izard, who had had her hands full since 1797 taking care of her ailing husband and Smith's two children, had found Smith "so very attentive, and so very agreeable a correspondent" that she wished to see him as

[59] Charles Cotesworth Pinckney to John Rutledge, junior, January 17, 1803, *John Rutledge, junior, Papers*, DUL. Henry William DeSaussure to John Rutledge, junior, January 1803, *John Rutledge, junior, Papers*, SHC.
[60] *City Gazette and Daily Advertiser*, February 4, 1803.
[61] Charles Cotesworth Pinckney to John Rutledge, junior, January 17, 1803, *John Rutledge, junior, Papers*, DUL.
[62] Henry William DeSaussure to John Rutledge, junior, February 14, 1803, *John Rutledge, junior, Papers*, SHC. *Biographical Directory of the American Congress, 1774-1949*, Washington, 1950, p. 82.
[63] The firm stopped payments on February 6, 1803, and was declared bankrupt on June 12, 1803. *South Carolina Circuit Court Records, 1790-1809*, FRC Georgia, pp. 326-327. *Also see* H. M. Bird to John Trumbull, April 8, 1804, *Gratz Collection*, PHS.

much on her own account, as on his children's account. She had expected him for Christmas dinner, but he did not arrive in Charleston until mid-January. He went straight to The Elms to distribute his presents and charm everyone with his conversation.[64] When he finally tore himself away from The Elms to go to town, Anne Izard Deas wrote her sister: "We won't see him for some time as he is much in demand there."[65]

In town, Smith stayed with the Gabriel Manigaults. There he stored his treasures: statues of Cupid and Psyche, Bacchus and Ariadne, the Apollo Belvedere, the three Graces, as well as busts of Bonaparte, Jefferson, and himself, two prints of Claude Lorraine paintings, three Canaletto views of Venice, and three pictures by a disciple of Vernet, one a magnificent view of Vesuvius. Margaret Manigault put these "pagan beauties and divinities" in her father's room, but told Smith they must be removed if her father wanted to come to town. One evening shortly after his arrival in town, Smith gave a full account of all his purchases to the Manigaults and the Deases.[66] Smith spent little time in the family circle, for he dined out continuously. Judge Thomas Bee had warned Mrs. Manigault while Smith was still at The Elms that many dinners were "*brewing* for him."[67] Judge Bee and Thomas Parker entertained him with talk of politics. Judge Grimké gave a large dinner party.[68] This was the frivolous, happy side of returning, and it continued in a round of parties and excursions for over a year.

He was one of the organizers of the Pique Nique Club.[69] Mrs. Manigault wrote of "taking a cold repast" to Accabee with Judge Bee, Smith, DeSaussure, Henry Rutledge, and the French consul, Soult.[70] The consul later honored them with a ball at which the waltz was introduced. The new dance was a subject of a great deal of comment. Mrs. Manigault was sure that it was not "the sedate and decent valse which we used to see at the Duchesse d'Aremberg's—*C'est une danse effreuse*."[71] Mrs. Henry Middleton was

[64] Alice Izard to Margaret Manigault, December 20, 1803; Margaret Izard to Alice Izard, January 19, 1804, *Izard Papers*, LC.

[65] Anne Izard Deas to Margaret Manigault, January 22, 1804, *Manigault Papers*, SCL.

[66] Margaret Manigault to Alice Izard, February 6, 1804, *Izard Papers*, LC. "List of Articles sold to General Benjamin Smith," *William Loughton Smith Papers*, SCHS.

[67] Margaret Manigault to Alice Izard, January 19, 1804, *Izard Papers*, LC.

[68] Margaret Manigault to Alice Izard, February 2, 1804, *Izard Papers*, LC.

[69] Margaret Manigault to Alice Izard, January 10, 1805, *Izard Papers*, LC.

[70] Margaret Manigault to Alice Izard, January 14, 1805, *Izard Papers*, LC.

[71] Margaret Manigault to Alice Izard, February 9, 1805, *Izard Papers*, LC.

equally sure that the waltz had never been danced in this fashion at Talleyrand's. Smith assured Mrs. Manigault that he had never seen the waltz danced in this "indecorous style" in France. "Indeed he says that the *ton* at the consul's was that of *la très mauvaise compagnie.*"[72] Smith went everywhere. At the Assembly he was "the gayest of the gay." At concerts he would take his Spanish guitar and accompany the singers. And on occasion he had to be helped home. "John R. gives a droll account of his vibrating between the two houses in Broad Street (Dr. Baron's, and Gen. McPherson's) and at last being drawn off to East Bay."[73]

SMITH WORKED as hard as he played. Feeling the need for a fresh start, he took a new name to set himself apart from his namesakes, a Charleston merchant and an upcountry politician. On February 1, 1804, in the colums of the *Courier,* he announced that henceforth he would be known as William Loughton Smith, thereby honoring his mother and undoubtedly the memory of his beloved elder brother.[74]

In 1804, it was not inflation that had depleted his fortune, but the financial indiscretions of his agent, David Campbell, who had managed Smith's affairs since 1789. Campbell had bought the Edisto Saw Mills in 1794, and Smith had endorsed Campbell's bonds.[75] Campbell, however, soon found himself in severe financial straits, and Smith became liable for a considerable amount, a situation that came to light while he was abroad. In 1800, in an attempt to extricate himself, Smith turned the management of his estate over to his brother-in-law William Allen Deas.[76] Mrs. Izard wrote Mrs. Manigault in August 1801 that Smith had received Deas's statement of his affairs and "was excessively hurt." Mrs. Izard wanted him to come home and take care of his own affairs, but his tour of Europe had intervened.[77] Deas was forced to sell Smith's four stores behind the Exchange and his houses in Broad Street in

[72] Margaret Manigault to Alice Izard, February 13, 1805, *Izard Papers,* LC.
[73] Margaret Manigault to Alice Izard, August 21, 1805, *Izard Papers,* LC.
[74] *See supra* Chapter I.
[75] David Campbell to William Smith, February 28, 1798, *William Loughton Smith Papers,* SCHS.
[76] Smith made out a power of attorney to Henry William DeSaussure and William Allen Deas on February 16, 1800. Deas was to perform the active duties; DeSaussure to advise. Henry William DeSaussure to William Allen Deas, May 21, 1800, *William Loughton Smith Papers,* SCHS. *Also see* William Allen Deas to William Smith, September 20, 1800, *William Loughton Smith Papers,* SCHS.
[77] Alice Izard to Margaret Manigault, August 31, 1801, *Manigault Papers,* SC Archives.

1802. According to Gabriel Manigault, Deas got "the enormous sum of near £4,000" for the former and only a rather modest £1,500 for the latter.[78] Deas had, of course, pressed Campbell for funds, but Smith was not the only creditor Campbell had to satisfy.[79] Smith, on his return, went to equity to establish himself at the top of the list of Campbell's creditors.[80] He finally succeeded in doing this, but it was several years before he recovered any of the money due him.[81]

Personal matters had once again drawn Smith into the practice of law, and the prospect of rebuilding his fortune kept him in it. He opened an office with Henry Bacot.[82] The prospects for one so familiar with commercial law and international trade were excellent in 1804, for war had again broken out in Europe. The most lucrative commerce for the past decade had been the indirect trade between the French West Indies and France, which the British had permitted to flow through American ports. The figures on drawbacks at the American customhouses describe the growth of this trade. In 1792, four per cent of all duties collected were drawbacks; in 1795, twenty-five per cent; in 1798 thirty-three per cent.[83] This was, of course, an artificial trade, for with the war's end these lines of commerce would snap back into place, and American ports like Charleston would be bereft of a major part of their trade. However, as long as the war lasted a lawyer could reap a harvest of fees by charting the course for a merchant through the myriad rules and regulations. William Smith could still find his profit, as his father before him had, in the Atlantic commercial world. Smith was retained by the French consul and, according to Mrs. Manigault, was soon "extremely busy" at the law.[84]

In Smith's drive to regain his fortune, he alienated some of his

[78] Gabriel Manigault to Margaret Manigault, September 3, 1802, *Manigault Papers*, SCL.
[79] William Allen Deas to William Smith, March 2, 1801, March 23, 1802, September 3, 1802; David Campbell to William Loughton Smith, July 16, 1804, *William Loughton Smith Papers*, SCHS.
[80] David Campbell to William Loughton Smith, February 28, 1805, *William Loughton Smith Papers*, SCHS.
[81] David Campbell to William Loughton Smith, October 13, 1807, August 17, November 12, 1809, *William Loughton Smith Papers*, SCHS.
[82] David Campbell to Smith and Bacot, June 29, 1805, *William Loughton Smith Papers*, SCHS.
[83] Robert Greenhalgh Albion, *Square Riggers on Schedule*, Princeton, 1938, pp. 77, 83.
[84] *See* case of *Benjamin Moodie Esq., Consul* v. *Mons. Soult, Commercial Agent of French Republic*, decided on January 23, 1805, by Judge William Johnson, *South Carolina Circuit Court Records, 1790-1809*, FRC Georgia, p. 246. Margaret Manigault to Alice Izard, January 19, 1805, *Izard Papers*, LC.

friends. The old ruthlessness he had displayed in politics became evident in his business dealings. Joseph Manigault wrote his brother, "William Smith is so fond of business, that he still keeps his former house in Tradd-Street, by way of an office; indeed he says, that he pities the idle fellows he sees about Charleston."[85] As a practicing attorney, he sued Mrs. Henry Middleton, and that ended that friendship.[86] When he took over a bond of John Bee's against Gabriel Manigault, he was quite willing to press his old friend for payment.[87] The sharpest dissensions occurred in the attempt to settle Ralph Izard's estate, one-seventh of which was his own children's share and the basis of their fortunes. Smith and Deas had divided the property into seven lots valued at £1,000 each. Smith then paid the estate £100 to have the choice of the lots and took the nine hundred fifty-eight acre plantation at Walnut Hill.[88] George Izard wrote Henry Izard: "S. I own has surprised me—I knew him attentive to his disbursements and fond of economy in his own person—but there has been a hestitating apprehension of not making the most of his children's property which I did not think in his character, and which is a very near neighbour to meanness."[89] Although Gabriel Manigault thought he had drawn the worst of the lots, he held no grudge against Smith.[90] Yet, in these transactions with those who were dearest and closest to him, there emerge some of those fundamental characteristics that kept Smith from being a lovable man. He must not have lost, however, his mother-in-law's respect and love, for he continued to manage her affairs.[91]

Smith's marriage to Charlotte Wragg had the appearance on the surface of being just another step in his scheme to re-establish his fortune. William Wragg, the distinguished loyalist, had left four children, a son and three daughters. William Wragg, the son, having been educated in England had returned to America in 1788 to look after the Wragg estates, which had not been confiscated. He died (without issue) in 1803 and his three sisters inherited his

[85] Joseph Manigault to Gabriel Manigault, December 21, 1806, *Manigault Papers*, SCL.
[86] Joseph Manigault to Gabriel Manigault, July 26, 1806, *Manigault Papers*, SCL.
[87] Joseph Manigault to Gabriel Manigault, June 16, 1807, *Manigault Papers*, SCL.
[88] Henry Izard to Gabriel Manigault, March 15, 1807; Alice Izard to Henry Izard, May 19, 1807, *Izard Papers*, SCL.
[89] George Izard to Henry Izard, May 27, 1807, *Izard Papers*, SCL.
[90] Gabriel Manigault to Joseph Manigault, September 13, 1808, *Manigault Papers*, SCL.
[91] John Vaughan to William Loughton Smith, May, September 8, 1808, March 3, 1810, *William Loughton Smith Papers*, SCHS.

estate, which considerably enhanced the charms of these three maiden ladies.[92] Their fortune was valued jointly at £8,000 sterling in bonds, stock, and notes; £15,000 in real estate; and two hundred seventy slaves. Harriet married the Reverend Milward Pogson in February 1805.[93] It is to Smith's credit that when he married Charlotte in December 1805, he offered to settle "the whole of her property on her but she would not consent to a settlement, of more than two thirds; and the other third, he will be at liberty to dispose of as he thinks proper by will."[94] By the property settlement at the time of the marriage, Charlotte Wragg Smith received the 4,060 acre Ashley Barony valued at £1,000, a town house at No. 82 East Bay valued at £4,000, and fifty-nine slaves, all of which would descend to the children of the marriage. Smith received in his own name four lots in Wraggborough and thirty-four slaves, besides Charlotte's share of £2,700 in English consols and annuities and her proportion of any other money due to the estate after the debts were paid.[95] The marriage had, to say the least, brought a sizeable addition to his fortune as well as two new economic roles, one as manager of the plantation and the other as developer of Wraggborough. DeSaussure had once written that Smith would never become a planter, but now, by marriage, he found himself one at last, the lord of Ashley Barony, which was to be one of his homes until his death in 1812.[96]

After his marriage, Smith became an active developer of Wraggborough, one of Charleston's first suburbs. Wraggborough had been laid out in 1802 and 1803. Smith had received four lots on his marriage and had bought others. As a means of developing the property, Smith projected the Wraggborough Canal Company to build a canal, twenty feet wide and six feet seven inches deep, which would pass through "Wrag Boro' to the east of King St.; & to the west thereof thro' land of the heirs of Thomas Radcliffe Esquire

[92] See genealogical chart, Henry A. M. Smith, "Wragg of South Carolina," SCHGM, XIX (1918), facing 121.
[93] "Abstract of Mr. Pogson's marriage bond, February 6, 1805," William Loughton Smith Papers, SCHS.
[94] Joseph Manigault to Gabriel Manigault, December 17, 1805, Manigault Papers, SCL.
[95] "Abstract of William Loughton Smith's marriage bond, December 10, 1805," William Loughton Smith Papers, SCHS. Thomas Parker charged $85.75 for drawing up the marriage settlement: "the same being uncommonly lengthy, and also very special, including many consultations upon the subject and alterations as required." "Thomas Parker's bill, December 1805," William Loughton Smith Papers, SCHS.
[96] Henry William DeSaussure to William Allen Deas, September 18, 1801, William Loughton Smith Papers, SCHS.

deceased, then across Cannon's Pond & along Hutson Street in Cannon Boro' to Mr. Lucas mill at a landing on a branch of Coming's creek out of Ashley River."[97] The canal was never built, but even without it Smith was able to dispose of his property for a good price—he had evidently gotten the choice lots. In 1807, he sold seven lots on the corner of King and John streets for £3,400 for one, two, and three years credit. The following year he sold Joseph Allen Smith's lot at King and Ann streets for £3,300. Joseph Manigault, who had his own home in Wraggborough, noted that Mr. Pogson's lots on Meeting Street did not sell—that there was a great deal of difference between the value of land on King Street and that in other parts of Wraggborough. Smith had evidently seen to it that his wife's share of the Wragg property was the most advantageously located.[98]

Smith had resumed his interest in canals on his return from Europe. He had planned to stop in Norfolk on his way to Charleston in 1803 to view the Dismal Swamp Canal, and although he missed seeing the canal, he kept up with its progress by letter.[99] The Santee Canal was now open, and he regularly attended the meetings, still contributed to the requisitions for additional work, and at his death was president of the company.[100] His most active work in these years, however, was with the Catawba Canal Company. By 1804, when Smith returned, only ten men could still be depended on to meet their requisitions. William Smith and his brother Joseph Allen Smith held two hundred thirty shares, Judge Grimké held fifty-four, the estate of Gabriel Manigault, I, fifty, General Pinckney, twenty, with sixty-six divided between Trescot, Cripps, Kean, Davie, and Hamilton.[101] This meant that Smith and his brother now bore half the financial burden of the company. Smith resumed the management of his brother's estate, so he and Judge Grimké took over the guidance of the work. Judge Grimké had a home at Belmont in Union District and his duties as circuit court judge often took him into the area, so he hired and super-

[97] See folder on "Wraggboro Canal Company," *William Loughton Smith Papers*, SCHS
[98] Joseph Manigault to Gabriel Manigault, July 26, 1806, June 16, 1807, *Manigault Papers*, SCL.
[99] Luke Wheeler to William Loughton Smith, February 17, 1804; Thomas Newton to William Loughton Smith, July 3, 1804; William Charles Lee to William Loughton Smith, February 26, 1807; William Cammach to William Loughton Smith, September 18, 1811, *William Loughton Smith Papers*, SCL.
[100] *Charleston Courier*, January 21, 1812.
[101] See list of stockholders, 1803, in folder on "Catawba Canal Company," *William Loughton Smith Papers*, SCHS.

vised the engineer, the surveyors, and the solicitors while Smith continued to supply funds from Charleston. In 1809, the upper part of the canal was opened. The rest of the work was to be paid for through the sale of lands, but it was not always easy to sell the land.[102] After a great spurt of activity in 1809 and 1810, which was a heavy drain upon the stockholders, General Pinckney authorized Smith to get the state to buy them out.[103] In 1818, when the state did buy the company, Smith's heirs received $3,855.75 for his shares, but he estimated before his death in 1812 that he had spent $15,554.07.[104] At the time of his death, Smith held canal shares which were valued at $33,000, one-fifth of his fortune.[105] No other South Carolinian had spent more on the state's canal ventures. Smith was a clever and an enterprising man, as his profits in stock speculation and Charleston real estate proved, but he could never make the canal experiments in his own state pay off.

WILLIAM LOUGHTON SMITH had by the successive steps of recovering his fortune, re-entering the practice of law, marrying, and developing the city and the state re-established himself. However, he still had political ambitions and wanted once again to hold a high public office. He had not been home long enough by the fall of 1804 to seek election. During that campaign he had actually been in the North. He would have gone to New York, but the shock of Hamilton's death had kept him near Philadelphia. He wrote Rufus King on October 18: "The loss of Washington and Hamilton and I must add, my respected friend, Mr. Izard, endears to me still more the few real worthies who remain. You cannot be ignorant that all the respectable men throughout the Continent look up to you and General Pinckney as their political saviours and that all their measures are predicated on a wish of and directed to the

[102] Judge Grimké to William Loughton Smith, October 11, 1809, March 4, May 26, 1812, *William Loughton Smith Papers*, SCHS. Colonel Christian Senf had been hired to superintend the work. Colonel Senf to Judge Grimké, May 25, 1803, *Society Collection*, PHS.
[103] Charles Cotesworth Pinckney to William Loughton Smith, June 21, 1811, *William Loughton Smith Papers*, SCHS.
[104] "Statement of Monies laid out and advanced by W. L. Smith for his shares in Catawba Co. with interest to 30 September 1811"; Judge Grimké to Mrs. William Loughton Smith, May 26, 1818, *William Loughton Smith Papers*, SCHS.
[105] His total fortune was estimated at $140,000, of which $25,000 consisted of 77 shares of Santee Canal stock, $5,000 of 100 shares of Catawba Canal stock, and $3,000 of Dismal Swamp Canal stock. "Statement of Smith's Fortune delivered into the Ordinary's Office, July 8, 1813," *William Loughton Smith Papers*, SCHS.

attainment of your future elevation to the Chief Magistracy."[106]
Smith hoped that Pinckney and King would be elected in 1804.

In Charleston, Thomas Lowndes had declined to run again for
Congress. Thomas Rhett Smith, the eldest son of Roger Smith, was
the choice of the Federalists. Frederick Rutledge wrote his brother
John: "I know no Person who can better afford to serve the Public.
He has a safe fortune and does not owe a six pence."[107] These
were not, however, the qualities admired by the voting public, and
he was defeated by Robert Marion. In Georgetown, Benjamin
Huger refused to stand. The elections, therefore, were swept by the
Republicans, who secured all eight seats in Congress.[108] With such
an overwhelming defeat for his party, could Smith ever hope to
stage a comeback as a Federalist?

By 1805, the four factions that had once supported Smith had
disappeared from the political stage. There were no Pinckneys or
Rutledges in public life. John Rutledge, junior, still moved behind
the scenes, corresponding with the northern leaders of the party,
but his public image had been undermined by a private disaster,
the scandalous breakup of his marriage.[109] Henry William DeSaussure was the only member of the old Smith-DeSaussure-Darrell
faction still active. Daniel DeSaussure and Edward Darrell were
dead, and Josiah Smith was bending with the political wind.[110]

Jacob Read of the Read-Simons faction now lived quietly at the
North.[111] He had failed to be re-elected senator and had been
deprived of his appointment as federal district judge.[112] James

[106] William Loughton Smith to Rufus King, October 18, 1804, "Letters from
Russia, 1802-1805," ed. George C. Rogers, Jr., *SCHGM*, LX (1959), 225.
[107] Frederick Rutledge to John Rutledge, junior, August 28, 1804, *John
Rutledge, junior, Papers*, SHC.
[108] *City Gazette and Daily Advertiser*, October 16, 20, 1804. Those elected
were William Butler, Levi Casey, Elias Earle, Robert Marion, Thomas Moore,
O'Brien Smith, David R. Williams, and Richard Winn. *Biographical Directory
of the American Congress, 1774-1949*, Washington, 1950, p. 87.
[109] There is an excellent series of letters between John Rutledge, junior, and
Harrison Gray Otis in the *Otis Papers*, MHS. There are also a number of Rut-
ledge-Wolcott letters in the *Wolcott Papers*, CHS. *Also see* Elizabeth Cometti,
"John Rutledge, Jr., Federalist," *Journal of Southern History*, XIII (1947),
186-219.
[110] Henry William DeSaussure to John Rutledge, junior, August 25, 1801,
John Rutledge, junior, Papers, SHC. DeSaussure to Jedediah Morse, May 24,
1802, copy in *Morse Papers*, YL. DeSaussure to Oliver Wolcott, July 17, 1802,
Wolcott Papers, CHS. DeSaussure to Josiah Smith, November 3, 1813, *Josiah
Edward Smith Letters*, DUL.
[111] Phineas Bond had urged Read to buy a house and live in Philadelphia.
Phineas Bond to Jacob Read, August 18, 1801, *Miscellaneous Manuscripts*,
NYPL. For Read's summer at Newport in 1803, *see* Jacob Read to George
Simpson, June 18, October 31, 1803, *Gratz Collection*, PHS.
[112] Anne King Gregorie, "Jacob Read," *DAB*.

Simons would give up his post as collector of the customs in 1805, and Thomas Simons died that year.[113] Jacob Read did not have enough influence left to secure the appointment of his brother Dr. William Read as a director of the branch bank when Thomas Simons died.[114]

Of the Izard-Manigault-Smith faction, Ralph Izard had died in 1804, and Gabriel Manigault, having sold his South Carolina plantation, planned to spend most of his time at Clifton, his estate near Philadelphia.[115] Many of the old Federalist leaders were actually living in the North or making plans to do so. Robert Goodloe Harper had settled in Baltimore in 1801. John Rutledge, junior, found Wethersfield, Connecticut, most congenial, and DeSaussure even spoke of joining him in the North.[116] William Loughton Smith himself considered settling in Philadelphia in 1804.[117] There were, in fact, very few leaders left around whom a party could be rebuilt. Young Rutledge and young DeSaussure with Judge Bee, Judge Grimké, and District Attorney Thomas Parker represented a working nucleus. The great merchants—Nathaniel Russell, Adam Gilchrist, Adam Tunno, Robert Hazlehurst, William Crafts—would stand in the background. The two Pinckneys were in the wings: Thomas at his Santee plantation, Charles Cotesworth on Pinckney Island. The *Courier*, founded in 1803, would be the mouthpiece. Yet this was essentially a local group, a remnant of a once great force. Smith's one chance was to re-establish his reputation as a spokesman on international affairs.

In 1805, Smith got the chance to resume his old role as expounder of English and American commercial policies; the *rapprochement* of 1795 had begun to fall apart. These ten years had brought great commercial success, but in 1805, the war in Europe moved into a more bitter phase. With Nelson's victory at Trafalgar in October 1805 and Napoleon's victory at Austerlitz that December, a stalemate had been reached in which England was supreme on the sea

[113] The new collector, Simeon Theus, was appointed by Jefferson on January 21, 1806, *Year Book, City of Charleston, 1883*, p. 458.

[114] Jacob Read to Thomas Willing, January 25, 1805, *Gratz Collection*, PHS.

[115] Izard died on May 30, 1804. Mabel L. Webber, "Ralph Izard," *DAB*. Gabriel Manigault sold all of his property in St. Thomas's Parish to Mrs. Nathaniel Heyward in 1805 for $100,000. Mrs. Manigault wrote, "We are now free to go to New York." Margaret Manigault to Alice Izard, March 14, 1805, *Izard Papers*, LC. For a description of Clifton, *see* Margaret Manigault to Alice Izard, January 20, 1811, *Izard Papers*, LC.

[116] Henry William DeSaussure to John Rutledge, junior, July 12, 1803, *John Rutledge, junior, Papers*, SHC.

[117] William Loughton Smith to Rufus King, October 18, 1804, "Letters from Russia, 1802-1805," ed. George C. Rogers, Jr., *SCHGM*, LX (1959), 225.

and France on the land. This was now a life and death struggle, and each country was forced to adopt measures characteristic of total war. Each set forth a plan of economic warfare; British orders in council matched French decrees. In order to tighten her blockade of France, England began to interpret very strictly those rules under which she permitted voyages. This was the gist of the decision in the admiralty court in the case of the *Essex* in 1805.[118] England stationed war vessels on the American side of the Atlantic in an attempt to enforce more rigorously these new interpretations of the maritime law. The winter of 1805-1806 was a gloomy one in the United States.

At this juncture Smith made a bid to re-establish himself with the thinking public. He published a series of letters in the Charleston *Courier*, the organ of the Federalist party.[119] His argument was the same as it had been in 1794. Smith was opposed not to negotiation, but to ultimata (threats of non-importation measures) before negotiations began, especially when the country had no navy or army to back up its threats. In the negotiations themselves, Smith warned that it would be wrong to demand the direct trade between the French colonies and their mother country. All the commercial interests had ever asked was the right to carry goods to the United States, land them, enter them at the customhouse, and then re-ship them. As a neutral, the United States had admitted the legality of the Rule of 1756. France on her part had only allowed Americans the direct trade out of her own necessity, not out of any concession of principles. Finally, it might be noted in all fairness to England, that if she had departed from the *Polly* decision (1800) it was under great duress—she was fighting for her life, her very existence. Furthermore, Congress in 1805 had done away with the bond in cases of re-exportation, an act which England might rightfully interpret as official encouragement for continuous voyages. The *Polly* decision stated that the duty must be paid, the goods landed and warehoused for "a considerable time," and if these things were done it would then devolve upon the captors to prove that the original intention had been to send the goods to the parent nation.[120]

Congress discussed these points in the spring of 1806 but ulti-

---

[118] For an argument that this decision brought a change in English policy, see Bradford Perkins, "Sir William Scott and the Essex," *William and Mary Quarterly*, XIII (1956), 169-183.

[119] *The Numbers of Phocion, which were originally published in the Charleston Courier, in 1806, on the subject of Neutral Rights,* Charleston, [1806].

[120] *Ibid.,* pp. 55-56.

mately decided in favor of non-importation, with Robert Marion and all the South Carolina representatives present voting in the affirmative. Non-importation was not to become effective until November 15, thereby giving to James Monroe and William Pinkney a bargaining point in their negotiations with Great Britain. These moves were contrary to Smith's views; he deprecated the use of non-importation as a threat during negotiations. He would have preferred a stronger army and navy as the basis for negotiating from strength. Congress, however, had just appropriated $2,000,000 to purchase West Florida, while doing very little to build up coastal defenses. Here were issues upon which Smith could attack Marion and the administration, appealing as before to the Charleston commercial interests for support.[121]

On September 17, 1806, Thomas Lowndes wrote John Rutledge, junior, that William Smith, John Ward, Henry Izard, and James Lowndes had each been mentioned to oppose Marion, but there had been no public announcement concerning their inclination to serve.[122] On October 6, James Lowndes was an announced candidate, and William Loughton Smith was presumably not a candidate. However, three days later, just four days before the election, Smith's name was presented, and Lowndes withdrew. A full Federalist-Republican ticket for the state legislature was announced at the same time: John Blake for state senator, and the following gentlemen for state representatives: John Dawson, junior, John Rutledge, junior, James Lowndes, Adam Gilchrist, Henry Deas, Henry Middleton, William Drayton, Keating L. Simons, William Lowndes, Thomas Baker, Langdon Cheves, James M. Ward, William Lee, Henry H. Bacot, and Thomas Campbell Cox. This was a strong ticket headed by the heirs of the most aristocratic families of Charleston. They were presented as "pupils of the Washington School."[123]

There was much electioneering in the four days before the election—a spate of letters to the editor and many broadsides. The Federalist strategy was to contrast the experience of Smith with the "back-woods youthful inexperience" of Marion. There was also an attempt to contrast the preparedness of 1798 with the unreadi-

[121] Irving Brant, *James Madison, Secretary of State, 1800-1809*, Indianapolis, 1953, pp. 316, 367. *Annals of the Congress of the United States*, Washington, 1852, XV (9th cong., 1st sess.), 877-878.
[122] Thomas Lowndes to John Rutledge, junior, September 17, 1806, *John Rutledge, junior, Papers*, SHC.
[123] *Charleston Courier*, October 6, 9, 1806.

ness of 1806. The Federalist campaign slogan was "Millions for Defense but not a cent for Tribute." Marion had voted to pay $2,000,000 for West Florida (some thought West Florida was part of the Louisiana Purchase and, therefore, that these millions constituted a bribe) and had done nothing for the defense of South Carolina. The neglect of Forts Johnson and Pinckney was highlighted. The commercial community was also reminded that Smith had consistently spoken out for their interests, that he had while in Congress kept in touch with a local commercial committee through whom the sentiments of the merchants were channeled to him.

The Democratic-Republicans tried to defeat Smith by raking up old scandals. He was, of course, charged with speculating. Smith had all the relevant documents put on public display at the *Courier* office. One Smith supporter pointed out that the assumption of the state's debts had brought in the new capital that had sparked Charleston's prosperity in the 1790's. His record of opposition to the abolition of slavery was also to his credit. Moreover, Smith was a great orator, and Marion never opened his mouth in Congress. The last retort by the Smith side was contained in an election-day broadside. Marion was pictured as "a citizen of a remote parish, holding no property in Charleston, never residing within its limits, and from the inactivity of whose character during the last session, it may be inferred, feeling no interest in it, or sympathy with its inhabitants." The following "Contrast" was made:

Citizens of Charleston, you have now the Choice!
"Look here upon *this* picture, and on *this*." Hamlet.

Washington Republican Candidate	Democratic Candidate
Great talents—great wisdom great experience—great eloquence—great political information.	No talents—no experience— no political information—as to eloquence—Mum!!!
Residence in Charleston, Property in Charleston, Relations in Charleston.	Residence, Property, Relations, } all at a distance from Charleston
While in Congress, Charleston was well fortified.	While in Congress, Charleston lies at the mercy of any Pirate.
While in Congress, Four Millions of Dollars paid out of the National Treasury to South-Carolina.	While in Congress, Two Millions of Dollars paid in Tribute to France.

When in Congress, Millions expended for national Defence.	When in Congress, Millions expended in National Tribute.
Personal merit—personal claims on your suffrages.	Hereditary merit—hereditary claims on your suffrages.
While a member of Congress, never absent from public duty.	While a Member of Congress, frequently absent, on very important occasions.

Say—"Have you eyes? Could you on this fair mountain leave to feed, and batten on this moor?"[124]

Smith did well, but he could not beat the nephew of the "Swamp Fox." Marion received five hundred twenty-one votes in Charleston to Smith's four hundred eighty-five. Smith carried a few of the country parishes but lost the parish of St. James Goose Creek by a vote of fifty-nine to eight. The power of the old Goose Creek families had definitely waned. In the Charleston delegation to the state legislature the Washington Republicans did quite well, securing eleven of the fifteen places, with only Rutledge, Gilchrist, Bacot, and Cox losing out. Their places were won by William Rouse, Thomas Hinds, Peter Freneau, and John Horlbeck, junior, of the Democratic-Republican ticket.[125]

In December, Congress voted to accede to the request of England to postpone non-importation. They gave to the President, however, the power to institute non-importation whenever he thought it necessary. This was the trump card that Jefferson held when the *Leopard* fired upon the *Chesapeake* in June 1807. This episode was as crucial in the shaping of American public opinion as the Boston Tea Party or Pearl Harbor. Jefferson could have had war, but he allowed time for passions to cool and only summoned Congress to meet in the fall when an embargo was ultimately passed.[126] This was to cut off all foreign trade and as such was the *coup de grace* for American commerce.

The Charleston merchants would have been hurt in any case, for on January 1, 1808, the slave trade came to an end. Robert Marion had tried to soften the blow by asking on December 29 for an exception for slaving vessels that had been sent out before the exclusion and had not yet returned. This was refused by a vote of thirty-nine to thirty-seven after a congressman pointed out that

[124] *Ibid.*, October 13, 14, 1806.
[125] *Ibid.*, October 15, 16, 18, 22, 24, 1806.
[126] The seven South Carolina members present voted for the embargo. *Annals of the Congress of the United States*, Washington, 1852, XVII (10th cong., 1st sess.), 1221-1222.

these petitioners had known when the prohibitory law was to go into effect, and therefore, "they were not entitled to relief by the laws of God or man."[127]

The merchants could not expect much sympathy any longer from Congress. When some Philadelphia merchants petitioned for exceptions to the embargo, John Taylor said that "they might be charged with being induced by foreign influence to endeavor to paralyze every measure for the good of their country, or might be supposed to be among the acquaintances of Mr. Cobbet in America, so taken up with their idol, Mammon, with their zeal after profit, that they cared not what became of the country if their coffers were filled. He [Taylor] would compare the conduct of the merchants of the city of Charleston, whose petition was scouted the other day, with that of these men, who might either be called the votaries of Mammon, or by a worse name."[128] If this were the attitude of a South Carolina upcountry leader, could the Charleston merchants be blamed for their despair? Only one of the merchants' legitimate problems got any helpful consideration. Robert Marion secured a government credit for them on duties paid which would ordinarily be drawn back when the goods were re-exported.[129] During the period of the embargo, the Charleston commercial interests were to suffer so seriously as never to revive. The basis of the Federalist party had been undermined. Smith began to assess the new economic forces and to tailor his politics accordingly.

WITH THE DECLINE of commerce, agriculture emerged supreme. By 1808 the planters in Carolina had become the unchallenged economic masters. The victory was, however, more the victory of cotton than of rice. Rice planters continued to flourish, but their numbers not only did not increase, but for a few years after 1800 actually declined as coastal planters found sea island cotton more profitable than rice.[130]

Indigo, which had supplemented rice as a Carolina staple, declined in importance with the Revolution. The loss of the British bounty had been disastrous; in the 1780's indigo planters were already looking for a new crop and cotton was the answer. A few

[127] *Ibid.,* p. 1243.
[128] *Ibid.,* p. 1274.
[129] *Ibid.,* pp. 1332-1333.
[130] Lewis Cecil Gray, *History of Agriculture in the Southern United States to 1860,* New York, 1941, II, 679, 1030-1031. *Also see* Barker and Lord to Brown and Ives, August 13, 1799, "Rogers, Barker, and Lord volume," *Brown Papers,* JCBL.

bags were shipped before 1790, and there was a small annual increase in production until the invention of the cotton gin in 1793. During the following decade, cotton swept the state; production increased eight-fold from 1794 to 1804.[131] Cotton actually came of age in 1799, for by that time indigo had almost completely disappeared and rice itself had yielded first place.

The letters of William Murrell, a Stateburg planter, to his Charleston factors in the year 1799 speak of "a considerable number of planters" embarking "in the cultivation of cotton" due to the losses suffered in the past "on the accursed article," indigo.[132] The letters of Barker and Lord, agents for the Browns of Rhode Island, in the same year, chart the rising importance of cotton. On April 16: "Cotton is being bought up as fast as it comes in. We never knew European freights so much in demand as at present—wanted mostly for some port in G.B."[133] On August 13, Barker and Lord observed that there was much more land being planted in cotton in the backcountry of Georgia and South Carolina than during the past year. With little rice being planted "in proportion to a few years back in the lowcountry owing to their attention to cotton the price of rice would stay up and the price of cotton would be going down."[134]

The political revolution of 1800 reflected this economic revolution of 1799. The Federalist party, when it had represented planters, had represented rice planters. The Jeffersonian party in South Carolina was to be dominated by the cotton planters. To go from rice to cotton was to change from Federalist to Republican. The clean, sharp, hard grain of rice symbolized the realism of the Federalist mind, while the round, soft, fluffy ball of cotton symbolized the vague idealism of the Jeffersonian mind.

Between 1800 and 1808 many of the backcountry farmers became cotton planters. The rapid increase in wealth brought a rapid change in status which brought a rapid change in political outlook. The greatest backcountry success story was that of Wade Hampton. He had come from Virginia to the South Carolina frontier just before the Revolution. At the end of the war Hampton had been a member of the Jacksonborough legislature, where the itch for lands and slaves had prompted great confiscations. He had gotten his

[131] Gray, op. cit., p. 681.
[132] William Murrell to Messrs. Cantey, Henry and Co., March 16, September 21, 1799, William Murrell Letterbook, 1795-1812, DUL.
[133] Barker and Lord to Brown and Ives, April 16, 1799, "Rogers, Barker, and Lord volume," Brown Papers, JCBL.
[134] Barker and Lord to Brown and Ives, August 13, 1799, "Rogers, Barker, and Lord volume," Brown Papers, JCBL.

share of both and had borrowed money to start his inland empire.[135] When the capital of the state was placed near his lands on the Congaree River, his fortune leaped forward. As a spokesman for the backcountry, he became a Jeffersonian. However, when in 1801 Jefferson offered him a reward for faithful support, the position of postmaster of the United States, Hampton refused, for, as he said, he would be sacrificing too much.[136] By 1809, his income was so vast that he stood to lose a possible $30,000 a year as a result of absence on military duty in the Southwest. In 1811, he was able to buy a great sugar estate on the Mississippi River for $300,000.[137]

The Hampton family was merely the most successful. Other families by 1808 had made the change in status from farmer to planter. The Sumters, the Calhouns, the Winns, the Taylors, the Pickenses, the Andersons, and the Mannings had been Jefferson's yeoman farmers but were now desirous of aping their "betters" on the coast. As these families grew rich, they married their sons and daughters into the lowcountry aristocracy. In this fashion the differences between the "prior immigrants" who had come in from the ocean and the "subsequent immigrants" who had come down from Virginia and Pennsylvania were rubbed out. It had been this difference in origin that Timothy Ford had pointed to in 1794 as the reason why there should be no change in representation at that time.[138] After the marriage of Wade Hampton's son to the daughter of Christopher Fitzsimons, a wealthy Charleston merchant of loyalist background; after the marriage of Langdon Cheves to the daughter of Joseph Dulles, a British merchant with world-wide connections; after the marriage of John C. Calhoun and Floride Bonneau Colhoun, a veritable union of cotton and rice, could there be a need much longer to distinguish the upcountry planter from the lowcountry planter?[139]

[135] Wade Hampton had written his brother from Jacksonborough: "All attempts to purchase negroes have been fruitless, owing to the flattering state of our affairs in this quarter. I proposed to have sent you *some* from a parcel which I recover'd at Combahee, but was disappointed in getting them off, however, I have yet hopes of securing them, and of purchasing *more;* but nothing can be done immediately. . . . *Confiscation* is likely to take place to a large amount." Wade Hampton to John Hampton, January 30, 1782, *Family Letters of the Three Wade Hamptons, 1782-1901*, ed. Charles E. Cauthen, Columbia, 1953, pp. 3-4.
[136] Wade Hampton to Thomas Jefferson, June 26, 1801, *Jefferson Papers*, LC.
[137] *Family Letters of the Three Wade Hamptons, 1782-1901*, ed. Charles E. Cauthen, Columbia, 1953, pp. xi-xiii.
[138] [Timothy Ford,] *The Constitutionalist*, Charleston, 1794, p. 11.
[139] Wade Hampton, III, was born in the Fitzsimons house in Charleston, the historic William Rhett house on Hasell Street. *Family Letters of the Three Wade Hamptons, 1782-1901*, ed. Charles E. Cauthen, Columbia, 1953, p. xv. Langdon Cheves married Mary Elizabeth Dulles in 1810. Samuel Gaillard

South Carolina College, which was established by the state legislature in 1801 and which opened its doors in 1805, was founded for the purpose of educating the backcountry leaders. Among those who sponsored the bill were Henry William DeSaussure and Thomas Rhett Smith in the House and Charles Cotesworth Pinckney in the Senate.[140] DeSaussure, the most important architect of the measure, said: "We of the lower country well knew that the power of the State was thence forward to be in the upper country, and we desired our future rulers to be educated men."[141] Schaper thought the lowcountry wanted to bring "a greater like mindedness through a common system of education before granting [the upcountry] any controlling influence in the legislature."[142] Daniel W. Hollis, the historian of the college, states, "It was the work of the Low Country aristocrats."[143] Petigru later called it "the last will and testament of the expiring" Federalist party.[144] Education would erase the differences in manners and ideas.

As the cotton plantations sprang up in the interior, slavery moved inland. Schaper's figures indicate that during the decade 1800-1810, slavery was spread much more evenly over the state.[145] After the Revolution it was the backcountry that had consistently urged the reopening of the slave trade. The new men won their point in 1803, and the trade flourished for the last time until 1808 marked the end of that business.[146] As the plantation with slave labor became the basic economic unit throughout the state, the lesser white men who had not made the change in status from farmer to planter moved westward. South Carolina became a hive of migration. In the 1790's, the white population of the state had increased forty per cent while in the first decade of the nineteenth century it increased only nine per cent. Many of those who moved had been small shopkeepers and manufacturers of household things.[147] There had been

Stoney, *The Dulles Family in South Carolina*, Columbia, 1955, pp. 9-10. Calhoun married Floride Colhoun on January 8, 1811. Charles M. Wiltse, *John C. Calhoun, Nationalist, 1782-1828*, Indianapolis, 1944, p. 51.

[140] Daniel Walker Hollis, *South Carolina College*, Columbia, 1951, pp. 3, 18-19.

[141] Quoted in *ibid.*, p. 17.

[142] William A. Schaper, "Sectionalism and Representation in South Carolina," *Annual Report of the American Historical Association for the Year 1900*, Washington, 1901, I, 402.

[143] Hollis, *op. cit.*, p. 5.

[144] Quoted in *ibid.*

[145] Schaper, *op. cit.*, p. 392.

[146] Elizabeth Donnan, *Documents Illustrative of the History of the Slave Trade to America*, Washington, 1935, IV, 502-587.

[147] Schaper, *op. cit.*, p. 395.

in existence a system of domestic manufacturing which had made the upcountry somewhat self-sufficient, but this system now gave way to the large plantations, specializing in one crop and demanding finished products from outside. Also among those leaving were Quakers who disapproved of slavery. Between 1805 and 1819, twelve hundred Quakers left for the Northwest.[148]

It was during this decade that two extremes in the old society disappeared. On one hand the merchants were declining, the men who had imported not only goods, but ideas, who had acted as ties with the great Atlantic community of Lisbon and London, of Bordeaux and Boston, of Rotterdam and Philadelphia, who had brought a sense of struggle and competition, who represented the thrust of the new middle class. On the other hand, the raw, untutored democrats, the element for which Aedanus Burke had spoken so forcefully, were drifting westward. This exodus of ardent democrats and early antislavery elements skimmed the milk of bitterness. Those who remained were fast forming into a society of almost feudal units, dominated by great planters. What was left was a planting world, drawn partly from tired Federalists and partly from Jeffersonians quite willing to forget their pure republicanism. Ironically, what was left was Shaftesbury's ideal of a neatly balanced agrarian society. And William Loughton Smith surveyed the new scene from Ashley Barony.[149]

In 1794, the lowcountry had told the upcountry that equality of representation would come when upcountrymen could think and act like gentlemen. The year of change came in 1808. In 1794, Timothy Ford had asserted that the rich men of the lowcountry could not possibly influence the poor voters of the upcountry, for a rich man could only influence those he came in contact with.[150] With the whole state carved into plantations and with the leading planter in each county now able to influence his neighbors, it was time for a change. Hampton is a good example of the altered farmer. In 1806, he confessed to Edward Hooker that he had come to agree with leading characters of the northern states, such as Governor Strong, Governor Treadwell, Mr. Tracy, Dr. Dwight, and the clergy in general, who thought "that the turbulent spirit of the people might lead to licentiousness" and that this tendency might

[148] *Ibid.*, pp. 384-385, 393.
[149] For Shaftesbury's agrarian law, *see* sections III and IV in "The First Set of the Fundamental Constitutions," B. R. Carroll, *Historical Collections of South Carolina*, New York, 1836, II, 363.
[150] [Timothy Ford,] *The Constitutionalist*, Charleston, 1794, pp. 37-38.

"weaken the government." He believed, however, that "there was more of the turbulent, licentious, fractious spirit in the common people of the northern states than of the Southern. . . . He thought there was more civility to strangers, to gentlemen riding in their carriages, more submission to the laws, and respect of authority in the South."[151] If the upcountry Hamptons held these views, what reason could the lowcountry have for denying them equality in representation? On June 28, 1808, the bill to alter representation was carried in the House by a vote of one hundred one to two.[152]

The first solid South Carolina had been formed.

JUST AS SOUTH CAROLINA took a step backward, the United States and the western world took a step forward. The age of commerce which had begun with Columbus came to an end in 1808, and in the western world it was succeeded by an age of industry, not by an age of agriculture as it was in South Carolina. The age of commerce died amid the Napoleonic struggles; as supply lines were cut, each western power was forced to build up its own industrial system in order to be as independent of England as possible. For the United States, the dividing line between the two ages was quite definitely 1808, a year more significant in American history than either 1776 or 1861.

The embargo provided American manufacturers (the industrialists, who were to become richer and more powerful than the merchants had ever been during the age of commerce) with a golden opportunity. The history of cotton manufacturing proves that many New Englanders perceived the advantages. Samuel Slater had come out to Rhode Island from England and successfully set up the first cotton manufacturing establishment in America before 1800. By 1803, there were still only four mills. By 1808, there were fifteen in operation with 8,000 spindles. By 1809, there were sixty-two with 31,000 spindles, and twenty-five more mills under construction. By 1815, there would be 500,000 spindles in operation in the United States.[153] This was a period when clever New England merchants transferred their fortunes to industry. Continental countries, as well

[151] "Diary of Edward Hooker, 1805-1808," ed. J. Franklin Jameson, *Annual Report of the American Historical Association for the Year 1896*, Washington, 1897, pp. 848-849.

[152] *JHR, November 23, 1807-June 29, 1808*, pp. 186-87. As Joseph Alston observed in the debates, the climax in the movement for a change in the representation had come since the upcountrymen "have assimilated so nearly to the privileged districts below." Quoted in Schaper, *op. cit.*, p. 433.

[153] F. W. Taussig, *The Tariff History of the United States*, New York, 1892, pp. 26-28.

as the United States, found a need to industrialize. A young Essen merchant named Friedrich Krupp began making steel when Napoleon's blockade cut off his supply of high-quality English steel.[154]

New England's factories needed the South's raw materials. The coastal trade was open and the South was grateful for a market. In 1800, New England used only five hundred bales of cotton; by 1815, she needed 90,000 bales.[155] Consequently there began to appear in southern ports northern agents to buy up cotton.

The Brown family of Rhode Island had realized at the time of the *Chesapeake* and *Leopard* affair that "the commercial capital of the country" was "greatly exposed," so they transferred more of their capital from commerce to manufacturing.[156] By January 1809, they were ordering two hundred fifty bales of sea-island cotton from their Charleston agent. "The cotton must be of the very first quality, it is intended to be manufactured by us and it is of importance that the first year, should be approved, to establish the credit of the manufactory."[157] In March 1809, they asked their agent to help Richard Waterman, a son of Rufus Waterman, who had just established a cotton manufacturing company in the vicinity of Providence, buy cotton.[158] Behind the embargo, the non-intercourse acts, and the War of 1812, South Carolina commerce began a slow but fundamental re-orientation. It was now to flow north to New York, Newport, and Boston under the direction of northern agents, and eventually the direct trade between Charleston and Europe would be destroyed.[159] This shift in lines of communication was to relegate the state to a backwater.

J. N. Cardozo, who was connected with Charleston's commercial life from 1794 until the Civil War, also considered 1808 as the great dividing line. He wrote that it would be convenient to divide the history of Charleston's commerce "into two epochs":

1. The period before the Berlin and Milan decrees, and British Orders in Council, and

---

[154] Gert von Klass, *Krupps, The Story of an Industrial Empire,* London, 1954, pp. 12-13.

[155] Taussig, *op. cit.,* p. 28.

[156] Brown and Ives to Joseph S. Barker, July 14, 1807, "Joseph S. Barker volume," *Brown Papers,* JCBL.

[157] Thomas P. Ives to Joseph S. Barker, January 31, 1809, "Joseph S. Barker volume," *Brown Papers,* JCBL.

[158] Brown and Ives to Joseph S. Barker, March 22, 1809, "Joseph S. Barker volume," *Brown Papers,* JCBL.

[159] For the rise of New York and the decline of the southern ports, *see* Robert Greenhalgh Albion, *The Rise of New York Port, 1815-1860,* New York, 1939, pp. 1-15.

2. The period subsequent to those measures which resulted in the war of 1812.

As a consequence of the neutral position of the United States, a large share of the carrying trade was thrown into the hands of the Americans, soon after the breaking out of the French revolution, and the Southern ports were made the depots, as we have said, of large quantities of European and West India merchandize—the produce of the latter, their bulky products—sugar, and coffee—requiring a large amount of shipping, being exchanged for the manufactures of Europe. Charleston, from her proximity to the former, became a convenient half-way house for the supplies indispensably necessary on both sides. She enjoyed, consequently, a lucrative commerce from 1792 until about 1807, when the embargo, and non-intercourse acts, followed by the war of 1812, took place. This was the great dividing line before and subsequent to this period.

Cardozo saw on each side of the line two distinct groups of merchants: "the Russells, Crafts, Winthrops, Tunnos, Hasletts, Hazelhursts," who were connected with the direct foreign trade of Charleston to the ports of Europe, disappeared and "were replaced by those who were connected with the indirect trade through Northern ports."[160]

New England took the place of old England. Those who had once railed against British influence would soon rail against Yankee influence. Thomas Shirley, a British merchant, had warned the Carolinians in 1773 that revolution would only mean an exchange of masters.[161] John Rutledge, in securing an exemption for rice in 1774 at the time of the non-exportation agreement, had recognized Carolina's peculiar economic position. In 1787, Charles Pinckney had not been satisfied with the protection for southern economic interests written into the Constitution; Rawlins Lowndes had found this lack the chief reason for opposing ratification. William Loughton Smith had frankly recognized the predominance of Britain in the Carolina trade in the 1790's. As late as 1806, he was explaining how American trade must dovetail with English trade. Yet the *Chesapeake* and *Leopard* affair, the embargo, and the arrival of northern agents—like three swift blows—altered his view. He grasped more clearly than any of his contemporaries the meaning of these events. The South must manufacture or stagnate.

Smith had long been interested in canals. He had the entrepreneurial spirit and he knew his northern magnates. Not only had he

[160] J. N. Cardozo, *Reminiscences of Charleston*, Charleston, 1866, pp. 11-13.
[161] "Journal of Josiah Quincy, Junior, 1773," *Proceedings of the Massachusetts Historical Society*, XLIX (1915-1916), 444-446.

seen the Duke of Bridgewater's canal, but also the manufactories of Manchester. In fact, wherever he had traveled he had stopped to inspect the local industries: the Carron Works in Scotland, the powder mills outside Wilmington, the glass factory in Portugal. Was it not time for South Carolina to venture into manufacturing? Smith no doubt shared his thoughts with fellow Carolinians who might be touched by the new signs. Jonathan Lucas, junior, whose father had come out from England to build Carolina rice mills, bringing with him the secrets of milling as Samuel Slater had brought the secrets of cotton milling, was such a man.[162] John Johnson, junior, Thomas Bennett, junior, and John Horlbeck, junior, the sons of master artisans, were also willing to carry their family skills a step further.[163] Lucas, Johnson, Bennett, and Horlbeck joined with Colonel Daniel Stevens, the supervisor of the excise, C. B. Cochran, intendant and former ship's captain, Major Robert Howard, and Dr. Joseph Kirkland to form the South Carolina Homespun Company of Charleston.[164] Dr. John L. E. W. Shecut was elected president of the company.[165] A petition was presented to the state legislature requesting a charter in these significant words:

> Agriculture, Commerce and Manufactures, have always been considered as the three Master-Links in the chain of Civil Society. The two first have already in the United States, compassed a growth, and flourished to a degree to astonish an admiring World. If the latter has been hitherto neglected and overlook'd, it is more owing to the propensity which mankind, in general, have to pursue those occupations, which promise the greatest returns of their labour, and capital than to any want of Spirit of enterprise, ingenuity, in the People, or local, or natural cause. It has indeed been said that the climate is unfriendly to such undertakings, but is it more so than India, and many other countries that could be named, and in what part of the hospitable globe are manufactures carried to a higher pitch of perfection? We are assured very few, and we believe moreover that the Glorious Memorable Epoch is near arrived, when the Genius of Manufactures, Phoenix-like will rise full of promise out of the ashes of our *Slaughtered Countrymen* and the *Death blow* aimed at our rights by *Orders of Counsel and Milan Decrees.*

The incorporators asked for a state subscription to sustain the manu-

---

[162] Anne King Gregorie, "Jonathan Lucas" and "Jonathan Lucas, Jr.," *DAB*.

[163] William Johnson was a blacksmith; Thomas Bennett and John Horlbeck were housewrights and architects. Donald G. Morgan, *Justice William Johnson, the First Dissenter*, Columbia, 1954, pp. 6, 24-25. Richard Walsh, *Charleston's Sons of Liberty, A Study of the Artisans, 1763-1789*, Columbia, 1959, p. 13.

[164] *Courier and Mercantile Daily Advertiser*, October 31, 1808.

[165] Robert Wilson, "A Sketch of the Life of J. L. E. W. Shecut," *Journal of the South Carolina Medical Association*, XXXVII (1941), 52-56.

facture of homespun so as to place *"that Independence* which their Fathers in their Revolutionary struggle sealed with their best blood, beyond the paralizing touch or control of any foreign power, accident or circumstance."[166] The legislature incorporated the company by an act of 1808.[167]

William Loughton Smith was asked to make the principal address at the laying of the cornerstone of the South Carolina Homespun Company. His address was the clearest statement of the changed conditions and the need for new departures:

> Amidst the inconveniences springing from an unavoidable measure, forced upon us by the rash councils of one belligerent and the miscalculating jealousy of another, we derive a most cheering consolation from anticipating the benefits of an Institution, which those councils and that jealousy have so essentially promoted.
>
> Whatever may be the artifical colourings of sophistry, or the real discontents of impatient cupidity, we may boldly predict, that history, clearing away the rubbish of party declamations and rending the veil of political deception, and in the spirit of truth recording those great events, will not fail to applaud America's neutral and pacifick system, and to announce to future ages, that if the year 1808 felt the pressure of a prolonged embargo, the year 1808 also gave birth to this beneficial Establishment.

Smith was quite sure that this twenty-fourth day of October would long be celebrated—in the style of a Fourth of July.

> We here see the triumph of reason over prejudice, of love of country over egotism, of perseverance over apathy; we here see, with exultation, the noble result of individual enthusiasm, a result, which exalts our national pride, and makes strong in the confidence of our own native means. We have long known that we possess, in the bosom of our soil, inexhaustible resources; we now know, and feel, that we have, in our own bosoms, a spirit of patriotism to call forth these resources, and to make them instrumental to the security of our rights and to the avenging of our wrongs. The shuttle and the loom, operating on the products of your fields and your flocks, will in this century, emancipate you from commercial thraldom, as the operations of your arsenals and foundries delivered you, in the last, from political slavery.

Smith then called attention to the spot on which they stood, a place which contained the hallowed remains of the ramparts of the Revolution and the bleached bones of the patriot heroes, for in Smith's

---

[166] "Petition of the President and Directors of the South Carolina Homespun Company," 1808, *Legislative Papers*, SC Archives.

[167] *SC Statutes*, VIII, 245-246. Richard W. Griffin, "An Origin of the New South: The South Carolina Homespun Company, 1808-1815," *Business History Review*, XXXV (1961), 402-414.

view they were now erecting another great and lasting monument to American independence.

> I would thus invoke the spirits of these immortal worthies: "sainted spirits of departed heroes!" here your throbbing veins poured forth the pure and patriotic streams—on this spot, you gladly sacrificed your lives to erect the bright temple of liberty, and to insure to your posterity their political independence; but your splendid fabrick remained incomplete, while your sons depended, for the essentials of life, on the very nation, from which you fondly believed that you had fully emancipated them. You laid the corner stone of that temple, which was to perpetuate your civil rights; your sons, emulating your virtuous deeds, have this day laid the cornerstone of that, which is to perpetuate our commercial rights—your great and glorious work is now consummated—now may our children shout and rejoice, for this day their independence is complete.[168]

In 1776, the united colonies had secured their political independence of Great Britain; in 1808, the united states secured their economic independence. Smith could discern American history in these terms even in 1808. His own life had been neatly divided by these crucial turning points. He had been educated in the period when Great Britain and the colonies were a political and economic unit; he had pursued his public career in the days when the United States was politically independent but was still economically dependent on the mother country. All of William Smith's speeches between 1789 and 1806 reflected this latter theme. Now a new era was beginning. America was ready to become a strong and self-reliant nation. The Federalist party had served its purpose, and new political courses had to be charted. Smith's speech of October 24, 1808, represented a profound change in his own thinking, a change based upon these altered circumstances. The change in Smith's attitudes had been foreshadowed by his political maneuverings during the preceding fall elections. To Smith's old political associates his turnabout seemed due merely to overweening personal ambition, but they missed the more important undercurrents.

JOHN RUTLEDGE, JUNIOR, had been active in the North during the summer. He had canvassed New England for General Pinckney and had secured his nomination to head the Federalist ticket at a

---

[168] *Charleston Courier*, October 31, 1808. Ramsay enclosed a copy of Smith's speech in the following letter to a London friend with this comment: "I expect that many factories will soon be established over this state & indeed all the states. The business . . . is to promote our own interests." David Ramsay to Dr. Lettsom, October 29, 1808, *Ramsay Letters*, SCL.

meeting of the leaders of the party in New York.[169] Pinckney did not expect to win, but he wanted it made known to the people of the country that "a formidable party of the old Washingtonian school" was still "alert to detect and expose any weak or visionary plans" which might "endanger the prosperity or safety" of the country—a last-gasp platform for a dying party.[170] General Pinckney, although he expected defeat in the national campaign, was quite sure that Thomas Lowndes, who had consented to come forward again, would win in Charleston District. The only possible obstacle in the way of Lowndes's victory was William Loughton Smith. It was rumored late in August that Smith planned to run independently, hoping for the support of the Democrats, even hoping that Robert Marion himself would step aside in favor of his old opponent and more famous contemporary.

Smith, according to the observations of some of his friends, had been toying with a change of political allegiance ever since the spring of 1807. Joseph Manigault wrote his brother Gabriel on May 24, 1807: "Among the strange things that happen, I must mention, that Mr. Owen informed me a few days ago that Charles Pinckney had employed W. L. Smith as his counsel in a chancery suit between his old friend Doyley and himself. That the former opponent of Pinckney in politics, should now defend him against his bosom friend, would have appeared very unlikely to happen some time ago; though I can see no impropriety in undertaking the cause. Lord Chesterfield's advice to his son (who was intended for a public character) appears very unamiable: 'To keep in mind that his friend may become his enemy, and his enemy his friend' and yet here is a case in point."[171] There is not enough information to explain precisely why Smith changed parties, but it is certain that in 1807 and in 1808 he was uneasy in his old beliefs. He, like most Americans, was jolted by the *Leopard* affair in June 1807. At the Fourth-of-July celebrations in 1807 and in 1808 he made himself most conspicuous; on the latter occasion he even wore a suit of homespun. In July 1807, he was elected vice-president, and a year later, president of the American Revolution Society.[172] In the fall

[169] Harrison Gray Otis to John Rutledge, junior, July 3, 1808; Charles Cotesworth Pinckney to John Rutledge, junior, August 24, 1808, *John Rutledge, junior, Papers*, SHC.

[170] Charles Cotesworth Pinckney to John Rutledge, junior, September 8, 1808, *John Rutledge, junior, Papers*, SHC.

[171] Joseph Manigault to Gabriel Manigault, May 24, 1807, *Manigault Papers*, SCL.

[172] *Charleston Courier*, July 7, 1807, July 6, 1808.

he spoke in favor of cutting all economic ties with Great Britain. In any complex personality the motives would be various; undoubtedly opportunism was present to a marked degree in Smith's character, but in 1808 it was not the only factor to be considered.

Regardless of his motives, Smith acted in such a way during September that he was blamed for the defeat of Lowndes and thereby earned the everlasting enmity of the Charleston Federalists. Early in the month, Lowndes, Smith, and Marion were all in the field. Marion, however, was expected to drop out in favor of Smith. When Smith received a message from the New York meeting of the Federalists he enclosed the message in a short note to the chairman of the local committee saying curtly: "I beg leave to transmit to you, to be disposed of as you may judge proper, a letter and communication which had been misdirected to me, and which were received this morning, yours, W.L.S."[173] Perhaps Smith wanted to prove to the Democrats that he would not associate with the Federalists. On September 28, Pinckney wrote Rutledge that Marion had refused to decline to run, but that Smith still intended to put forward his own name. Pinckney felt that if Smith ran he would take enough votes in the middle to permit Lowndes to win.[174] In the end, Smith did not let his name go before the voters, and he threw his strength to the Democrats. Marion got seven hundred seventy-five votes in Charleston to Lowndes's three hundred ninety-one.[175] Smith was promptly blamed for Lowndes's defeat, and his disaffection was looked upon as a betrayal of everything he had ever stood for.

Oliver Wolcott wrote Rutledge: "What you write respecting Mr. Smith is astonishing—It is an unbecoming thing in any Federalist, to turn Democrat, but less proper in Mr. Smith, than any other person of my acquaintance."[176] Harrison Gray Otis wrote Rutledge: "How humiliating is the conduct of such men as W.S.— Among the young, the dependent, the unprincipled, one might naturally look for defection and apostasy, but it is nauseating to see a man of a certain age, turn sycophant to those he has abused, and offer incense to those who have been the objects of his deliberate

[173] John Rutledge, junior, to Oliver Wolcott, October 15, 1808, *Wolcott Papers*, CHS.

[174] Charles Cotesworth Pinckney to John Rutledge, junior, September 28, 1808, *John Rutledge, junior, Papers*, SHC.

[175] *Charleston Courier*, October 13, 1808.

[176] Oliver Wolcott to John Rutledge, junior, October 24, 1808, *Wolcott Papers*, CHS.

reprobation."[177] George Izard wrote his brother Henry: "But what
is this Metamorphosis of WLS? The accounts we have here, must
be exaggerated—it is impossible he should be Fool enough, as well
as scoundrel, to hold himself up forever to Hatred and Contempt."[178] Even Mrs. Izard, his devoted mother-in-law, wrote: "It
is a thousand pities that at the age of fifty he should mar his happiness, and destroy his character as he has done."[179]

But was it a matter of sheer opportunism or had he seen that the
Federalists had nothing left to offer the country? His association
with the men of the Homespun Company is one proof of a new
view. Charlestonians elected to the state legislature in 1808 were
all on the Democratic ticket, and among these were John Johnson,
junior, John Horlbeck, junior, and Thomas Bennett, junior, all directors of the Homespun Company.[180] Smith might not be betray-
ing the old cause. He merely realized that with the embargo the old
cause was gone. Any new departure must come from within the
Jeffersonian phalanx.

IN WESTERN EUROPE a defeated aristocracy has usually retreated
into an "Establishment." The French aristocrats with the rise of the
bourgeoisie sought refuge in their chateaux, in the army, and in the
church. The English aristocrats have had their country houses, colleges, and clubs, as well as crack regiments. The rice aristocrats of
South Carolina built their own "Establishment" of plantations,
select societies, and a church.

The plantations after a hundred years were handsome estates;
some of them, beyond twisting creeks and forbidding swamps, were
almost inaccessible. General Pinckney achieved the most splendid
isolation on Pinckney Island, where he lived for the greater part
of each year until his death in 1825. Pinckney Island was lost amid
the sea islands that stretched from Charleston to Savannah, reached
only by a wayward boat stopping upon call.[181] Mrs. Pinckney,
when she went to spend the day with a neighbor, usually "expected
to be an hour upon the water."[182] Mrs. Gabriel Manigault captured
the remoteness of this retreat in her description of how the Pinck-

[177] Harrison Gray Otis to John Rutledge, junior, December 15, 1808, *John Rutledge, junior, Papers*, SHC.
[178] George Izard to Henry Izard, October 24, 1808, *Izard Papers*, SCL.
[179] Alice Izard to Margaret Manigault, February 6, 1809, *Manigault Papers*, SC Archives.
[180] *Charleston Courier*, October 14, 1808.
[181] Margaret Manigault to Alice Izard, March 24, 1805, *Izard Papers*, LC.
[182] Margaret Manigault to Alice Izard, February 5, 1809, *Izard Papers*, LC.

ney ladies spent their days, almost as if the family were in exile: "Mrs. P. is sadly altered—yet she is in high spirits, and seems to have caught her husband's happy temper. She reads, and writes, and keeps the accounts at Pinckney Island—General P. is farmer, and housekeeper there. Eliza reads, and works, and papers the rooms and puts up curtains, and amuses herself perhaps as well as she would do there. Yet I think that at her age, with her fortune, it is too solitary a life."[183]

The South Carolina Jockey Club, which had built the Washington Race Course in 1792, was one citadel of the old society.[184] Among the original members and proprietors of the course were General Pinckney, General William Washington, General Jacob Read, General William Moultrie, Gabriel Manigault, Edward Fenwick, Wade Hampton, and William Alston. General Pinckney, the club's president, brought his family to town each February for Race Week, which was the highlight of the social season.[185]

During Race Week many balls were given. Mrs. Manigault, whose letters give a glimpse of the innermost citadels of society, described a "complete Ball" given in February 1809:

> Mrs. Radcliffe's ball attracted all the Town. It was really a splendid and well conducted affair. The house was well lighted. . . . The stair case is very pretty, and the passage above remarkably large and well finished. It was furnished with handsome girandoles, & ornamented with festoons of flowers, & flower pots from her green house shedding fragrant odours. The drawing room retained its carpet and card tables were ready to accommodate those who did not prefer dancing. Mr. R. did the honours with great attention and great ease—so that every body was pleased. Hers was a complete Ball—for it concluded with a magnificent supper at which near eighty persons were seated. The centre of it was adorned with an accumulation of iced plumb cakes in a kind of bower of natural flowers which gave the whole a very gay appearance—the table was loaded with every dainty that could be thought of, & every precaution was taken for the accommodation of so large a party. We slipped away immediately after, at about one o'clock, and got home safe.[186]

"All the Town" meant "near eighty persons" who were, of course,

---

[183] Margaret Manigault to Alice Izard, November 29, 1808, *Izard Papers*, LC. Eliza, General Pinckney's daughter, married Ralph Izard, the third surviving son of Senator Ralph Izard, who followed a career in the United States Navy. "Izard of South Carolina," *SCHGM*, II (1901), 225-226.

[184] *The John's Island Stud (South Carolina) 1750-1788*, n.p., 1931.

[185] John B. Irving, *The South Carolina Jockey Club*, Charleston, 1857, p. 14. *The John's Island Stud (South Carolina) 1750-1788*, n.p., 1931, pp. 39-40, 98-99.

[186] Margaret Manigault to Alice Izard, February 19, 1809, *Izard Papers*, LC.

the cream of society. This select group was composed of planters and professional men whose families had long been connected with Carolina. Before the Revolution such a group would have included many merchants, but the merchants who had arrived after the Revolution were not welcome in the inner society. Thomas, in his *Reminiscences,* wrote that "the door of the St. Cecilia Society was shut to the plebeian and the man of business, with two exceptions: Adam Tunno, king of the Scotch, and William Crafts, vice-king of the Yankees under their legitimate head, Nathaniel Russell, than whom there was no better man."[187]

Russell was Charleston's best example of a self-made man of business. With no education and with only a few New England products to peddle, he came to South Carolina in 1765. In 1788, he married Sarah Hopton, daughter of a loyalist merchant, and by her he had two daughters.[188] By 1795, he was the prince of Charleston merchants. In order to provide a proper setting for his daughters he built on Meeting Street one of Charleston's grandest mansions, more pretentious than the exquisite Joseph Manigault mansion at the other end of Meeting Street.[189] The elder daughter, Alicia, married Arthur Middleton in 1809.[190] Mrs. Manigault wrote: "Arthur has made for himself a very snug nest—and his example is not without imitators. The little sister, Sarah Russell has had several suitors already, although scarcely grown up. . . ." During the festivities surrounding this marriage, the two worlds met. Adam Gilchrist "with whom we never before had any intercourse did us the honor to invite us to a ball on Tuesday."[191] The younger daughter, Sarah, married Bishop Theodore Dehon in 1813. Although his daughters had entered local society, Nathaniel Russell retained his status as a northern man. In 1819 he became the first president of the New England Society of Charleston, a society founded by gentlemen who were agents of northern firms.[192]

[187] E. S. Thomas, *Reminiscences of the Last Sixty-Five Years,* Hartford, 1840, I, 33-34, 40.
[188] "Historical Notes," *SCHGM,* V (1904), 120. William Way, *History of The New England Society of Charleston, South Carolina, for One Hundred Years, 1819-1919,* Charleston, 1920, p. 27.
[189] The Joseph Manigault mansion was built *c.* 1802; the Russell mansion *c.* 1809. Samuel Gaillard Stoney, *This Is Charleston,* Charleston, 1960, pp. 73, 80.
[190] "Middleton of South Carolina," *SCHGM,* I (1900), 253-254.
[191] Margaret Manigault to Alice Izard, March 12, 1808, *Izard Papers,* LC. Mrs. Manigault did not attend the ball given by Gilchrist nor one given for the young couple by William Loughton Smith. Margaret Manigault to Alice Izard, March 19, 1809, *Izard Papers,* LC.
[192] Way, *op. cit.,* pp. 3, 5, 27.

It was during this period that the St. Cecilia Society was transformed from an organization dedicated to music to a preserve of social privilege. The society, founded in 1735, had been famous for its concerts. Josiah Quincy was impressed in 1773.[193] An influx of French musicians in the 1790's had brought the level of performance to its highest peak. In 1793 a concert for the benefit of the Orphan House consisted of the following pieces: "*Grand overture* of Haydn, *sinfonie concertante* of Davaux, *concerto grosso* of Corelli, *sinfonie* of the celebrated Pleyel, and *quartette* of Pleyel." By 1819 the ties between Charleston and Europe had been so completely cut that it was impossible to make up an orchestra in the city, and after 1822 concerts were given up.[194] The society had been drained of its original purpose, and the shell of its former self refurbished as the citadel of the old society.

William Loughton Smith was vice-president of the St. Cecilia Society, a position which meant that his social position was impregnable.[195] Yet even in the old society any deviation might be punished by social ostracism as far as it was possible to carry this out against a member of the family circle. After William Loughton Smith's betrayal of the party in 1808, a blanket of disapproval was tucked in around his daily life. This disapproval affected something as personal, and usually so jubilant, as the christening of Smith's son, born on October 2, 1808, Smith's own fiftieth birthday. The "great Christening" was by Dr. William Percy on the evening of November 28, after which there was "a magnificent dinner where nothing was wanting but heart." Mrs. Gabriel Manigault summed up Smith's new position: "The master of that house must now feel awkward in the company of all his former friends. . . . He is exceedingly ridiculed here, & must feel ashamed of himself I am sure—*d'autant plus* that he has not succeeded, & that he is a suspicious character among the party he has joined. To be respected in one party unto the age of 50 & then to turn, & be an object of derision—It is melancholy, & really pains me."[196] On December 6, Mrs. Manigault wrote her son: "Mr. Smith who used to be the life of all parties—is now not invited to them or a word of apology is

---

[193] Josiah Quincy, *Memoirs of the life of Josiah Quincy, Junior, of Massachusetts Bay, 1744-1775*, Boston, 1875, pp. 73-74.

[194] Elizabeth P. Simons, *Music in Charleston from 1732 to 1919*, Charleston, 1927, pp. 16, 24-25.

[195] *Charleston Courier*, February 20, 1808.

[196] Margaret Manigault to Alice Izard, November 29, 1808, *Izard Papers*, LC.

made to the company privately if he is—and gentlemen who have
been invited by him decline going to his house without assigning
any reason."[197] The Manigaults wanted to be sympathetic, wanted
to help, but did not know how. Mrs. Manigault wrote on December
27: "Mr. Smith is in town, but we never see him. Mr. M. wishes
to ask him to dine with us & knows not who to invite to meet him—
It is to me highly disgusting, as well as to Mr. M. to see party spirit
carried to such a length."[198]

The great days of the Federalists were over, but the aristocrats
could not forgive Smith for telling them the truth. An aristocracy
without power tends to be ridiculous. General and Mrs. Jacob Read,
who returned to make their home in South Carolina in December
1808 after many years in the North, were symbols of deflated Federalist power. Mrs. Manigault described their return:

> Mrs. Read whom I have not yet seen—is in great distress—she is
> condemned to occupy her old house on East Bay—and as you sup-
> pose, that is not improved, and her eyes, accustomed to the splen-
> did mansions of her Sisters in New York see it perhaps even more
> dirty, more misshapen, and frightful than it is. Then she com-
> plains more than most of the servants here. She is come she says
> with the hope of spending time pleasantly with her friends—& she
> is obliged to employ it in *contending* with negroes. She has no
> cook. All their servants we know, left them in Philadelphia, or at
> Rhode Island. Thus she amuses the ladies with her rain of com-
> plaints & he the gentleman with his wonderful pomposity—but he
> is a sensible, as well as a very good natured man—and although
> one may laugh, one cannot *dis*like him. I am really sorry for her.
> She must feel sadly mortified.[199]

The Charleston society that could spurn Smith's warnings and
fail to see how absurd and pathetic Read had become was prepared
to fete America's greatest tin soldier. Charleston was galvanized into
social activity by the arrival of General James Wilkinson and his
suite (George Izard was an aide-de-camp) in February 1809. "He
was ushered into the harbor and announced to the citizens by the
brazen throats of the Forts' guns."[200] Where Washington was once
the hero, now strutted General Wilkinson. Miss Claudia Smith, who

[197] Margaret Manigault to Henry Manigault, December 6, 1808, *Louis Manigault Papers*, DUL.
[198] Margaret Manigault to Alice Izard, December 27, 1808, *Izard Papers*, LC.
[199] *Ibid.*
[200] Margaret Manigault to Alice Izard, February 19, 1809, *Izard Papers*, LC.
Wilkinson arrived from Baltimore in the sloop of war *Hornet* on February 17
and stayed a week. He was on his way to Havana and New Orleans. James
Ripley Jacobs, *Tarnished Warrior, Major-General James Wilkinson*, New York,
1938, pp. 249-250.

had sat at the right hand of Washington, was "still a Belle" and "charmed General Wilkinson," who was "a great admirer of the ladies." Mrs. Manigault was sure "frivolity" was "a working trait in the commander in chief's character. He dresses most splendidly—covered with embroidery and lace—every seam in his coat laced—his boots edged with gold—with a gold tassel—gold spurs—a white sattin sash embroidered with gold." He professed to be a "great gallant—and is as most people of his age who do, very absurd. Anecdotes without number, fly about upon the occasion. I hope he is more discreet in his military maneuvers than he is in those of gallantry. He writes the most burlesque notes."[201] Here was a "fighting cock," a Jean Anouilh general, whom all Charleston turned out to "fête a l'infini." Mrs. Radcliffe gave a ball even more outstanding than her last. "General Wilkinson's band charmed us with some well executed military pieces—during which we paced up, & down the spacious corridor which was brilliantly illuminated, & into her handsome bed room, which was likewise lighted. A variety of cake, and wine, and fruit, and jellies, and all the nice things that could be collected were handed about."[202] General Benjamin Smith from North Carolina, Colonel Wade Hampton, some American and French naval officers were all in town to honor the "great general." Moving among the guests at all the parties were two English admirals, Sir Isaac Coffin and Sir Thomas Graves; as Mrs. Manigault herself wrote, "was there ever a more sinister coincidence of names."[203]

THE ARISTOCRATS were not without fears. Indeed this would have been the natural psychological bent of a declining aristocracy. With

---

[201] Margaret Manigault to Alice Izard, February 26, March 5, 1809, *Izard Papers*, LC.

[202] Margaret Manigault to Alice Izard, March 12, 1809, *Izard Papers*, LC. James Wilkinson gave Smith at this time a very odd pamphlet: *Memoir of the Northern Kingdom, Written, A. D. 1872, by the late Rev. Williamson Jahnsenykes, LL.D. and Hon. Member of the Royal American Board of Literature, In Six Letters to His Son*, Quebec, 1901. See *William Loughton Smith Pamphlets*, CLS, IV, number 1.

[203] Margaret Manigault to Alice Izard, February 26, 1809, *Izard Papers*, LC. Admirals Graves and Coffin had been charmed with Pinckney Island. Margaret Manigault to Mrs. Charles Cotesworth Pinckney, March 20, 1809, *Manigault Papers*, SCL. Sir Isaac Coffin (1759-1839) was a Boston loyalist who rose to the rank of admiral in the British navy. Smith knew him as naval commissioner in Lisbon. "Correspondence of William Smith, American Minister to Portugal," ed. Bernard C. Steiner, *Sewanee Review*, XIV (1906), 78. Sir Thomas Graves (1747-1814) should not be confused with his more famous cousin, Lord Thomas Graves (1725-1802), also an admiral. Sir John Knox Loughton, "Sir Thomas Graves," *DNB*.

democracy tending to rear its ugly head in the sphere of politics, the rice aristocrats were determined to construct one safe refuge where form and order and authority might be duly respected. Before it was too late, the Anglican Church in South Carolina had to be transformed from congregationalism to episcopalianism. This battle was fought between 1804 and 1812. William Loughton Smith was the most important lay figure in the contest, his career in this instance mirroring his career in national politics. He fought for episcopacy until 1808 and then shifted his support to those who wished to curb the power of the clergy.

The South Carolina Constitution of 1778 had disestablished the Anglican Church and had at the same time put the seal of approval on congregationalism by permitting each Protestant congregation to acquire a charter of incorporation from the state, guaranteeing the right of each congregation to elect its own minister.[204] With all the Protestant churches in South Carolina reduced to autonomous congregations by the Revolution, it was up to each denomination to construct voluntarily a state or national organization, if such were desired. For most Episcopalians, state and national organizations seemed imperative. A national organization was achieved in Philadelphia in 1789 with the adoption of the Constitution and Canons of the Protestant Episcopal Church in the United States. In October 1790, the South Carolina Episcopal Church made a perfunctory gesture to join the national church. Jacob Read and William Loughton Smith had been the two laymen most interested in this movement, but perhaps their overwhelming concern in the political sphere during the 1790's made their efforts fall short of a final victory in the religious sphere. At any rate, South Carolina got along without a bishop until 1795, when Robert Smith was selected, rather ironically, more to prevent having a bishop superimposed from the outside than from any burning desire to have bishops in South Carolina. After Bishop Smith's death in 1801, there was a hiatus.[205]

In 1803, the attempt to revitalize the Episcopal Church in South Carolina began.[206] The vestries of St. Philip's and St. Michael's sent out a call in January 1804 for a state convention. The old Federalist

---

[204] George C. Rogers, Jr., "Church and State in Eighteenth-Century South Carolina," *Publications of the Dalcho Historical Society*, number 12 (1959), pp. 22-23.

[205] *Ibid.*, pp. 24-29.

[206] *See particularly* Thomas Frost to Theodore Dehon, August 16, 1803, *Trapier Papers*, SHC.

pockets of strength at Goose Creek, Georgetown, and Beaufort responded quickly. In this movement William Loughton Smith, Robert Barnwell, Harry Laurens, Samuel Wragg, John and Thomas Parker, Francis Kinloch, and Peter Smith took the lead. This convention elected the Reverend Edward Jenkins, who had once served as chaplain to the royal troops in Charleston, as the new bishop, but he refused to serve.[207]

In 1805, there was a move to have the annual state convention draw up a new state constitution for the church, but some of the delegates challenged the authority of the convention. They felt that a special convention should be called to draw up a constitution, which should then be approved by each congregation; such was the guarantee of their charters of incorporation, such was "a first principle" of American democracy.[208]

The convention that was held in Charleston at St. Michael's from February 17 through February 20, 1806, was called for this purpose and was, therefore, the most important that had yet been held. William Loughton Smith, representing St. Philip's, took the chair. Robert Barnwell of St. Helena's moved that prayers be read each morning. These two former Federalist Congressmen were ably assisted by the Messrs. William Percy, Edward Jenkins, Nathaniel Bowen, and Milward Pogson, representing the clergy, as well as by prominent merchants (Robert Hazlehurst and David Alexander) and great planters (Harry Laurens of St. John's Berkeley and Samuel Wragg of Prince George's, Winyaw). Seventeen rules were eventually agreed to as the new constitution. Congregationalism, however, was still an issue. A standing committee was to make recommendations and help secure clergymen for the parishes, but the vestry and congregation of each parish were to have the right of final approval. Furthermore, in every case the charters of the churches were to be the ultimate source of authority. Rule 14 even upheld the charters against any violation by national action: "No article, canon, rule or other regulation, of any general or state convention, shall be obligatory on any Epis. church within this state, where the same shall be found to infringe on any of its chartered rights." The Book of Common Prayer and the sacraments,

---

[207] Rogers, op. cit., pp. 30-32. "The Journal of Alexander Chesney, a South Carolina Loyalist in the Revolution and After," ed. E. Alfred Jones, Ohio State University Bulletin, XXVI (1921), number 4, p. 111.

[208] Rogers, op. cit., pp. 30-31.

rites, and ceremonies of the Protestant Episcopal Church in the United States were to be used.[209]

At the February 1807 convention, the crucial question was the recognition of the authority of the national church. The Hon. Thomas Waties, the Reverend Samuel Lilly, the Reverend Nathaniel Bowen, Thomas Parker, Robert Barnwell, William Loughton Smith, Francis Kinloch, Thomas Roper, and Peter Smith were appointed a committee to discover if the Constitution and Canons of the Protestant Episcopal Church in the United States of America had been adopted by the church in South Carolina. This committee unanimously reported that five delegates had been appointed by South Carolina to attend the General Convention of 1789, that three had attended and had signed the constitution there agreed upon, and that on October 19, 1790, the state convention of South Carolina had unanimously agreed to accept that constitution and those canons. There was no objection to adopting the constitution and original canons, but there was some objection to ratifying all of the canons passed by the national church since 1790, especially the second and fourth canons of 1804. The second canon concerned the dismissal of pastors by congregations; the fourth concerned differences between ministers and their congregations.[210]

William Loughton Smith moved to divide the committee report so as to take a vote first on the constitution and canons of 1789 and then to take a second vote on the canons passed since 1789. The first part was adopted unanimously. On the second, Barnwell moved: "Provided such canons be not repugnant to the constitutions." Smith, seeing that the crux of the matter was still the second and fourth canons of 1804, moved that the convention instruct their delegates to the next general convention of the national church to move for the repeal or modification of the objectionable canons. This was then agreed to.[211] The general convention in May 1808 met the demands of the southern churches by attaching the following clause to both the second and fourth canons of 1804: "This canon shall not be obligatory upon the church, in those states or Dioceses with whose usages, laws or charters it interferes."[212] In this manner the ties with the national church were reaffirmed.

The democratic point of view in the conventions had been main-

[209] *Ibid.*, pp. 31-32.
[210] *Ibid.*, pp. 32-33.
[211] *Ibid.*, pp. 33-34.
[212] *Ibid.*, p. 37. *See* Nathaniel Bowen to John Henry Hobart, April 20, 1808, *Hobart Papers*, NYHS.

tained by a strong, outspoken minority from St. Philip's Church led by Thomas Roper. The only ones who had wanted to uphold the episcopal authority over the clergy and laity were the clergy themselves and the old-guard Federalists. Smith stood with the second group at first, but changed his views at the same time that he changed his political position. After 1808, he became the spokesman for the element in St. Philip's that wanted to curtail the power of clerical delegates in state conventions. He led the fight in each convention, but the battle was finally lost in 1812, when the clergy was granted an unlimited right to vote in the conventions.[213] The 1812 convention also finally selected a second bishop for South Carolina, the Reverend Theodore Dehon.[214]

After 1812, the Protestant Episcopal Church in South Carolina became a citadel of the lowcountry aristocrats. It was, like the English Church of the eighteenth century, to emphasize form more than content. This may be a harsh verdict, for a wave of enthusiasm did sweep through the church in 1810, and in that year, the Protestant Episcopal Society for the Advancement of Christianity in South Carolina was founded to convert the upcountry.[215] General Pinckney, who had helped found the South Carolina College to educate upcountry men, now gave his time and money to the society that meant to convert them.[216] John Henry Hobart writing in the *Churchman's Magazine* compared this organization to the English Society for the Propagation of the Gospel in Foreign Parts of the previous century.[217] Just as the victorious English Church in 1701 had established the SPG to win back the American Dissenters, so now the newly re-established Episcopal Church in South Carolina hoped to win back the dissenters of the upcountry.

One thing missing in this "Establishment" was a select university— neither the College of Charleston nor the South Carolina College took the role of an Oxford or a Cambridge to give special polish to the local society.[218] Perhaps more indicative of the educational

---

[213] Rogers, *op. cit.*, p. 37, n. 76.

[214] *Ibid.*, p. 38.

[215] *Address and Constitution of the P.E.S. for the Advancement of Christianity in South-Carolina*, Charleston, 1810.

[216] For Pinckney's interest in religion, *see* Charles Cotesworth Pinckney to Jedediah Morse, December 1, 1810, *Gratz Collection*, PHS.

[217] *The Churchman's Magazine*, VII (1810), 208-213.

[218] The Smiths had been loyal supporters of the College of Charleston since its inception. Benjamin Smith had left £500 sterling to found the college. William Loughton Smith served as a trustee, 1785-1797, 1805-1812; Roger Smith, 1791-1805; Thomas Rhett Smith, 1800-1813. J. H. Easterby, *A History of the College of Charleston*, n. p., 1935, pp. 12, 261-262.

tone of this society is the fact that when a new institution of higher learning was set up in Charleston it was a military institution and it was called The Citadel.[219]

Those within the old Federalist society might have considered the new "Establishment" complete, sufficient to preserve their way of life against the encroachments of democracy and the transforming winds of the nineteenth century. For Smith, who by birth and former allegiance belonged to this group, it contained everything—everything, that is, but power and national prestige. It was his ambition for these two things that goaded him to take his new political course.

IN THE YEAR 1810 a new generation of leaders was elected to Congress. Henry Clay and John C. Calhoun were merely the best known of these young men who became the War Hawks. The generation of the Founding Fathers had almost completely passed from the scene. Men who had been educated in Europe, who knew England and France intimately, who were more aristocratic than any American group to follow—more cosmopolitan, more worldly, more civilized—were no longer around. Gone with them were their doubts about the success of the new American venture and the need for compromise with Old World powers. The new generation has been perfectly described by Kendric Babcock:

> They were the first ripened product of the generation which had grown up since the Revolutionary War. They were patriotic by inheritance, optimistic and self-reliant by force of their surroundings; they had seen the nation grow at a marvelous rate, and they had the most uncompromising faith in the republic's strength and future. Their patriotism was untroubled by fear of war and its horrors, and untrammelled by any traditional obligations or sentiments regarding foreign relations, unless it were a chronic suspicion of England, bordering on unreason. The insults heaped upon the United States by both France and England they felt keenly, and with the fine and ready resentment of youth, they scorned the vacillations and delays of Madison and led him and his administration speedily out of the devious labyrinth into which Jefferson had first guided the Republican party.[220]

These were the chauvinists of the new America.

[219] The Citadel was founded in 1842, but it was established at the arsenal which had been used as a rallying point for the municipal guard since the abortive Denmark Vesey insurrection of 1822. Colonel O. J. Bond, *The Story of The Citadel*, Richmond, 1936, pp. 1-5, 17.

[220] Kendric Charles Babcock, *The Rise of American Nationality, 1811-1819*, New York, 1906, pp. 51-52.

Smith watched this new America take shape. Why then did he fail to find a place in the Republican party in 1810? He had been writing a series of articles for the *City Gazette*, the chief Republican newspaper in Charleston, and certainly hoped once again to represent South Carolina in Congress. The nomination was in the hands of four men: Charles Pinckney, Colonel Thomas Lehre, and Peter Freneau, Jefferson's three correspondents in Charleston, and E. S. Thomas, the editor of the *City Gazette*, who conferred every Wednesday evening at Freneau's House on George Street.[221] During 1810 they had come to realize that the people of South Carolina were generally discouraged with the do-nothing attitude of the Eleventh Congress.[222] The people wanted a change, and these leaders looked for likely candidates; William Loughton Smith and Langdon Cheves were the leading contenders for the nomination.

Smith's articles in the *City Gazette* had attracted attention, and Thomas, the editor, was for Smith.[223] Thomas felt that Smith had been "ill-used and neglected by both political parties. . . . When Doctor Shecut wrote up the cotton manufacturing business, and Mr. Smith was appointed orator of the day, at the laying of the cornerstone of the building, he came out in terms so plain, upon the republican side, that he did not leave a loop to hang a doubt upon." Yet Smith had not been taken up, "so that he remained in a complete political purgatory, suspended between the two parties, and acknowledged by neither." Thomas, however, considered Smith the first statesman in the state and among the first in the nation. "By far the greater portion of the men of 'sober second thoughts' were" for Smith, but "the huzza boys" were for Cheves.[224]

Thomas tried hard to persuade Pinckney, Lehre, and Freneau to support Smith, but some of the Republicans backing Cheves got to Freneau, "whose only fault was he could not withstand the solici-

[221] E. S. Thomas, *Reminiscences of the Last Sixty-Five Years*, Hartford, 1840, II, 51-52. There are a number of letters from these three men to Jefferson in the *Jefferson Papers*, LC.

[222] In June 1810, Thomas wrote in an editorial: "If my father were a member of the present Congress, and his bread depended upon his reelection, I would not give him my vote." *City Gazette and Commercial Daily Advertiser*, June 25, 1810. *Also see* Thomas, *op. cit.*, II, 51.

[223] It has been impossible to identify Smith's articles in this newspaper. Thomas had come to Charleston as a bookseller and had prospered until the slave trade was reopened in 1803 when the planters began to buy slaves rather than books Thomas transferred his funds to a cotton manufactory in Rhode Island, but later sold his shares and moved to Baltimore. The embargo ruined his attempt at farming, and so he returned to Charleston and bought Freneau's paper. *Ibid.*, pp. 35-36.

[224] *Ibid.*, pp. 50-53.

tations of his friends." Freneau yielded and then worked on Thomas, whose paper was an important element in Republican strength in the city. Thomas admitted that Freneau "was a man I loved next Heaven"; he could deny him nothing. Thus the four were unanimous in their support of Cheves. Although Thomas had made no promises to Smith, Smith was hurt, and the two men "were never upon the same friendly footing afterwards."[225] Smith's attempt to emerge from political limbo failed, and the failure was a bitter blow. Cheves was elected without opposition.

Among the South Carolina War Hawks, John C. Calhoun was the most prominent; through him the long-smoldering hostility of the upcountry towards Britain emerged at the national level. No longer would any improper British action be ignored in the hope that negotiation would remove the evil. Calhoun considered diplomacy too slow—the tool of the effete coastal aristocrat. Calhoun summed up the new attitude in Congress in December 1811: "When we contend, let us contend for all our rights; the doubtful and the certain, the unimportant and essential."[226] This was American nationalism, full-blown, blatant, and uncompromising. It had been much too much a luxury for the age of commerce, but because of the luck of geography it was to be *the American view* for over a hundred years.[227] Internationalism seemed necessary during the age of commerce, but during the age of industry, nationalism burned brightly. Calhoun refused to listen to the merchants' arguments; he would banish "calculating avarice" from affairs of state. The basing of policy on a profits-and-loss calculation was, he felt, "only fit for shops and counting-houses, and ought not to disgrace the seat of sovereignty by its squalid and vile appearance."[228] Calhoun said that he would resent every injury like a Chatham. One Congressman pointed out that if "it is a principle of honor in a nation, as in an individual, to resist a first insult—when should we have had a moment's peace?"[229] America was, however, by 1811, safe enough to be foolish, to act on the basis of what she would like the world to be, rather than on the basis of what the world really was. This

---

[225] *Ibid.* In November 1830 Thomas, however, could still write of Smith as "a name that will long dwell in sweet remembrance with all the admirers of patriotism and talent." *Ibid.*, p. 228.

[226] *Annals of the Congress of the United States,* Washington, 1853, XXIII (12th cong., 1st sess.), 477.

[227] See George Kennan, *American Diplomacy, 1900-1950,* Chicago, 1951, p. 11.

[228] *Annals of the Congress of the United States,* Washington, 1853, XXIII (12th cong., 1st sess.), 479.

[229] *Ibid.*, pp. 483, 513.

was the foreign policy of the America that lay above the fall line, and as Frank Thistlethwaite has pointed out, of that America that lay beyond the commercial world of the eighteenth century.[230]

What did these sons of the frontier know about international law? Nothing indeed. Recall the toast that was given to Andrew Jackson in Nashville in 1819 upon his return from Pensacola: "The Floridas—Ours without 16 years of negotiation."[231] "The reason of the university was rejected in behalf of the higher reason of nature."[232] One of their contemporaries saw this as the difference between John Quincy Adams and Andrew Jackson. "Jackson was the very man to d--n Grotius, Puffendorf, and Vattel; and Adams was the very man to condemn him for that above all other things as a great malefactor. Jackson cared only for his justification, but Adams was horrified at its mode. Jackson made law; Adams quoted it."[233]

This was also the difference between William Loughton Smith and John C. Calhoun in 1811. One need only compare Smith's *Phocion* letters of 1806 with Calhoun's speech of December 1811. Smith quoted law; Calhoun spoke from the heart. Was there any wonder that "the huzza boys" were not for Smith in 1810? And this was the reason why Smith, although he could no longer follow the old Federalists, was unable to fall in with the new chauvinists. His education, his commercial contacts, his federal career had imbued him with a sense of realism in international relations, a sense of history. Of this he could not divest himself. Many Americans had tried to ever since Tom Paine had flamed forth in his *Common Sense.* Jefferson wrote Count Diodati on March 29, 1807: "Were I in Europe, *pax et panis* would certainly be my motto. Wars and contentions, indeed, fill the pages of history with more matter. But more blest is that nation whose silent course of happiness furnishes nothing for history to say. This is what I ambition for my own country. . . ."[234] Smith, on the other hand, could not admit that America could escape from history—to admit it would be to sacrifice the one quality that had made the Federalists great, the quality

---

[230] Frank Thistlethwaite, *The Anglo-American Connection in the Early Nineteenth Century,* Philadelphia, 1959, p. 7.

[231] Quoted in John William Ward, *Andrew Jackson, Symbol for an Age,* New York, 1955, p. 61.

[232] *Ibid.,* pp. 49-50.

[233] The words of Henry A. Wise quoted in *ibid.,* p. 63.

[234] Thomas Jefferson to Monsieur le Comte Diodati, March 29, 1807, *The Writings of Thomas Jefferson,* ed. Andrew A. Lipscomb, Washington, 1904, XI, 181-182.

that had edged the thoughts of John Adams and Alexander Hamilton, the sense of history. When the rice aristocrats exchanged this quality of mind for Calhoun's patriotism, not the nationalist blend, but the later sectionalist blend, the South Carolina mind was set.

PERHAPS IT IS FITTING that William Loughton Smith died in 1812, the year that finally brought war with Great Britain. Smith was living the life of an ordinary citizen, unable to influence the course of events, dividing his time between Ashley Barony and his town house on the corner of East Bay and Amen Alley.[235] He still practiced law, but his cases represented the remnants of eighteenth century litigation: Luxembourg claims, maritime disputes arising out of the classic struggle between England and France, and family quarrels over the Wragg estate.[236] He was president of the Santee Canal Company and the most important figure in the Catawba Canal Company, but the age of canal building in South Carolina by private capital was almost over.[237] Smith wrote Judge Grimké in 1812 that he had been the only person present at a meeting of the Catawba Canal Company.[238] After his death, this company was sold to the state.

He was Grand Master of the Masons, but the Masons were soon to be under attack in America as an organization slightly alien, slightly aristocratic.[239] The Masons would never again recover their exalted position in the world.

The Smith family itself, at least in William Loughton's line, had lost its vigor. The third generation of Smiths lacked the push and power of the grandfather-founder. If any talent remained it flowed

[235] William Loughton Smith to Judge Grimké, April 23, 1812, *William Loughton Smith Papers*, SCHS. "Marriage and Death Notices from the *City Gazette* of Charleston, S. C.," *SCHGM*, XLIV (1943), 151.
[236] For his interest in the Luxembourg claims, *see* William Patterson and Sons to William Loughton Smith, April 9, 1812; William Loughton Smith to William Patterson and Sons, June 8, 1812, *William Loughton Smith Papers*, SCHS. Smith was engaged in a prize-money case as late as November 1812. *Admiralty Journal, 1806-1814*, FRC Georgia. For Wragg estate, *see* William Loughton Smith to Edward Penman, June 27, 1812, *William Loughton Smith Papers*, SCHS.
[237] *Charleston Courier*, January 21, 1812.
[238] William Loughton Smith to Judge Grimké, April 23, 1812, *William Loughton Smith Papers*, SCHS.
[239] Smith was Grand Master of the Ancient Yorks in 1808. He presided over a meeting in his home on September 5, 1808, at which the Ancient Yorks and the Modern Masons agreed to form one Grand Lodge of South Carolina Smith became the grand master and Judge Grimké the deputy grand master of the new United Grand Lodge. Albert G. Mackey, *The History of Freemasonry in South Carolina, From its Origin in the year 1736 to the present time*, Columbia, 1861, pp. 92-97.

in a thin, fine line of aesthetic appreciation. Thomas Loughton and Ann Caroline, William's children by his first marriage, who had been brought up by their grandmother Mrs. Ralph Izard while their father served his country in Philadelphia and Lisbon, must have been singularly unattractive.[240] Mrs. Izard wrote in 1807 that "they might both be remarkably pleasing if they were ignited, at present they are heavy companions."[241] A year later, this loving grandmother commented that it was surprising that the son and daughter "of so animated, so lovely a woman as their Mother was, should be of such torpid natures as they both are."[242] Tom was a shy, withdrawn boy with "an unpleasant temper."[243] Mrs. Gabriel Manigault, wanting her son to be "a respectable independent gentleman," held Tom up as all that her son should not be.[244] She wrote of Tom as one "deprived in his early years of his Mother—neglected by his Father—& disliked by all those to whom he ought to be dear. Think of this et plaignez le."[245] There were faults on both sides. The father should have had "more tenderness in his disposition," but the son did "not like good company, and il s'est encanaille." The father had accused the son "of very serious misconduct—of negligence in his studies, of disrespect to him, & the ladies—of fondness for bad company—of disregard to his advice—of irreligion—and here is the source of all the rest."[246] The result of this incompatibility between father and son was that the father shipped the son off to Philadelphia to study law in the office of William Rawle and to be looked after by Smith's agent, John Vaughan.[247] Apparently Tom never reformed, and his unhappy life was ended by his early death in

[240] Alice Izard to Margaret Manigault, December 20, 1803, Izard Papers, LC.

[241] Alice Izard to Margaret Manigault, October 28, 1807, Manigault Papers, SC Archives.

[242] Alice Izard to Margaret Manigault, December 18, 1808, Manigault Papers, SC Archives.

[243] Margaret Manigault to Alice Izard, March 15, 1808, Manigault Papers, SC Archives. Margaret Manigault to Henry Manigault, January 20, 1809, Louis Manigault Papers, DUL.

[244] Margaret Manigault to Henry Manigault, December 17, 1808, Louis Manigault Papers, DUL.

[245] Margaret Manigault to Henry Manigault, January 20, 1809, Louis Manigault Papers, DUL.

[246] Margaret Manigault to Henry Manigault, December 17, 28, 1808, Louis Manigault Papers, DUL.

[247] John Vaughan to William Loughton Smith, May, September 8, 1808, March 3, July 5, 1810; William Loughton Smith in account with John Vaughan, November 24, 1809, William Loughton Smith Papers, SCHS. Rawle was a Philadelphia loyalist who had studied at the Middle Temple at the same time as Smith. T. I. Wharton, "A Memoir of William Rawle," Memoirs of the Historical Society of Pennsylvania, Philadelphia, 1840, IV, part 1, 33-91.

1817.[248] Little is known of Ann Caroline except that she made her debut in 1809 and was married in 1820 to Peter Pederson, the Danish minister to the United States.[249]

Smith had two more children by his second marriage: Elizabeth Wragg Smith and William Wragg Smith. Elizabeth married Thomas Osborn Lowndes in 1824 and left a distinguished family.[250] William devoted himself to planting and poetry. In 1842 he published *The Last Canto of Childe Harold's Pilgrimage*, which he had translated and amplified from the French of Alphonse de Lamartine.[251]

William Loughton Smith died on December 19, 1812.[252] His devoted sister-in-law Mrs. Gabriel Manigault wrote to her daughter:

> You may suppose that we heard with sensations of pain and surprize that Mr. Smith had so suddenly left this world. He seems to have been spared all pain—and to have left his affairs in good order. Those are two great consolations. His wife cannot be supposed to feel those agonies which call forth compassion. Yet I dare say that his loss will be severely felt in his family. He has treated his wife with a respect which must raise her in the opinion of all those who know of it. I mean in his will.[253]

Smith left $140,000. Except for a few bequests to nieces and godchildren, the entire estate of real and personal property was left to his widow. His children by his first wife had been provided for out of the Izard estate.[254]

Smith's only extant comment on the war then in progress is in a letter of June 27, 1812: "I hope that a speedy restoration of harmony between this country & G.B. will revive an intercourse formerly so beneficial to both."[255] Among those who had been Federalists in the 1790's—always strongly pro-English—there was very little enthusiasm for the war. Judge William Johnson wrote Monroe in 1813

[248] Margaret Manigault to Alice Izard, November 24, 1811, *Izard Papers*, LC. "Marriage and Death Notices from the *City Gazette* of Charleston, S. C.," *SCHGM*, XLIV (1943), 151.

[249] Margaret Manigault to Alice Izard, February 26, 1809, *Izard Papers*, LC. A. S. Salley, Jr., "William Smith and Some of His Descendants," *SCHGM*, IV (1903), 256.

[250] Elizabeth Wragg Smith is not mentioned by Salley, *ibid.* She was born on September 23, 1806. Annie Elizabeth Miller, *Our Family Circle*, Macon, 1931, pp. 55-56.

[251] A. S. Salley, Jr., "William Smith and Some of His Descendants," *SCHGM*, IV (1903), 256, n. 68.

[252] *City Gazette*, December 21, 1812. Anne King Gregorie, "William Loughton Smith," *DAB*.

[253] Margaret Manigault to Mrs Lewis Morris, junior, January 3, 1813, *Manigault-Morris-Grimball Papers*, SHC.

[254] The will can be found in the *William Loughton Smith Papers*, RC.

[255] William Loughton Smith to Thomas Nicholls, June 27, 1812, *William Loughton Smith Papers*, SCHS.

that half the people of Charleston were "disaffected to the Administration, and would very reluctantly draw a trigger upon an Englishman." Judge Johnson had little faith that the city would be defended, since General Jacob Read was the commander and Colonel John Rutledge, junior, was his chief lieutenant. "It is well known that both of them as well as most others of their politics, instead of endeavouring to encourage and inspirit our citizens; are in the habit of haranguing eternally upon our defenceless and exposed situation. . . ."[256] Fortunately the city and its inhabitants were not put to the test.

In the period after 1815, the old Federalist leaders slipped gradually into oblivion. Their devotion to the Union was replaced by a devotion to state rights. Charles Pinckney, who had helped to make the Constitution, yet who had almost immediately pointed out its dangers, now got his chance. In Congress at the time of the Missouri controversy, he pointed out the threats to the South and emphasized the limitations of the Constitution, paving the way for Calhoun's exposition of the doctrine of nullification.[257] Yet this dress rehearsal was soon over, and the final halcyon years of the Revolutionary leaders were at hand.

A last revival of enthusiasm burst forth with Lafayette's visit to Charleston in 1825. Two old Revolutionary heroes briefly emerged from retirement. Charles Cotesworth and Thomas Pinckney clasped hands with the French general and departed.[258] Joseph Allen Smith wrote Joel Roberts Poinsett: "His reception has been warm and animated, and appeared to be justly appreciated on his part. In the midst of all this joy, there was a propriety of conduct throughout the whole which does Honour to Charleston."[259] Shortly afterwards

[256] Judge William Johnson to James Monroe, July 25, 1813, Monroe Papers, NYPL.

[257] See Charles Pinckney to Robert Y. Hayne, March 31, 1821, Miscellaneous Manuscripts, NYPL. Hayne was Pinckney's son-in-law. A controversy has raged over Pinckney's supposed authorship of the Constitution. See Charles C. Nott, The Mystery of the Pinckney Draught, New York, 1908. The important point is not whether he contributed greatly to the original document, but why he should have been willing to put forth claims to superior knowledge concerning that document in the years 1819-1821. He was obviously desirous of putting forth his own interpretation of key passages to counteract the misinterpretations of thirty years.

[258] Yates Snowden, "Incidents in Lafayette's Two Visits to S. C.," typed manuscript, SCL, pp. 8-12.

[259] Joseph Allen Smith to Joel Roberts Poinsett, March 1, 1825, quoted in "Letters from Russia, 1802-1805," ed. George C. Rogers, Jr., SCHGM, LX (1959), 227.

the stage was swept almost bare. Charles Cotesworth Pinckney died on August 16, 1825, and Thomas Pinckney, on November 2, 1828.[260]

With the death of the old leaders and the corrosion of economic change at work, the state began to exhibit a new public face. Henry William DeSaussure, one of the few remaining Federalist shades, wrote in 1830 of the new possibilities:

> There is great and almost universal discontent in this state at the imposition of enormous duties for protection, greatly beyond the actual wants of the government for legitimate purposes, such as the payment of the debt, the civil list, the army, navy, & other indispensable objects. It is believed that a tariff for protection is against the spirit of the constitution, & that it is oppressive, unequal & unjust—It is therefore very generally odious, & is weakening the attachment of the South to the Union, tho' the value of that is felt & appreciated: for you may be assured that all charges of a desire to separate from the Union are fables of a distempered imagination. It may ultimately come to that, because our people would prefer even that deplorable measure, to having a Government of unlimited powers. At present we are divided into nearly equal parts, not at all as to the evil, but as to the remedy, & to the degree of forebearance—If the tariff of protection, & vast expenditure, for internal improvements, become the settled policy of the government, beyond all hope of redress, the separation of the Union will inevitably follow; which I pray God I may not live to see.[261]

[260] J. G. de Roulhac Hamilton, "Charles Cotesworth Pinckney" and "Thomas Pinckney," *DAB.*

[261] Henry William DeSaussure to Benjamin Silliman, November 1, 1830, *Gratz Collection,* PHS.

GENEALOGICAL CHARTS

Chart I. The Schenckingh-Smiths

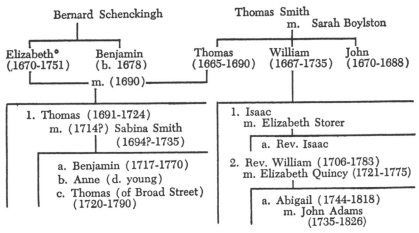

Bernard Schenckingh | Thomas Smith m. Sarah Boylston

Elizabeth* (1670-1751) — Benjamin (b. 1678) — m. (1690) | Thomas (1665-1690) — William (1667-1735) — John (1670-1688)

1. Thomas (1691-1724)
   m. (1714?) Sabina Smith
   (1694?-1735)

   a. Benjamin (1717-1770)
   b. Anne (d. young)
   c. Thomas (of Broad Street)
      (1720-1790)

1. Isaac
   m. Elizabeth Storer

   a. Rev. Isaac

2. Rev. William (1706-1783)
   m. Elizabeth Quincy (1721-1775)

   a. Abigail (1744-1818)
      m. John Adams
      (1735-1826)

* Elizabeth Schenckingh Smith married secondly William Smith, merchant, and had six children by this second marriage.

Chart II. The Family of Josiah Smith

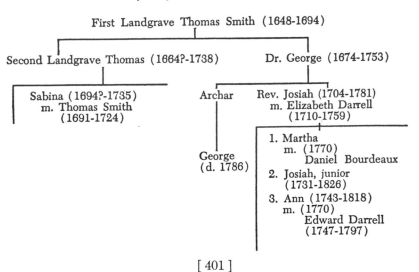

First Landgrave Thomas Smith (1648-1694)

Second Landgrave Thomas (1664?-1738) | Dr. George (1674-1753)

Sabina (1694?-1735)
m. Thomas Smith
(1691-1724)

Archar

Rev. Josiah (1704-1781)
m. Elizabeth Darrell
(1710-1759)

George
(d. 1786)

1. Martha
   m. (1770)
      Daniel Bourdeaux
2. Josiah, junior
   (1731-1826)
3. Ann (1743-1818)
   m. (1770)
      Edward Darrell
      (1747-1797)

Chart III.   The Family of Benjamin Smith

Benjamin Smith (1717-1770)
m. 1st   Anne Loughton (d. 1760)

1. Thomas Loughton (1741-1773)
     m. (1763) Elizabeth Inglis

     a. Elizabeth
          m. (1784) David Campbell
     b. Ann Loughton (d. 1835)
          m. (1782) Thomas Fraser (1755-1820)
     c. Claudia   (d. 1855)
          m. Henry Izard (1771-1826)
     d. Maria
          m. 1st   John Deas, junior
          m. 2nd John Ramsay
2. John (1743-d. young)
3. Anne (1745-1772)
     m. (1763) Isaac Motte
4. Susannah
     m. 1st   Barnard Elliott (d. 1778)

     a. Barnard, junior
     m. 2nd Capt. Patrick Carnes (d. 1786)
5. William (1758-1812)
     m. 1st   (1786) Charlotte Izard (1770-1792)

     a. Thomas Loughton (d. 1817)
     b. Anne Caroline (b. 1791)
          m. (1820) Peter Pederson
     m. 2nd (1805) Charlotte Wragg

     c. Elizabeth Wragg (b. 1806)
          m. (1824) Thomas Osborn Lowndes
     d. William Wragg (b. 1808)
6. Catherine (1759-1760)

          m. 2nd (1760) Mary Wragg

7. Judith (1762-1820)
     m. (1778) James Ladson
8. Benjamin Wragg (d. young)
9. Mary
     m. (1787) John Gibbes (b. 1765)
10. Sabina (d. young)
11. Charlotte (d. young)
12. Joseph Allen (1769-1828)
     m. (1809) Charlotte Georgina Izard (1792-1832)

Chart IV. The Family of Thomas Smith of Broad Street

Thomas Smith (1720-1790)
m. (1744) Sarah Moore (1728-1774)

1. Roger Moore (1745-1805)
   m. (1768) Mary Rutledge (1747-1832)

      a. Thomas Rhett (1768-1829)
      b. Benjamin Burgh (1776-1823)

2. Thomas (1748-1749)
3. Benjamin (1749-1750)
4. William (1751-1751)
5. Sarah (b. 1752)
   m. 1st (1769) John Mackenzie (d. 1771)
   m. 2nd (1773) Thomas Bee (1729?-1812)
6. Peter (1754-1821)
   m. (1776) Mary Middleton (1757-1825)
7. Benjamin (1757-1826)
   m. (1777) Sarah Dry (d. 1821)
8. Rhett (1759-1760)
9. James (1761-1835)
   m. (1791) Mariana Gough (1773-1837)

      a. 15 children—his sons changed their name to Rhett
      b. Robert Barnwell (1800-1876)

10. Mary (1764-1839)
    m. (1784) John Faucheraud Grimké (1752-1819)

      a. Thomas Smith (1786-1834)
      b. Sarah Moore (1792-1873)
      c. Angelina Emily (1805-1879)

11. Ann (1765-1799?)
    m. (1783) Hugh Rutledge (1745-1811)
12. Rhett (1767-1767)

Chart V. The Family of Ralph Izard

Ralph Izard (1742-1804)
m. (1767) Alice DeLancey (1745-1832)

1. Margaret (1768-1824)
   m. (1785) Gabriel Manigault, II
2. Charlotte (1770-1792)
   m. (1786) William Loughton Smith (1758-1812)
3. Henry (1771-1826)
   m. 1st (1795) Emma Middleton (1776-1813)
   m. 2nd Claudia Smith (d. 1855)
4. George (1776-1828)
5. Anne (1779-1863)
   m. William Allen Deas
6. Ralph (1785-1824)
   m. 1st (1808) Elizabeth Middleton (1787-1822)
   m. 2nd Eliza Lucas Pinckney (d. 1851)
7. Charlotte Georgina (1792-1832)
   m. (1809) Joseph Allen Smith (1769-1828)

Chart VI. The Family of James Read (Reid)

James Read (d. 1778)
m. (1750) Rebecca Bond (1730-1786)

1. Jacob (1752-1816)
   m. (1785) Catherine Van Horn
2. William (1754-1845)
   m. Sarah Harleston
3. Elizabeth
   m. (1787) Thomas Simons (1765-1805)
4. Susannah
   m. (1784) Hugh Rose (1756-1841), son of John Rose, loyalist

Chart VII. The Family of Dr. John Rutledge

Dr. John Rutledge (d. 1750)
m. (1738) Sarah Hext (1724-1792)

1. John Rutledge (1739-1800)
   m. (1763) Elizabeth Grimké (d. 1792)

   a. Martha (1764-1806)
      m. (1785) Francis Kinloch (1755-1826)
   b. John (1766-1819)
      m. (1791) Sarah Smith, daughter of Bishop Robert
         Smith
   c. Edward (1767-1811)
   d. Elizabeth (1776-1842)
      m. (1792) Harry Laurens (1763-1821)
         (Henry Laurens, junior)
   e. States (1783-1829)
2. Hugh (1745-1811)
   m. (1783) Ann Smith (1765-1787)
3. Mary (1747-1832)
   m. (1768) Roger Smith (1745-1805)
4. Edward (1749-1800)
   m. 1st (1774) Henrietta Middleton (1750-1792)

   a. Henry Middleton (1775-1844)
   b. Sarah (1782-1855)
   m. 2nd (1792) Mary (Shubrick) Everleigh (1753-1837)

Chart VIII. The Family of Benjamin Simons, II

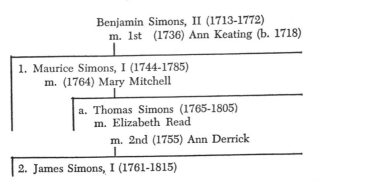

Benjamin Simons, II (1713-1772)
m. 1st (1736) Ann Keating (b. 1718)

1. Maurice Simons, I (1744-1785)
   m. (1764) Mary Mitchell

   a. Thomas Simons (1765-1805)
      m. Elizabeth Read
   m. 2nd (1755) Ann Derrick
2. James Simons, I (1761-1815)

Chart IX. The Family of Thomas Pinckney

Thomas Pinckney (1629-1705)
m. (1698) Mary Cotesworth (d. 1745)

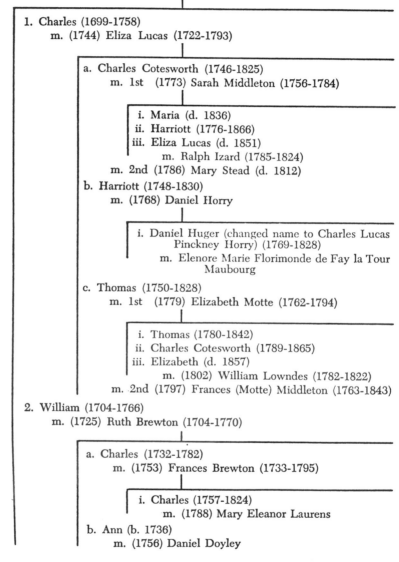

1. Charles (1699-1758)
   m. (1744) Eliza Lucas (1722-1793)

   a. Charles Cotesworth (1746-1825)
      m. 1st (1773) Sarah Middleton (1756-1784)

      i. Maria (d. 1836)
      ii. Harriott (1776-1866)
      iii. Eliza Lucas (d. 1851)
           m. Ralph Izard (1785-1824)
      m. 2nd (1786) Mary Stead (d. 1812)
   b. Harriott (1748-1830)
      m. (1768) Daniel Horry

      i. Daniel Huger (changed name to Charles Lucas
         Pinckney Horry) (1769-1828)
         m. Elenore Marie Florimonde de Fay la Tour
         Maubourg
   c. Thomas (1750-1828)
      m. 1st (1779) Elizabeth Motte (1762-1794)

      i. Thomas (1780-1842)
      ii. Charles Cotesworth (1789-1865)
      iii. Elizabeth (d. 1857)
           m. (1802) William Lowndes (1782-1822)
      m. 2nd (1797) Frances (Motte) Middleton (1763-1843)
2. William (1704-1766)
   m. (1725) Ruth Brewton (1704-1770)

   a. Charles (1732-1782)
      m. (1753) Frances Brewton (1733-1795)

      i. Charles (1757-1824)
         m. (1788) Mary Eleanor Laurens
   b. Ann (b. 1736)
      m. (1756) Daniel Doyley

BIBLIOGRAPHY

Manuscripts

American Antiquarian Society
    Andrew Craigie Papers

Boston Public Library
    Chamberlain Collection

John Carter Brown Library
    Brown Family Papers

Charleston Library Society
    Manuscript Collection
    Shoolbred Business Letter Book, 1793-1796

Colonial Williamsburg
    Coleman-Tucker Papers

Connecticut Historical Society
    Trumbull Papers
    Wadsworth Papers
    Wolcott Papers

Duke University Library
    Louis Manigault Papers
    William Murrell Letterbook, 1795-1812
    Charles Cotesworth Pinckney Papers
    Jacob Read Papers
    John Rutledge, junior, Papers
    Josiah Edward Smith Letters
    William Loughton Smith Papers

Essex Institute
    Pickering Papers

Henry E. Huntington Library
    William Loughton Smith Papers

Library of Congress
    Thomas Bee Papers
    Papers of Lt. Col. Henry Bouquet
    Genêt Papers
    Hamilton Papers
    Izard Papers
    Jefferson Papers
    Richard Bland Lee Papers

James McHenry Papers
Monroe Papers
Pinckney Papers
William Loughton Smith Papers

Library Company of Philadelphia
Ramsay Papers

Long Island Historical Society
Laurens Papers (now in private hands)

Massachusetts Historical Society
Andrews-Eliot Papers
Caleb Davis Papers
C. E. French Collection
Henry Knox Papers
Otis Papers
Pickering Papers
Sedgwick Papers
Smith-Carter Papers

Department of Archives and History, Raleigh, North Carolina
William R. Davie Papers
Miscellaneous Manuscripts

The New-York Historical Society
William Duer Papers
John Henry Hobart Papers
Rufus King Papers
John Lamb Papers
Miscellaneous Manuscripts

New York Public Library
Emmet Collection
Letter-Book of Nalbro' Frazier, 1783-1799
Miscellaneous Manuscripts
Monroe Papers
Myers Collection
State Boxes (South Carolina)

The Historical Society of Pennsylvania
Dreer Collection
Etting Papers
Gratz Collection
Pemberton Papers
Society Collection

The Pierpont Morgan Library
Autographs of the Signers of the Declaration of
Independence
William Vans Murray Correspondence

Rosenbach Foundation
>William Loughton Smith Papers

South Carolina Archives Department
>Manigault Papers

South Carolina Historical Society
>Laurens Letter-Books, 1767-1774
>Manigault Papers
>Miscellaneous Manuscripts
>William Loughton Smith Papers

South Caroliniana Library
>Izard Papers
>Manigault Papers
>Charles Cotesworth Pinckney Papers
>Ramsay Letters
>Read Papers
>William Loughton Smith Papers

Southern Historical Collection
>Preston Davie Papers
>Hayes Collection
>Louis Manigault Papers
>Manigault-Morris-Grimball Papers
>John Rutledge, junior, Papers
>Josiah Smith, junior, Letter-Book, 1771-1784
>Trapier Papers

University of Virginia Library
>Edgehill-Randolph Papers

William L. Clements Library
>James McHenry Papers
>William Loughton Smith Papers

Yale University Library
>Jedediah Morse Papers

Government Documents

Federal Records Center, East Point, Georgia
>Admiralty Journal, 1806-1814
>South Carolina Circuit Court Records, 1790-1809

National Archives
>Consular Dispatches from Lisbon, 1791-1802
>Ledger of Assumed Debt, vol. 1258
>Miscellaneous Letters, Department of State, 1789-1796
>Senate Papers, Claims, 1791-1796
>Senate Papers, Various, 1791-1796

South Carolina Archives Department
>   Manuscript Journals. of the Council of South Carolina
>   Manuscript Journals of the Commons House of Assembly
>   of South Carolina
>   Manuscript Journals of the House of Representatives of
>   South Carolina
>   Copies of the Manuscript Records in the British Public
>   Record Office Relating to South Carolina
>   Records of Confiscated Estates
>   Legislative Papers
>   Miscellaneous Records
>   Ship Register, 1734-1765
>   Will Books

Newspapers

Charleston, South Carolina
>   *South-Carolina Gazette*, 1732-1776
>   *South-Carolina Weekly Gazette*, 1783, 1784
>   *South-Carolina Gazette and Public Advertiser*, 1784, 1785
>   *Columbian Herald*, 1786
>   *Charleston Morning Post and Daily Advertiser*, 1786, 1787
>   *City Gazette*, 1788-1812
>   *State Gazette of South-Carolina*, 1788-1796
>   *Charleston Courier*, 1803-1812

Newport, Rhode Island
>   *Newport Herald*, 1790

New York, New York
>   *Minerva*, 1796

Philadelphia, Pennsylvania
>   *Philadelphia Daily Advertiser*, 1791
>   *Aurora*, 1795
>   *Gazette of the United States*, 1796

Providence, Rhode Island
>   *Providence Gazette and Country Journal*, 1790

Pamphlets

Address and Constitution of the P. E. S. for the Advancement of Christianity in South-Carolina.   Charleston, 1810.

A Few Salutary Hints, Pointing out the Policy and Consequences of admitting British Subjects to Engross our trade and become our Citizens. Addressed to those who either risqued or lost their all in bringing about the Revolution.   Charleston, 1786.

The Original Institution of the General Society of the Cincinnati, as formed by the Officers of the Army of the United States, at the conclusion of the Revolutionary War, which gave Independence to America. Charleston, 1808.

Rules of the Company for Opening the Inland Navigation, between the Santee and Cooper Rivers, Agreed to on March the 23rd, 1786. Charleston, 1786.

[Bird, Henry M.] *A View of the Relative Situation of Great Britain and the United States of North America.* London, 1794.

[Burke, Aedanus.] *Considerations on the Society or Order of Cincinnati; lately instituted by the Major-Generals, Brigadier-Generals, and other Officers of the American Army, Proving that it creates a Race of Hereditary Patricians, or Nobility.* Philadelphia, 1783.

Callender, James Thomson. *Sedgwick & Co. or a Key to the Six Per Cent Cabinet.* Philadelphia, 1798.

[Drayton, William Henry.] *Letter from Freeman of South Carolina, to the Deputies of North-America, Assembled in the High Court of Congress at Philadelphia.* Charles-Town, 1774.

Drayton, John. *A View of South Carolina, As Respects Her Natural and Civil Concerns.* Charleston, 1802.

[Ford, Timothy.] *The Constitutionalist.* Charleston, 1794.

Harper, Robert Goodloe. *An Address from Robert Goodloe Harper, of South-Carolina, to His Constituents. Containing His Reasons for Approving the Treaty of Amity, Commerce, and Navigation, with Great-Britain.* Philadelphia, 1795.

[Harper, Robert Goodloe.] *An Address to the People of South-Carolina, By the General Committee of the Representative Reform Association, at Columbia.* Columbia, 1794.

[Madison, James.] *Speech, in the House of Representatives of the Congress of the United States, Delivered January 14, 1794, by James Madison, of Virginia, in support of his Propositions for the Promotion of the Commerce of the United States, and in Reply to William Smith, of South-Carolina.* New York, 1794.

Ramsay, David. *An Oration on the Advantages of American Independence: spoken before a publick assembly of the inhabitants of Charleston in South-Carolina, on the second anniversary of that glorious aera.* Charlestown, 1778.

Ramsay, David. *Observations on the Decision of the House of Representatives of the United States, on the 22nd Day of May, 1789; Respecting the Eligibility of the Hon. William Smith, of South-Carolina, to a Seat in that House.* New York, 1789.

Sheffield, John, Lord. *Observations on the Commerce of the American States.* London, 1784.

[Smith, William.] *An Address from William Smith, of South-Carolina, to his Constituents.* Philadelphia, 1794.

[Smith, William.] *A Candid Examination of the Objections to the Treaty of Amity, Commerce, and Navigation, between the United States and Great Britain, as stated in the report of the committee, appointed by the citizens of the United States, in Charleston, South-Carolina.* Charleston, 1795.

Smith, William. *A Comparative View of the Constitutions of the Several States with each other, and with that of the United States: Exhibiting in Tables the Prominent Features of each Constitution, and Classing together their most important Provisions under the Several Heads of Administration; with Notes and Observations.* Philadelphia, 1796.

[Smith, William.] *The Numbers of Phocion, which were originally published in the Charleston Courier, in 1806, on the subject of Neutral Rights.* Charleston, [1806].

Smith, William. *An Oration, Delivered in St. Philip's Church, Before the Inhabitants of Charleston, South-Carolina, on the Fourth of July, 1796, in Commemoration of American Independence.* Charleston, 1796.

[Smith, William.] *The Politicks and Views of a Certain Party, Displayed.* n. p., 1792.

[Smith, William.] *The Pretensions of Thomas Jefferson to the Presidency Examined; and the Charges against John Adams Refuted. Addressed to the Citizens of America in general; and particularly to the Electors of the President.* n. p., 1796.

[Smith, William.] *The Speeches of Mr. Smith, of South-Carolina, Delivered in the House of Representatives of the United States, in January, 1794, on the subject of certain Commercial Regulations, proposed by Mr. Madison, in the Committee of the Whole, on the Report of the Secretary of State.* Philadelphia, [1794].

Southey, Robert. *Letters Written During a Short Residence in Spain and Portugal.* Bristol, 1799.

Taylor, John. *An Examination of the Late Proceedings in Congress, Respecting the Official Conduct of the Secretary of Treasury.* n. p., n. d.

INDEX

349; secretary of the treasury, 185, 188, 218, 238, 241n, 245, 304; secretary of war, 319, 349

Cabot, George, 230, 236, 281, 299

Cadiz, Spain, 307, 316, 317

Caesar, Julius, 69, 328

Calder, General, 323

Calhoun; see Presstman and Calhoun

Calhoun, Floride Bonneau (Colhoun), 371

Calhoun, Gustavus, 202, 204

Calhoun, John C., 147, 371, 392, 394-396, 399

Calhoun, Patrick, 140, 150

Calhouns, the, 371

Callender, James T., 205

Cambridge, Duke of, 66

Cambridge University, 64, 68, 391

Camden, S. C., 101, 109, 130n, 133, 134, 143, 225, 245, 247, 282, 283

Cammach, William, 361n

Campbell; see McCartan and Campbell

Campbell, Lieutenant David, 120, 121, 189n, 206, 227, 235, 239, 240, 243n, 265, 306, 357, 358

Campbell, Dougal, 46

Campbell, Elizabeth (Smith), 120, 121

Campbell, Laurence, 100, 108n

Campbell, Macartan, 243

Campbell, Nancy (Motte), 121n

Campbell, Sarah (Fenwick), 243n

Campbell, Lady Sarah (Izard), 30n

Campbell, Lord William, 30n, 36, 78

Campbells, the, 93

Canaletto, 356

Canals, 129-134, 223, 235, 242, 361, 362, 376, 377; see also Catawba Canal Company; Dismal Swamp Canal Company; Santee Canal Company; Susquehanna Canal Company; Wraggborough Canal Company

Cannon, Daniel, 76

Canterbury, Archbishop of, 32

Cantey, Messrs. Henry, and Company, 370n

Cape Finisterre, 16

Capital: of South Carolina, 168, 233, 350, 371; of the United States, 196, 198, 222

Capitalists, 125, 134

Capitol, of Virginia, 222

Cardozo, J. N., 375-376

Carlisle Commission, 84n

Carmarthen, Marquis of, 149, 159-162, 166n, 167n

Carnes, Captain Patrick, 104n

Carnes, Susannah (Smith), 104, 243

Carroll, Charles, 230, 353

Carron Works, 377

Casadeux, General, 249

Casey, Levi, 355, 363n

Castlereagh, Lord, 339

Catawba Canal Company, 133-134, 235, 245n, 361, 362, 396

Cathcart, James Leander, 333, 334, 341n

Cazenove, Théophile, 202, 206, 207, 229, 236

Census, 182-183, 239, 354

Chais, M., 67

Chamber of Commerce, 76n, 99, 137, 152, 225

Champneys, John, 82, 203, 204

Chapman; see Brailsford and Chapman

Charles Town (after 1783, Charleston), 3, 13, 16, 20, 22, 24, 25, 31, 32, 36, 44, 45, 48, 49, 53, 54, 56, 61, 70, 73, 75, 78, 80, 84, 85, 105, 107, 108, 112, 114, 118, 130-133, 136, 137, 144, 145, 154, 156, 162, 163, 166, 169, 189, 191, 195, 200, 203, 204, 220, 225, 226, 231, 232, 240, 242, 245-247, 250-252, 255, 258, 259, 266, 267, 275, 276, 278, 279, 282, 286, 304, 307, 346, 348, 350, 355, 356, 359, 363, 367-371, 375, 376, 381, 382, 385, 387, 389, 392, 399; description of, 233-234; evacuation of, 97, 98, 100, 102, 103, 109, 110, 113, 135; fall of, 86, 116, 120, 165; harbor, 6, 43, 104, 301; siege of, 86-88

Charlestown Library Society, 130

Charlotte, N. C., 225

Charters, 77; of 1663 and 1665, 3, 42

Chauvet, M., 67, 71, 72, 80

Chauvet, Madame, 67

Chauvets, the, 72

Cheraw District, S. C., 130, 246n; see also Districts

Cheraw Hill, 131

Chesnut, John, 101, 131, 293, 294

Chesterfield, Lord, 66, 380